MATTHEW ARNOLD

MATTHEW ARNOLD

Poetry and Prose

edited by

JOHN BRYSON

HARVARD UNIVERSITY PRESS
CAMBRIDGE MASSACHUSETTS

SBN 674-67870-2
1970 Importation
PRINTED IN GREAT BRITAIN

CONTENTS

I. POETRY

EARLY POEMS

NARRATIVE POEMS

5

6   CONTENTS

SONNETS

LYRIC POEMS

ELEGIAC POEMS

DRAMATIC POEMS

LATER POEMS

II. PROSE

CONTENTS

III. LETTERS

INTRODUCTION

I

MATTHEW ARNOLD, poet and critic, should be seen steadily and seen whole. The poet is familiar and his reputation is not in doubt. While Arnold has never had the popular appeal of his great contemporaries, his verse, less mannered and less voluminous, has withstood change of taste and fashion better than much of theirs. But the poetry is only a part of his varied achievement, and Arnold the prose-writer is not well known. In his Harvard lectures of 1930 Mr. Garrod remarked that clever young men no longer read Arnold's criticism and that they would be wiser and no less clever if they did. *Essays in Criticism* and the Introduction to Ward's *English Poets* may still provide critical counters like "high seriousness", "the grand style" and "poetry as criticism of life", but the lectures on Homer and the mass of his social, religious and educational writings remain scattered and largely unread. There are to-day signs of a change of heart and of a growing sense that these writings are worth rediscovering, because Arnold has a way of anticipating problems which are our concern as well as his. Here is a writer whose main object was to make the critical study of literature a guide to the business of living; one who saw in this study a training ground for clear thought and a field for the free play of ideas—and the ideas thus acquired he brings to bear on the wider issues of education, politics and religion. A critic of European outlook who believed in a culture based on the attempt "to learn and propagate the best that is known and thought in the world" is likely to furnish tracts for our time as well as for his own.

In range, sanity and intelligence Arnold's critical writings are outstanding in Victorian literature. His temper is no less serious than Carlyle's or Ruskin's, but the touch is lighter and the tone less hysterical. The spirit of gaiety so signally absent from his poetry found its natural outlet in his prose. Nor is it fair to isolate the purely literary criticism from the rest. Literature is not for Arnold a thing apart; it must take its place beside religion, politics and education in establishing the enlightened way of life for which he fought. That is the special quality of his writings about it. Culture, a term we have come to regard with some

13

suspicion, is for Arnold the study of perfection moving "by the force, not merely or primarily of the scientific passion for pure knowledge, but also of the moral and social passion for doing good". He is as far removed as Dr. Johnson from the the the sterile position of the aesthete. "A fine culture is the complement of a high reason: it is in the conjunction of both with character and energy, that the ideal for men and nations is to be placed." Great poetry must be a criticism of life because a poetry of revolt against, or indifference towards, moral ideas is a poetry of indifference towards life.

Some aspects of his criticism may have less importance for us than they had for him. He places too much value on the great poetic subject, and too little on poetic treatment, and his test of merit by "touchstone lines" can be unfair. His leisurely repetitive method of exposition is that of one who tends to lay more stress on precept than on appreciation and enjoyment—but in that respect Pater and his school have taught us how to set the balance right, and criticism nowadays is reverting to the austerer approach. If Arnold seemed supercilious about the early claims of science to a place in education, we can to-day well afford to listen once more to his reasoned plea for the humanities. He did not bother much about historical method, and was ready to found theories of literature on an inadequate basis of fact—notoriously in his generalizations about Celtic literature and in his treatment of Gray. Since his time, however, the historical method and the scientific have more than asserted their rights, and an academic criticism all too skilled in numbering the streaks of the tulip is turning again to the large general appearances. When there is danger of new schools, semi-philosophical and semi-propaganda, invading criticism and falsifying literary perspective, Arnold's plea for disinterestedness in criticism, his refusal to confound literary and non-literary issues, is all-important. He remains the sure defender of Art "from its eternal enemy Caprice", and his rejection of the grand name without the grand thing is consistent alike in literature and life. "Whoever talks of excellence as common and abundant, is on the way to lose all right standards of excellence", he says in the essay on Milton. To distinguish the good from the *faux bon* is more than ever necessary at a time when education has spread widely, if not always deeply, beyond the limits of Arnold's dreams.

As a young Fellow of Oriel, Arnold came back from Paris with the latest *chanson* of Béranger on his lips, and shocked the Oxford common-rooms by the fashionable length of his hair and his neglect of attendance at chapel. All his life indeed,

> Somewhat of worldling mingled still
> With bard and sage.

He retained his early love of the theatre, and even at the height of his fame did not scorn to combine dramatic criticism with the graver activities of reformer and prophet. And he remained proud of the fine head of hair even in old age. This mixture of professor and man of the world is reflected in the famous Arnoldian manner, with its dandyism, its Olympian superiority, its polite irony. His characteristic play with proper names can be devastating: Wragg, Roebuck, and Lowe; Professors Anderson, Pepper and Frickel; Miss Cobbe and the British College of Health— even Sir Walter Raleigh, who liked him little, can praise the adorable insolence of that manner. Others who only appreciate a plain piece of work, a bare hanging, have liked it less. When his patience is tried it is true that the accents become more those of the lecture-room than the city, and what he said about Burns can be applied to himself—when he is not speaking from the heart he is more or less preaching. Yet the essential Arnold manner is more than didacticism and more than mere insolence. We too can be aggressive, but urbanity and amenity are the rarer virtues in our criticism, and it is these qualities that Arnold teaches— "the tone of the city, of the centre, the tone which always aims at a spiritual and intellectual effect, and not excluding the use of banter, never disjoins banter itself from politeness, from felicity".

II

Arnold was a critic almost as soon as he was a poet, and the critic outlived the poet. Already in the Preface to the *Poems* of 1853 he is asserting one of the cardinal articles of his belief—the importance of the great poetic subject. He there puts appreciation of the larger unity of design above beauties of individual detail, and in one of his latest essays he returns to this *symmetria prisca*: "Fit details strictly combined, in view of a large general result nobly conceived . . . it is just where we English fail, where all our art fails." In 1857 his inaugural lecture as Professor of Poetry was on *The Modern Element in Literature*; by a comparison of Greek and Roman civilization he shows that what most enlightens us in a study of the past is the revelation of the co-existence of a great epoch and a great literature. "For the creation of a master-work of literature two powers must concur, the power of the man and the power of the moment, and the man is not enough without the moment." There followed the *Lectures on Translating Homer*, with their emphasis on the Grand Style, and *The Study of Celtic Literature*, with its discovery of "natural magic" in poetry. The lovely tribute to Oxford which closes the

introduction to *Essays in Criticism* of 1865 is universally known:
but its full magic and its deeper significance are only realized—
as with so many of Arnold's pronouncements—when the passage
is taken in its setting, and seen as a tribute to other ideals than
those of the world of Wragg and Roebuck and the science of
Tübingen. Two major essays in this collection, *The Function of
Criticism at the Present Time* and *The Use of Academies*, are key-
pieces for the understanding of Arnold's wide conception of criticism and of the value he sets on an established critical tradition.
This he finds in France, with his idol Sainte-Beuve ever in mind,
but not yet in England. And here he starts that crusade for the
free play of unprejudiced ideas which in *Culture and Anarchy* and
Literature and Dogma and his later writings he was to bring to
bear on the widest social and religious issues.

Within the limits of a brief introduction it is not possible to
treat Arnold adequately as a social, political and religious
thinker. The war-cries of his campaign, the famous motto
phrases, indicate the direction of his reform—Barbarian and
Philistine, Hebraism and Hellenism, Sweetness and Light.
Disraeli once told him that the currency of these phrases had
made him a classic already in his own lifetime. His hope for the
future lies with the great middle-classes; aware of what they can
contribute if guided aright he is fighting to break down narrow
interests and barriers of prejudice—"to pull out a few more stops
in that powerful but at present somewhat narrow-toned organ
the modern Englishman". He wants to give them an openness
of mind aware of the best that has been known and thought in
the world. The result of enlarged knowledge will be the growth
of a tolerant spirit, patient of the diversities of habits and opinions.
"The judgement which almost insensibly forms itself in a fair
and clear mind, along with fresh knowledge, is the valuable
one." In the essay on Wordsworth he pictures a poetry-reading
at a Social Science Congress in a provincial town:

> One can call up the whole scene. A great room in one of
> our dismal provincial towns; dusty air and jaded afternoon
> daylight; benches full of men with bald heads and women in
> spectacles; an orator lifting up his face from a manuscript
> written within and without to declaim these lines of Words-
> worth; and in the soul of any poor child of nature who may
> have wandered in thither, an unutterable sense of lamenta-
> tion, and mourning, and woe!

That is a public that Arnold the school-inspector knew only too
well; the earnest public "one has a chance of getting at . . . and
such a work as one wants to do with it". The sketch is written
from his inmost heart.

There is no better introduction to Arnold as a political thinker than the two essays *Democracy* and *Equality*. They show the sureness of his convictions and all the lucidity and flexibility of his own mind. "It is a very great thing to be able to think as you like", he tells his readers, "but after all the important question remains: what you think." He is no root-and-branch innovator. It is his strength and his sanity that, while as a moralist he can plead for enlightenment and reform, as a poet he is ever conscious of the living value of tradition and the past. His conception of truth is wide enough to embrace the dreaming spires and the poetry—if not the facts—of the Bible. "Religious emotion has the power to *light up* morality."

He made his last general pronouncement on poetry in the Introduction to the collection of *English Poets* edited by his son-in-law Thomas Humphry Ward in 1880. This sweeping survey is a personal and controversial performance, which should be judged in the light of what he had written on poetry elsewhere. His attitude to certain poets—Chaucer, Pope and Burns—becomes understandable, and the questionable general propositions fall into proper perspective, when related to the pattern of his criticism as a whole. Taken in isolation his definition of poetry as a criticism of life can lead to endless and fruitless argument, as many a later critic has demonstrated his ingenuity in showing. That great poetry (the term embracing all high creative art) must have moral standards in its interpretation of human conduct is the very basis of Arnold's conception of an art which has the power "of forming, sustaining, and delighting us, as nothing else can". This may be a truism, but it was worth stating. And, as he said elsewhere of the "grand style", this is the last matter in the world for verbal definition to deal with adequately: "One may say of it, as is said of faith, 'one must feel it in order to know what it is'."

His many essays on individual authors, ranging from Theocritus and Marcus Aurelius to Byron and Goethe, demonstrate the value of that comparative study of literature which he advocated, and show his power of seizing the qualities of a writer. Dislike may sometimes lead to prejudice, as in his treatment of Shelley, and he is capable of over-valuing minor finds like the de Guérins. But on the great writers he is always great, and the *Wordsworth* and the *Byron* remain unsurpassed as critical estimates of two poets he admired and understood. His range is surprisingly wide, and it should not be forgotten that he was one of the first English critics to appreciate the poetry of Leopardi and the novels of Tolstoy.

The prose writings have delicate pages of landscape description which come naturally from the pen of one who can in his poetry bring before us the Alpine mountains, the Cumnor hill-side, the Thames valley, and the wet, bird-haunted English lawn. He paints the clear Berry countryside in August, "a region of broad light, and fresh breezes, and wide horizons", when this "Milton jeune et voyageant" made his pilgrimage to George Sand at Nohant, and found Chopin of the wonderful eyes at mid-day breakfast with her and her family. The scenery of the Gorge-du-Tarn around Sorrèze is the setting for the visit to Lacordaire so vividly described in *A French Eton*, that early work which the author accounted one of his best. The distant Welsh mountains across the Bay of Anglesey form the background for his study of Celtic literature. And in a beautiful passage at the close of the essay on Falkland—a martyr to Arnold's own ideal of lucidity of mind and largeness of temper—he returns to the much-loved countryside of the Scholar Gipsy which he had made his own:

> In the end it will prevail; only we must have patience. The day will come when this nation shall be renewed by it. But, O lime-trees of Tew, and quiet Oxfordshire field-banks where the first violets are even now raising their heads!—how often, ere that day arrive for Englishmen, shall your renewal be seen!

III

"The period between forty and fifty," Arnold wrote in 1861, "is not a bad ten years of one's life for poetry, if one resolutely uses it, but it is a time in which, if one does not use it, one dries up and becomes prosaic." He was then thirty-nine, a professor of poetry, and embarking on the career of social reformer. Most of his best poetry was already written. For Arnold, as for Wordsworth and Coleridge, the years of intense poetic activity were brief. There are fine things after the *Poems* of 1855, but they are occasional, and, like *Thyrsis*, most often inspired by the moods of earlier years. The professor and the moralist no doubt played their part in killing the poet, but that is not the complete answer. A deeper reason for his unproductiveness lay in the nature of his poetic talent. A poetic vein which runs deep and full is not so easily diverted from its course by alien activities. Arnold was pre-eminently strong in the intellectual power which he found wanting in Tennyson, but he lacked Tennyson's abundance, and the words he applies so sympathetically to Gray's poetry—"so distinguished, so rare, but so stinted"—are an apt description of his own. It is remarkable how often the images of the full flowing river and the ocean occur in his poetry, but when he comes to write the allegory of his own poetic progress the stream is one which all too soon runs dry in its channel.

Youth rambles on life's arid mount,
And strikes the rock and finds the vein,
And brings the water from the fount,
The fount which shall not flow again.

The man mature with labour chops
For the bright steam a channel grand,
And sees not that the sacred drops
Ran off and vanished out of hand.

And then the old man totters nigh,
And freely rakes among the stones.
The mount is mute, the channel dry;
And down he lays his weary bones.

All his life he gave much attention to the revision of his poems,
and was continually altering and regrouping them. They did not
reach the final pattern till the collected edition of 1885. In the
edition of 1869 the lyrics inspired by his most intense emotional
experience are given their authoritative shape. We are not likely
now to know more about Marguerite than we can guess from the
poems and from what Arnold told Clough in two letters from
Switzerland; one written in September 1848, the other on his
return visit a year later, in "a curious and not altogether comfortable state".[1] Mr. Garrod has acutely observed that "when he
made his final arrangement of his poems [Arnold] was willing
that she should appear in his poetry as a diversion; he did not
wish that she should look like an obsession, even an obsession of
youth." But Marguerite was not forgotten. She haunts his poetry,
and her presence can be felt in many a poem outside the group of
seven lyrics entitled "Switzerland", and even in the prose. Is it
altogether fanciful to find her ghost still lingering years later in
such a sentence as this from *St. Paul and Protestantism*?

Of such a mysterious power and its operation some clear
notion may be got by anyone who has ever had any overpowering attachment, or has been, according to the common
expression, in love. Everyone knows how being in love
changes for a time a man's spiritual atmosphere, and makes
animation and buoyancy where before there was flatness
and dullness.

Arnold felt that his poems represented the main movement of
mind of the mid-century, and foresaw that they would have their
day as people became conscious of what that movement was and
interested in the productions which reflect it. Writing to his
mother in 1869 he says:

It might be fairly urged that I have less poetical sentiment
than Tennyson, and less intellectual vigour and abundance
than Browning; yet because I have perhaps more of a fusion

[1] pp. 734 and 739.

of the two than either of them, and have more regularly applied that fusion to the main line of modern development, I am likely enough to have my turn.

Both his strength and his weakness have been plain to critical admirers from the beginning, and as a poet he stands in less need of reassessment than any of the great Victorians. Reviewing the *Poems* of 1869, Swinburne praised the large and clear and calm utterance, the power and perfection of landscape, and at the same time found fault with mere dejection and what he calls 'misty mental weather'. Lionel Johnson in a discriminating essay recognized Arnold's main technical faults—discordant lines where the sense of melody fails, and poems where, for all the loftiness of conception, the thought is unadorned and the austerity far from radiant. But he answers Swinburne's charge of mere dejection by a just, if one-sided, comparison with Clough's mournful, homesick and desultory poems. Arnold too is touched by the Zeitgeist of the later nineteenth century, but the best of his meditative poetry is more than the record of transitory emotion, more than the phase and habit of an age. His melancholy brings the eternal note of sadness in; " of ample power to chasten and subdue ", it leaves us calm.

The dominant mood of elegiac meditation in which Arnold is indeed at his best is accompanied by another strain—a strain of realism and toughness which is ready to make the best of things as they are. This dogged Stoic quality saw him through the

> Strange disease of modern life
> With its sick hurry, its divided aims.

This was the mental fibre Clough lacked, but which enabled Arnold to carry out a life's duty of school-inspectorship and yet remain a poet. In his letters there are frequent glimpses of the wearing dreariness of that common round and daily task. The author of *The Last Word* is no Rabbi Ben Ezra with a message of easy comfort to leave : he has seen a bleaker truth :

> They out-talk'd thee, hiss'd thee, tore thee ?
> Better men fared thus before thee;
> Fired their ringing shot and pass'd,
> Hotly charged—and sank at last.
>
> Charge once more, then, and be dumb!
> Let the victors when they come,
> When the forts of folly fall,
> Find thy body by the wall!

They are the last words of a fighter, one who nurses no extravagant hope and yet is convinced

"Because thou must not dream, thou need's not then despair."

Each new age takes from the older poets what it needs. Arnold the Stoic and realist may have a significance for our generation more to its purpose than Browning's all-too-confident optimism, or the Tennysonian hope that somehow good will be the end of ill.

IV

If it is important to see Arnold whole, that is not easy. His collected works are out of print, and many of the prose writings are not easily available in any convenient form. There may then be room for a volume which attempts to bring together the best of his poetry, a representative body of his prose, and a selection of his letters.

Each poem is printed in its entirety, and consequent limitation of space has caused the omission of some longer pieces which have reasonable claims to inclusion. *Tristan and Iseult* and *The Sick King in Bokhara* are instances. Of the Dramatic Poems *Empedocles on Etna* is given complete, while *Merope* is omitted. The latter need not be regretted ; its appeal is to the student of that sparse and specialized field, Greek tragedy in English. The author had a special affection for it and even hoped to present it on the stage, but he got nearer the true Sophoclean vein in the *Fragment of an Antigone* and *Fragment of Chorus of a Dejaneira*. Of the "Dejaneira" Swinburne wrote, "That must be a noble statue which could match this massive fragment". Selection is a matter of personal taste, and no choice can satisfy every reader; but it is hoped that this volume may have achieved what Arnold claimed for his own selection of Wordsworth— "The volume contains, I think, everything, or nearly everything, which may best serve him with the majority of lovers of poetry, nothing which may disserve him . . . I don't think any of his *best* work will be left out, though a great deal must be left out which is *good* work."

The arrangement follows Arnold's classification of his poems by kind. A chronological method would help in tracing his poetic development, but it presents difficulties which only a critical edition could properly solve. His own arrangement, while not always logical, has the merits of familiarity and use, and it is comparatively simple; it has not the complexity and artificiality to which he rightly objected in Wordsworth's. The notes record the date of composition or first publication of each poem, and details of textual history are given where of interest. The reader who wishes to make a full study of Arnold's text and of his habit of revising and regrouping his poems is referred to the critical edition of the *Poetical Works*, edited by C. B. Tinker and H. F. Lowry (Oxford University Press, 1950). The text is

that of the three-volume edition of 1888, published in the year
of the poet's death, and the last which could have had his own
supervision.

The selection of prose attempts to cover most of Arnold's varied
interests as a prose writer, but more emphasis is laid on the
critic of literature than on the social and religious reformer.
The prose writings are arranged chronologically, and the text
is usually that of the first edition. Arnold tended to make minor
changes of slight importance in subsequent editions, but some
works, like *Culture and Anarchy*, he revised and abbreviated
considerably. Here the later text is used. For convenience of
reference editorial subtitles have been added in some cases to
indicate the subject-matter or nature of the passages selected.
The more important of Arnold's own notes are retained : editor's
notes are indicated by square brackets. Not all the essays are
printed *in extenso*, but as Arnold had a fondness for lengthy and
repetitive development, this is not entirely a disadvantage.

Arnold expressed a wish that no official biography should be
written; but the general background of his life can be adequately
filled in from his letters. It cannot be claimed that he is one of
the great letter-writers, and the interest of his correspondence
lies mainly in the impression of the man it presents; an impression less formal and more human than that left by his other
writings or current in popular tradition. His was not an eventful
or varied career, but he was in close touch with all main intellectual movements of his time. Extracts have been chosen to
illustrate both his day-to-day activities and interests, and the
opinions, frankly given, of his own work and that of his contemporaries.

JOHN BRYSON

September, 1953.

CHRONOLOGICAL TABLE

MATTHEW ARNOLD'S LIFE AND WRITINGS

1822	Born at Laleham, Surrey, 24 December. Eldest son of Rev. Thomas Arnold, later headmaster of Rugby, and Mary Penrose.
1833	The Arnolds acquire a home at Fox How, Ambleside.
1836–40	Educated at Winchester and later at Rugby where in 1840 he won the poetry prize with *Alaric at Rome*.
1840	Elected to an open classical scholarship at Balliol.
	Friendship at Oxford with Arthur Hugh Clough, also at Balliol.
1842	Death of Dr. Arnold.
1843	Awarded the Newdigate prize for poem on *Cromwell*.
1844	Awarded a 'second' in Literae Humaniores.
1845	Elected to a Fellowship at Oriel, where Clough had preceded him in 1842.
1846–7	Travels in France and Switzerland. Visits George Sand at Nohant, and sees Rachel act both in London and Paris.
1847	Becomes private secretary to the Marquis of Lansdowne, Lord President of the Council.
1848–49	Further visits to Switzerland.
1849	*The Strayed Reveller, and Other Poems.*
1851	Appointed to an Inspectorship of Schools under the Department of Education. Held this office till his retirement in 1886, two years before his death.
	Marriage to Frances Lucy Wightman (June 10).
1852	*Empedocles on Etna, and Other Poems.*
1853	*Poems. A New Edition.*

1855	*Poems. Second Series.*
1857	May 5—elected to the Professorship of Poetry at Oxford which he held for ten years.
1858	*Merope.*
	Takes house 2 Chester Square, London.
1859	*England and the Italian Question.*
	Visits schools in France, Holland and Switzerland as Foreign Assistant Commissioner to Education Commission.
1861	*The Popular Education of France with notices of that of Holland and Switzerland.*
	November 13, Clough died at Florence.
	On Translating Homer : Three Lectures given at Oxford.
1862	*On Translating Homer: Last Words.*
1864	*A French Eton.*
1865	*Essays in Criticism. (First Series.)*
	Thyrsis published in Macmillan's Magazine for April.
1867	*New Poems.*
1868	*On the Study of Celtic Literature.*
	Moves to Byron House, Harrow.
1869	*Poems. First collected edition : in two vols.*
	Culture and Anarchy.
1870	*St. Paul and Protestantism.*
	Honorary degree of D.C.L. conferred at Oxford.
1871	*Friendship's Garland.*
1873	*Literature and Dogma.*
	Moves to Pain's Hill Cottage, Cobham, Surrey.
1875	*God and the Bible.*
1877	*Last Essays on Church and Religion.*
	Poems. Second collected edition : in two vols.
1879	*Mixed Essays.*
1880	Introduction and contributions to Ward's *English Poets.*
1881	*Poems* (a re-issue of the 1877 edition with slight alterations).
1882	*Irish Essays and others.*

1883	Civil List pension of £250 conferred by Gladstone.
	Lecture-tour in America.
1885	*Discourses in America.*
	Poems. In three volumes: classified—Early Poems, Narrative Poems and Sonnets.—Lyric and Elegiac Poems—Dramatic and Later Poems. Re-issued without change in 1888.
	Refuses re-nomination for the Oxford Professorship.
1886	Second visit to America. Resigns Inspectorship.
1888	April 15, died suddenly at Liverpool, where he had gone to meet his married daughter Mrs. Whitridge arriving from America.
	Buried at All Saints, Laleham.
	Essays in Criticism, Second Series, issued posthumously.

A drawing by Frederick Sandys executed in 1882 is in the possession of Messrs. Macmillan, and a portrait painted by G. F. Watts in 1880 is in the National Portrait Gallery.

ACKNOWLEDGMENTS

I wish to express my indebtedness to *The Poetry of Matthew Arnold: A Commentary*, by C. B. Tinker and H. F. Lowry (Oxford University Press, 1940): without its help my notes would have been the poorer. *Matthew Arnold: A Study*, by Sir E. K. Chambers (Clarendon Press, 1947), has provided biographical material, and use has been made of *The Bibliography of Matthew Arnold*, by T. B. Smart, 1892. (Revised and extended in Vol. XV of *The Works of Matthew Arnold*, Macmillan, 1904.) I am grateful to the Warden of All Souls for much valuable criticism and advice, and to Mr. V. Quinn for his help in preparing the text.

POETRY

EARLY POEMS

Notes on Early Poems, pp. 782–5.

EARLY POEMS

Sonnets

Quiet Work

ONE lesson, Nature, let me learn of thee,
One lesson which in every wind is blown,
One lesson of two duties kept at one
Though the loud world proclaim their enmity—

Of toil unsever'd from tranquillity!
Of labour, that in lasting fruit outgrows
Far noisier schemes, accomplish'd in repose,
Too great for haste, too high for rivalry!

Yes, while on earth a thousand discords ring,
Man's fitful uproar mingling with his toil,
Still do thy sleepless ministers move on,

Their glorious tasks in silence perfecting;
Still working, blaming still our vain turmoil,
Labourers that shall not fail, when man is gone.

To a Friend

WHO prop, thou ask'st, in these bad days, my mind?—
He much, the old man, who, clearest-soul'd of men,
Saw The Wide Prospect, and the Asian Fen,
And Tmolus hill, and Smyrna bay, though blind.

Much he, whose friendship I not long since won,
That halting slave, who in Nicopolis
Taught Arrian, when Vespasian's brutal son
Clear'd Rome of what most shamed him. But be his

My special thanks, whose even-balanced soul,
From first youth tested up to extreme old age,
Business could not make dull, nor passion wild;

31

Who saw life steadily, and saw it whole;
The mellow glory of the Attic stage,
Singer of sweet Colonus, and its child.

Shakespeare

OTHERS abide our question. Thou art free.
We ask and ask—Thou smilest and art still,
Out-topping knowledge. For the loftiest hill,
Who to the stars uncrowns his majesty,

Planting his steadfast footsteps in the sea,
Making the heaven of heavens his dwelling-place,
Spares but the cloudy border of his base
To the foil'd searching of mortality;

And thou, who didst the stars and sunbeams know,
Self-school'd, self-scann'd, self-honour'd, self-secure,
Didst tread on earth unguess'd at.—Better so!

All pains the immortal spirit must endure,
All weakness which impairs, all griefs which bow,
Find their sole speech in that victorious brow.

In Harmony with Nature

To a Preacher

"IN harmony with Nature?" Restless fool,
Who with such heat dost preach what were to thee,
When true, the last impossibility—
To be like Nature strong, like Nature cool!

Know, man hath all which Nature hath, but more,
And in that *more* lie all his hopes of good.
Nature is cruel, man is sick of blood;
Nature is stubborn, man would fain adore;

Nature is fickle, man hath need of rest;
Nature forgives no debt, and fears no grave;
Man would be mild, and with safe conscience blest.

Man must begin, know this, where Nature ends;
Nature and man can never be fast friends.
Fool, if thou canst not pass her, rest her slave!

Mycerinus

"NOT by the justice that my father spurn'd,
Not for the thousands whom my father slew,
Altars unfed and temples overturn'd,
Cold hearts and thankless tongues, where thanks are due;
Fell this dread voice from lips that cannot lie,
Stern sentence of the Powers of Destiny.

"I will unfold my sentence and my crime.
My crime—that, rapt in reverential awe,
I sate obedient, in the fiery prime
Of youth, self-govern'd, at the feet of Law;
Ennobling this dull pomp, the life of kings,
By contemplation of diviner things.

"My father loved injustice, and lived long;
Crowned with gray hairs he died, and full of sway.
I loved the good he scorn'd, and hated wrong—
The Gods declare my recompence to-day.
I look'd for life more lasting, rule more high;
And when six years are measured, lo, I die!

"Yet surely, O my people, did I deem
Man's justice from the all-just Gods was given;
A light that from some upper fount did beam,
Some better archetype, whose seat was heaven;
A light that, shining from the blest abodes,
Did shadow somewhat of the life of Gods.

"Mere phantoms of man's self-tormenting heart,
Which on the sweets that woo it dares not feed!
Vain dreams, which quench our pleasures, then depart,
When the duped soul, self-master'd, claims its meed;
When, on the strenuous just man, Heaven bestows,
Crown of his struggling life, an unjust close!

"Seems it so light a thing, then, austere Powers,
To spurn man's common lure, life's pleasant things?
Seems there no joy in dances crown'd with flowers,
Love, free to range, and regal banquetings?
Bend ye on these, indeed, an unmoved eye,
Not Gods but ghosts, in frozen apathy?

B

"Or is it that some Force, too wise, too strong,
Even for yourselves to conquer or beguile,
Sweep earth, and heaven, and men, and gods along,
Like the broad volume of the insurgent Nile?
And the great powers we serve, themselves may be
Slaves of a tyrannous necessity?

"Or in mid-heaven, perhaps, your golden cars,
Where earthly voice climbs never, wing their flight,
And in wild hunt, through mazy tracts of stars,
Sweep in the sounding stillness of the night?
Or in deaf ease, on thrones of dazzling sheen,
Drinking deep draughts of joy, ye dwell serene?

"Oh, wherefore cheat our youth, if thus it be,
Of one short joy, one lust, one pleasant dream?
Stringing vain words of powers we cannot see,
Blind divinations of a will supreme;
Lost labour! when the circumambient gloom
But hides, if Gods, Gods careless of our doom?

"The rest I give to joy. Even while I speak,
My sand runs short; and—as yon star-shot ray,
Hemm'd by two banks of cloud, peers pale and weak,
Now, as the barrier closes, dies away—
Even so do past and future intertwine,
Blotting this six years' space, which yet is mine.

"Six years—six little years—six drops of time!
Yet suns shall rise, and many moons shall wane,
And old men die, and young men pass their prime,
And languid pleasure fade and flower again,
And the dull Gods behold, ere these are flown,
Revels more deep, joy keener than their own.

"Into the silence of the groves and woods
I will go forth; though something would I say—
Something—yet what, I know not; for the Gods
The doom they pass revoke not, nor delay;
And prayers, and gifts, and tears, are fruitless all,
And the night waxes, and the shadows fall.

"Ye men of Egypt, ye have heard your king!
I go, and I return not. But the will
Of the great Gods is plain; and ye must bring
Ill deeds, ill passions, zealous to fulfil
Their pleasure, to their feet; and reap their praise,
The praise of Gods, rich boon! and length of days."

—So spake he, half in anger, half in scorn;
And one loud cry of grief and of amaze
Broke from his sorrowing people; so he spake,
And turning, left them there; and with brief pause,
Girt with a throng of revellers, bent his way
To the cool region of the groves he loved.
There by the river-banks he wander'd on,
From palm-grove on to palm-grove, happy trees,
Their smooth tops shining sunward, and beneath
Burying their unsunn'd stems in grass and flowers;
Where in one dream the feverish time of youth
Might fade in slumber, and the feet of joy
Might wander all day long and never tire.
Here came the king, holding high feast, at morn,
Rose-crown'd; and ever, when the sun went down,
A hundred lamps beam'd in the tranquil gloom,
From tree to tree all through the twinkling grove,
Revealing all the tumult of the feast—
Flush'd guests, and golden goblets foam'd with wine
While the deep-burnish'd foliage overhead
Splinter'd the silver arrows of the moon.

It may be that sometimes his wondering soul
From the loud joyful laughter of his lips
Might shrink half startled, like a guilty man
Who wrestles with his dream; as some pale shape
Gliding half hidden through the dusky stems,
Would thrust a hand before the lifted bowl,
Whispering: *A little space, and thou art mine!*
It may be on that joyless feast his eye
Dwelt with mere outward seeming; he, within,
Took measure of his soul, and knew its strength,
And by that silent knowledge, day by day,
Was calm'd, ennobled, comforted, sustain'd.
It may be; but not less his brow was smooth,
And his clear laugh fled ringing through the gloom,
And his mirth quail'd not at the mild reproof
Sigh'd out by winter's sad tranquillity;
Nor, pall'd with its own fulness, ebb'd and died
In the rich languor of long summer-days;
Nor wither'd when the palm-tree plumes, that roof'd
With their mild dark his grassy banquet-hall,
Bent to the cold winds of the showerless spring;
No, nor grew dark when autumn brought the clouds.

So six long years he revell'd, night and day.
And when the mirth wax'd loudest, with dull sound

Sometimes from the grove's centre echoes came,
To tell his wondering people of their king;
In the still night, across the steaming flats,
Mix'd with the murmur of the moving Nile.

The Church of Brou

I

𝕿𝖍𝖊 𝕮𝖆𝖘𝖙𝖑𝖊

DOWN the Savoy valleys sounding,
  Echoing round this castle old,
'Mid the distant mountain-chalets
  Hark! what bell for church is toll'd?

In the bright October morning
  Savoy's Duke had left his bride.
From the castle, past the drawbridge,
  Flow'd the hunters' merry tide.

Steeds are neighing, gallants glittering;
  Gay, her smiling lord to greet,
From her mullion'd chamber-casement
  Smiles the Duchess Marguerite.

From Vienna, by the Danube,
  Here she came, a bride, in spring.
Now the autumn crisps the forest;
  Hunters gather, bugles ring.

Hounds are pulling, prickers swearing,
  Horses fret, and boar-spears glance.
Off!—They sweep the marshy forests,
  Westward, on the side of France.

Hark! the game's on foot; they scatter!—
  Down the forest-ridings lone,
Furious, single horsemen gallop—
  Hark! a shout—a crash—a groan!

Pale and breathless, came the hunters;
  On the turf dead lies the boar—
God! the Duke lies stretch'd beside him,
  Senseless, weltering in his gore.

*   *   *   *

In the dull October evening,
   Down the leaf-strewn forest-road,
To the castle, past the drawbridge,
   Came the hunters with their load.

In the hall, with sconces blazing,
   Ladies waiting round her seat,
Clothed in smiles, beneath the daïs
   Sate the Duchess Marguerite.

Hark! below the gates unbarring!
   Tramp of men and quick commands!
"—'Tis my lord come back from hunting—"
   And the Duchess claps her hands.

Slow and tired, came the hunters—
   Stopp'd in darkness in the court.
"—Ho, this way, ye laggard hunters!
   To the hall! What sport? What sport?"—

Slow they enter'd with their master;
   In the hall they laid him down.
On his coat were leaves and blood-stains,
   On his brow an angry frown.

Dead her princely youthful husband
   Lay before his youthful wife,
Bloody, 'neath the flaring sconces—
   And the sight froze all her life.

  *   *   *   *

In Vienna, by the Danube,
   Kings hold revel, gallants meet.
Gay of old amid the gayest
   Was the Duchess Marguerite.

In Vienna, by the Danube,
   Feast and dance her youth beguiled.
Till that hour she never sorrow'd;
   But from then she never smiled.

'Mid the Savoy mountain valleys
   Far from town or haunt of man,
Stands a lonely church, unfinish'd,
   Which the Duchess Maud began;

Old, that Duchess stern began it,
  In gray age, with palsied hands;
But she died while it was building,
  And the Church unfinish'd stands—

Stands as erst the builders left it,
  When she sank into her grave;
Mountain greensward paves the chancel,
  Harebells flower in the nave.

"—In my castle all is sorrow,"
  Said the Duchess Marguerite then;
"Guide me, some one, to the mountain!
  We will build the Church again."—

Sandall'd palmers, faring homeward,
  Austrian knights from Syria came.
"—Austrian wanderers bring, O warders!
  Homage to your Austrian dame."—

From the gate the warders answer'd:
  "—Gone, O knights, is she you knew!
Dead our Duke, and gone his Duchess;
  Seek her at the Church of Brou!"

Austrian knights and much-worn palmers
  Climb the winding mountain-way—
Reach the valley, where the Fabric
  Rises higher day by day.

Stones are sawing, hammers ringing;
  On the work the bright sun shines,
In the Savoy mountain-meadows,
  By the stream, below the pines.

On her palfrey white the Duchess
  Sate and watch'd her working train—
Flemish carvers, Lombard gilders,
  German masons, smiths from Spain.

Clad in black, on her white palfrey,
  Her old architect beside—
There they found her in the mountains,
  Morn and noon and eventide.

There she sate, and watch'd the builders,
  Till the Church was roof'd and done.
Last of all, the builders rear'd her
  In the nave a tomb of stone.

On the tomb two forms they sculptured,
  Lifelike in the marble pale—
One, the Duke in helm and armour;
  One, the Duchess in her veil.

Round the tomb the carved stone fretwork
  Was at Easter-tide put on.
Then the Duchess closed her labours;
  And she died at the St. John.

II

The Church

UPON the glistening leaden roof
Of the new Pile, the sunlight shines;
    The stream goes leaping by.
The hills are clothed with pines sun-proof;
'Mid bright green fields, below the pines,
    Stands the Church on high.
What Church is this, from men aloof?—
'Tis the Church of Brou.

At sunrise, from their dewy lair
Crossing the stream, the kine are seen
    Round the wall to stray—
The churchyard wall that clips the square
Of open hill-sward fresh and green
    Where last year they lay.
But all things now are order'd fair
Round the Church of Brou.

On Sundays, at the matin-chime,
The Alpine peasants, two and three,
    Climb up here to pray;
Burghers and dames, at summer's prime,
Ride out to church from Chambery,
    Dight with mantles gay.
But else it is a lonely time
Round the Church of Brou.

On Sundays, too, a priest doth come
From the wall'd town beyond the pass,
    Down the mountain-way;
And then you hear the organ's hum,
You hear the white-robed priest say mass,
    And the people pray.
But else the woods and fields are dumb
Round the Church of Brou.

And after church, when mass is done,
The people to the nave repair
    Round the tomb to stray;
And marvel at the Forms of stone,
And praise the chisell'd broideries rare—
    Then they drop away.
The princely Pair are left alone
In the Church of Brou.

III

The Tomb

So rest, for ever rest, O princely Pair!
In your high church, 'mid the still mountain-air,
Where horn, and hound, and vassals, never come.
Only the blessed Saints are smiling dumb,
From the rich painted windows of the nave,
On aisle, and transept, and your marble grave;
Where thou, young Prince! shalt never more arise
From the fringed mattress where thy Duchess lies,
On autumn-mornings, when the bugle sounds,
And ride across the drawbridge with thy hounds
To hunt the boar in the crisp woods till eve;
And thou, O Princess! shalt no more receive,
Thou and thy ladies, in the hall of state,
The jaded hunters with their bloody freight,
Coming benighted to the castle-gate.
    So sleep, for ever sleep, O marble Pair!
Or, if ye wake, let it be then, when fair
On the carved western front a flood of light
Streams from the setting sun, and colours bright
Prophets, transfigured Saints, and Martyrs brave,
In the vast western window of the nave;
And on the pavement round the Tomb there glints
A chequer-work of glowing sapphire-tints,

And amethyst, and ruby—then unclose
Your eyelids on the stone where ye repose,
And from your broider'd pillows lift your heads,
And rise upon your cold white marble beds;
And, looking down on the warm rosy tints,
Which chequer, at your feet, the illumined flints,
Say: *What is this? we are in bliss—forgiven—*
Behold the pavement of the courts of Heaven!
Or let it be on autumn nights, when rain
Doth rustlingly above your heads complain
On the smooth leaden roof, and on the walls
Shedding her pensive light at intervals
The moon through the clere-story windows shines,
And the wind washes through the mountain-pines.
Then, gazing up 'mid the dim pillars high,
The foliaged marble forest where ye lie,
Hush, ye will say, *it is eternity!*
This is the glimmering verge of Heaven, and these
The columns of the heavenly palaces!
And, in the sweeping of the wind, your ear
The passage of the Angels' wings will hear,
And on the lichen-crusted leads above
The rustle of the eternal rain of love.

A Modern Sappho

THEY are gone—all is still! Foolish heart, dost thou quiver?
    Nothing stirs on the lawn but the quick lilac-shade.
Far up shines the house, and beneath flows the river—
    Here lean, my head, on this cold balustrade!

Ere he come—ere the boat by the shining-branch'd border
    Of dark elms shoot round, dropping down the proud stream,
Let me pause, let me strive, in myself make some order,
    Ere their boat-music sound, ere their broider'd flags gleam.

Last night we stood earnestly talking together;
    She enter'd—that moment his eyes turn'd from me!
Fasten'd on her dark hair, and her wreath of white heather—
    As yesterday was, so to-morrow will be.

Their love, let me know, must grow strong and yet stronger,
    Their passion burn more, ere it ceases to burn.
They must love—while they must! but the hearts that love
        longer
    Are rare—ah! most loves but flow once, and return.

I shall suffer—but they will outlive their affection;
  I shall weep—but their love will be cooling; and he,
As he drifts to fatigue, discontent, and dejection,
  Will be brought, thou poor heart, how much nearer to thee!

For cold is his eye to mere beauty, who, breaking
  The strong band which passion around him hath furl'd,
Disenchanted by habit, and newly awaking,
  Looks languidly round on a gloom-buried world.

Through that gloom he will see but a shadow appearing,
  Perceive but a voice as I come to his side—
But deeper their voice grows, and nobler their bearing,
  Whose youth in the fires of anguish hath died.

So, to wait!—But what notes down the wind, hark! are driving?
  'Tis he! 'tis their flag, shooting round by the trees!
—Let my turn, if it *will* come, be swift in arriving!
  Ah! hope cannot long lighten torments like these.

Hast thou yet dealt him, O life, thy full measure?
  World, have thy children yet bow'd at his knee?
Hast thou with myrtle-leaf crown'd him, O pleasure?
  —Crown, crown him quickly, and leave him for me!

Requiescat

STREW on her roses, roses,
  And never a spray of yew!
In quiet she reposes;
  Ah, would that I did too!

Her mirth the world required;
  She bathed it in smiles of glee.
But her heart was tired, tired,
  And now they let her be.

Her life was turning, turning,
  In mazes of heat and sound.
But for peace her soul was yearning,
  And now peace laps her round.

Her cabin'd, ample spirit,
  It flutter'd and fail'd for breath.
To-night it doth inherit
  The vasty hall of death.

Youth and Calm

'Tis death! and peace, indeed, is here,
And ease from shame, and rest from fear.
There's nothing can dismarble now
The smoothness of that limpid brow.
But is a calm like this, in truth,
The crowning end of life and youth,
And when this boon rewards the dead,
Are all debts paid, has all been said?
And is the heart of youth so light,
Its step so firm, its eyes so bright,
Because on its hot brow there blows
A wind of promise and repose
From the far grave, to which it goes;
Because it hath the hope to come,
One day, to harbour in the tomb?
Ah no, the bliss youth dreams is one
For daylight, for the cheerful sun,
For feeling nerves and living breath—
Youth dreams a bliss on this side death.
It dreams a rest, if not more deep,
More grateful than this marble sleep;
It hears a voice within it tell:
Calm's not life's crown, though calm is well.
'Tis all perhaps which man acquires,
But 'tis not what our youth desires.

A Memory-Picture

LAUGH, my friends, and without blame
Lightly quit what lightly came;
Rich to-morrow as to-day,
Spend as madly as you may!
I, with little land to stir,
Am the exacter labourer.
  Ere the parting hour go by,
  Quick, thy tablets, Memory!

Once I said: "A face is gone
If too hotly mused upon;
And our best impressions are
Those that do themselves repair."

Many a face I so let flee,
Ah! is faded utterly.
  Ere the parting hour go by,
  Quick, thy tablets, Memory!

Marguerite says: "As last year went,
So the coming year'll be spent;
Some day next year, I shall be,
Entering heedless, kiss'd by thee."
Ah, I hope!—yet, once away,
What may chain us, who can say?
  Ere the parting hour go by,
  Quick, thy tablets, Memory!

Paint that lilac kerchief, bound
Her soft face, her hair around;
Tied under the archest chin
Mockery ever ambush'd in.
Let the fluttering fringes streak
All her pale, sweet-rounded cheek.
  Ere the parting hour go by,
  Quick, thy tablets, Memory!

Paint that figure's pliant grace
As she tow'rd me lean'd her face,
Half refused and half resign'd,
Murmuring: "Art thou still unkind?"
Many a broken promise then
Was new made—to break again.
  Ere the parting hour go by,
  Quick, thy tablets, Memory!

Paint those eyes, so blue, so kind,
Eager tell-tales of her mind;
Paint, with their impetuous stress
Of inquiring tenderness,
Those frank eyes, where deep I see
An angelic gravity.
  Ere the parting hour go by,
  Quick, thy tablets, Memory!

What, my friends, these feeble lines
Show, you say, my love declines?
To paint ill as I have done,
Proves forgetfulness begun?

Time's gay minions, pleased you see,
Time, your master, governs me;
 Pleased, you mock the fruitless cry:
 "Quick, thy tablets, Memory!"

Ah, too true! Time's current strong
Leaves us fixt to nothing long.
Yet, if little stays with man,
Ah, retain we all we can!
If the clear impression dies,
Ah, the dim remembrance prize!
 Ere the parting hour go by,
 Quick, thy tablets, Memory!

A Dream

WAS it a dream? We sail'd, I thought we sail'd,
Martin and I, down a green Alpine stream,
Border'd, each bank, with pines; the morning sun,
On the wet umbrage of their glossy tops,
On the red pinings of their forest-floor,
Drew a warm scent abroad; behind the pines
The mountain-skirts, with all their sylvan change
Of bright-leaf'd chestnuts and moss'd walnut-trees
And the frail scarlet-berried ash, began.
Swiss chalets glitter'd on the dewy slopes,
And from some swarded shelf, high up, there came
Notes of wild pastoral music—over all
Ranged, diamond-bright, the eternal wall of snow.
Upon the mossy rocks at the stream's edge,
Back'd by the pines, a plank-built cottage stood,
Bright in the sun; the climbing gourd-plant's leaves
Muffled its walls, and on the stone-strewn roof
Lay the warm golden gourds; golden, within,
Under the eaves, peer'd rows of Indian corn.
We shot beneath the cottage with the stream.
On the brown, rude-carved balcony, two forms
Came forth—Olivia's Marguerite! and thine.
Clad were they both in white, flowers in their breast;
Straw hats bedeck'd their heads, with ribbons blue,
Which danced, and on their shoulders, fluttering, play'd.
They saw us, they conferr'd; their bosoms heaved,
And more than mortal impulse fill'd their eyes.
Their lips moved; their white arms, waved eagerly,

Flash'd once, like falling streams; we rose, we gazed.
One moment, on the rapid's top, our boat
Hung poised—and then the darting river of Life
(Such now, methought, it was), the river of Life,
Loud thundering, bore us by; swift, swift it foam'd,
Black under cliffs it raced, round headlands shone.
Soon the plank'd cottage by the sun-warm'd pines
Faded—the moss—the rocks; us burning plains,
Bristled with cities, us the sea received.

Youth's Agitations

WHEN I shall be divorced, some ten years hence,
From this poor present self which I am now;
When youth has done its tedious vain expense
Of passions that for ever ebb and flow;

Shall I not joy youth's heats are left behind,
And breathe more happy in an even clime?—
Ah no, for then I shall begin to find
A thousand virtues in this hated time!

Then I shall wish its agitations back,
And all its thwarting currents of desire;
Then I shall praise the heat which then I lack,
And call this hurrying fever, generous fire;

And sigh that one thing only has been lent
To youth and age in common—discontent.

Human Life

WHAT mortal, when he saw,
Life's voyage done, his heavenly Friend,
Could ever yet dare tell him fearlessly:
"I have kept uninfringed my nature's law;
The inly-written chart thou gavest me,
To guide me, I have steer'd by to the end"?

Ah! let us make no claim,
On life's incognisable sea,
To too exact a steering of our way;
Let us not fret and fear to miss our aim,
If some fair coast have lured us to make stay,
Or some friend hail'd us to keep company.

Ay! we would each fain drive
At random, and not steer by rule.
Weakness! and worse, weakness bestow'd in vain
Winds from our side the unsuiting consort rive,
We rush by coasts where we had lief remain;
Man cannot, though he would, live chance's fool.

No! as the foaming swath
Of torn-up water, on the main,
Falls heavily away with long-drawn roar
On either side the black deep-furrow'd path
Cut by an onward-labouring vessel's prore,
And never touches the ship-side again;

Even so we leave behind,
As, charter'd by some unknown Powers,
We stem across the sea of life by night,
The joys which were not for our use design'd;—
The friends to whom we had no natural right,
The homes that were not destined to be ours.

To a Gipsy Child by the Sea-Shore

Douglas, Isle of Man

WHO taught this pleading to unpractised eyes?
Who hid such import in an infant's gloom?
Who lent thee, child, this meditative guise?
Who mass'd, round that slight brow, these clouds of
  doom?

Lo! sails that gleam a moment and are gone;
The swinging waters, and the cluster'd pier.
Not idly Earth and Ocean labour on,
Nor idly do these sea-birds hover near.

But thou, whom superfluity of joy
Wafts not from thine own thoughts, nor longings vain,
Nor weariness, the full-fed soul's annoy—
Remaining in thy hunger and thy pain;

Thou, drugging pain by patience; half averse
From thine own mother's breast, that knows not thee;
With eyes which sought thine eyes thou didst converse,
And that soul-searching vision fell on me.

Glooms that go deep as thine I have not known:
Moods of fantastic sadness, nothing worth.
Thy sorrow and thy calmness are thine own:
Glooms that enhance and glorify this earth.

What mood wears like complexion to thy woe?
His, who in mountain glens, at noon of day,
Sits rapt, and hears the battle break below?
—Ah! thine was not the shelter, but the fray.

Some exile's, mindful how the past was glad?
Some angel's, in an alien planet born?
—No exile's dream was ever half so sad,
Nor any angel's sorrow so forlorn.

Is the calm thine of stoic souls, who weigh
Life well, and find it wanting, nor deplore;
But in disdainful silence turn away,
Stand mute, self-centred, stern, and dream no more?

Or do I wait, to hear some gray-hair'd king
Unravel all his many-colour'd lore;
Whose mind hath known all arts of governing,
Mused much, loved life a little, loathed it more?

Down the pale cheek long lines of shadow slope,
Which years, and curious thought, and suffering give.
—Thou hast foreknown the vanity of hope,
Foreseen thy harvest—yet proceed'st to live.

O meek anticipant of that sure pain
Whose sureness gray-hair'd scholars hardly learn!
What wonder shall time breed, to swell thy strain?
What heavens, what earth, what sun shalt thou discern?

Ere the long night, whose stillness brooks no star,
Match that funereal aspect with her pall,
I think, thou wilt have fathom'd life too far,
Have known too much——or else forgotten all.

The Guide of our dark steps a triple veil
Betwixt our senses and our sorrow keeps;
Hath sown with cloudless passages the tale
Of grief, and eased us with a thousand sleeps.

Ah! not the nectarous poppy lovers use,
Not daily labour's dull, Lethæan spring,
Oblivion in lost angels can infuse
Of the soil'd glory, and the trailing wing.

And though thou glean, what strenuous gleaners may,
In the throng'd fields where winning comes by strife;
And though the just sun gild, as mortals pray,
Some reaches of thy storm-vext stream of life;

Though that blank sunshine blind thee; though the cloud
That sever'd the world's march and thine, be gone;
Though ease dulls grace, and Wisdom be too proud
To halve a lodging that was all her own—

Once, ere the day decline, thou shalt discern,
Oh once, ere night, in thy success, thy chain!
Ere the long evening close, thou shalt return,
And wear this majesty of grief again.

In Utrumque Paratus

IF, in the silent mind of One all-pure,
    At first imagined lay
The sacred world; and by procession sure
From those still deeps, in form and colour drest,
Seasons alternating, and night and day,
The long-mused thought to north, south, east, and west,
    Took then its all-seen way;

O waking on a world which thus-wise springs!
    Whether it needs thee count
Betwixt thy waking and the birth of things
Ages or hours—O waking on life's stream!
By lonely pureness to the all-pure fount
(Only by this thou canst) the colour'd dream
    Of life remount!

Thin, thin the pleasant human noises grow,
    And faint the city gleams;
Rare the lone pastoral huts—marvel not thou!
The solemn peaks but to the stars are known,
But to the stars, and the cold lunar beams;
Alone the sun arises, and alone
    Spring the great streams.

But, if the wild unfather'd mass no birth
     In divine seats hath known;
In the blank, echoing solitude if Earth,
Rocking her obscure body to and fro,
Ceases not from all time to heave and groan,
Unfruitful oft, and at her happiest throe
     Forms, what she forms, alone;

O seeming sole to awake, thy sun-bathed head
     Piercing the solemn cloud
Round thy still dreaming brother-world outspread!
O man, whom Earth, thy long-vext mother, bare
Not without joy—so radiant, so endow'd
(Such happy issue crown'd her painful care)—
     Be not too proud!

Oh when most self-exalted most alone,
     Chief dreamer, own thy dream!
Thy brother-world stirs at thy feet unknown,
Who hath a monarch's hath no brother's part;
Yet doth thine inmost soul with yearning teem.
—Oh, what a spasm shakes the dreamer's heart!
     "*I, too, but seem.*"

Resignation

To Fausta

To die be given us, or attain!
Fierce work it were, to do again.
So pilgrims, bound for Mecca, pray'd
At burning noon; so warriors said,
Scarf'd with the cross, who watch'd the miles
Of dust which wreathed their struggling files
Down Lydian mountains; so, when snows
Round Alpine summits, eddying, rose,
The Goth, bound Rome-wards; so the Hun,
Crouch'd on his saddle, while the sun
Went lurid down o'er flooded plains
Through which the groaning Danube strains
To the drear Euxine;—so pray all,
Whom labours, self-ordain'd, enthrall;
Because they to themselves propose
On this side the all-common close
A goal which, gain'd, may give repose.

So pray they; and to stand again
Where they stood once, to them were pain;
Pain to thread back and to renew
Past straits, and currents long steer'd through.

But milder natures, and more free—
Whom an unblamed serenity
Hath freed from passions, and the state
Of struggle these necessitate;
Whom schooling of the stubborn mind
Hath made, or birth hath found, resign'd—
These mourn not, that their goings pay
Obedience to the passing day.
These claim not every laughing Hour
For handmaid to their striding power;
Each in her turn, with torch uprear'd,
To await their march; and when appear'd,
Through the cold gloom, with measured race,
To usher for a destined space
(Her own sweet errands all forgone)
The too imperious traveller on.
These, Fausta, ask not this; nor thou,
Time's chafing prisoner, ask it now!

We left, just ten years since, you say,
That wayside inn we left to-day.
Our jovial host, as forth we fare,
Shouts greeting from his easy chair.
High on a bank our leader stands,
Reviews and ranks his motley bands,
Makes clear our goal to every eye—
The valley's western boundary.
A gate swings to! our tide hath flow'd
Already from the silent road.
The valley-pastures, one by one,
Are threaded, quiet in the sun;
And now beyond the rude stone bridge
Slopes gracious up the western ridge.
Its woody border, and the last
Of its dark upland farms is past—
Cool farms, with open-lying stores,
Under their burnish'd sycamores;
All past! and through the trees we glide,
Emerging on the green hill-side.
There climbing hangs, a far-seen sign,
Our wavering, many-colour'd line;

There winds, upstreaming slowly still
Over the summit of the hill.
And now, in front, behold outspread
Those upper regions we must tread!
Mild hollows, and clear heathy swells,
The cheerful silence of the fells.
Some two hours' march with serious air,
Through the deep noontide heats we fare;
The red-grouse, springing at our sound,
Skims, now and then, the shining ground;
No life, save his and ours, intrudes
Upon these breathless solitudes.
O joy! again the farms appear.
Cool shade is there, and rustic cheer;
There springs the brook will guide us down,
Bright comrade, to the noisy town.
Lingering, we follow down; we gain
The town, the highway, and the plain.
And many a mile of dusty way,
Parch'd and road-worn, we made that day;
But, Fausta, I remember well,
That as the balmy darkness fell
We bathed our hands with speechless glee,
That night, in the wide-glimmering sea.

Once more we tread this self-same road,
Fausta, which ten years since we trod;
Alone we tread it, you and I,
Ghosts of that boisterous company.
Here, where the brook shines, near its head,
In its clear, shallow, turf-fringed bed;
Here, whence the eye first sees, far down,
Capp'd with faint smoke, the noisy town;
Here sit we, and again unroll,
Though slowly, the familiar whole.
The solemn wastes of heathy hill
Sleep in the July sunshine still;
The self-same shadows now, as then,
Play through this grassy upland glen;
The loose dark stones on the green way
Lie strewn, it seems, where then they lay;
On this mild bank above the stream,
(You crush them!) the blue gentians gleam.
Still this wild brook, the rushes cool,
The sailing foam, the shining pool!

These are not changed; and we, you say,
Are scarce more changed, in truth, than they.

The gipsies, whom we met below,
They, too, have long roam'd to and fro;
They ramble, leaving, where they pass,
Their fragments on the cumber'd grass.
And often to some kindly place
Chance guides the migratory race,
Where, though long wanderings intervene,
They recognise a former scene.
The dingy tents are pitch'd; the fires
Give to the wind their wavering spires;
In dark knots crouch round the wild flame
Their children, as when first they came;
They see their shackled beasts again
Move, browsing, up the grey-wall'd lane.
Signs are not wanting, which might raise
The ghost in them of former days—
Signs are not wanting, if they would;
Suggestions to disquietude.
For them, for all, time's busy touch,
While it mends little, troubles much.
Their joints grow stiffer—but the year
Runs his old round of dubious cheer;
Chilly they grow—yet winds in March,
Still, sharp as ever, freeze and parch;
They must live still—and yet, God knows,
Crowded and keen the country grows;
It seems as if, in their decay,
The law grew stronger every day.
So might they reason, so compare,
Fausta, times past with times that are.
But no!—they rubb'd through yesterday
In their hereditary way,
And they will rub through, if they can,
To-morrow on the self-same plan,
Till death arrive to supersede,
For them, vicissitude and need.

The poet, to whose mighty heart
Heaven doth a quicker pulse impart,
Subdues that energy to scan
Not his own course, but that of man.
Though he moves mountains, though his day
Be pass'd on the proud heights of sway,

Though he hath loosed a thousand chains,
Though he hath borne immortal pains,
Action and suffering though he know—
He hath not lived, if he lives so.
He sees, in some great-historied land,
A ruler of the people stand,
Sees his strong thought in fiery flood
Roll through the heaving multitude
Exults—yet for no moment's space
Envies the all-regarded place.
Beautiful eyes meet his—and he
Bears to admire uncravingly;
They pass—he, mingled with the crowd,
Is in their far-off triumphs proud.
From some high station he looks down,
At sunset, on a populous town;
Surveys each happy group, which fleets,
Toil ended, through the shining streets,
Each with some errand of its own—
And does not say: *I am alone.*
He sees the gentle stir of birth
When morning purifies the earth;
He leans upon a gate and sees
The pastures, and the quiet trees.
Low, woody hill, with gracious bound,
Folds the still valley almost round;
The cuckoo, loud on some high lawn,
Is answer'd from the depth of dawn;
In the hedge straggling to the stream,
Pale, dew-drench'd, half-shut roses gleam;
But, where the farther side slopes down,
He sees the drowsy new-waked clown
In his white quaint-embroider'd frock
Make, whistling, tow'rd his mist-wreathed flock—
Slowly, behind his heavy tread,
The wet, flower'd grass heaves up its head.
Lean'd on his gate, he gazes—tears
Are in his eyes, and in his ears
The murmur of a thousand years.
Before him he sees life unroll,
A placid and continuous whole—
That general life, which does not cease,
Whose secret is not joy, but peace;
That life, whose dumb wish is not miss'd
If birth proceeds, if things subsist;

The life of plants, and stones, and rain,
The life he craves—if not in vain
Fate gave, what chance shall not control,
His sad lucidity of soul.

You listen—but that wandering smile,
Fausta, betrays you cold the while!
Your eyes pursue the bells of foam
Wash'd, eddying, from this bank, their home.
Those gipsies, so your thoughts I scan,
Are less, the poet more, than man.
They feel not, though they move and see;
Deeper the poet feels; but he
Breathes, when he will, immortal air,
Where Orpheus and where Homer are.
In the day's life, whose iron round
Hems us all in, he is not bound;
He leaves his kind, o'erleaps their pen,
And flees the common life of men.
He escapes thence, but we abide—
Not deep the poet sees, but wide.

The world in which we live and move
Outlasts aversion, outlasts love,
Outlasts each effort, interest, hope,
Remorse, grief, joy;—and were the scope
Of these affections wider made,
Man still would see, and see dismay'd,
Beyond his passion's widest range,
Far regions of eternal change.
Nay, and since death, which wipes out man,
Finds him with many an unsolved plan,
With much unknown, and much untried,
Wonder not dead, and thirst not dried,
Still gazing on the ever full
Eternal mundane spectacle—
This world in which we draw our breath,
In some sense, Fausta, outlasts death.

Blame thou not, therefore, him who dares
Judge vain beforehand human cares;
Whose natural insight can discern
What through experience others learn;
Who needs not love and power, to know
Love transient, power an unreal show;

Who treads at ease life's uncheer'd ways—
Him blame not, Fausta, rather praise!
Rather thyself for some aim pray
Nobler than this, to fill the day;
Rather that heart, which burns in thee,
Ask, not to amuse, but to set free;
Be passionate hopes not ill resign'd
For quiet, and a fearless mind.
And though fate grudge to thee and me
The poet's rapt security,
Yet they, believe me, who await
No gifts from chance, have conquer'd fate.
They, winning room to see and hear,
And to men's business not too near,
Through clouds of individual strife
Draw homeward to the general life.
Like leaves by suns not yet uncurl'd;
To the wise, foolish; to the world,
Weak;—yet not weak, I might reply,
Not foolish, Fausta, in His eye,
To whom each moment in its race,
Crowd as we will its neutral space,
Is but a quiet watershed
Whence, equally, the seas of life and death are fed.

Enough, we live!—and if a life,
With large results so little rife,
Though bearable, seem hardly worth
This pomp of worlds, this pain of birth;
Yet, Fausta, the mute turf we tread,
The solemn hills around us spread,
This stream which falls incessantly,
The strange-scrawl'd rocks, the lonely sky,
If I might lend their life a voice,
Seem to bear rather than rejoice.
And even could the intemperate prayer
Man iterates, while these forbear,
For movement, for an ampler sphere,
Pierce Fate's impenetrable ear;
Not milder is the general lot
Because our spirits have forgot,
In action's dizzying eddy whirl'd,
The something that infects the world.

NARRATIVE POEMS

Notes on Narrative Poems, pp. 785-6.

NARRATIVE POEMS

Sohrab and Rustum

An Episode

AND the first grey of morning fill'd the east,
And the fog rose out of the Oxus stream.
But all the Tartar camp along the stream
Was hush'd, and still the men were plunged in sleep;
Sohrab alone, he slept not; all night long
He had lain wakeful, tossing on his bed;
But when the grey dawn stole into his tent,
He rose, and clad himself, and girt his sword,
And took his horseman's cloak, and left his tent,
And went abroad into the cold wet fog,
Through the dim camp to Peran-Wisa's tent.
    Through the black Tartar tents he pass'd, which stood
Clustering like bee-hives on the low flat strand
Of Oxus, where the summer-floods o'erflow
When the sun melts the snows in high Pamere;
Through the black tents he pass'd, o'er that low strand,
And to a hillock came, a little back
From the stream's brink—the spot where first a boat,
Crossing the stream in summer, scrapes the land.
The men of former times had crown'd the top
With a clay fort; but that was fall'n, and now
The Tartars built there Peran-Wisa's tent,
A dome of laths, and o'er it felts were spread.
And Sohrab came there, and went in, and stood
Upon the thick piled carpets in the tent,
And found the old man sleeping on his bed
Of rugs and felts, and near him lay his arms.
And Peran-Wisa heard him, though the step
Was dull'd; for he slept light, an old man's sleep;
And he rose quickly on one arm, and said:—
    "Who art thou? for it is not yet clear dawn.
Speak! is there news, or any night alarm?"
    But Sohrab came to the bedside, and said:—
"Thou know'st me, Peran-Wisa! it is I.

The sun is not yet risen, and the foe
Sleep; but I sleep not; all night long I lie
Tossing and wakeful, and I come to thee.
For so did King Afrasiab bid me seek
Thy counsel, and to heed thee as thy son,
In Samarcand, before the army march'd;
And I will tell thee what my heart desires.
Thou know'st if, since from Ader-baijan first
I came among the Tartars and bore arms,
I have still served Afrasiab well, and shown,
At my boy's years, the courage of a man.
This too thou know'st, that while I still bear on
The conquering Tartar ensigns through the world,
And beat the Persians back on every field,
I seek one man, one man, and one alone—
Rustum, my father; who I hoped should greet,
Should one day greet, upon some well-fought field,
His not unworthy, not inglorious son.
So I long hoped, but him I never find.
Come then, hear now, and grant me what I ask.
Let the two armies rest to-day; but I
Will challenge forth the bravest Persian lords
To meet me, man to man; if I prevail,
Rustum will surely hear it; if I fall—
Old man, the dead need no one, claim no kin.
Dim is the rumour of a common fight,
Where host meets host, and many names are sunk;
But of a single combat fame speaks clear."
      He spoke; and Peran-Wisa took the hand
Of the young man in his, and sigh'd, and said:—
      "O Sohrab, an unquiet heart is thine!
Canst thou not rest among the Tartar chiefs,
And share the battle's common chance with us
Who love thee, but must press for ever first,
In single fight incurring single risk,
To find a father thou hast never seen?
That were far best, my son, to stay with us
Unmurmuring; in our tents, while it is war,
And when 'tis truce, then in Afrasiab's towns.
But, if this one desire indeed rules all,
To seek out Rustum—seek him not through fight!
Seek him in peace, and carry to his arms,
O Sohrab, carry an unwounded son!
But far hence seek him, for he is not here.
For now it is not as when I was young,

When Rustum was in front of every fray;
But now he keeps apart, and sits at home,
In Seistan, with Zal, his father old.
Whether that his own mighty strength at last
Feels the abhorr'd approaches of old age,
Or in some quarrel with the Persian King.
There go!—Thou wilt not? Yet my heart forebodes
Danger or death awaits thee on this field.
Fain would I know thee safe and well, though lost
To us; fain therefore send thee hence, in peace
To seek thy father, not seek single fights
In vain;—but who can keep the lion's cub
From ravening, and who govern Rustum's son?
Go, I will grant thee what thy heart desires."

   So said he, and dropp'd Sohrab's hand, and left
His bed, and the warm rugs whereon he lay;
And o'er his chilly limbs his woollen coat
He pass'd, and tied his sandals on his feet,
And threw a white cloak round him, and he took
In his right hand a ruler's staff, no sword;
And on his head he set his sheep-skin cap,
Black, glossy, curl'd, the fleece of Kara-Kul;
And raised the curtain of his tent, and call'd
His herald to his side, and went abroad.

   The sun by this had risen, and clear'd the fog
From the broad Oxus and the glittering sands.
And from their tents the Tartar horseman filed
Into the open plain; so Haman bade—
Haman, who next to Peran-Wisa ruled
The host, and still was in his lusty prime.
From their black tents, long files of horse, they stream'd;
As when some grey November morn the files,
In marching order spread, of long-neck'd cranes
Stream over Casbin and the southern slopes
Or Elburz, from the Aralian estuaries,
Or some frore Caspain reed-bed, southward bound
For the warm Persian sea-board—so they stream'd.
The Tartars of the Oxus, the King's guard,
First, with black sheep-skin caps and with long spears;
Large men, large steeds; who from Bokhara come
And Khiva, and ferment the milk of mares.
Next, the more temperate Toorkmuns of the south,
The Tukas, and the lances of Salore,
And those from Attruck and the Caspian sands;
Light men and on light steeds, who only drink

The acrid milk of camels, and their wells.
And then a swarm of wandering horse, who came
From far, and a more doubtful service own'd;
The Tartars of Ferghana, from the banks
Of the Jaxartes, men with scanty beards
And close-set skull-caps; and those wilder hordes
Who roam o'er Kipchak and the northern waste,
Kalmucks and unkempt Kuzzaks, tribes who stray
Nearest the Pole, and wandering Kirghizzes,
Who come on shaggy ponies from Pamere;
These all filed out from camp into the plain.
And on the other side the Persians form'd;—
First a light cloud of horse, Tartars they seem'd,
The Ilyats of Khorassan; and behind,
The royal troops of Persia, horse and foot,
Marshall'd battalions bright in burnish'd steel.
But Peran-Wisa with his herald came,
Threading the Tartar squadrons to the front,
And with his staff kept back the foremost ranks.
And when Ferood, who led the Persians, saw
That Peran-Wisa kept the Tartars back,
He took his spear, and to the front he came,
And check'd his ranks, fix'd them where they stood.
And the old Tartar came upon the sand
Betwixt the silent hosts, and spake, and said:—
    "Ferood, and ye, Persians and Tartars, hear!
Let there be truce between the hosts to-day.
But choose a champion from the Persian lords
To fight our champion Sohrab, man to man."
    As, in the country, on a morn in June,
When the dew glistens on the pearled ears,
A shiver runs through the deep corn for joy—
So, when they heard what Peran-Wisa said,
A thrill through all the Tartar squadrons ran
Of pride and hope for Sohrab, whom they loved.
    But as a troop of pedlars, from Cabool,
Cross underneath the Indian Caucasus,
That vast sky-neighbouring mountain of milk snow;
Crossing so high, that, as they mount, they pass
Long flocks of travelling birds dead on the snow,
Choked by the air, and scarce can they themselves
Slake their parch'd throats with sugar'd mulberries—
In single file they move, and stop their breath
For fear they should dislodge the o'erhanging snows—
So the pale Persians held their breath with fear.

And to Ferood his brother chiefs came up
To counsel; Gudurz and Zoarrah came,
And Feraburz, who ruled the Persian host
Second, and was the uncle of the King;
These came and counsell'd, and then Gudurz said:—
"Ferood, shame bids us take their challenge up,
Yet champion have we none to match this youth.
He has the wild stag's foot, the lion's heart.
But Rustum came last night; aloof he sits
And sullen, and has pitch'd his tents apart.
Him will I seek, and carry to his ear
The Tartar challenge, and this young man's name.
Haply he will forget his wrath, and fight.
Stand forth the while, and take their challenge up."
So spake he; and Ferood stood forth and cried:—
"Old man, be it agreed as thou hast said!
Let Sohrab arm, and we will find a man."
He spake: and Peran-Wisa turn'd, and strode
Back through the opening squadrons to his tent.
But through the anxious Persians Gudurz ran,
And cross'd the camp which lay behind, and reach'd,
Out on the sands beyond it, Rustum's tents.
Of scarlet cloth they were, and glittering gay,
Just pitch'd; the high pavilion in the midst
Was Rustum's, and his men lay camp'd around.
And Gudurz enter'd Rustum's tent, and found
Rustum; his morning meal was done, but still
The table stood before him, charged with food—
A side of roasted sheep, and cakes of bread,
And dark green melons; and there Rustum sate
Listless, and held a falcon on his wrist,
And play'd with it; but Gudurz came and stood
Before him; and he look'd, and saw him stand,
And with a cry sprang up and dropp'd the bird,
And greeted Gudurz with both hands, and said:—
"Welcome! these eyes could see no better sight.
What news? but sit down first, and eat and drink."
But Gudurz stood in the tent-door, and said:—
"Not now! a time will come to eat and drink,
But not to-day; to-day has other needs.
The armies are drawn out, and stand at gaze;
For from the Tartars is a challenge brought
To pick a champion from the Persian lords
To fight their champion—and thou know'st his name—
Sohrab men call him, but his birth is hid.

O Rustum, like thy might is this young man's!
He has the wild stag's foot, and lion's heart;
And he is young, and Iran's chiefs are old,
Or else too weak; and all eyes turn to thee.
Come down and help us, Rustum, or we lose!"
    He spoke; but Rustum answer'd with a smile:—
"Go to! if Iran's chiefs are old, then I
Am older; if the young are weak, the King
Errs strangely; for the King, for Kai Khosroo,
Himself is young, and honours younger men,
And lets the aged moulder to their graves.
Rustum he loves no more, but loves the young—
The young may rise at Sohrab's vaunts, not I.
For what care I, though all speak Sohrab's fame?
For would that I myself had such a son,
And not that one slight helpless girl I have—
A son so famed, so brave, to send to war,
And I to tarry with the snow-hair'd Zal,
My father, whom the robber Afghans vex,
And clip his borders short, and drive his herds,
And he has none to guard his weak old age.
There would I go, and hang my armour up,
And with my great name fence that weak old man,
And spend the goodly treasures I have got,
And rest my age, and hear of Sohrab's fame,
And leave to death the hosts of thankless kings,
And with these slaughterous hands draw sword no more."
    He spoke, and smiled; and Gudurz made reply:—
"What then, O Rustum, will men say to this,
When Sohrab dares our bravest forth, and seeks
Thee most of all, and thou, whom most he seeks,
Hidest thy face? Take heed lest men should say:
Like some old miser, Rustum hoards his fame,
And shuns to peril it with younger men."
    And, greatly moved, then Rustum made reply:—
"O Gudurz, wherefore dost thou say such words?
Thou knowest better words than this to say.
What is one more, one less, obscure or famed,
Valiant or craven, young or old, to me?
Are not they mortal, am not I myself?
But who for men of nought would do great deeds?
Come, thou shalt see how Rustum hoards his fame!
But I will fight unknown, and in plain arms;
Let not men say of Rustum, he was match'd
In single fight with any mortal man."

He spoke, and frown'd; and Gudurz turn'd, and ran
Back quickly through the camp in fear and joy—
Fear at his wrath, but joy that Rustum came.
But Rustum strode to his tent-door, and call'd
His followers in, and bade them bring his arms,
And clad himself in steel; the arms he chose
Were plain, and on his shield was no device,
Only his helm was rich, inlaid with gold,
And, from the fluted spine atop, a plume
Of horsehair waved, a scarlet horsehair plume.
So arm'd, he issued forth; and Ruksh, his horse,
Follow'd him like a faithful hound at heel—
Ruksh, whose renown was noised through all the earth,
The horse, whom Rustum on a foray once
Did in Bokhara by the river find
A colt beneath its dam, and drove him home
And rear'd him; a bright bay, with lofty crest,
Dight with a saddle-cloth of broider'd green
Crusted with gold, and on the ground were work'd
All beasts of chase, all bears which hunters know.
So follow'd, Rustum left his tents, and cross'd
The camp, and to the Persian host appear'd.
And all the Persians knew him, and with shouts
Hail'd; but the Tartars knew not who he was.
And dear as the wet diver to the eyes
Of his pale wife who waits and weeps on shore,
By sandy Bahrein, in the Persian Gulf,
Plunging all day in the blue waves, at night,
Having made up his tale of precious pearls,
Rejoins her in their hut upon the sands—
So dear to the pale Persians Rustum came.

And Rustum to the Persian front advanced,
And Sohrab arm'd in Haman's tent, and came.
And as afield the reapers cut a swath
Down through the middle of a rich man's corn,
And on each side are squares of standing corn,
And in the midst a stubble, short and bare—
So on each side were squares of men, with spears
Bristling, and in the midst, the open sand.
And Rustum came upon the sand, and cast
His eyes toward the Tartar tents, and saw
Sohrab come forth, and eyed him as he came.

As some rich woman, on a winter's morn,
Eyes through her silken curtains the poor drudge
Who with numb blacken'd fingers makes her fire—

C

At cock-crow, on a starlit winter's morn,
When the frost flowers the whiten'd window-panes—
And wonders how she lives, and what the thoughts
Of that poor drudge may be; so Rustum eyed
The unknown adventurous youth, who from afar
Came seeking Rustum, and defying forth
All the most valiant chiefs; long he perused
His spirited air, and wonder'd who he was.
For very young he seem'd, tenderly rear'd;
Like some young cypress, tall, and dark, and straight,
Which in a queen's secluded garden throws
Its slight dark shadow on the moonlit turf,
By midnight, to a bubbling fountain's sound—
So slender Sohrab seem'd, so softly rear'd.
And a deep pity enter'd Rustum's soul
As he beheld him coming; and he stood,
And beckon'd to him with his hand, and said:—

"O thou young man, the air of Heaven is soft,
And warm, and pleasant; but the grave is cold!
Heaven's air is better than the cold dead grave.
Behold me! I am vast, and clad in iron,
And tried; and I have stood on many a field
Of blood, and I have fought with many a foe—
Never was that field lost, or that foe saved.
O Sohrab, wherefore wilt thou rush on death?
Be govern'd! quit the Tartar host, and come
To Iran, and be as my son to me,
And fight beneath my banner till I die!
There are no youths in Iran brave as thou."

So he spake, mildly; Sohrab heard his voice,
The mighty voice of Rustum, and he saw
His giant figure planted on the sand,
Sole, like some single tower, which a chief
Hath builded on the waste in former years
Against the robbers; and he saw that head,
Streak'd with its first grey hairs;—hope filled his soul,
And he ran forward and embraced his knees,
And clasp'd his hand within his own, and said:—

'O, by thy father's head! by thine own soul!
Art thou not Rustum? speak! art thou not he?"

But Rustum eyed askance the kneeling youth,
And turn'd away, and spake to his own soul:—

"Ah me, I muse what this young fox may mean!
False, wily, boastful, are these Tartar boys.
For if I now confess this thing he asks,

And hide it not, but say: *Rustum is here!*
He will not yield indeed, nor quit our foes,
But he will find some pretext not to fight,
And praise my fame, and proffer courteous gifts
A belt or sword perhaps, and go his way.
And on a feast-tide, in Afrasiab's hall,
In Samarcand, he will arise and cry:
'I challenged once, when the two armies camp'd
Beside the Oxus, all the Persian lords
To cope with me in single fight; but they
Shrank, only Rustum dared; then he and I
Changed gifts, and went on equal terms away.'
So will he speak, perhaps, while men applaud;
Then were the chiefs of Iran shamed through me."

   And then he turn'd, and sternly spake aloud:—
"Rise! wherefore dost thou vainly question thus
Of Rustum? I am here, whom thou hast call'd
By challenge forth; make good thy vaunt, or yield!
Is it with Rustum only thou wouldst fight?
Rash boy, men look on Rustum's face and flee!
For well I know, that did great Rustum stand
Before thy face this day, and were reveal'd,
There would be then no talk of fighting more.
But being what I am, I tell thee this—
Do thou record it in thine inmost soul:
Either thou shalt renounce thy vaunt, and yield,
Or else thy bones shall strew this sand, till winds
Bleach them, or Oxus with his summer-floods,
Oxus in summer wash them all away."

   He spoke; and Sohrab answer'd, on his feet:—
"Art thou so fierce? Thou wilt not fright me so!
I am no girl, to be made pale by words.
Yet this thou hast said well, did Rustum stand
Here on this field, there were no fighting then.
But Rustum is far hence, and we stand here.
Begin! thou art more vast, more dread than I,
And thou art proved, I know, and I am young—
But yet success sways with the breath of Heaven.
And though thou thinkest that thou knowest sure
Thy victory, yet thou canst not surely know.
For we are all, like swimmers in the sea,
Poised on the top of a huge wave of fate,
Which hangs uncertain to which side to fall.
And whether it will heave us up to land,
Or whether it will roll us out to sea,

Back out to sea, to the deep waves of death,
We know not, and no search will make us know;
Only the event will teach us in its hour."
   He spoke, and Rustum answer'd not, but hurl'd
His spear; down from the shoulder, down it came,
As on some partridge in the corn a hawk,
That long has tower'd in the airy clouds,
Drops like a plummet; Sohrab saw it come,
And sprang aside, quick as a flash; the spear
Hiss'd, and went quivering down into the sand,
Which it sent flying wide;—then Sohrab threw
In turn, and full struck Rustum's shield; sharp rang,
The iron plates rang sharp, but turn'd the spear.
And Rustum seized his club, which none but he
Could wield; an unlopp'd trunk it was, and huge,
Still rough—like those which men in treeless plains
To build them boats fish from the flooded rivers,
Hyphasis or Hydaspes, when, high up
By their dark springs, the wind in winter-time
Hath made in Himalayan forests wrack,
And strewn the channels with torn boughs—so huge
The club which Rustum lifted now, and struck
One stroke; but again Sohrab sprang aside,
Lithe as the glancing snake, and the club came
Thundering to earth, and leapt from Rustum's hand.
And Rustum follow'd his own blow, and fell
To his knees, and with his fingers clutch'd the sand;
And now might Sohrab have unsheathed his sword,
And pierced the mighty Rustum while he lay
Dizzy, and on his knees, and choked with sand;
But he look'd on, and smiled, nor bared his sword,
But courteously drew back, and spoke, and said:—
   "Thou strik'st too hard! that club of thine will float
Upon the summer-floods, and not my bones.
But rise, and be not wroth! not wroth am I;
No, when I see thee, wrath forsakes my soul.
Thou say'st, thou art not Rustum; be it so!
Who art thou then, that canst so touch my soul?
Boy as I am, I have seen battles too—
Have waded foremost in their bloody waves,
And heard their hollow roar of dying men;
But never was my heart thus touch'd before.
Are they from Heaven, these softenings of the heart?
O thou old warrior, let us yield to Heaven!
Come, plant we here in earth our angry spears,

And make a truce, and sit upon this sand,
And pledge each other in red wine, like friends,
And thou shalt talk to me of Rustum's deeds.
There are enough foes in the Persian host,
Whom I may meet, and strike, and feel no pang;
Champions enough Afrasiab has, whom thou
Mayst fight; fight *them*, when they confront thy spear!
But oh, let there be peace 'twixt thee and me!"
   He ceased, but while he spake, Rustum had risen,
And stood erect, trembling with rage; his club
He left to lie, but had regain'd his spear,
Whose fiery point now in his mail'd right-hand
Blazed bright and baleful, like that autumn-star,
The baleful sign of fevers; dust had soil'd
His stately crest, and dimm'd his glittering arms.
His breast heaved, his lips foam'd, and twice his voice
Was choked with rage; at last these words broke way:—
   "Girl! nimble with thy feet, not with thy hands!
Curl'd minion, dancer, coiner of sweet words!
Fight, let me hear thy hateful voice no more!
Thou art not in Afrasiab's gardens now
With Tartar girls, with whom thou art wont to dance;
But on the Oxus-sands, and in the dance
Of battle, and with me, who make no play
Of war; I fight it out, and hand to hand.
Speak not to me of truce, and pledge, and wine!
Remember all thy valour; try thy feints
And cunning! all the pity I had is gone;
Because thou hast shamed me before both the hosts
With thy light skipping tricks, and thy girl's wiles."
   He spoke, and Sohrab kindled at his taunts,
And he too drew his sword; at once they rush'd
Together, as two eagles on one prey
Come rushing down together from the clouds,
One from the east, one from the west; their shields
Dash'd with a clang together, and a din
Rose, such as that the sinewy woodcutters
Make often in the forest's heart at morn,
Of hewing axes, crashing trees—such blows
Rustum and Sohrab on each other hail'd.
And you would say that sun and stars took part
In that unnatural conflict; for a cloud
Grew suddenly in Heaven, and dark'd the sun
Over the fighters' heads; and a wind rose
Under their feet, and moaning swept the plain,

And in a sandy whirlwind wrapp'd the pair.
In gloom they twain were wrapp'd, and they alone;
For both the on-looking hosts on either hand
Stood in broad daylight, and the sky was pure,
And the sun sparkled on the Oxus stream.
But in the gloom they fought, with bloodshot eyes
And labouring breath; first Rustum struck the shield
Which Sohrab held stiff out; the steel-spiked spear
Rent the tough plates, but fail'd to reach the skin,
And Rustum pluck'd it back with angry groan.
Then Sohrab with his sword smote Rustum's helm,
Nor clove its steel quite through; but all the crest
He shore away, and that proud horsehair plume,
Never till now defiled, sank to the dust;
And Rustum bow'd his head; but then the gloom
Grew blacker, thunder rumbled in the air,
And lightnings rent the cloud; and Ruksh, the horse,
Who stood at hand, utter'd a dreadful cry;—
No horse's cry was that, most like the roar
Of some pain'd desert-lion, who all day
Hath trail'd the hunter's javelin in his side,
And comes at night to die upon the sand.
The two hosts heard that cry, and quaked for fear,
And Oxus curdled as it cross'd his stream.
But Sohrab heard, and quail'd not, but rush'd on,
And struck again; and again Rustum bow'd
His head; but this time all the blade, like glass,
Sprang in a thousand shivers on the helm,
And in the hand the hilt remain'd alone.
Then Rustum raised his head; his dreadful eyes
Glared, and he shook on high his menacing spear,
And shouted: *Rustum!*—Sohrab heard that shout,
And shrank amazed; back he recoil'd one step,
And scann'd with blinking eyes the advancing form;
And then he stood bewilder'd; and he dropp'd
His covering shield, and the spear pierced his side.
He reel'd, and staggering back, sank to the ground;
And then the gloom dispersed, and the wind fell,
And the bright sun broke forth, and melted all
The cloud; and the two armies saw the pair—
Saw Rustum standing, safe upon his feet,
And Sohrab, wounded, on the bloody sand.
   Then, with a bitter smile, Rustum began:—
"Sohrab, thou thoughtest in thy mind to kill
A Persian lord this day, and strip his corpse,

And bear thy trophies to Afrasiab's tent.
Or else that the great Rustum would come down
Himself to fight, and that thy wiles would move
His heart to take a gift, and let thee go.
And then that all the Tartar host would praise
Thy courage or thy craft, and spread thy fame,
To glad thy father in his weak old age.
Fool, thou art slain, and by an unknown man!
Dearer to the red jackals shalt thou be
Than to thy friends, and to thy father old."
    And, with a fearless mien, Sohrab replied:—
"Unknown thou art; yet thy fierce vaunt is vain.
Thou dost not slay me, proud and boastful man!
No! Rustum slays me, and this filial heart.
For were I match'd with ten such men as thee,
And I were that which till to-day I was,
They should be lying here, I standing there.
But that belovéd name unnerved my arm—
That name, and something, I confess, in thee,
Which troubles all my heart, and made my shield
Fall; and thy spear transfix'd an unarm'd foe.
And now thou boastest, and insult'st my fate.
But hear thou this, fierce man, tremble to hear
The mighty Rustum shall avenge my death!
My father, whom I seek through all the world,
He shall avenge my death, and punish thee!"
    As when some hunter in the spring hath found
A breeding eagle sitting on her nest,
Upon the craggy isle of a hill-lake,
And pierced her with an arrow as she rose,
And follow'd her to find her where she fell
Far off;—anon her mate comes winging back
From hunting, and a great way off descries
His huddling young left sole; at that, he checks
His pinion, and with short uneasy sweeps
Circles above his eyry, with loud screams
Chiding his mate back to her nest; but she
Lies dying, with the arrow in her side,
In some far stony gorge out of his ken,
A heap of fluttering feathers—never more
Shall the lake glass her, flying over it;
Never the black and dripping precipices
Echo her stormy scream as she sails by—
As that poor bird flies home, nor knows his loss,
So Rustum knew not his own loss, but stood

Over his dying son, and knew him not.
    But, with a cold incredulous voice, he said:—
"What prate is this of fathers and revenge?
The mighty Rustum never had a son."
    And, with a failing voice, Sohrab replied:—
"Ah yes, he had! and that lost son am I.
Surely the news will one day reach his ear,
Reach Rustum, where he sits, and tarries long,
Somewhere, I know not where, but far from here;
And pierce him like a stab, and make him leap
To arms, and cry for vengeance upon thee.
Fierce man, bethink thee, for an only son!
What will that grief, what will that vengeance be?
Oh, could I live, till I that grief had seen!
Yet him I pity not so much, but her,
My mother, who in Ader-baijan dwells
With that old king, her father, who grows grey
With age, and rules over the valiant Koords.
Her most I pity, who no more will see
Sohrab returning from the Tartar camp,
With spoils and honour, when the war is done.
But a dark rumour will be bruited up,
From tribe to tribe, until it reach her ear;
And then will that defenceless woman learn
That Sohrab will rejoice her sight no more,
But that in battle with a nameless foe,
By the far-distant Oxus, he is slain."
    He spoke; and as he ceased, he wept aloud,
Thinking of her he left, and his own death.
He spoke; but Rustum listen'd, plunged in thought.
Nor did he yet believe it was his son
Who spoke, although he call'd back names he knew;
For he had had sure tidings that the babe,
Which was in Ader-baijan born to him,
Had been a puny girl, no boy at all—
So that sad mother sent him word, for fear
Rustum should seek the boy, to train in arms
And so he deem'd that either Sohrab took,
By a false boast, the style of Rustum's son;
Or that men gave it him, to swell his fame.
So deem'd he; yet he listen'd, plunged in thought
And his soul set to grief, as the vast tide
Of the bright rocking Ocean sets to shore
At the full moon; tears gather'd in his eyes;
For he remember'd his own early youth,

And all its bounding rapture; as, at dawn,
The shepherd from his mountain-lodge descries
A far, bright city, smitten by the sun,
Through many rolling clouds—so Rustum saw
His youth; saw Sohrab's mother, in her bloom;
And that old king, her father, who loved well
His wandering guest, and gave him his fair child
With joy; and all the pleasant life they led,
They three, in that long-distant summer-time—
The castle, and the dewy woods, and hunt
And hound, and morn on those delightful hills
In Ader-baijan. And he saw that youth,
Of age and looks to be his own dear son,
Piteous and lovely, lying on the sand,
Like some rich hyacinth which by the scythe
Of an unskilful gardener has been cut,
Mowing the garden grass-plots near its bed,
And lies, a fragrant tower of purple bloom,
On the mown, dying grass—so Sohrab lay,
Lovely in death, upon the common sand.
And Rustum gazed on him with grief, and said:—
    "O Sohrab, thou indeed art such a son
Whom Rustum, wert thou his, might well have loved.
Yet here thou errest, Sohrab, or else men
Have told thee false—thou art not Rustum's son.
For Rustum had no son; one child he had—
But one—a girl; who with her mother now
Plies some light female task, nor dreams of us—
Of us she dreams not, nor of wounds, nor war."
    But Sohrab answer'd him in wrath; for now
The anguish of the deep-fix'd spear grew fierce,
And he desired to draw forth the steel,
And let the blood flow free, and so to die—
But first he would convince his stubborn foe;
And, rising sternly on one arm, he said:—
    "Man, who art thou who dost deny my words?
Truth sits upon the lips of dying men,
And falsehood, while I lived, was far from mine.
I tell thee, prick'd upon this arm I bear
That seal which Rustum to my mother gave,
That she might prick it on the babe she bore."
    He spoke; and all the blood left Rustum's cheeks,
And his knees totter'd, and he smote his hand
Against his breast, his heavy mailed hand,
That the hard iron corslet clank'd aloud;

And to his heart be press'd the other hand,
And in a hollow voice he spake, and said:—
  "Sohrab, that were a proof which could not lie!
If thou show this, then art thou Rustum's son."
  Then, with weak hasty fingers, Sohrab loosed
His belt, and near the shoulder bared his arm,
And show'd a sign in faint vermilion points
Prick'd; as a cunning workman, in Pekin,
Pricks with vermilion some clear porcelain vase,
An emperor's gift—at early morn he paints,
And all day long, and, when night comes, the lamp
Lights up his studious forehead and thin hands—
So delicately prick'd the sign appear'd
On Sohrab's arm, the sign of Rustum's seal.
It was that griffin, which of old rear'd Zal,
Rustum's great father, whom they left to die,
A helpless babe, among the mountain-rocks;
Him that kind creature found, and rear'd, and loved—
Then Rustum took it for his glorious sign.
And Sohrab bared that image on his arm,
And himself scann'd it long with mournful eyes,
And then he touch'd it with his hand and said:—
  "How say'st thou? Is that sign the proper sign
Of Rustum's son, or of some other man's?"
  He spoke; but Rustum gazed, and gazed, and stood
Speechless; and then he utter'd one sharp cry:
O boy—thy father!—and his voice choked there.
And then a dark cloud pass'd before his eyes,
And his head swam, and he sank down to earth.
But Sohrab crawl'd to where he lay, and cast
His arms about his neck, and kiss'd his lips,
And with fond faltering fingers stroked his cheeks,
Trying to call him back to life; and life
Came back to Rustum, and he oped his eyes,
And they stood wide with horror; and he seized
In both his hands the dust which lay around,
And threw it on his head, and smirch'd his hair,—
His hair, and face, and beard, and glittering arms;
And strong convulsive groanings shook his breast,
And his sobs choked him; and he clutch'd his sword,
To draw it, and for ever let life out.
But Sohrab saw his thought, and held his hands,
And with a soothing voice he spake, and said:—
  "Father, forbear! for I but meet to-day
The doom which at my birth was written down

In Heaven, and thou art Heaven's unconscious hand.
Surely my heart cried out that it was thou,
When first I saw thee; and thy heart spoke too,
I know it! but fate trod those promptings down
Under its iron heel; fate, fate engaged
The strife, and hurl'd me on my father's spear.
But let us speak no more of this! I find
My father; let me feel that I have found!
Come, sit beside me on this sand, and take
My head betwixt thy hands, and kiss my cheeks,
And wash them with thy tears, and say: *My son!*
Quick! quick! for number'd are my sands of life,
And swift; for like the lightning to this field
I came, and like the wind I go away—
Sudden, and swift, and like a passing wind.
But it was writ in Heaven that this should be."

So said he, and his voice released the heart
Of Rustum, and his tears broke forth; he cast
His arms round his son's neck, and wept aloud,
And kiss'd him. And awe fell on both the hosts,
When they saw Rustum's grief; and Ruksh, the horse,
With his head bowing to the ground and mane
Sweeping the dust, came near, and in mute woe
First to the one then to the other moved
His head, as if inquiring what their grief
Might mean; and from his dark, compassionate eyes,
The big warm tears roll'd down, and caked the sand.
But Rustum chid him with stern voice, and said:—

"Ruksh, now thou grievest; but, O Ruksh, thy feet
Should first have rotted on their nimble joints,
Or ere they brought thy master to this field!"

But Sohrab look'd upon the horse and said;—
"Is this, then, Ruksh? How often, in past days,
My mother told me of thee, thou brave steed,
My terrible father's terrible horse! and said,
That I should one day find thy lord and thee.
Come, let me lay my hand upon thy mane!
O Ruksh, thou art more fortunate than I;
For thou hast gone where I shall never go,
And snuff'd the breezes of my father's home.
And thou hast trod the sands of Seistan,
And seen the River of Helmund, and the Lake
Of Zirrah; and the aged Zal himself
Has often stroked thy neck, and given thee food,
Corn in a golden platter soak'd with wine,

And said; *O Ruksh! bear Rustum well!*—but I
Have never known my grandsire's furrow'd face,
Nor seen his lofty house in Seistan,
Nor slaked my thirst at the clear Helmund stream;
But lodged among my father's foes, and seen
Afrasiab's cities only, Samarcand,
Bokhara, and lone Khiva in the waste,
And the black Toorkmun tents; and only drunk
The desert rivers, Moorghab and Tejend,
Kohik, and where the Kalmuks feed their sheep,
The northern Sir; and this great Oxus stream,
The yellow Oxus, by whose brink I die."

    Then, with a heavy groan, Rustum bewail'd:—
"Oh, that its waves were flowing over me!
Oh, that I saw its grains of yellow silt
Roll tumbling in the current o'er my head!"

    But, with a grave mild voice, Sohrab replied:—
"Desire not that, my father! thou must live.
For some are born to do great deeds, and live,
As some are born to be obscured, and die.
Do thou the deeds I die too young to do,
And reap a second glory in thine age;
Thou art my father, and thy gain is mine.
But come! thou seest this great host of men
Which follow me; I pray thee, slay not these!
Let me entreat for them; what have they done?
They follow'd me, my hope, my fame, my star.
Let them all cross the Oxus back in peace.
But me thou must bear hence, not send with them,
But carry me with thee to Seistan,
And place me on a bed, and mourn for me,
Thou, and the snow-hair'd Zal and all thy friends.
And thou must lay me in that lovely earth,
And heap a stately mound above my bones,
And plant a far-seen pillar over all.
That so the passing horseman on the waste
May see my tomb a great way off, and cry:
*Sohrab, the mighty Rustum's son, lies there,
Whom his great father did in ignorance kill!*
And I be not forgotten in my grave."

    And, with a mournful voice, Rustum replied:—
"Fear not! as thou hast said, Sohrab, my son,
So shall it be; for I will burn my tents,
And quit the host, and bear thee hence with me,
And carry thee away to Seistan,

And place thee on a bed, and mourn for thee,
With the snow-headed Zal, and all my friends.
And I will lay thee in that lovely earth,
And heap a stately mound above thy bones,
And plant a far-seen pillar over all,
And men shall not forget thee in thy grave.
And I will spare thy host; yea, let them go!
Let them all cross the Oxus back in peace!
What should I do with slaying any more?
For would that all that I have ever slain
Might be once more alive; my bitterest foes,
And they who were call'd champions in their time,
And through whose death I won that fame I have—
And I were nothing but a common man,
A poor, mean soldier, and without renown,
So thou mightest live too, my son, my son!
Or rather would that I, even I myself,
Might now be lying on this bloody sand,
Near death, and by an ignorant stroke of thine,
Not thou of mine! and I might die, not thou;
And I, not thou, be borne to Seistan;
And Zal might weep above my grave, not thine;
And say: *O son, I weep thee not too sore,*
For willingly, I know, thou met'st thine end!
But now in blood and battles was my youth,
And full of blood and battles is my age,
And I shall never end this life of blood."
    Then, at the point of death, Sohrab replied:—
"A life of blood indeed, thou dreadful man!
But thou shalt yet have peace; only not now,
Not yet! but thou shalt have it on that day,
When thou shalt sail in a high-masted ship,
Thou and the other peers of Kai Khosroo,
Returning home over the salt blue sea,
From laying thy dear master in his grave."
    And Rustum gazed in Sohrab's face, and said:—
"Soon be that day, my son, and deep that sea!
Till then, if fate so wills, let me endure."
    He spoke; and Sohrab smiled on him, and took
The spear, and drew it from his side, and eased
His wound's imperious anguish; but the blood
Came welling from the open gash, and life
Flow'd with the stream;—all down his cold white side
The crimson torrent ran, dim now and soil'd,
Like the soil'd tissue of white violets

Left, freshly gather'd, on their native bank,
By children whom their nurses call with haste
Indoors from the sun's eye; his head droop'd low,
His limbs grew slack; motionless, white, he lay—
White, with eyes closed; only when heavy gasps,
Deep heavy gasps quivering through all his frame,
Convulsed him back to life, he open'd them,
And fix'd them feebly on his father's face;
Till now all strength was ebb'd, and from his limbs
Unwillingly the spirit fled away,
Regretting the warm mansion which it left,
And youth, and bloom, and this delightful world.

So, on the blody sand, Sohrab lay dead;
And the great Rustum drew his horseman's cloak
Down o'er his face, and sate by his dead son.
As those black granite pillars, once high-rear'd
By Jemshid in Persepolis, to bear
His house, now 'mid their broken flights of steps
Lie prone, enormous, down the mountain side—
So in the sand lay Rustum by his son.

And night came down over the solemn waste,
And the two gazing hosts, and that sole pair,
And darken'd all; and a cold fog, with night,
Crept from the Oxus. Soon a hum arose,
As of a great assembly loosed, and fires
Began to twinkle through the fog; for now
Both armies moved to camp, and took their meal;
The Persians took it on the open sands
Southward, the Tartars by the river marge;
And Rustum and his son were left alone.

But the majestic river floated on,
Out of the mist and hum of that low land,
Into the frosty starlight, and there moved,
Rejoicing, through the hush'd Chorasmian waste,
Under the solitary moon;—he flow'd
Right for the polar star, past Orgunjè,
Brimming, and bright, and large; then sands begin
To hem his watery march, and dam his streams,
And split his currents; and for many a league
The shorn and parcell'd Oxus strains along
Through beds of sand and matted rushy isles—
Oxus, forgetting the bright speed he had
In his high mountain-cradle in Pamere,
A foil'd circuitous wanderer—till at last
The long'd-for dash of waves is heard, and wide

His luminous home of waters opens, bright
And tranquil, from whose floor the new-bathed stars
Emerge, and shine upon the Aral Sea.

Balder Dead

1. Sending

So on the floor lay Balder dead; and round
Lay thickly strewn swords, axes, darts, and spears,
Which all the Gods in sport had idly thrown
At Balder, whom no weapon pierced or clove;
But in his breast stood fixt the fatal bough
Of mistletoe, which Lok the Accuser gave
To Hoder, and unwitting Hoder threw—
'Gainst that alone had Balder's life no charm.

And all the Gods and all the Heroes came,
And stood round Balder on the bloody floor,
Weeping and wailing; and Valhalla rang
Up to its golden roof with sobs and cries;
And on the tables stood the untasted meats,
And in the horns and gold-rimm'd skulls the wine.
And now would night have fall'n, and found them yet
Wailing; but otherwise was Odin's will.
And thus the father of the ages spake:—
  "Enough of tears, ye Gods, enough of wail!
Not to lament in was Valhalla made.
If any here might weep for Balder's death,
I most might weep, his father; such a son
I lose to-day, so bright, so loved a God.
But he has met that doom, which long ago
The Nornies, when his mother bare him, spun,
And fate set seal, that so his end must be.
Balder has met his death, and ye survive—
Weep him an hour, but what can grief avail?
For ye yourselves, ye Gods, shall meet your doom,
All ye who hear me, and inhabit Heaven,
And I too, Odin too, the Lord of all.
But ours we shall not meet, when that day comes,
With women's tears and weak complaining cries—
Why should we meet another's portion so?
Rather it fits you, having wept your hour,
With cold dry eyes, and hearts composed and stern,
To live, as erst, your daily life in Heaven.

By me shall vengeance on the murderer Lok,
The foe, the accuser, whom, though Gods, we hate,
Be strictly cared for, in the appointed day.
Meanwhile, to-morrow, when the morning dawns,
Bring wood to the seashore to Balder's ship,
And on the deck build high a funeral-pile,
And on the top lay Balder's corpse, and put
Fire to the wood, and send him out to sea
To burn; for that is what the dead desire."
　　So spake the King of Gods, and straightway rose,
And mounted his horse Sleipner, whom he rode;
And from the hall of Heaven he rode away
To Lidskialf, and sate upon his throne,
The mount, from whence his eye surveys the world.
And far from Heaven he turn'd his shining orbs
To look on Midgard, and the earth, and men.
And on the conjuring Lapps he bent his gaze
Whom antler'd reindeer pull over the snow;
And on the Finns, the gentlest of mankind,
Fair men, who live in holes under the ground;
Nor did he look once more to Ida's plain,
Nor tow'rd Valhalla, and the sorrowing Gods;
For well he knew the Gods would heed his word,
And cease to mourn, and think of Balder's pyre.
　　But in Valhalla all the Gods went back
From around Balder, all the Heroes went;
And left his body stretch'd upon the floor.
And on their golden chairs they sate again,
Beside the tables, in the hall of Heaven;
And before each the cooks who served them placed
New messes of the boar Serimner's flesh,
And the Valkyries crown'd their horns with mead.
So they, with pent-up hearts and tearless eyes,
Wailing no more, in silence ate and drank,
While twilight fell, and sacred night came on.
　　But the blind Hoder left the feasting Gods
In Odin's hall, and went through Asgard streets,
And past the haven where the Gods have moor'd
Their ships, and through the gate, beyond the wall;
Though sightless, yet his own mind led the God.
Down to the margin of the roaring sea
He came, and sadly went along the sand,
Between the waves and black o'erhanging cliffs
Where in and out the screaming seafowl fly;
Until he came to where a gully breaks

Through the cliff-wall, and a fresh stream runs down
From the high moors behind, and meets the sea.
There, in the glen, Fensaler stands, the house
Of Frea, honour'd mother of the Gods,
And shows its lighted windows to the main.
There he went up, and pass'd the open doors;
And in the hall he found those women old,
The prophetesses, who by rite eterne
On Frea's hearth feed high the sacred fire
Both night and day; and by the inner wall
Upon her golden chair the Mother sate,
With folded hands, revolving things to come.
To her drew Hoder near, and spake, and said:—
    "Mother, a child of bale thou bar'st in me!
For, first, thou barest me with blinded eyes,
Sightless and helpless, wandering weak in Heaven;
And, after that, of ignorant witless mind
Thou barest me, and unforeseeing soul;
That I alone must take the branch from Lok,
The foe, the accuser, whom, though Gods, we hate,
And cast it at the dear-loved Balder's breast
At whom the Gods in sport their weapons threw—
'Gainst that alone had Balder's life no charm.
Now therefore what to attempt, or whither fly,
For who will bear my hateful sight in Heaven?
Can I, O mother, bring them Balder back?
Or—for thou know'st the fates, and things allow'd—
Can I with Hela's power a compact strike,
And make exchange, and give my life for his?"
    He spoke: the mother of the Gods replied:—
"Hoder, ill-fated, child of bale, my son,
Sightless in soul and eye, what words are these?
That one, long portion'd with his doom of death,
Should change his lot, and fill another's life,
And Hela yield to this, and let him go!
On Balder Death hath laid her hand, not thee;
Nor doth she count this life a price for that.
For many Gods in Heaven, not thou alone,
Would freely die to purchase Balder back,
And wend themselves to Hela's gloomy realm.
For not so gladsome is that life in Heaven
Which Gods and heroes lead, in feast and fray,
Waiting the darkness of the final times,
That one should grudge its loss for Balder's sake,
Balder their joy, so bright, so loved a God.

But fate withstands, and laws forbid this way.
Yet in my secret mind one way I know,
Nor do I judge if it shall win or fail;
But much must still be tried, which shall but fail."
    And the blind Hoder answer'd her, and said:—
"What way is this, O mother, that thou show'st?
Is it a matter which a God might try?"
    And straight the mother of the Gods replied:—
"There is a road which leads to Hela's realm,
Untrodden, lonely, far from light and Heaven.
Who goes that way must take no other horse
To ride, but Sleipner, Odin's horse, alone.
Nor must he choose that common path of Gods
Which every day they come and go in Heaven,
O'er the bridge Bifrost, where is Heimdall's watch,
Past Midgard fortress, down to earth and men.
But he must tread a dark untravell'd road
Which branches from the north of Heaven, and ride
Nine days, nine nights, toward the northern ice,
Through valleys deep-engulph'd, with roaring streams.
And he will reach on the tenth morn a bridge
Which spans with golden arches Giall's stream,
Not Bifrost, but that bridge a damsel keeps,
Who tells the passing troops of dead their way
To the low shore of ghosts, and Hela's realm.
And she will bid him northward steer his course.
Then he will journey through no lighted land,
Nor see the sun arise, nor see it set;
But he must ever watch the northern Bear,
Who from her frozen height with jealous eye
Confronts the Dog and Hunter in the south,
And is alone not dipt in Ocean's stream.
And straight he will come down to Ocean's strand—
Ocean, whose watery ring enfolds the world,
And on whose marge the ancient giants dwell.
But he will reach its unknown northern shore,
Far, far beyond the outmost giant's home,
At the chink'd fields of ice, the waste of snow.
And he must fare across the dismal ice
Northward, until he meets a stretching wall
Barring his way, and in the wall a grate.
But then he must dismount, and on the ice
Tighten the girths of Sleipner, Odin's horse,
And make him leap the grate, and come within.
And he will see stretch round him Hela's realm,

The plains of Niflheim, where dwell the dead,
And hear the roaring of the streams of Hell.
And he will see the feeble, shadowy tribes,
And Balder sitting crown'd, and Hela's throne.
Then must he not regard the wailful ghosts
Who all will flit, like eddying leaves, around;
But he must straight accost their solemn queen,
And pay her homage, and entreat with prayers,
Telling her all that grief they have in Heaven
For Balder, whom she holds by right below;
If haply he may melt her heart with words,
And make her yield, and give him Balder back."

   She spoke; but Hoder answer'd her and said:—
"Mother, a dreadful way is this thou show'st;
No journey for a sightless God to go!"

   And straight the mother of the Gods replied:—
"Therefore thyself thou shalt not go, my son.
But he whom first thou meetest when thou com'st
To Asgard, and declar'st this hidden way,
Shall go; and I will be his guide unseen."

   She spoke, and on her face let fall her veil,
And bow'd her head, and sate with folded hands,
But at the central hearth those women old,
Who while the Mother spake had ceased their toil,
Began again to heap the sacred fire.
And Hoder turn'd, and left his mother's house,
Fensaler, whose lit windows look to sea;
And came again down to the roaring waves,
And back along the beach to Asgard went,
Pondering on that which Frea said should be.

   But night came down, and darken'd Asgard streets
Then from their loathéd feasts the Gods arose,
And lighted torches, and took up the corpse
Of Balder from the floor of Odin's hall,
And laid it on a bier, and bare him home
Through the fast-darkening streets to his own house,
Breidablik, on whose columns Balder graved
The enchantments that recall the dead to life.
For wise he was, and many curious arts,
Postures of runes, and healing herbs he knew;
Unhappy! but that art he did not know,
To keep his own life safe, and see the sun.
There to his hall the Gods brought Balder home,
And each bespake him as he laid him down:—

   "Would that ourselves, O Balder, we were borne

Home to our halls, with torchlight, by our kin,
So thou might'st live, and still delight the Gods!"
　　They spake; and each went home to his own house.
But there was one, the first of all the Gods
For speed, and Hermod was his name in Heaven;
Most fleet he was, but now he went the last,
Heavy in heart for Balder, to his house,
Which he in Asgard built him, there to dwell,
Against the harbour, by the city-wall.
Him the blind Hoder met, as he came up
From the sea cityward, and knew his step;
Nor yet could Hermod see his brother's face,
For it grew dark; but Hoder touch'd his arm.
And as a spray of honeysuckle flowers
Brushes across a tired traveller's face
Who shuffles through the deep dew-moisten'd dust,
On a May evening, in the darken'd lanes,
And starts him, that he thinks a ghost went by—
So Hoder brush'd by Hermod's side, and said:—
　　"Take Sleipner, Hermod, and set forth with dawn
To Hela's kingdom, to ask Balder back;
And they shall be thy guides, who have the power."
　　He spake, and brush'd soft by, and disappear'd.
And Hermod gazed into the night, and said:—
　　"Who is it utters through the dark his hest
So quickly, and will wait for no reply?
The voice was like the unhappy Hoder's voice.
Howbeit I will see, and do his hest;
For there rang note divine in that command."
　　So speaking, the fleet-footed Hermod came
Home, and lay down to sleep in his own house;
And all the Gods lay down in their own homes.
And Hoder too came home, distraught with grief,
Loathing to meet, at dawn, the other Gods;
And he went in, and shut the door, and fixt
His sword upright, and fell on it, and died.
　　But from the hill of Lidskialf Odin rose,
The throne, from which his eye surveys the world;
And mounted Sleipner, and in darkness rode
To Asgard.　And the stars came out in heaven,
High over Asgard, to light home the King.
But fiercely Odin gallop'd, moved in heart;
And swift to Asgard, to the gate, he came.
And terribly the hoofs of Sleipner rang
Along the flinty floor of Asgard streets,

And the Gods trembled on their golden beds
Hearing the wrathful Father coming home—
For dread, for like a whirlwind, Odin came.
And to Valhalla's gate he rode, and left
Sleipner; and Sleipner went to his own stall;
And in Valhalla Odin laid him down.
　But in Breidablik, Nanna, Balder's wife,
Came with the Goddesses who wrought her will,
And stood by Balder lying on his bier.
And at his head and feet she station'd Scalds
Who in their lives were famous for their song;
These o'er the corpse intoned a plaintive strain,
A dirge—and Nanna and her train replied.
And far into the night they wail'd their dirge.
But when their souls were satisfied with wail,
They went, and laid them down, and Nanna went
Into an upper chamber, and lay down;
And Frea seal'd her tired lids with sleep.
　And 'twas when night is bordering hard on dawn,
When air is chilliest, and the stars sunk low;
Then Balder's spirit through the gloom drew near,
In garb, in form, in feature as he was,
Alive; and still the rays were round his head
Which were his glorious mark in Heaven; he stood
Over against the curtain of the bed,
And gazed on Nanna as she slept, and spake:—
　"Poor lamb, thou sleepest, and forgett'st thy woe!
Tears stand upon the lashes of thine eyes,
Tears wet the pillow by thy cheek; but thou,
Like a young child, hast cried thyself to sleep.
Sleep on; I watch thee, and am here to aid.
Alive I kept not far from thee, dear soul!
Neither do I neglect thee now, though dead.
For with to-morrow's dawn the Gods prepare
To gather wood, and build a funeral-pile
Upon my ship, and burn my corpse with fire,
That sad, sole honour of the dead; and thee
They think to burn, and all my choicest wealth,
With me, for thus ordains the common rite.
But it shall not be so; but mild, but swift,
But painless shall a stroke from Frea come,
To cut thy thread of life, and free thy soul,
And they shall burn thy corpse with mine, not thee.
And well I know that by no stroke of death,
Tardy or swift, would'st thou be loath to die,

So it restored thee, Nanna, to my side,
Whom thou so well hast loved; but I can smooth
Thy way, and this, at least, my prayers avail.
Yes, and I fain would altogether ward
Death from thy head, and with the Gods in Heaven
Prolong thy life, though not by thee desired—
But right bars this, not only thy desire.
Yet dreary, Nanna, is the life they lead
In that dim world, in Hela's mouldering realm;
And doleful are the ghosts, the troops of dead,
Whom Hela with austere control presides.
For of the race of Gods is no one there,
Save me alone, and Hela, solemn queen;
And all the nobler souls of mortal men
On battle-field have met their death, and now
Feast in Valhalla, in my father's hall;
Only the inglorious sort are there below,
The old, the cowards, and the weak are there—
Men spent by sickness, or obscure decay.
But even there, O Nanna, we might find
Some solace in each other's look and speech,
Wandering together through that gloomy world,
And talking of the life we led in Heaven,
While we yet lived, among the other Gods.''
   He spake, and straight his lineaments began
To fade; and Nanna in her sleep stretch'd out
Her arms towards him with a cry—but he
Mournfully shook his head, and disappear'd.
And as the woodman sees a little smoke
Hang in the air, afield, and disappear,
So Balder faded in the night away.
And Nanna on her bed sank back; but then
Frea, the mother of the Gods, with stroke
Painless and swift, set free her airy soul,
Which took, on Balder's track, the way below;
And instantly the sacred morn appear'd.

2. *Journey to the Dead*

FORTH from the east, up the ascent of Heaven,
Day drove his courser with the shining mane;
And in Valhalla, from his gable-perch,
The golden-crested cock began to crow.
Hereafter, in the blackest dead of night,
With shrill and dismal cries that bird shall crow,

Warning the Gods that foes draw nigh to Heaven;
But now he crew at dawn, a cheerful note,
To wake the Gods and Heroes to their tasks.
And all the Gods and all the Heroes, woke.
And from their beds the Heroes rose, and donn'd
Their arms, and led their horses from the stall,
And mounted them, and in Valhalla's court
Were ranged; and then the daily fray began.
And all day long they there are hack'd and hewn,
'Mid dust, and groans, and limbs lopp'd off, and blood;
But all at night return to Odin's hall,
Woundless and fresh; such lot is theirs in Heaven.
And the Valkyries on their steeds went forth
Tow'rd earth and fights of men; and at their side
Skulda, the youngest of the Nornies, rode;
And over Bifrost, where is Heimdall's watch,
Past Midgard fortress, down to earth they came;
There through some battle-field, where men fall fast,
Their horses fetlock-deep in blood, they ride,
And pick the bravest warriors out for death,
Whom they bring back with them at night to Heaven
To glad the Gods, and feast in Odin's hall.
    But the Gods went not now, as otherwhile,
Into the tilt-yard, where the Heroes fought,
To feast their eyes with looking on the fray;
Nor did they to their judgment-place repair
By the ash Igdrasil, in Ida's plain,
Where they hold council, and give laws for men.
But they went, Odin first, the rest behind,
To the hall Gladheim, which is built of gold;
Where are in circle ranged twelve golden chairs,
And in the midst one higher, Odin's throne.
There all the Gods in silence sate them down;
And thus the Father of the ages spake:—
    "Go quickly, Gods, bring wood to the seashore,
With all, which it beseems the dead to have,
And make a funeral-pile on Balder's ship;
On the twelfth day the Gods shall burn his corpse.
But Hermod, thou, take Sleipner, and ride down
To Hela's kingdom, to ask Balder back."
    So said he; and the Gods arose, and took
Axes and ropes, and at their head came Thor,
Shouldering his hammer, which the giants know.
Forth wended they, and drave their steeds before.
And up the dewy mountain-tracks they fared

To the dark forests, in the early dawn;
And up and down, and side and slant they roam'd.
And from the glens all day an echo came
Of crashing falls; for with his hammer Thor
Smote 'mid the rocks the lichen-bearded pines,
And burst their roots, while to their tops the Gods
Made fast the woven ropes, and haled them down,
And lopp'd their boughs, and clove them on the sward,
And bound the logs behind their steeds to draw,
And drave them homeward; and the snorting steeds
Went straining through the crackling brushwood down,
And by the darkling forest-paths the Gods
Follow'd, and on their shoulders carried boughs.
And they came out upon the plain, and pass'd
Asgard, and led their horses to the beach,
And loosed them of their loads on the seashore,
And ranged the wood in stacks by Balder's ship;
And ever God went home to his own house.
    But when the Gods were to the forest gone,
Hermod led Sleipner from Valhalla forth
And saddled him; before that, Sleipner brook'd
No meaner hand than Odin's on his mane,
On his broad back no lesser rider bore;
Yet docile now he stood at Hermod's side,
Arching his neck, and glad to be bestrode,
Knowing the God they went to seek, how dear.
But Hermod mounted him, and sadly fared
In silence up the dark untravell'd road
Which branches from the north of Heaven, and went
All day; and daylight waned, and night came on.
And all that night he rode, and journey'd so,
Nine days, nine nights, towards the northern ice,
Through valleys deep-engulph'd, by roaring streams.
And on the tenth morn he beheld the bridge
Which spans with golden arches Giall's stream,
And on the bridge a damsel watching arm'd,
In the strait passage, at the farther end,
Where the road issues between walling rocks.
Scant space that warder left for passers by;—
But as when cowherds in October drive
Their kine across a snowy mountain-pass
To winter-pasture on the southern side,
And on the ridge a waggon chokes the way,
Wedged in the snow; then painfully the hinds
With goad and shouting urge their cattle past,

Plunging through deep untrodden banks of snow
To right and left, and warm steam fills the air—
So on the bridge that damsel block'd the way,
And question'd Hermod as he came, and said:—
"Who art thou on thy black and fiery horse
Under whose hoofs the bridge o'er Giall's stream
Rumbles and shakes? Tell me thy race and home.
But yestermorn, five troops of dead pass'd by,
Bound on their way below to Hela's realm,
Nor shook the bridge so much as thou alone.
And thou hast flesh and colour on thy cheeks,
Like men who live, and draw the vital air;
Nor look'st thou pale and wan, like men deceased,
Souls bound below, my daily passers here."
    And the fleet-footed Hermod answer'd her:—
"O damsel, Hermod am I call'd, the son
Of Odin; and my high-roof'd house is built
Far hence, in Asgard, in the city of Gods;
And Sleipner, Odin's horse, is this I ride.
And I come, sent this road on Balder's track;
Say then, if he hath cross'd thy bridge or no?"
    He spake; the warder of the bridge replied:—
"O Hermod, rarely do the feet of Gods
Or of the horses of the Gods resound
Upon my bridge; and, when they cross, I know.
Balder hath gone this way, and ta'en the road
Below there, to the north, tow'rd Hela's realm.
From here the cold white mist can be discern'd,
Nor lit with sun, but through the darksome air
By the dim vapour-blotted light of stars,
Which hangs over the ice where lies the road.
For in that ice are lost those northern streams,
Freezing and ridging in their onward flow,
Which from the fountain of Vergelmer run,
The spring that bubbles up by Hela's throne.
There are the joyless seats, the haunt of ghosts,
Hela's pale swarms; and there was Balder bound.
Ride on! pass free! but he by this is there."
    She spake, and stepp'd aside, and left him room.
And Hermod greeted her, and gallop'd by
Across the bridge; then she took post again.
But northward Hermod rode, the way below;
And o'er a darksome tract, which knows no sun,
But by the blotted light of stars, he fared.
And he came down to Ocean's northern strand,

At the drear ice, beyond the giants' home.
Thence on he journey'd o'er the fields of ice
Still north, until he met a stretching wall
Barring his way, and in the wall a grate.
Then he dismounted, and drew tight the girths,
On the smooth ice, of Sleipner, Odin's horse,
And made him leap the grate, and came within.
And he beheld spread round him Hela's realm,
The plains of Niflheim, where dwell the dead,
And heard the thunder of the streams of Hell.
For near the wall the river of Roaring flows,
Outmost; the others near the centre run—
The Storm, the Abyss, the Howling, and the Pain;
These flow by Hela's throne, and near their spring.
And from the dark flock'd up the shadowy tribes;—
And as the swallows crowd the bulrush-beds
Of some clear river, issuing from a lake,
On autumn-days, before they cross the sea;
And to each bulrush-crest a swallow hangs
Quivering, and others skim the river-streams,
And their quick twittering fills the banks and shores—
So around Hermod swarm'd the twittering ghosts.
Women, and infants, and young men who died
Too soon for fame, with white ungraven shields;
And old men, known to glory, but their star
Betray'd them, and of wasting age they died,
Not wounds; yet, dying, they their armour wore,
And now have chief regard in Hela's realm.
Behind flock'd wrangling up a piteous crew,
Greeted of none, disfeatured and forlorn—
Cowards, who were in sloughs interr'd alive;
And round them still the wattled hurdles hung,
Wherewith they stamp'd them down, and trod them deep,
To hide their shameful memory from men.
But all he pass'd unhail'd, and reach'd the throne
Of Hela, and saw, near it, Balder crown'd,
And Hela set thereon, with countenance stern
And thus bespake him first the solemn queen:—
    "Unhappy, how hast thou endured to leave
The light, and journey to the cheerless land
Where idly flit about the feeble shades?
How didst thou cross the bridge o'er Giall's stream,
Being alive, and come to Ocean's shore?
Or how o'erleap the grate that bars the wall?"
    She spake: but down off Sleipner Hermod sprang,

And fell before her feet, and clasp'd her knees:
And spake, and mild entreated her, and said:—
    "O Hela, wherefore should the Gods declare
Their errands to each other, or the ways
They go? the errand and the way is known.
Thou know'st, thou know'st, what grief we have in Heaven
For Balder, whom thou hold'st by right below.
Restore him! for what part fulfils he here?
Shall he shed cheer over the cheerless seats,
And touch the apathetic ghosts with joy?
Not for such end, O queen, thou hold'st thy realm.
For Heaven was Balder born, the city of Gods
And Heroes, where they live in light and joy.
Thither restore him, for his place is there!"
    He spoke; and grave replied the solemn queen:—
"Hermod, for he thou art, thou son of Heaven!
A strange unlikely errand, sure, is thine.
Do the Gods send to me to make them blest?
Small bliss my race hath of the Gods obtained.
Three mighty children to my father Lok
Did Angerbode, the giantess, bring forth—
Fenris the wolf, the Serpent huge, and me.
Of these the Serpent in the sea ye cast,
Who since in your despite hath wax'd amain,
And now with gleaming ring enfolds the world;
Me on this cheerless nether world ye threw,
And gave me nine unlighted realms to rule;
While on his island in the lake afar,
Made fast to the bored crag, by wile not strength
Subdued, with limber chains lives Fenris bound.
Lok still subsists in Heaven, our father wise,
Your mate, though loathed, and feasts in Odin's hall;
But him too foes await, and netted snares,
And in a cave a bed of needle-rocks,
And o'er his visage serpents dropping gall.
Yet he shall one day rise, and burst his bonds,
And with himself set us his offspring free,
When he guides Muspel's children to their bourne.
Till then in peril or in pain we live,
Wrought by the Gods—and ask the Gods our aid?
Howbeit, we abide our day; till then,
We do not as some feebler haters do—
Seek to afflict our foes with petty pangs,
Helpless to better us, or ruin them.
Come then! if Balder was so dear beloved,

And this is true, and such a loss is Heaven's—
Hear, how to Heaven may Balder be restored.
Show me through all the world the signs of grief!
Fails but one thing to grieve, here Balder stops!
Let all that lives and moves upon the earth
Weep him, and all that is without life weep;
Let Gods, men, brutes, beweep him; plants and stones!
So shall I know the lost was dear indeed,
And bend my heart, and give him back to Heaven."

She spake; and Hermod answer'd her, and said:—
"Hela, such as thou say'st, the terms shall be.
But come, declare me this, and truly tell:
May I, ere I depart, bid Balder hail,
Or is it here withheld to greet the dead?"

He spake, and straightway Hela answered him:—
"Hermod, greet Balder if thou wilt, and hold
Converse; his speech remains, though he be dead."

And straight to Balder Hermod turn'd, and spake:—
"Even in the abode of death, O Balder, hail!
Thou hear'st, if hearing, like as speech, is thine,
The terms of thy releasement hence to Heaven;
Fear nothing but that all shall be fulfill'd.
For not unmindful of thee are the Gods,
Who see the light, and blest in Asgard dwell;
Even here they seek thee out, in Hela's realm.
And sure of all the happiest far art thou
Who ever have been known in earth or Heaven;
Alive, thou wast of Gods the most beloved,
And now thou sittest crown'd by Hela's side,
Here, and hast honour among all the dead."

He spake; and Balder utter'd him reply,
But feebly, as a voice far off; he said:—
"Hermod the nimble, gild me not my death!
Better to live a serf, a captured man,
Who scatters rushes in a master's hall,
Than be a crown'd king here, and rule the dead.
And now I count not of these terms as safe
To be fulfill'd, nor my return as sure,
Though I be loved, and many mourn my death;
For double-minded ever was the seed
Of Lok, and double are the gifts they give.
Howbeit, report thy message; and therewith,
To Odin, to my father, take this ring,
Memorial of me, whether saved or no;
And tell the Heaven-born Gods how thou hast seen

Me sitting here below by Hela's side,
Crown'd, having honour among all the dead."
　He spake, and raised his hand, and gave the ring.
And with inscrutable regard the queen
Of Hell beheld them, and the ghosts stood dumb.
But Hermod took the ring, and yet once more
Kneel'd and did homage to the solemn queen;
Then mounted Sleipner, and set forth to ride
Back, through the astonish'd tribes of dead, to Heaven.
And to the wall he came, and found the grate
Lifted, and issued on the fields of ice.
And o'er the ice he fared to Ocean's strand,
And up from thence, a wet and misty road,
To the arm'd damsel's bridge, and Giall's stream.
Worse was that way to go than to return,
For him;—for others all return is barr'd.
Nine days he took to go, two to return,
And on the twelfth morn saw the light of Heaven.
And as a traveller in the early dawn
To the steep edge of some great valley comes,
Through which a river flows, and sees, beneath,
Clouds of white rolling vapours fill the vale,
But o'er them, on the farther slope, descries
Vineyards, and crofts, and pastures, bright with sun—
So Hermod, o'er the fog between, saw Heaven.
And Sleipner snorted, for he smelt the air
Of Heaven; and mightily, as wing'd, he flew.
And Hermod saw the towers of Asgard rise;
And he drew near, and heard no living voice
In Asgard; and the golden halls were dumb.
Then Hermod knew what labour held the Gods;
And through the empty streets he rode, and pass'd
Under the gate-house to the sands, and found
The Gods on the sea-shore by Balder's ship.

3. *Funeral*

The Gods held talk together, group'd in knots,
Round Balder's corpse, which they had thither borne;
And Hermod came down tow'rds them from the gate.
And Lok, the father of the serpent, first
Beheld him come, and to his neighbour spake:—
　"See, here is Hermod, who comes single back
From Hell; and shall I tell thee how he seems?
Like as a farmer, who hath lost his dog,

Some morn, at market, in a crowded town—
Through many streets the poor beast runs in vain,
And follows this man after that, for hours;
And, late at evening, spent and panting, falls
Before a stranger's threshold, not his home,
With flanks a-tremble, and his slender tongue
Hangs quivering out between his dust-smear'd jaws,
And piteously he eyes the passers by;
But home his master comes to his own farm,
Far in the country, wondering where he is—
So Hermod comes to-day unfollow'd home."
    And straight his neighbour, moved with wrath, replied:—
"Deceiver! fair in form, but false in heart!
Enemy, mocker, whom, though Gods, we hate—
Peace, lest our father Odin hear thee gibe!
Would I might see him snatch thee in his hand,
And bind thy carcase, like a bale, with cords,
And hurl thee in a lake, to sink or swim!
If clear from plotting Balder's death, to swim;
But deep, if thou devisedst it, to drown,
And perish, against fate, before thy day."
    So they two soft to one another spake.
But Odin look'd toward the land, and saw
His messenger; and he stood forth, and cried.
And Hermod came, and leapt from Sleipner down,
And in his father's hand put Sleipner's rein,
And greeted Odin and the Gods, and said:—
    "Odin, my father, and ye, Gods of Heaven!
Lo, home, having perform'd your will, I come.
Into the joyless kingdom have I been,
Below, and look'd upon the shadowy tribes
Of ghosts, and commix'd with their solemn queen;
And to your prayer she sends you this reply:
Show her through all the world the signs of grief!
Fails but one thing to grieve, there Balder stops!
Let Gods, men, brutes, beweep him; plants and stones:
So shall she know your loss was dear indeed,
And bend her heart, and give you Balder back."
    He spoke; and all the Gods to Odin look'd;
And straight the Father of the ages said:—
    "Ye Gods, these terms may keep another day.
But now, put on your arms, and mount your steeds,
And in procession all come near, and weep
Balder; for that is what the dead desire.
When ye enough have wept, then build a pile

Of the heap'd wood, and burn his corpse with fire
Out of our sight; that we may turn from grief,
And lead, as erst, our daily life in Heaven."
    He spoke, and the Gods arm'd; and Odin donn'd
His dazzling corslet and his helm of gold,
And led the way on Sleipner; and the rest
Follow'd, in tears, their father and their king.
And thrice in arms around the dead they rode,
Weeping; the sand were wetted, and their arms,
With their thick-falling tears—so good a friend
They mourn'd that day, so bright, so loved a God.
And Odin came, and laid his kingly hands
On Balder's breast, and thus began the wail:—
    "Farewell, O Balder, bright and loved, my son!
In that great day, the twilight of the Gods,
When Muspel's children shall beleaguer Heaven,
Then we shall miss thy counsel and thy arm."
    Thou camest near the next, O warrior Thor!
Shouldering thy hammer, in thy chariot drawn,
Swaying the long-hair'd goats with silver'd rein;
And over Balder's corpse these words didst say:—
    "Brother, thou dwellest in the darksome land,
And talkest with the feeble tribes of ghosts,
Now, and I know not how they prize thee there—
But here, I know, thou wilt be miss'd and mourn'd.
For haughty spirits and high wraths are rife
Among the Gods and Heroes here in Heaven,
As among those whose joy and work is war;
And daily strifes arise, and angry words.
But from thy lips, O Balder, night or day,
Heard no one ever an injurious word
To God or Hero, but thou keptest back
The others, labouring to compose their brawls.
Be ye then kind, as Balder too was kind!
For we lose him, who smoothed all strife in Heaven."
    He spake, and all the Gods assenting wail'd.
And Freya next came nigh, with golden tears;
The loveliest Goddess she in Heaven, by all
Most honour'd after Frea, Odin's wife.
Her long ago the wandering Oder took
To mate, but left her to roam distant lands;
Since then she seeks him, and weeps tears of gold.
Names hath she many; Vanadis on earth
They call her, Freya is her name in Heaven;
She in her hands took Balder's head, and spake:—·

"Balder, my brother, thou art gone a road
Unknown and long, and haply on that way
My long-lost wandering Oder thou hast met,
For in the paths of Heaven he is not found.
Oh, if it be so, tell him what thou wast
To his neglected wife, and what he is,
And wring his heart with shame, to hear thy word!
For he, my husband, left me here to pine,
Not long a wife, when his unquiet heart
First drove him from me into distant lands;
Since then I vainly seek him through the world,
And weep from shore to shore my golden tears,
But neither god nor mortal heeds my pain.
Thou only, Balder, wast for ever kind,
To take my hand, and wipe my tears, and say:
Weep not, O Freya, weep no golden tears!
One day the wandering Oder will return,
Or thou wilt find him in thy faithful search
On some great road, or resting in an inn,
Or at a ford, or sleeping by a tree.
So Balder said;—but Oder, well I know,
My truant Oder I shall see no more
To the world's end; and Balder now is gone,
And I am left uncomforted in Heaven."

She spake; and all the Goddesses bewail'd.
Last from among the Heroes one came near,
No God, but of the hero-troop the chief—
Regner, who swept the northern sea with fleets,
And ruled o'er Denmark and the heathy isles,
Living; but Ella captured him and slew;—
A king whose fame then fill'd the vast of Heaven,
Now time obscures it, and men's later deeds.
He last approach'd the corpse, and spake, and said:—

"Balder, there yet are many Scalds in Heaven
Still left, and that chief Scald, thy brother Brage,
Whom we may bid to sing, though thou art gone.
And all these gladly, while we drink, we hear,
After the feast is done, in Odin's hall;
But they harp ever on one string, and wake
Remembrance in our soul of wars alone,
Such as on earth we valiantly have waged,
And blood, and ringing blows, and violent death.
But when thou sangest, Balder, thou didst strike
Another note, and, like a bird in spring,
Thy voice of joyance minded us, and youth,

And wife, and children, and our ancient home.
Yes, and I, too, remember'd then no more
My dungeon, where the serpents stung me dead,
Nor Ella's victory on the English coast—
But I heard Thora laugh in Gothland Isle,
And saw my shepherdess, Aslauga, tend
Her flock along the white Norwegian beach.
Tears started to mine eyes with yearning joy.
Therefore with grateful heart I mourn thee dead."
    So Regner spake, and all the Heroes groan'd.
But now the sun had pass'd the height of Heaven,
And soon had all that day been spent in wail;
But then the Father of the ages said:—
    "Ye Gods, there well may be too much of wail!
Bring now the gather'd wood to Balder's ship;
Heap on the deck the logs, and build the pyre."
    But when the Gods and Heroes heard, they brought
The wood to Balder's ship, and built a pile,
Full the deck's breadth, and lofty; then the corpse
Of Balder on the highest top they laid,
With Nanna on his right, and on his left
Hoder, his brother, whom his own hand slew.
And they set jars of wine and oil to lean
Against the bodies, and stuck torches near,
Splinters of pine-wood, soak'd with turpentine;
And brought his arms and gold, and all his stuff,
And slew the dogs who at his table fed,
And his horse, Balder's horse, whom most he loved,
And placed them on the pyre, and Odin threw
A last choice gift thereon, his golden ring.
The mast they fixt, and hoisted up the sails,
Then they put fire to the wood; and Thor
Set his stout shoulder hard against the stern
To push the ship through the thick sand;—sparks flew
From the deep trench she plough'd, so strong a God
Furrow'd it; and the water gurgled in.
And the ship floated on the waves, and rock'd.
But in the hills a strong east-wind arose,
And came down moaning to the sea; first squalls
Ran black o'er the sea's face, then steady rush'd
The breeze, and fill'd the sails, and blew the fire.
And wreathed in smoke the ship stood out to sea.
Soon with a roaring rose the mighty fire,
And the pile crackled; and between the logs
Sharp quivering tongues of flame shot out, and leapt,

D

Curling and darting, higher, until they lick'd
The summit of the pile, the dead, the mast,
And ate the shrivelling sails; but still the ship
Drove on, ablaze above her hull with fire.
And the Gods stood upon the beach, and gazed.
And while they gazed, the sun went lurid down
Into the smoke-wrapt sea, and night came on.
Then the wind fell, with night, and there was calm;
But through the dark they watch'd the burning ship
Still carried o'er the distant waters on,
Farther and farther, like an eye of fire.
And long, in the far dark, blazed Balder's pile;
But fainter, as the stars rose high, it flared,
The bodies were consumed, ash choked the pile.
And as, in a decaying winter-fire,
A charr'd log, falling, makes a shower of sparks—
So with a shower of sparks the pile fell in,
Reddening the sea around; and all was dark.

    But the Gods went by starlight up the shore
To Asgard, and sate down in Odin's hall
At table, and the funeral-feast began.
All night they ate the boar Serimner's flesh,
And from their horns, with silver rimm'd, drank mead,
Silent, and waited for the sacred morn.

    And morning over all the world was spread.
Then from their loathéd feast the Gods arose,
And took their horses, and set forth to ride
O'er the bridge Bifrost, where is Heimdall's watch,
To the ash Igdrasil, and Ida's plain;
Thor came on foot, the rest on horseback rode.
And they found Mimir sitting by his fount
Of wisdom, which beneath the ashtree springs;
And saw the Nornies watering the roots
Of that world-shadowing tree with honey-dew.
There came the Gods, and sate them down on stones;
And thus the Father of the ages said:—
    "Ye Gods, the terms ye know, which Hermod brought.
Accept them or reject them! both have grounds.
Accept them, and they bind us, unfulfill'd,
To leave for ever Balder in the grave,
An unrecover'd prisoner, shade with shades.
But how, ye say, should the fulfilment fail?—
Smooth sound the terms, and light to be fulfill'd;
For dear-beloved was Balder while he lived
In Heaven and earth, and who would grudge him tears?

But from the traitorous seed of Lok they come,
These terms, and I suspect some hidden fraud.
Bethink ye, Gods, is there no other way?—
Speak, were not this a way, the way for Gods?
If I, if Odin, clad in radiant arms,
Mounted on Sleipner, with the warrior Thor
Drawn in his car beside me, and my sons.
All the strong brood of Heaven, to swell my train,
Should make irruption into Hela's realm,
And set the fields of gloom ablaze with light,
And bring in triumph Balder back to Heaven?"
 He spake, and his fierce sons applauded loud.
But Frea, mother of the Gods, arose,
Daughter and wife of Odin; thus she said:—
 "Odin, thou whirlwind, what a threat is this!
Thou threatenest what transcends thy might, even thine.
For of all powers the mightiest far art thou,
Lord over men on earth, and Gods in Heaven;
Yet even from thee thyself hath been withheld
One thing—to undo what thou thyself hast ruled.
For all which hath been fixt, was fixt by thee.
In the beginning, ere the Gods were born,
Before the Heavens were builded, thou didst slay
The giant Ymir, whom the abyss brought forth,
Thou and thy brethren fierce, the sons of Bor,
And cast his trunk to choke the abysmal void.
But of his flesh and members thou didst build
The earth and Ocean, and above them Heaven.
And from the flaming world, where Muspel reigns,
Thou sent'st and fetched'st fire, and madest lights,
Sun, moon, and stars, which thou hast hung in Heaven,
Dividing clear the paths of night and day.
And Asgard thou didst build, and Midgard fort;
Then me thou mad'st; of us the Gods were born.
Last, walking by the sea, thou foundest spars
Of wood, and framed'st men, who till the earth,
Or on the sea, the field of pirates, sail.
And all the race of Ymir thou didst drown,
Save one, Bergelmer;—he on shipboard fled
Thy deluge, and from him the giants sprang.
But all that brood thou hast removed far off,
And set by Ocean's utmost marge to dwell;
But Hela into Niflheim thou threw'st,
And gav'st her nine unlighted worlds to rule,
A queen, and empire over all the dead.

That empire wilt thou now invade, light up
Her darkness, from her grasp a subject tear?—
Try it; but I, for one, will not applaud.
Nor do I merit, Odin, thou should'st slight
Me and my words, though thou be first in Heaven;
For I too am a Goddess, born of thee,
Thine eldest, and of me the Gods are sprung;
And all that is to come I know, but lock
In mine own breast, and have to none reveal'd.
Come then! since Hela holds by right her prey,
But offers terms for his release to Heaven,
Accept the chance; thou canst no more obtain.
Send through the world thy messengers; entreat
All living and unliving things to weep
For Balder; if thou haply thus may'st melt
Hela, and win the loved one back to Heaven."

　　She spake, and on her face let fall her veil,
And bow'd her head, and sate with folded hands.
Nor did the all-ruling Odin slight her word;
Straightway he spake, and thus address'd the Gods:
　　"Go quickly forth through all the world, and pray
All living and unliving things to weep
Balder, if haply he may thus be won."

　　When the Gods heard they straight arose, and took
Their horses, and rode forth through all the world;
North, south, east, west, they struck, and roam'd the world,
Entreating all things to weep Balder's death.
And all that lived, and all without life, wept.
And as in winter, when the frost breaks up,
At winter's end, before the spring begins,
And a warm west-wind blows, and thaw sets in—
After an hour a dripping sound is heard
In all the forests, and the soft-strewn snow
Under the trees is dibbled thick with holes,
And from the boughs the snowloads shuffle down;
And, in fields sloping to the south, dark plots
Of grass peep out amid surrounding snow,
And widen, and the peasant's heart is glad—
So through the world was heard a dripping noise
Of all things weeping to bring Balder back;
And there fell joy upon the Gods to hear.

　　But Hermod rode with Niord, whom he took
To show him spits and beaches of the sea
Far off, where some unwarn'd might fail to weep—
Niord, the God of storms, whom fishers know;

Not born in Heaven; he was in Vanheim rear'd,
With men, but lives a hostage with the Gods;
He knows each frith, and every rocky creek
Fringed with dark pines, and sands where seafowl scream—
They two scour'd every coast, and all things wept.
And they rode home together, through the wood
Of Jarnvid, which to east of Midgard lies
Bordering the giants, where the trees are iron;
There in the wood before a cave they came,
Where sate, in the cave's mouth, a skinny hag,
Toothless and old; she gibes the passers by.
Thok is she call'd, but now Lok wore her shape;
She greeted them the first, and laugh'd, and said:—
"Ye Gods, good lack, is it so dull in Heaven,
That ye come pleasuring to Thok's iron wood?
Lovers of change ye are, fastidious sprites.
Look, as in some boor's yard a sweet-breath'd cow,
Whose manger is stuff'd full of good fresh hay,
Snuffs at it daintily, and stoops her head
To chew the straw, her litter, at her feet—
So ye grow squeamish, Gods, and sniff at Heaven!"

    She spake; but Hermod answer'd her and said:—
"Thok, not for gibes we come, we come for tears.
Balder is dead, and Hela holds her prey,
But will restore, if all things give him tears.
Begrudge not thine! to all was Balder dear."

    Then, with a louder laugh, the hag replied:—
"Is Balder dead? and do ye come for tears?
Thok with dry eyes will weep o'er Balder's pyre.
Weep him all other things, if weep they will—
I weep him not! let Hela keep her prey."

    She spake, and to the cavern's depth she fled,
Mocking; and Hermod knew their toil was vain.
And as seafaring men, who long have wrought
In the great deep for gain, at last come home,
And towards evening see the headlands rise
Of their dear country, and can plain descry
A fire of wither'd furze which boys have lit
Upon the cliffs, or smoke of burning weeds
Out of a till'd field inland;—then the wind
Catches them, and drives out again to sea;
And they go long days tossing up and down
Over the grey sea-ridges, and the glimpse
Of port they had makes bitterer far their toil—
So the Gods' cross was bitterer for their joy.

Then, sad at heart, to Niord Hermod spake:—
"It is the accuser Lok, who flouts us all!
Ride back, and tell in Heaven this heavy news;
I must again below, to Hela's realm."
     He spoke; and Niord set forth back to Heaven.
But northward Hermod rode, the way below,
The way he knew; and traversed Giall's stream,
And down to Ocean groped, and cross'd the ice,
And came beneath the wall, and found the grate
Still lifted; well was his return foreknown.
And once more Hermod saw around him spread
The joyless plains, and heard the streams of Hell.
But as he enter'd, on the extremest bound
Of Niflheim, he saw one ghost come near,
Hovering, and stopping oft, as if afraid—
Hoder, the unhappy, whom his own hand slew.
And Hermod look'd, and knew his brother's ghost,
And call'd him by his name, and sternly said:—
     "Hoder, ill-fated, blind in heart and eyes!
Why tarriest thou to plunge thee in the gulph
Of the deep inner gloom, but flittest here,
In twilight, on the lonely verge of Hell,
Far from the other ghosts, and Hela's throne?
Doubtless thou fearest to meet Balder's voice,
Thy brother, whom through folly thou didst slay."
     He spoke; but Hoder answer'd him, and said:—
"Hermod the nimble, dost thou still pursue
The unhappy with reproach, even in the grave?
For this I died, and fled beneath the gloom,
Not daily to endure abhorring Gods,
Nor with a hateful presence cumber Heaven;
And canst thou not, even here, pass pitying by?
No less than Balder have I lost the light
Of Heaven, and communion with my kin;
I too had once a wife, and once a child,
And substance, and a golden house in Heaven—
But all I left of my own act, and fled
Below, and dost thou hate me even here?
Balder upbraids me not, nor hates at all,
Though he has cause, have any cause; but he,
When that with downcast looks I hither came,
Stretch'd forth his hand, and with benignant voice,
Welcome, he said, *if there be welcome here,*
Brother and fellow-sport of Lok with me!
And not to offend thee, Hermod, nor to force

My hated converse on thee, came I up
From the deep gloom, where I will now return;
But earnestly I long'd to hover near,
Not too far off, when that thou camest by;
To feel the presence of a brother God,
And hear the passage of a horse of Heaven,
For the last time—for here thou com'st no more."
   He spake, and turn'd to go to the inner gloom.
But Hermod stay'd him with mild words, and said:—
   "Thou doest well to chide me, Hoder blind!
Truly thou say'st, the planning guilty mind
Was Lok's; the unwitting hand alone was thine.
But Gods are like the sons of men in this—
When they have woe, they blame the nearest cause.
Howbeit stay, and be appeased! and tell:
Sits Balder still in pomp by Hela's side,
Or is he mingled with the unnumber'd dead?"
   And the blind Hoder answer'd him and spake:—
"His place of state remains by Hela's side,
But empty; for his wife, for Nanna came
Lately below, and join'd him; and the pair
Frequent the still recesses of the realm
Of Hela, and hold converse undisturb'd.
But they too, doubtless, will have breathed the balm,
Which floats before a visitant from Heaven,
And have drawn upward to this verge of Hell."
   He spake; and, as he ceased, a puff of wind
Roll'd heavily the leaden mist aside
Round where they stood, and they beheld two forms
Make toward them o'er the stretching cloudy plain.
And Hermod straight perceived them, who they were
Balder and Nanna; and to Balder said:—
   "Balder, too truly thou foresaw'st a snare!
Lok triumphs still, and Hela keeps her prey.
No more to Asgard shalt thou come, nor lodge
In thy own house, Breidablik, nor enjoy
The love all bear toward thee, nor train up
Forset, thy son, to be beloved like thee.
Here must thou lie, and wait an endless age.
Therefore for the last time, O Balder, hail!"
   He spake; and Balder answer'd him, and said:—
"Hail and farewell! for here thou com'st no more.
Yet mourn not for me, Hermod, when thou sitt'st
In Heaven, nor let the other Gods lament,
As wholly to be pitied, quite forlorn.

For Nanna hath rejoin'd me, who, of old,
In Heaven, was seldom parted from my side;
And still the acceptance follows me, which crown'd
My former life, and cheers me even here.
The iron frown of Hela is relax'd
When I draw nigh, and the wan tribes of dead
Love me, and gladly bring for my award
Their ineffectual feuds and feeble hates—
Shadows of hates, but they distress them still."
    And the fleet-footed Hermod made reply:—
"Thou hast then all the solace death allows,
Esteem and function; and so far is well.
Yet here thou liest, Balder, underground,
Rusting for ever; and the years roll on,
The generations pass, the ages grow,
And bring us nearer to the final day
When from the south shall march the fiery band
And cross the bridge of Heaven, with Lok for guide,
And Fenris at his heel with broken chain;
While from the east the giant Rymer steers
His ship, and the great serpent makes to land;
And all are marshall'd in one flaming square
Against the Gods, upon the plains of Heaven,
I mourn thee, that thou canst not help us then."
    He spake; but Balder answer'd him, and said:—
"Mourn not for me! Mourn, Hermod, for the Gods;
Mourn for the men on earth, the Gods in Heaven,
Who live, and with their eyes shall see that day!
The day will come, when fall shall Asgard's towers,
And Odin, and his sons, the seed of Heaven;
But what were I, to save them in that hour?
If strength might save them, could not Odin save,
My father, and his pride, the warrior Thor,
Vidar the silent, the impetuous Tyr?
I, what were I, when these can nought avail?
Yet, doubtless, when the day of battle comes,
And the two hosts are marshall'd, and in Heaven
The golden-crested cock shall sound alarm,
And his black brother-bird from hence reply,
And bucklers clash, and spears begin to pour—
Longing will stir within my breast, though vain.
But not to me so grievous, as, I know,
To other Gods it were, is my enforced
Absence from fields where I could nothing aid;
For I am long since weary of your storm

Of carnage, and find, Hermod, in your life
Something too much of war and broils, which make
Life one perpetual fight, a bath of blood.
Mine eyes are dizzy with the arrowy hail;
Mine ears are stunn'd with blows, and sick for calm.
Inactive therefore let me lie, in gloom,
Unarm'd, inglorious; I attend the course
Of ages, and my late return to light,
In times less alien to a spirit mild,
In new-recover'd seats, the happier day."
    He spake; and the fleet Hermod thus replied:—
"Brother, what seats are these, what happier day?
Tell me, that I may ponder it when gone."
    And the ray-crowned Balder answer'd him:—
"Far to the south, beyond the blue, there spreads
Another Heaven, the boundless—no one yet
Hath reach'd it; there hereafter shall arise
The second Asgard, with another name.
Thither, when o'er this present earth and Heavens
The tempest of the latter days hath swept,
And they from sight have disappear'd, and sunk,
Shall a small remnant of the Gods repair;
Hoder and I shall join them from the grave.
There re-assembling we shall see emerge
From the bright Ocean at our feet an earth
More fresh, more verdant than the last, with fruits
Self-springing, and a seed of man preserved,
Who then shall live in peace, as now in war.
But we in Heaven shall find again with joy
The ruin'd palaces of Odin, seats
Familiar, halls where we have supp'd of old;
Re-enter them with wonder, never fill
Our eyes with gazing, and rebuild with tears.
And we shall tread once more the well-known plain
Of Ida, and among the grass shall find
The golden dice wherewith we play'd of yore ;
And that will bring to mind the former life
And pastime of the Gods, the wise discourse
Of Odin, the delights of other days,
O Hermod, pray that thou may'st join us then!
Such for the future is my hope; meanwhile,
I rest the thrall of Hela, and endure
Death, and the gloom which round me even now
Thickens, and to its inner gulph recalls.
Farewell, for longer speech is not allow'd!"

He spoke, and waved farewell, and gave his hand
To Nanna; and she gave their brother blind
Her hand, in turn, for guidance; and the three
Departed o'er the cloudy plain, and soon
Faded from sight into the interior gloom.
But Hermod stood beside his drooping horse,
Mute, gazing after them in tears; and fain,
Fain had he follow'd their receding steps,
Though they to death were bound, and he to Heaven,
Then; but a power he could not break withheld.
And as a stork which idle boys have trapp'd,
And tied him in a yard, at autumn sees
Flocks of his kind pass flying o'er his head
To warmer lands, and coasts that keep the sun;—
He strains to join their flight, and from his shed
Follows them with a long complaining cry—
So Hermod gazed, and yearn'd to join his kin.

At last he sigh'd, and set forth back to Heaven.

The Forsaken Merman

COME, dear children, let us away;
Down and away below!
Now my brothers call from the bay,
Now the great winds shoreward blow,
Now the salt tides seaward flow;
Now the wild white horses play,
Champ and chafe and toss in the spray.
Children dear, let us away!
This way, this way!

Call her once before you go—
Call once yet!
In a voice that she will know:
"Margaret! Margaret!"
Children's voices should be dear
(Call once more) to a mother's ear;
Children's voices, wild with pain—
Surely she will come again!
Call her once and come away;
This way, this way!
"Mother dear, we cannot stay!
The wild white horses foam and fret."
Margaret! Margaret!

Come, dear children, come away down;
Call no more!
One last look at the white-wall'd town,
And the little grey church on the windy shore;
Then come down!
She will not come though you call all day;
Come away, come away!

Children dear, was it yesterday
We heard the sweet bells over the bay?
In the caverns where we lay,
Through the surf and through the swell,
The far-off sound of a silver bell?
Sand-strewn caverns, cool and deep,
Where the winds are all asleep;
Where the spent lights quiver and gleam,
Where the salt weed sways in the stream,
Where the sea-beasts, ranged all round,
Feed in the ooze of their pasture-ground;
Where the sea-snakes coil and twine,
Dry their mail and bask in the brine;
Where great whales come sailing by,
Sail and sail, with unshut eye,
Round the world for ever and aye?
When did music come this way?
Children dear, was it yesterday?

Children dear, was it yesterday
(Call yet once) that she went away?
Once she sate with you and me,
On a red gold throne in the heart of the sea,
And the youngest sate on her knee.
She comb'd its bright hair, and she tended it well,
When down swung the sound of a far-off bell.
She sigh'd, she look'd up through the clear green sea;
She said: "I must go, for my kinsfolk pray
In the little grey church on the shore to-day.
'Twill be Easter-time in the world—ah me!
And I lose my poor soul, Merman! here with thee."
I said: "Go up, dear heart, through the waves;
Say thy prayer, and come back to the kind sea-caves!"
She smiled, she went up through the surf in the bay.
Children dear, was it yesterday?

Children dear, were we long alone?
"The sea grows stormy, the little ones moan;
Long prayers," I said, "in the world they say;
Come!" I said; and we rose through the surf in the bay.
We went up the beach, by the sandy down
Where the sea-stocks bloom, to the white-wall'd town;
Through the narrow paved streets, where all was still,
To the little grey church on the windy hill.
From the church came a murmur of folk at their prayers,
But we stood without in the cold blowing airs.
We climb'd on the graves, on the stones worn with rains,
And we gazed up the aisle through the small leaded panes.
She sate by the pillar; we saw her clear:
"Margaret, hist! come quick, we are here!
Dear heart," I said, "we are long alone;
The sea grows stormy, the little ones moan."
But, ah, she gave me never a look,
For her eyes were seal'd to the holy book!
Loud prays the priest; shut stands the door.
Come away, children, call no more!
Come away, come down, call no more!

Down, down, down!
Down to the depths of the sea!
She sits at her wheel in the humming town,
Singing most joyfully.
Hark what she sings: "O joy, O joy,
For the humming street, and the child with its toy!
For the priest, and the bell, and the holy well;
For the wheel where I spun,
And the blessed light of the sun!"
And so she sings her fill,
Singing most joyfully,
Till the spindle drops from her hand,
And the whizzing wheel stands still.
She steals to the window, and looks at the sand,
And over the sand at the sea;
And her eyes are set in a stare;
And anon there breaks a sigh,
And anon there drops a tear,
From a sorrow-clouded eye,
And a heart sorrow-laden,
A long, long sigh;
For the cold strange eyes of a little Mermaiden
And the gleam of her golden hair.

Come away, away children;
Come children, come down!
The hoarse wind blows coldly;
Lights shine in the town.
She will start from her slumber
When gusts shake the door;
She will hear the winds howling,
Will hear the waves roar.
We shall see, while above us
The waves roar and whirl,
A ceiling of amber,
A pavement of pearl.
Singing: "Here came a mortal,
But faithless was she!
And alone dwell for ever
The kings of the sea."

But, children, at midnight,
When soft the winds blow,
When clear falls the moonlight,
When spring-tides are low;
When sweet airs come seaward
From heaths starr'd with broom,
And high rocks throw mildly
On the blanch'd sands a gloom;
Up the still, glistening beaches,
Up the creeks we will hie,
Over banks of bright seaweed
The ebb-tide leaves dry.
We will gaze, from the sand-hills,
At the white, sleeping town;
At the church on the hill-side —
And then come back down.
Singing: "There dwells a loved one,
But cruel is she!
She left lonely for ever
The kings of the sea."

SONNETS

Notes on Sonnets, pp. 786–7.

SONNETS

Austerity of Poetry

THAT son of Italy who tried to blow,
Ere Dante came, the trump of sacred song,
In his light youth amid a festal throng
Sate with his bride to see a public show.

Fair was the bride, and on her front did glow
Youth like a star; and what to youth belong—
Gay raiment, sparkling gauds, elation strong.
A prop gave way! crash fell a platform! lo,

'Mid struggling sufferers, hurt to death, she lay!
Shuddering, they drew her garments off—and found
A robe of sackcloth next the smooth, white skin.

Such, poets, is your bride, the Muse! young, gay,
Radiant, adorn'd outside; a hidden ground
Of thought and of austerity within.

Rachel

I

IN Paris all look'd hot and like to fade.
Sere, in the garden of the Tuileries,
Sere with September, droop'd the chestnut-trees.
'Twas dawn; a brougham roll'd through the streets
    and made

Halt at the white and silent colonnade
Of the French Theatre. Worn with disease,
Rachel, with eyes no gazing can appease,
Sate in the brougham and those blank walls survey'd.

She follows the gay world, whose swarms have fled
To Switzerland, to Baden, to the Rhine;
Why stops she by this empty play-house drear?

Ah, where the spirit its highest life hath led,
All spots, match'd with that spot, are less divine;
And Rachel's Switzerland, her Rhine, is here!

II

UNTO a lonely villa, in a dell
Above the fragrant warm Provençal shore,
The dying Rachel in a chair they bore
Up the steep pine-plumed paths of the Estrelle,

And laid her in a stately room, where fell
The shadow of a marble Muse of yore,
The rose-crown'd queen of legendary lore,
Polymnia, full on her death-bed.—'Twas well!

The fret and misery of our northern towns,
In this her life's last day, our poor, our pain,
Our jangle of false wits, our climate's frowns,

Do for this radiant Greek-soul'd artist cease;
Sole object of her dying eyes remain
The beauty and the glorious art of Greece.

III

SPRUNG from the blood of Israel's scatter'd race,
At a mean inn in German Aarau born,
To forms from antique Greece and Rome uptorn,
Trick'd out with a Parisian speech and face,

Imparting life renew'd, old classic grace;
Then, soothing with thy Christian strain forlorn,
A-Kempis! her departing soul outworn,
While by her bedside Hebrew rites have place—

Ah, not the radiant spirit of Greece alone
She had—one power, which made her breast its home!
In her, like us, there clash'd, contending powers,

Germany, France, Christ, Moses, Athens, Rome.
The strife, the mixture in her soul, are ours;
Her genius and her glory are her own.

Worldly Place

EVEN *in a palace, life may be led well!*
So spake the imperial sage, purest of men,
Marcus Aurelius. But the stifling den
Of common life, where, crowded up pell-mell,

Our freedom for a little bread we sell,
And drudge under some foolish master's ken
Who rates us if we peer outside our pen—
Match'd with a palace, is not this a hell?

Even in a palace! On his truth sincere,
Who spoke these words, no shadow ever came;
And when my ill-school'd spirit is aflame

Some nobler, ampler stage of life to win,
I'll stop, and say: "There were no succour here!
The aids to noble life are all within."

Immortality

FOIL'D by our fellow-men, depress'd, outworn,
We leave the brutal world to take its way,
And, *Patience! in another life*, we say,
The world shall be thrust down, and we up-borne.

And will not, then, the immortal armies scorn
The world's poor, routed leavings? or will they,
Who fail'd under the heat of this life's day,
Support the fervours of the heavenly morn?

No, no! the energy of life may be
Kept on after the grave, but not begun;
And he who flagg'd not in the earthly strife,

From strength to strength advancing—only he,
His soul well-knit, and all his battles won,
Mounts, and that hardly, to eternal life.

The Good Shepherd with the Kid

HE *saves the sheep, the goats he doth not save.*
So rang Tertullian's sentence, on the side
Of that unpitying Phrygian sect which cried:
"Him can no fount of fresh forgiveness lave,

"Who sins, once wash'd by the baptismal wave."—
So spake the fierce Tertullian. But she sigh'd,
The infant Church! of love she felt the tide
Stream on her from her Lord's yet recent grave.

And then she smiled; and in the Catacombs,
With eye suffused but heart inspired true,
On those walls subterranean, where she hid

Her head 'mid ignominy, death, and tombs,
She her Good Shepherd's hasty image drew—
And on his shoulders, not a lamb, a kid.

Monica's Last Prayer

"Ah, could thy grave at home, at Carthage, be!"
Care not for that, and lay me where I fall!
Everywhere heard will be the judgment-call;
But at God's altar, oh! remember me.

Thus Monica, and died in Italy.
Yet fervent had her longing been, through all
Her course, for home at last, and burial
With her own husband, by the Libyan sea.

Had been! but at the end, to her pure soul
All tie with all beside seem'd vain and cheap,
And union before God the only care.

Creeds pass, rites change, no altar standeth whole.
Yet we her memory, as she pray'd, will keep,
Keep by this: *Life in God, and union there!*

LYRIC POEMS

Notes on Lyric Poems, pp. 787–90.

LYRIC POEMS

Switzerland

1. *Meeting*

AGAIN I see my bliss at hand,
The town, the lake are here;
My Marguerite smiles upon the strand,
Unalter'd with the year.

I know that graceful figure fair,
That cheek of languid hue;
I know that soft, enkerchief'd hair,
And those sweet eyes of blue.

Again I spring to make my choice;
Again in tones of ire
I hear a God's tremendous voice:
"Be counsell'd, and retire."

Ye guiding Powers who join and part,
What would ye have with me?
Ah, warn some more ambitious heart,
And let the peaceful be!

2. *Parting*

YE storm-winds of Autumn!
Who rush by, who shake
The window, and ruffle
The gleam-lighted lake;
Who cross to the hill-side
Thin-sprinkled with farms,
Where the high woods strip sadly
Their yellowing arms—
Ye are bound for the mountains!
Ah! with you let me go
Where your cold, distant barrier,
The vast range of snow,

Through the loose clouds lifts dimly
Its white peaks in air—
How deep is their stillness!
Ah, would I were there!

But on the stairs what voice is this I hear,
Buoyant as morning, and as morning clear?
Say, has some wet bird-haunted English lawn
Lent it the music of its trees at dawn?
Or was it from some sun-fleck'd mountain-brook
That the sweet voice its upland clearness took?
      Ah! it comes nearer—
      Sweet notes, this way!

Hark! fast by the window
The rushing winds go,
To the ice-cumber'd gorges,
The vast seas of snow!
There the torrents drive upward
Their rock-strangled hum;
There the avalanche thunders
The hoarse torrent dumb.
—I come, O ye mountains!
Ye torrents, I come!

But who is this, by the half-open'd door,
Whose figure casts a shadow on the floor?
The sweet blue eyes—the soft, ash-colour'd hair—
The cheeks that still their gentle paleness wear—
The lovely lips, with their arch smile that tells
The unconquer'd joy in which her spirit dwells—
      Ah! they bend nearer—
      Sweet lips, this way!

Hark! the wind rushes past us!
Ah! with that let me go
To the clear, waning hill-side,
Unspotted by snow,
There to watch, o'er the sunk vale,
The frore mountain-wall,
Where the niched snow-bed sprays down
Its powdery fall.
There its dusky blue clusters
The aconite spreads;
There the pines slope, the cloud-strips

Hung soft in their heads.
No life but, at moments,
The mountain-bee's hum.
—I come, O ye mountains!
Ye pine-woods, I come!

Forgive me! forgive me!
  Ah, Marguerite, fain
Would these arms reach to clasp thee!
  But see! 'tis in vain.

In the void air, towards thee,
  My stretch'd arms are cast;
But a sea rolls between us—
  Our different past!

To the lips, ah! of others
  Those lips have been prest,
And others, ere I was,
  Were strain'd to that breast;

Far, far from each other
  Our spirits have grown;
And what heart knows another?
  Ah! who knows his own?

Blow, ye winds! lift me with you!
  I come to the wild.
Fold closely, O Nature!
  Thine arms round thy child.

To thee only God granted
  A heart ever new—
To all always open,
  To all always true.

Ah! calm me, restore me;
  And dry up my tears
On thy high mountain-platforms,
  Where morn first appears;

Where the white mists, for ever,
  Are spread and upfurl'd—
In the stir of the forces
  Whence issued the world.

3. *A Farewell*

MY horse's feet beside the lake,
Where sweet the unbroken moonbeams lay,
Sent echoes through the night to wake
Each glistening strand, each heath-fringed bay.

The poplar avenue was pass'd,
And the roof'd bridge that spans the stream;
Up the steep street I hurried fast,
Led by thy taper's starlike beam.

I came! I saw thee rise!—the blood
Pour'd flushing to thy languid cheek.
Lock'd in each other's arms we stood,
In tears, with hearts too full to speak.

Days flew;—ah, soon I could discern
A trouble in thine alter'd air!
Thy hand lay languidly in mine,
Thy cheek was grave, thy speech grew rare.

I blame thee not!—this heart, I know,
To be long loved was never framed;
For something in its depths doth glow
Too strange, too restless, too untamed.

And women—things that live and move
Mined by the fever of the soul—
They seek to find in those they love
Stern strength, and promise of control.

They ask not kindness, gentle ways—
These they themselves have tried and known;
They ask a soul which never sways
With the blind gusts that shake their own.

I too have felt the load I bore
In a too strong emotion's sway;
I too have wish'd, no woman more,
This starting, feverish heart away.

I too have long'd for trenchant force,
And will like a dividing spear;
Have praised the keen, unscrupulous course,
Which knows no doubt, which feels no fear.

But in the world I learnt, what there
Thou too wilt surely one day prove,
That will, that energy, though rare,
Are yet far, far less rare than love.

Go, then!—till time and fate impress
This truth on thee, be mine no more!
They will!—for thou, I feel, not less
Than I, wast destined to this lore.

We school our manners, act our parts—
But He, who sees us through and through,
Knows that the bent of both our hearts
Was to be gentle, tranquil, true.

And though we wear out life, alas!
Distracted as a homeless wind,
In beating where we must not pass,
In seeking what we shall not find;

Yet we shall one day gain, life past,
Clear prospect o'er our being's whole;
Shall see ourselves, and learn at last
Our true affinities of soul.

We shall not then deny a course
To every thought the mass ignore;
We shall not then call hardness force,
Nor lightness wisdom any more.

Then, in the eternal Father's smile,
Our soothed, encouraged souls will dare
To seem as free from pride and guile,
As good, as generous, as they are.

Then we shall know our friends!—though much
Will have been lost—the help in strife,
The thousand sweet, still joys of such
As hand in hand face earthly life—

Though these be lost, there will be yet
A sympathy august and pure;
Ennobled by a vast regret,
And by contrition seal'd thrice sure.

And we, whose ways were unlike here,
May then more neighbouring courses ply;
May to each other be brought near,
And greet across infinity.

How sweet, unreach'd by earthly jars,
My sister! to maintain with thee
The hush among the shining stars,
The calm upon the moonlit sea!

How sweet to feel, on the boon air,
All our unquiet pulses cease!
To feel that nothing can impair
The gentleness, the thirst for peace—

The gentleness too rudely hurl'd
On this wild earth of hate and fear;
The thirst for peace a raving world
Would never let us satiate here.

4. *Isolation. To Marguerite*

WE were apart; yet, day by day,
I bade my heart more constant be.
I bade it keep the world away,
And grow a home for only thee;
Nor fear'd but thy love likewise grew,
Like mine, each day, more tried, more true.

The fault was grave! I might have known,
What far too soon, alas! I learn'd—
The heart can bind itself alone,
And faith may oft be unreturn'd.
Self-sway'd our feelings ebb and swell—
Thou lov'st no more;—Farewell! Farewell!

Farewell!—and thou, thou lonely heart,
Which never yet without remorse
Even for a moment didst depart
From thy remote and spheréd course
To haunt the place where passions reign—
Back to thy solitude again!

Back! with the conscious thrill of shame
Which Luna felt, that summer-night,
Flash through her pure immortal frame,
When she forsook the starry height
To hang over Endymion's sleep
Upon the pine-grown Latmian steep.

Yet she, chaste queen, had never proved
How vain a thing is mortal love,
Wandering in Heaven, far removed.
But thou hast long had place to prove
This truth—to prove, and make thine own:
"Thou hast been, shalt be, art, alone."

Or, if not quite alone, yet they
Which touch thee are unmating things—
Ocean and clouds and night and day;
Lorn autumns and triumphant springs;
And life, and others' joy and pain,
And love, if love, of happier men.

Of happier men—for they, at least,
Have *dream'd* two human hearts might blend
In one, and were through faith released
From isolation without end
Prolong'd; nor knew, although not less
Alone than thou, their loneliness.

5. *To Marguerite—Continued*

YES! in the sea of life enisled,
With echoing straits between us thrown,
Dotting the shoreless watery wild,
We mortal millions live *alone*.
The islands feel the enclasping flow,
And then their endless bounds they know.

But when the moon their hollows lights,
And they are swept by balms of spring,
And in their glens, on starry nights,
The nightingales divinely sing;
And lovely notes, from shore to shore,
Across the sounds and channels pour—

Oh! then a longing like despair
Is to their farthest caverns sent;
For surely once, they feel, we were
Parts of a single continent!
Now round us spreads the watery plain—
Oh might our marges meet again!

Who order'd, that their longing's fire
Should be, as soon as kindled, cool'd?
Who renders vain their deep desire?—
A God, a God their severance ruled!
And bade betwixt their shores to be
The unplumb'd, salt, estranging sea.

6. *Absence*

In this fair stranger's eyes of grey
Thine eyes, my love! I see.
I shiver; for the passing day
Had borne me far from thee.

This is the curse of life! that not
A nobler, calmer train
Of wiser thoughts and feelings blot
Our passions from our brain;

But each day brings its petty dust
Our soon-choked souls to fill,
And we forget because we must
And not because we will.

I struggle towards the light; and ye,
Once-long'd-for storms of love!
If with the light ye cannot be,
I bear that ye remove.

I struggle towards the light—but oh,
While yet the night is chill,
Upon time's barren, stormy flow,
Stay with me, Marguerite, still!

7. *The Terrace at Berne*

(*Composed Ten Years after the Preceding*)

TEN years!—and to my waking eye
Once more the roofs of Berne appear;
The rocky banks, the terrace high,
The stream!—and do I linger here?

The clouds are on the Oberland,
The Jungfrau snows look faint and far;
But bright are those green fields at hand,
And through those fields comes down the Aar,

And from the blue twin-lakes it comes,
Flows by the town, the churchyard fair;
And 'neath the garden-walk it hums,
The house!—and is my Marguerite there?

Ah, shall I see thee, while a flush
Of startled pleasure floods thy brow,
Quick through the oleanders brush,
And clap thy hands, and cry: '*Tis thou!*

Or hast thou long since wander'd back,
Daughter of France! to France, thy home;
And flitted down the flowery track
Where feet like thine too lightly come?

Doth riotous laughter now replace
Thy smile; and rouge, with stony glare,
Thy cheek's soft hue; and fluttering lace
The kerchief that enwound thy hair?

Or is it over?—art thou dead?—
Dead!—and no warning shiver ran
Across my heart, to say thy thread
Of life was cut, and closed thy span!

Could from earth's ways that figure slight
Be lost, and I not feel 'twas so?
Of that fresh voice the gay delight
Fail from earth's air, and I not know?

Or shall I find thee still, but changed,
But not the Marguerite of thy prime?
With all thy being re-arranged,
Pass'd through the crucible of time;

With spirit vanish'd, beauty waned,
And hardly yet a glance, a tone,
A gesture—anything—retain'd
Of all that was my Marguerite's own?

I will not know! For wherefore try,
To things by mortal course that live,
A shadowy durability,
For which they were not meant, to give?

Like driftwood spars, which meet and pass
Upon the boundless ocean-plain,
So on the sea of life, alas!
Man meets man—meets, and quits again.

I knew it when my life was young;
I feel it still, now youth is o'er.
—The mists are on the mountain hung,
And Marguerite I shall see no more.

The Strayed Reveller

THE PORTICO OF CIRCE'S PALACE.   EVENING

A Youth.   Circe

The Youth

FASTER, faster,
O Circe, Goddess,
Let the wild, thronging train,
The bright procession
Of eddying forms,
Sweep through my soul!

Thou standest, smiling
Down on me! thy right arm,
Lean'd up against the column there,
Props thy soft cheek;
Thy left holds, hanging loosely,
The deep cup, ivy-cinctured,
I held but now.

Is it, then, evening
So soon? I see, the night-dews,
Cluster'd in thick beads, dim
The agate brooch-stones
On thy white shoulder;
The cool night-wind, too,
Blows through the portico,
Stirs thy hair, Goddess,
Waves thy white robe!

Circe

Whence art thou, sleeper?

The Youth

When the white dawn first
Through the rough fir-planks
Of my hut, by the chestnuts,
Up at the valley-head,
Came breaking, Goddess!
I sprang up, I threw round me
My dappled fawn-skin;
Passing out, from the wet turf,
Where they lay, by the hut door,
I snatch'd up my vine-crown, my fir-staff,
All drench'd in dew—
Came swift down to join
The rout early gather'd
In the town, round the temple,
Iacchus' white fane
On yonder hill.

Quick I pass'd, following
The wood-cutters' cart-track
Down the dark valley;—I saw
On my left, through the beeches
Thy palace, Goddess,
Smokeless, empty!
Trembling, I enter'd; beheld
The court all silent,
The lions sleeping,
On the altar this bowl.
I drank, Goddess!
And sank down here, sleeping,
On the steps of thy portico.

E

Circe

Foolish boy! Why tremblest thou?
Thou lovest it, then, my wine?
Wouldst more of it? See, how glows,
Through the delicate, flush'd marble,
The red, creaming liquor,
Strown with dark seeds!
Drink, then! I chide thee not,
Deny thee not my bowl.
Come, stretch forth thy hand, then—so!
Drink—drink again!

The Youth

Thanks, gracious one!
Ah, the sweet fumes again!
More soft, ah me,
More subtle-winding
Than Pan's flute-music!
Faint—faint! Ah me,
Again the sweet sleep!

Circe

Hist! Thou—within there!
Come forth, Ulysses!
Art tired with hunting?
While we range the woodland,
See what the day brings.

Ulysses

Ever new magic!
Hast thou then lured hither,
Wonderful Goddess, by thy art,
The young, languid-eyed Ampelus,
Iacchus' darling—
Or some youth beloved of Pan,
Of Pan and the Nymphs?
That he sits, bending downward
His white, delicate neck
To the ivy-wreathed marge
Of thy cup; the bright, glancing vine-leaves
That crown his hair,
Falling forward, mingling
With the dark ivy-plants—
His fawn-skin, half untied,

Smear'd with red wine-stains? Who is he,
That he sits, overweigh'd
By fumes of wine and sleep,
So late, in thy portico?
What youth, Goddess,—what guest
Of Gods or mortals?

Circe

Hist! he wakes!
I lured him not hither, Ulysses.
Nay, ask him!

The Youth

Who speaks? Ah, who comes forth
To thy side, Goddess, from within?
How shall I name him?
This spare, dark-featured,
Quick-eyed stranger?
Ah, and I see too
His sailor's bonnet,
His short coat, travel-tarnish'd,
With one arm bare!—
Art thou not he, whom fame
This long time rumours
The favour'd guest of Circe, brought by the waves?
Art thou he, stranger?
The wise Ulysses,
Laertes' son?

Ulysses

I am Ulysses.
And thou, too, sleeper?
Thy voice is sweet.
It may be thou hast follow'd
Through the islands some divine bard,
By age taught many things,
Age and the Muses;
And heard him delighting
The chiefs and people
In the banquet, and learn'd his songs,
Of Gods and Heroes,
Of war and arts,
And peopled cities,
Inland, or built
By the grey sea.—If so, then hail!
I honour and welcome thee.

The Youth

The Gods are happy.
They turn on all sides
Their shining eyes,
And see below them
The earth and men.

They see Tiresias
Sitting, staff in hand,
On the warm, grassy
Asopus bank,
His robe drawn over
His old, sightless head,
Revolving inly
The doom of Thebes.

They see the Centaurs
In the upper glens
Of Pelion, in the streams,
Where red-berried ashes fringe
The clear-brown shallow pools,
With streaming flanks, and heads
Rear'd proudly, snuffing
The mountain wind.

They see the Indian
Drifting, knife in hand,
His frail boat moor'd to
A floating isle thick-matted
With large-leaved, low-creeping melon-plants,
And the dark cucumber.
He reaps, and stows them,
Drifting—drifting;—round him,
Round his green harvest-plot,
Flow the cool lake-waves,
The mountains ring them.

They see the Scythian
On the wide stepp, unharnessing
His wheel'd house at noon.
He tethers his beast down, and makes his meal—
Mares' milk, and bread
Baked on the embers;—all around
The boundless, waving grass-plains stretch, thick-
    starr'd

With saffron and the yellow hollyhock
And flag-leaved iris-flowers.
Sitting in his cart
He makes his meal; before him, for long miles,
Alive with bright green lizards,
And the springing bustard-fowl,
The track, a straight black line,
Furrows the rich soil; here and there
Clusters of lonely mounds
Topp'd with rough-hewn,
Grey, rain-blear'd statues, overpeer
The sunny waste.

They see the ferry
On the broad, clay-laden
Lone Chorasmian stream;—thereon,
With snort and strain,
Two horses, strongly swimming, tow
The ferry-boat, with woven ropes
To either bow
Firm harness'd by the mane; a chief,
With shout and shaken spear,
Stands at the prow, and guides them; but astern
The cowering merchants, in long robes,
Sit pale beside their wealth
Of silk-bales and of balsam-drops,
Of gold and ivory,
Of turquoise-earth and amethyst,
Jasper and chalcedony,
And milk-barr'd onyx-stones.
The loaded boat swings groaning
In the yellow eddies;
The Gods behold them.
They see the Heroes
Sitting in the dark ship
On the foamless, long-heaving
Violet sea,
At sunset nearing
The Happy Islands.

These things, Ulysses,
The wise bards also
Behold and sing.
But oh, what labour!
O prince, what pain!

They too can see
Tiresias;—but the Gods,
Who give them vision,
Added this law:
That they should bear too
His groping blindness,
His dark foreboding,
His scorn'd white hairs;
Bear Hera's anger
Through a life lengthen'd
To seven ages.

They see the Centaurs
On Pelion;—then they feel,
They too, the maddening wine
Swell their large veins to bursting; in wild pain
They feel the biting spears
Of the grim Lapithæ, and Theseus, drive,
Drive crashing through their bones; they feel
High on a jutting rock in the red stream
Alcmena's dreadful son
Ply his bow;—such a price
The Gods exact for song:
To become what we sing.

They see the Indian
On his mountain lake; but squalls
Make their skiff reel, and worms
In the unkind spring have gnawn
Their melon-harvest to the heart.—They see
The Scythian; but long frosts
Parch them in winter-time on the bare stepp,
Till they too fade like grass; they crawl
Like shadows forth in spring.

They see the merchants
On the Oxus stream;—but care
Must visit first them too, and make them pale.
Whether, through whirling sand,
A cloud of desert robber-horse have burst
Upon their caravan; or greedy kings,
In the wall'd cities the way passes through,
Crush'd them with tolls; or fever-airs,
On some great river's marge,
Mown them down, far from home.

They see the Heroes
Near harbour;—but they share
Their lives, and former violent toil in Thebes,
Seven-gated Thebes, or Troy;
Or where the echoing oars
Of Argo first
Startled the unknown sea.

The old Silenus
Came, lolling in the sunshine,
From the dewy forest-coverts,
This way, at noon.
Sitting by me, while his Fauns
Down at the water-side
Sprinkled and smoothed
His drooping garland,
He told me these things.

But I, Ulysses,
Sitting on the warm steps,
Looking over the valley,
All day long, have seen,
Without pain, without labour,
Sometimes a wild-hair'd Mænad—
Sometimes a Faun with torches—
And sometimes, for a moment,
Passing through the dark stems
Flowing-robed, the beloved,
The desired, the divine,
Beloved Iacchus.

Ah, cool night-wind, tremulous stars!
Ah, glimmering water,
Fitful earth-murmur,
Dreaming woods!
Ah, golden-hair'd, strangely smiling Goddess,
And thou, proved, much enduring,
Wave-toss'd Wanderer!
Who can stand still?
Ye fade, ye swim, ye waver before me—
The cup again!

Faster, faster,
O Circe, Goddess,
Let the wild, thronging train,
The bright procession
Of eddying forms,
Sweep through my soul!

Fragment of an "Antigone"

The Chorus

WELL hath he done who hath seized happiness!
For little do the all-containing hours,
    Though opulent, freely give.
    Who, weighing that life well
    Fortune presents unpray'd,
Declines her ministry, and carves his own;
    And, justice not infringed,
  Makes his own welfare his unswerved-from law.

He does well too, who keeps that clue the mild
Birth-Goddess and the austere Fates first gave.
    For from the day when these
    Bring him, a weeping child,
    First to the light, and mark
A country for him, kinsfolk, and a home,
    Unguided he remains,
Till the Fates come again, this time with death.

    In little companies,
    And, our own place once left,
Ignorant where to stand, or whom to avoid,
By city and household group'd, we live; and many shocks
    Our order heaven-ordain'd
    Must every day endure:
Voyages, exiles, hates, dissensions, wars.
    Besides what waste *he* makes,
    The all-hated, order-breaking,
    Without friend, city, or home,
    Death, who dissevers all.

    Him then I praise, who dares
    To self-selected good
Prefer obedience to the primal law,
Which consecrates the ties of blood; for these, indeed,
    Are to the Gods a care;
    That touches but himself.
For every day man may be link'd and loosed
    With strangers; but the bond
    Original, deep-inwound,
    Of blood, can he not bind,
    Nor, if Fate binds, not bear.

But hush! Hæmon, whom Antigone,
Robbing herself of life in burying,
Against Creon's law, Polynices,
Robs of a loved bride—pale, imploring,
  Waiting her passage,
Forth from the palace hitherward comes.

Hæmon

No, no, old men, Creon, I curse not!
  I weep, Thebans,
  One than Creon crueller far!
For he, he, at least, by slaying her,
August laws doth mightily vindicate;
But thou, too-bold, headstrong, pitiless!
Ah me!—honourest more than thy lover,
  O Antigone!
A dead, ignorant, thankless corpse.

The Chorus

Nor was the love untrue
Which the Dawn-Goddess bore
To that fair youth she erst,
Leaving the salt sea-beds
And coming flush'd over the stormy frith
Of loud Euripus, saw—
Saw and snatch'd, wild with love,
From the pine-dotted spurs
Of Parnes, where thy waves,
Asopus! gleam rock-hemm'd—
The Hunter of the Tanagræan Field.

But him, in his sweet prime,
By severance immature,
By Artemis' soft shafts,
She, though a Goddess born,
Saw in the rocky isle of Delos die.
Such end o'ertook that love.
For she desired to make
Immortal mortal man,
And blend his happy life,
Far from the Gods, with hers;
To him postponing an eternal law.

Hæmon

But like me, she, wroth, complaining,
Succumb'd to the envy of unkind Gods;
And, her beautiful arms unclasping,
Her fair youth unwillingly gave.

The Chorus

Nor, though enthroned too high
To fear assault of envious Gods,
His beloved Argive seer would Zeus retain
From this appointed end

In this our Thebes; but when
His flying steeds came near
To cross the steep Ismenian glen,
The broad earth open'd, and whelm'd them and him;
And through the void air sang
At large his enemy's spear.

And fain would Zeus have saved his tired son
Beholding him where the Two Pillars stand
O'er the sun-redden'd western straits,
Or at his work in that dim lower world.
Fain would he have recall'd
The fraudulent oath which bound
To a much feebler wight the heroic man.

But he preferr'd Fate to his strong desire.
Nor did there need less than the burning pile
Under the towering Trachis crags,
And the Spercheios vale, shaken with groans,
And the roused Maliac gulph,
And scared Œtæan snows,
To achieve his son's deliverance, O my child!

Fragment of Chorus of a "Dejaneira"

O FRIVOLOUS mind of man,
Light ignorance, and hurrying, unsure thoughts!
Though man bewails you not,
How *I* bewail you!

Little in your prosperity
Do you seek counsel of the Gods.
Proud, ignorant, self-adored, you live alone.
In profound silence stern,
Among their savage gorges and cold springs,
Unvisited remain
The great oracular shrines.

Thither in your adversity
Do you betake yourselves for light,
But strangely misinterpret all you hear.
For you will not put on
New hearts with the enquirer's holy robe,
And purged, considerate minds.

And him on whom, at the end
Of toil and dolour untold,
The Gods have said that repose
At last shall descend undisturb'd—
Him you expect to behold
In an easy old age, in a happy home;
No end but this you praise.

But him, on whom, in the prime
Of life, with vigour undimm'd,
With unspent mind, and a soul
Unworn, undebased, undecay'd,
Mournfully grating, the gates
Of the city of death have for ever closed—
Him, I count *him*, well-starr'd.

Philomela

HARK! ah, the nightingale—
The tawny-throated!
Hark, from that moonlit cedar what a burst!
What triumph! hark!—what pain!

O wanderer from a Grecian shore,
Still, after many years, in distant lands,
Still nourishing in thy bewilder'd brain
That wild, unquench'd, deep-sunken, old-world pain—

Say, will it never heal?
And can this fragrant lawn
With its cool trees, and night,
And the sweet, tranquil Thames,
And moonshine, and the dew,
To thy rack'd heart and brain
Afford no balm?

Dost thou to-night behold,
Here, through the moonlight on this English grass,
The unfriendly palace in the Thracian wild?
Dost thou again peruse
With hot cheeks and sear'd eyes
The too clear web, and thy dumb sister's shame?
Dost thou once more assay
Thy flight, and feel come over thee,
Poor fugitive, the feathery change
Once more, and once more seem to make resound
With love and hate, triumph and agony,
Lone Daulis, and the high Cephissian vale?
Listen, Eugenia—
How thick the bursts come crowding through the leaves!
Again—thou hearest?
Eternal passion!
Eternal pain!

Calais Sands

A THOUSAND knights have rein'd their steeds
To watch this line of sand-hills run,
Along the never-silent Strait,
To Calais glittering in the sun;

To look tow'rd Ardres' Golden Field
Across this wide aërial plain,
Which glows as if the Middle Age
Were gorgeous upon earth again.

Oh, that to share this famous scene,
I saw, upon the open sand,
Thy lovely presence at my side,
Thy shawl, thy look, thy smile, thy hand!

How exquisite thy voice would come,
My darling, on this lonely air!
How sweetly would the fresh sea-breeze
Shake loose some band of soft brown hair!

Yet now my glance but once hath roved
O'er Calais and its famous plain;
To England's cliffs my gaze is turn'd,
On the blue strait mine eyes I strain.

Thou comest! Yes! the vessel's cloud
Hangs dark upon the rolling sea.
Oh, that yon sea-bird's wings were mine,
To win one instant's glimpse of thee!

I must not spring to grasp thy hand,
To woo thy smile, to seek thine eye;
But I may stand far off, and gaze,
And watch thee pass unconscious by,

And spell thy looks, and guess thy thoughts,
Mixt with the idlers on the pier.—
Ah, might I always rest unseen,
So I might have thee always near!

To-morrow hurry through the fields
Of Flanders to the storied Rhine!
To-night those soft-fringed eyes shall close
Beneath one roof, my queen! with mine.

Faded Leaves

1. *The River*

STILL glides the stream, slow drops the boat
Under the rustling poplars' shade;
Silent the swans beside us float—
None speaks, none heeds; ah, turn thy head!

Let those arch eyes now softly shine,
That mocking mouth grow sweetly bland;
Ah, let them rest, those eyes, on mine!
On mine let rest that lovely hand!

My pent-up tears oppress my brain,
My heart is swoln with love unsaid.
Ah, let me weep, and tell my pain,
And on thy shoulder rest my head!

Before I die—before the soul,
Which now is mine, must re-attain
Immunity from my control,
And wander round the world again;

Before this teased o'erlabour'd heart
For ever leaves its vain employ,
Dead to its deep habitual smart,
And dead to hopes of future joy.

2. *Too Late*

EACH on his own strict line we move,
And some find death ere they find love;
So far apart their lives are thrown
From the twin soul which halves their own.

And sometimes, by still harder fate,
The lovers meet, but meet too late.
—Thy heart is mine!—*True, true! ah, true!*
—Then, love, thy hand!—*Ah no! adieu!*

3. *Separation*

STOP!—not to me, at this bitter departing,
  Speak of the sure consolations of time!
Fresh be the wound, still-renew'd be its smarting,
  So but thy image endure in its prime.

But, if the stedfast commandment of Nature
  Wills that remembrance should always decay—
If the loved form and the deep-cherish'd feature
  Must, when unseen, from the soul fade away—

Me let no half-effaced memories cumber!
  Fled, fled at once, be all vestige of thee!
Deep be the darkness and still be the slumber—
  Dead be the past and its phantoms to me!

Then, when we meet, and thy look strays toward me,
  Scanning my face and the changes wrought there:
Who, let me say, is this stranger regards me,
  With the grey eyes, and the lovely brown hair?

4. *On the Rhine*

VAIN is the effort to forget.
Some day I shall be cold, I know,
As is the eternal moonlit snow
Of the high Alps, to which I go—
But ah, not yet, not yet!

Vain is the agony of grief.
'Tis true, indeed, an iron knot
Ties straitly up from mine thy lot,
And were it snapt—thou lov'st me not!
But is despair relief?

Awhile let me with thought have done.
And as this brimm'd unwrinkled Rhine,
And that far purple mountain-line,
Lie sweetly in the look divine
Of the slow-sinking sun;

So let me lie, and, calm as they,
Let beam upon my inward view
Those eyes of deep, soft, lucent hue—
Eyes too expressive to be blue,
Too lovely to be grey.

Ah, Quiet, all things feel thy balm!
Those blue hills, too, this river's flow,
Were restless once, but long ago.
Tamed is their turbulent youthful glow;
Their joy is in their calm.

5. *Longing*

COME to me in my dreams, and then
By day I shall be well again!
For then the night will more than pay
The hopeless longing of the day.

Come, as thou cam'st a thousand times,
A messenger from radiant climes,
And smile on thy new world, and be
As kind to others as to me!

Or, as thou never cam'st in sooth,
Come now, and let me dream it truth
And part my hair, and kiss my brow,
And say: *My love! why sufferest thou?*

Come to me in my dreams, and then
By day I shall be well again!
For then the night will more than pay
The hopeless longing of the day.

Dover Beach

THE sea is calm to-night.
The tide is full, the moon lies fair
Upon the straits;—on the French coast the light
Gleams and is gone; the cliffs of England stand,
Glimmering and vast, out in the tranquil bay.
Come to the window, sweet is the night-air!
Only, from the long line of spray
Where the sea meets the moon-blanch'd land,
Listen! you hear the grating roar
Of pebbles which the waves draw back, and fling,
At their return, up the high strand,
Begin, and cease, and then again begin,
With tremulous cadence slow, and bring
The eternal note of sadness in.

Sophocles long ago
Heard it on the Ægæan, and it brought
Into his mind the turbid ebb and flow
Of human misery; we
Find also in the sound a thought,
Hearing it by this distant northern sea.

The Sea of Faith
Was once, too, at the full, and round earth's shore
Lay like the folds of a bright girdle furl'd.
But now I only hear
Its melancholy, long, withdrawing roar,
Retreating, to the breath
Of the night-wind, down the vast edges drear
And naked shingles of the world.

Ah, love, let us be true
To one another! for the world, which seems
To lie before us like a land of dreams,
So various, so beautiful, so new,
Hath really neither joy, nor love, nor light,
Nor certitude, nor peace, nor help for pain;
And we are here as on a darkling plain
Swept with confused alarms of struggle and flight,
Where ignorant armies clash by night.

Growing Old

WHAT is it to grow old?
Is it to lose the glory of the form,
The lustre of the eye?
Is it for beauty to forego her wreath?
—Yes, but not this alone.

Is it to feel our strength—
Not our bloom only, but our strength—decay?
Is it to feel each limb
Grow stiffer, every function less exact,
Each nerve more loosely strung?

Yes, this, and more; but not
Ah, 'tis not what in youth we dream'd 'twould be!
'Tis not to have our life
Mellow'd and soften'd as with sunset-glow,
A golden day's decline.

'Tis not to see the world
As from a height, with rapt prophetic eyes,
And heart profoundly stirr'd;
And weep, and feel the fulness of the past,
The years that are no more.

It is to spend long days
And not once feel that we were ever young;
It is to add, immured
In the hot prison of the present, month
To month with weary pain.

It is to suffer this,
And feel but half, and feebly, what we feel.
Deep in our hidden heart
Festers the dull remembrance of a change,
But no emotion—none.

It is—last stage of all—
When we are frozen up within, and quite
The phantom of ourselves,
To hear the world applaud the hollow ghost
Which blamed the living man.

The Progress of Poesy

A Variation

YOUTH rambles on life's arid mount,
And strikes the rock, and finds the vein,
And brings the water from the fount,
The fount which shall not flow again.

The man mature with labour chops
For the bright stream a channel grand,
And sees not that the sacred drops
Ran off and vanish'd out of hand.

And then the old man totters nigh,
And feebly rakes among the stones.
The mount is mute, the channel dry;
And down he lays his weary bones.

The Last Word

CREEP into thy narrow bed,
Creep, and let no more be said!
Vain thy onset! all stands fast.
Thou thyself must break at last.

Let the long contention cease!
Geese are swans, and swans are geese.
Let them have it how they will!
Thou art tired; best be still.

They out-talk'd thee, hiss'd thee, tore thee?
Better men fared thus before thee;
Fired their ringing shot and pass'd,
Hotly charged—and sank at last.

Charge once more, then, and be dumb!
Let the victors, when they come,
When the forts of folly fall,
Find thy body by the wall!

Bacchanalia;
or, *The New Age*

I

THE evening comes, the fields are still.
The tinkle of the thirsty rill,
Unheard all day, ascends again;
Deserted is the half-mown plain,
Silent the swaths! the ringing wain,
The mower's cry, the dog's alarms,
All housed within the sleeping farms!
The business of the day is done,
The last-left haymaker is gone.
And from the thyme upon the height,
And from the elder-blossom white
And pale dog-roses in the hedge,
And from the mint-plant in the sedge,
In puffs of balm the night-air blows
The perfume which the day forgoes.
And on the pure horizon far,
See, pulsing with the first-born star,
The liquid sky above the hill!
The evening comes, the fields are still.

Loitering and leaping,
With saunter, with bounds—
Flickering and circling
In files and in rounds—
Gaily their pine-staff green
Tossing in air,
Loose o'er their shoulders white
Showering their hair—

See! the wild Mænads
Break from the wood,
Youth and Iacchus
Maddening their blood.
See! through the quiet land
Rioting they pass—
Fling the fresh heaps about,
Trample the grass.
Tear from the rifled hedge
Garlands, their prize;
Fill with their sports the field,
Fill with their cries.

Shepherd, what ails thee, then?
Shepherd, why mute?
Forth with thy joyous song!
Forth with thy flute!
Tempts not the revel blithe?
Lure not their cries?
Glow not their shoulders smooth?
Melt not their eyes?
Is not, on cheeks like those,
Lovely the flush?
—*Ah, so the quiet was!*
So was the hush!

II

The epoch ends, the world is still.
The age has talk'd and work'd its fill—
The famous orators have shone,
The famous poets sung and gone,
The famous men of war have fought,
The famous speculators thought,
The famous players, sculptors, wrought,
The famous painters fill'd their wall,
The famous critics judged it all.
The combatants are parted now—
Uphung the spear, unbent the bow,
The puissant crown'd, the weak laid low.
And in the after-silence sweet,
Now strifes are hush'd, our ears doth meet,
Ascending pure, the bell-like fame
Of this or that down-trodden name,

Delicate spirits, push'd away
In the hot press of the noon-day.
And o'er the plain, where the dead age
Did its now silent warfare wage—
O'er that wide plain, now wrapt in gloom,
Where many a splendour finds its tomb,
Many spent fames and fallen mights—
The one or two immortal lights
Rise slowly up into the sky
To shine there everlastingly,
Like stars over the bounding hill.
The epoch ends, the world is still.

Thundering and bursting
In torrents, in waves—
Carolling and shouting
Over tombs, amid graves—
See! on the cumber'd plain
Clearing a stage,
Scattering the past about,
Comes the new age.
Bards make new poems,
Thinkers new schools,
Statesmen new systems,
Critics new rules.
All things begin again;
Life is their prize;
Earth with their deeds they fill,
Fill with their cries.

Poet, what ails thee, then?
Say, why so mute?
Forth with thy praising voice!
Forth with thy flute!
Loiterer! why sittest thou
Sunk in thy dream?
Tempts not the bright new age?
Shines not its stream?
Look, ah, what genius,
Art, science, wit!
Soldiers like Cæsar,
Statesmen like Pitt!
Sculptors like Phidias,
Raphaels in shoals,
Poets like Shakespeare—
Beautiful souls!

See, on their glowing cheeks
Heavenly the flush!
—*Ah, so the silence was!*
So was the hush!

The world but feels the present's spell,
The poet feels the past as well;
Whatever men have done, might do,
Whatever thought, might think it too.

Epilogue
to Lessing's Laocoön

ONE morn as through Hyde Park we walk'd,
My friend and I, by chance we talk'd
Of Lessing's famed Laocoön;
And after we awhile had gone
In Lessing's track, and tried to see
What painting is, what poetry—
Diverging to another thought,
"Ah," cries my friend, "but who hath taught
Why music and the other arts
Oftener perform aright their parts
Than poetry? why she, than they,
Fewer fine successes can display?

"For 'tis so, surely! Even in Greece,
Where best the poet framed his piece,
Even in that Phœbus-guarded ground
Pausanias on his travels found
Good poems, if he look'd, more rare
(Though many) than good statues were—
For these, in truth, were everywhere.
Of bards full many a stroke divine
In Dante's, Petrarch's, Tasso's line,
The land of Ariosto show'd;
And yet, e'en there, the canvas glow'd
With triumphs, a yet ampler brood,
Of Raphael and his brotherhood.
And nobly perfect, in our day
Of haste, half-work, and disarray,
Profound yet touching, sweet yet strong,
Hath risen Goethe's, Wordsworth's song;

Yet even I (and none will bow
Deeper to these) must needs allow,
They yield us not, to soothe our pains,
Such multitude of heavenly strains
As from the kings of sound are blown,
Mozart, Beethoven, Mendelssohn."

While thus my friend discoursed, we pass
Out of the path, and take the grass.
The grass had still the green of May,
And still the unblacken'd elms were gay;
The kine were resting in the shade,
The flies a summer-murmur made.
Bright was the morn and south the air;
The soft-couch'd cattle were as fair
As those which pastured by the sea,
That old-world morn, in Sicily,
When on the beach the Cyclops lay,
And Galatea from the bay
Mock'd her poor lovelorn giant's lay.
"Behold," I said, "the painter's sphere!
The limits of his art appear.
The passing group, the summer-morn,
The grass, the elms, that blossom'd thorn—
Those cattle couch'd, or, as they rise,
Their shining flanks, their liquid eyes—
These, or much greater things, but caught
Like these, and in one aspect brought!
In outward semblance he must give
A moment's life of things that live!
Then let him choose his moment well,
With power divine its story tell."

Still we walk'd on, in thoughtful mood,
And now upon the bridge we stood.
Full of sweet breathings was the air,
Of sudden stirs and pauses fair.
Down o'er the stately bridge the breeze
Came rustling from the garden-trees
And on the sparkling waters play'd;
Light-plashing waves an answer made,
And mimic boats their haven near'd.
Beyond, the Abbey-towers appear'd,
By mist and chimneys unconfined,
Free to the sweep of light and wind;

While through their earth-moor'd nave below
Another breath of wind doth blow,
Sound as of wandering breeze—but sound
In laws by human artists bound.
"The world of music!" I exclaim'd:—
"This breeze that rustles by, that famed
Abbey recall it! what a sphere
Large and profound, hath genius here!
The inspired musician what a range,
What power of passion, wealth of change!
Some source of feeling he must choose
And its lock'd fount of beauty use,
And through the stream of music tell
Its else unutterable spell;
To choose it rightly is his part,
And press into its inmost heart.

"*Miserere, Domine!*
The words are utter'd, and they flee.
Deep is their penitential moan,
Mighty their pathos, but 'tis gone.
They have declared the spirit's sore
Sore load, and words can do no more.
Beethoven takes them then—those two
Poor, bounded words—and makes them new;
Infinite makes them, makes them young;
Transplants them to another tongue,
Where they can now, without constraint,
Pour all the soul of their complaint,
And roll adown a channel large
The wealth divine they have in charge.
Page after page of music turn,
And still they live and still they burn,
Eternal, passion-fraught, and free—
Miserere, Domine!"

Onward we moved, and reach'd the Ride
Where gaily flows the human tide.
Afar, in rest the cattle lay;
We heard, afar, faint music play;
But agitated, brisk, and near,
Men, with their stream of life, were here.
Some hang upon the rails, and some
On foot behind them go and come.
This through the Ride upon his steed
Goes slowly by, and this at speed.

The young, the happy, and the fair,
The old, the sad, the worn, were there;
Some vacant, and some musing went,
And some in talk and merriment.
Nods, smiles, and greetings, and farewells!
And now and then, perhaps, there swells
A sigh, a tear—but in the throng
All changes fast, and hies along.
Hies, ah, from whence, what native ground?
And to what goal, what ending, bound?
"Behold, at last the poet's sphere!
But who," I said, "suffices here?

"For, ah! so much he has to do;
Be painter and musician too!
The aspect of the moment show,
The feeling of the moment know!
The aspect not, I grant, express
Clear as the painter's art can dress;
The feeling not, I grant, explore
So deep as the musician's lore—
But clear as words can make revealing,
And deep as words can follow feeling.
But, ah! then comes his sorest spell
Of toil—he must life's *movement* tell!
The thread which binds it all in one,
And not its separate parts alone.
The *movement* he must tell of life,
Its pain and pleasure, rest and strife;
His eye must travel down, at full,
The long, unpausing spectacle;
With faithful unrelaxing force
Attend it from its primal source,
From change to change and year to year
Attend it of its mid career,
Attend it to the last repose
And solemn silence of its close.

"The cattle rising from the grass
His thought must follow where they pass;
The penitent with anguish bow'd
His thought must follow through the crowd.
Yes! all this eddying, motley throng
That sparkles in the sun along,
Girl, statesman, merchant, soldier bold,
Master and servant, young and old,

Grave, gay, child, parent, husband, wife,
He follows home, and lives their life.

"And many, many are the souls
Life's movement fascinates, controls;
It draws them on, they cannot save
Their feet from its alluring wave;
They cannot leave it, they must go
With its unconquerable flow.
But ah! how few, of all that try
This mighty march, do aught but die!
For ill-endow'd for such a way,
Ill-stored in strength, in wits, are they.
They faint, they stagger to and fro,
And wandering from the stream they go;
In pain, in terror, in distress,
They see, all round, a wilderness.
Sometimes a momentary gleam
They catch of the mysterious stream;
Sometimes, a second's space, their ear
The murmur of its waves doth hear.
That transient glimpse in song they say,
But not as painter can pourtray—
That transient sound in song they tell,
But not, as the musician, well.
And when at last their snatches cease,
And they are silent and at peace,
The stream of life's majestic whole
Hath ne'er been mirror'd on their soul.

"Only a few the life-stream's shore
With safe unwandering feet explore;
Untired its movement bright attend,
Follow its windings to the end.
Then from its brimming waves their eye
Drinks up delighted ecstasy,
And its deep-toned, melodious voice
For ever makes their ear rejoice.
They speak! the happiness divine
They feel, runs o'er in every line;
Its spell is round them like a shower—
It gives them pathos, gives them power.
No painter yet hath such a way,
Nor no musician made, as they,
And gather'd on immortal knolls
Such lovely flowers for cheering souls.

Beethoven, Raphael, cannot reach
The charm which Homer, Shakespeare, teach
To these, to these, their thankful race
Gives, then, the first, the fairest place;
And brightest is their glory's sheen,
For greatest hath their labour been."

The Youth of Nature

RAISED are the dripping oars,
Silent the boat! the lake,
Lovely and soft as a dream,
Swims in the sheen of the moon.
The mountains stand at its head
Clear in the pure June-night,
But the valleys are flooded with haze.
Rydal and Fairfield are there;
In the shadow Wordsworth lies dead.
So it is, so it will be for aye.
Nature is fresh as of old,
Is lovely; a mortal is dead.

The spots which recall him survive,
For he lent a new life to these hills.
The Pillar still broods o'er the fields
Which border Ennerdale Lake,
And Egremont sleeps by the sea.
The gleam of The Evening Star
Twinkles on Grasmere no more,
But ruin'd and solemn and grey
The sheepfold of Michael survives;
And, far to the south, the heath
Still blows in the Quantock coombs,
By the favourite waters of Ruth.
These survive!—yet not without pain,
Pain and dejection to-night,
Can I feel that their poet is gone.

He grew old in an age he condemn'd.
He look'd on the rushing decay
Of the times which had shelter'd his youth.
Felt the dissolving throes
Of a social order he loved;
Outlived his brethren, his peers;
And, like the Theban seer,
Died in his enemies' day.

Cold bubbled the spring of Tilphusa,
Copais lay bright in the moon,
Helicon glass'd in the lake
Its firs, and afar rose the peaks
Of Parnassus, snowily clear;
Thebes was behind him in flames,
And the clang of arms in his ear,
When his awe-struck captors led
The Theban seer to the spring.
Tiresias drank and died.
Nor did reviving Thebes
See such a prophet again.

Well may we mourn, when the head
Of a sacred poet lies low
In an age which can rear them no more!
The complaining millions of men
Darken in labour and pain;
But he was a priest to us all
Of the wonder and bloom of the world,
Which we saw with his eyes, and were glad.
He is dead, and the fruit-bearing day
Of his race is past on the earth;
And darkness returns to our eyes.

For, oh! is it you, is it you,
Moonlight, and shadow, and lake,
And mountains, that fill us with joy,
Or the poet who sings you so well?
Is it you, O beauty, O grace,
O charm, O romance, that we feel,
Or the voice which reveals what you are?
Are ye, like daylight and sun,
Shared and rejoiced in by all?
Or are ye immersed in the mass
Of matter, and hard to extract,
Or sunk at the core of the world
Too deep for the most to discern?
Like stars in the deep of the sky,
Which arise on the glass of the sage,
But are lost when their watcher is gone.

"They are here"—I heard, as men heard
In Mysian Ida the voice
Of the Mighty Mother, or Crete,
The murmur of Nature reply—

"Loveliness, magic, and grace,
They are here! they are set in the world,
They abide; and the finest of souls
Hath not been thrill'd by them all,
Nor the dullest been dead to them quite.
The poet who sings them may die,
But they are immortal and live,
For they are the life of the world.
Will ye not learn it, and know,
When ye mourn that a poet is dead,
That the singer was less than his themes,
Life, and emotion, and I?

"More than the singer are these.
Weak is the tremor of pain
That thrills in his mournfullest chord
To that which once ran through his soul.
Cold the elation of joy
In his gladdest, airiest song,
To that which of old in his youth
Fill'd him and made him divine.
Hardly his voice at its best
Gives us a sense of the awe,
The vastness, the grandeur, the gloom
Of the unlit gulph of himself.

"Ye know not yourselves; and your bards—
The clearest, the best, who have read
Most in themselves—have beheld
Less than they left unreveal'd.
Ye express not yourselves;—can you make
With marble, with colour, with word,
What charm'd you in others re-live?
Can thy pencil, O artist! restore
The figure, the bloom of thy love,
As she was in her morning of spring?
Canst thou paint the ineffable smile
Of her eyes as they rested on thine?
Can the image of life have the glow,
The motion of life itself?

"Yourselves and your fellows ye know not; and me,
The mateless, the one, will ye know?
Will ye scan me, and read me, and tell
Of the thoughts that ferment in my breast,

My longing, my sadness, my joy?
Will ye claim for your great ones the gift
To have render'd the gleam of my skies,
To have echoed the moan of my seas,
Utter'd the voice of my hills?
When your great ones depart, will ye say:
All things have suffer'd a loss,
Nature is hid in their grave?

"Race after race, man after man,
Have thought that my secret was theirs,
Have dream'd that I lived but for them,
That they were my glory and joy.
—They are dust, they are changed, they are gone!
I remain."

The Youth of Man

WE, O Nature, depart,
Thou survivest us! this,
This, I know, is the law.
Yes! but more than this,
Thou who seest us die
Seest us change while we live;
Seest our dreams, one by one,
Seest our errors depart;
Watchest us, Nature! throughout,
Mild and inscrutably calm.

Well for us that we change!
Well for us that the power
Which in our morning-prime
Saw the mistakes of our youth,
Sweet, and forgiving, and good,
Sees the contrition of age!

Behold, O Nature, this pair!
See them to-night where they stand,
Not with the halo of youth
Crowning their brows with its light,
Not with the sunshine of hope,
Not with the rapture of spring,
Which they had of old, when they stood
Years ago at my side

In this self-same garden, and said:
"We are young, and the world is ours;
Man, man is the king of the world!
Fools that these mystics are
Who prate of Nature! for she
Hath neither beauty, nor warmth,
Nor life, nor emotion, nor power.
But man has a thousand gifts,
And the generous dreamer invests
The senseless world with them all.
Nature is nothing; her charm
Lives in our eyes which can paint,
Lives in our hearts which can feel."

Thou, O Nature, wast mute,
Mute as of old! days flew,
Days and years; and Time
With the ceaseless stroke of his wings
Brush'd off the bloom from their soul.
Clouded and dim grew their eye,
Languid their heart—for youth
Quicken'd its pulses no more.
Slowly, within the walls
Of an ever-narrowing world,
They droop'd, they grew blind, they grew old.
Thee and their youth in thee,
Nature! they saw no more.

Murmur of living,
Stir of existence,
Soul of the world!
Make, oh, make yourselves felt
To the dying spirit of youth!
Come, like the breath of the spring!
Leave not a human soul
To grow old in darkness and pain!
Only the living can feel you,
But leave us not while we live!

Here they stand to-night—
Here, where this grey balustrade
Crowns the still valley; behind
Is the castled house, with its woods,
Which shelter'd their childhood—the sun
On its ivied windows; a scent

From the grey-wall'd gardens, a breath
Of the fragrant stock and the pink,
Perfumes the evening air.
Their children play on the lawns.
They stand and listen; they hear
The children's shouts, and at times,
Faintly, the bark of a dog
From a distant farm in the hills.
Nothing besides! in front
The wide, wide valley outspreads
To the dim horizon, reposed
In the twilight, and bathed in dew,
Corn-field and hamlet and copse
Darkening fast; but a light,
Far off, a glory of day,
Still plays on the city spires;
And there in the dusk by the walls,
With the grey mist marking its course
Through the silent, flowery land,
On, to the plains, to the sea,
Floats the imperial stream.

　　Well I know what they feel!
They gaze, and the evening wind
Plays on their faces; they gaze—
Airs from the Eden of youth
Awake and stir in their soul;
The past returns—they feel
What they are, alas! what they were.
They, not Nature, are changed.
Well I know what they feel!

Hush, for tears
Begin to steal to their eyes!
Hush, for fruit
Grows from such sorrow as theirs!

And they remember,
With piercing, untold anguish,
The proud boasting of their youth.
And they feel how Nature was fair.
And the mists of delusion,
And the scales of habit,
Fall away from their eyes;
And they see, for a moment,
Stretching out, like the desert

In its weary, unprofitable length,
Their faded, ignoble lives.

While the locks are yet brown on thy head,
While the soul still looks through thine eyes,
While the heart still pours
The mantling blood to thy cheek,
Sink, O youth, in thy soul!
Yearn to the greatness of Nature;
Rally the good in the depths of thyself!

Palladium

SET where the upper streams of Simois flow
Was the Palladium, high 'mid rock and wood;
And Hector was in Ilium, far below,
And fought, and saw it not—but there it stood!

It stood, and sun and moonshine rain'd their light
On the pure columns of its glen-built hall.
Backward and forward roll'd the waves of fight
Round Troy—but while this stood, Troy could not fall.

So, in its lovely moonlight, lives the soul.
Mountains surround it, and sweet virgin air;
Cold plashing, past it, crystal waters roll;
We visit it by moments, ah, too rare!

We shall renew the battle in the plain
To-morrow;—red with blood will Xanthus be;
Hector and Ajax will be there again,
Helen will come upon the wall to see.

Then we shall rust in shade, or shine in strife,
And fluctuate 'twixt blind hopes and blind despairs,
And fancy that we put forth all our life,
And never know how with the soul it fares.

Still doth the soul, from its lone fastness high,
Upon our life a ruling effluence send.
And when it fails, fight as we will, we die;
And while it lasts, we cannot wholly end.

F

Morality

WE cannot kindle when we will
The fire which in the heart resides;
The spirit bloweth and is still,
In mystery our soul abides.
   But tasks in hours of insight will'd
   Can be through hours of gloom fulfill'd.

With aching hands and bleeding feet
We dig and heap, lay stone on stone;
We bear the burden and the heat
Of the long day, and wish 'twere done.
   Not till the hours of light return,
   All we have built do we discern.

Then, when the clouds are off the soul,
When thou dost bask in Nature's eye,
Ask, how *she* view'd thy self-control,
Thy struggling, task'd morality—
   Nature, whose free, light, cheerful air,
   Oft made thee, in thy gloom, despair.

And she, whose censure thou dost dread,
Whose eye thou wast afraid to seek,
See, on her face a glow is spread,
A strong emotion on her cheek!
   "Ah, child!" she cries, "that strife divine,
   Whence was it, for it is not mine?

"There is no effort on *my* brow—
I do not strive, I do not weep;
I rush with the swift spheres and glow
In joy, and when I will, I sleep.
   Yet that severe, that earnest air,
   I saw, I felt it once—but where?

"I knew not yet the gauge of time,
Nor wore the manacles of space;
I felt it in some other clime,
I saw it in some other place.
   'Twas when the heavenly house I trod,
   And lay upon the breast of God."

A Summer Night

IN the deserted, moon-blanch'd street,
How lonely rings the echo of my feet!
Those windows, which I gaze at, frown,
Silent and white, unopening down,
Repellent as the world;—but see,
A break between the housetops shows
The moon! and, lost behind her, fading dim
Into the dewy dark obscurity
Down at the far horizon's rim,
Doth a whole tract of heaven disclose!

And to my mind the thought
Is on a sudden brought
Of a past night, and a far different scene.
Headlands stood out into the moonlit deep
As clearly as at noon;
The spring-tide's brimming flow
Heaved dazzlingly between;
Houses, with long white sweep,
Girdled the glistening bay;
Behind, through the soft air,
The blue haze-cradled mountains spread away,
That night was far more fair—
But the same restless pacings to and fro,
And the same vainly throbbing heart was there,
And the same bright, calm moon.

And the calm moonlight seems to say:
Hast thou then still the old unquiet breast,
Which neither deadens into rest,
Nor ever feels the fiery glow
That whirls the spirit from itself away,
But fluctuates to and fro,
Never by passion quite possess'd
And never quite benumb'd by the world's sway?—
And I, I know not if to pray
Still to be what I am, or yield and be
Like all the other men I see.

For most men in a brazen prison live,
Where, in the sun's hot eye,
With heads bent o'er their toil, they languidly
Their lives to some unmeaning taskwork give,

Dreaming of nought beyond their prison-wall.
And as, year after year,
Fresh products of their barren labour fall
From their tired hands, and rest
Never yet comes more near,
Gloom settles slowly down over their breast;
And while they try to stem
The waves of mournful thought by which they are prest
Death in their prison reaches them,
Unfreed, having seen nothing, still unblest.

And the rest, a few,
Escape their prison and depart
On the wide ocean of life anew.
There the freed prisoner, where'er his heart
Listeth, will sail;
Nor doth he know how there prevail,
Despotic on that sea,
Trade-winds which cross it from eternity.
Awhile he holds some false way, undebarr'd
By thwarting signs, and braves
The freshening wind and blackening waves.
And then the tempest strikes him; and between
The lightning-bursts is seen
Only a driving wreck,
And the pale master on his spar-strewn deck
With anguish'd face and flying hair
Grasping the rudder hard,
Still bent to make some port he knows not where,
Still standing for some false, impossible shore.
And sterner comes the roar
Of sea and wind, and through the deepening gloom
Fainter and fainter wreck and helmsman loom,
And he too disappears, and comes no more.

Is there no life, but these alone?
Madman or slave must man be one?

Plainness and clearness without shadow of stain!
Clearness divine!
Ye heavens, whose pure dark regions have no sign
Of languor, though so calm, and, though so great,
Are yet untroubled and unpassionate;
Who, though so noble, share in the world's toil,
And, though so task'd, keep free from dust and soil!

I will not say that your mild deeps retain
A tinge, it may be, of their silent pain
Who have long'd deeply once, and long'd in vain—
But I will rather say that you remain
A world above man's head, to let him see
How boundless might his soul's horizons be,
How vast, yet of what clear transparency!
How it were good to abide there, and breathe free;
How fair a lot to fill
Is left to each man still!

The Buried Life

LIGHT flows our war of mocking words, and yet,
Behold, with tears mine eyes are wet!
I feel a nameless sadness o'er me roll.
Yes, yes, we know that we can jest,
We know, we know that we can smile!
But there's a something in this breast,
To which thy light words bring no rest.
And thy gay smiles no anodyne.
Give me thy hand, and hush awhile,
And turn those limpid eyes on mine,
And let me read there, love! thy inmost soul.

Alas! is even love too weak
To unlock the heart, and let it speak?
Are even lovers powerless to reveal
To one another what indeed they feel?
I knew the mass of men conceal'd
Their thoughts, for fear that if reveal'd
They would by other men be met
With blank indifference, or with blame reproved;
I knew they lived and moved
Trick'd in disguises, alien to the rest
Of men, and alien to themselves—and yet
The same heart beats in every human breast!

But we, my love!—doth a like spell benumb
Our hearts, our voices?—must we too be dumb?

Ah! well for us, if even we,
Even for a moment, can get free
Our heart, and have our lips unchain'd;
For that which seals them hath been deep-ordain'd!

Fate, which foresaw
How frivolous a baby man would be—
By what distractions he would be possess'd,
How he would pour himself in every strife,
And well-nigh change his own identity—
That it might keep from his capricious play
His genuine self, and force him to obey
Even in his own despite his being's law,
Bade through the deep recesses of our breast
The unregarded river of our life
Pursue with indiscernible flow its way;
And that we should not see
The buried stream, and seem to be
Eddying at large in blind uncertainty,
Though driving on with it eternally.

But often, in the world's most crowded streets,
But often, in the din of strife,
There rises an unspeakable desire
After the knowledge of our buried life;
A thirst to spend our fire and restless force
In tracking out our true, original course;
A longing to inquire
Into the mystery of this heart which beats
So wild, so deep in us—to know
Whence our lives come and where they go.
And many a man in his own breast then delves,
But deep enough, alas! none ever mines.
And we have been on many thousand lines,
And we have shown, on each, spirit and power;
But hardly have we, for one little hour,
Been on our own line, have we been ourselves—
Hardly had skill to utter one of all
The nameless feelings that course through our breast,
But they course on for ever unexpress'd.
And long we try in vain to speak and act
Our hidden self, and what we say and do
Is eloquent, is well—but 'tis not true!
And then we will no more be rack'd
With inward striving, and demand
Of all the thousand nothings of the hour
Their stupefying power;
Ah yes, and they benumb us at our call!
Yet still, from time to time, vague and forlorn,
From the soul's subterranean depth upborne

As from an infinitely distant land,
Come airs, and floating echoes, and convey
A melancholy into all our day.

Only—but this is rare—
When a belovéd hand is laid in ours.
When, jaded with the rush and glare
Of the interminable hours,
Our eyes can in another's eyes read clear,
When our world-deafen'd ear
Is by the tones of a loved voice caress'd—
A bolt is shot back somewhere in our breast,
And a lost pulse of feeling stirs again.
The eye sinks inward, and the heart lies plain,
And what we mean, we say, and what we would, we know
A man becomes aware of his life's flow,
And hears its winding murmur; and he sees
The meadows where it glides, the sun, the breeze

And there arrives a lull in the hot race
Wherein he doth for ever chase
That flying and elusive shadow, rest.
An air of coolness plays upon his face,
And an unwonted calm pervades his breast
And then he thinks he knows
The hills where his life rose,
And the sea where it goes.

A Wish

I ASK not that my bed of death
From bands of greedy heirs be free;
For these besiege the latest breath
Of fortune's favour'd sons, not me.

I ask not each kind soul to keep
Tearless, when of my death he hears.
Let those who will, if any, weep!
There are worse plagues on earth than tears.

I ask but that my death may find
The freedom to my life denied;
Ask but the folly of mankind
Then, then at last, to quit my side.

Spare me the whispering, crowded room,
The friends who come, and gape, and go;
The ceremonious air of gloom—
All, which makes death a hideous show!

Nor bring, to see me cease to live,
Some doctor full of phrase and fame,
To shake his sapient head, and give
The ill he cannot cure a name.

Nor fetch, to take the accustom'd toll
Of the poor sinner bound for death,
His brother-doctor of the soul,
To canvass with official breath

The future and its viewless things—
That undiscover'd mystery
Which one who feels death's winnowing wings
Must needs read clearer, sure, than he!

Bring none of these; but let me be,
While all around in silence lies,
Moved to the window near, and see
Once more, before my dying eyes,

Bathed in the sacred dews of morn
The wide aerial landscape spread—
The world which was ere I was born,
The world which lasts when I am dead;

Which never was the friend of *one*,
Nor promised love it could not give,
But lit for all its generous sun,
And lived itself, and made us live.

There let me gaze, till I become
In soul, with what I gaze on, wed!
To feel the universe my home;
To have before my mind—instead

Of the sick room, the mortal strife,
The turmoil for a little breath—
The pure eternal course of life,
Not human combatings with death!

Thus feeling, gazing, might I grow
Composed, refresh'd, ennobled, clear;
Then willing let my spirit go
To work or wait elsewhere or here!

The Future

A WANDERER is man from his birth.
He was born in a ship
On the breast of the river of Time;
Brimming with wonder and joy
He spreads out his arms to the light,
Rivets his gaze on the banks of the stream.

As what he sees is, so have his thoughts been.
Whether he wakes,
Where the snowy mountainous pass,
Echoing the screams of the eagles,
Hems in its gorges the bed
Of the new-born clear-flowing stream;
Whether he first sees light
Where the river in gleaming rings
Sluggishly winds through the plain;
Whether in sound of the swallowing sea—
As is the world on the banks,
So is the mind of the man.

Vainly does each, as he glides,
Fable and dream
Of the lands which the river of Time
Had left ere he woke on its breast,
Or shall reach when his eyes have been closed.
Only the tract where he sails
He wots of; only the thoughts,
Raised by the objects he passes, are his.

Who can see the green earth any more
As she was by the sources of Time?
Who imagines her fields as they lay
In the sunshine, unworn by the plough?
Who thinks as they thought,
The tribes who then roam'd on her breast,
Her vigorous, primitive sons?

What girl
Now reads in her bosom as clear
As Rebekah read, when she sate
At eve by the palm-shaded well?
Who guards in her breast
As deep, as pellucid a spring
Of feeling, as tranquil, as sure?

   What bard,
At the height of his vision, can deem
Of God, of the world, of the soul,
With a plainness as near,
As flashing as Moses felt
When he lay in the night by his flock
On the starlit Arabian waste?
Can rise and obey
The beck of the Spirit like him?

This tract which the river of Time
Now flows through with us, is the plain.
Gone is the calm of its earlier shore.
Border'd by cities and hoarse
With a thousand cries is its stream.
And we on its breast, our minds
Are confused as the cries which we hear,
Changing and shot as the sights which we see.

And we say that repose has fled
For ever the course of the river of Time.
That cities will crowd to its edge
In a blacker, incessanter line;
That the din will be more on its banks,
Denser the trade on its stream,
Flatter the plain where it flows,
Fiercer the sun overhead.
That never will those on its breast
See an ennobling sight,
Drink of the feeling of quiet again.

But what was before us we know not,
And we know not what shall succeed.

Haply, the river of Time—
As it grows, as the towns on its marge
Fling their wavering lights

On a wider, statelier stream—
May acquire, if not the calm
Of its early mountainous shore,
Yet a solemn peace of its own.

And the width of the waters, the hush
Of the grey expanse where he floats,
Freshening its current and spotted with foam
As it draws to the Ocean, may strike
Peace to the soul of the man on its breast—
As the pale waste widens around him,
As the banks fade dimmer away,
As the stars come out, and the night-wind
Brings up the stream
Murmurs and scents of the infinite sea.

ELEGIAC POEMS

Notes on Elegiac Poems, pp. 790–4.

ELEGIAC POEMS

The Scholar-Gipsy

Go, for they call you, shepherd, from the hill;
  Go, shepherd, and untie the wattled cotes!
    No longer leave thy wistful flock unfed,
    Nor let thy bawling fellows rack their throats,
      Nor the cropp'd herbage shoot another head.
      But when the fields are still,
    And the tired men and dogs all gone to rest,
      And only the white sheep are sometimes seen
      Cross and recross the strips of moon-blanch'd green,
    Come, shepherd, and again begin the quest!

Here, where the reaper was at work of late—
  In this high field's dark corner, where he leaves
    His coat, his basket, and his earthen cruse,
    And in the sun all morning binds the sheaves,
      Then here, at noon, comes back his stores to use—
      Here will I sit and wait,
    While to my ear from uplands far away
      The bleating of the folded flocks is borne,
      With distant cries of reapers in the corn—
    All the live murmur of a summer's day.

Screen'd is this nook o'er the high, half-reap'd field,
  And here till sun-down, shepherd! will I be.
    Through the thick corn the scarlet poppies peep,
    And round green roots and yellowing stalks I see
      Pale pink convolvulus in tendrils creep;
      And air-swept lindens yield
    Their scent, and rustle down their perfumed showers
      Of bloom on the bent grass where I am laid,
      And bower me from the August sun with shade;
    And the eye travels down to Oxford's towers.

And near me on the grass lies Glanvil's book—
  Come, let me read the oft-read tale again!
    The story of the Oxford scholar poor,
    Of pregnant parts and quick inventive brain,

Who, tired of knocking at preferment's door,
   One summer-morn forsook
His friends, and went to learn the gipsy-lore,
   And roam'd the world with that wild brotherhood,
   And came, as most men deem'd, to little good,
But came to Oxford and his friends no more.

But once, years after, in the country-lanes,
   Two scholars, whom at college erst he knew,
   Met him, and of his way of life enquired;
Whereat he answer'd, that the gipsy-crew,
   His mates, had arts to rule as they desired
   The workings of men's brains,
And they can bind them to what thoughts they will.
"And I," he said, "the secret of their art,
   When fully learn'd, will to the world impart;
But it needs heaven-sent moments for this skill."

This said, he left them, and return'd no more.—
   But rumours hung about the country-side,
   That the lost Scholar long was seen to stray,
Seen by rare glimpses, pensive and tongue-tied,
   In hat of antique shape, and cloak of grey,
   The same the gipsies wore.
Shepherds had met him on the Hurst in spring;
   At some lone alehouse in the Berkshire moors,
   On the warm ingle-bench, the smock-frock'd boors
Had found him seated at their entering,

But, 'mid their drink and clatter, he would fly.
   And I myself seem half to know thy looks,
   And put the shepherds, wanderer! on thy trace;
And boys who in lone wheatfields scare the rooks
   I ask if thou hast pass'd their quiet place;
   Or in my boat I lie
Moor'd to the cool bank in the summer-heats,
   'Mid wide grass meadows which the sunshine fills,
   And watch the warm, green-muffled Cumner hills,
And wonder if thou haunt'st their shy retreats.

For most, I know, thou lov'st retired ground!
   Thee at the ferry Oxford riders blithe,
   Returning home on summer-nights, have met
Crossing the stripling Thames at Bab-lock-hithe,
   Trailing in the cool stream thy fingers wet,
   As the punt's rope chops round;

And leaning backward in a pensive dream,
  And fostering in thy lap a heap of flowers
  Pluck'd in shy fields and distant Wychwood bowers,
And thine eyes resting on the moonlit stream.

And then they land, and thou art seen no more!—
  Maidens, who from the distant hamlets come
    To dance around the Fyfield elm in May,
Oft through the darkening fields have seen thee roam,
    Or cross a stile into the public way.
      Oft thou hast given them store
Of flowers—the frail-leaf'd, white anemony,
  Dark bluebells drench'd with dews of summer eves,
  And purple orchises with spotted leaves—
But none hath words she can report of thee.

And, above Godstow Bridge, when hay-time's here
  In June, and many a scythe in sunshine flames,
  Men who through those wide fields of breezy grass
Where black-wing'd swallows haunt the glittering Thames,
    To bathe in the abandon'd lasher pass,
      Have often pass'd thee near
Sitting upon the river bank o'ergrown;
  Mark'd thine outlandish garb, thy figure spare,
  Thy dark vague eyes, and soft abstracted air—
But, when they came from bathing, thou wast gone!

At some lone homestead in the Cumner hills,
  Where at her open door the housewife darns,
    Thou hast been seen, or hanging on a gate
To watch the threshers in the mossy barns.
    Children, who early range these slopes and late
      For cresses from the rills,
Have known thee eying, all an April-day,
  The springing pastures and the feeding kine;
  And mark'd thee, when the stars come out and shine,
Through the long dewy grass move slow away.

In autumn, on the skirts of Bagley Wood—
  Where most the gipsies by the turf-edged way
    Pitch their smoked tents, and every bush you see
With scarlet patches tagg'd and shreds of grey,
    Above the forest-ground called Thessaly—
      The blackbird, picking food,

Sees thee, nor stops his meal, nor fears at all;
    So often has he known thee past him stray,
    Rapt, twirling in thy hand a wither'd spray,
And waiting for the spark from heaven to fall.

And once, in winter, on the causeway chill
    Where home through flooded fields foot-travellers go,
        Have I not pass'd thee on the wooden bridge,
    Wrapt in thy cloak and battling with the snow,
        Thy face tow'rd Hinksey and its wintry ridge?
            And thou hast climb'd the hill,
    And gain'd the white brow of the Cumner range;
        Turn'd once to watch, while thick the snowflakes fall,
        The line of festal light in Christ-Church hall—
Then sought thy straw in some sequester'd grange.

But what—I dream! Two hundred years are flown
    Since first thy story ran through Oxford halls,
        And the grave Glanvil did the tale inscribe
    That thou wert wander'd from the studious walls
        To learn strange arts, and join a gipsy-tribe;
            And thou from earth art gone
    Long since, and in some quiet churchyard laid—
        Some country-nook, where o'er thy unknown grave
        Tall grasses and white flowering nettles wave,
Under a dark, red-fruited yew-tree's shade.

—No, no, thou hast not felt the lapse of hours!
    For what wears out the life of mortal men?
        'Tis that from change to change their being rolls;
    'Tis that repeated shocks, again, again,
        Exhaust the energy of strongest souls
            And numb the elastic powers.
    Till having used our nerves with bliss and teen,
        And tired upon a thousand schemes our wit,
        To the just-pausing Genius we remit
Our worn-out life, and are—what we have been.

Thou hast not lived, why should'st thou perish, so?
    Thou hadst *one* aim, *one* business, *one* desire;
        Else wert thou long since number'd with the dead!
    Else hadst thou spent, like other men, thy fire!
        The generations of thy peers are fled,
            And we ourselves shall go;

But thou possessest an immortal lot,
  And we imagine thee exempt from age
  And living as thou liv'st on Glanvil's page,
Because thou hadst—what we, alas! have not.

For early didst thou leave the world, with powers
  Fresh, undiverted to the world without,
    Firm to their mark, not spent on other things;
  Free from the sick fatigue, the languid doubt,
    Which much to have tried, in much been baffled, brings.
      O life unlike to ours!
  Who fluctuate idly without term or scope,
    Of whom each strives, nor knows for what he strives,
    And each half lives a hundred different lives;
  Who wait like thee, but not, like thee, in hope.

Thou waitest for the spark from heaven! and we,
  Light half-believers of our casual creeds,
    Who never deeply felt, nor clearly will'd,
  Whose insight never has borne fruit in deeds,
    Whose vague resolves never have been fulfill'd;
      For whom each year we see
  Breeds new beginnings, disappointments new;
    Who hesitate and falter life away,
    And lose to-morrow the ground won to-day—
Ah! do not we, wanderer! await it too?

Yes, we await it!—but it still delays,
  And then we suffer! and amongst us one,
    Who most has suffer'd, takes dejectedly
  His seat upon the intellectual throne;
    And all his store of sad experience he
      Lays bare of wretched days;
  Tells us his misery's birth and growth and signs,
    And how the dying spark of hope was fed,
    And how the breast was soothed, and how the head,
  And all his hourly varied anodynes.

This for our wisest! and we others pine,
  And wish the long unhappy dream would end,
    And waive all claim to bliss, and try to bear;
  With close-lipp'd patience for our only friend,
    Sad patience, too near neighbour to despair—
      But none has hope like thine!

Thou through the fields and through the woods dost stray,
  Roaming the country-side, a truant boy,
  Nursing thy project in unclouded joy,
And every doubt long blown by time away.

O born in days when wits were fresh and clear,
  And life ran gaily as the sparkling Thames;
    Before this strange disease of modern life,
  With its sick hurry, its divided aims,
    Its heads o'ertax'd, its palsied hearts, was rife—
      Fly hence, our contact fear!
  Still fly, plunge deeper in the bowering wood!
    Averse, as Dido did with gesture stern
    From her false friend's approach in Hades turn,
Wave us away, and keep thy solitude!

Still nursing the unconquerable hope,
  Still clutching the inviolable shade,
    With a free, onward impulse brushing through,
  By night, the silver'd branches of the glade—
    Far on the forest-skirts, where none pursue,
      On some mild pastoral slope
  Emerge, and resting on the moonlit pales
    Freshen thy flowers as in former years
    With dew, or listen with enchanted ears,
From the dark dingles, to the nightingales!

But fly our paths, our feverish contact fly!
  For strong the infection of our mental strife,
    Which, though it gives no bliss, yet spoils for rest;
  And we should win thee from thy own fair life,
    Like us distracted, and like us unblest.
      Soon, soon thy cheer would die,
  Thy hopes grow timorous, and unfix'd thy powers,
    And thy clear aims be cross and shifting made;
    And then thy glad perennial youth would fade,
Fade, and grow old at last, and die like ours.

Then fly our greetings, fly our speech and smiles!
  —As some grave Tyrian trader, from the sea,
    Descried at sunrise an emerging prow
  Lifting the cool-hair'd creepers stealthily,
    The fringes of a southward-facing brow
      Among the Ægæan isles;

And saw the merry Grecian coaster come,
　　Freighted with amber grapes, and Chian wine,
　　Green, bursting figs, and tunnies steep'd in brine—
And knew the intruders on his ancient home,

The young light-hearted masters of the waves—
　　And snatch'd his rudder, and shook out more sail;
　　And day and night held on indignantly
O'er the blue Midland waters with the gale,
　　Betwixt the Syrtes and soft Sicily,
　　　　To where the Atlantic raves
Outside the western straits; and unbent sails
　　There, where down cloudy cliffs, through sheets of foam,
　　Shy traffickers, the dark Iberians come;
And on the beach undid his corded bales.

Thyrsis

A Monody, to commemorate the author's friend,
Arthur Hugh Clough, who died at Florence, 1861.

How changed is here each spot man makes or fills!
　　In the two Hinkseys nothing keeps the same;
　　The village street its haunted mansion lacks,
And from the sign is gone Sibylla's name,
　　And from the roofs the twisted chimney-stacks—
　　　　Are ye too changed, ye hills?
See, 'tis no foot of unfamiliar men
　　To-night from Oxford up your pathway strays!
　　Here came I often, often, in old days—
Thyrsis and I; we still had Thyrsis then.

Runs it not here, the track by Childsworth Farm,
　　Past the high wood, to where the elm-tree crowns
　　The hill behind whose ridge the sunset flames?
The signal-elm, that looks on Ilsley Downs,
　　The Vale, the three lone weirs, the youthful Thames?—
　　　　This winter-eve is warm,
Humid the air! leafless, yet soft as spring,
　　The tender purple spray on copse and briers!
　　And that sweet city with her dreaming spires,
She needs not June for beauty's heightening,

Lovely all times she lies, lovely to-night!—
　　Only, methinks, some loss of habit's power
　　Befalls me wandering through this upland dim.
Once pass'd I blindfold here, at any hour;

Now seldom come I, since I came with him.
That single elm-tree bright
Against the west—I miss it! is it gone?
We prized it dearly; while it stood, we said,
Our friend, the Gipsy-Scholar, was not dead;
While the tree lived, he in these fields lived on.

Too rare, too rare, grow now my visits here,
But once I knew each field, each flower, each stick;
And with the country-folk acquaintance made
By barn in threshing-time, by new-built rick.
Here, too, our shepherd-pipes we first assay'd.
Ah me! this many a year
My pipe is lost, my shepherd's holiday!
Needs must I lose them, needs with heavy heart
Into the world and wave of men depart;
But Thyrsis of his own will went away.

It irked him to be here, he could not rest.
He loved each simple joy the country yields,
He loved his mates; but yet he could not keep,
For that a shadow lour'd on the fields,
Here with the shepherds and the silly sheep.
Some life of men unblest
He knew, which made him droop, and fill'd his head.
He went; his piping took a troubled sound
Of storms that rage outside our happy ground;
He could not wait their passing, he is dead.

So, some tempestuous morn in early June,
When the year's primal burst of bloom is o'er,
Before the roses and the longest day—
When garden-walks and all the grassy floor
With blossoms red and white of fallen May
And chestnut-flowers are strewn—
So have I heard the cuckoo's parting cry,
From the wet field, through the vext garden-trees,
Come with the volleying rain and tossing breeze:
The bloom is gone, and with the bloom go I!

Too quick despairer, wherefore wilt thou go?
Soon will the high Midsummer pomps come on,
Soon will the musk carnations break and swell,
Soon shall we have gold-dusted snapdragon,
Sweet-William with his homely cottage-smell,
And stocks in fragrant blow;

Roses that down the alleys shine afar,
    And open, jasmine-muffled lattices,
    And groups under the dreaming garden-trees,
And the full moon, and the white evening-star.

He hearkens not! light comer, he is flown!
    What matters it? next year he will return,
    And we shall have him in the sweet spring-days,
    With whitening hedges, and uncrumpling fern,
    And blue-bells trembling by the forest-ways,
      And scent of hay new-mown.
But Thyrsis never more we swains shall see;
    See him come back, and cut a smoother reed,
    And blow a strain the world at last shall heed—
For Time, not Corydon, hath conquer'd thee!

Alack, for Corydon no rival now!—
    But when Sicilian shepherds lost a mate,
    Some good survivor with his flute would go,
    Piping a ditty sad for Bion's fate;
    And cross the unpermitted ferry's flow,
      And relax Pluto's brow,
And make leap up with joy the beauteous head
    Of Proserpine, among whose crowned hair
    Are flowers first open'd on Sicilian air,
And flute his friend, like Orpheus, from the dead.

O easy access to the hearer's grace
    When Dorian shepherds sang to Prosperpine!
    For she herself had trod Sicilian fields,
    She knew the Dorian water's gush divine,
    She knew each lily white which Enna yields,
      Each rose with blushing face;
She loved the Dorian pipe, the Dorian strain.
    But ah, of our poor Thames she never heard!
    Her foot the Cumner cowslips never stirr'd;
And we should tease her with our plaint in vain!

Well! wind-dispersed and vain the words will be,
    Yet, Thyrsis, let me give my grief its hour
    In the old haunt, and find our tree-topp'd hill!
Who, if not I, for questing here hath power?
    I know the wood which hides the daffodil,
      I know the Fyfield tree,

  I know what white, what purple fritillaries
   The grassy harvest of the river-fields,
   Above by Ensham, down by Sandford, yields,
  And what sedged brooks are Thames's tributaries;

 I know these slopes; who knows them if not I?—
  But many a dingle on the loved hill-side,
   With thorns once studded, old, white-blossom'd trees,
  Where thick the cowslips grew, and far descried
   High tower'd the spikes of purple orchises,
    Hath since our day put by
  The coronals of that forgotten time;
   Down each green bank hath gone the ploughboy's team,
   And only in the hidden brookside gleam
  Primroses, orphans of the flowery prime.

Where is the girl, who by the boatman's door,
  Above the locks, above the boating throng,
   Unmoor'd our skiff when through the Wytham flats,
  Red loosestrife and blond meadow-sweet among
   And darting swallows and light water-gnats,
    We track'd the shy Thames shore?
  Where are the mowers, who, as the tiny swell
   Of our boat passing heaved the river-grass,
   Stood with suspended scythe to see us pass?—
  They all are gone, and thou art gone as well!

Yes, thou art gone! and round me too the night
  In ever-nearing circle weaves her shade.
   I see her veil draw soft across the day,
  I feel her slowly chilling breath invade
   The cheek grown thin, the brown hair sprent with grey;
    I feel her finger light
  Laid pausefully upon life's headlong train;—
   The foot less prompt to meet the morning dew,
   The heart less bounding at emotion new,
  And hope, once crush'd, less quick to spring again.

And long the way appears, which seem'd so short
  To the less practised eye of sanguine youth;
   And high the mountain-tops, in cloudy air,
  The mountain-tops where is the throne of Truth,
   Tops in life's morning-sun so bright and bare!
    Unbreachable the fort

Of the long-batter'd world uplifts its wall;
　　And strange and vain the earthly turmoil grows,
　　And near and real the charm of thy repose,
And night as welcome as a friend would fall.

But hush! the upland hath a sudden loss
　　Of quiet!—Look, adown the dusk hill-side,
　　A troop of Oxford hunters going home,
As in old days, jovial and talking, ride!
　　　From hunting with the Berkshire hounds they come.
　　　　Quick! let me fly, and cross
Into yon farther field!—'Tis done; and see,
　　Back'd by the sunset, which doth glorify
　　The orange and pale violet evening-sky,
Bare on its lonely ridge, the Tree! the Tree!

I take the omen! Eve lets down her veil,
　　The white fog creeps from bush to bush about,
　　The west unflushes, the high stars grow bright,
And in the scatter'd farms the lights come out.
　　　I cannot reach the signal-tree to-night,
　　　　Yet, happy omen, hail!
Hear it from thy broad lucent Arno-vale
　　(For there thine earth-forgetting eyelids keep
　　The morningless and unawakening sleep
Under the flowery oleanders pale),

Hear it, O Thyrsis, still our tree is there!—
　　Ah, vain! These English fields, this upland dim,
　　These brambles pale with mist engarlanded,
That lone, sky-pointing tree, are not for him;
　　　To a boon southern country he is fled,
　　　　And now in happier air,
Wandering with the great Mother's train divine
　　(And purer or more subtle soul than thee,
　　I trow the mighty Mother doth not see)
Within a folding of the Apennine,

Thou hearest the immortal chants of old!—
　　Putting his sickle to the perilous grain
　　In the hot cornfield of the Phrygian king,
For thee the Lityerses-song again
　　　Young Daphnis with his silver voice doth sing;
　　　　Sings his Sicilian fold,

His sheep, his hapless love, his blinded eyes—
  And how a call celestial round him rang,
  And heavenward from the fountain-brink he sprang,
And all the marvel of the golden skies.

There thou art gone, and me thou leavest here
  Sole in these fields! yet will I not despair.
    Despair I will not, while I yet descry
  'Neath the mild canopy of English air
    That lonely tree against the western sky.
      Still, still these slopes,' tis clear,
  Our Gipsy-Scholar haunts, outliving thee!
    Fields where soft sheep from cages pull the hay,
    Woods with anemonies in flower till May,
Know him a wanderer still; then why not me?

A fugitive and gracious light he seeks,
  Shy to illumine; and I seek it too.
    This does not come with houses or with gold,
  With place, with honour, and a flattering crew;
    'Tis not in the world's market bought and sold—
      But the smooth-slipping weeks
  Drop by, and leave its seeker still untired;
    Out of the heed of mortals he is gone,
    He wends unfollow'd, he must house alone;
Yet on he fares, by his own heart inspired.

Thou too, O Thyrsis, on like quest wast bound;
  Thou wanderedst with me for a little hour!
    Men gave thee nothing; but this happy quest,
  If men esteem'd thee feeble, gave thee power,
    If men procured thee trouble, gave thee rest.
    And this rude Cumner ground,
  Its fir-topped Hurst, its farms, its quiet fields,
    Here cam'st thou in thy jocund youthful time,
    Here was thine height of strength, thy golden prime!
And still the haunt beloved a virtue yields.

What though the music of thy rustic flute
  Kept not for long its happy, country tone;
    Lost it too soon, and learnt a stormy note
  Of men, contention-tost, of men who groan,
    Which task'd thy pipe too sore, and tired thy throat—
      It fail'd, and thou wast mute!

Yet hadst thou alway visions of our light,
   And long with men of care thou couldst not stay,
   And soon thy foot resumed its wandering way,
Left human haunt, and on alone till night.

Too rare, too rare, grow now my visits here!
   'Mid city-noise, not, as with thee of yore,
    Thyrsis! in reach of sheep-bells is my home.
   —Then through the great town's harsh, heart-wearying
      roar,
    Let in thy voice a whisper often come,
     To chase fatigue and fear:
Why faintest thou? I wander'd till I died.
   Roam on! The light we sought is shining still.
   Dost thou ask proof? Our tree yet crowns the hill,
Our Scholar travels yet the loved hill-side.

Memorial Verses

April, 1850

GOETHE in Weimar sleeps, and Greece,
Long since, saw Byron's struggle cease.
But one such death remain'd to come;
The last poetic voice is dumb—
We stand to-day by Wordsworth's tomb.

When Byron's eyes were shut in death,
We bow'd our head and held our breath.
He taught us little; but our soul
Had *felt* him like the thunder's roll.
With shivering heart the strife we saw
Of passion with eternal law;
And yet with reverential awe
We watch'd the fount of fiery life
Which served for that Titanic strife.

When Goethe's death was told, we said:
Sunk, then, is Europe's sagest head.
Physician of the iron age,
Goethe has done his pilgrimage.
He took the suffering human race,
He read each wound, each weakness clear;
And struck his finger on the place,
And said: *Thou ailest here, and here!*

He look'd on Europe's dying hour
Of fitful dream and feverish power;
His eye plunged down the weltering strife,
The turmoil of expiring life—
He said: *The end is everywhere,*
Art still has truth, take refuge there!
And he was happy, if to know
Causes of things, and far below
His feet to see the lurid flow
Of terror, and insane distress,
And headlong fate, be happiness.

And Wordsworth!—Ah, pale ghosts, rejoice!
For never has such soothing voice
Been to your shadowy world convey'd,
Since erst, at morn, some wandering shade
Heard the clear song of Orpheus come
Through Hades, and the mournful gloom.
Wordsworth has gone from us—and ye,
Ah, may ye feel his voice as we!
He too upon a wintry clime
Had fallen—on this iron time
Of doubts, disputes, distractions, fears.
He found us when the age had bound
Our souls in its benumbing round;
He spoke, and loosed our heart in tears.
He laid us as we lay at birth
On the cool flowery lap of earth,
Smiles broke from us and we had ease;
The hills were round us, and the breeze
Went o'er the sun-lit fields again;
Our foreheads felt the wind and rain.
Our youth return'd; for there was shed
On spirits that had long been dead,
Spirits dried up and closely furl'd,
The freshness of the early world.

Ah! since dark days still bring to light
Man's prudence and man's fiery might,
Time may restore us in his course
Goethe's sage mind and Byron's force;
But where will Europe's latter hour
Again find Wordsworth's healing power?
Others will teach us how to dare,

And against fear our breast to steel;
Others will strengthen us to bear—
But who, ah! who, will make us feel?
The cloud of mortal destiny,
Others will front it fearlessly—
But who, like him, will put it by?

Keep fresh the grass upon his grave
O Rotha, with thy living wave!
Sing him thy best! for few or none
Hears thy voice right, now he is gone.

A Southern Night

THE sandy spits, the shore-lock'd lakes,
    Melt into open, moonlit sea;
The soft Mediterranean breaks
    At my feet, free.

Dotting the fields of corn and vine,
    Like ghosts the huge, gnarl'd olives stand.
Behind, that lovely mountain-line!
    While, by the strand,

Cette, with its glistening houses white,
    Curves with the curving beach away
To where the lighthouse beacons bright
    Far in the bay.

Ah! such a night, so soft, so lone,
    So moonlit, saw me once of yore
Wander unquiet, and my own
    Vext heart deplore.

But now that trouble is forgot;
    Thy memory, thy pain, to-night,
My brother! and thine early lot,
    Possess me quite.

The murmur of this Midland deep
    Is heard to-night around thy grave,
There, where Gibraltar's cannon'd steep
    O'erfrowns the wave.

For there, with bodily anguish keen,
   With Indian heats at last fordone,
With public toil and private teen—
    Thou sank'st, alone.

Slow to a stop, at morning grey,
   I see the smoke-crown'd vessel come;
Slow round her paddles dies away
    The seething foam.

A boat is lower'd from her side;
   Ah, gently place him on the bench!
That spirit—if all have not yet died—
    A breath might quench.

Is this the eye, the footstep fast,
   The mien of youth we used to see,
Poor, gallant boy!—for such thou wast,
    Still art, to me.

The limbs their wonted tasks refuse;
   The eyes are glazed, thou canst not speak;
And whiter than thy white burnous
    That wasted cheek!

Enough! The boat, with quiet shock,
   Unto its haven coming nigh,
Touches, and on Gibraltar's rock
    Lands thee to die.

Ah me! Gibraltar's strand is far,
   But farther yet across the brine
Thy dear wife's ashes buried are,
    Remote from thine.

For there, where morning's sacred fount
   Its golden rain on earth confers,
The snowy Himalayan Mount
    O'ershadows hers.

Strange irony of fate, alas,
   Which, for two jaded English, saves,
When from their dusty life they pass,
    Such peaceful graves!

In cities should we English lie,
 Where cries are rising ever new,
And men's incessant stream goes by—
  We who pursue

Our business with unslackening stride,
 Traverse in troops, with care-fill'd breast,
The soft Mediterranean side,
  The Nile, the East,

And see all sights from pole to pole,
 And glance, and nod, and bustle by,
And never once possess our soul
  Before we die.

Not by those hoary Indian hills,
 Not by this gracious Midland sea
Whose floor to-night sweet moonshine fills,
  Should our graves be.

Some sage, to whom the world was dead,
 And men were specks, and life a play;
Who made the roots of trees his bed,
  And once a day

With staff and gourd his way did bend
 To villages and homes of man,
For food to keep him till he end
  His mortal span

And the pure goal of being reach;
 Hoar-headed, wrinkled, clad in white,
Without companion, without speech,
  By day and night

Pondering God's mysteries untold,
 And tranquil as the glacier-snows
He by those Indian mountains old
  Might well repose.

Some grey crusading knight austere,
 Who bore Saint Louis company,
And came home hurt to death, and here
  Landed to die;

Some youthful troubadour, whose tongue
  Fill'd Europe once with his love-pain,
Who here outworn had sunk, and sung
      His dying strain;

Some girl, who here from castle-bower,
  With furtive step and cheek of flame,
'Twixt myrtle-hedges all in flower
      By moonlight came

To meet her pirate-lover's ship;
  And from the wave-kiss'd marble stair
Beckon'd him on, with quivering lip
      And floating hair;

And lived some moons in happy trance,
  Then learnt his death and pined away—
Such by these waters of romance
      'Twas meet to lay.

But you—a grave for knight or sage.
  Romantic, solitary, still,
O spent ones of a work-day age!
      Befits you ill.

So sang I; but the midnight breeze,
  Down to the brimm'd, moon-charmed main,
Comes softly through the olive-trees,
      And checks my strain.

I think of her, whose gentle tongue
  All plaint in her own cause controll'd;
Of thee I think, my brother! young
      In heart, high-soul'd—

That comely face, that cluster'd brow,
  That cordial hand, that bearing free,
I see them still, I see them now,
      Shall always see!

And what but gentleness untired,
  And what but noble feeling warm,
Wherever shown, howe'er inspired,
      Is grace, is charm?

What else is all these waters are,
    What else is steep'd in lucid sheen,
What else is bright, what else is fair,
        What else serene?

Mild o'er her grave, ye mountains, shine!
    Gently by his, ye waters, glide!
To that in you which is divine
        They were allied.

Haworth Churchyard

April, 1855

WHERE, under Loughrigg, the stream
Of Rotha sparkles through fields
Vested for ever with green,
Four years since, in the house
Of a gentle spirit now dead—
Wordsworth's son-in-law, friend—
I saw the meeting of two
Gifted women.   The one,
Brilliant with recent renown,
Young, unpractised, had told
With a master's accent her feign'd
Story of passionate life;
The other, maturer in fame,
Earning, she too, her praise
First in fiction, had since
Widen'd her sweep, and survey'd
History, politics, mind.

    The two held converse; they wrote
In a book which of world-famous souls
Kept the memorial;—bard,
Warrior, statesman, had sign'd
Their names; chief glory of all,
Scott had bestow'd there his last
Breathings of song, with a pen
Tottering, a death-stricken hand.

Hope at that meeting smiled fair.
Years in number, it seem'd,
Lay before both, and a fame
Heighten'd, and multiplied power,—

G

Behold! The elder, to-day,
Lies expecting from death,
In mortal weakness, a last
Summons! the younger is dead!

First to the living we pay
Mournful homage;—the Muse
Gains not an earth-deafen'd ear.

Hail to the steadfast soul,
Which, unflinching and keen,
Wrought to erase from its depth
Mist and illusion and fear!
Hail to the spirit which dared
Trust its own thoughts, before yet
Echoed her back by the crowd!
Hail to the courage which gave
Voice to its creed, ere the creed
Won consecration from time!

Turn we next to the dead.
—How shall we honour the young,
The ardent, the gifted? how mourn?
Console we cannot, her ear
Is deaf.　Far northward from here,
In a churchyard high 'mid the moors
Of Yorkshire, a little earth
Stops it for ever to praise.

Where, behind Keighley, the road
Up to the heart of the moors
Between heath-clad showery hills
Runs, and colliers' carts
Poach the deep ways coming down,
And a rough, grimed race have their homes—
There on its slope is built
The moorland town.　But the church
Stands on the crest of the hill,
Lonely and bleak;—at its side
The parsonage-house and the graves.

Strew with laurel the grave
Of the early-dying! Alas,
Early she goes on the path
To the silent country, and leaves
Half her laurels unwon,

Dying too soon!—yet green
Laurels she had, and a course
Short, but redoubled by fame.

And not friendless, and not
Only with strangers to meet,
Faces ungreeting and cold,
Thou, O mourn'd one, to-day
Enterest the house of the grave!
Those of thy blood, whom thou lov'dst,
Have preceded thee—young,
Loving, a sisterly band;
Some in art, some in gift
Inferior—all in fame.
They, like friends, shall receive
This comer, greet her with joy;
Welcome the sister, the friend;
Hear with delight of thy fame!

Round thee they lie—the grass
Blows from their graves to thy own!
She, whose genius, though not
Puissant like thine, was yet
Sweet and graceful;—and she
(How shall I sing her?) whose soul
Knew no fellow for might,
Passion, vehemence, grief,
Daring, since Byron died,
That world-famed son of fire—she, who sank
Baffled, unknown, self-consumed;
Whose too bold dying song
Stirr'd, like a clarion-blast, my soul.

Of one, too, I have heard,
A brother—sleeps he here?
Of all that gifted race
Not the least gifted; young,
Unhappy, eloquent—the child
Of many hopes, of many tears.
O boy, if here thou sleep'st, sleep well!
On thee too did the Muse
Bright in thy cradle smile;
But some dark shadow came
(I know not what) and interposed.

Sleep, O cluster of friends,
Sleep!—or only when May,
Brought by the west-wind, returns
Back to your native heaths,
And the plover is heard on the moors,
Yearly awake to behold
The opening summer, the sky,
The shining moorland—to hear
The drowsy bee, as of old,
Hum o'er the thyme, the grouse
Call from the heather in bloom!
Sleep, or only for this
Break your united repose!

Epilogue

So I sang; but the Muse,
Shaking her head, took the harp—
Stern interrupted my strain,
Angrily smote on the chords.

April showers
Rush o'er the Yorkshire moors.
Stormy, through driving mist,
Loom the blurr'd hills; the rain
Lashes the newly-made grave.

Unquiet souls!
—In the dark fermentation of earth,
In the never idle workshop of nature,
In the eternal movement,
Ye shall find yourselves again!

Rugby Chapel

November, 1857

COLDLY, sadly descends
The autumn-evening. The field
Strewn with its dank yellow drifts
Of wither'd leaves, and the elms,
Fades into dimness apace,
Silent;—hardly a shout
From a few boys late at their play!

The lights come out in the street,
In the school-room windows;—but cold,
Solemn, unlighted, austere,
Through the gathering darkness, arise
The chapel-walls, in whose bound
Thou, my father! art laid.

There thou dost lie, in the gloom
Of the autumn evening. But ah!
That word, *gloom*, to any mind
Brings thee back, in the light
Of thy radiant vigour, again;
In the gloom of November we pass'd
Days not dark at thy side;
Seasons impair'd not the ray
Of thy buoyant cheerfulness clear.
Such thou wast! and I stand
In the autumn evening, and think
Of bygone autumns with thee.

Fifteen years have gone round
Since thou arosest to tread,
In the summer-morning, the road
Of death, at a call unforeseen,
Sudden. For fifteen years,
We who till then in thy shade
Rested as under the boughs
Of a mighty oak, have endured
Sunshine and rain as we might,
Bare, unshaded, alone,
Lacking the shelter of thee.

O strong soul, by what shore
Tarriest thou now? For that force,
Surely, has not been left vain!
Somewhere, surely, afar,
In the sounding labour-house vast
Of being, is practised that strength,
Zealous, beneficent, firm!

Yes, in some far-shining sphere,
Conscious or not of the past,
Still thou performest the word
Of the Spirit in whom thou dost live—
Prompt, unwearied, as here!

Still thou upraised with zeal
The humble good from the ground,
Sternly repressest the bad!
Still, like a trumpet, dost rouse
Those who with half-open eyes
Tread the border-land dim
'Twixt vice and virtue; reviv'st,
Succourest!—this was thy work,
This was thy life upon earth.

What is the course of the life
Of mortal men on the earth?—
Most men eddy about
Here and there—eat and drink,
Chatter and love and hate,
Gather and squander, are raised
 Aloft, are hurl'd in the dust,
Striving blindly, achieving
Nothing; and then they die—
Perish;—and no one asks
Who or what they have been,
More than he asks what waves,
In the moonlit solitudes mild
Of the midmost Ocean, have swell'd,
Foam'd for a moment, and gone.

And there are some, whom a thirst
Ardent, unquenchable, fires,
Not with the crowd to be spent,
Not without aim to go round
In an eddy of purposeless dust,
Effort unmeaning and vain.
Ah yes! some of us strive
Not without action to die
Fruitless, but something to snatch
From dull oblivion, nor all
Glut the devouring grave!
We, we have chosen our path—
Path to a clear-purposed goal,
Path of advance!—but it leads
A long, steep journey, through sunk
Gorges, o'er mountains in snow.
Cheerful, with friends, we set forth—
Then, on the height, comes the storm.

Thunder crashes from rock
To rock, the cataracts reply,
Lightnings dazzle our eyes.
Roaring torrents have breach'd
The track, the stream-bed descends
In the place where the wayfarer once
Planted his footstep—the spray
Boils o'er its borders! aloft
The unseen snow-beds dislodge
Their hanging ruin; alas,
Havoc is made in our train!
Friends, who set forth at our side,
Falter, are lost in the storm.
We, we only are left!
With frowning foreheads, with lips
Sternly compress'd, we strain on,
On—and at nightfall at last
Come to the end of our way,
To the lonely inn 'mid the rocks;
Where the gaunt and taciturn host
Stands on the threshold, the wind
Shaking his thin white hairs—
Holds his lantern to scan
Our storm-beat figures, and asks:
Whom in our party we bring?
Whom we have left in the snow?

Sadly we answer: We bring
Only ourselves! we lost
Sight of the rest in the storm.
Hardly ourselves we fought through,
Stripp'd, without friends, as we are.
Friends, companions, and train,
The avalanche swept from our side.

But thou would'st not *alone*
Be saved, my father! *alone*
Conquer and come to thy goal,
Leaving the rest in the wild.
We were weary, and we
Fearful, and we in our march
Fain to drop down and to die.
Still thou turnedst, and still
Beckonedst the trembler, and still
Gavest the weary thy hand.

If, in the paths of the world,
Stones might have wounded thy feet,
Toil or dejection have tried
Thy spirit, of that we saw
Nothing—to us thou wast still
Cheerful, and helpful, and firm!
Therefore to thee it was given
Many to save with thyself;
And, at the end of thy day,
O faithful shepherd! to come,
Bringing thy sheep in thy hand.
And through thee I believe
In the noble and great who are gone;
Pure souls honour'd and blest
By former ages, who else—
Such, so soulless, so poor,
Is the race of men whom I see—
Seem'd but a dream of the heart,
Seem'd but a cry of desire.
Yes! I believe that there lived
Others like thee in the past,
Not like the men of the crowd
Who all round me to-day
Bluster or cringe, and make life
Hideous, and arid, and vile;
But souls temper'd with fire,
Fervent, heroic, and good,
Helpers and friends of mankind.

Servants of God!—or sons
Shall I not call you? because
Not as servants ye knew
Your Father's innermost mind,
His, who unwillingly sees
One of his little ones lost—
Yours is the praise, if mankind
Hath not as yet in its march
Fainted, and fallen, and died!

See! In the rocks of the world
Marches the host of mankind,
A feeble, wavering line.
Where are they tending?—A God
Marshall'd them, gave them their goal.

Ah, but the way is so long!
Years they have been in the wild!
Sore thirst plagues them, the rocks,
Rising all round, overawe;
Factions divide them, their host
Threatens to break, to dissolve.
—Ah, keep, keep them combined!
Else, of the myriads who fill
That army, not one shall arrive;
Sole they shall stray; in the rocks
Stagger for ever in vain,
Die one by one in the waste.

Then, in such hour of need
Of your fainting, dispirited race,
Ye, like angels, appear,
Radiant with ardour divine!
Beacons of hope, ye appear!
Languor is not in your heart,
Weakness is not in your word,
Weariness not on your brow.
Ye alight in our van! at your voice,
Panic, despair, flee away.
Ye move through the ranks, recall
The stragglers, refresh the outworn,
Praise, re-inspire the brave!
Order, courage, return.
Eyes rekindling, and prayers,
Follow your steps as ye go.
Ye fill up the gaps in our files,
Strengthen the wavering line,
Stablish, continue our march,
On, to the bound of the waste,
On, to the City of God.

Stanzas from the Grande Chartreuse

THROUGH Alpine meadows soft-suffused
With rain, where thick the crocus blows,
Past the dark forges long disused,
The mule-track from Saint Laurent goes.
The bridge is cross'd, and slow we ride,
Through forest, up the mountain-side.

The autumnal evening darkens round,
The wind is up, and drives the rain;
While, hark! far down, with strangled sound
Doth the Dead Guier's stream complain,
Where that wet smoke, among the woods,
Over his boiling cauldron broods.

Swift rush the spectral vapours white
Past limestone scars with ragged pines,
Showing—then blotting from our sight!—
Halt—through the cloud-drift something shines!
High in the valley, wet and drear,
The huts of Courrerie appear.

Strike leftward! cries our guide; and higher
Mounts up the stony forest-way.
At last the encircling trees retire;
Look! through the showery twilight grey
What pointed roofs are these advance?—
A palace of the Kings of France?

Approach, for what we seek is here!
Alight, and sparely sup, and wait
For rest in this outbuilding near;
Then cross the sward and reach that gate.
Knock; pass the wicket!   Thou art come
To the Carthusians' world-famed home.

The silent courts, where night and day
Into their stone-carved basins cold
The splashing icy fountains play—
The humid corridors behold!
Where, ghostlike in the deepening night,
Cowl'd forms brush by in gleaming white.

The chapel, where no organ's peal
Invests the stern and naked prayer—
With penitential cries they kneel
And wrestle; rising then, with bare
And white uplifted faces stand,
Passing the Host from hand to hand;

Each takes, and then his visage wan
Is buried in his cowl once more.
The cells!—the suffering Son of Man
Upon the wall—the knee-worn floor—
And where they sleep, that wooden bed
Which shall their coffin be, when dead!

The library, where tract and tome
Not to feed priestly pride are there,
To hymn the conquering march of Rome,
Nor yet to amuse, as ours are!
They paint of souls the inner strife,
Their drops of blood, their death in life.

The garden, overgrown—yet mild,
See, fragrant herbs are flowering there!
Strong children of the Alpine wild
Whose culture is the brethren's care;
Of human tasks their only one,
And cheerful works beneath the sun.

Those halls, too, destined to contain
Each its own pilgrim-host of old,
From England, Germany, or Spain—
All are before me! I behold
The House, the Brotherhood austere!
—And what am I, that I am here?

For rigorous teachers seized my youth,
And purged its faith, and trimm'd its fire,
Show'd me the high, white star of Truth,
There bade me gaze, and there aspire.
Even now their whispers pierce the gloom:
What dost thou in this living tomb?

Forgive me, masters of the mind!
At whose behest I long ago
So much unlearnt, so much resign'd—
I come not here to be your foe!
I seek these anchorites, not in ruth,
To curse and to deny your truth;

Not as their friend, or child, I speak!
But as, on some far northern strand,
Thinking of his own Gods, a Greek
In pity and mournful awe might stand
Before some fallen Runic stone—
For both were faiths, and both are gone.

Wandering between two worlds, one dead,
The other powerless to be born,
With nowhere yet to rest my head,
Like these, on earth I wait forlorn.
Their faith, my tears, the world deride—
I come to shed them at their side.

Oh, hide me in your gloom profound,
Ye solemn seats of holy pain!
Take me, cowl'd forms, and fence me round
Till I possess my soul again;
Till free my thoughts before me roll,
Not chafed by hourly false control!

For the world cries your faith is now
But a dead time's exploded dream;
My melancholy, sciolists say,
Is a pass'd mode, an outworn theme—
As if the world had ever had
A faith, or sciolists been sad!

As, if it *be* pass'd, take away,
At least, the restlessness, the pain;
Be man henceforth no more a prey
To these out-dated stings again!
The nobleness of grief is gone—
Ah, leave us not the fret alone!

But—if you cannot give us ease—
Last of the race of them who grieve
Here leave us to die out with these
Last of the people who believe!
Silent, while years engrave the brow;
Silent—the best are silent now.

Achilles ponders in his tent,
The kings of modern thought are dumb;
Silent they are, though not content,
And wait to see the future come.
They have the grief men had of yore,
But they contend and cry no more.

Our fathers water'd with their tears
This sea of time whereon we sail,
Their voices were in all men's ears
Who pass'd within their puissant hail.
Still the same ocean round us raves,
But we stand mute, and watch the waves.

For what avail'd it, all the noise
And outcry of the former men?—
Say, have their sons achieved more joys,
Say, is life lighter now than then?
The sufferers died, they left their pain—
The pangs which tortured them remain.

What helps it now, that Byron bore,
With haughty scorn which mock'd the smart,
Through Europe to the Ætolian shore
The pageant of his bleeding heart?
That thousands counted every groan,
And Europe made his woe her own?

What boots it, Shelley! that the breeze
Carried thy lovely wail away,
Musical through Italian trees
Which fringe thy soft blue Spezzian bay?
Inheritors of thy distress
Have restless hearts one throb the less?

Or are we easier, to have read,
O Obermann! the sad, stern page,
Which tells us how thou hidd'st thy head
From the fierce tempest of thine age
In the lone brakes of Fontainebleau,
Or chalets near the Alpine snow?

Ye slumber in your silent grave!—
The world, which for an idle day
Grace to your mood of sadness gave,
Long since hath flung her weeds away.
The eternal trifler breaks your spell;
But we—we learnt your lore too well!

Years hence, perhaps, may dawn an age,
More fortunate, alas! than we,
Which without hardness will be sage,
And gay without frivolity.
Sons of the world, oh, speed those years;
But, while we wait, allow our tears!

Allow them! We admire with awe
The exulting thunder of your race;
You give the universe your law,
You triumph over time and space!
Your pride of life, your tireless powers,
We laud them, but they are not ours.

We are like children rear'd in shade
Beneath some old-world abbey wall,
Forgotten in a forest-glade,
And secret from the eyes of all.
Deep, deep the greenwood round them waves,
Their abbey, and its close of graves!

But, where the road runs near the stream,
Oft through the trees they catch a glance
Of passing troops in the sun's beam—
Pennon, and plume, and flashing lance!
Forth to the world those soldiers fare,
To life, to cities, and to war!

And through the wood, another way,
Faint bugle-notes from far are borne,
Where hunters gather, staghounds bay,
Round some fair forest-lodge at morn.
Gay dames are there, in sylvan green;
Laughter and cries—those notes between!

The banners flashing through the trees
Make their blood dance and chain their eyes
That bugle-music on the breeze
Arrests them with a charm'd surprise.
Banner by turns and bugle woo:
Ye shy recluses, follow too!

O children, what do ye reply?—
" Action and pleasure, will ye roam
Through these secluded dells to cry
And call us?—but too late ye come!
Too late for us your call ye blow,
Whose bent was taken long ago.

"Long since we pace this shadow'd nave;
We watch those yellow tapers shine,
Emblems of hope over the grave,
In the high altar's depth divine;
The organ carries to our ear
Its accents of another sphere.

"Fenced early in this cloistral round
Of reverie, of shade, of prayer,
How should we grow in other ground?
How can we flower in foreign air?
—Pass, banners, pass, and bugles, cease;
And leave our desert to its peace! "

Stanzas in Memory of the Author of "Obermann"
November, 1849

IN front the awful Alpine track
Crawls up its rocky stair;
The autumn storm-winds drive the rack,
Close o'er it, in the air.

Behind are the abandon'd baths
Mute in their meadows lone;
The leaves are on the valley-paths,
The mists are on the Rhone—

The white mists rolling like a sea!
I hear the torrents roar.
—Yes, Obermann, all speaks of thee;
I feel thee near once more!

I turn thy leaves! I feel their breath
Once more upon me roll;
That air of languor, cold, and death,
Which brooded o'er thy soul.

Fly hence, poor wretch, whoe'er thou art,
Condemn'd to cast about,
All shipwreck in thy own weak heart,
For comfort from without!

A fever in these pages burns
Beneath the calm they feign;
A wounded human spirit turns,
Here, on its bed of pain.

Yes, though the virgin mountain-air
Fresh through these pages blows;
Though to these leaves the glaciers spare
The soul of their white snows;

Though here a mountain-murmur swells
Of many a dark-bough'd pine;
Though, as you read, you hear the bells
Of the high-pasturing kine—

Yet, through the hum of torrent lone,
And brooding mountain-bee,
There sobs I know not what ground-tone
Of human agony.

Is it for this, because the sound
Is fraught too deep with pain,
That, Obermann! the world around
So little loves thy strain?

Some secrets may the poet tell,
For the world loves new ways;
To tell too deep ones is not well—
It knows not what he says.

Yet, of the spirits who have reign'd
In this our troubled day,
I know but two, who have attain'd,
Save thee, to see their way.

By England's lakes, in grey old age,
His quiet home one keeps;
And one, the strong much-toiling sage,
In German Weimar sleeps.

But Wordsworth's eyes avert their ken
From half of human fate;
And Goethe's course few sons of men
May think to emulate.

For he pursued a lonely road,
His eyes on Nature's plan;
Neither made man too much a God,
Nor God too much a man.

Strong was he, with a spirit free
From mists, and sane, and clear;
Clearer, how much! than ours—yet we
Have a worse course to steer.

For though his manhood bore the blast
Of a tremendous time,
Yet in a tranquil world was pass'd
His tenderer youthful prime.

But we, brought forth and rear'd in hours
Of change, alarm, surprise—
What shelter to grow ripe is ours?
What leisure to grow wise?

Like children bathing on the shore,
Buried a wave beneath,
The second wave succeeds, before
We have had time to breathe.

Too fast we live, too much are tried,
Too harass'd, to attain
Wordsworth's sweet calm, or Goethe's wide
And luminous view to gain.

And then we turn, thou sadder sage,
To thee! we feel thy spell!
—The hopeless tangle of our age,
Thou too hast scann'd it well!

Immoveable thou sittest, still
As death, composed to bear!
Thy head is clear, thy feeling chill,
And icy thy despair.

Yes, as the son of Thetis said,
I hear thee saying now:
Greater by far than thou are dead ;
Strive not ! die also thou !

Ah! two desires toss about
The poet's feverish blood.
One drives him to the world without,
And one to solitude.

The glow, he cries, *the thrill of life,*
Where, where do these abound?—
Not in the world, not in the strife
Of men, shall they be found.

He who hath watch'd, not shared, the strife,
Knows how the day hath gone.
He only lives with the world's life,
Who hath renounced his own.

To thee we come, then! Clouds are roll'd
Where thou, O seer! art set;
Thy realm of thought is drear and cold—
The world is colder yet!

And thou hast pleasures, too, to share
With those who come to thee—
Balms floating on thy mountain-air,
And healing sights to see.

How often, where the slopes are green
On Jaman, hast thou sate
By some high chalet-door, and seen
The summer-day grow late;

And darkness steal o'er the wet grass
With the pale crocus starr'd,
And reach that glimmering sheet of glass
Beneath the piny sward,

Lake Leman's waters, far below!
And watch'd the rosy light
Fade from the distant peaks of snow;
And on the air of night

Heard accents of the eternal tongue
Through the pine branches play—
Listen'd, and felt thyself grow young!
Listen'd and wept——Away!

Away the dreams that but deceive
And thou, sad guide, adieu!
I go, fate drives me; but I leave
Half of my life with you.

We, in some unknown Power's employ,
Move on a rigorous line;
Can neither, when we will, enjoy.
Nor, when we will, resign.

I in the world must live; but thou,
Thou melancholy shade!
Wilt not, if thou canst see me now,
Condemn me, nor upbraid.

For thou art gone away from earth,
And place with those dost claim,
The Children of the Second Birth,
Whom the world could not tame;

And with that small, transfigured band,
Whom many a different way
Conducted to their common land,
Thou learn'st to think as they.

Christian and pagan, king and slave,
Soldier and anchorite,
Distinctions we esteem so grave,
Are nothing in their sight.

They do not ask, who pined unseen,
Who was on action hurl'd,
Whose one bond is, that all have been
Unspotted by the world.

There without anger thou wilt see
Him who obeys thy spell
No more, so he but rest, like thee,
Unsoil'd!—and so, farewell.

Farewell!—Whether thou now liest near
That much-loved inland sea,
The ripples of whose blue waves cheer
Vevey and Meillerie:

And in that gracious region bland,
Where with clear-rustling wave
The scented pines of Switzerland
Stand dark round thy green grave,

Between the dusty vineyard-walls
Issuing on that green place
The early peasant still recalls
The pensive stranger's face,

And stoops to clear thy moss-grown date
Ere he plods on again;—
Or whether, by maligner fate,
Among the swarms of men,

Where between granite terraces
The blue Seine rolls her wave,
The Capital of Pleasure sees
The hardly-heard-of grave;—

Farewell! Under the sky we part,
In this stern Alpine dell.
O unstrung will! O broken heart!
A last, a last farewell!

Obermann Once More

(*Composed many years after the preceding*)

Savez-vous quelque bien qui console du regret d'un monde?
OBERMANN.

GLION?——Ah, twenty years, it cuts
All meaning from a name!
White houses prank where once were huts.
Glion, but not the same!

And yet I know not! All unchanged
The turf, the pines, the sky!
The hills in their old order ranged;
The lake, with Chillon by!

And, 'neath those chestnut-trees, where stiff
And stony mounts the way,
The crackling husk-heaps burn, as if
I left them yesterday!

Across the valley, on that slope,
The huts of Avant shine!
Its pines, under their branches, ope
Ways for the pasturing kine.

Full-foaming milk-pails, Alpine fare,
Sweet heaps of fresh-cut grass,
Invite to rest the traveller there
Before he climb the pass—

The gentian-flower'd pass, its crown
With yellow spires aflame;
Whence drops the path to Allière down,
And walls where Byron came,

By their green river, who doth change
His birth-name just below;
Orchard, and croft, and full-stored grange
Nursed by his pastoral flow.

But stop!—to fetch back thoughts that stray
Beyond this gracious bound,
The cone of Jaman, pale and grey,
See, in the blue profound!

Ah, Jaman! delicately tall
Above his sun-warm'd firs—
What thoughts to me his rocks recall,
What memories he stirs!

And who but thou must be, in truth,
Obermann! with me here?
Thou master of my wandering youth,
But left this many a year!

Yes, I forget the world's work wrought,
Its warfare waged with pain;
An eremite with thee, in thought
Once more I slip my chain,

And to thy mountain-chalet come,
And lie beside its door,
And hear the wild bee's Alpine hum,
And thy sad, tranquil lore!

Again I feel the words inspire
Their mournful calm; serene,
Yet tinged with infinite desire
For all that *might* have been—

The harmony from which man swerved
Made his life's rule once more!
The universal order served,
Earth happier than before!

—While thus I mused, night gently ran
Down over hill and wood.
Then, still and sudden, Obermann
On the grass near me stood.

Those pensive features well I knew,
On my mind, years before,
Imagined so oft! imaged so true!
—A shepherd's garb he wore,

A mountain-flower was in his hand,
A book was in his breast.
Bent on my face, with gaze which scann'd
My soul, his eyes did rest.

"And is it thou," he cried, "so long
Held by the world which we
Loved not, who turnest from the throng
Back to thy youth and me?

"And from thy world, with heart opprest,
Choosest thou *now* to turn?—
Ah me! we anchorites read things best,
Clearest their course discern!

"Thou fledst me when the ungenial earth,
Man's work-place, lay in gloom.
Return'st thou in her hour of birth,
Of hopes and hearts in bloom?

"Perceiv'st thou not the change of day?
  Ah! Carry back thy ken,
What, some two thousand years! Survey
The world as it was then!

"Like ours it look'd in outward air.
Its head was clear and true,
Sumptuous its clothing, rich its fare,
No pause its action knew;

"Stout was its arm, each thew and bone
Seem'd puissant and alive—
But, ah! its heart, its heart was stone,
And so it could not thrive!

"On that hard Pagan world disgust
And secret loathing fell.
Deep weariness and sated lust
Made human life a hell.

"In his cool hall, with haggard eyes,
The Roman noble lay;
He drove abroad, in furious guise,
Along the Appian way.

"He made a feast, drank fierce and fast,
And crown'd his hair with flowers—
No easier nor no quicker pass'd
The impracticable hours.

"The brooding East with awe beheld
Her impious younger world.
The Roman tempest swell'd and swell'd,
And on her head was hurl'd.

"The East bow'd low before the blast
In patient, deep disdain;
She let the legions thunder past,
And plunged in thought again.

"So well she mused, a morning broke
Across her spirit grey;
A conquering, new-born joy awoke,
And fill'd her life with day.

" 'Poor world,' she cried, 'so deep accurst,
That runn'st from pole to pole
To seek a draught to slake thy thirst—
Go, seek it in thy soul!

"She heard it, the victorious West,
In crown and sword array'd!
She felt the void which mined her breast,
She shiver'd and obey'd.

"She veil'd her eagles, snapp'd her sword,
And laid her sceptre down;
Her stately purple she abhorr'd,
And her imperial crown.

"She broke her flutes, she stopp'd her sports,
Her artists could not please;
She tore her books, she shut her courts,
She fled her palaces;

"Lust of the eye and pride of life
She left it all behind,
And hurried, torn with inward strife,
The wilderness to find.

"Tears wash'd the trouble from her face!
She changed into a child!
'Mid weeds and wrecks she stood—a place
Of ruin—but she smiled!

"Oh, had I lived in that great day,
How had its glory new
Fill'd earth and heaven, and caught away
My ravish'd spirit too!

"No thoughts that to the world belong
Had stood against the wave
Of love which set so deep and strong
From Christ's then open grave.

"No cloister-floor of humid stone
Had been too cold for me.
For me no Eastern desert lone
Had been too far to flee.

"No lonely life had pass'd too slow,
When I could hourly scan
Upon his Cross, with head sunk low,
That nail'd, thorn-crowned Man!

"Could see the Mother with her Child
Whose tender winning arts
Have to his little arms beguiled
So many wounded hearts!

"And centuries came and ran their course,
And unspent all that time
Still, still went forth that Child's dear force,
And still was at its prime.

"Ay, ages long endured his span
Of life—'tis true received—
That gracious Child, that thorn-crown'd Man!
—He lived while we believed.

"While we believed, on earth he went,
And open stood his grave.
Men call'd from chamber, church, and tent;
And Christ was by to save.

"Now he is dead!   Far hence he lies
In the lorn Syrian town;
And on his grave, with shining eyes,
The Syrian stars look down.

"In vain men still, with hoping new,
Regard his death-place dumb,
And say the stone is not yet to,
And wait for words to come.

"Ah, o'er that silent sacred land,
Of sun, and arid stone,
And crumbling wall, and sultry sand,
Sounds now one word alone!

"*Unduped of fancy, henceforth man*
Must labour!—must resign
His all too human creeds, and scan
Simply the way divine!

"But slow that tide of common thought.
Which bathed our life, retired;
Slow, slow the old world wore to nought,
And pulse by pulse expired.

"Its frame yet stood without a breach
When blood and warmth were fled;
And still it spake its wonted speech—
But every word was dead.

"And oh, we cried, that on this corse
Might fall a freshening storm!
Rive its dry bones, and with new force
A new-sprung world inform!

"—Down came the storm! O'er France it pass'd
In sheets of scathing fire;
All Europe felt that fiery blast,
And shook as it rush'd by her.

"Down came the storm! In ruins fell
The worn-out world we knew.
　　It pass'd, that elemental swell!
Again appear'd the blue;

"The sun shone in the new-wash'd sky,
And what from heaven saw he?
Blocks of the past, like icebergs high,
Float on a rolling sea!

"Upon them plies the race of man
All it before endeavour'd;
'Ye live,' I cried, 'ye work and plan,
And know not ye are sever'd!

" 'Poor fragments of a broken world
Whereon men pitch their tent!
Why were ye too to death not hurl'd
When your world's day was spent?

" 'That glow of central fire is done
Which with its fusing flame
Knit all your parts, and kept you one—
But ye, ye are the same!

" 'The past, its mask of union on,
Had ceased to live and thrive.
The past, its mask of union gone,
Say, is it more alive?

" 'Your creeds are dead, your rites are dead,
Your social order too!
Where tarries he, the Power who said:
See, I make all things new?

" 'The millions suffer still, and grieve,
And what can helpers heal
With old-world cures men half believe
For woes they wholly feel?

" 'And yet men have such need of joy!
But joy whose grounds are true;
And joy that should all hearts employ
As when the past was new.

" 'Ah, not the emotion of that past,
Its common hope, were vain!
Some new such hope must dawn at last,
Or man must toss in pain.

" 'But now the old is out of date,
The new is not yet born,
And who can be *alone* elate,
While the world lies forlorn?'

"Then to the wilderness I fled.—
There among Alpine snows
And pastoral huts I hid my head,
And sought and found repose.

"It was not yet the appointed hour.
Sad, patient, and resign'd,
I watch'd the crocus fade and flower,
I felt the sun and wind.

"The day I lived in was not mine,
Man gets no second day.
In dreams I saw the future shine—
But ah! I could not stay!

"Action I had not, followers, fame;
I pass'd obscure, alone.
The after-world forgets my name,
Nor do I wish it known.

"Composed to bear, I lived and died,
And knew my life was vain,
With fate I murmur not, nor chide,
At Sèvres by the Seine

"(If Paris that brief flight allow)
My humble tomb explore!
It bears: *Eternity, be thou
My refuge!* and no more.

"But thou, whom fellowship of mood
Did make from haunts of strife
Come to my mountain-solitude,
And learn my frustrate life;

"O thou, who, ere thy flying span
Was past of cheerful youth,
Didst find the solitary man
And love his cheerless truth—

"Despair not thou as I despair'd,
Nor be cold gloom thy prison!
Forward the gracious hours have fared,
And see! the sun is risen!

"He breaks the winter of the past;
A green, new earth appears.
Millions, whose life in ice lay fast,
Have thoughts, and smiles, and tears.

"What though there still need effort, strife?
Though much be still unwon?
Yet warm it mounts, the hour of life!
Death's frozen hour is done!

"The world's great order dawns in sheen,
After long darkness rude,
Divinelier imaged, clearer seen,
With happier zeal pursued.

"With hope extinct and brow composed
I mark'd the present die;
Its term of life was nearly closed,
Yet it had more than I.

"But thou, though to the world's new hour
Thou come with aspect marr'd,
Shorn of the joy, the bloom, the power
Which best befits its bard—

"Though more than half thy years be past,
And spent thy youthful prime;
Though, round thy firmer manhood cast,
Hang weeds of our sad time

"Whereof thy youth felt all the spell,
And traversed all the shade—
Though late, though dimm'd, though weak, yet tell
Hope to a world new-made!

"Help it to fill that deep desire,
The want which rack'd our brain,
Consumed our heart with thirst like fire,
Immedicable pain;

"Which to the wilderness drove out
Our life, to Alpine snow,
And palsied all our word with doubt,
And all our work with woe—

"What still of strength is left, employ
That end to help attain:
*One common wave of thought and joy
Lifting mankind again!*"

—The vision ended. I awoke
As out of sleep, and no
Voice moved;—only the torrent broke
The silence, far below.

Soft darkness on the turf did lie.
Solemn, o'er hut and wood,
In the yet star-sown nightly sky,
The peak of Jaman stood.

Still in my soul the voice I heard
Of Obermann!——away
I turned; by some vague impulse stirr'd,
Along the rocks of Naye

Past Sonchaud's piny flanks I gaze
And the blanch'd summit bare
Of Malatrait, to where in haze
The Valais opens fair,

And the domed Velan, with his snows,
Behind the upcrowding hills,
Doth all the heavenly opening close
Which the Rhone's murmur fills;—

And glorious there, without a sound,
Across the glimmering lake,
High in the Valais-depth profound,
I saw the morning break.

DRAMATIC POEMS

Notes on Dramatic Poems, p. 794.

DRAMATIC POEMS

Empedocles on Etna

A Dramatic Poem

PERSONS

EMPEDOCLES.
PAUSANIAS, *a Physician.*
CALLICLES, *a young Harp-player.*

The Scene of the Poem is on Mount Etna; at first in the forest region, afterwards on the summit of the mountain.

ACT I. SCENE I.

Morning. A Pass in the forest region of Etna.

CALLICLES

(Alone, resting on a rock by the path.)

THE mules, I think, will not be here this hour;
They feel the cool wet turf under their feet
By the stream-side, after the dusty lanes
In which they have toil'd all night from Catana,
And scarcely will they budge a yard. O Pan,
How gracious is the mountain at this hour!
A thousand times have I been here alone,
Or with the revellers from the mountain-towns,
But never on so fair a morn;—the sun
Is shining on the brilliant mountain-crests,
And on the highest pines; but farther down,
Here in the valley, is in shade; the sward
Is dark, and on the stream the mist still hangs;
One sees one's footprints crush'd in the wet grass,
One's breath curls in the air; and on these pines
That climb from the stream's edge, the long grey tufts,
Which the goats love, are jewell'd thick with dew.
Here will I stay till the slow litter comes.

I have my harp too—that is well.—Apollo!
What mortal could be sick or sorry here?
I know not in what mind Empedocles,
Whose mules I follow'd, may be coming up,
But if, as most men say, he is half mad
With exile, and with brooding on his wrongs,
Pausanias, his sage friend, who mounts with him,
Could scarce have lighted on a lovelier cure.
The mules must be below far down. I hear
Their tinkling bells, mix'd with the song of birds,
Rise faintly to me—now it stops!—Who's here?
Pausanias! and on foot? alone?

Pausanias

            And thou, then?
I left thee supping with Peisianax,
With thy head full of wine and thy hair crown'd,
Touching thy harp as the whim came on thee,
And praised and spoil'd by master and by guests
Almost as much as the new dancing-girl.
Why hast thou follow'd us?

Callicles

            The night was hot,
And the feast past its prime; so we slipp'd out,
Some of us, to the portico to breathe;—
Peisianax, thou know'st, drinks late;—and then,
As I was lifting my soil'd garland off,
I saw the mules and litter in the court,
And in the litter sate Empedocles;
Thou, too, wast with him. Straightway I sped home;
I saddled my white mule, and all night long
Through the cool lovely country follow'd you,
Pass'd you a little since as morning dawn'd,
And have this hour sate by the torrent here,
Till the slow mules should climb in sight again.
And now?

Pausanias

       And now, back to the town with speed!
Crouch in the wood first, till the mules have pass'd;
They do but halt, they will be here anon.
Thou must be viewless to Empedocles;
Save mine, he must not meet a human eye.
One of his moods is on him that thou know'st;
I think, thou wouldst not vex him.

Callicles

No—and yet

I would fain stay, and help thee tend him. Once
He knew me well, and would oft notice me;
And still, I know not how, he draws me to him,
And I could watch him with his proud sad face,
His flowing locks and gold-encircled brow
And kingly gait, for ever; such a spell
In his severe looks, such a majesty
As drew of old the people after him,
In Agrigentum and Olympia,
When his star reign'd, before his banishment,
Is potent still on me in his decline.
But oh! Pausanias he is changed of late;
There is a settled trouble in his air
Admits no momentary brightening now,
And when he comes among his friends at feasts,
'Tis as an orphan among prosperous boys.
Thou know'st of old he loved this harp of mine,
When first he sojourn'd with Peisianax;
He is now always moody, and I fear him;
But I would serve him, soothe him, if I could,
Dared one but try.

Pausanias

Thou wast a kind child ever!

He loves thee, but he must not see thee now.
Thou hast indeed a rare touch on thy harp,
He loves that in thee, too;—there was a time
(But that is pass'd), he would have paid thy strain
With music to have drawn the stars from heaven.
He hath his harp and laurel with him still,
But he has laid the use of music by,
And all which might relax his settled gloom.
Yet thou may'st try thy playing, if thou wilt—
But thou must keep unseen; follow us on,
But at a distance! in these solitudes,
In this clear mountain-air, a voice will rise,
Though from afar, distinctly; it may soothe him.
Play when we halt, and, when the evening comes
And I must leave him (for his pleasure is
To be left musing these soft nights alone
In the high unfrequented mountain-spots),
Then watch him, for he ranges swift and far,
Sometimes to Etna's top, and to the cone;

But hide thee in the rocks a great way down,
And try thy noblest strains, my Callicles,
With the sweet night to help thy harmony!
Thou wilt earn my thanks sure, and perhaps his.

Callicles

More than a day and night, Pausanias,
Of this fair summer-weather, on these hills,
Would I bestow to help Empedocles.
That needs no thanks; one is far better here
Than in the broiling city in these heats.
But tell me, how hast thou persuaded him
In this his present fierce, man-hating mood,
To bring thee out with him alone on Etna?

Pausanias

Thou hast heard all men speaking of Pantheia
The woman who at Agrigentum lay
Thirty long days in a cold trance of death,
And whom Empedocles call'd back to life.
Thou art too young to note it, but his power
Swells with the swelling evil of this time,
And holds men mute to see where it will rise.
He could stay swift diseases in old days,
Chain madmen by the music of his lyre,
Cleanse to sweet airs the breath of poisonous streams,
And in the mountain-chinks inter the winds.
This he could do of old; but now, since all
Clouds and grows daily worse in Sicily,
Since broils tear us in twain, since this new swarm
Of sophists has got empire in our schools
Where he was paramount, since he is banish'd
And lives a lonely man in triple gloom—
He grasps the very reins of life and death.
I ask'd him of Pantheia yesterday,
When we were gather'd with Peisianax,
And he made answer, I should come at night
On Etna here, and be alone with him,
And he would tell me, as his old, tried friend,
Who still was faithful, what might profit me;
That is, the secret of this miracle.

Callicles

Bah! Thou a doctor! Thou art superstitious.
Simple Pausanias, 'twas no miracle!

Pantheia, for I know her kinsmen well,
Was subject to these trances from a girl.
Empedocles would say so, did he deign;
But he still lets the people, whom he scorns,
Gape and cry *wizard* at him, if they list.
But thou, thou art no company for him!
Thou art as cross, as sour'd as himself!
Thou hast some wrong from thine own citizens,
And then thy friend is banish'd, and on that,
Straightway thou fallest to arraign the times,
As if the sky was impious not to fall.
The sophists are no enemies of his;
I hear, Gorgias, their chief, speaks nobly of him,
As of his gifted master, and once friend.
He is too scornful, too high-wrought, too bitter.
'Tis not the times, 'tis not the sophists vex him;
There is some root of suffering in himself,
Some secret and unfollow'd vein of woe,
Which makes the time look black and sad to him.
Pester him not in this his sombre mood
With questionings about an idle tale,
But lead him through the lovely mountain-paths,
And keep his mind from preying on itself,
And talk to him of things at hand and common,
Not miracles! thou art a learned man,
But credulous of fables as a girl.

Pausanias

And thou, a boy whose tongue outruns his knowledge,
And on whose lightness blame is thrown away.
Enough of this! I see the litter wind
Up by the torrent-side, under the pines.
I must rejoin Empedocles. Do thou
Crouch in the brushwood till the mules have pass'd;
Then play thy kind part well. Farewell till night!

SCENE II

Noon. A Glen on the highest skirts of the woody region of Etna.

EMPEDOCLES—PAUSANIAS

Pausanias

The noon is hot. When we have cross'd the stream,
We shall have left the woody tract, and come

Upon the open shoulder of the hill.
See how the giant spires of yellow bloom
Of the sun-loving gentian, in the heat,
Are shining on those naked slopes like flame!
Let us rest here; and now, Empedocles,
Pantheia's history!

[A harp-note below is heard.

Empedocles

Hark! what sound was that
Rose from below? If it were possible,
And we were not so far from human haunt,
I should have said that some one touch'd a harp
Hark! there again!

Pausanias

'Tis the boy Callicles,
The sweetest harp-player in Catana.
He is for ever coming on these hills,
In summer, to all country-festivals,
With a gay revelling band; he breaks from them
Sometimes, and wanders far among the glens.
But heed him not, he will not mount to us;
I spoke with him this morning. Once more, therefore,
Instruct me of Pantheia's story, Master,
As I have pray'd thee.

Empedocles

That? and to what end?

Pausanias

It is enough that all men speak of it.
But I will also say, that when the Gods
Visit us as they do with sign and plague,
To know those spells of thine which stay their hand
Were to live free from terror.

Empedocles

Spells? Mistrust them!
Mind is the spell which governs earth and heaven.
Man has a mind with which to plan his safety;
Know that, and help thyself!

Pausanias

But thine own words?
"The wit and counsel of man was never clear,
Troubles confound the little wit he has."
Mind is a light which the Gods mock us with,
To lead those false who trust it.

[*The harp sounds again.*

Empedocles

Hist! once more!
Listen, Pausanias!—Ay, 'tis Callicles;
I know these notes among a thousand. Hark!

Callicles

(*Sings unseen, from below*).

The track winds down to the clear stream,
To cross the sparkling shallows; there
The cattle love to gather, on their way
To the high mountain-pastures, and to stay,
Till the rough cow-herds drive them past,
Knee-deep in the cool ford; for 'tis the last
Of all the woody, high, well-water'd dells
On Etna; and the beam
Of noon is broken there by chestnut-boughs
Down its steep verdant sides; the air
Is freshen'd by the leaping stream, which throws
Eternal showers of spray on the moss'd roots
Of trees, and veins of turf, and long dark shoots
Of ivy-plants, and fragrant hanging bells
Of hyacinths, and on late anemonies,
That muffle its wet banks; but glade,
And stream, and sward, and chestnut-trees,
End here; Etna beyond, in the broad glare
Of the hot noon, without a shade,
Slope behind slope, up to the peak, lies bare;
The peak, round which the white clouds play.

In such a glen, on such a day,
On Pelion, on the grassy ground,
Chiron, the aged Centaur lay,
The young Achilles standing by.
The Centaur taught him to explore
The mountains; where the glens are dry

And the tired Centaurs come to rest,
And where the soaking springs abound
And the straight ashes grow for spears,
And where the hill-goats come to feed,
And the sea-eagles build their nest.
He show'd him Phthia far away,
And said: O boy, I taught this lore
To Peleus, in long distant years!
He told him of the Gods, the stars,
The tides;—and then of mortal wars,
And of the life which heroes lead
Before they reach the Elysian place
And rest in the immortal mead;
And all the wisdom of his race.

The music below ceases, and EMPEDOCLES *speaks, accompanying himself in a solemn manner on his harp.*

The out-spread world to span
A cord the Gods first slung,
And then the soul of man
There, like a mirror, hung,
And bade the winds through space impel the gusty toy.

Hither and thither spins
The wind-borne, mirroring soul,
A thousand glimpses wins,
And never sees a whole;
Looks once, and drives elsewhere, and leaves its last employ.

The Gods laugh in their sleeve
To watch man doubt and fear,
Who knows not what to believe
Since he sees nothing clear,
And dares stamp nothing false where he finds nothing sure.

Is this, Pausanias, so?
And can our souls not strive,
But with the winds must go,
And hurry where they drive?
Is fate indeed so strong, man's strength indeed so poor?

I will not judge. That man,
Howbeit, I judge as lost,
Whose mind allows a plan,
Which would degrade it most;
And he treats doubt the best who tries to see least ill.

Be not, then, fear's blind slave!
Thou art my friend; to thee,
All knowledge that I have,
All skill I wield, are free.
Ask not the latest news of the last miracle,

Ask not what days and nights
In trance Pantheia lay,
But ask how thou such sights
May'st see without dismay;
Ask what most helps when known, thou son of Anchitus!

What? hate, and awe, and shame
Fill thee to see our time;
Thou feelest thy soul's frame
Shaken and out of chime?
What? life and chance go hard with thee too, as with us;

Thy citizens, 'tis said,
Envy thee and oppress,
Thy goodness no men aid,
All strive to make it less;
Tyranny, pride, and lust, fill Sicily's abodes;

Heaven is with earth at strife,
Signs make thy soul afraid,
The dead return to life,
Rivers are dried, winds stay'd;
Scarce can one think in calm, so threatening are the Gods;

And we feel, day and night,
The burden of ourselves—
Well, then, the wiser wight
In his own bosom delves,
And asks what ails him so, and gets what cure he can.

The sophist sneers: Fool, take
Thy pleasure, right or wrong.
The pious wail: Forsake
A world these sophists throng.
Be neither saint nor sophist-led, but be a man!

These hundred doctors try
To preach thee to their school.
We have the truth! they cry;
And yet their oracle,
Trumpet it as they will, is but the same as thine.

Once read thy own breast right,
And thou hast done with fears;
Man gets no other light,
Search he a thousand years.
Sink in thyself! there ask what ails thee, at that shrine!

What makes thee struggle and rave?
Why are men ill at ease?—
'Tis that the lot they have
Fails their own will to please;
For man would make no murmuring, were his will obey'd.

And why is it, that still
Man with his lot thus fights?—
'Tis that he makes this *will*
The measure of his *rights*,
And believes Nature outraged if his will's gainsaid.

Couldst thou, Pausanias, learn
How deep a fault is this;
Couldst thou but once discern
Thou hast no *right* to bliss,
No title from the Gods to welfare and repose;

Then thou wouldst look less mazed
Whene'er of bliss debarr'd,
Nor think the Gods were crazed
When thy own lot went hard.
But we are all the same—the fools of our own woes!

For, from the first faint morn
Of life, the thirst for bliss
Deep in man's heart is born;
And, sceptic as he is,
He fails not to judge clear if this be quench'd or no.

Nor is the thirst to blame.
Man errs not that he deems
His welfare his true aim,
He errs because he dreams
The world does but exist that welfare to bestow.

We mortals are no kings
For each of whom to sway
A new-made world up-springs,
Meant merely for his play;
No, we are strangers here; the world is from of old.

In vain our pent wills fret,
And would the world subdue.
Limits we did not set
Condition all we do;
Born into life we are, and life must be our mould.

Born into life!—man grows
Forth from his parents' stem,
And blends their bloods, as those
Of theirs are blent in them;
So each new man strikes root into a far fore-time.

Born into life!—we bring
A bias with us here,
And, when here, each new thing
Affects us we come near;
To tunes we did not call our being must keep chime.

Born into life!—in vain,
Opinions, those or these,
Unalter'd to retain
The obstinate mind decrees;
Experience, like a sea, soaks all-effacing in.

Born into life!—who lists
May what is false hold dear,
And for himself make mists
Through which to see less clear;
The world is what it is, for all our dust and din.

Born into life!—'tis we,
And not the world, are new;
Our cry for bliss, our plea,
Others have urged it too—
Our wants have all been felt, our errors made before.

No eye could be too sound
To observe a world so vast,
No patience too profound
To sort what's here amass'd;
How man may here best live no care too great to explore.

But we—as some rude guest
Would change, where'er he roam,
The manners there profess'd
To those he brings from home—
We mark not the world's course, but would have *it* take *ours*.

The world's course proves the terms
On which man wins content;
Reason the proof confirms—
We spurn it, and invent
A false course for the world, and for ourselves, false powers.

Riches we wish to get,
Yet remain spendthrifts still;
We would have health, and yet
Still use our bodies ill;
Bafflers of our own prayers, from youth to life's last scenes.

We would have inward peace,
Yet will not look within;
We would have misery cease,
Yet will not cease from sin;
We want all pleasant ends, but will use no harsh means;

We do not what we ought,
What we ought not, we do,
And lean upon the thought
That chance will bring us through;
But our own acts, for good or ill, are mightier powers.

Yet, even when man forsakes
All sin,—is just, is pure,
Abandons all which makes
His welfare insecure,—
Other existences there are, that clash with ours.

Like us, the lightning-fires
Love to have scope and play;
The stream, like us, desires
An unimpeded way;
Like us, the Libyan wind delights to roam at large.

Streams will not curb their pride
The just man not to entomb,
Nor lightnings go aside
To give his virtues room;
Nor is that wind less rough which blows a good man's barge.

Nature, with equal mind,
Sees all her sons at play;
Sees man control the wind,
The wind sweep man away;
Allows the proudly-riding and the foundering bark.

And, lastly, though of ours
No weakness spoil our lot,
Though the non-human powers
Of Nature harm us not,
The ill deeds of other men make often *our* life dark.

What were the wise man's plan?—
Through this sharp, toil-set life,
To work as best he can,
And win what's won by strife.—
But we an easier way to cheat our pains have found.

Scratch'd by a fall, with moans
As children of weak age
Lend life to the dumb stones
Whereon to vent their rage,
And bend their little fists, and rate the senseless ground;

So, loath to suffer mute,
We, peopling the void air,
Make Gods to whom to impute
The ills we ought to bear;
With God and Fate to rail at, suffering easily.

Yet grant—as sense long miss'd
Things that are now perceived,
And much may still exist
Which is not yet believed—
Grant that the world were full of Gods we cannot see;

All things the world which fill
Of but one stuff are spun,
That we who rail are still,
With what we rail at, one;
One with the o'erlabour'd Power that through the breadth
and length

Of earth, and air, and sea,
In men, and plants, and stones,
Hath toil perpetually,
And travails, pants, and moans;
Fain would do all things well, but sometimes fails in strength.

And patiently exact
This universal God
Alike to any act
Proceeds at any nod,
And quietly declaims the cursings of himself.

This is not what man hates,
Yet he can curse but this.
Harsh Gods and hostile Fates
Are dreams! this only *is*—
Is everywhere; sustains the wise, the foolish elf.

Nor only, in the intent
To attach blame elsewhere,
Do we at will invent
Stern Powers who make their care
To embitter human life, malignant Deities;

But, next, we would reverse
The scheme ourselves have spun,
And what we made to curse
We now would lean upon,
And feign kind Gods who perfect what man vainly tries.

Look, the world tempts our eye,
And we would know it all!
We map the starry sky,
We mine this earthen ball,
We measure the sea-tides, we number the sea-sands;

We scrutinise the dates
Of long-past human things,
The bounds of effaced states,
The lines of deceased kings;
We search out dead men's words, and works of dead men's
hands;

We shut our eyes, and muse
How our own minds are made,
What springs of thought they use,
How righten'd, how betray'd—
And spend our wit to name what most employ unnamed.

But still, as we proceed
The mass swells more and more
Of volumes yet to read,
Of secrets yet to explore.
Our hair grows grey, our eyes are dimm'd, our heat is tamed;

We rest our faculties,
And thus address the Gods:
"True science if there is,
It stays in your abodes!
Man's measures cannot mete the immeasurable All.

"You only can take in
The world's immense design.
Our desperate search was sin,
Which henceforth we resign,
Sure only that your mind sees all things which befal."

Fools! That in man's brief term
He cannot all things view,
Afford no ground to affirm
That there are Gods who do;
Nor does being weary prove that he has where to rest.

Again.—Our youthful blood
Claims rapture as its right;
The world, a rolling flood
Of newness and delight,
Draws in the enamour'd gazer to its shining breast;

Pleasure, to our hot grasp,
Gives flowers, after flowers;
With passionate warmth we clasp
Hand after hand in ours;
Now do we soon perceive how fast our youth is spent.

At once our eyes grow clear!
We see, in blank dismay,
Year posting after year,
Sense after sense decay;
Our shivering heart is mined by secret discontent;

Yet still, in spite of truth,
In spite of hopes entomb'd,
That longing of our youth
Burns ever unconsumed,
Still hungrier for delight as delights grow more rare.

We pause; we hush our heart,
And thus address the Gods:
"The world hath fail'd to impart
The joy our youth forebodes,
Fail'd to fill up the void which in our breasts we bear.

"Changeful till now, we still
Look'd on to something new;
Let us, with changeless will,
Henceforth look on to you,
To find with you the joy we in vain here require!'

Fools! That so often here
Happiness mock'd our prayer,
I think, might make us fear
A like event elsewhere;
Make us, not fly to dreams, but moderate desire.

And yet, for those who know
Themselves, who wisely take
Their way through life, and bow
To what they cannot break,
Why should I say that life need yield but *moderate* bliss?

Shall we, with temper spoil'd,
Health sapp'd by living ill,
And judgment all embroil'd
By sadness and self-will,
Shall *we* judge what for man is not true bliss or is?

Is it so small a thing
To have enjoy'd the sun,
To have lived light in the spring,
To have loved, to have thought, to have done;
To have advanced true friends, and beat down baffling foes—

That we must feign a bliss
Of doubtful future date,
And, while we dream on this,
Lose all our present state,
And relegate to worlds yet distant our repose?

Not much, I know, you prize
What pleasures may be had,
Who look on life with eyes
Estranged, like mine, and sad;
And yet the village-churl feels the truth more than you,

Who's loath to leave this life
Which to him little yields—
His hard-task'd sunburnt wife,
His often-labour'd fields,
The boors with whom he talk'd, the country-spots he knew.

But thou, because thou hear'st
Men scoff at Heaven and Fate,
Because the Gods thou fear'st
Fail to make blest thy state,
Tremblest, and wilt not dare to trust the joys there are!

I say: Fear not! Life still
Leaves human effort scope.
But, since life teems with ill,
Nurse no extravagant hope;
Because thou must not dream, thou need'st not then despair!

*A long pause. At the end of it the notes of a harp below are
again heard, and* CALLICLES *sings :—*

Far, far from here,
The Adriatic breaks in a warm bay
Among the green Illyrian hills; and there
The sunshine in the happy glens is fair,
And by the sea, and in the brakes.
The grass is cool, the sea-side air
Buoyant and fresh, the mountain flowers
More virginal and sweet than ours.

And there, they say, two bright and aged snakes,
Who once were Cadmus and Harmonia,
Bask in the glens or on the warm sea-shore,
In breathless quiet, after all their ills;
Nor do they see their country, nor the place
Where the Sphinx lived among the frowning hills,
Nor the unhappy palace of their race,
Nor Thebes, nor the Ismenus, any more.

There those two live, far in the Illyrian brakes!
They had stay'd long enough to see,
In Thebes, the billow of calamity
Over their own dear children roll'd,
Curse upon curse, pang upon pang,
For years, they sitting helpless in their home,
A grey old man and woman; yet of old
The Gods had to their marriage come,
And at the banquet all the Muses sang.

Therefore they did not end their days
In sight of blood; but were rapt, far away,
To where the west-wind plays,
And murmurs of the Adriatic come
To those untrodden mountain-lawns; and there
Placed safely in changed forms, the pair
Wholly forget their first sad life, and home,
And all that Theban woe, and stray
For ever through the glens, placid and dumb.

Empedocles

That was my harp-player again!—where is he?
Down by the stream?

Pausanias

Yes, Master, in the wood.

Empedocles

He ever loved the Theban story well!
But the day wears. Go now, Pausanias,
For I must be alone.   Leave me one mule;
Take down with thee the rest to Catana.
And for young Callicles, thank him from me;
Tell him, I never fail'd to love his lyre—
But he must follow me no more to-night.

Pausanias

Thou wilt return to-morrow to the city?

Empedocles

Either to-morrow or some other day,
In the sure revolutions of the world,
Good friend, I shall revisit Catana.
I have seen many cities in my time,
Till mine eyes ache with the long spectacle,
And I shall doubtless see them all again;
Thou know'st me for a wanderer from of old.
Meanwhile, stay me not now. Farewell, Pausanias!

He departs on his way up the mountain.

Pausanias (alone)

I dare not urge him further—he must go;
But he is strangely wrought!—I will speed back
And bring Peisianax to him from the city;
His counsel could once soothe him.   But, Apollo!
How his brow lighten'd as the music rose!
Callicles must wait here, and play to him;
I saw him through the chestnuts far below,
Just since, down at the stream.—Ho! Callicles!

He descends, calling.

ACT II

Evening. The Summit of Etna.

EMPEDOCLES

Alone!—
On this charr'd, blacken'd, melancholy waste,
Crown'd by the awful peak, Etna's great mouth.
Round which the sullen vapour rolls—alone!
Pausanias is far hence, and that is well,
For I must henceforth speak no more with man
He hath his lesson too, and that debt's paid;
And the good, learned, friendly, quiet man,
May bravelier front his life, and in himself
Find henceforth energy and heart. But I—
The weary man, the banish'd citizen,
Whose banishment is not his greatest ill,
Whose weariness no energy can reach,
And for whose hurt courage is not the cure—
What should I do with life and living more?

No, thou art come too late, Empedocles!
And the world hath the day, and must break thee,
Not thou the world. With men thou canst not live,
Their thoughts, their ways, their wishes, are not thine;
And being lonely thou art miserable,
For something has impair'd thy spirit's strength,
And dried its self-sufficing fount of joy.
Thou canst not live with men nor with thyself—
O sage! O sage!—Take then the one way left;
And turn thee to the elements, thy friends,
Thy well-tried friends, thy willing ministers,
And say: Ye helpers, hear Empedocles,
Who asks this final service at your hands!
Before the sophist-brood hath overlaid
The last spark of man's consciousness with words—
Ere quite the being of man, ere quite the world
Be disarray'd of their divinity—
Before the soul lose all her solemn joys,
And awe be dead, and hope impossible,
And the soul's deep eternal night come on—
Receive me, hide me, quench me, take me home!

He advances to the edge of the crater. Smoke and
fire break forth with a loud noise, and CALLICLES
is heard below singing:—

The lyre's voice is lovely everywhere;
In the court of Gods, in the city of men,
And in the lonely rock-strewn mountain-glen,
In the still mountain air.

Only to Typho it sounds hatefully;
To Typho only, the rebel o'erthrown,
Through whose heart Etna drives her roots of stone,
To imbed them in the sea.

Wherefore dost thou groan so loud?
Wherefore do thy nostrils flash,
Through the dark night, suddenly,
Typho, such red jets of flame?—
Is thy tortured heart still proud?
Is thy fire-scathed arm still rash?
Still alert thy stone-crush'd frame?
Doth thy fierce soul still deplore
Thine ancient rout by the Cilician hills,
And that curst treachery on the Mount of Gore?
Do thy bloodshot eyes still weep
The fight which crown'd thine ills,
Thy last mischance on this Sicilian deep?
Hast thou sworn, in thy sad lair,
Where erst the strong sea-currents suck'd thee down,
Never to cease to writhe, and try to rest,
Letting the sea-stream wander through thy hair?
That thy groans, like thunder prest,
Begin to roll, and almost drown
The sweet notes whose lulling spell
Gods and the race of mortals love so well,
When through thy caves thou hearest music swell?

But an awful pleasure bland
Spreading o'er the Thunderer's face,
When the sound climbs near his seat,
The Olympian council sees;
As he lets his lax right hand,
Which the lightnings doth embrace,
Sink upon his mighty knees.

And the eagle, at the beck
Of the appeasing, gracious harmony,
Droops all his sheeny, brown, deep-feather'd neck,
Nestling nearer to Jove's feet;
While o'er his sovran eye
The curtains of the blue films slowly meet
And the white Olympus-peaks
Rosily brighten, and the soothed Gods smile
At one another from their golden chairs,
And no one round the charmed circle speaks.
Only the loved Hebe bears
The cup about, whose draughts beguile
Pain and care, with a dark store
Of fresh-pull'd violets wreathed and nodding o'er;
And her flush'd feet glow on the marble floor.

Empedocles

He fables, yet speaks truth!
The brave, impetuous heart yields everywhere
To the subtle, contriving head;
Great qualities are trodden down,
And littleness united
Is become invincible.

These rumblings are not Typho's groans, I know!
These angry smoke-bursts
Are not the passionate breath
Of the mountain-crush'd, tortured, intractable Titan
      king—
But over all the world
What suffering is there not seen
Of plainness oppress'd by cunning,
As the well-counsell'd Zeus oppress'd
That self-helping son of earth!
What anguish of greatness,
Rail'd and hunted from the world,
Because its simplicity rebukes
This envious, miserable age!

I am weary of it.
—Lie there, ye ensigns
Of my unloved preëminence
In an age like this!
Among a people of children,
Who throng'd me in their cities,

Who worshipp'd me in their houses,
And ask'd, not wisdom,
But drugs to charm with,
But spells to mutter—
All the fool's-armoury of magic!—Lie there,
My golden circlet,
My purple robe!

Callicles (from below)

As the sky-brightening south-wind clears the day,
And makes the mass'd clouds roll,
The music of the lyre blows away
The clouds which wrap the soul.

Oh! that Fate had let me see
That triumph of the sweet persuasive lyre,
That famous, final victory,
When jealous Pan with Marsyas did conspire.

When, from far Parnassus' side,
Young Apollo, all the pride
Of the Phrygian flutes to tame,
To the Phrygian highlands came;
Where the long green reed-beds sway
In the rippled waters grey
Of that solitary lake
Where Mæander's springs are born;
Whence the ridged pine-wooded roots
Of Messogis westward break,
Mounting westward, high and higher.
There was held the famous strife;
There the Phrygian brought his flutes,
And Apollo brought his lyre;
And, when now the westering sun
Touch'd the hills, the strife was done.
And the attentive Muses said:
"Marsyas, thou art vanquished!"
Then Apollo's minister
Hang'd upon a branching fir
Marsyas, that unhappy Faun,
And began to whet his knife.
But the Mænads, who were there,
Left their friend, and with robes flowing
In the wind, and loose dark hair
O'er their polish'd bosoms blowing,

Each her ribbon'd tambourine
Flinging on the mountain-sod,
With a lovely frighten'd mien
Came about the youthful God.
But he turn'd his beauteous face
Haughtily another way,
From the grassy sun-warm'd place
Where in proud repose he lay,
With one arm over his head,
Watching how the whetting sped.

But aloof, on the lake-strand,
Did the young Olympus stand,
Weeping at his master's end;
For the Faun had been his friend.
For he taught him how to sing,
And he taught him flute-playing,
Many a morning had they gone
To the glimmering mountain-lakes,
And had torn up by the roots
The tall crested water-reeds
With long plumes and soft brown seeds,
And had carved them into flutes,
Sitting on a tabled stone
Where the shoreward ripple breaks.
And he taught him how to please
The red-snooded Phrygian girls,
Whom the summer evening sees
Flashing in the dance's whirls
Underneath the starlit trees
In the mountain-villages.
Therefore now Olympus stands,
At his master's piteous cries
Pressing fast with both his hands
His white garment to his eyes,
Not to see Apollo's scorn;—
Ah, poor Faun, poor Faun! ah, poor Faun!

Empedocles

And lie thou there,
My laurel bough!
Scornful Apollo's ensign, lie thou there!
Though thou hast been my shade in the world's heat—
Though I have loved thee, lived in honouring thee—
Yet lie thou there,
My laurel bough!

I am weary of thee.
I am weary of the solitude
Where he who bears thee must abide—
Of the rocks of Parnassus,
Of the rocks of Delphi,
Of the moonlit peaks, and the caves.
Thou guardest them, Apollo!
Over the grave of the slain Pytho,
Though young, intolerably severe!
Thou keepest aloof the profane,
But the solitude oppresses thy votary!
The jars of men reach him not in thy valley—
But can life reach him?
Thou fencest him from the multitude—
Who will fence him from himself?
He hears nothing but the cry of the torrents,
And the beating of his own heart.
The air is thin, the veins swell,
The temples tighten and throb there—
Air! air!

Take thy bough, set me free from my solitude;
I have been enough alone!

Where shall thy votary fly then? back to men?—
But they will gladly welcome him once more,
And help him to unbend his too tense thought,
And rid him of the presence of himself,
And keep their friendly chatter at his ear,
And haunt him, till the absence from himself,
That other torment, grow unbearable;
And he will fly to solitude again,
And he will find its air too keen for him,
And so change back; and many thousand times
Be miserably bandied to and fro
Like a sea-wave, betwixt the world and thee,
Thou young, implacable God! and only death
Can cut his oscillations short, and so
Bring him to poise. There is no other way.
And yet what days were those, Parmenides!
When we were young, when we could number friends
In all the Italian cities like ourselves,
When with elated hearts we join'd your train.
Ye Sun-born Virgins! on the road of truth.
Then we could still enjoy, then neither thought
Nor outward things were closed and dead to us

But we received the shock of mighty thoughts
On simple minds with a pure natural joy;
And if the sacred load oppress'd our brain,
We had the power to feel the pressure eased,
The brow unbound, the thoughts flow free again,
In the delightful commerce of the world.
We had not lost our balance then, nor grown
Thought's slaves, and dead to every natural joy.
The smallest thing could give us pleasure then—
The sports of the country-people,
A flute-note from the woods,
Sunset over the sea;
Seed-time and harvest,
The reapers in the corn,
The vinedresser in his vineyard,
The village-girl at her wheel.

Fulness of life and power of feeling, ye
Are for the happy, for the souls at ease,
Who dwell on a firm basis of content!
But he, who has outlived his prosperous days—
But he, whose youth fell on a different world
From that on which his exiled age is thrown—
Whose mind was fed on other food, was train'd
By other rules than are in vogue to-day—
Whose habit of thought is fix'd, who will not change,
But, in a world he loves not, must subsist
In ceaseless opposition, be the guard
Of his own breast, fetter'd to what he guards,
That the world win no mastery over him—
Who has no friend, no fellow left, not one;
Who has no minute's breathing space allow'd
To nurse his dwindling faculty of joy——
Joy and the outward world must die to him,
As they are dead to me.

> *A long pause, during which* EMPEDOCLES *remains
> motionless, plunged in thought. The night deepens.
> He moves forward and gazes round him, and
> proceeds:—*

And you, ye stars,
Who slowly begin to marshal,
As of old, in the fields of heaven,
Your distant, melancholy lines!
Have you, too, survived yourselves?
Are you, too, what I fear to become?

You, too, once lived;
You too moved joyfully
Among august companions,
In an older world, peopled by Gods,
In a mightier order,
The radiant, rejoicing, intelligent Sons of Heaven.
But now, ye kindle
Your lonely, cold-shining lights,
Unwilling lingerers
In the heavenly wilderness,
For a younger, ignoble world;
And renew, by necessity,
Night after night your courses,
In echoing, unnear'd silence,
Above a race you know not—
Uncaring and undelighted,
Without friend and without home;
Weary like us, though not
Weary with our weariness.

No, no, ye stars! there is no death with you,
No languor, no decay! languor and death,
They are with me, not you! ye are alive—
Ye, and the pure dark ether where ye ride
Brilliant above me! And thou, fiery world,
That sapp'st the vitals of this terrible mount
Upon whose charr'd and quaking crust I stand—
Thou, too, brimmest with life!—the sea of cloud,
That heaves its white and billowy vapours up
To moat this isle of ashes from the world,
Lives; and that other fainter sea, far down,
O'er whose lit floor a road of moonbeams leads
To Etna's Liparëan sister-fires
And the long dusky line of Italy—
That mild and luminous floor of waters lives,
With held-in joy swelling its heart; I only,
Whose spring of hope is dried, whose spirit has fail'd,
I, who have not, like these, in solitude
Maintain'd courage and force, and in myself
Nursed an immortal vigour—I alone
Am dead to life and joy, therefore I read
In all things my own deadness.

A long silence. He continues:—

Oh, that I could glow like this mountain!
Oh, that my heart bounded with the swell of the sea!

Oh, that my soul were full of light as the stars!
Oh, that it brooded over the world like the air!

But no, this heart will glow no more; thou art
A living man no more, Empedocles!
Nothing but a devouring flame of thought—
But a naked, eternally restless mind!

After a pause:—

To the elements it came from
Everything will return—
Our bodies to earth,
Our blood to water,
Heat to fire,
Breath to air.
They were well born, they will be well entomb'd—
But mind? . . .

And we might gladly share the fruitful stir
Down in our mother earth's miraculous womb;
Well would it be
With what roll'd of us in the stormy main;
We might have joy, blent with the all-bathing air,
Or with the nimble, radiant life of fire.

But mind, but thought—
If these have been the master part of us—
Where will *they* find their parent element?
What will receive *them*, who will call *them* home?
But we shall still be in them, and they in us,
And we shall be the strangers of the world,
And they will be our lords, as they are now;
And keep us prisoners of our consciousness,
And never let us clasp and feel the All
But through their forms, and modes, and stifling veils.
And we shall be unsatisfied as now;
And we shall feel the agony of thirst,
The ineffable longing for the life of life
Baffled for ever; and still thought and mind
Will hurry us with them on their homeless march,
Over the unallied unopening earth,
Over the unrecognising sea; while air
Will blow us fiercely back to sea and earth,
And fire repel us from its living waves.
And then we shall unwillingly return
Back to this meadow of calamity,
This uncongenial place, this human life;

And in our individual human state
Go through the sad probation all again,
To see if we will poise our life at last,
To see if we will now at last be true
To our own only true, deep-buried selves,
Being one with which we are one with the whole world;
Or whether we will once more fall away
Into some bondage of the flesh or mind,
Some slough of sense, or some fantastic maze
Forged by the imperious lonely thinking-power.
And each succeeding age in which we are born
Will have more peril for us than the last;
Will goad our senses with a sharper spur,
Will fret our minds to an intenser play,
Will make ourselves harder to be discern'd.
And we shall struggle awhile, gasp and rebel—
And we shall fly for refuge to past times,
Their soul of unworn youth, their breath of greatness;
And the reality will pluck us back,
Knead us in its hot hand, and change our nature
And we shall feel our powers of effort flag,
And rally them for one last fight—and fail;
And we shall sink in the impossible strife,
And be astray for ever.

                    Slave of sense
I have in no wise been;—but slave of thought? . . .
And who can say: I have been always free,
Lived ever in the light of my own soul?—
I cannot; I have lived in wrath and gloom,
Fierce, disputatious, ever at war with man,
Far from my own soul, far from warmth and light.
But I have not grown easy in these bonds—
But I have not denied what bonds these were.
Yea, I take myself to witness,
That I have loved no darkness,
Sophisticated no truth,
Nursed no delusion,
Allow'd no fear!

    And therefore, O ye elements! I know—
Ye know it too—it hath been granted me
Not to die wholly, not to be all enslaved.
I feel it in this hour. The numbing cloud
Mounts off my soul; I feel it, I breathe free.

Is it but for a moment?
—Ah, boil up, ye vapours!
Leap and roar, thou sea of fire!
My soul glows to meet you.
Ere it flag, ere the mists
Of despondency and gloom
Rush over it again,
Receive me, save me!

[*He plunges into the crater.*

Callicles

(*from below*)

Through the black, rushing smoke-bursts,
Thick breaks the red flame;
All Etna heaves fiercely
Her forest-clothed frame.

Not here, O Apollo!
Are haunts meet for thee.
But, where Helicon breaks down
In cliff to the sea,

Where the moon-silver'd inlets
Send far their light voice
Up the still vale of Thisbe,
O speed, and rejoice!

On the sward at the cliff-top
Lie strewn the white flocks,
On the cliff-side the pigeons
Roost deep in the rocks.

In the moonlight the shepherds,
Soft lull'd by the rills,
Lie wrapt in their blankets
Asleep on the hills.

—What forms are these coming
So white through the gloom?
What garments out-glistening
The gold-flower'd broom?

What sweet-breathing presence
Out-perfumes the thyme?
What voices enrapture
The night's balmy prime?—

'Tis Apollo comes leading
His choir, the Nine.
—The leader is fairest,
But all are divine.

They are lost in the hollows!
They stream up again!
What seeks on this mountain
The glorified train?—

They bathe on this mountain,
In the spring by their road;
Then on to Olympus,
Their endless abode.

—Whose praise do they mention?
Of what is it told?—
What will be for ever;
What was from of old.

First hymn they the Father
Of all things; and then,
The rest of immortals,
The action of men.

The day in his hotness,
The strife with the palm;
The night in her silence,
The stars in their calm.

LATER POEMS

Notes on Later Poems, pp. 794–5.

LATER POEMS

Geist's Grave

FOUR years!—and didst thou stay above
The ground, which hides thee now, but four?
And all that life, and all that love,
Were crowded, Geist! into no more?

Only four years those winning ways,
Which make me for thy presence yearn,
Call'd us to pet thee or to praise,
Dear little friend! at every turn?

That loving heart, that patient soul,
Had they indeed no longer span,
To run their course, and reach their goal,
And read their homily to man?

That liquid, melancholy eye,
From whose pathetic, soul-fed springs
Seem'd surging the Virgilian cry,[1]
The sense of tears in mortal things- -

That steadfast, mournful strain, consoled
By spirits gloriously gay,
And temper of heroic mould—
What, was four years their whole short day?

Yes, only four!—and not the course
Of all the centuries yet to come,
And not the infinite resource
Of Nature, with her countless sum

Of figures, with her fulness vast
Of new creation, evermore,
Can ever quite repeat the past,
Or just thy little self restore.

[1] *Sunt lacrimæ rerum!*

Stern law of every mortal lot!
Which man, proud man, finds hard to bear,
And builds himself I know not what
Of second life I know not where.

But thou, when struck thine hour to go,
On us, who stood despondent by,
A meek last glance of love didst throw,
And humbly lay thee down to die.

Yet would we keep thee in our heart—
Would fix our favourite on the scene,
Nor let thee utterly depart
And be as if thou ne'er hadst been.

And so there rise these lines of verse
On lips that rarely form them now;
While to each other we rehearse:
Such ways, such arts, such looks hadst thou!

We stroke thy broad brown paws again,
We bid thee to thy vacant chair,
We greet thee by the window-pane,
We hear thy scuffle on the stair.

We see the flaps of thy large ears
Quick raised to ask which way we go;
Crossing the frozen lake, appears
Thy small black figure on the snow!

Nor to us only art thou dear
Who mourn thee in thine English home;
Thou hast thine absent master's tear,
Dropt by the far Australian foam.

Thy memory lasts both here and there,
And thou shalt live as long as we.
And after that—thou dost not care!
In us was all the world to thee.

Yet, fondly zealous for thy fame,
Even to a date beyond our own
We strive to carry down thy name,
By mounded turf, and graven stone.

We lay thee, close within our reach,
Here, where the grass is smooth and warm,
Between the holly and the beech,
Where oft we watch'd thy couchant form,

Asleep, yet lending half an ear
To travellers on the Portsmouth road;—
There build we thee, O guardian dear,
Mark'd with a stone, thy last abode!

Then some, who through this garden pass,
When we too, like thyself, are clay,
Shall see thy grave upon the grass,
And stop before the stone, and say:

People who lived here long ago
Did by this stone, it seems, intend
To name for future times to know
The dachs-hound, Geist, their little friend.

Poor Matthias

Poor Matthias!—Found him lying
Fall'n beneath his perch and dying?
Found him stiff, you say, though warm—
All convulsed his little form?
Poor canary! many a year
Well he knew his mistress dear;
Now in vain you call his name,
Vainly raise his rigid frame,
Vainly warm him in your breast,
Vainly kiss his golden crest,
Smooth his ruffled plumage fine,
Touch his trembling beak with wine.
One more gasp—it is the end!
Dead and mute our tiny friend!
—Songster thou of many a year,
Now thy mistress brings thee here,
Says, it fits that I rehearse,
Tribute due to thee, a verse,
Meed for daily song of yore
Silent now for evermore.

Poor Matthias! Wouldst thou have
More than pity? claim'st a stave?
—Friends more near us than a bird
We dismiss'd without a word.
Rover, with the good brown head,
Great Atossa, they are dead;
Dead, and neither prose nor rhyme
Tells the praises of their prime.
Thou didst know them old and grey,
Know them in their sad decay.
Thou hast seen Atossa sage
Sit for hours beside thy cage;
Thou wouldst chirp, thou foolish bird,
Flutter, chirp—she never stirr'd!
What were now these toys to her?
Down she sank amid her fur;
Eyed thee with a soul resign'd—
And thou deemedst cats were kind!
—Cruel, but composed and bland,
Dumb, inscrutable and grand,
So Tiberius might have sat,
Had Tiberius been a cat.

Rover died—Atossa too.
Less than they to us are you!
Nearer human were their powers,
Closer knit their life with ours.
Hands had stroked them, which are cold,
Now for years, in churchyard mould;
Comrades of our past were they,
Of that unreturning day.
Changed and aging, they and we
Dwelt, it seem'd, in sympathy.
Alway from their presence broke
Somewhat which remembrance woke
Of the loved, the lost, the young—
Yet they died, and died unsung.

Geist came next, our little friend;
Geist had verse to mourn his end.
Yes, but that enforcement strong
Which compell'd for Geist a song—
All that gay courageous cheer,
All that human pathos dear;

Soul-fed eyes with suffering worn,
Pain heroically borne,
Faithful love in depth divine—
Poor Matthias, were they thine?

Max and Kaiser we to-day
Greet upon the lawn at play;
Max a dachshound without blot—
Kaiser should be, but is not.
Max, with shining yellow coat,
Prinking ears and dewlap throat—
Kaiser, with his collie face,
Penitent for want of race.
—Which may be the first to die,
Vain to augur, they or I!
But, as age comes on, I know,
Poet's fire gets faint and low;
If so be that travel they
First the inevitable way,
Much I doubt if they shall have
Dirge from me to crown their grave.

Yet, poor bird, thy tiny corse
Moves me, somehow, to remorse;
Something haunts my conscience, brings
Sad, compunctious visitings.
Other favourites, dwelling here,
Open lived to us, and near;
Well we knew when they were glad,
Plain we saw if they were sad,
Joy'd with them when they were gay,
Soothed them in their last decay;
Sympathy could feel and show
Both in weal of theirs and woe.

Birds, companions more unknown,
Live beside us, but alone;
Finding not, do all they can,
Passage from their souls to man.
Kindness we bestow, and praise,
Laud their plumage, greet their lays;
Still, beneath their feather'd breast,
Stirs a history unexpress'd.
Wishes there, and feelings strong,
Incommunicably throng;

What they want, we cannot guess,
Fail to track their deep distress—
Dull look on when death is nigh,
Note no change, and let them die.
Poor Matthias! couldst thou speak,
What a tale of thy last week!
Every morning did we pay
Stupid salutations gay,
Suited well to health, but how
Mocking, how incongruous now!
Cake we offer'd, sugar, seed,
Never doubtful of thy need;
Praised, perhaps, thy courteous eye,
Praised thy golden livery.
Gravely thou the while, poor dear!
Sat'st upon thy perch to hear,
Fixing with a mute regard
Us, thy human keepers hard,
Troubling, with our chatter vain,
Ebb of life, and mortal pain—
Us, unable to divine
Our companion's dying sign,
Or o'erpass the severing sea
Set betwixt ourselves and thee,
Till the sand thy feathers smirch
Fallen dying off thy perch!

Was it, as the Grecian sings,
Birds were born the first of things,
Before the sun, before the wind,
Before the gods, before mankind,
Airy, ante-mundane throng—
Witness their unworldly song!
Proof they give, too, primal powers,
Of a prescience more than ours—
Teach us, while they come and go,
When to sail, and when to sow.
Cuckoo calling from the hill,
Swallow skimming by the mill,
Swallows trooping in the sedge,
Starlings swirling from the hedge,
Mark the seasons, map our year,
As they show and disappear.
But, with all this travail sage
Brought from that anterior age,

Goes an unreversed decree
Whereby strange are they and we,
Making want of theirs, and plan,
Indiscernible by man.

No, away with tales like these
Stol'n from Aristophanes!
Does it, if we miss your mind,
Prove us so remote in kind?
Birds! we but repeat on you
What amongst ourselves we do.
Somewhat more or somewhat less,
'Tis the same unskilfulness.
What you feel, escapes our ken—
Know we more our fellow men?
Human suffering at our side,
Ah, like yours is undescried!
Human longings, human fears,
Miss our eyes and miss our ears.
Little helping, wounding much,
Dull of heart, and hard of touch,
Brother man's despairing sign
Who may trust us to divine?
Who assure us, sundering powers
Stand not 'twixt his soul and ours?

Poor Matthias! See, thy end
What a lesson doth it lend!
For that lesson thou shalt have,
Dead canary bird, a stave!
Telling how, one stormy day,
Stress of gale and showers of spray
Drove my daughter small and me
Inland from the rocks and sea.
Driv'n inshore, we follow down
Ancient streets of Hastings town—
Slowly thread them—when behold,
French canary-merchant old
Shepherding his flock of gold
In a low dim-lighted pen
Scann'd of tramps and fishermen!
There a bird, high-coloured, fat,
Proud of port, though something squat—
Pursy, play'd-out Philistine—
Dazzled Nelly's youthful eyne.

But, far in, obscure, there stirr'd
On his perch a sprightlier bird,
Courteous-eyed, erect and slim;
And I whisper'd: "Fix on *him!*"
Home we brought him, young and fair,
Songs to trill in Surrey air.
Here Matthias sang his fill,
Saw the cedars of Pains Hill;
Here he pour'd his little soul,
Heard the murmur of the Mole.
Eight in number now the years
He hath pleased our eyes and ears;
Other favourites he hath known
Go, and now himself is gone.
—Fare thee well, companion dear!
Fare for ever well, nor fear,
Tiny though thou art, to stray
Down the uncompanion'd way!
We without thee, little friend,
Many years have not to spend;
What are left, will hardly be
Better than we spent with thee.

PROSE

ON THE MODERN ELEMENT
IN LITERATURE

1857

On the Modern Element in Literature

ARNOLD'S inaugural lecture as Professor of Poetry at Oxford, delivered in the autumn of 1857. It was the introduction to an uncompleted course of lectures, and Arnold did not include it in any collection of his essays. It was printed in *Macmillan's Magazine*, February 1869, with an introductory note:

> What follows was delivered as an inaugural lecture in the Poetry Chair at Oxford. It was never printed, but there appeared at the time several comments on it, from critics who had either heard it, or heard reports about it. It was meant to be followed and completed by a course of lectures developing the subject entirely, and some of these were given. But the course was broken off because I found my knowledge insufficient for treating in a solid way many portions of the subject chosen. . . .

The lecture was reprinted posthumously in *Essays in Criticism* (Third Series), and in *Essays* by Matthew Arnold (Oxford, 1914). The present text is complete except for the two introductory paragraphs which are omitted.

Some information about the missing lectures may be gleaned from the "University Intelligence" columns of *The Times*. Six additional lectures in continuation of the introductory course "On the Modern Element in Literature" were announced at intervals—the last on 29 March 1862. The titles of two only are given: "The Claim of the Celtic Race and the Claim of the Christian Religion to have Originated Chivalrous Sentiment" on 8 June 1861, and "The Modern Element in Dante" on 29 March 1862. During 1860–61 the course was interrupted by the Homer lectures.

A full list of Arnold's professorial lectures is given by Miss Marion Mainwaring in *Notes Toward a Matthew Arnold Bibliography* (*Modern Philology*, Vol. 49, 1952).

ON THE MODERN ELEMENT
IN LITERATURE

... An intellectual deliverance is the peculiar demand of those ages which are called modern; and those nations are said to be imbued with the modern spirit most eminently in which the demand for such a deliverance has been made with most zeal, and satisfied with most completeness. Such a deliverance is emphatically, whether we will or no, the demand of the age in which we ourselves live. All intellectual pursuits our age judges according to their power of helping to satisfy this demand; of all studies it asks, above all, the question, how far they can contribute to this deliverance.

I propose, on this my first occasion of speaking here, to attempt such a general survey of ancient classical literature and history as may afford us the conviction—in presence of the doubts so often expressed of the profitableness, in the present day, of our study of this literature—that, even admitting to their fullest extent the legitimate demands of our age, the literature of ancient Greece is, even for modern times, a mighty agent of intellectual deliverance; even for modern times, therefore, an object of indestructible interest.

But first let us ask ourselves why the demand for an intellectual deliverance arises in such an age as the present, and in what the deliverance itself consists? The demand arises, because our present age has around it a copious and complex present, and behind it a copious and complex past; it arises, because the present age exhibits to the individual man who contemplates it the spectacle of a vast multitude of facts awaiting and inviting his comprehension. The deliverance consists in man's comprehension of this present and past. It begins when our mind begins to enter into possession of the general ideas which are the law of this vast multitude of facts. It is perfect when we have acquired that harmonious acquiescence of mind which we feel in contemplating a grand spectacle that is intelligible to us; when we have lost that impatient irritation of mind which we feel in presence of an immense, moving, confused spectacle which, while it perpetually excites our curiosity, perpetually baffles our comprehension.

This, then, is what distinguishes certain epochs in the history

269

of the human race, and our own amongst the number;—on the one hand, the presence of a significant spectacle to contemplate; on the other hand, the desire to find the true point of view from which to contemplate this spectacle. He who has found that point of view, he who adequately comprehends this spectacle, has risen to the comprehension of his age: he who communicates that point of view to his age, he who interprets to it that spectacle, is one of his age's intellectual deliverers.

The spectacle, the facts, presented for the comprehension of the present age, are indeed immense. The facts consist of the events, the institutions, the sciences, the arts, the literatures, in which human life has manifested itself up to the present time: the spectacle is the collective life of humanity. And everywhere there is connexion, everywhere there is illustration: no single event, no single literature, is adequately comprehended except in its relation to other events, to other literatures. The literature of ancient Greece, the literature of the Christian Middle Age, so long as they are regarded as two isolated literatures, two isolated growths of the human spirit, are not adequately comprehended; and it is adequate comprehension which is the demand of the present age. "We must compare,"— the illustrious Chancellor of Cambridge [1] said the other day to his hearers at Manchester,—"we must compare the works of other ages with those of our own age and country; that, while we feel proud of the immense development of knowledge and power of production which we possess, we may learn humility in contemplating the refinement of feeling and intensity of thought manifested in the works of the older schools." To know how others stand, that we may know how we ourselves stand; and to know how we ourselves stand, that we may correct our mistakes and achieve our deliverance—that is our problem.

But all facts, all the elements of the spectacle before us, have not an equal value—do not merit a like attention: and it is well that they do not, for no man would be adequate to the task of thoroughly mastering them all. Some have more significance for us, others have less; some merit our utmost attention in all their details, others it is sufficient to comprehend in their general character, and then they may be dismissed.

What facts, then, let us ask ourselves, what elements of the spectacle before us, will naturally be most interesting to a highly developed age like our own, to an age making the demand which we have described for an intellectual deliverance by means of the complete intelligence of its own situation? Evidently, the other ages similarly developed, and making the same demand.

[1] The late Prince Consort.

And what past literature will naturally be most interesting to such an age as our own? Evidently, the literatures which have most successfully solved for *their* ages the problem which occupies ours: the literatures which in their day and for their own nation have adequately comprehended, have adequately represented, the spectacle before them. A significant, a highly-developed, a culminating epoch, on the one hand,—a comprehensive, a commensurate, an adequate literature, on the other, — these will naturally be the objects of deepest interest to our modern age. Such an epoch and such a literature are, in fact, *modern*, in the same sense in which our own age and literature are modern; they are founded upon a rich past and upon an instructive fulness of experience.

It may, however, happen that a great epoch is without a perfectly adequate literature; it may happen that a great age, a great nation, has attained a remarkable fulness of political and social development, without intellectually taking the complete measure of itself, without adequately representing that development in its literature. In this case, the *epoch*, the *nation* itself, will still be an object of the greatest interest to us; but the *literature* will be an object of less interest to us: the facts, the material spectacle, are there; but the contemporary view of the facts, the intellectual interpretation, are inferior and inadequate.

It may happen, on the other hand, that great authors, that a powerful literature, are found in an age and nation less great and powerful than themselves; it may happen that a literature, that a man of genius, may arise adequate to the representation of a greater, a more highly-developed age than that in which they appear; it may happen that a literature completely interprets its epoch, and yet has something over; that it has a force, a richness, a geniality, a power of view which the materials at its disposition are insufficient adequately to employ. In such a case, the literature will be more interesting to us than the epoch. The interpreting power, the illuminating and revealing intellect, are there; but the spectacle on which they throw their light is not fully worthy of them.

And I shall not, I hope, be thought to magnify too much my office if I add, that it is to the poetical literature of an age that we must, in general, look for the most perfect, the most adequate interpretation of that age,—for the performance of a work which demands the most energetic and harmonious activity of all the powers of the human mind. Because that activity of the whole mind, that genius, as Johnson nobly describes it, "without which judgment is cold and knowledge is inert; that

energy which collects, combines, amplifies, and animates,"
is in poetry at its highest stretch and in its most energetic
exertion.

What we seek, therefore, what will most enlighten us, most
contribute to our intellectual deliverance, is the union of two
things; it is the co-existence, the simultaneous appearance, of a
great epoch and a great literature.

Now the culminating age in the life of ancient Greece I call,
beyond question, a great epoch; the life of Athens in the fifth
century before our era I call one of the highly-developed, one
of the marking, one of the modern periods in the life of the whole
human race. It has been said that the "Athens of Pericles was a
vigorous man, at the summit of his bodily strength and mental
energy." There was the utmost energy of life there, public and
private; the most entire freedom, the most unprejudiced and
intelligent observation of human affairs. Let us rapidly examine
some of the characteristics which distinguish modern epochs;
let us see how far the culminating century of ancient Greece
exhibits them; let us compare it, in respect of them, with a much
later, a celebrated century; let us compare it with the age of
Elizabeth in our own country.

To begin with what is exterior. One of the most characteristic
outward features of a *modern* age, of an age of advanced civilization, is the banishment of the ensigns of war and bloodshed
from the intercourse of civil life. Crime still exists, and wars are
still carried on; but within the limits of civil life a circle has been
formed within which man can move securely, and develop the
arts of peace uninterruptedly. The private man does not go
forth to his daily occupation prepared to assail the life of his
neighbour or to have to defend his own. With the disappearance
of the constant means of offence the occasions of offence
diminish; society at last acquires repose, confidence, and free
activity. An important inward characteristic, again, is the growth
of a tolerant spirit; that spirit which is the offspring of an enlarged knowledge; a spirit patient of the diversities of habits
and opinions. Other characteristics are the multiplication of the
conveniences of life, the formation of taste, the capacity for refined pursuits. And this leads us to the supreme characteristic of
all: the intellectual maturity of man himself; the tendency to observe facts with a critical spirit; to search for their law, not to
wander among them at random; to judge by the rule of reason,
not by the impulse of prejudice or caprice.

Well, now, with respect to the presence of all these characteristics in the age of Pericles, we possess the explicit testimony of an immortal work,—of the history of Thucydides.

"The Athenians first," he says—speaking of the gradual development of Grecian society up to the period when the Peloponnesian war commenced—"the Athenians first left off the habit of wearing arms:" that is, this mark of superior civilization had, in the age of Pericles, become general in Greece, had long been visible at Athens. In the time of Elizabeth, on the other hand, the wearing of arms was universal in England and throughout Europe. Again, the conveniences, the ornaments, the luxuries of life, had become common at Athens at the time of which we are speaking. But there had been an advance even beyond this; there had been an advance to that perfection, that propriety of taste which prescribes the excess of ornament, the extravagance of luxury. The Athenians had given up, Thucydides says, had given up, although not very long before, an extravagance of dress and an excess of personal ornament which, in the first flush of newly discovered luxury, had been adopted by some of the richer classes. The height of civilization in this respect seems to have been attained; there was general elegance and refinement of life, and there was simplicity. What was the case in this respect in the Elizabethan age? The scholar Casaubon, who settled in England in the reign of James I, bears evidence to the want here, even at that time, of conveniences of life which were already to be met with on the continent of Europe. On the other hand, the taste for fantastic, for excessive personal adornment, to which the portraits of the time bear testimony, is admirably set forth in the work of a great novelist, who was also a very truthful antiquarian—in the *Kenilworth* of Sir Walter Scott. We all remember the description, in the thirteenth and fourteenth chapters of the second volume of *Kenilworth*, of the barbarous magnificence, the "fierce vanities," of the dress of the period.

Pericles praises the Athenians that they had discovered sources of recreation for the spirit to counterbalance the labours of the body: compare these, compare the pleasures which charmed the whole body of the Athenian people through the yearly round of their festivals with the popular shows and pastimes in *Kenilworth*. "We have freedom," says Pericles, "for individual diversities of opinion and character; we do not take offence at the tastes and habits of our neighbour if they differ from our own." Yes, in Greece, in the Athens of Pericles, there is toleration; but in England, in the England of the sixteenth century?—the Puritans are then in full growth. So that with regard to these characteristics of civilization of a modern spirit which we have hitherto enumerated, the superiority, it will be admitted, rests with the age of Pericles.

Let us pass to what we said was the supreme characteristic

of a highly developed, a modern age—the manifestation of a critical spirit, the endeavour after a rational arrangement and appreciation of facts. Let us consider one or two of the passages in the masterly introduction which Thucydides, the contemporary of Pericles, has prefixed to his history. What was his motive in choosing the Peloponnesian War for his subject? Because it was, in his opinion, the most important, the most instructive event which had, up to that time, happened in the history of mankind. What is his effort in the first twenty-three chapters of his history? To place in their correct point of view all the facts which had brought Grecian society to the point at which that dominant event found it; to strip these facts of their exaggeration, to examine them critically. The enterprises undertaken in the early times of Greece were on a much smaller scale than had been commonly supposed. The Greek chiefs were induced to combine in the expedition against Troy, not by their respect for an oath taken by them all when suitors to Helen, but by their respect for the preponderating influence of Agamemnon; the siege of Troy had been protracted not so much by the valour of the besieged as by the inadequate mode of warfare necessitated by the want of funds of the besiegers. No doubt Thucydides' criticism of the Trojan war is not perfect; but observe how in these and many other points he labours to correct popular errors, to assign their true character to facts, complaining, as he does so, of men's habit of *uncritical* reception of current stories. "So little a matter of care to most men," he says, "is the search after truth, and so inclined are they to take up any story which is ready to their hand." "He himself," he continues, "has endeavoured to give a true picture, and believes that in the main he has done so. For some readers his history may want the charm of the uncritical, half-fabulous narratives of earlier writers; but for such as desire to gain a clear knowledge of the past, and thereby of the future also, which will surely, after the course of human things, represent again hereafter, if not the very image, yet the near resemblance of the past —if such shall judge my work to be profitable, I shall be well content."

What language shall we properly call this? It is *modern* language; it is the language of a thoughtful philosophic man of our own days; it is the language of Burke or Niebuhr assigning the true aim of history. And yet Thucydides is no mere literary man; no isolated thinker, speaking far over the heads of his hearers to a future age—no: he was a man of action, a man of the world, a man of his time. He represents, at its best indeed, but he represents, the general intelligence of his age and nation;

of a nation the meanest citizens of which could follow with comprehension the profoundly thoughtful speeches of Pericles.

Let us now turn for a contrast to a historian of the Elizabethan age, also a man of great mark and ability, also a man of action, also a man of the world, Sir Walter Ralegh. Sir Walter Ralegh writes the *History of the World*, as Thucydides has written the *History of the Peloponnesian War*; let us hear his language; let us mark his point of view; let us see what problems occur to him for solution. "Seeing," he says, "that we digress in all the ways of our lives—yea, seeing the life of man is nothing else but digression—I may be the better excused in writing their lives and actions." What are the preliminary facts which he discusses, as Thucydides discusses the Trojan War and the early naval power of Crete, and which are to lead up to his main inquiry? Open the table of contents of his first volume. You will find:—"Of the firmament, and of the waters above the firmament, and whether there be any crystalline Heaven, or any primum mobile." You will then find:—"Of Fate, and that the stars have great influence, and that their operations may diversely be prevented or furthered." Then you come to two entire chapters on the place of Paradise, and on the two chief trees in the garden of Paradise. And in what style, with what power of criticism, does Ralegh treat the subjects so selected? I turn to the seventh section of the third chapter of his first book, which treats "Of their opinion which make Paradise as high as the moon, and of others which make it higher than the middle region of the air." Thus he begins the discussion of this opinion:—"Whereas Beda saith, and as the schoolmen affirm Paradise to be a place altogether removed from the knowledge of men ("locus a cognitione hominum remotissimus"), and Barcephas conceived that Paradise was far in the east, but mounted above the ocean and all the earth, and near the orb of the moon (which opinion, though the schoolmen charge Beda withal, yet Pererius lays it off from Beda and his master Rabanus); and whereas Rupertus in his geography of Paradise doth not much differ from the rest, but finds it seated next or nearest Heaven——" So he states the error, and now for his own criticism of it. "First, such a place cannot be commodious to live in, for being so near the moon it had been too near the sun and other heavenly bodies. Secondly, it must have been too joint a neighbour to the element of fire. Thirdly, the air in that region is so violently moved and carried about with such swiftness as nothing in that place can consist or have abiding. Fourthly,"—but what has been quoted is surely enough, and there is no use in continuing.

Which is the ancient here, and which is the modern? Which

uses the language of an intelligent man of our own days? which a language wholly obsolete and unfamiliar to us? Which has the rational appreciation and control of his facts? which wanders among them helplessly and without a clue? Is it our own countryman, or is it the Greek? And the language of Ralegh affords a fair sample of the critical power, of the point of view, possessed by the majority of intelligent men of his day; as the language of Thucydides affords us a fair sample of the critical power of the majority of intelligent men in the age of Pericles.

Well, then, in the age of Pericles we have, in spite of its antiquity, a highly-developed, a modern, a deeply interesting epoch. Next comes the question: Is this epoch adequately interpreted by its highest literature? Now, the peculiar characteristic of the highest literature—the poetry—of the fifth century in Greece before the Christian era, is its *adequacy*; the peculiar characteristic of the poetry of Sophocles is its consummate, its unrivalled *adequacy*; that it represents the highly developed human nature of that age—human nature developed in a number of directions, politically, socially, religiously, morally developed—in its completest and most harmonious development in all these directions; while there is shed over this poetry the charm of that noble serenity which always accompanies true insight. If in the body of Athenians of that time there was, as we have said, the utmost energy of mature manhood, public and private; the most entire freedom, the most unprejudiced and intelligent observation of human affairs— in Sophocles there is the same energy, the same maturity, the same freedom, the same intelligent observation; but all these idealized and glorified by the grace and light shed over them from the noblest poetical feeling. And therefore I have ventured to say of Sophocles, that he "saw life steadily, and saw it whole." Well may we understand how Pericles—how the great statesman whose aim was, it has been said, "to realize in Athens the idea which he had conceived of human greatness," and who partly succeeded in his aim—should have been drawn to the great poet whose works are the noblest reflection of his success.

I assert, therefore, though the detailed proof of the assertion must be reserved for other opportunities, that, if the fifth century in Greece before our era is a significant and modern epoch, the poetry of that epoch—the poetry of Pindar, Aeschylus, and Sophocles—is an adequate representation and interpretation of it.

The poetry of Aristophanes is an adequate representation of it also. True, this poetry regards humanity from the comic side; but there is a comic side from which to regard humanity as well as a tragic one; and the distinction of Aristophanes is to have regarded it from the true point of view on the comic side. He too, like Sophocles, regards the human nature of his time in its fullest development; the boldest creations of a riotous imagination are in Aristophanes, as has been justly said, based always upon the foundation of a serious thought: politics, education, social life, literature—all the great modes in which the human life of his day manifested itself—are the subjects of his thoughts, and of his penetrating comment. There is shed, therefore, over his poetry the charm, the vital freshness, which is felt when man and his relations are from any side adequately, and therefore genially, regarded. Here is the true difference between Aristophanes and Menander. There has been preserved an epitome of a comparison by Plutarch between Aristophanes and Menander, in which the grossness of the former, the exquisite truth to life and felicity of observation of the latter, are strongly insisted upon; and the preference of the refined, the learned, the intelligent men of a later period for Menander loudly proclaimed. "What should take a man of refinement to the theatre," asks Plutarch, "except to see one of Menander's plays? When do you see the theatre filled with cultivated persons, except when Menander is acted? and he is the favourite refreshment," he continues, "to the overstrained mind of the laborious philosopher." And every one knows the famous line of tribute to this poet by an enthusiastic admirer in antiquity:—"O Life and Menander, which of you painted the other?" We remember, too, how a great English statesman is said to have declared that there was no lost work of antiquity which he so ardently desired to recover as a play of Menander. Yet Menander has perished, and Aristophanes has survived. And to what is this to be attributed? To the instinct of self-preservation in humanity. The human race has the strongest, the most invincible tendency to *live*, to *develop* itself. It retains, it clings to what fosters its life, what favours its development, to the literature which exhibits it in its vigour; it rejects, it abandons what does not foster its development, the literature which exhibits it arrested and decayed. Now, between the times of Sophocles and Menander a great check had befallen the development of Greece;—the failure of the Athenian expedition to Syracuse, and the consequent termination of the Peloponnesian War in a result unfavourable to Athens. The free expansion of her growth was checked; one of the noblest channels of Athenian life, that of political activity, had begun to narrow and to dry up. That was the true catastrophe of the ancient world; it was then that the oracles of the ancient world should have become silent, and that its gods should have forsaken their temples; for from that date the intellectual and spiritual life of Greece was left without an adequate material basis of political and practical life; and both began inevitably to decay. The opportunity of the ancient world was then lost, never to return; for neither the Macedonian nor the Roman world, which possessed an adequate material basis, possessed, like the Athens of earlier times, an adequate intellect and soul to inform and inspire them; and there was left of the ancient world, when Christianity arrived, of Greece only a head without a body, and of Rome only a body without a soul.

It is Athens after this check, after this diminution of vitality,— it is man with part of his life shorn away, refined and intelligent indeed, but sceptical, frivolous, and dissolute,—which the poetry of Menander represented. The cultivated, the accomplished might applaud the dexterity, the perfection of the representation—might prefer it to the free genial delineation of a more living time with which they were no longer in sympathy. But the instinct of humanity taught it, that in the one poetry there was the seed of life, in the other poetry the seed of death; and it had rescued Aristophanes, while it has left Menander to his fate.

In the flowering period of the life of Greece, therefore, we have a culminating age, one of the flowering periods of the life of the human race: in the poetry of that age we have a literature commensurate with its epoch. It is most perfectly commensurate in the poetry of Pindar, Aeschylus, Sophocles, Aristophanes; these, therefore, will be the supremely interesting objects in this literature; but the stages in literature which led up to this point of perfection, the stages in literature which led downward from it, will be deeply interesting also. A distinguished person,[1] who has lately been occupying himself with Homer, has remarked that an undue preference is given, in the studies of Oxford, to these poets over Homer. The justification of such a preference even if we put aside all philological considerations, lies, perhaps, in what I have said. Homer himself is eternally interesting; he is a greater poetical power than even Sophocles or Aeschylus; but his age is less interesting than himself. Aeschylus and Sophocles represent an age as interesting as themselves; the names, indeed, in their dramas are the names of the old heroic world, from which they were far separated; but these names are taken, because the use of them permits to the poet that free and ideal treatment of his characters which the highest tragedy demands; and into these figures of the old world is poured all

[1] Mr. Gladstone.

the fulness of life and of thought which the new world had accumulated. This new world in its maturity of reason resembles our own; and the advantage over Homer in their greater significance for *us*, which Aeschylus and Sophocles gain by belonging to this new world, more than compensates for their poetical inferiority to him.

Let us now pass to the Roman world. There is no necessity to accumulate proofs that the culminating period of Roman history is to be classed among the leading, the significant, the modern periods of the world. There is universally current, I think, a pretty correct appreciation of the high development of the Rome of Cicero and Augustus; no one doubts that material civilization and the refinements of life were largely diffused in it; no one doubts that cultivation of mind and intelligence were widely diffused in it. Therefore, I will not occupy time by showing that Cicero corresponded with his friends in the style of the most accomplished, the most easy letter-writers of modern times; that Caesar did not write history like Sir Walter Ralegh. The great period of Rome is, perhaps, on the whole, the greatest, the fullest, the most significant period on record; it is certainly a greater, a fuller period than the age of Pericles. It is an infinitely larger school for the men reared in it; the relations of life are immeasurably multiplied, the events which happen are on an immeasurably grander scale. The facts, the spectacle of this Roman world, then, are immense: let us see how far the literature, the interpretation of the facts, has been adequate.

Let us begin with a great poet, a great philosopher, Lucretius. In the case of Thucydides I called attention to the fact that his habit of mind, his mode of dealing with questions, were modern; that they were those of an enlightened, reflecting man among ourselves. Let me call attention to the exhibition in Lucretius of a modern *feeling* not less remarkable than the modern *thought* in Thucydides. The predominance of thought, of reflection, in modern epochs is not without its penalties; in the unsound, in the over-tasked, in the over-sensitive, it has produced the most painful, the most lamentable results; it has produced a state of feeling unknown to less enlightened but perhaps healthier epochs—the feeling of depression, the feeling of *ennui*. Depression and *ennui*; these are the characteristics stamped on how many of the representative works of modern times! they are also the characteristics stamped on the poem of Lucretius. One of the most powerful, the most solemn passages of the work of Lucretius, one of the most powerful, the most solemn passages in the literature of the whole world, is the well-known conclusion of the third book. With masterly touches he exhibits the lassitude, the incurable tedium which pursue men in their amusements; with indignant irony he upbraids them for the cowardice with which they cling to a life which for most is miserable; to a life which contains, for the most fortunate, nothing but the old dull round of the same unsatisfying objects for ever presented. "A man rushes abroad," he says, "because he is sick of being at home; and suddenly comes home again because he finds himself no whit easier abroad. He posts as fast as his horses can take him to his country-seat: when he has got there he hesitates what to do; or he throws himself down moodily to sleep, and seeks forgetfulness in that; or he makes the best of his way back to town again with the same speed as he fled from it. Thus every one flies from himself." What a picture of *ennui*! of the disease of the most modern societies, the most advanced civilizations! "O man," he exclaims again, "the lights of the world, Scipio, Homer, Epicurus, are dead; wilt thou hesitate and fret at dying, whose life is wellnigh dead whilst thou art yet alive; who consumest in sleep the greater part of thy span, and when awake dronest and ceasest not to dream; and carriest about a mind troubled with baseless fear, and canst not find what it is that aileth thee when thou staggerest like a drunken wretch in the press of thy cares, and welterest hither and thither in the unsteady wandering of thy spirit!" And again: "I have seen nothing more than you have already seen," he makes Nature say to man, "to invent for your amusement; *eadem sunt omnia semper*—all things continue the same for ever."

Yes, Lucretius is modern; but is he adequate? And how can a man adequately interpret the activity of his age when he is not in sympathy with it? Think of the varied, the abundant, the wide spectacle of the Roman life of his day; think of its fulness of occupation, its energy of effort. From these Lucretius withdraws himself, and bids his disciples to withdraw themselves; he bids them to leave the business of the world, and to apply themselves *"naturam cognoscere rerum*—to learn the nature of things;" but there is no peace, no cheerfulness for him either in the world from which he comes, or in the solitude to which he goes. With stern effort, with gloomy despair, he seems to rivet his eyes on the elementary reality, the naked framework of the world, because the world in its fulness and movement is too exciting a spectacle for his discomposed brain. He seems to feel the spectacle of it at once terrifying and alluring; and to deliver himself from it he has to keep perpetually repeating his formula of disenchantment and annihilation. In reading him, you understand the tradition which represents him as having been driven mad by a poison administered as a love-charm by his mistress, and as having composed his great work in the intervals of his madness. Lucretius is, therefore, overstrained, gloom-weighted, morbid; and he who is morbid is no adequate interpreter of his age.

I pass to Virgil; to the poetical name which of all poetical names has perhaps had the most prodigious fortune; the name which for Dante, for the Middle Age, represented the perfection of classical antiquity. The perfection of classical antiquity Virgil does not represent; but far be it from me to add my voice to those which have decried his genius; nothing that I shall say is, or can ever be, inconsistent with a profound, an almost affectionate veneration for him. But with respect to him, as with respect to Lucretius, I shall freely ask the question, *Is he adequate*? Does he represent the epoch in which he lived, the mighty Roman world of his time, as the great poets of the great epoch of Greek life represented theirs, in all its fulness, in all its significance?

From the very form itself of his great poem, the *Aeneid*, one would be led to augur that this was impossible. The epic form, as a form for representing contemporary or nearly contemporary events, has attained, in the poems of Homer, an unmatched, an immortal success; the epic form as employed by learned poets for the reproduction of the events of a past age has attained a very considerable success. But for *this* purpose, for the poetic treatment of the events of a *past* age, the epic form is a less vital form than the dramatic form. The great poets of the modern period of Greece are accordingly, as we have seen, the *dramatic* poets. The chief of these—Aeschylus, Sophocles, Euripides, Aristophanes—have survived: the distinguished epic poets of the same period—Panyasis, Choerilus, Antimachus—though praised by the Alexandrian critics, have perished in a common destruction with the undistinguished. And what is the reason of this? It is, that the dramatic form exhibits, above all, *the actions of man as strictly determined by his thoughts and feelings*; it exhibits, therefore, what may be always accessible, always intelligible, always interesting. But the epic form takes a wider range; it represents not only the thought and passion of man, that which is universal and eternal, but also the forms of outward life, the fashion of manners, the aspects of nature, that which is local or transient. To exhibit adequately what is local and transient, only a witness, a contemporary, can suffice. In the *reconstruction*, by learning and antiquarian ingenuity, of the local and transient features of a past age, in their representation by one who is not a witness or contemporary, it is impossible to feel the liveliest kind of interest. What, for instance, is the most interesting portion of the *Aeneid*,—the portion where Virgil seems to be moving most freely, and therefore to be most animated, most forcible? Precisely that portion which has most a *dramatic* character; the episode of Dido; that portion where locality and manners are nothing— where persons and characters are everything. We might presume beforehand, therefore, that if Virgil, at a time when contemporary epic poetry was no longer possible, had been inspired to represent human life in its fullest significance, he would not have selected the epic form. Accordingly, what is, in fact, the character of the poem, the frame of mind of the poet? Has the poem depth, the completeness of the poems of Aeschylus or Sophocles, of those adequate and consummate representations of human life? Has the poet the serious cheerfulness of Sophocles, of a man who has mastered the problem of human life, who knows its gravity, and is therefore serious, but who knows that he comprehends it, and is therefore cheerful? Over the whole of the great poem of Virgil, over the whole *Aeneid*, there rests an ineffable melancholy: not a rigid, a moody gloom, like the melancholy of Lucretius; no, a sweet, a touching sadness, but still a sadness; a melancholy which is at once a source of charm in the poem, and a testimony to its incompleteness. Virgil, as Niebuhr has well said, expressed no affected self-disparagement, but the haunting, the irresistible self-dissatisfaction of his heart, when he desired on his deathbed that his poem might be destroyed. A man of the most delicate genius, the most rich learning, but of weak health, of the most sensitive nature, in a great and overwhelming world; conscious, at heart, of his inadequacy for the thorough spiritual mastery of that world and its interpretation in a work of art; conscious of this inadequacy—the one inadequacy, the one weak place in the mighty Roman nature! This suffering, this graceful-minded, this finely-gifted man is the most beautiful, the most attractive figure in literary history; but he is not the adequate interpreter of the great period of Rome.

We come to Horace: and if Lucretius, if Virgil want cheerfulness, Horace wants seriousness. I go back to what I said of Menander: as with Menander so it is with Horace: the men of taste, the men of cultivation, the men of the world are enchanted with him; he has not a prejudice, not an illusion, not a blunder. True! yet the best men in the best ages have never been thoroughly satisfied with Horace. If human life were complete without faith, without enthusiasm, without energy, Horace, like Menander, would be the perfect interpreter of human life:

but it is not; to the best, to the most living sense of humanity, it is not; and because it is not, Horace is inadequate. Pedants are tiresome, men of reflection and enthusiasm are unhappy and morbid; therefore Horace is a sceptical man of the world. Men of action are without ideas, men of the world are frivolous and sceptical; therefore Lucretius is plunged in gloom and in stern sorrow. So hard, nay, so impossible for most men is it to develop themselves in their entireness; to rejoice in the variety, the movement of human life with the children of the world; to be serious over the depth, the significance of human life with the wise! Horace warms himself before the transient fire of human animation and human pleasure while he can, and is only serious when he reflects that the fire must soon go out:—

> "Damna tamen celeres reparant coelestia lunae:
>   Nos, ubi decidimus——"

"For nature there is renovation, but for man there is none!"—it is exquisite, but it is not interpretative and fortifying.

In the Roman world, then, we have found a highly modern, a deeply significant, an interesting period—a period more significant and more interesting, because fuller, than the great period of Greece; but we have not a commensurate literature. In Greece we have seen a highly modern, a most significant and interesting period, although on a scale of less magnitude and importance than the great period of Rome; but then, co-existing with the great epoch of Greece there is what is wanting to that of Rome, a commensurate, an interesting literature.

The intellectual history of our race cannot be clearly understood without applying to other ages, nations, and literatures the same method of inquiry which we have been here imperfectly applying to what is called classical antiquity. But enough has at least been said, perhaps, to establish the absolute, the enduring interest of Greek literature, and, above all, of Greek poetry.

ON TRANSLATING HOMER
1861

On Translating Homer. Three Lectures given at Oxford by Matthew Arnold, M.A., Professor of Poetry in the University of Oxford, and formerly Fellow of Oriel College. London. Longman, Green, Longman, and Roberts. 1861.

ARNOLD's inaugural lecture as Professor of Poetry was delivered in the autumn term of 1857. The subjects of his lectures for the following three years are uncertain but in the autumn of 1860 he gave two lectures on Homer and another in January 1861; he was cheered by his audience at the end of the third lecture. The three were printed with the title *On Translating Homer* early in 1861. For Arnold's reply to criticism of the tone of these lectures see a letter to his sister Mrs. Forster, February 1861 (p. 753).

ON TRANSLATING HOMER

.... Nunquamne reponam?

From *Lecture I*

I. *Advice to the Translator*

IT has more than once been suggested to me that I should translate Homer. That is a task for which I have neither the time nor the courage; but the suggestion led me to regard yet more closely a poet whom I had already long studied, and for one or two years the works of Homer were seldom out of my hands. The study of classical literature is probably on the decline; but, whatever may be the fate of this study in general, it is certain that, as instruction spreads and the number of readers increases, attention will be more and more directed to the poetry of Homer, not indeed as a part of a classical course, but as the most important poetical monument existing. Even within the last ten years two fresh translations of the *Iliad* have appeared in England: one by a man of great ability and genuine learning, Professor Newman;[1] the other by Mr. Wright,[2] the conscientious and painstaking translator of Dante. It may safely be asserted that neither of these works will take rank as the standard translation of Homer; that the task of rendering him will still be attempted by other translators. It may perhaps be possible to render to these some service, to save them some loss of labour, by pointing out rocks on which their predecessors have split, and the right objects on which a translator of Homer should fix his attention.

It is disputed what aim a translator should propose to him-

---

[1] [Francis William Newman was a younger brother of John Henry Newman. Fellow of Balliol 1826–30, Professor of Latin, University College London 1846–69. Controversialist on subjects ranging from unitarianism to vivisection. The Cardinal said of his brother: "Much as we love each other, neither would like to be mistaken for the other."]

[2] [Ichabod Charles Wright (1795–1871), Fellow of Magdalen College, Oxford, which he left in 1825 to join his family banking business at Nottingham. Published verse translations of Dante and of Homer's *Iliad*. Wright replied in print to Arnold's remarks, thus provoking both the additional references to himself and the famous defence of Oxford in the Preface to *Essays in Criticism*.]

287

self in dealing with his original. Even this preliminary is not
yet settled. On one side it is said that the translation ought to be
such "that the reader should, if possible, forget that it is a translation at all, and be lulled into the illusion that he is reading an
original work,—something original" (if the translation be in
English), "from an English hand." The real original is in this
case, it is said, "taken as a basis on which to rear a poem that
shall affect our countrymen as the original may be conceived
to have affected its natural hearers." On the other hand, Mr.
Newman, who states the foregoing doctrine only to condemn it,
declares that he "aims at precisely the opposite: to retain every
peculiarity of the original, so far as he is able, *with the greater
care the more foreign it may happen to be*;" so that it may "never
be forgotten that he is imitating, and imitating in a different
material." The translator's "first duty," says Mr. Newman, "is a
historical one—to be *faithful*." Probably both sides would agree
that the translator's "first duty is to be faithful"; but the question
at issue between them is, in what faithfulness consists.

My one object is to give practical advice to a translator; and
I shall not in the least concern myself with theories of translation
as such. But I advise the translator not to try "to rear on the
basis of the *Iliad*, a poem that shall affect our countrymen as
the original may be conceived to have affected its natural
hearers"; and for this simple reason, that we cannot possibly
tell *how* the *Iliad* "affected its natural hearers." It is probably
meant merely that he should try to affect Englishmen powerfully, as Homer affected Greeks powerfully; but this direction
is not enough, and can give no real guidance. For all great poets
affect their hearers powerfully, but the effect of one poet is one
thing, that of another poet another thing: it is our translator's
business to reproduce the effect of Homer, and the most
powerful emotion of the unlearned English reader can never
assure him whether he has *re*produced this, or whether he has
produced something else. So, again, he may follow Mr. Newman's directions, he may try to be "faithful," he may "retain every
peculiarity of his original"; but who is to assure him, who is to
assure Mr. Newman himself, that, when he has done this, he has
done that for which Mr. Newman enjoins this to be done,
"adhered closely to Homer's manner and habit of thought"?
Evidently the translator needs some more practical directions
than these. No one can tell him how Homer affected the Greeks;
but there are those who can tell him how Homer affects *them*.
These are scholars; who possess, at the same time with knowledge of Greek, adequate poetical taste and feeling. No translation will seem to them of much worth compared with the

original; but they alone can say whether the translation produces more or less the same effect upon them as the original. They are the only competent tribunal in this matter: the Greeks are dead; the unlearned Englishman has not the data for judging; and no man can safely confide in his own single judgment of his own work. Let not the translator, then, trust to his notions of what the ancient Greeks would have thought of him; he will lose himself in the vague. Let him not trust to what the ordinary English reader thinks of him; he will be taking the blind for his guide. Let him not trust to his own judgment of his own work; he may be misled by individual caprices. Let him ask how his work affects those who both know Greek and can appreciate poetry; whether to read it gives the Provost of Eton, or Professor Thompson at Cambridge, or Professor Jowett here in Oxford, at all the same feeling which to read the original gives them. I consider that when Bentley said of Pope's translation, "It was a pretty poem, but must not be called Homer," the work, in spite of all its power and attractiveness, was judged.

' Ὡς ἂν ὁ φρόνιμος ὁρίσειεν,—"as the judicious would determine,"—that is a test to which every one professes himself willing to submit his works. Unhappily, in most cases, no two persons agree as to who "the judicious" are. In the present case the ambiguity is removed: I suppose the translator at one with me as to the tribunal to which alone he should look for judgment; and he has thus obtained a practical test by which to estimate the real success of his work. How is he to proceed, in order that his work, tried by this test, may be found most successful?

First of all, there are certain negative counsels which I will give him. Homer has occupied men's minds so much, such a literature has arisen about him, that every one who approaches him should resolve strictly to limit himself to that which may directly serve the object for which he approaches him. I advise the translator to have nothing to do with the questions, whether Homer ever existed; whether the poet of the *Iliad* be one or many; whether the *Iliad* be one poem or an *Achilleis* and an *Iliad* stuck together; whether the Christian doctrine of the Atonement is shadowed forth in the Homeric mythology; whether the Goddess Latona in any way prefigures the Virgin Mary, and so on. These are questions which have been discussed with learning, with ingenuity, nay, with genius; but they have two inconveniences,—one general for all who approach them, one particular for the translator. The general inconvenience is that there really exist no data for determining them. The particular inconvenience is that their solution by the

K

translator, even were it possible, could be of no benefit to his translation.

I advise him, again, not to trouble himself with constructing a special vocabulary for his use in translation; with excluding a certain class of English words, and with confining himself to another class, in obedience to any theory about the peculiar qualities of Homer's style. Mr. Newman says that "the entire dialect of Homer being essentially archaic, that of a translator ought to be as much Saxo-Norman as possible, and owe as little as possible to the elements thrown into our language by classical learning." Mr. Newman is unfortunate in the observance of his own theory; for I continually find in his translation words of Latin origin, which seem to me quite alien to the simplicity of Homer,—"responsive," for instance, which is a favourite word of Mr. Newman, to represent the Homeric ἀμειβόμενος :

> Great Hector of the motley helm thus spake to her *responsive*.
> But thus *responsively* to him spake god-like Alexander.

And the word "celestial," again, in the grand address of Zeus to the horses of Achilles,

> You, who are born *celestial*, from Eld and Death exempted!

seems to me in that place exactly to jar upon the feeling as too bookish. But, apart from the question of Mr. Newman's fidelity to his own theory, such a theory seems to me both dangerous for a translator and false in itself. Dangerous for a translator; because, wherever one finds such a theory announced (and one finds it pretty often), it is generally followed by an explosion of pedantry; and pedantry is of all things in the world the most un-Homeric. False in itself; because, in fact, we owe to the Latin element in our language most of that very rapidity and clear decisiveness by which it is contradistinguished from the German, and in sympathy with the languages of Greece and Rome: so that to limit an English translator of Homer to words of Saxon origin is to deprive him of one of his special advantages for translating Homer. In Voss's well-known translation of Homer, it is precisely the qualities of his German language itself, something heavy and trailing both in the structure of its sentences and in the words of which it is composed, which prevent his translation, in spite of the hexameters, in spite of the fidelity, from creating in us the impression created by the Greek. Mr. Newman's prescription, if followed, would just strip the English translator of the advantage which he has over Voss.

The frame of mind in which we approach an author influences

our correctness of appreciation of him; and Homer should be approached by a translator in the simplest frame of mind possible. Modern sentiment tries to make the ancient not less than the modern world its own; but against modern sentiment in its applications to Homer the translator, if he would feel Homer truly—and unless he feels him truly, how can he render him truly?—cannot be too much on his guard. For example: the writer of an interesting article on English translations of Homer, in the last number of the *National Review*, quotes, I see, with admiration, a criticism of Mr. Ruskin on the use of the epithet φυσίζοος, "life-giving," in that beautiful passage in the third book of the *Iliad*, which follows Helen's mention of her brothers Castor and Pollux as alive, though they were in truth dead:

> ὣς φάτο · τοὺς δ᾽ ἤδη κατέχεν φυσίζοος αἶα
> ἐν Λακεδαίμονι αὖθι, φίλῃ ἐν πατρίδι γαίῃ.[1]

"The poet," says Mr. Ruskin, "has to speak of the earth in sadness; but he will not let that sadness affect or change his thought of it. No; though Castor and Pollux be dead, yet the earth is our mother still,—fruitful, life-giving." This is a just specimen of that sort of application of modern sentiment to the ancients, against which a student, who wishes to feel the ancients truly, cannot too resolutely defend himself. It reminds one, as, alas! so much of Mr. Ruskin's writing reminds one, of those words of the most delicate of living critics: "Comme tout genre de composition a son écueil particulier, *celui du genre romanesque, c'est le faux*." The reader may feel moved as he reads it; but it is not the less an example of "le faux" in criticism; it is false. It is not true, as to that particular passage, that Homer called the earth φυσίζοος because, "though he had to speak of the earth in sadness, he would not let that sadness change or affect his thought of it," but consoled himself by considering that "the earth is our mother still,—fruitful, life-giving." It is not true, as a matter of general criticism, that this kind of sentimentality, eminently modern, inspires Homer at all. "From Homer and Polygnotus I every day learn more clearly," says Goethe, "that in our life here above ground we have, properly speaking, to enact Hell:" [2]—if the student must absolutely have a keynote to the *Iliad*, let him take this of Goethe, and see what he can do with it; it will not, at any rate, like the tender pantheism of Mr. Ruskin, falsify for him the whole strain of Homer.

These are negative counsels; I come to the positive. When I

---

[1] *Iliad*, iii. 243.
[2] *Briefwechsel zwischen Schiller und Goethe*, vi. 230.

say, the translator of Homer should above all be penetrated by a sense of four qualities of his author;—that he is eminently rapid; that he is eminently plain and direct, both in the evolution of his thought and in the expression of it, that is, both in his syntax and in his words; that he is eminently plain and direct in the substance of his thought, that is, in his matter and ideas; and, finally, that he is eminently noble;—I probably seem to be saying what is too general to be of much service to anybody. Yet it is strictly true that, for want of duly penetrating themselves with the first-named quality of Homer, his rapidity, Cowper and Mr. Wright have failed in rendering him; that, for want of duly appreciating the second-named quality, his plainness and directness of style and dictation, Pope and Mr. Sotheby have failed in rendering him; that for want of appreciating the third, his plainness and directness of ideas, Chapman has failed in rendering him; while for want of appreciating the fourth, his nobleness, Mr. Newman, who has clearly seen some of the faults of his predecessors, has yet failed more conspicuously than any of them.

Coleridge says, in his strange language, speaking of the union of the human soul with the divine essence, that this takes place

> Whene'er the mist, which stands 'twixt God and thee,
> Defecates to a pure transparency;

and so, too, it may be said of that union of the translator with his original, which alone can produce a good translation, that it takes place when the mist which stands between them—the mist of alien modes of thinking, speaking, and feeling on the translator's part—"defecates to a pure transparency," and disappears. But between Cowper and Homer—(Mr. Wright repeats in the main Cowper's manner, as Mr. Sotheby repeats Pope's manner, and neither Mr. Wright's translation nor Mr. Sotheby's has, I must be forgiven for saying, any proper reason for existing)—between Cowper and Homer there is interposed the mist of Cowper's elaborate Miltonic manner, entirely alien to the flowing rapidity of Homer; between Pope and Homer there is interposed the mist of Pope's literary artificial manner, entirely alien to the plain naturalness of Homer's manner; between Chapman and Homer there is interposed the mist of the fancifulness of the Elizabethan age, entirely alien to the plain directness of Homer's thought and feeling; while between Mr. Newman and Homer is interposed a cloud of more than Egyptian thickness—namely, a manner, in Mr. Newman's version, eminently ignoble, while Homer's manner is eminently noble.

II. *Lord Granville*

Robert Wood, whose *Essay on the Genius of Homer* is mentioned by Goethe as one of the books which fell into his hands when his powers were first developing themselves, and strongly interested him, relates of this passage [1] a striking story. He says that in 1762, at the end of the Seven Years' War, being then Under-Secretary of State, he was directed to wait upon the President of the Council, Lord Granville, a few days before he died, with the preliminary articles of the Treaty of Paris. "I found him," he continues, "so languid, that I proposed postponing my business for another time; but he insisted that I should stay, saying, it could not prolong his life to neglect his duty; and repeating the following passage out of Sarpedon's speech, he dwelt with particular emphasis on the third line, which recalled to his mind the distinguishing part he had taken in public affairs:—

> ὦ πέπον, εἰ μὲν γὰρ, πόλεμον περὶ τόνδε φυγόντε,
> αἰεὶ δὴ μέλλοιμεν ἀγήρω τ' ἀθανάτω τε
> ἔσσεσθ', οὔτε κεν αὐτὸς ἐνὶ πρώτοισι μαχοίμην, [2]
> οὔτε κέ σε στέλλοιμι μάχην ἐς κυδιάνειραν·
> νῦν δ'—ἔμπης γὰρ Κῆρες ἐφεστᾶσιν θανάτοιο
> μυρίαι, ἃς οὐκ ἔστι φυγεῖν βρότον, οὐδ' ὑπαλύξαι—
> ἴομεν.

His Lordship repeated the last word several times with a calm and determinate resignation; and, after a serious pause of some minutes, he desired to hear the Treaty read, to which he listened with great attention, and recovered spirits enough to declare the approbation of a dying statesman (I use his own words) 'on the most glorious war, and most honourable peace, this nation ever saw.' " [3]

I quote this story, first, because it is interesting as exhibiting the English aristocracy at its very height of culture, lofty spirit, and greatness, towards the middle of the last century. I quote it, secondly, because it seems to me to illustrate Goethe's saying which I mentioned, that our life, in Homer's view of it, represents a conflict and a hell; and it brings out, too, what there is tonic and fortifying in this doctrine. I quote it, lastly, because it shows that the passage is just one of those in translating which

---

[1] [Sarpedon's speech to Glaucus: *Iliad*, xii, 322.]
[2] These are the words on which Lord Granville "dwelt with particular emphasis."
[3] Robert Wood, *Essay on the Original Genius and Writings of Homer*, London, 1775, p. vii.

Pope will be at his best, a passage of strong emotion and oratorical movement, not of simple narrative or description.

Pope translates the passage thus:—

> Could all our care elude the gloomy grave
> Which claims no less the fearful than the brave,
> For lust of fame I should not vainly dare
> In fighting fields, nor urge thy soul to war:
> But since, alas! ignoble age must come,
> Disease, and death's inexorable doom;
> The life which others pay, let us bestow,
> And give to fame what we to nature owe.

Nothing could better exhibit Pope's prodigious talent; and nothing, too, could be better in its own way. But, as Bentley said, "You must not call it Homer." One feels that Homer's thought has passed through a literary and rhetorical crucible, and come out highly intellectualised; come out in a form which strongly impresses us, indeed, but which no longer impresses us in the same way as when it was uttered by Homer. The antithesis of the last two lines—

> The life which others pay, let us bestow,
> And give to fame what we to nature owe—

is excellent, and is just suited to Pope's heroic couplet; but neither the antithesis itself, nor the couplet which conveys it, is suited to the feeling or to the movement of the Homeric ἴομεν.

A literary and intellectualised language is, however, in its own way well suited to grand matters; and Pope, with a language of this kind and his own admirable talent, comes off well enough as long as he has passion, or oratory, or a great crisis to deal with. Even here, as I have been pointing out, he does not render Homer; but he and his style are in themselves strong. It is when he comes to level passages—passages of narrative or description—that he and his style are sorely tried, and prove themselves weak. A perfectly plain direct style can, of course, convey the simplest matter as naturally as the grandest; indeed, it must be harder for it, one would say, to convey a grand matter worthily and nobly, than to convey a common matter, as alone such a matter should be conveyed, plainly and simply. But the style of Rasselas is incomparably better fitted to describe a sage philosophising than a soldier lighting his camp-fire. The style of Pope is not the style of Rasselas; but it is equally a literary style, equally unfitted to describe a simple matter with the plain naturalness of Homer.

III. *Plainness and Directness*

I said that there were four things which eminently distinguished Homer, and with a sense of which Homer's translator should penetrate himself as fully as possible. One of these four things was, the plainness and directness of Homer's ideas. I have just been speaking of the plainness and directness of his style; but the plainness and directness of the contents of his style, of his ideas themselves, is not less remarkable. But as eminently as Homer is plain, so eminently is the Elizabethan literature in general, and Chapman in particular, fanciful. Steeped in humours and fantasticality up to its very lips, the Elizabethan age, newly arrived at the free use of the human faculties after their long term of bondage, and delighting to exercise them freely, suffers from its own extravagance in this first exercise of them, can hardly bring itself to see an object quietly or to describe it temperately. Happily, in the translation of the Bible, the sacred character of their original inspired the translators with such respect that they did not dare to give the rein to their own fancies in dealing with it. But, in dealing with works of profane literature, in dealing with poetical works above all, which highly stimulated them, one may say that the minds of the Elizabethan translators were *too* active; that they could not forbear importing so much of their own, and this of a most peculiar and Elizabethan character, into their original, that they effaced the character of the original itself.

IV. *Nobility*

And yet, in spite of this perfect plainness and directness of Homer's style, in spite of this perfect plainness and directness of his ideas, he is eminently *noble*; he works as entirely in the grand style, he is as grandiose, as Phidias, or Dante, or Michael Angelo. This is what makes his translators despair. "To give relief," says Cowper, "to prosaic subjects" (such as dressing, eating, drinking, harnessing, travelling, going to bed), that is to treat such subjects nobly, in the grand style, "without seeming unreasonably tumid, is extremely difficult." It *is* difficult, but Homer has done it. Homer is precisely the incomparable poet he is, because he has done it. His translator must not be tumid, must not be artificial, must not be literary,—true: but then also he must not be commonplace, must not be ignoble. I have shown you how translators of Homer fail by wanting rapidity, by wanting simplicity of style, by wanting plainness of thought: in a second lecture I will show you how a translator fails by wanting nobility.

From *Lecture II*

I. *The Homeric Qualities*

Well, then, Homer is neither quaint, nor garrulous, nor prosaic, nor mean: and Mr. Newman, in seeing him so, sees him differently from those who are to judge Mr. Newman's rendering of him. By pointing out how a wrong conception of Homer affects Mr. Newman's translation, I hope to place in still clearer light those four cardinal truths which I pronounce essential for him who would have a right conception of Homer: that Homer is rapid, that he is plain and direct in word and style, that he is plain and direct in his ideas, and that he is noble.

II. *The Grand Style*

For Homer is not only rapid in movement, simple in style, plain in language, natural in thought; he is also, and above all, *noble*. I have advised the translator not to go into the vexed question of Homer's identity. Yet I will just remind him that the grand argument—or rather, not argument, for the matter affords no data for arguing, but the grand source from which conviction, as we read the *Iliad*, keeps pressing in upon us, that there is one poet of the *Iliad*, one Homer—is precisely this nobleness of the poet, this grand manner: we feel that the analogy drawn from other joint compositions does not hold good here, because those works do not bear, like the *Iliad*, the magic stamp of a master; and the moment you have *anything* less than a masterwork, the co-operation or consolidation of several poets becomes possible, for talent is not uncommon; the moment you have *much* less than a masterwork, they become easy, for mediocrity is everywhere. I can imagine fifty Bradies joined with as many Tates to make the New Version of the Psalms. I can imagine several poets having contributed to any one of the old English ballads in Percy's collection. I can imagine several poets, possessing, like Chapman, the Elizabethan vigour and the Elizabethan mannerism, united with Chapman to produce his version of the *Iliad*. I can imagine several poets, with the literary knack of the twelfth century, united to produce the *Nibelungen Lay* in the form in which we have it,—a work which the Germans, in their joy at discovering a national epic of their own, have rated vastly higher than it deserves. And lastly, though Mr. Newman's translation of Homer bears the strong mark of his own idiosyncrasy, yet I can imagine Mr. Newman and a school of adepts trained by him in his art of poetry,

jointly producing that work, so that Aristarchus himself should
have difficulty in pronouncing which line was the master's, and
which a pupil's. But I cannot imagine several poets, or one poet,
joined with Dante in the composition of his *Inferno*, though
many poets have taken for their subject a descent into Hell.
Many artists, again, have represented Moses; but there is only
one Moses of Michael Angelo. So the insurmountable obstacle
to believing the *Iliad* a consolidated work of several poets is
this: that the work of great masters is unique; and the *Iliad* has
a great master's genuine stamp, and that stamp is *the grand style*.

Poets who cannot work in the grand style instinctively seek a
style in which their comparative inferiority may feel itself at
ease, a manner which may be, so to speak, indulgent to their
inequalities. The ballad-style offers to an epic poet, quite
unable to fill the canvas of Homer, or Dante, or Milton, a
canvas which he is capable of filling. The ballad-measure is
quite able to give due effect to the vigour and spirit which its
employer, when at his very best, may be able to exhibit; and,
when he is not at his best, when he is a little trivial or a little
dull, it will not betray him, it will not bring out his weaknesses
into broad relief. This is a convenience; but it is a convenience
which the ballad-style purchases by resigning all pretensions
to the highest, to the grand manner. It is true of its movement,
as it is *not* true of Homer's, that it is "liable to degenerate into
doggerel." It is true of its "moral qualities," as it is *not* true of
Homer's, that "quaintness" and "garrulity" are among them.
It is true of its employers, as it is *not* true of Homer, that they
"rise and sink with their subject, are prosaic when it is tame, are
low when it is mean." For this reason the ballad-style and the
ballad-measure are eminently *in*appropriate to render Homer.
Homer's manner and movement are always both noble and
powerful: the ballad-manner and movement are often either
jaunty and smart, so not noble; or jog-trot and humdrum, so not
powerful.

III. *Ballad Poetry and the Grand Style*

But so deeply seated is the difference between the ballad-
manner and Homer's, that even a man of the highest powers,
even a man of the greatest vigour of spirit and of true genius—
the Coryphæus of balladists, Sir Walter Scott—fails with a
manner of this kind to produce an effect at all like the effect of
Homer. "I am not so rash," declares Mr. Newman, "as to say
that if *freedom* be given to rhyme as in Walter Scott's poetry"—
Walter Scott, "by far the most Homeric of our poets," as in

another place he calls him—"a genius may not arise who will
translate Homer into the melodies of *Marmion*." "The *truly*
classical and *truly* romantic," says Dr. Maginn,[1] "are one; the
moss-trooping Nestor reappears in the moss-trooping heroes of
Percy's *Reliques*"; and a description by Scott, which he quotes, he
calls "graphic, and therefore Homeric." He forgets our fourth
axiom—that Homer is not *only* graphic; he is also noble, and
has the grand style. Human nature under like circumstances is
probably in all stages much the same; and so far it may be said
that "the truly classical and the truly romantic are one"; but
it is of little use to tell us this, because we know the human
nature of other ages only through the representations of them
which have come down to us, and the classical and the romantic
modes of representation are so far from being "one," that they
remain eternally distinct, and have created for us a separation
between the two worlds which they respectively represent.
Therefore to call Nestor the "moss-trooping Nestor" is absurd,
because, though Nestor may possibly have been much the same
sort of man as many a moss-trooper, he has yet come to us
through a mode of representation so unlike that of Percy's
Reliques, that instead of "reappearing in the moss-trooping
heroes" of these poems, he exists in our imagination as something utterly unlike them, and as belonging to another world.
So the Greeks in Shakspeare's *Troilus and Cressida* are no
longer the Greeks whom we have known in Homer, because
they come to us through a mode of representation of the
romantic world. But I must not forget Scott.

I suppose that when Scott is in what may be called full ballad
swing, no one will hesitate to pronounce his manner neither
Homeric nor the grand manner. When he says, for instance,

> I do not rhyme to that dull elf
> Who cannot image to himself,[2]

and so on, any scholar will feel that *this* is not Homer's manner.
But let us take Scott's poetry at its best; and when it is at its
best, it is undoubtedly very good indeed:

> Tunstall lies dead upon the field,
> His life-blood stains the spotless shield:
> Edmund is down,—my life is reft,—
> The Admiral alone is left.

---

[1] [William Maginn (1793–1842). Contributor to *Blackwood's*
and founder of *Fraser's Magazine*, in which he published his
"Homeric Ballads" 1838. The original of Thackeray's Captain
Shandon.]

[2] *Marmion*, canto vi. 38.

> Let Stanley charge with spur of fire,—
> With Chester charge, and Lancashire,
> Full upon Scotland's central host,
> Or victory and England's lost.[1]

That is, no doubt, as vigorous as possible, as spirited as possible; it is exceedingly fine poetry. And still I say, it is not in the grand manner, and therefore it is not like Homer's poetry. Now, how shall I make him who doubts this feel that I say true; that these lines of Scott are essentially neither in Homer's style nor in the grand style? I may point out to him that the movement of Scott's lines, while it is rapid, is also at the same time what the French call *saccadé*, its rapidity is "jerky"; whereas Homer's rapidity is a flowing rapidity. But this is something external and material; it is but the outward and visible sign of an inward and spiritual diversity. I may discuss what, in the abstract, constitutes the grand style; but that sort of general discussion never much helps our judgment of particular instances. I may say that the presence or absence of the grand style can only be spiritually discerned; and this is true, but to plead this looks like evading the difficulty. My best way is to take eminent specimens of the grand style, and to put them side by side with this of Scott. For example, when Homer says:

> ἀλλά, φίλος, θάνε καὶ σύ· τίη ὀλυφύρεαι οὕτως;
> κάτθανε καὶ Πάτροκλος, ὅπερ σέο πολλὸν ἀμείνων,[2]

that is in the grand style. When Virgil says:

> Disce, puer, virtutem ex me verumque laborem,
> Fortunam ex aliis,[3]

that is in the grand style. When Dante says:

> Lascio lo fele, et vo pei dolci pomi
> Promessi a me per lo verace Duca;
> Ma fino al centro pria convien ch' io tomi,[4]

that is in the grand style. When Milton says:

> His form had yet not lost
> All her original brightness, nor appeared
> Less than archangel ruined, and the excess
> Of glory obscured,

---

[1] *Marmion*, canto vi. 29.

[2] " Be content, good friend, die also thou! why lamentest thou thyself on this wise? Patroclus, too, died, who was a far better than thou."—*Iliad*, xxi. 106.

[3] " From me, young man, learn nobleness of soul and true effort: learn success from others."—*Æneid*, xii. 435.

[4] " I leave the gall of bitterness, and I go for the apples of sweetness promised unto me by my faithful Guide; but far as the centre it behoves me first to fall."—*Hell*, xvi. 61.

that, finally, is in the grand style. Now let any one after repeating to himself these four passages, repeat again the passage of Scott, and he will perceive that there is something in style which the four first have in common, and which the last is without; and this something is precisely the grand manner. It is no disrespect to Scott to say that he does not attain to this manner in his poetry; to say so, is merely to say that he is not among the five or six supreme poets of the world. Among these he is not; but, being a man of far greater powers than the ballad poets, he has tried to give to their instrument a compass and an elevation which it does not naturally possess, in order to enable him to come nearer to the effect of the instrument used by the great epic poets—an instrument which he felt he could not truly use— and in this attempt he has but imperfectly succeeded. The poetic style of Scott is—(it becomes necessary to say so when it is proposed to "translate Homer into the melodies of *Marmion*")— it is, tried by the highest standard, a bastard epic style; and that is why, out of his own powerful hands, it has had so little success. It is a less natural, and therefore a less good style, than the original ballad-style; while it shares with the ballad-style the inherent incapacity of rising into the grand style, of adequately rendering Homer. Scott is certainly at his best in his battles. Of Homer you could not say this: he is not better in his battles than elsewhere; but even between the battle-pieces of the two there exists all the difference which there is between an able work and a masterpiece.

> Tunstall lies dead upon the field,
> His life-blood stains the spotless shield:
> Edmund is down,—my life is reft,—
> The Admiral alone is left.

—"For not in the hands of Diomede the son of Tydeus rages the spear, to ward off destruction from the Danaans; neither as yet have I heard the voice of the son of Atreus, shouting out of his hated mouth; but the voice of Hector the slayer of men bursts round me, as he cheers on the Trojans; and they with their yellings fill all the plain, overcoming the Achaians in the battle."—I protest that, to my feeling, Homer's performance, even through that pale and far-off shadow of a prose translation, still has a hundred times more of the grand manner about it than the original poetry of Scott.

Well, then, the ballad-manner and the ballad-measure, whether in the hands of the old ballad poets, or arranged by Chapman, or arranged by Mr. Newman, or, even, arranged by Sir Walter Scott, cannot worthily render Homer. And for one reason: Homer is plain, so are they; Homer is natural, so are they; Homer is spirited, so are they; but Homer is sustainedly noble, and they are not. Homer and they are both of them natural, and therefore touching and stirring; but the grand style, which is Homer's, is something more than touching and stirring; it can form the character, it is edifying. The old English balladist may stir Sir Philip Sidney's heart like a trumpet, and this is much; but Homer, but the few artists in the grand style, can do more: they can refine the raw natural man, they can transmute him. So it is not without cause that I say, and say again, to the translator of Homer: "Never for a moment suffer yourself to forget our fourth fundamental proposition, *Homer is noble*." For it is seen how large a share this nobleness has in producing that general effect of his, which it is the main business of a translator to *re*produce.

From *Lecture III*

I. *Metrical Vehicles*

Homer is rapid in his movement, Homer is plain in his words and style, Homer is simple in his ideas, Homer is noble in his manner. Cowper renders him ill because he is slow in his movement, and elaborate in his style; Pope renders him ill because he is artificial both in his style and in his words; Chapman renders him ill because he is fantastic in his ideas; Mr. Newman renders him ill because he is odd in his words and ignoble in his manner. All four translators diverge from their original at other points besides those named; but it is at the points thus named that their divergence is greatest. For instance Cowper's diction is not as Homer's diction, nor his nobleness as Homer's nobleness; but it is in movement and grammatical style that he is most unlike Homer. Pope's rapidity is not of the same sort as Homer's rapidity, nor are his plainness of ideas and his nobleness as Homer's plainness of ideas and nobleness; but it is in the artificial character of his style and diction that he is most unlike Homer. Chapman's movement, words, style, and manner are often far enough from resembling Homer's movement, words, style, and manner; but it is the fantasticality of his ideas which puts him farthest from resembling Homer. Mr. Newman's movement, grammatical style, and ideas are a thousand times in strong contrast with Homer's; still it is by the oddness of his diction and the ignobleness of his manner that he contrasts with Homer the most violently.

Therefore the translator must not say to himself: "Cowper is

noble, Pope is rapid, Chapman has a good diction, Mr. Newman
has a good cast of sentence: I will avoid Cowper's slowness,
Pope's artificiality, Chapman's conceits, Mr. Newman's oddity;
I will take Cowper's dignified manner, Pope's impetuous
movement, Chapman's vocabulary, Mr. Newman's syntax, and
so make a perfect translation of Homer." Undoubtedly in
certain points the versions of Chapman, Cowper, Pope, and Mr.
Newman, all of them have merit; some of them very high
merit, others a lower merit; but even in these points they have
none of them precisely the same kind of merit as Homer, and
therefore the new translator, even if he can imitate them in
their good points, will still not satisfy his judge, the scholar, who
asks him for Homer and Homer's kind of merit, or, at least, for
as much of them as it is possible to give.

So the translator really has no good model before him for
any part of his work, and has to invent everything for himself.
He is to be rapid in movement, plain in speech, simple in
thought, and noble; and *how* he is to be either rapid, or plain, or
simple, or noble, no one yet has shown him. I shall try to-day
to establish some practical suggestions which may help the
translator of Homer's poetry to comply with the four grand
requirements which we make of him.

His version is to be rapid; and, of course, to make a man's
poetry rapid, as to make it noble, nothing can serve him so much
as to have, in his own nature, rapidity and nobleness. *It is the
spirit that quickeneth*; and no one will so well render Homer's
swift-flowing movement as he who has himself something of the
swift-moving spirit of Homer. Yet even this is not quite enough.
Pope certainly had a quick and darting spirit, and he had, also,
real nobleness; yet Pope does not render the movement of
Homer. To render this the translator must have, besides his
natural qualifications, an appropriate metre.

I have sufficiently shown why I think all forms of our ballad-
metre unsuited to Homer. It seems to me to be beyond question
that, for epic poetry, only three metres can seriously claim to be
accounted capable of the grand style. Two of these will at once
occur to every one,—the ten-syllable, or so-called *heroic*,
couplet, and blank verse. I do not add to these the Spenserian
stanza, although Dr. Maginn, whose metrical eccentricities I
have already criticised, pronounces this stanza the one right
measure for a translation of Homer. It is enough to observe that
if Pope's couplet, with the simple system of correspondence that
its rhymes introduce, changes the movement of Homer, in
which no such correspondences are found, and is therefore a bad
measure for a translator of Homer to employ, Spenser's stanza,

with its far more intricate system of correspondences, must change Homer's movement far more profoundly, and must therefore be for the translator a far worse measure than the couplet of Pope. Yet I will say, at the same time, that the verse of Spenser is more fluid, slips more easily and quickly along, than the verse of almost any other English poet.

> By this the northern wagoner had set
> His seven-fold team behind the steadfast star
> That was in ocean waves yet never wet,
> But firm is fixt, and sendeth light from far
> To all that in the wide deep wandering are.[1]

One cannot but feel that English verse has not often moved with the fluidity and sweet ease of these lines. It is possible that it may have been this quality of Spenser's poetry which made Dr. Maginn think that the stanza of *The Faery Queen* must be a good measure for rendering Homer. This it is not: Spenser's verse is fluid and rapid, no doubt, but there are more ways than one of being fluid and rapid, and Homer is fluid and rapid in quite another way than Spenser. Spenser's manner is no more Homeric than is the manner of the one modern inheritor of Spenser's beautiful gift,—the poet, who evidently caught from Spenser his sweet and easy-slipping movement, and who has exquisitely employed it; a Spenserian genius, nay, a genius by natural endowment richer probably than even Spenser; that light which shines so unexpected and without fellow in our century, an Elizabethan born too late, the early lost and admirably gifted Keats.

I say, then, that there are really but three metres,—the ten-syllable couplet, blank verse, and a third metre which I will not yet name, but which is neither the Spenserian stanza nor any form of ballad-verse,—between which, as vehicles for Homer's poetry, the translator has to make his choice. Every one will at once remember a thousand passages in which both the ten-syllable couplet and blank verse prove themselves to have nobleness. Undoubtedly the movement and manner of this,—

> Still raise for good the supplicating voice,
> But leave to Heaven the measure and the choice,—

are noble. Undoubtedly, the movement and manner of this,—

> High on a throne of royal state, which far
> Outshone the wealth of Ormus and of Ind,—

are noble also. But the first is in a rhymed metre; and the unfitness of a rhymed metre for rendering Homer I have

[1] *The Faery Queen*, canto ii. stanza 1.

already shown. I will observe, too, that the fine couplet which I
have quoted comes out of a satire, a didactic poem; and that it
is in didactic poetry that the ten-syllable couplet has most
successfully essayed the grand style. In narrative poetry this
metre has succeeded best when it essayed a sensibly lower style,
the style of Chaucer, for instance; whose narrative manner,
though a very good and sound manner, is certainly neither the
grand manner nor the manner of Homer.

The rhymed ten-syllable couplet being thus excluded, blank
verse offers itself for the translator's use. The first kind of blank
verse which naturally occurs to us is the blank verse of Milton,
which has been employed, with more or less modification, by
Mr. Cary in translating Dante, by Cowper, and by Mr. Wright
in translating Homer. How noble this metre is in Milton's
hands, how completely it shows itself capable of the grand, nay,
of the grandest, style, I need not say. To this metre, as used in
the *Paradise Lost*, our country owes the glory of having produced
one of the only two poetical works in the grand style which are
to be found in the modern languages; the *Divine Comedy* of
Dante is the other. England and Italy here stand alone; Spain,
France, and Germany have produced great poets, but neither
Calderon, nor Corneille, nor Schiller, nor even Goethe, has
produced a body of poetry in the true grand style, in the sense in
which the style of the body of Homer's poetry, or Pindar's, or
Sophocles', is grand. But Dante has, and so has Milton; and in
this respect Milton possesses a distinction which even Shakspeare, undoubtedly the supreme poetical power in our literature, does not share with him. Not a tragedy of Shakspeare
but contains passages in the worst of all styles, the affected
style; and the grand style, although it may be harsh, or obscure,
or cumbrous, or over-laboured, is never affected. In spite,
therefore, of objections which may justly be urged against the
plan and treatment of the *Paradise Lost*, in spite of its possessing,
certainly, a far less enthralling force of interest to attract and to
carry forward the reader than the *Iliad* or the *Divine Comedy*, it
fully deserves, it can never lose, its immense reputation; for,
like the *Iliad* and the *Divine Comedy*, nay, in some respects to a
higher degree than either of them, it is in the grand style.

But the grandeur of Milton is one thing, and the grandeur
of Homer is another. Homer's movement, I have said again and
again, is a flowing, a rapid movement; Milton's, on the other
hand, is a laboured, a self-retarding movement. In each case,
the movement, the metrical cast, corresponds with the mode
of evolution of the thought, with the syntactical cast, and is
indeed determined by it. Milton charges himself so full with

thought, imagination, knowledge, that his style will hardly contain them. He is too full-stored to show us in much detail one conception, one piece of knowledge; he just shows it to us in a pregnant, allusive way, and then he presses on to another; and all this fulness, this pressure, this condensation, this self-constraint, enters into his movement, and makes it what it is,— noble, but difficult and austere. Homer is quite different: he says a thing, and says it to the end, and then begins another, while Milton is trying to press a thousand things into one. So that whereas, in reading Milton, you never lose the sense of laborious and condensed fulness, in reading Homer you never lose the sense of flowing and abounding ease. With Milton line runs into line, and all is straitly bound together: with Homer line runs off from line, and all hurries away onward. Homer begins, Μῆνιν ἄειδε, Φεά,—at the second word announcing the proposed action: Milton begins:

> Of man's first disobedience, and the fruit
> Of that forbidden tree, whose mortal taste
> Brought death into the world, and all our woe,
> With loss of Eden, till one greater Man
> Restore us, and regain the blissful seat,
> Sing, heavenly muse.

So chary of a sentence is he, so resolute not to let it escape him till he has crowded into it all he can, that it is not till the thirty-ninth word in the sentence that he will give us the key to it, the word of action, the verb. Milton says:

> O for that warning voice, which he, who saw
> The Apocalypse, heard cry in heaven aloud.

He is not satisfied, unless he can tell us, all in one sentence, and without permitting himself actually to mention the name, that the man who had the warning voice was the same man who saw the Apocalypse. Homer would have said, "O for that warning voice, which *John* heard"—and if it had suited him to say that John also saw the Apocalypse, he would have given us that in another sentence. The effect of this allusive and com-pressed manner of Milton is, I need not say, often very powerful; and it is an effect which other great poets have often sought to obtain much in the same way: Dante is full of it, Horace is full of it; but wherever it exists, it is always an un-Homeric effect. "The losses of the heavens," says Horace, "fresh moons speedily repair; we, when we have gone down where the pious Æneas, where the rich Tullus and Ancus are,—*pulvis et umbra sumus.*"[1]

[1] *Odes*, IV. vii. 13.

He never actually says *where* we go to; he only indicates it by saying that it is that place where Æneas, Tullus and Ancus are. But Homer, when he has to speak of going down to the grave, says, definitely, ἐς 'Ηλύσιον πεδίον—ἀθάνατοι πέμψουσιν,[1]—"The immortals shall send thee *to the Elysian plain*;" and it is not till after he has definitely said this, that he adds, that it is there that the abode of departed worthies is placed: ὅθι ξανθὸς 'Ραδάμανθυς —"Where the yellow-haired Rhadamanthus is." Again; Horace, having to say that punishment sooner or later overtakes crime, says it thus:

> Raro antecedentem scelestum
> Deseruit pede Pœna claudo.[2]

The thought itself of these lines is familiar enough to Homer and Hesiod; but neither Homer nor Hesiod, in expressing it, could possibly have so complicated its expression as Horace complicates it, and purposely complicates it, by his use of the word *deseruit*. I say that this complicated evolution of the thought necessarily complicates the movement and rhythm of a poet; and that the Miltonic blank verse, of course the first model of blank verse which suggests itself to an English translator of Homer, bears the strongest marks of such complication, and is therefore entirely unfit to render Homer.

If blank verse is used in translating Homer, it must be a blank verse of which English poetry, naturally swayed much by Milton's treatment of this metre, offers at present hardly any examples. It must not be Cowper's blank verse, who has studied Milton's pregnant manner with such effect, that, having to say of Mr. Throckmorton that he spares his avenue, although it is the fashion with other people to cut down theirs, he says that Benevolus "reprieves The obsolete prolixity of shade." It must not be Mr. Tennyson's blank verse.

> For all experience is an arch, wherethrough
> Gleams that untravelled world, whose distance fades
> For ever and for ever, as we gaze.

It is no blame to the thought of those lines, which belongs to another order of ideas than Homer's, but it is true, that Homer would certainly have said of them, "It is to consider too curiously to consider so." It is no blame to their rhythm, which belongs to another order of movement than Homer's, but it is true that these three lines by themselves take up nearly as much time as a whole book of the *Iliad*. No; the blank verse used in rendering Homer must be a blank verse of which perhaps the best speci-

---

[1] *Odyssey*, iv. 563.   [2] *Odes*, III. ii. 31.

mens are to be found in some of the most rapid passages of Shakspeare's plays,—a blank verse which does not dovetail its lines into one another, and which habitually ends its lines with monosyllables. Such a blank verse might no doubt be very rapid in its movement, and might perfectly adapt itself to a thought plainly and directly evolved; and it would be interesting to see it well applied to Homer. But the translator who determines to use it, must not conceal from himself that in order to pour Homer into the mould of this metre, he will have entirely to break him up and melt him down, with the hope of then successfully composing him afresh; and this is a process which is full of risks. It may, no doubt, be the real Homer that issues new from it; it is not certain beforehand that it cannot be the real Homer, as it is certain that from the mould of Pope's couplet or Cowper's Miltonic verse it cannot be the real Homer that will issue; still, the chances of disappointment are great. The result of such an attempt to renovate the old poet may be an Æson; but it may also, and more probably will be a Pelias.

When I say this, I point to the metre which seems to me to give the translator the best chance of preserving the general effect of Homer,—that third metre which I have not yet expressly named, the hexameter. I know all that is said against the use of hexameters in English poetry; but it comes only to this, that, among us, they have not yet been used on any considerable scale with success. *Solvitur ambulando*: this is an objection which can best be met by *producing* good English hexameters. And there is no reason in the nature of the English language why it should not adapt itself to hexameters as well as the German language does; nay, the English language, from its greater rapidity, is in itself better suited than the German for them. The hexameter, whether alone or with the pentameter, possesses a movement, an expression, which no metre hitherto in common use amongst us possesses, and which I am convinced English poetry, as our mental wants multiply, will not always be content to forego. Applied to Homer, this metre affords to the translator the immense support of keeping him more nearly than any other metre to Homer's movement; and, since a poet's movement makes so large a part of his general effect, and to reproduce this general effect is at once the translator's indispensable business and so difficult for him, it is a great thing to have this part of your model's general effect already given you in your metre, instead of having to get it entirely for yourself.

These are general considerations; but there are also one or two particular considerations which confirm me in the opinion

that for translating Homer into English verse the hexameter
should be used. The most successful attempt hitherto made at
rendering Homer into English, the attempt in which Homer's
general effect has been best retained, is an attempt made in the
hexameter measure. It is a version of the famous lines in the
third book of the *Iliad*, which end with that mention of Castor
and Pollux from which Mr. Ruskin extracts the sentimental
consolation already noticed by me. The author is the accomplished Provost of Eton, Dr. Hawtrey; and this performance of
his must be my excuse for having taken the liberty to single him
out for mention, as one of the natural judges of a translation of
Homer, along with Professor Thompson and Professor Jowett,
whose connection with Greek literature is official. The passage
is short; [1] and Dr. Hawtrey's version of it is suffused with a
pensive grace which is, perhaps, rather more Virgilian than

[1] So short, that I quote it entire:—

Clearly the rest I behold of the dark-eyed sons of Achaia;
Known to me well are the faces of all; their names I remember;
Two, two only remain, whom I see not among the commanders,
Castor fleet in the car,—Polydeukes brave with the cestus,—
Own dear brethren of mine,—one parent loved us as infants.
Are they not here in the host, from the shores of loved Lacedæmon,
Or, though they came with the rest in ships that bound through the
    waters,
Dare they not enter the fight or stand in the council of Heroes,
All for fear of the shame and the taunts my crime has awakened!
    So said she;—they long since in Earth's soft arms were reposing,
There, in their own dear land, their Fatherland, Lacedæmon.
        English Hexameter Translations, London, 1847; p. 242.

I have changed Dr. Hawtrey's "Kastor," "Lakedaimon," back to
the familiar "Castor," "Lacedæmon," in obedience to my own rule
that everything *odd* is to be avoided in rendering Homer, the most
natural and least odd of poets. I see Mr. Newman's critic in the
National Review urges our generation to bear with the unnatural
effect of these rewritten Greek names, in the hope that by this means
the effect of them may have to the next generation become natural.
For my part, I feel no disposition to pass all my own life in the
wilderness of pedantry, in order that a posterity which I shall never
see may one day enter an orthographical Canaan; and, after all, the
real question is this: whether our living apprehension of the Greek
word is more checked by meeting in an English book about the
Greeks, names not spelt letter for letter as in the original Greek, or by
meeting names which make us rub our eyes and call out, "How
exceedingly odd!"
    The Latin names of the Greek deities raise in most cases the idea of
quite distinct personages from the personages whose idea is raised by
the Greek names. Hera and Juno are actually, to every scholar's
imagination, two different people. So in all these cases the Latin
names must, at any inconvenience, be abandoned when we are dealing
with the Greek world. But I think it can be in the sensitive imagination of Mr. Grote only, that "Thucydides" raises the idea of a different
man from Θουκυδίδης.

Homeric; still it is the one version of any part of the *Iliad* which in some degree reproduces for me the original effect of Homer: it is the best, and it is in hexameters.

This is one of the particular considerations that incline me to prefer the hexameter, for translating Homer, to our established metres. There is another. Most of you, probably, have some knowledge of a poem by Mr. Clough, *The Bothie of Toper-na-fuosich*, a long-vacation pastoral, in hexameters. The general merits of that poem I am not going to discuss: it is a serio-comic poem, and therefore of essentially different nature from the *Iliad*. Still in two things it is, more than any other English poem which I can call to mind, like the *Iliad*: in the rapidity of its movement, and the plainness and directness of its style. The thought in this poem is often curious and subtle, and that is not Homeric; the diction is often grotesque, and that is not Homeric. Still by its rapidity of movement, and plain and direct manner of presenting the thought, however curious in itself, this poem, which, being as I say a serio-comic poem, has a right to be grotesque, is grotesque *truly*, not, like Mr. Newman's version of the *Iliad*, *falsely*. Mr. Clough's odd epithets, "The grave man nicknamed Adam," "The hairy Aldrich," and so on, grow vitally and appear naturally in their place; while Mr. Newman's "dapper-greaved Achaians," and "motley-helmed Hector," have all the air of being mechanically elaborated and artificially stuck in. Mr. Clough's hexameters are excessively, needlessly rough; still, owing to the native rapidity of this measure, and to the directness of style which so well allies itself with it, his composition produces a sense in the reader which Homer's composition also produces, and which Homer's translator ought to *re*produce—the sense of having, within short limits of time, a large portion of human life presented to him, instead of a small portion.

Mr. Clough's hexameters are, as I have just said, too rough and irregular; and indeed a good model, on any considerable scale, of this metre, the English translator will nowhere find. He must not follow the model offered by Mr. Longfellow in his pleasing and popular poem of *Evangeline*; for the merit of the manner and movement of *Evangeline*, when they are at their best, is to be tenderly elegant; and their fault, when they are at their worst, is to be lumbering; but Homer's defect is not lumberingness, neither is tender elegance his excellence. The lumbering effect of most English hexameters is caused by their being much too dactylic; the translator must learn to use spondees freely. Mr. Clough has done this, but he has not sufficiently observed another rule which the translator cannot follow too strictly; and that is, to have no lines which will not, as it is familiarly said, *read themselves*. This is of the last importance for rhythms with which the ear of the English public is not thoroughly acquainted. Lord Redesdale,[1] in two papers on the subject of Greek and Roman metres, has some good remarks on the outrageous disregard of quantity in which English verse, trusting to its force of accent, is apt to indulge itself. The predominance of accent in our language is so great, that it would be pedantic not to avail one's self of it; and Lord Redesdale suggests rules which might easily be pushed too far. Still, it is undeniable that in English hexameters we generally force the quantity far too much; we rely on justification by accent with a security which is excessive. But not only do we abuse accent by shortening long syllables and lengthening short ones; we perpetually commit a far worse fault, by requiring the removal of the accent from its natural place to an unnatural one, in order to make our line scan. This is a fault, even when our metre is one which every English reader knows, and when he can see what we want and can correct the rhythm according to our wish; although it is a fault which a great master may sometimes commit knowingly to produce a desired effect, as Milton changes the natural accent on the word *Tirésias* in the line—

And Tíresias and Phineus, prophets old;

and then it ceases to be a fault, and becomes a beauty. But it is a real fault, when Chapman has:—

By him the golden-throned Queen slept, the Queen of Deities;

for in this line, to make it scan, you have to take away the accent from the word *Queen*, on which it naturally falls, and to place it on *throned*, which would naturally be unaccented; and yet, after all, you get no peculiar effect or beauty of cadence to reward you.

It is a real fault, when Mr. Newman has:

Infatuate! O that thou wert lord to some other army—

for here again the reader is required, not for any special advantage to himself, but simply to save Mr. Newman trouble, to place the accent on the insignificant word *wert*, where it has no business whatever. But it is still a great fault, when Spenser has (to take a striking instance):

Wot ye why his mother with a veil hath covered his face?

[1] [John Thomas Freeman-Mitford (1805–1886), cr. Earl of Redesdale 1877. Author of 'Thoughts on English Prosody and Translations from Horace' and 'Further Thoughts on English Prosody' (1859).]

for a hexameter; because here not only is the reader causelessly required to make havoc with the natural accentuation of the line in order to get it to run as a hexameter; but also he, in nine cases out of ten, will be utterly at a loss how to perform the process required, and the line will remain a mere monster for him. I repeat, it is advisable to construct *all* verses so that by reading them naturally—that is, according to the sense and legitimate accent,—the reader gets the right rhythm; but, for English hexameters, that they be so constructed is indispensable.

If the hexameter best helps the translator to the Homeric rapidity, what style may best help him to the Homeric plainness and directness? It is the merit of a metre appropriate to your subject, that it in some degree suggests and carries with itself a style appropriate to the subject; the elaborate and self-retarding style, which comes so naturally when your metre is the Miltonic blank verse, does not come naturally with the hexameter; is, indeed, alien to it. On the other hand, the hexameter has a natural dignity which repels both the jaunty style and the jog-trot style, to both of which the ballad-measure so easily lends itself. These are great advantages; and, perhaps, it is nearly enough to say to the translator who uses the hexameter that he cannot too religiously follow, in style, the inspiration of his metre. He will find that a loose and idiomatic grammar—a grammar which follows the essential rather than the formal logic of the thought—allies itself excellently with the hexameter; and that, while this sort of grammar ensures plainness and naturalness, it by no means comes short in nobleness. It is difficult to pronounce, certainly, what is idiomatic in the ancient literature of a language which, though still spoken, has long since entirely adopted, as modern Greek had adopted, modern idioms. Still one may, I think, clearly perceive that Homer's grammatical style is idiomatic,—that it may even be called, not improperly, a loose grammatical style. Examples, however, of what I mean by a loose grammatical style, will be of more use to the translator if taken from English poetry than if taken from Homer. I call it, then, a loose and idiomatic grammar which Shakspeare uses in the last line of the following three:—

> He's here in double trust:
> First, as I am his kinsman and his subject,
> *Strong both against the deed,*—

or in this:—

> Wilt, *whither wilt?*

What Shakspeare means is perfectly clear—clearer, probably, than if he had said it in a more formal and regular manner;

but his grammar is loose and idiomatic, because he leaves out the subject of the verb "wilt" in the second passage quoted, and because, in the first, a prodigious addition to the sentence has to be, as we used to say in our old Latin grammar days, *understood*, before the word "both" can be properly parsed. So, again, Chapman's grammar is loose and idiomatic where he says,

> Even share hath he that keeps his tent, and *he to field* doth go,—

because he leaves out, in the second clause, the relative which in formal writing would be required. But Chapman here does not lose dignity by this idiomatic way of expressing himself, any more than Shakspeare loses it by neglecting to confer on "both" the blessings of a regular government: neither loses dignity, but each gives that impression of a plain, direct, and natural mode of speaking, which Homer, too, gives, and which is so important, as I say, that Homer's translator should succeed in giving. Cowper calls blank verse "a style further removed than rhyme from the vernacular idiom, both in the language itself and in the arrangement of it;" and just in proportion as blank verse is removed from the vernacular idiom, from that idiomatic style which is of all styles the plainest and most natural, blank verse is unsuited to render Homer.

Shakspeare is not only idiomatic in his grammar or style, he is also idiomatic in his words or diction; and here too, his example is valuable for the translator of Homer. The translator must not, indeed, allow himself all the liberty that Shakspeare allows himself; for Shakspeare sometimes uses expressions which pass perfectly well as he uses them, because Shakspeare thinks so fast and so powerfully, that in reading him we are borne over single words as by a mighty current; but, if our mind were less excited,—and who may rely on exciting our mind like Shakspeare?—they would check us. "To grunt and sweat under a weary load"; —that does perfectly well where it comes in Shakspeare; but if the translator of Homer, who will hardly have wound our minds up to the pitch at which these words of Hamlet find them, were to employ, when he has to speak of one of Homer's heroes under the load of calamity, this figure of "grunting" and "sweating," we should say, *He Newmanises*, and his diction would offend us. For he is to be noble; and no plea of wishing to be plain and natural can get him excused from being this: only, as he is to be also, like Homer, perfectly simple and free from artificiality, and as the use of idiomatic expressions undoubtedly gives this effect, he should be as idiomatic as he can be without ceasing to be noble. Therefore the idiomatic language of Shakspeare—such language as "prate of his *where-about*;" *jump* the life to come;" "the damnation of his *taking-off*;" "his *quietus make* with a bare *bodkin*"—should be carefully observed by the translator of Homer, although in every case he will have to decide for himself whether the use, by him, of Shakspeare's liberty will or will not clash with his indispensable duty of nobleness. He will find one English book, and one only, where as in the *Iliad* itself, perfect plainness of speech is allied with perfect nobleness; and that book is the Bible. No one could see this more clearly than Pope saw it: "This pure and noble simplicity," he says, "is nowhere in such perfection as in the Scripture and Homer:" yet even with Pope a woman is a "fair," a father is a "sire," and an old man a "reverend sage," and so on through all the phrases of that pseudo-Augustan, and most unbiblical, vocabulary. The Bible, however, is undoubtedly the grand mine of diction for the translator of Homer; and, if he knows how to discriminate truly between what will suit him and what will not, the Bible may afford him also invaluable lessons of style.

I said that Homer, besides being plain in style and diction, was plain in the quality of his thought. It is possible that a thought may be expressed with idiomatic plainness, and yet not be in itself a plain thought. For example, in Mr. Clough's poem, already mentioned, the style and diction is almost always idiomatic and plain, but the thought itself is often of a quality which is not plain; it is *curious*. But the grand instance of the union of idiomatic expression with curious or difficult thought is in Shakspeare's poetry. Such, indeed, is the force and power of Shakspeare's idiomatic expression, that it gives an effect of clearness and vividness even to a thought which is imperfect and incoherent: for instance, when Hamlet says,—

> To take arms against a sea of troubles,—

the figure there is undoubtedly most faulty, it by no means runs on four legs; but the thing is said so freely and idiomatically, that it passes. This, however, is not a point to which I now want to call your attention; I want you to remark, in Shakspeare and others, only that which we may directly apply to Homer. I say, then, that in Shakspeare the thought is often, while most idiomatically uttered, nay, while good and sound in itself, yet of a quality which is curious and difficult, and that this quality of thought is something entirely un-Homeric. For example, when Lady Macbeth says,—

> Memory, the warder of the brain,
> Shall be a fume, and the receipt of reason
> A limbeck only,—

this figure is a perfectly sound and correct figure, no doubt; Mr. Knight even calls it a "happy" figure; but it is a *difficult* figure: Homer would not have used it. Again, when Lady Macbeth says,—

> When you durst do it, then you were a man;
> And, to be more than what you were, you would
> Be so much more the man,—

the thought in the two last of these lines is, when you seize it, a perfectly clear thought, and a fine thought; but it is a *curious* thought: Homer would not have used it. These are favourable instances of the union of plain style and words with a thought not plain in quality; but take stronger instances of this union,— let the thought be not only not plain in quality, but highly fanciful: and you have the Elizabethan conceits; you have, in spite of idiomatic style and idiomatic diction, everything which is most un-Homeric: you have such atrocities as this of Chapman:—

> Fate shall fail to vent her gall
> Till mine vent thousands.

I say, the poets of a nation which has produced such conceit as that, must purify themselves seven times in the fire before they can hope to render Homer. They must expel their nature with a fork, and keep crying to one another night and day: "Homer not only moves rapidly, not only speaks idiomatically; he is, also, *free from fancifulness*."

So essentially characteristic of Homer is his plainness and naturalness of thought, that to the preservation of this in his own version the translator must without scruple sacrifice, where it is necessary, verbal fidelity to his original, rather than run any risk of producing, by literalness, an odd and unnatural effect. The double epithets so constantly occurring in Homer must be dealt with according to this rule; these epithets come quite naturally in Homer's poetry; in English poetry they, in nine cases out of ten, come, when literally rendered, quite un-naturally. I will not now discuss why this is so, I assume it as an indisputable fact that it is so; that Homer's μερόπων ἀνθρώπων comes to the reader as something perfectly natural, while Mr. Newman's "voice-dividing mortals" comes to him as something perfectly unnatural. Well then, as it is Homer's general effect which we are to reproduce, it is to be false to Homer to be so verbally faithful to him as that we lose this effect; and by the English translator Homer's double epithets must be, in many places, renounced altogether; in all places where they are rendered, rendered by equivalents which come naturally.

Instead of rendering Θέτι τανύπεπλε by Mr. Newman's "Thetis trailing-robed," which brings to one's mind long petticoats sweeping a dirty pavement, the translator must render the Greek by English words which come as naturally to us as Milton's words when he says, "Let gorgeous Tragedy With sceptred pall come sweeping by." Instead of rendering μώνυχας ἵππους by Chapman's "one-hoofed steeds," or Mr. Newman's "single-hoofed horses," he must speak of horses in a way which surprises us as little as Shakspeare surprises when he says, "Gallop apace, you fiery-footed steeds." Instead of rendering μελιηδέα θυμόν by "life as honey pleasant," he must characterise life with the simple pathos of Gray's "warm precincts of the cheerful day." Instead of converting μοῖόν σε ἔπος φύγεν ἕρκος ὀδόντων; into the portentous remonstrance, "Betwixt the outwork of thy teeth what word hath split?" he must remonstrate in English as straightforward as this of St. Peter, "Be it far from thee, Lord: this shall not be unto thee;" or as this of the disciples, "What is this that he saith, a little while? we cannot tell what he saith." Homer's Greek, in each of the places quoted, reads as naturally as any of those English passages: the expression no more calls away the attention from the sense in the Greek than in the English. But when, in order to render literally in English one of Homer's double epithets, a strange unfamiliar adjective is invented—such as "voice-dividing" for μέροψ,—an improper share of the reader's attention is necessarily diverted to this ancillary word, to this word which Homer never intended should receive so much notice; and a total effect quite different from Homer's is thus produced. Therefore Mr. Newman, though he does not purposely import, like Chapman, conceits of his own into the *Iliad*, does actually import them; for the result of his singular diction is to raise ideas, and odd ideas, not raised by the corresponding diction in Homer; and Chapman himself does no more. Cowper says: "I have cautiously avoided all terms of new invention, with an abundance of which persons of more ingenuity than judgment have not enriched our language but encumbered it;" and this criticism so exactly hits the diction of Mr. Newman that one is irresistibly led to imagine his present appearance in the flesh to be at least his second.

A translator cannot well have a Homeric rapidity, style, diction, and quality of thought, without at the same time having what is the result of these in Homer,—nobleness. Therefore I do not attempt to lay down any rules for obtaining this effect of nobleness,—the effect, too, of all others the most impalpable, the most irreducible to rule, and which most depends on the individual personality of the artist.

II. *Conclusion*

Here I stop. I have said so much, because I think that the task of translating Homer into English verse both will be re-attempted, and may be re-attempted successfully. There are great works composed of parts so disparate that one translator is not likely to have the requisite gifts for poetically rendering all of them. Such are the works of Shakspeare, and Goethe's *Faust*; and these it is best to attempt to render in prose only. People praise Tieck and Schlegel's version of Shakspeare: I, for my part, would sooner read Shakspeare in the French prose translation, and that is saying a great deal; but in the German poets' hands Shakspeare so often gets, especially where he is humorous, an air of what the French call *niaiserie*! and can anything be more un-Shakspearian than that? Again; Mr. Hayward's prose translation of the first part of *Faust* [1]—so good that it makes one regret Mr. Hayward should have abandoned the line of translation for a kind of literature which is, to say the least, somewhat slight—is not likely to be surpassed by any translation in verse. But poems like the *Iliad*, which, in the main, are in one manner, may hope to find a poetical translator so gifted and so trained as to be able to learn that one manner, and to reproduce it. Only, the poet who would reproduce this must cultivate in himself a Greek virtue by no means common among the moderns in general, and the English in particular,— *moderation*. For Homer has not only the English vigour, he has the Greek grace; and when one observes the boistering, rollicking way in which his English admirers—even men of genius, like the late Professor Wilson—love to talk of Homer and his poetry, one cannot help feeling that there is no very deep community of nature between them and the object of their enthusiasm. "It is very well, my good friends," I always imagine Homer saying to them—if he could hear them: "you do me a great deal of honour, but somehow or other you praise me too like barbarians." For Homer's grandeur is not the mixed and turbid grandeur of the great poets of the north, of the authors of *Othello* and *Faust*; it is a perfect, a lovely grandeur. Certainly his poetry has all the energy and power of the poetry of our ruder climates; but it has, besides, the pure lines of an Ionian horizon, the liquid clearness of an Ionian sky.

[1] [Abraham Hayward (1801–1884), essayist. Published his translation of *Faust* 1833.]

ON TRANSLATING HOMER
LAST WORDS
1862

On translating Homer. Last Words. A Lecture given at Oxford
by Matthew Arnold M.A. Professor of Poetry in the University of Oxford and formerly Fellow of Oriel College.
London. Longman, Green, Longman, and Roberts. 1862.

THE lectures on Homer were attacked in the *Saturday Review*, July
1861, in an article entitled *Homeric Translators and Critics*. (Sir
Edmund Chambers has suggested that the author may have been
James Spedding.) Francis Newman published his own defence—
*Homeric Translation in Theory and Practice: A Reply to Matthew
Arnold Esq.* 1861. To this *Last Words on Homer*, the first Oxford
lecture of 1862, was a reply. It was published in the same year. In
1896 the four lectures were printed together in a "Popular Edition"
which is in effect the second edition of both works.

ON TRANSLATING HOMER
LAST WORDS

I. *The Grand Style*

BUT the supreme poet is he who is thoroughly sound and poetical, alike when his subject is grand, and when it is plain: with him the subject may sink, but never the poet. But a Dutch painter does not rise and sink with his subject,—Defoe, in *Moll Flanders*, does not rise and sink with his subject,—in so far as an artist cannot be said to sink who is sound in his treatment of his subject, however plain it is; yet Defoe, yet a Dutch painter, may in one sense be said to sink with their subject, because though sound in their treatment of it, they are not *poetical*,—poetical in the true, not the false sense of the word; because, in fact, they are not in the grand style. Homer can in no sense be said to sink with his subject, because his soundness has something more than literal naturalness about it; because his soundness is the soundness of Homer, of a great epic poet; because, in fact, he is in the grand style. So he sheds over the simplest matter he touches the charm of his grand manner; he makes everything noble. Nothing has raised more questioning among my critics than these words,—*noble, the grand style*. People complain that I do not define these words sufficiently, that I do not tell them enough about them. "The grand style,—but what *is* the grand style?"—they cry; some with an inclination to believe in it, but puzzled; others mockingly and with incredulity. Alas: the grand style is the last matter in the world for verbal definition to deal with adequately. One may say of it, as is said of faith: "One must feel it in order to know what it is." But, as of faith, so too one may say of nobleness, of the grand style: "Woe to those who know it not!" Yet this expression, though indefinable, has a charm; one is the better for considering it; *bonum est, nos hic esse*; nay, one loves to try to explain it, though one knows that one must speak imperfectly. For those, then, who ask the question,—What is the grand style?—with sincerity, I will try to make some answer, inadequate as it must be. For those who ask it mockingly I have no answer, except to repeat to them, with compassionate sorrow, the Gospel words: *Moriemini in peccatis vestris*,—Ye shall die in your sins.

But let me, at any rate, have the pleasure of again giving, before I begin to try and define the grand style, a specimen of what it *is*.

> Standing on earth, not rapt above the pole,
> More safe I sing with mortal voice, unchanged
> To hoarse or mute, though fall'n on evil days,
> On evil days though fall'n, and evil tongues. . . .

There is the grand style in perfection; and any one who has a sense for it, will feel it a thousand times better from repeating those lines than from hearing anything I can say about it.

Let us try, however, what *can* be said, controlling what we say by examples. I think it will be found that the grand style arises in poetry, *when a noble nature, poetically gifted, treats with simplicity or with severity a serious subject*. I think this definition will be found to cover all instances of the grand style in poetry which present themselves. I think it will be found to exclude all poetry which is not in the grand style. And I think it contains no terms which are obscure, which themselves need defining. Even those who do not understand what is meant by calling poetry noble, will understand, I imagine, what is meant by speaking of a noble nature in a man. But the noble or powerful nature—the *bedeutendes Individuum* of Goethe—is not enough. For instance, Mr. Newman has zeal for learning, zeal for thinking, zeal for liberty, and all these things are noble, they ennoble a man; but he has not the poetical gift: there must be the poetical gift, the "divine faculty," also. And, besides all this, the subject must be a serious one (for it is only by a kind of licence that we can speak of the grand style in comedy); and it must be treated *with simplicity or severity*. Here is the great difficulty: the poets of the world have been many; there has been wanting neither abundance of poetical gift nor abundance of noble natures; but a poetical gift so happy, in a noble nature so circumstanced and trained, that the result is a continuous style, perfect in simplicity or perfect in severity, has been extremely rare. One poet has had the gifts of nature and faculty in unequalled fulness, without the circumstances and training which make this sustained perfection of style possible. Of other poets, some have caught this perfect strain now and then, in short pieces or single lines, but have not been able to maintain it through considerable works; others have composed all their productions in a style which, by comparison with the best, one must call secondary.

The best model of the grand style simple is Homer; perhaps the best model of the grand style severe is Milton. But Dante

is remarkable for affording admirable examples of both styles;
he has the grand style which arises from simplicity, and he has
the grand style which arises from severity; and from him I will
illustrate them both. In a former lecture I pointed out what that
severity of poetical style is, which comes from saying a thing
with a kind of intense compression, or in an allusive, brief,
almost haughty way, as if the poet's mind were charged with
so many and such grave matters, that he would not deign to
treat any one of them explicitly. Of this severity the last line
of the following stanza of the *Purgatory* is a good example.
Dante has been telling Forese that Virgil had guided him
through Hell, and he goes on:[1]

> Indi m' han tratto su gli suoi conforti,
> Salendo e rigirando la Montagna
> *Che drizza voi che il mondo fece torti.*

"Thence hath his comforting aid led me up, climbing and
circling the Mountain, *which straightens you whom the world
made crooked.*" These last words, "la Montagna *che drizza voi
che il mondo fece torti,*"—"the Mountain *which straightens you
whom the world made crooked,*"—for the Mountain of Purgatory,
I call an excellent specimen of the grand style in severity, where
the poet's mind is too full charged to suffer him to speak more
explicitly. But the very next stanza is a beautiful specimen of
the grand style in simplicity, where a noble nature and a poetical
gift unite to utter a thing with the most limpid plainness and
clearness:[2]

> Tanto dice di farmi sua compagna
> Ch' io sarò là dove fia Beatrice;
> Quivi convien che senza lui rimagna.

"So long," Dante continues, "so long he (Virgil) saith he will
bear me company, until I shall be there where Beatrice is: there
it behoves that without him I remain." But the noble simplicity
of that in the Italian no words of mine can render.

Both these styles, the simple and the severe, are truly grand;
the severe seems, perhaps, the grandest, so long as we attend
most to the great personality, to the noble nature, in the poet its
author; the simple seems the grandest when we attend most to
the exquisite faculty, to the poetical gift. But the simple is no
doubt to be preferred. It is the more *magical*: in the other there
is something intellectual, something which gives scope for a
play of thought which may exist where the poetical gift is either
wanting or present in only inferior degree: the severe is much

---

[1] *Purgatory*, xxiii. 124.   [2] *Ibid.*, xxiii. 127.

more imitable, and this a little spoils its charm. A kind of semblance of this style keeps Young going, one may say, through all the nine parts of that most indifferent production, the *Night Thoughts*. But the grand style in simplicity is inimitable:

αἰὼν ἀσφαλὴς
οὐκ ἔγεντ' οὔτ' Αἰακίδᾳ παρὰ Πηλεί,
οὔτε οαρ ἀντιθέῳ Κάδμῳ · λέγονται μὰν βροτῶν
ὄλβον ὑπέρτατον οἱ σχεῖν, οἵ τε καὶ χρυσαμπύκων
μελπομενᾶν ἐν ὄρει Μοισᾶν, καὶ ἐν ἑπταπύλοις
ἄϊον Θήβαις . . .[1]

There is a limpidness in that, a want of salient points to seize and transfer, which makes imitation impossible, except by a genius akin to the genius which produced it.

II. *Tribute to Clough*

The successful translator of Homer will have (or he cannot succeed) that true sense for his subject, and that disinterested love of it, which are, both of them, so rare in literature, and so precious; he will not be led off by any false scent; he will have an eye for the real matter, and, where he thinks he may find any indication of this, no hint will be too slight for him, no shade will be too fine, no imperfections will turn him aside,—he will go before his adviser's thought, and help it out with his own. This is the sort of student that a critic of Homer should always have in his thoughts; but students of this sort are indeed rare.

And now, then, can I help being reminded what a student of this sort we have just lost in Mr. Clough, whose name I have already mentioned in these lectures? He, too, was busy with Homer; but it is not on that account that I now speak of him. Nor do I speak of him in order to call attention to his qualities and powers in general, admirable as these were. I mention him because, in so eminent a degree, he possessed these two invaluable literary qualities,—a true sense for his object of study, and a single-hearted care for it. He had both; but he had the second even more eminently than the first. He greatly developed the first through means of the second. In the study of art, poetry, or philosophy, he had the most undivided and disinterested love for his object in itself, the greatest aversion to mixing up with it anything accidental or personal. His interest

---

[1] " A secure time fell to the lot neither of Peleus the son of Æacus, nor of the godlike Cadmus; howbeit these are said to have had, of all mortals, the supreme of happiness, who heard the golden-snooded Muses sing, one of them on the mountain (Pelion), the other in seven-gated Thebes." [Pindar, *Pyth.* iii. 86.]

was in literature itself; and it was this which gave so rare a stamp to his character, which kept him so free from all taint of littleness. In the saturnalia of ignoble personal passions, of which the struggle for literary success, in old and crowded communities, offers so sad a spectacle, he never mingled. He had not yet traduced his friends, nor flattered his enemies, nor disparaged what he admired, nor praised what he despised. Those who knew him well had the conviction that, even with time, these literary arts would never be his. His poem, of which I before spoke, has some admirable Homeric qualities; out-of-doors freshness, life, naturalness, buoyant rapidity. Some of the expressions in that poem,—"*Dangerous Corrievreckan . . Where roads are unknown to Loch Nevish*," [1]— come back now to my ear with the true Homeric ring. But that in him of which I think oftenest is the Homeric simplicity of his literary life.

[1] [Arnold is here quoting from two separate passages of the *Bothie*: iv. 12, and ix. 79.]

A FRENCH ETON
1864

A French Eton; or, Middle Class Education and the State. By
Matthew Arnold. London and Cambridge. Macmillan
and Co. 1864.

IN 1859 Arnold visited the Continent at the request of the Royal
Commission on Education in order to enquire into the state of French
primary schools. He published his observations in 1861 as *The Popular
Education of France, with notices of that of Holland and Switzerland.*
At the same time he took the opportunity of seeing something of the
secondary schools too, and the result was *A French Eton.* Arnold
later said of it, "I have written, to my own mind, nothing better."

Jean Baptiste Henri Lacordaire (1802–1861), friend of Lamennais
and Montalembert, was associated with them in the attempt to combine Catholicism with free democratic principles. The most eloquent
preacher of his age, his sermons at Notre Dame were of European
fame. Failing in his attempt to re-establish the Dominican order in
France, in 1854 he retired from public life to direct the college at
Sorèze on lines akin to English public school principles, and this
Arnold here describes.

On his one visit to England in 1852 Lacordaire, returning from
Oscott, spent a night alone and unknown in Oxford: from there he
sent his impressions to a young friend in France. When, after his
death, the *Lettres à des jeunes gens* were published in 1862, this letter
caught the attention of William Cory and inspired him to write his
poem "Lacordaire at Oxford." It is of some interest to place this side
by side with Arnold's first-hand impressions. Cory wrote to Charles
Wood from Eton, 1 February, 1863:—

> I read with great interest an extract from the great preacher
> Lacordaire's letters: it was about Oxford: perhaps I have already
> mentioned it to you. When you come here I will show you some
> lines I wrote at Torquay on that text . . .

Lacordaire at Oxford

> Lost to the Church and deaf to me, this town
> Yet wears a reverend garniture of peace.
> Set in a land of trade, like Gideon's fleece
> Bedewed where all is dry; the Pope may frown;
> But, if this city is the shrine of youth,
> How shall the Preacher lord of virgin souls,
> When by glad streams and laughing lawns he strolls,
> How can he bless them not? Yet in sad sooth,
> When I would love these English gownsmen, sighs
> Heave my frail breast, and weakness dims mine eyes.
>
> These strangers heed me not. Far off in France
> Are young men not so fair, and not so cold,
> My listeners. Were they here, their greeting glance
> Might charm me to forget that I were old.

A FRENCH ETON

OR, MIDDLE-CLASS EDUCATION AND THE STATE

I. *A Visit to Lacordaire*

A day or two after I had seen the Toulouse Lyceum, I started for Sorèze. Sorèze is a village in the department of the Tarn, a department bordering upon that in which Toulouse stands; it contains one of the most successful private schools in France, and of this school, in 1859, the celebrated Father Lacordaire was director. I left Toulouse by railway in the middle of the day; in two hours I was at Castelnaudary, an old Visigoth place, on a hill rising out of the great plain of Languedoc, with immense views towards the Pyrenees on one side and the Cevennes on the other. After rambling about the town for an hour, I started for Sorèze in a vehicle exactly like an English coach; I was outside with the driver, and the other places, inside and outside, were occupied by old pupils of the Sorèze school, who were going there for the annual *fête*, the *Speeches*, to take place the next day. They were, most of them, young men from the universities of Toulouse and Montpellier; two or three were settled in Paris, but, happening to be just then at their homes, at Béziers or Narbonne, they had come over like the rest: they seemed a good set, all of them, and their attachment to their old school and master was more according to one's notions of English school-life than French. We had to cross the *Montagne Noire*, an outlier of the Cevennes; the elevation was not great, but the air, even on the 18th of May in Languedoc, was sharp, the vast distance looked grey and chill, and the whole landscape was severe, lonely, and desolate. Sorèze is in the plain on the other side of the *Montagne Noire*, at the foot of gorges running up into the Cevennes; at the head of these gorges are the basins from which the *Canal du Midi*—the great canal uniting the Mediterranean with the Atlantic—is fed. It was seven o'clock when we drove up the street, shaded with large trees, of Sorèze; my fellow-travellers showed me the way to the school, as I was obliged to get away early the next morning, and wanted, therefore, to make my visit that evening. The school occupies the place of an old abbey, founded in 757 by Pepin the Little; for several hundred years the abbey had been in the possession of

the Dominicans, when, in Louis the Sixteenth's reign, a schoo
was attached to it. In this school the king took great interest,
and himself designed the dress for the scholars. The establishment was saved at the Revolution by the tact of the Dominican
who was then at its head; he resumed the lay dress, and returned,
in all outward appearance, to the secular life, and his school was
allowed to subsist. Under the Restoration it was one of the
most famous and most aristocratic schools in France, but it had
much declined when Lacordaire, in 1854, took charge of it.
I waited in the monastic-looking court (much of the old abbey
remains as part of the present building) while my card, with a
letter which the Papal Nuncio at Paris, to whom I had been
introduced through Sir George Bowyer's kindness,[1] had obtained
for me from the Superior of the Dominicans, was taken up to
Lacordaire; he sent down word directly that he would see me;
I was shown across the court, up an old stone staircase, into a
vast corridor; a door in this corridor was thrown open, and in a
large bare room, with no carpet or furniture of any kind, except a
small table, one or two chairs, a small book-case, a crucifix, and
some religious pictures on the walls, Lacordaire, in the dress of
his order, white-robed, hooded, and sandalled, sat before me.

The first public appearance of this remarkable man was in the
cause of education. The Charter of 1830 had promised liberty
of instruction; liberty, that is, for persons outside the official
hierarchy of public instruction to open schools. This promise M.
Guizot's celebrated school law of 1833 finally performed; but,
in the meantime, the authorities of public instruction refused to
give effect to it. Lacordaire and M. de Montalembert opened in
Paris, on the 7th of May, 1831, an independent free school, of
which they themselves were the teachers; it was closed in a
day or two by the police and its youthful conductors were tried
before the Court of Peers and fined. This was Lacordaire's first
public appearance; twenty-two years later his last sermon in
Paris was preached in the same cause; it was a sermon on behalf
of the schools of the Christian Brethren. During that space of
twenty-two years he had run a conspicuous career, but on
another field than that of education; he had become the most
renowned preacher in Europe, and he had re-established in
France, by his energy, conviction, and patience, the religious
orders banished thence since the Revolution. Through this
career I cannot now attempt to follow him; with the heart of
friendship and the eloquence of genius, M. de Montalembert

[1] [Sir George Bowyer (1811–1883), jurist, converted to Roman
Catholicism in 1850, he became a strong supporter of the Catholic
cause in England.]

has recently written its history; but I must point out two characteristics which distinguished him in it, and which created in
him the force by which, as an educator, he worked, the force by
which he most impressed and commanded the young. One of
these was his passion for firm order, for solid government. He
called our age an age "which does not know how to obey—
qui ne sait guère obéir." It is easy to see that this is not so absolutely a matter of reproach as Lacordaire made it; in an epoch of
transition society may and must say to its governors, "Govern
me according to my spirit, if I am to obey you." One cannot
doubt that Lacordaire erred in making absolute devotion to the
Church (*malheur a qui trouble l'Église!*) the watch-word of a
gifted man in our century; one cannot doubt that he erred in
affirming that "the greatest service to be rendered to Christianity in our day was to do something for the revival of the
mediæval religious orders." Still, he seized a great truth when
he proclaimed the intrinsic weakness and danger of a state of
anarchy; above all, when he applied this truth in the moral
sphere he was incontrovertible, fruitful for his nation, especially fruitful for the young. He dealt vigorously with himself,
and he told others that the first thing for them was to do the
same; he placed character above everything else. "One may
have spirit, learning, even genius," he said, "and not *character*;
for want of character our age is the age of miscarriages. Let us
form Christians in our schools, but, first of all, let us form
Christians in our own hearts; the one great thing is *to have a
life of one's own.*"

Allied to this characteristic was his other—his passion, in an
age which seems to think that progress can be achieved only by
our herding together and making a noise, for the antique discipline of retirement and silence. His plan of life for himself,
when he first took orders, was to go and be a village curé in a
remote province in France. M. de Quélen, the Archbishop of
Paris, kept him in the capital as chaplain to the Convent of the
Visitation; he had not then commenced the *conférences* which
made his reputation; he lived perfectly isolated and obscure,
and he was never so happy. "It is with delight," he wrote at
this time, "that I find my solitude deepening round me; 'one
can do nothing without solitude,' is my grand maxim. A man
is formed from within, and not from without. To withdraw
and be with oneself and with God, is the greatest strength there
can be in the world." It is impossible not to feel the serenity and
sincerity of these words. Twice he refused to edit the *Univers*;
he refused a chair in the University of Louvain. In 1836,
when his fame filled France, he disappeared for five years, and

these years he passed in silence and seclusion at Rome. He came back in 1841 a Dominican monk; again, at Notre Dame, that eloquence, that ineffable *accent*, led his countrymen and foreigners captive; he achieved his cherished purpose of re-establishing in France the religious orders. Then once more he disappeared, and after a short station at Toulouse consigned himself, for the rest of his life, to the labour and obscurity of Sorèze. "One of the great consolations of my present life," he writes from Sorèze, "is, that I have now God and the young for my sole companions." The young, with their fresh spirit, as they instinctively feel the presence of a great character, so, too, irresistibly receive an influence from souls which live habitually with God.

Lacordaire received me with great kindness. He was above the middle height, with an excellent countenance; great dignity in his look and bearing, but nothing ascetic; his manners animated, and every gesture and movement showing the orator. He asked me to dine with him the next day, and to see the school festival, the *fête des anciens élèves*; but I could not stop. Then he ordered lights, for it was growing dark, and insisted on showing me all over the place that evening. While we were waiting for lights he asked me much about Oxford; I had already heard from his old pupils that Oxford was a favourite topic with him, and that he held it up to them as a model of everything that was venerable. Lights came, and we went over the establishment; the school then contained nearly three hundred pupils—a great rise since Lacordaire first came in 1854, but not so many as the school has had in old days. It is said that Lacordaire at one time resorted so frequently to expulsion as rather to alarm people.

Sorèze, under his management, chiefly created interest by the sort of competition which it maintained with the lyceums, or State schools. A private school, in France, cannot be opened without giving notice to the public authorities; the consent of these authorities is withheld if the premises of the proposed school are improper, or if its director fails to produce a certificate of probation and a certificate of competency—that is, if he has not served for five years in a secondary school, and passed the authorised public examination for secondary teachers. Finally, the school is always subject to State-inspection, to ascertain that the pupils are properly lodged and fed, and that the teaching contains nothing contrary to public morality and to the laws; and the school may be closed by the public authorities on an inspector's report, duly verified. Still, for an establishment like the Sorèze school, the actual State-interference comes to very little; the Minister has the power of dispensing with the certificate of probation, and holy orders are accepted in the place of the certificate of competency (the examination in the seminary being more difficult than the examination for this latter). In France the State (Machiavel as we English think it), in naming certain matters as the objects of its supervision in private schools, means what it says, and does not go beyond these matters; and, for these matters, the name of a man like Lacordaire serves as a guarantee, and is readily accepted as such.

All the boys at Sorèze are boarders, and a boarder's expenses here exceed by about 8*l.* or 10*l.* a year his expenses at a lyceum. The programme of studies differs little from that of the lyceums, but the military system of these State schools Lacordaire repudiated. Instead of the vast common dormitories of the lyceums, every boy had his little cell to himself; that was, after all, as it seemed to me, the great difference. But immense stress was laid, too, upon physical education, which the lyceums are said too much to neglect. Lacordaire showed me with great satisfaction the stable, with more than twenty horses, and assured me that all the boys were taught to ride. There was the *salle d'escrime*, where they fenced, the armoury full of guns and swords, the shooting gallery, and so on. All this is in our eyes a little fantastic, and does not replace the want of cricket and football in a good field, and of freedom to roam over the country out of school-hours; in France, however, it is a good deal; and then twice a week all the boys used to turn out with Lacordaire upon the mountains, to their great enjoyment as the Sorèze people said, the Father himself being more vigorous than any of them. And the old abbey school has a small park adjoining it, with the mountains rising close behind, and it has beautiful trees in its courts, and by no means the dismal barrack-look of a lyceum. Lacordaire had a staff of more than fifty teachers and helpers, about half of these being members of his own religious order—Dominicans; all co-operated in some way or other in conducting the school. Lacordaire used never to give school-lessons himself, but scarcely a Sunday passed without his preaching in the chapel. The highest and most distinguished boys formed a body called *the Institute*, with no governing powers like those of our sixth form, but with a sort of common-room to themselves, and with the privilege of having their meals with Lacordaire and his staff. I was shown, too, a *Salle d'Illustres*, or Hall of Worthies, into which the boys are introduced on high days and holidays; we should think this fanciful, but I found it impressive. The hall is decorated with busts of the chief of the former scholars, some of them very distinguished.

Among these busts was that of Henri de Larochejacquelin [1] (who was brought up here at Sorèze), with his noble, speaking countenance, his Vendean hat, and the heart and cross on his breast. There was, besides, a theatre for public recitations. We ended with the chapel, in which we found all the school assembled; a Dominican was reading to them from the pulpit an edifying life of a scapegrace converted to seriousness by a bad accident, much better worth listening to than most sermons. When it was over, Lacordaire whispered to me to ask if I would stay for the prayers or go at once. I stayed; they were very short and simple; and I saw the boys disperse afterwards. The gaiety of the little ones and their evident fondness for the *Père* was a pretty sight. As we went out of chapel, one of them, a little fellow of ten or eleven, ran from behind us, snatched, with a laughing face, Lacordaire's hand, and kissed it; Lacordaire smiled, and patted his head. When I read the other day in M. de Montalembert's book how Lacordaire had said, shortly before his death, "I have always tried to serve God, the Church, and our Lord Jesus Christ; besides these, I have loved—oh, dearly loved!—children and young people," I thought of this incident.

Lacordaire knew absolutely nothing of our great English schools, their character, or recent history; but then no Frenchman, except a very few at Paris who know more than anybody in the world, knows anything about anything. However, I have seen few people more impressive; he was not a great modern thinker, but a great Christian orator of the fourth century, born in the nineteenth; playing his part in the nineteenth century not so successfully as he would have played it in the fourth, but still nobly. I would have given much to stay longer with him, as he kindly pressed me; I was tempted, too, by hearing that it was likely he would make a speech the next day. Never did any man so give one the sense of his being a natural orator, perfect in ease and simplicity; they told me that on Sunday, when he preached, he hardly ever went up into the pulpit, but spoke to them from his place "*sans façon.*" But I had an engagement to keep at Carcassone at a certain hour, and I was obliged to go. At nine I took leave of Lacordaire and returned to the village inn, clean, because it is frequented by the relations of pupils. There I supped with my fellow-travellers, the old scholars; charming companions they proved themselves. Late we sat, much *vin de Cahors* we drank, and great friends we became.

---

[1] [Henri du Vergier, Comte de La Rochejacquelin (1772–1794), member of an intensely royalist French family. Both he and his younger brothers were leaders in the Vendean uprising.]

Before we parted, one of them, the Béziers youth studying at Paris, with the amiability of his race assured me (God forgive him!) that he was well acquainted with my poems. By five the next morning I had started to return to Castelnaudary. Recrossing the *Montagne Noire* in the early morning was very cold work, but the view was inconceivably grand. I caught the train at Castelnaudary, and was at Carcassone by eleven; there I saw a school, and I saw the old *city* of Carcassone. I am not going to describe either the one or the other, but I cannot forbear saying, Let everybody see the *cité de Carcassone*. It is, indeed, as the antiquarians call it, the Middle Age Herculaneum. When you first get sight of the old city, which is behind the modern town—when you have got clear of the modern town, and come out upon the bridge over the Aude, and see the walled *cité* upon its hill before you—you rub your eyes and think that you are looking at a vignette in *Ivanhoe*.

II. *Education for the Middle Classes*

Such institutions are the great public schools of England and the great Universities; with these influences, and some others to which I just now pointed, they have formed the upper class of this country—a class with many faults, with many shortcomings, but imbued, on the whole, and mainly through these influences, with a high, magnanimous, governing spirit, which has long enabled them to rule, not ignobly, this great country, and which will still enable them to rule it until they are equalled or surpassed. These institutions had their origin in endowments; and the age of endowments is gone. Beautiful and venerable as are many of the aspects under which it presents itself, this form of public establishment of education, with its limitations, its preferences, its ecclesiastical character, its inflexibility, its inevitable want of foresight, proved, as time rolled on, to be subject to many inconveniences, to many abuses. On the Continent of Europe a clean sweep has in general been made of this old form of establishment, and new institutions have arisen upon its ruins. In England we have kept our great school and college foundations, introducing into their system what correctives and palliatives were absolutely necessary. Long may we so keep them! but no such palliatives or correctives will ever make the public establishment of education which sufficed for earlier ages suffice for this, nor persuade the stream of endowment, long since failing and scanty, to flow again for our present needs as it flowed in the middle ages. For public establishments modern societies have to betake themselves to the State; that is, to *themselves in their collective and corporate character*. On the Continent, society has thus betaken itself to the State for the establishment of education. The result has been the formation of institutions like the Lyceum of Toulouse; institutions capable of great improvement, by no means to be extolled absolutely, by no means to be imitated just as they are; but institutions formed by modern society, with modern modes of operation, to meet modern wants; and in some important respects, at any rate, meeting those wants. These institutions give to a whole new class—to the middle class taken at its very widest—not merely an education for whose teaching and boarding there is valid security, but something—not so much I admit, but something—of the same enlarging, liberalising sense, the sense of belonging to a great and honourable public institution, which Eton and our three or four great public schools give to our upper class only, and to a small fragment broken off from the top of our middle class. That is where England is weak, and France, Holland, and Germany are strong. Education is and must be a matter of public establishment. Other countries have replaced the defective public establishment made by the middle ages for their education with a new one, which provides for the actual condition of things. We in England keep our old public establishment for education. That is very well; but then we must not forget to supplement it where it falls short. We must not neglect to provide for the actual condition of things.

III. *Education and the State*

But there is a catchword which, I know, will be used against me. England is the country of cries and catchwords; a country where public life is so much carried on by means of parties must be. That English public life should be carried on as it is, I believe to be an excellent thing; but it is certain that all modes of life have their special inconveniences, and every sensible man, however much he may hold a particular way of life to be the best, and may be bent on adhering to it, will yet always be sedulous to guard himself against its inconveniences. One of these is, certainly, in English public life, the prevalence of cries and catchwords, which are very apt to receive an application, or to be used with an absoluteness, which do not belong to them; and then they tend to narrow our spirit and to hurt our practice. It is good to make a catchword of this sort come down from its stronghold of commonplace, to force it to move about before us in the open country, and to show us its real strength. Such a catchword as this: *The State had better leave things alone.* One constantly hears that as an absolute maxim; now, as an absolute maxim, it has really no force at all. The absolute maxims are those which carry to man's spirit their own demonstration with them; such propositions as, *Duty is the law of human life, Man is morally free*, and so on. The proposition, *The State had better leave things alone*, carries no such demonstration with it; it has, therefore, no absolute force; it merely conveys a notion which certain people have generalised from certain facts which have come under their observation, and which, by a natural vice of the human mind, they are then prone to apply absolutely. Some things the State had better leave alone, others it had better not. Is this particular thing one of these, or one of those?—that, as to any particular thing, is the right question. Now, I say, that education is one of those things which the State ought not to leave alone, which it ought to establish. It is said that in education given, wholly or in part, by the State, there is something eleemosynary, pauperising, degrading; that the self-respect and manly energy of those receiving it are likely to become impaired, as I have said that the manly energy of those who are too much made to feel their dependence upon a parental benefactor, is apt to become impaired. Well, now, is this so? Is a citizen's relation to the State that of a dependent to a parental benefactor? By no means; it is that of a member in a partnership to the whole firm. The citizens of a State, the members of a society, are really a partnership; "a partnership," as Burke nobly says, "in all science, in all art, in every virtue, in all perfection." Towards this great final design of their connexion, they apply the aids which co-operative association can give them. This applied to education will, undoubtedly, give the middling person a better schooling than his own individual unaided resources could give him; but he is not thereby humiliated, he is not degraded; he is wisely and usefully turning his associated condition to the best account. Considering his end and destination, he is bound so to turn it; certainly he has a right so to turn it. Certainly he has a right— to quote Burke again—"to a fair portion of all which society, *with all its combinations of skill and force*, can do in his favour." Men in civil society have the right—to quote Burke yet once more (one cannot quote him too often)—as "to the acquisitions of their parents and to the fruits of their own industry," so also "*to the improvement of their offspring, to instruction in life*, and to consolation in death."

How vain, then, and how meaningless, to tell a man who, for

the instruction of his offspring, receives aid from the State, that he is humiliated! Humiliated by receiving help for himself as an individual from himself in his corporate and associated capacity! help to which his own money, as a tax-payer, contributes, and for which, as a result of the joint energy and intelligence of the whole community in employing its powers, he himself deserves some of the praise! He is no more humiliated than one is humiliated by being on the foundation of the Charterhouse or of Winchester, or by holding a scholarship or fellowship at Oxford or Cambridge. Nay (if there be any humiliation here), not so much. For the amount of benefaction, the amount of obligation, the amount, therefore, I suppose, of humiliation, diminishes as the public character of the aid becomes more undeniable. He is no more humiliated than when he crosses London Bridge, or walks down the King's Road, or visits the British Museum. But it is one of the extraordinary inconsistencies of some English people in this matter, that they keep all their cry of humiliation and degradation for help which the State offers. A man is not pauperised, is not degraded, is not oppressively obliged, by taking aid for his son's schooling from Mr. Woodard's [1] subscribers, or from the next squire, or from the next rector, or from the next ironmonger, or from the next druggist; he is only pauperised when he takes it from the State, when he helps to give it himself!

IV. *Ferment and Stir in the Middle Classes*

Two things must, I think, strike any one who attentively regards the English middle class at this moment. One is the intellectual ferment which is taking place, or rather, which is beginning to take place, amongst them. It is only in its commencement as yet; but it shows itself at a number of points, and bids fair to become a great power. The importance of a change, placing in the great middle class the centre of the intellectual life of this country, can hardly be over-estimated. I have been reproved for saying that the culture and intellectual life of our highest class seem to me to have somewhat flagged since the last century. That is my opinion, indeed, and all that I see and hear strengthens rather than shakes it. The culture of this class is

---

[1] [Nathaniel Woodard (1811–1891), educational reformer who devoted himself to putting an education on public-school lines within the means of the middle classes. Founder of the Woodard Schools, Lancing, Hurstpierpoint, Denstone and others.]

not what it used to be. Their value for high culture, their belief in its importance, is not what it used to be. One may see it in the public schools, one may see it in the universities. Whence come the deadness, the want of intellectual life, the poverty of acquirement after years of schooling, which the Commissioners, in their remarkable and interesting report, show us so prevalent in our most distinguished public schools? What gives to play and amusement, both there and at the universities, their present overweening importance, so that home critics cry out: "The real studies of Oxford are its games," and foreign critics cry out: "At Oxford the student is still the mere school-boy"? The most experienced and acute of Oxford heads of houses told me himself, that when he spoke to an undergraduate the other day about trying for some distinguished scholarship, the answer he got was: "Oh, the men from the great schools don't care for those things now; the men who care about them are the men from Marlborough, Cheltenham, and the second-rate schools." Whence, I say, does this slackness, this sleep of the mind, come, except from a torpor of intellectual life, a dearth of ideas, an indifference to fine culture or disbelief in its necessity, spreading through the bulk of our highest class, and influencing its rising generation? People talk as if the culture of this class had only changed; the Greek and Roman classics, they say, are no longer in vogue as they were in Lord Chesterfield's time. Well, if this class had only gone from one source of high culture to another; if only, instead of reading Homer and Cicero, it now read Goethe and Montesquieu;—but it does not; it reads the *Times* and the *Agricultural Journal*. And it devotes itself to practical life. And it amuses itself. It is not its rising generation only which loves play; never in all its history has our whole highest class shown such zeal for enjoying life, for amusing itself. It would be absurd to make this a matter of reproach against it. The triumphs of material progress multiply the means of material enjoyment; they attract all classes, more and more, to taste of this enjoyment; on the highest class, which possesses in the amplest measure these means, they must needs exercise this attraction very powerfully. But every thoughtful observer can perceive that the ardour for amusement and enjoyment, often educative and quickening to a toil-numbed working class or a strait-laced middle class, whose great want is expansion, tends to become enervative and weakening to an aristocratic class—a class which must rule by superiority of all kinds, superiority not to be won without contention of spirit and a certain severity. I think, therefore, both that the culture of our highest class has declined, and that this declension, though natural and venial, impairs its power.

Yet in this vigorous country everything has a wonderful ability for self-restoration, and he would be a bold prophet who should deny that the culture of our highest class may recover itself. But however this may be, there is no doubt that a liberal culture, a fulness of intellectual life, in the middle class, is a far more important matter, a far more efficacious stimulant to national progress, than the same powers in an aristocratic class. Whatever may be its culture, an aristocratic class will always have at bottom, like the young man in Scripture with great possessions, an inaptitude for ideas; but, besides this, high culture or ardent intelligence, pervading a large body of the community, acquire a breadth of basis, a sum of force, an energy of central heat for radiating further, which they can never possess when they pervade a small upper class only. It is when such a broad basis is obtained, that individual genius gets its proper nutriment, and is animated to put forth its best powers; this is the secret of rich and beautiful epochs in national life; the epoch of Pericles in Greece, the epoch of Michael Angelo in Italy, the epoch of Shakspeare in England. Our actual middle class has not yet, certainly, the fine culture, or the living intelligence, which quickened great bodies of men at these epochs; but it has the forerunner, the preparer, the indispensable initiator; it is traversed by a strong intellectual ferment. It is the middle class which has real mental ardour, real curiosity; it is the middle class which is the great reader; that immense literature of the day which we see surging up all round us,— literature the absolute value of which it is almost impossible to rate too humbly, literature hardly a word of which will reach, or deserves to reach, the future,—it is the middle class which calls it forth, and its evocation is at least a sign of a widespread mental movement in that class. Will this movement go on and become fruitful: will it conduct the middle class to a high and commanding pitch of culture and intelligence? That depends on the sensibility which the middle class has for *perfection*; that depends on its power to *transform itself*.

And it is not yet manifest how far it possesses this power. For—and here I pass to the second of those two things which particularly, I have said, strike any one who observes the English middle class just now—in its public action this class has hitherto shown only the power and disposition to *affirm itself*, not at all the power and disposition to *transform itself*. That, indeed, is one of the deep-seated instincts of human nature, but of vulgar human nature—of human nature not high-souled and aspiring after perfection—to esteem itself for what it is, to try to establish itself just as it is, to try even to impose itself with its stock of habitudes, pettinesses, narrownesses, shortcomings of every kind, on the rest of the world as a conquering power. But nothing has really a right to be satisfied with itself, to be and remain itself, except that which has reached perfection; and nothing has the right to impose itself on the rest of the world as a conquering force, except that which is of higher perfection than the rest of the world. And such is the fundamental constitution of human affairs, that the measure of right proves also, in the end, the measure of power. Before the English middle class can have the right or the power to assert itself absolutely, it must have greatly perfected itself. It has been jokingly said of this class, that all which the best of it cared for was summed up in this alliterative phrase—*Business and Bethels*: and that all which the rest of it cared for was the *Business* without the *Bethels*. No such jocose and slighting words can convey any true sense of what the religion of the English middle class has really been to it; what a source of vitality, energy, and persistent vigour. "They who wait on the Lord," says Isaiah, in words not less true than they are noble, "*shall renew their strength*;" and the English middle class owes to its religion not only comfort in the past, but also a vast latent force of unworn life and strength for future progress. But the Puritanism of the English middle class, which has been so great an element of strength to them, has by no means brought them to perfection; nay, by the rigid mould in which it has cast their spirit, it has kept them back from perfection. The most that can be said of it is, that it has supplied a stable basis on which to build perfection; it has given them character, though it has not given them culture. But it is in making endless additions to itself, in the endless expansion of its powers, in endless growth in wisdom and beauty, that the spirit of the human race finds its ideal; to reach this ideal, culture is an indispensable aid, and that is the true value of culture. The life of aristocracies, with its large and free use of the world, its conversance with great affairs, its exemption from sordid cares, its liberation from the humdrum provincial round, its external splendour and refinement, is a kind of outward shadow of this ideal, a prophecy of it; and there lies the secret of the charm of aristocracies, and of their power over men's minds. In a country like England, the middle class, with its industry and its Puritanism, and nothing more, will never be able to make way beyond a certain point, will never be able to divide power with the aristocratic class, much less to win for itself a preponderance of power. While it only tries to affirm its actual self, to impose its actual self, it has no charm for men's minds, and can achieve no great triumphs. And this is all it attempts at present. The Conservative reaction, of which we hear so much just now, is in great part merely a general indisposition to let the middle-class spirit, working by its old methods, and having only its old self to give us, establish itself at all points and become master of the situation. Particularly on Church questions is this true. In this sphere of religion, where feeling and beauty are so all-important, we shrink from giving to the middle-class spirit, limited as we see it, with its sectarianism, its under-culture, its intolerance, its bitterness, its unloveliness, too much its own way. Before we give it quite its own way, we insist on its making itself into something larger, newer, more fruitful. This is what the recent Church-Rate divisions really mean, and the lovers of perfection, therefore, may accept them without displeasure. They are the voice of the nation crying to the *untransformed* middle class (if it will receive it) with a voice of thunder: "The future is not yours!"

· · · · · · · · · ·

In the Crusade of Peter the Hermit, where the hosts that marched were not filled after the usual composition of armies, but contained along with the fighters whole families of people— old men, women, and children, swept by the universal torrent of enthusiasm towards the Holy Land—the marches, as might have been expected, were tedious and painful. Long before Asia was reached, long before even Europe was half traversed, the little children in that travelling multitude began to fancy, with a natural impatience, that their journey must surely be drawing to an end; and every evening, as they came in sight of some town which was the destination of that day's march, they cried out eagerly to those who were with them, "*Is this Jerusalem?*" No, poor children, not this town, nor the next, nor yet the next, is Jerusalem; Jerusalem is far off, and it needs time, and strength, and much endurance to reach it. Seas and mountains, labour and peril, hunger and thirst, disease and death, are between Jerusalem and you.

So, when one marks the ferment and stir of life in the middle class at this moment, and sees this class impelled to take possession of the world, and to assert itself and its own actual spirit absolutely, one is disposed to exclaim to it, "*Jerusalem is not yet.*" Your present spirit is not Jerusalem, is not the goal you have to reach, the place you may be satisfied in. And when one says this, they sometimes fancy that one has the same object as others who say the same to them; that one means that they are to yield themselves to be moulded by some existing force, their rival; that one wishes Nonconformity to take the law from actual Anglicanism, and the middle class from the present governing class; that one thinks Anglicanism Jerusalem, and the English aristocratic class Jerusalem.

I do not mean, or wish, or think this, though many, no doubt, do. It is not easy for a reflecting man, who had studied its origin, to feel any vehement enthusiasm for Anglicanism; Henry the Eighth and his parliaments have taken care of that. One may esteem it as a beneficent social and civilising agent. One may have an affection for it from life-long associations, and for the sake of much that is venerable and interesting which it has inherited from antiquity. One may cherish gratitude to it—and here, I think, Mr. Goldwin Smith,[1] who fights against it the battle of the Nonconformists with so much force and so much ability, is a little ungrateful—for the shelter and basis for culture which this, like other great nationally established forms of religion, affords; those who are born in them can get forward on their road, instead of always eyeing the ground on which they stand and disputing about it. But actual Anglicanism is certainly not Jerusalem, and I should be sorry to think it the end which Nonconformity and the middle class are to reach. The actual governing class, again, the English aristocratic class (in the widest sense of the word *aristocratic*)—I cannot wish that the rest of the nation, the new and growing part of the nation, should be transformed in spirit exactly according, to the image of that class. The merits and services of that class no one rates higher than I do; no one appreciates higher than I do the value of the relative standard of elevation, refinement and grandeur, which they have exhibited; no one would more strenuously oppose the relinquishing of this for any lower standard. But I cannot hide from myself that while modern societies increasingly tend to find their best life in a free and heightened spiritual and intellectual activity, to this tendency aristocracies offer at least a strong passive resistance, by their secular prejudices, their incurable dearth of ideas. In modern, rich, and industrial societies, they tend to misplace the ideal for the classes below them; the immaterial chivalrous ideal of high descent and honour is, by the very nature of the case, of force only for aristocracies themselves; the immaterial modern ideal of spiritual and intellectual perfection through culture, they have not to communicate. What they can and do communicate

---

[1] [Goldwin Smith (1823–1910), Liberal controversialist, reformer and philanthropist. Regius professor of history at Oxford (1858–66): professor of history at Cornell University 1868, and thenceforward resided in America and Canada.]

is the material ideal of splendour of wealth, and weight of property. And this ideal is the ideal truly operative upon our middle classes at this moment. To be as rich as they can, that they may reach the splendour of wealth and weight of property, and, with time, the importance of the actual heads of society, is their ambition. I do not blame them, or the class from which they get their ideal; all I say is, that the good ideal for humanity, the true Jerusalem, is an ideal more spiritual than brilliant wealth and boundless property, an ideal in which more can participate. The beloved friends of humanity have been those who made it feel its ideal to be in the things of the mind and spirit, to be in an internal condition separable from wealth and accessible to all—men like St. Francis, the ardent bridegroom of poverty; men like the great personages of antiquity, almost all of them, as Lacordaire was so fond of saying, poor. Therefore, that the middle class should simply take its ideal from the aristocratic class, I do not wish. That the aristocratic class should be able absolutely to assert itself and its own spirit, is not my desire. No, no; they are not Jerusalem.

The truth is, the English spirit has to accomplish an immense evolution; nor, as that spirit at this moment presents itself in any class or description amongst us, can one be perfectly satisfied with it, can one wish it to prevail just as it is.

But in a transformed middle class, in a middle class raised to a higher and more genial culture, we may find, not perhaps Jerusalem, but, I am sure, a notable stage towards it. In that great class, strong by its numbers, its energy, its industry, strong by its freedom from frivolity, not by any law of nature prone to immobility of mind, actually at this moment agitated by a spreading ferment of mind, in that class, liberalised by an ampler culture, admitted to a wider sphere of thought, living by larger ideas, with its provincialism dissipated, its intolerance cured, its pettinesses purged away,—what a power there will be, what an element of new life for England! Then let the middle class rule, then let it affirm its own spirit, when it has thus perfected itself.

And I cannot see any means so direct and powerful for developing this great and beneficent power as the public establishment of schools for the middle class. By public establishment they may be made cheap and accessible to all. By public establishment they may give securities for the culture offered in them being really good and sound, and the best that our time knows. By public establishment they may communicate to those reared in them the sense of being brought in contact with their country, with the national life, with the life of the world;

and they will expand and dignify their spirits by communicating this sense to them. I can see no other mode of institution which will offer the same advantages in the same degree.

V. *Conclusion*

I hope the middle class will not much longer delay to take a step on which its future value and dignity and influence so much depend. By taking this step they will indirectly confer a great boon upon the lower class also. This obscure embryo, only just beginning to move, travailing in labour and darkness, so much left out of account when we celebrate the glories of our Atlantis, now and then, by so mournful a glimpse, showing itself to us in Lambeth, or Spitalfields, or Dorsetshire; this immense working class, now so without a practicable passage to all the joy and beauty of life, for whom in an aristocratic class, which is unattainable by them, there is no possible ideal, for whom in a middle class, narrow, ungenial, and unattractive, there is no adequate ideal, will have, in a cultured, liberalised, ennobled, transformed middle class, a point towards which it may hopefully work, a goal towards which it may with joy direct its aspirations.

Children of the future, whose day has not yet dawned, you, when that day arrives, will hardly believe what obstructions were long suffered to prevent its coming! You who, with all your faults, have neither the aridity of aristocracies, nor the narrow-mindedness of middle classes, you, whose power of simple enthusiasm is your great gift, will not comprehend how progress towards man's best perfection—the adorning and ennobling of his spirit—should have been reluctantly undertaken; how it should have been for years and years retarded by barren commonplaces, by worn-out clap-traps. You will wonder at the labour of its friends in proving the self-proving; you will know nothing of the doubts, the fears, the prejudices they had to dispel; nothing of the outcry they had to encounter; of the fierce protestations of life from policies which were dead and did not know it, and the shrill querulous upbraiding from publicists in their dotage. But you, in your turn, with difficulties of your own, will then be mounting some new step in the arduous ladder whereby man climbs towards his perfection; towards that unattainable but irresistible lode-star, gazed after with earnest longing, and invoked with bitter tears; the longing of thousands of hearts, the tears of many generations.

ESSAYS IN CRITICISM

1865

Essays in Criticism. By Matthew Arnold, Professor of Poetry in the University of Oxford. London and Cambridge. Macmillan and Co. 1865.

Second edition 1869.
Third edition, revised and enlarged, 1875.

ALL these essays had previously appeared in periodical form. In the second edition the Preface is condensed, the essay on Spinoza enlarged, and its title changed. In the third edition an additional essay, *A Persian Passion Play*, was added.

The text used is that of the second edition. Arnold's footnotes are mostly omitted.

The following essays are omitted from the present selection: *Maurice de Guérin, Eugénie de Guérin, Spinoza.*

ESSAYS IN CRITICISM

Preface

SEVERAL of the Essays which are here collected and reprinted had the good or the bad fortune to be much criticised at the time of their first appearance. I am not now going to inflict upon the reader a reply to those criticisms; for one or two explanations which are desirable, I shall elsewhere, perhaps, be able some day to find an opportunity; but, indeed it is not in my nature,—some of my critics would rather say, not in my power, —to dispute on behalf of any opinion, even my own, very obstinately. To try and approach truth on one side after another, not to strive or cry, nor to persist in pressing forward, on any one side, with violence and self-will—it is only thus, it seems to me, that mortals may hope to gain any vision of the mysterious Goddess, whom we shall never see except in outline, but only thus even in outline. He who will do nothing but fight impetuously towards her on his own, one, favourite, particular line, is inevitably destined to run his head into the folds of the black robe in which she is wrapped.

So it is not to reply to my critics that I write this preface, but to prevent a misunderstanding, of which certain phrases that some of them use make me apprehensive. Mr. Wright,[1] one of the many translators of Homer, has published a letter to the Dean of Canterbury, complaining of some remarks of mine, uttered now a long while ago, on his version of the *Iliad*. One cannot be always studying one's own works, and I was really under the impression, till I saw Mr. Wright's complaint, that I had spoken of him with all respect. The reader may judge of my astonishment, therefore, at finding, from Mr. Wright's pamphlet, that I had "declared with much solemnity that there is not any proper reason for his existing." That I never said; but, on looking back at my Lectures on translating Homer, I find that I did say, not that Mr. Wright, but that Mr. Wright's version of the *Iliad*, repeating in the main the merits and defects of Cowper's version, as Mr. Sotheby's repeated those of Pope's version, had, if I might be pardoned for saying so, no proper reason for existing. Elsewhere I expressly spoke of the merit of

---

[1] [See note p. 287.]

his version; but I confess that the phrase, qualified as I have shown, about its want of a proper reason for existing, I used. Well, the phrase had, perhaps, too much vivacity; we have all of us a right to exist, we and our works; an unpopular author should be the last person to call in question this right. So I gladly withdraw the offending phrase, and I am sorry for having used it; Mr. Wright, however, would perhaps be more indulgent to my vivacity, if he considered that we are none of us likely to be lively much longer. My vivacity is but the last sparkle of flame before we are all in the dark, the last glimpse of colour before we all go into drab,—the drab of the earnest, prosaic, practical, austerely literal future. Yes, the world will soon be the Philistines'! and then, with every voice, not of thunder, silenced, and the whole earth filled and ennobled every morning by the magnificent roaring of the young lions of the *Daily Telegraph*, we shall all yawn in one another's faces with the dismallest, the most unimpeachable gravity.

But I return to my design in writing this Preface. That design was, after apologising to Mr. Wright for my vivacity of five years ago, to beg him and others to let me bear my own burdens, without saddling the great and famous University to which I have the honour to belong with any portion of them. What I mean to deprecate is such phrases as, "his professorial assault," "his assertions issued *ex cathedrâ*," "the sanction of his name as the representative of poetry," and so on. Proud as I am of my connection with the University of Oxford, I can truly say, that knowing how unpopular a task one is undertaking when one tries to pull out a few more stops in that powerful but at present somewhat narrow-toned organ, the modern Englishman, I have always sought to stand by myself, and to compromise others as little as possible. Besides this, my native modesty is such, that I have always been shy of assuming the honourable style of Professor, because this is a title I share with so many distinguished men,—Professor Pepper, Professor Anderson, Professor Frickel, and others,[1]—who adorn it, I feel, much more than I do.

However, it is not merely out of modesty that I prefer to stand alone, and to concentrate on myself, as a plain citizen of the republic of letters, and not as an office-bearer in a hierarchy, the whole responsibility for all I write; it is much more out of

[1] [The references are ironical. Pepper was lecturer at the Royal Polytechnic and famed for his exhibition of the optical illusion known as 'Pepper's Ghost'. Anderson was a popular actor and conjurer, known as 'The Wizard of the North'. Frickel I am unable to trace.]

genuine devotion to the University of Oxford, for which I feel, and always must feel, the fondest, the most reverential attachment. In an epoch of dissolution and transformation, such as that on which we are now entered, habits, ties, and associations are inevitably broken up, the action of individuals becomes more distinct, the shortcomings, errors, heats, disputes, which necessarily attend individual action, are brought into greater prominence. Who would not gladly keep clear, from all these passing clouds, an august institution which was there before they arose, and which will be there when they have blown over?

It is true, the *Saturday Review* maintains that our epoch of transformation is finished; that we have found our philosophy; that the British nation has searched all anchorages for the spirit, and has finally anchored itself, in the fulness of perfected knowledge, on Benthamism. This idea at first made a great impression on me; not only because it is so consoling in itself, but also because it explained a phenomenon which in the summer of last year had, I confess, a good deal troubled me. At that time my avocations led me travel almost daily on one of the Great Eastern Lines,—the Woodford Branch. Every one knows that the murderer, Müller, perpetrated his detestable act on the North London Railway, close by. The English middle-class, of which I am myself a feeble unit, travel on the Woodford Branch in large numbers. Well, the demoralisation of our class,—the class which (the newspapers are constantly saying it, so I may repeat it without vanity) has done all the great things which have ever been done in England,—the demoralisation, I say, of our class, caused by the Bow tragedy, was something bewildering. Myself a transcendentalist (as the *Saturday Review* knows), I escaped the infection; and, day after day, I used to ply my agitated fellow-travellers with all the consolations which my transcendentalism would naturally suggest to me. I reminded them how Cæsar refused to take precautions against assassination, because life was not worth having at the price of an ignoble solicitude for it. I reminded them what insignificant atoms we all are in the life of the world. "Suppose the worst to happen," I said, addressing a portly jeweller from Cheapside; "suppose even yourself to be the victim; *il n'y a pas d'homme nécessaire.* We should miss you for a day or two upon the Woodford Branch; but the great mundane movement would still go on, the gravel walks of your villa would still be rolled, dividends would still be paid at the Bank, omnibuses would still run, there would still be the old crush at the corner of Fenchurch Street." All was of no avail. Nothing could moderate, in the bosom of the great English middle-class, their passionate, absorbing, almost blood-thirsty clinging to life. At the moment I thought this over-concern a little unworthy; but the *Saturday Review* suggests a touching explanation of it. What I took for the ignoble clinging to life of a comfortable worldling, was, perhaps, only the ardent longing of a faithful Benthamite, traversing an age still dimmed by the last mists of transcendentalism, to be spared long enough to see his religion in the full and final blaze of its triumph. This respectable man, whom I imagined to be going up to London to serve his shop, or to buy shares, or to attend an Exeter Hall meeting, or to assist at the deliberations of the Marylebone Vestry, was even, perhaps, in real truth, on a pious pilgrimage, to obtain from Mr. Bentham's executors a secret bone of his great, dissected master.

And yet, after all, I cannot but think that the *Saturday Review* has here, for once, fallen a victim to an idea,—a beautiful but deluding idea,—and that the British nation has not yet, so entirely as the reviewer seems to imagine, found the last word of its philosophy. No, we are all seekers still! seekers often make mistakes, and I wish mine to redound to my own discredit only, and not to touch Oxford. Beautiful city! so venerable, so lovely, so unravaged by the fierce intellectual life of our century, so serene!

"There are our young barbarians, all at play!"

And yet, steeped in sentiment as she lies, spreading her gardens to the moonlight, and whispering from her towers the last enchantments of the Middle Age, who will deny that Oxford, by her ineffable charm, keeps ever calling us nearer to the true goal of all of us, to the ideal, to perfection,—to beauty, in a word, which is only truth seen from another side?—nearer, perhaps, than all the science of Tübingen. Adorable dreamer, whose heart has been so romantic! who hast given thyself so prodigally, given thyself to sides and to heroes not mine, only never to the Philistines! home of lost causes, and forsaken beliefs, and unpopular names, and impossible loyalties! what example could ever so inspire us to keep down the Philistine in ourselves, what teacher could ever so save us from that bondage to which we are all prone, that bondage which Goethe, in his incomparable lines on the death of Schiller, makes it his friend's highest praise (and nobly did Schiller deserve the praise) to have left miles out of sight behind him;—the bondage of "*was uns alle bändigt, DAS GEMEINE!*" She will forgive me, even if I have unwittingly drawn upon her a shot or two aimed at her unworthy son; for she is generous, and the cause in which I fight is, after all, hers. Apparitions of a day, what is our puny

warfare against the Philistines, compared with the warfare
which this queen of romance has been waging against them for
centuries, and will wage after we are gone? [1]

The Function of Criticism at the Present Time

MANY objections have been made to a proposition which, in
some remarks of mine on translating Homer, I ventured to put
forth; a proposition about criticism, and its importance at
the present day. I said: "Of the literature of France and Germany, as of the intellect of Europe in general, the main effort,
for now many years, has been a critical effort; the endeavour, in
all branches of knowledge, theology, philosophy, history, art,
science, to see the object as in itself it really is." I added, that
owing to the operation in English literature of certain causes,
"almost the last thing for which one would come to English
literature is just that very thing which now Europe most
desires,—criticism;" and that the power and value of English
literature was thereby impaired. More than one rejoinder
declared that the importance I here assigned to criticism was
excessive, and asserted the inherent superiority of the creative
effort of the human spirit over its critical effort. And the other
day, having been led by a Mr. Shairp's excellent notice of
Wordsworth to turn again to his biography, I found, in the
words of this great man, whom I, for one, must always listen to
with the profoundest respect, a sentence passed on the critic's
business, which seems to justify every possible disparagement
of it. Wordsworth says in one of his letters:—

"The writers in these publications" (the Reviews), "while
they prosecute their inglorious employment, can not be supposed to be in a state of mind very favourable for being affected
by the finer influences of a thing so pure as genuine poetry."

And a trustworthy reporter of his conversation quotes a
more elaborate judgment to the same effect:—

"Wordsworth holds the critical power very low, infinitely
lower than the inventive; and he said to-day that if the quantity
of time consumed in writing critiques on the works of others
were given to original composition, of whatever kind it might
be, it would be much better employed; it would make a man
find out sooner his own level, and it would do infinitely less

---

[1] [In *Culture and its Enemies*, his last lecture as Professor of Poetry
which was delivered in the summer of 1867, Arnold said: "Perhaps
none but Oxford men can know how much truth there really is in the
praise I have given to Oxford for her sentiment."]

mischief. A false or malicious criticism may do much injury to the minds of others, a stupid invention, either in prose or verse, is quite harmless."

It is almost too much to expect of poor human nature, that a man capable of producing some effect in one line of literature, should, for the greater good of society, voluntarily doom himself to impotence and obscurity in another. Still less is this to be expected from men addicted to the composition of the "false or malicious criticism" of which Wordsworth speaks. However, everybody would admit that a false or malicious criticism had better never have been written. Everybody, too, would be willing to admit, as a general proposition, that the critical faculty is lower than the inventive. But is it true that criticism is really, in itself, a baneful and injurious employment; is it true that all time given to writing critiques on the works of others would be much better employed if it were given to original composition, of whatever kind this may be? Is it true that Johnson had better have gone on producing more *Irenes* instead of writing his *Lives of the Poets*; nay, is it certain that Wordsworth himself was better employed in making his Ecclesiastical Sonnets than when he made his celebrated Preface, so full of criticism, and criticism of the works of others? Wordsworth was himself a great critic, and it is to be sincerely regretted that he has not left us more criticism; Goethe was one of the greatest of critics, and we may sincerely congratulate ourselves that he has left us so much criticism. Without wasting time over the exaggeration which Wordsworth's judgment on criticism clearly contains, or over an attempt to trace the causes,—not difficult, I think, to be traced,—which may have led Wordsworth to this exaggeration, a critic may with advantage seize an occasion for trying his own conscience, and for asking himself of what real service at any given moment the practice of criticism either is or may be made to his own mind and spirit, and to the minds and spirits of others.

The critical power is of lower rank than the creative. True; but in assenting to this proposition, one or two things are to be kept in mind. It is undeniable that the exercise of a creative power, that a free creative activity, is the highest function of man; it is proved to be so by man's finding in it his true happiness. But it is undeniable, also, that men may have the sense of exercising this free creative activity in other ways than in producing great works of literature or art; if it were not so, all but a very few men would be shut out from the true happiness of all men. They may have it in well-doing, they may have it in learning, they may have it even in criticising. This is one thing to be kept in mind. Another is, that the exercise of the creative power in the production of great works of literature or art, however high this exercise of it may rank, is not at all epochs and under all conditions possible; and that therefore labour may be vainly spent in attempting it, which might with more fruit be used in preparing for it, in rendering it possible. This creative power works with elements, with materials; what if it has not those materials, those elements, ready for its use? In that case it must surely wait till they are ready. Now, in literature,—I will limit myself to literature, for it is about literature that the question arises,—the elements with which the creative power works are ideas; the best ideas on every matter which literature touches, current at the time. At any rate we may lay it down as certain that in modern literature no manifestation of the creative power not working with these can be very important or fruitful. And I say *current* at the time, not merely accessible at the time; for creative literary genius does not principally show itself in discovering new ideas, that is rather the business of the philosopher. The grand work of literary genius is a work of synthesis and exposition, not of analysis and discovery; its gift lies in the faculty of being happily inspired by a certain intellectual and spiritual atmosphere, by a certain order of ideas, when it finds itself in them; of dealing divinely with these ideas, presenting them in the most effective and attractive combinations,—making beautiful works with them, in short. But it must have the atmosphere, it must find itself amidst the order of ideas, in order to work freely; and these it is not so easy to command. This is why great creative epochs in literature are so rare, this is why there is so much that is unsatisfactory in the productions of many men of real genius; because, for the creation of a master-work of literature two powers must concur, the power of the man and the power of the moment, and the man is not enough without the moment; the creative power has, for its happy exercise, appointed elements, and those elements are not in its own control.

Nay, they are more within the control of the critical power. It is the business of the critical power, as I said in the words already quoted, "in all branches of knowledge, theology, philosophy, history, art, science, to see the object as in itself it really is." Thus it tends, at last, to make an intellectual situation of which the creative power can profitably avail itself. It tends to establish an order of ideas, if not absolutely true, yet true by comparison with that which it displaces; to make the best ideas prevail. Presently these new ideas reach society, the touch of truth is the touch of life, and there is a stir and growth

M

everywhere; out of this stir and growth come the creative epochs of literature.

Or, to narrow our range, and quit these considerations of the general march of genius and of society,—considerations which are apt to become too abstract and impalpable,—every one can see that a poet, for instance, ought to know life and the world before dealing with them in poetry; and life and the world being in modern times very complex things, the creation of a modern poet, to be worth much, implies a great critical effort behind it; else it must be a comparatively poor, barren, and short-lived affair. This is why Byron's poetry had so little endurance in it, and Goethe's so much; both Byron and Goethe had a great productive power, but Goethe's was nourished by a great critical effort providing the true materials for it, and Byron's was not; Goethe knew life and the world, the poet's necessary subjects, much more comprehensively and thoroughly than Byron. He knew a great deal more of them, and he knew them much more as they really are.

It has long seemed to me that the burst of creative activity in out literature, through the first quarter of this century, had about it in fact something premature; and that from this cause its productions are doomed, most of them, in spite of the sanguine hopes which accompanied and do still accompany them, to prove hardly more lasting than the productions of far less splendid epochs. And this prematureness comes from its having proceeded without having its proper data, without sufficient materials to work with. In other words, the English poetry of the first quarter of this century, with plenty of energy, plenty of creative force, did not know enough. This makes Byron so empty of matter, Shelley so incoherent, Wordsworth even, profound as he is, yet so wanting in completeness and variety. Wordsworth cared little for books, and disparaged Goethe. I admire Wordsworth, as he is, so much that I cannot wish him different; and it is vain, no doubt, to imagine such a man different from what he is, to suppose that he *could* have been different. But surely the one thing wanting to make Wordsworth an even greater poet than he is,—his thought richer, and his influence of wider application,—was that he should have read more books, among them, no doubt, those of that Goethe whom he disparaged without reading him.

But to speak of books and reading may easily lead to a mis-understanding here. It was not really books and reading that lacked to our poetry at this epoch; Shelley had plenty of reading, Coleridge had immense reading. Pindar and Sophocles—as we all say so glibly, and often with so little discernment of the real import of what we are saying—had not many books; Shakspeare was no deep reader. True; but in the Greece of Pindar and Sophocles, in the England of Shakspeare, the poet lived in a current of ideas in the highest degree animating and nourishing to the creative power; society was, in the fullest measure, permeated by fresh thought, intelligent and alive. And this state of things is the true basis for the creative power's exercise, in this it finds its data, its materials, truly ready for its hand; all the books and reading in the world are only valuable as they are helps to this. Even when this does not actually exist, books and reading may enable a man to construct a kind of semblance of it in his own mind, a world of knowledge and intelligence in which he may live and work. This is by no means an equivalent to the artist for the nationally diffused life and thought of the epochs of Sophocles or Shakspeare; but, besides that it may be a means of preparation for such epochs, it does really constitute, if many share in it, a quickening and sustaining atmosphere of great value. Such an atmosphere the many-sided learning and the long and widely-combined critical effort of Germany formed for Goethe, when he lived and worked. There was no national glow of life and thought there as in the Athens of Pericles or the England of Elizabeth. That was the poet's weakness. But there was a sort of equivalent for it in the complete culture and unfettered thinking of a large body of Germans. That was his strength. In the England of the first quarter of this century there was neither a national glow of life and thought, such as we had in the age of Elizabeth, nor yet a culture and a force of learning and criticism such as were to be found in Germany. Therefore the creative power of poetry wanted, for success in the highest sense, materials and a basis; a thorough interpretation of the world was necessarily denied to it.

At first sight it seems strange that out of the immense stir of the French Revolution and its age should not have come a crop of works of genius equal to that which came out of the stir of the great productive time of Greece, or out of that of the Renascence, with its powerful episode the Reformation. But the truth is that the stir of the French Revolution took a character which essentially distinguished it from such movements as these. These were, in the main, disinterestedly intellectual and spiritual movements; movements in which the human spirit looked for its satisfaction in itself and in the increased play of its own activity. The French Revolution took a political, practical character. The movement which went on in France under the old *régime*, from 1700 to 1789, was far more really akin than that of the Revolution itself to the movement of the Renascence; the France of Voltaire and Rousseau told far more powerfully upon the mind of Europe than the France of the Revolution. Goethe reproached this last expressly with having "thrown quiet culture back." Nay, and the true key to how much in our Byron, even in our Wordsworth, is this!—that they had their source in a great movement of feeling, not in a great movement of mind. The French Revolution, however,—that object of so much blind love and so much blind hatred,—found undoubtedly its motive-power in the intelligence of men, and not in their practical sense; that is what distinguishes it from the English Revolution of Charles the First's time. This is what makes it a more spiritual event than our Revolution, an event of much more powerful and world-wide interest, though practically less successful; it appeals to an order of ideas which are universal, certain, permanent. 1789 asked of a thing, Is it rational? 1642 asked of a thing, Is it legal? or, when it went furthest, Is it according to conscience? This is the English fashion, a fashion to be treated, within its own sphere, with the highest respect; for its success, within its own sphere, has been prodigious. But what is law in one place is not law in another; what is law here to-day is not law even here to-morrow; and as for conscience, what is binding on one man's conscience is not binding on another's. The old woman who threw her stool at the head of the surpliced minister in St. Giles's Church at Edinburgh obeyed an impulse to which millions of the human race may be permitted to remain strangers. But the prescriptions of reason are absolute, unchanging, of universal validity; *to count by tens is the easiest way of counting*—that is a proposition of which every one, from here to the Antipodes, feels the force; at least I should say so if we did not live in a country where it is not impossible that any morning we may find a letter in the *Times* declaring that a decimal coinage is an absurdity. That a whole nation should have been penetrated with an enthusiasm for pure reason, and with an ardent zeal for making its prescriptions triumph, is a very remarkable thing, when we consider how little of mind, or anything so worthy and quickening as mind, comes into the motives which alone, in general, impel great masses of men. In spite of the extravagant direction given to this enthusiasm, in spite of the crimes and follies in which it lost itself, the French Revolution derives from the force, truth, and universality of the ideas which it took for its law, and from the passion with which it could inspire a multitude for these ideas, a unique and still living power; it is—it will probably long remain —the greatest, the most animating event in history. And as no sincere passion for the things of the mind, even though it turn out in many respects an unfortunate passion, is ever quite thrown away and quite barren of good, France has reaped from hers one fruit—the natural and legitimate fruit, though not precisely the grand fruit she expected: she is the country in Europe where *the people* is most alive.

But the mania for giving an immediate political and practical application to all these fine ideas of the reason was fatal. Here an Englishman is in his element: on this theme we can all go on for hours. And all we are in the habit of saying on it has undoubtedly a great deal of truth. Ideas cannot be too much prized in and for themselves, cannot be too much lived with; but to transport them abruptly into the world of politics and practice, violently to revolutionise this world to their bidding,— that is quite another thing. There is the world of ideas and there is the world of practice; the French are often for suppressing the one and the English the other; but neither is to be suppressed. A member of the House of Commons said to me the other day: "That a thing is an anomaly, I consider to be no objection to it whatever." I venture to think he was wrong; that a thing is an anomaly *is* an objection to it, but absolutely and in the sphere of ideas: it is not necessarily, under such and such circumstances, or at such and such a moment, an objection to it in the sphere of politics and practice. Joubert has said beautifully: "C'est la force et le droit qui règlent toutes choses dans le monde; la force en attendant le droit." (Force and right are the governors of this world; force till right is ready.) *Force till right is ready*; and till right is ready, force, the existing order of things, is justified, is the legitimate ruler. But right is something moral, and implies inward recognition, free assent of the will; we are not ready for right—*right*, so far as we are concerned, *is not ready*,—until we have attained this sense of seeing it and willing it. The way in which for us it may change and transform force, the existing order of things, and become, in its turn, the legitimate ruler of the world, should depend on the way in which, when our time comes, we see it and will it. Therefore for other people enamoured of their own newly discerned right, to attempt to impose it upon us as ours, and violently to substitute their right for our force, is an act of tyranny, and to be resisted. It sets at nought the second great half of our maxim, *force till right is ready*. This was the grand error of the French Revolution, and its movements of ideas, by quitting the intellectual sphere and rushing furiously into the political sphere, ran, indeed, a prodigious and memorable course, but produced no such intellectual fruit as the movement of ideas of the Renascence, and created, in opposition to itself, what I may call an *epoch of concentration*. The great force of that epoch of concentration was England; and the great voice of that epoch of concentration was Burke. It is the fashion to treat Burke's writings on the French Revolution as super-annuated and conquered by the event; as the eloquent but un-philosophical tirades of bigotry and prejudice. I will not deny that they are often disfigured by the violence and passion of the moment, and that in some directions Burke's view was bounded, and his observation therefore at fault. But on the whole, and for those who can make the needful corrections, what dis-tinguishes these writings is their profound, permanent, fruitful, philosophical truth. They contain the true philosophy of an epoch of concentration, dissipate the heavy atmosphere which its own nature is apt to engender round it, and make its resistance rational instead of mechanical.

But Burke is so great because, almost alone in England, he brings thought to bear upon politics, he saturates politics with thought. It is his accident that his ideas were at the service of an epoch of concentration, not of an epoch of expansion; it is his characteristic that he so lived by ideas, and had such a source of them welling up within him, that he could float even an epoch of concentration and English Tory politics with them. It does not hurt him that Dr. Price and the Liberals were enraged with him; it does not even hurt him that George the Third and the Tories were enchanted with him. His greatness is that he lived in a world which neither English Liberalism nor English Toryism is apt to enter;—the world of ideas, not the world of catchwords and party habits. So far is it from being really true of him that he "to party gave up what was meant for mankind," that at the very end of his fierce struggle with the French Revolution, after all his invectives against its false pretensions, hollowness, and madness, with his sincere conviction of its mischievousness, he can close a memorandum on the best means of combating it, some of the last pages he ever wrote,—the *Thoughts on French Affairs*, in December 1791,—with these striking words:—

"The evil is stated, in my opinion, as it exists. The remedy must be where power, wisdom, and information, I hope, are more united with good intentions than they can be with me. I have done with this subject, I believe, for ever. It has given me many anxious moments for the last two years. *If a great change is to be made in human affairs, the minds of men will be fitted to it; the general opinions and feelings will draw that way. Every fear, every hope will forward it, and then they who persist in opposing this mighty current in human affairs, will appear rather to resist the decrees of Providence itself, than the mere designs of men. They will not be resolute and firm, but perverse and obstinate.*"

That return of Burke upon himself has always seemed to me one of the finest things in English literature, or indeed in any literature. That is what I call living by ideas: when one side of a question has long had your earnest support, when all your feelings are engaged, when you hear all round you no language but one, when your party talks this language like a steam-engine and can imagine no other,—still to be able to think, still to be irresistibly carried, if so it be, by the current of thought to the opposite side of the question and, like Balaam, to be unable to speak anything *but what the Lord has put in your mouth.* I know nothing more striking, and I must add that I know nothing more un-English.

For the Englishman in general is like my friend the Member of Parliament, and believes, point-blank, that for a thing to be an anomaly is absolutely no objection to it whatever. He is like the Lord Auckland of Burke's day, who, in a memorandum on the French Revolution, talks of "certain miscreants, assuming the name of philosophers, who have presumed themselves capable of establishing a new system of society." The Englishman has been called a political animal, and he values what is political and practical so much that ideas easily become objects of dislike in his eyes, and thinkers "miscreants," because ideas and thinkers have rashly meddled with politics and practice. This would be all very well if the dislike and neglect confined themselves to ideas transported out of their own sphere, and meddling rashly with practice; but they are inevitably extended to ideas as such, and to the whole life of intelligence; practice is everything, a free play of the mind is nothing. The notion of the free play of the mind upon all subjects being a pleasure in itself, being an object of desire, being an essential provider of elements without which a nation's spirit, whatever compensations it may have for them, must, in the long run, die of inanition, hardly enters into an Englishman's thoughts. It is noticeable that the word *curiosity*, which in other languages is used in a good sense, to mean, as a high and fine quality of man's nature, just this disinterested love of a free play of the mind on all subjects, for its own sake,—it is noticeable, I say, that this word has in our language no sense of the kind, no sense but a rather bad and disparaging one. But criticism, real criticism, is essentially the exercise of this very quality. It obeys an instinct prompting it to try to know the best that is known and thought in the world, irrespectively of practice, politics, and everything of the kind; and to value knowledge and thought as they approach this best, without the intrusion of any other considerations whatever. This is an instinct for which there is, I think, little original sympathy in the practical English nature, and what there was of it has undergone a long benumbing period of blight and suppression in the epoch of concentration which followed the French Revolution.

But epochs of concentration cannot well endure for ever; epochs of expansion, in the due course of things, follow them. Such an epoch of expansion seems to be opening in this country. In the first place all danger of a hostile forcible pressure of foreign ideas upon our practice has long disappeared; like the traveller in the fable, therefore, we begin to wear our cloak a little more loosely. Then, with a long peace, the ideas of Europe steal gradually and amicably in, and mingle, though in infinitesimally small quantities at a time, with our own notions. Then, too, in spite of all that is said about the absorbing and brutalising influence of our passionate material progress, it seems to me indisputable that this progress is likely, though not certain, to lead in the end to an apparition of intellectual life; and that man, after he has made himself perfectly comfortable and has now to determine what to do with himself next, may begin to remember that he has a mind, and that the mind may be made the source of great pleasure. I grant it is mainly the privilege of faith, at present, to discern this end to our railways, our business, and our fortune-making; but we shall see if, here as elsewhere, faith is not in the end the true prophet. Our ease, our travelling, and our unbounded liberty to hold just as hard and securely as we please to the practice to which our notions have given birth, all tend to beget an inclination to deal a little more freely with these notions themselves, to canvass them a little, to penetrate a little into their real nature. Flutterings of curiosity, in the foreign sense of the word, appear amongst us, and it is in these that criticism must look to find its account. Criticism first; a time of true creative activity, perhaps,—which, as I have said, must inevitably be preceded amongst us by a time of criticism,—hereafter, when criticism has done its work.

It is of the last importance that English criticism should clearly discern what rule for its course, in order to avail itself of the field now opening to it, and to produce fruit for the future, it ought to take. The rule may be summed up in one word,—*disinterestedness*. And how is criticism to show disinterestedness? By keeping aloof from what is called "the practical view of things;" by resolutely following the law of its own nature, which is to be a free play of the mind on all subjects which it touches. By steadily refusing to lend itself to any of those ulterior, political, practical considerations about ideas, which plenty of people will be sure to attach to them, which perhaps ought often to be attached to them, which in this country at any rate are certain to be attached to them quite sufficiently, but which criticism has really nothing to do with. Its business is, as I have said, simply to know the best that is known and thought in the world, and by in its turn making this known, to create a current of true and fresh ideas. Its business is to do this with inflexible honesty, with due ability; but its business is to do no more, and to leave alone all questions of practical consequences and applications, questions which will never fail to have due prominence given to them. Else criticism, besides being really false to its own nature, merely continues in the old rut which it has hitherto followed in this country, and will certainly miss the chance now given to it. For what is at present the banc of criticism in this country? It is that practical considerations cling to it and stifle it. It subserves interests not its own. Our organs of criticism are organs of men and parties having practical ends to serve, and with them those practical ends are the first thing and the play of mind the second; so much play of mind as is compatible with the prosecution of those practical ends is all that is wanted. An organ like the *Revue des Deux Mondes*, having for its main function to understand and utter the best that is known and thought in the world, existing, it may be said, as just an organ for a free play of the mind, we have not. But we have the *Edinburgh Review*, existing as an organ of the old Whigs, and for as much play of the mind as may suit its being that; we have the *Quarterly Review*, existing as an organ of the Tories and for as much play of mind as may suit its being that; we have the *British Quarterly Review*, existing as an organ of the political Dissenters, and for as much play of mind as may suit its being that; we have the *Times*, existing as an organ of the common, satisfied, well-to-do Englishman, and for as much play of mind as may suit its being that. And so on through all the various fractions, political and religious, of our society; every fraction has, as such, its organ of criticism, but the notion of combining all fractions in the common pleasure of a free disinterested play of mind meets with no favour. Directly this play of mind wants to have more scope, and to forget the pressure of practical considerations a little, it is checked, it is made to feel the chain. We saw this the other day in the extinction, so much to be regretted, of the *Home and Foreign Review*. Perhaps in no organ of criticism in this country was there so much knowledge, so much play of mind; but these could not save it. The *Dublin*

Review subordinates play of mind to the practical business of English and Irish Catholicism, and lives. It must needs be that men should act in sects and parties, that each of these sects and parties should have its organ, and should make this organ subserve the interests of its action; but it would be well, too, that there should be a criticism not the minister of these interests, not their enemy, but absolutely and entirely independent of them. No other criticism will ever attain any real authority or make any real way towards its end,—the creating a current of true and fresh ideas.

It is because criticism has so little kept in the pure intellectual sphere, has so little detached itself from practice, has been so directly polemical and controversial, that it has so ill accomplished, in this country, its best spiritual work; which is to keep man from a self-satisfaction which is retarding and vulgarising, to lead him towards perfection, by making his mind dwell upon what is excellent in itself, and the absolute beauty and fitness of things. A polemical practical criticism makes men blind even to the ideal imperfection of their practice, makes them willingly assert its ideal perfection, in order the better to secure it against attack; and clearly this is narrowing and baneful for them. If they were reassured on the practical side, speculative considerations of ideal perfection they might be brought to entertain, and their spiritual horizon would thus gradually widen. Sir Charles Adderley [1] says to the Warwickshire farmers:—

"Talk of the improvement of breed! Why, the race we ourselves represent, the men and women, the old Anglo-Saxon race, are the best breed in the whole world. . . . The absence of a too enervating climate, too unclouded skies, and a too luxurious nature, has produced so vigorous a race of people, and has rendered us so superior to all the world."

Mr. Roebuck [2] says to the Sheffield cutlers:—

"I look around me and ask what is the state of England? Is not property safe? Is not every man able to say what he likes? Can you not walk from one end of England to the other in perfect security? I ask you whether, the world over or in past history, there is anything like it? Nothing. I pray that our unrivalled happiness may last."

Now obviously there is a peril for poor human nature in

---

[1] [Sir Charles Bowyer Adderley, first Baron Norton, 1814–1905. M.P. for North Staffordshire 1841–1878. Held various government offices. A pioneer in the causes of colonial self-government, elementary education, and prison reform.]

[2] [John Arthur Roebuck, 1801–1879. M.P. for Sheffield 1849–68 and 1874–79. Chairman of the Commission of Inquiry into the Conduct of the Crimean War. An original member of the Reform Club.]

words and thoughts of such exuberant self-satisfaction, until we find ourselves safe in the streets of the Celestial City.

"Das wenige verschwindet leicht dem Blicke
        Der vorwärts sieht, wie viel noch übrig bleibt—"

says Goethe; "the little that is done seems nothing when we look forward and see how much we have yet to do." Clearly this is a better line of reflection for weak humanity, so long as it remains on this earthly field of labour and trial.

But neither Sir Charles Adderley nor Mr. Roebuck is by nature inaccessible to considerations of this sort. They only lose sight of them owing to the controversial life we all lead, and the practical form which all speculation takes with us. They have in view opponents whose aim is not ideal, but practical; and in their zeal to uphold their own practice against these innovators, they go so far as even to attribute to this practice an ideal perfection. Somebody has been wanting to introduce a six-pound franchise, or to abolish church-rates, or to collect agricultural statistics by force, or to diminish local self-government. How natural, in reply to such proposals, very likely improper or ill-timed, to go a little beyond the mark, and to say stoutly, "Such a race of people as we stand, so superior to all the world! The old Anglo-Saxon race, the best breed in the whole world! I pray that our unrivalled happiness may last! I ask you whether, the world over or in past history, there is anything like it?" And so long as criticism answers this dithyramb by insisting that the old Anglo-Saxon race would be still more superior to all others if it had no church-rates, or that our unrivalled happiness would last yet longer with a six-pound franchise, so long will the strain, "The best breed in the whole world!" swell louder and louder everything ideal and refining will be lost out of sight, and both the assailed and their critics will remain in a sphere, to say the truth, perfectly unvital, a sphere in which spiritual progression is impossible. But let criticism leave church-rates and the franchise alone, and in the most candid spirit, without a single lurking thought of practical innovation, confront with our dithyramb this paragraph on which I stumbled in a newspaper immediately after reading Mr. Roebuck:—

"A shocking child murder has just been committed at Nottingham. A girl named Wragg left the workhouse there on Saturday morning with her young illegitimate child. The child was soon afterwards found dead on Mapperly Hills, having been strangled. Wragg is in custody."

Nothing but that; but, in juxtaposition with the absolute euologies of Sir Charles Adderley and Mr. Roebuck, how eloquent, how suggestive are those few lines! "Our old Anglo-Saxon breed, the best in the whole world!"—how much that is harsh and ill-favoured there is in this best! *Wragg!* If we are to talk of ideal perfection, of "the best in the whole world," has any one reflected what a touch of grossness in our race, what an original shortcoming in the more delicate spiritual perceptions, is shown by the natural growth amongst us of such hideous names,—Higginbottom, Stiggins, Bugg! In Ionia and Attica they were luckier in this respect than "the best race in the world;" by the Ilissus there was no Wragg, poor thing! And "our unrivalled happiness;"—what an element of grimness, bareness, and hideousness mixes with it and blurs it? the work-house, the dismal Mapperly Hills,—how dismal those who have seen them will remember;—the gloom, the smoke, the cold, the strangled illegitimate child! "I ask you whether, the world over or in past history, there is anything like it?" Perhaps not, one is inclined to answer; but at any rate, in that case, the world is very much to be pitied. And the final touch,—short, bleak and inhuman: *Wragg is in custody.* The sex lost in the confusion of our unrivalled happiness; or (shall I say?) the superfluous Christian name lopped off by the straightforward vigour of our old Anglo-Saxon breed! There is profit for the spirit in such contrasts as this; criticism serves the cause of perfection by establishing them. By eluding sterile conflict, by refusing to remain in the sphere where alone narrow and relative concep-tions have any worth and validity, criticism may diminish its momentary importance, but only in this way has it a chance of gaining admittance for those wider and more perfect conceptions to which all its duty is really owed. Mr. Roebuck will have a poor opinion of an adversary who replies to his defiant songs of triumph only by murmuring under his breath, *Wragg is in custody*; but in no other way will these songs of triumph be induced gradually to moderate themselves, to get rid of what in them is excessive and offensive, and to fall into a softer and truer key.

It will be said that it is a very subtle and indirect action which I am thus prescribing for criticism, and that, by embracing in this manner the Indian virtue of detachment and abandoning the sphere of practical life, it condemns itself to a slow and obscure work. Slow and obscure it may be, but it is the only proper work of criticism. The mass of mankind will never have any ardent zeal for seeing things as they are; very inadequate ideas will always satisfy them. On these inadequate ideas reposes, and must repose, the general practice of the world. That is as much as saying that whoever sets himself to see things as they are will find himself one of a very small circle; but it is only by this small circle resolutely doing its own work that adequate ideas will ever get current at all. The rush and roar of practical life will always have a dizzying and attracting effect upon the most collected spectator, and tend to draw him into its vortex; most of all will this be the case where that life is so powerful as it is in England. But it is only by remaining collected, and refusing to lend himself to the point of view of the practical man, that the critic can do the practical man any service; and it is only by the greatest sincerity in pursuing his own course, and by at last convincing even the practical man of his sincerity, that he can escape misunderstandings which perpetually threaten him.

For the practical man is not apt for fine distinctions, and yet in these distinctions truth and the highest culture greatly find their account. But it is not easy to lead a practical man,—unless you reassure him as to your practical intentions, you have no chance of leading him,—to see that a thing which he has always been used to look at from one side only, which he greatly values, and which, looked at from that side, quite deserves, perhaps, all the prizing and admiring which he bestows upon it,—that this thing, looked at from another side, may appear much less beneficent and beautiful, and yet retain all its claims to our practical allegiance. Where shall we find language innocent enough, how shall we make the spotless purity of our intentions evident enough, to enable us to say to the political Englishman that the British Constitution itself, which, seen from the practical side, looks such a magnificent organ of progress and virtue, seen from the speculative side,—with its compromises, its love of facts, its horror of theory, its studied avoidance of clear thoughts,—that, seen from this side, our august Constitution sometimes looks,—forgive me, shade of Lord Somers!—a colossal machine for the manufacture of Philistines? How is Cobbett to say this and not be misunderstood, blackened as he is with the smoke of a lifelong conflict in the field of political practice? how is Mr. Carlyle to say it and not be misunderstood, after his furious raid into this field with his *Latter-day Pamphlets?* how is Mr. Ruskin, after his pugnacious political economy? I say, the critic must keep out of the region of immediate practice in the political, social, humanitarian sphere, if he wants to make a beginning for that more free speculative treatment of things, which may perhaps one day make its benefits felt even in this sphere, but in a natural and thence irresistible manner.

Do what he will, however, the critic will still remain exposed to frequent misunderstandings, and nowhere so much as in this country. For here people are particularly indisposed even to comprehend that without this free disinterested treatment of things, truth and the highest culture are out of the question. So immersed are they in practical life, so accustomed to take all their notions from this life and its processes, that they are apt to think that truth and culture themselves can be reached by the processes of this life, and that it is an impertinent singularity to think of reaching them in any other. "We are all *terræ filii*," cries their eloquent advocate; "all Philistines together. Away with the notion of proceeding by any other course than the course dear to the Philistines; let us have a social movement, let us organise and combine a party to pursue truth and new thought, let us call it *the liberal party*, and let us all stick to each other, and back each other up. Let us have no nonsense about independent criticism, and intellectual delicacy, and the few and the many. Don't let us trouble ourselves about foreign thought; we shall invent the whole thing for ourselves as we go along. If one of us speaks well, applaud him; if one of us speaks ill, applaud him too; we are all in the same movement, we are all liberals, we are all in pursuit of truth." In this way the pursuit of truth becomes really a social, practical, pleasurable affair, almost requiring a chairman, a secretary, and advertisements; with the excitement of an occasional scandal, with a little resistance to give the happy sense of difficulty overcome; but, in general, plenty of bustle and very little thought. To act is so easy, as Goethe says; to think is so hard! It is true that the critic has many temptations to go with the stream, to make one of the party movement, one of these *terræ filii*; it seems ungracious to refuse to be a *terræ filius*, when so many excellent people are; but the critic's duty is to refuse, or, if resistance is vain, at least to cry with Obermann: *Périssons en résistant.*

How serious a matter it is to try and resist, I had ample opportunity of experiencing when I ventured some time ago to criticise the celebrated first volume of Bishop Colenso.[1] The

---

[1] So sincere is my dislike to all personal attack and controversy, that I abstain from reprinting, at this distance of time from the occasion which called them forth, the essays in which I criticised Dr. Colenso's book; I feel bound, however, after all that has passed, to make here a final declaration of my sincere impenitence for having published them. Nay, I cannot forbear repeating yet once more, for his benefit and that of his readers, this sentence from my original remarks upon him: *There is truth of science and truth of religion; truth of science does not become truth of religion till it is made religious.* And I will add: Let us have all the science there is from the men of science; from the men of religion let us have religion.

[J. W. Colenso, Bishop of Natal, was the author of *A Commentary on St. Paul's Epistle to the Romans* (1861) and of a critical commentary on

echoes of the storm which was then raised I still, from time to time, hear grumbling round me. That storm arose out of a misunderstanding almost inevitable. It is a result of no little culture to attain to a clear perception that science and religion are two wholly different things. The multitude will for ever confuse them; but happily that is of no great real importance, for while the multitude imagines itself to live by its false science, it does really live by its true religion. Dr. Colenso, however, in his first volume did all he could to strengthen the confusion,[1] and to make it dangerous. He did this with the best intentions, I freely admit, and with the most candid ignorance that this was the natural effect of what he was doing; but, says Joubert, "Ignorance, which in matters of morals extenuates the crime, is itself, in intellectual matters, a crime of the first order." I criticised Bishop Colenso's speculative confusion. Immediately there was a cry raised: "What is this? here is a liberal attacking a liberal. Do not you belong to the movement? are not you a friend of truth? Is not Bishop Colenso in pursuit of truth? then speak with proper respect of his book. Dr. Stanley is another friend of truth, and you speak with proper respect of his book; why make these invidious differences? both books are excellent, admirable, liberal; Bishop Colenso's perhaps the most so, because it is the boldest, and will have the best practical consequences for the liberal cause. Do you want to encourage to the attack of a brother liberal his, and your, and our implacable enemies, the *Church and State Review* or the *Record*,— the High Church rhinoceros and the Evangelical hyæna? Be silent, therefore; or rather speak, speak as loud as ever you can! and go into ecstasies over the eighty and odd pigeons."

But criticism cannot follow this coarse and indiscriminate method. It is unfortunately possible for a man in pursuit of truth to write a book which reposes upon a false conception. Even the practical consequences of a book are to genuine criticism no recommendation of it, if the book is, in the highest

---

the Pentateuch (1862–79). The latter work, questioning the dates and historical value of Old Testament writings, provoked heated religious controversy. Colenso was criticized by A. P. Stanley in his *History of the Jewish Church*, and attacked by Arnold in an article called *The Bishop and the Philosopher* contributed to Macmillan's Magazine, January 1863. Arnold approached the problem of Biblical interpretation in the spirit of Spinoza, and parts of this article he later worked into the essay on *Spinoza and the Bible* in the 2nd edition of *Essays in Criticism.*]

[1] It has been said I make it "a crime against literary criticism and the higher culture to attempt to inform the ignorant." Need I point out that the ignorant are not informed by being confirmed in a confusion?

sense, blundering. I see that a lady who herself, too, is in pursuit of truth, and who writes with great ability, but a little too much, perhaps, under the influence of the practical spirit of the English liberal movement, classes Bishop Colenso's book and M. Renan's together, in her survey of the religious state of Europe, as facts of the same order, works, both of them, of "great importance;" "great ability, power, and skill;" Bishop Colenso's, perhaps, the most powerful; at least, Miss Cobbe gives special expression to her gratitude that to Bishop Colenso "has been given the strength to grasp, and the courage to teach, truths of such deep import." In the same way, more than one popular writer has compared him to Luther. Now it is just this kind of false estimate which the critical spirit is, it seems to me, bound to resist. It is really the strongest possible proof of the low ebb at which, in England, the critical spirit is, that while the critical hit in the religious literature of Germany is Dr. Strauss's book, in that of France M. Renan's book, the book of Bishop Colenso is the critical hit in the religious literature of England. Bishop Colenso's book reposes on a total misconception of the essential elements of the religious problem, as that problem is now presented for solution. To criticism, therefore, which seeks to have the best that is known as thought on this problem, it is, however well meant, of no importance whatever. M. Renan's book attempts a new synthesis of the elements furnished to us by the Four Gospels. It attempts, in my opinion, a synthesis, perhaps premature, perhaps impossible, certainly not successful. Up to the present time, at any rate, we must acquiesce in Fleury's sentence on such recastings of the Gospel-story: *Quiconque s'imagine la pourvoir mieux écrire, ne l'entend pas.* M. Renan had himself passed by anticipation a like sentence on his own work, when he said: "If a new presentation of the character of Jesus were offered to me, I would not have it; its very clearness would be, in my opinion, the best proof of its insufficiency." His friends may with perfect justice rejoin that at the sight of the Holy Land, and of the actual scene of the Gospel-story, all the current of M. Renan's thoughts may have naturally changed, and a new casting of that story irresistibly suggested itself to him; and that this is just a case for applying Cicero's maxim: Change of mind is not inconsistency—*nemo doctus unquam mutationem consilii inconstantiam dixit esse.* Nevertheless, for criticism, M. Renan's first thought must still be the truer one, as long as his new casting so fails more fully to commend itself, more fully (to use Coleridge's happy phrase about the Bible) to *find* us. Still M. Renan's attempt is, for criticism, of the most real interest and importance, since, with

all its difficulty, a fresh synthesis of the New Testament *data*,—
not a making war on them, in Voltaire's fashion, not a leaving
them out of mind, in the world's fashion, but the putting a new
construction upon them, the taking them from under the old,
traditional, conventional point of view and placing them under
a new one,—is the very essence of the religious problem, as
now presented; and only by efforts in this direction can it
receive a solution.

Again, in the same spirit in which she judges Bishop Colenso,
Miss Cobbe, like so many earnest liberals of our practical race,
both here and in America, herself sets vigorously about a
positive reconstruction of religion, about making a religion of
the future out of hand, or at least setting about making it. We
must not rest, she and they are always thinking and saying, in
negative criticism, we must be creative and constructive;
hence we have such works as her recent *Religious Duty*, and
works still more considerable, perhaps, by others, which will
be in every one's mind. These works often have much ability;
they often spring out of sincere convictions, and a sincere wish
to do good; and they sometimes, perhaps, do good. Their fault
is (if I may be permitted to say so) one which they have in
common with the British College of Health, in the New Road.
Every one knows the British College of Health; it is that building with the lion and the statue of the Goddess Hygeia before
it; at least I am sure about the lion, though I am not absolutely
certain about the Goddess Hygeia. This building does credit,
perhaps, to the resources of Dr. Morrison and his disciples;
but it falls a good deal short of one's idea of what a British
College of Health ought to be. In England, where we hate
public interference and love individual enterprise, we have a
whole crop of places like the British College of Health; the grand
name without the grand thing. Unluckily, creditable to individual enterprise as they are, they tend to impair our taste by
making us forget what more grandiose, noble, or beautiful character properly belongs to a public institution. The same may be
said of the religions of the future of Miss Cobbe and others.
Creditable, like the British College of Health, to the resources of
their authors, they yet tend to make us forget what more
grandiose, noble, or beautiful character properly belongs to
religious constructions. The historic religions, with all their
faults, have had this; it certainly belongs to the religious sentiment, when it truly flowers, to have this; and we impoverish
our spirit if we allow a religion of the future without it. What
then is the duty of criticism here? To take the practical point
of view, to applaud the liberal movement and all its works,—

its New Road religions of the future into the bargain,—for their general utility's sake? By no means; but to be perpetually dissatisfied with these works, while they perpetually fall short of a high and perfect ideal.

For criticism, these are elementary laws; but they never can be popular, and in this country they have been very little followed, and one meets with immense obstacles in following them. That is a reason for asserting them again and again. Criticism must maintain its independence of the practical spirit and its aims. Even with well-meant efforts of the practical spirit it must express dissatisfaction, if in the sphere of the ideal they seem impoverishing and limiting. It must not hurry on to the goal because of its practical importance. It must be patient, and know how to wait; and flexible, and know how to attach itself to things and how to withdraw from them. It must be apt to study and praise elements that for the fulness of spiritual perfection are wanted, even though they belong to a power which in the practical sphere may be maleficent. It must be apt to discern the spiritual shortcomings or illusions of powers that in the practical sphere may be beneficent. And this without any notion of favouring or injuring, in the practical sphere, one power or the other; without any notion of playing off, in this sphere, one power against the other. When one looks, for instance, at the English Divorce Court,—an institution which perhaps has its practical conveniences, but which in the ideal sphere is so hideous; an institution which neither makes divorce impossible nor makes it decent, which allows a man to get rid of his wife, or a wife of her husband, but makes them drag one another first, for the public edification, through a mire of unutterable infamy,—when one looks at this charming institution, I say, with its crowded trials, its newspaper reports, and its money compensations, this institution in which the gross unregenerate British Philistine has indeed stamped an image of himself,—one may be permitted to find the marriage theory of Catholicism refreshing and elevating. Or when Protestantism, in virtue of its supposed rational and intellectual origin, gives the law to criticism too magisterially, criticism may and must remind it that its pretensions, in this respect, are illusive and do it harm; that the Reformation was a moral rather than an intellectual event; that Luther's theory of grace no more exactly reflects the mind of the spirit than Bossuet's philosophy of history reflects it; and that there is no more antecedent probability of the Bishop of Durham's stock of ideas being agreeable to perfect reason than of Pope Pius the Ninth's. But criticism will not on that account forget the achievements of Protestantism in the practical and moral sphere; nor that, even in the intellectual sphere, Protestantism, though in a blind and stumbling manner, carried forward the Renascence, while Catholicism threw itself violently across its path.

I lately heard a man of thought and energy contrasting the want of ardour and movement which he now found amongst young men in this country with what he remembered in his own youth, twenty years ago. "What reformers we were then!" he exclaimed; "what a zeal we had! how we canvassed every institution in Church and State, and were prepared to remodel them all on first principles!" He was inclined to regret, as a spiritual flagging, the lull which he saw. I am disposed rather to regard it as a pause in which the turn to a new mode of spiritual progress is being accomplished. Everything was long seen, by the young and ardent amongst us, in inseparable connection with politics and practical life. We have pretty well exhausted the benefits of seeing things in this connection, we have got all that can be got by so seeing them. Let us try a more disinterested mode of seeing them; let us betake ourselves more to the serener life of the mind and spirit. This life, too, may have its excesses and dangers; but they are not for us at present. Let us think of quietly enlarging our stock of true and fresh ideas, and not, as soon as we get an idea or half an idea, be running out with it into the street, and trying to make it rule there. Our ideas will, in the end, shape the world all the better for maturing a little. Perhaps in fifty years' time it will in the English House of Commons be an objection to an institution that it is an anomaly, and my friend the Member of Parliament will shudder in his grave. But let us in the meanwhile rather endeavour that in twenty years' time it may, in English literature, be an objection to a proposition that it is absurd. That will be a change so vast, that the imagination almost fails to grasp it. *Ab integro sæclorum nascitur ordo.*

If I have insisted so much on the course which criticism must take where politics and religion are concerned, it is because, where these burning matters are in question, it is most likely to go astray. I have wished, above all, to insist on the attitude which criticism should adopt towards things in general; on its right tone and temper of mind. But then comes another question as to the subject-matter which literary criticism should most seek. Here, in general, its course is determined for it by the idea which is the law of its being; the idea of a disinterested endeavour to learn and propagate the best that is known and thought in the world, and thus to establish a current of fresh and true ideas. By the very nature of things, as England is not all the world, much of the best that is known and thought in the world cannot be of English growth, must be foreign; by the nature of things, again, it is just this that we are least likely to know, while English thought is streaming in upon us from all sides, and takes excellent care that we shall not be ignorant of its existence. The English critic of literature, therefore, must dwell much on foreign thought, and with particular heed on any part of it, which, while significant and fruitful in itself, is for any reason specially likely to escape him. Again, judging is often spoken of as the critic's one business, and so in some sense it is; but the judgment which almost insensibly forms itself in a fair and clear mind, along with fresh knowledge, is the valuable one; and thus knowledge, and ever fresh knowledge, must be the critic's great concern for himself. And it is by communicating fresh knowledge, and letting his own judgment pass along with it,—but insensibly, and in the second place, not the first, as a sort of companion and clue, not as an abstract lawgiver,—that the critic will generally do most good to his readers. Sometimes, no doubt, for the sake of establishing an author's place in literature, and his relation to a central standard (and if this is not done, how are we to get at our *best in the world*?) criticism may have to deal with a subject-matter so familiar that fresh knowledge is out of the question, and then it must be all judgment; an enunciation and detailed application of principles. Here the great safeguard is never to let oneself become abstract, always to retain an intimate and lively consciousness of the truth of what one is saying, and, the moment this fails us, to be sure that something is wrong. Still, under all circumstances, this mere judgment and application of principles is, in itself, not the most satisfactory work to the critic; like mathematics, it is tautological, and cannot well give us, like fresh learning, the sense of creative activity.

But stop, some one will say; all this talk is of no practical use to us whatever; this criticism of yours is not what we have in our minds when we speak of criticism; when we speak of critics and criticism, we mean critics and criticism of the current English literature of the day; when you offer to tell criticism its function, it is to this criticism that we expect you to address yourself. I am sorry for it, for I am afraid I must disappoint these expectations. I am bound by my own definition of criticism: *a disinterested endeavour to learn and propagate the best that is known and thought in the world.* How much of current English literature comes into this "best that is known and thought in the world?" Not very much, I fear; certainly less, at this moment, than of the current literature of France or

Germany. Well, then, am I to alter my definition of criticism, in order to meet the requirements of a number of practising English critics, who, after all, are free in their choice of a business? That would be making criticism lend itself just to one of those alien practical considerations, which, I have said, are so fatal to it. One may say, indeed, to those who have to deal with the mass—so much better disregarded—of current English literature, that they may at all events endeavour, in dealing with this, to try it, so far as they can, by the standard of the best that is known and thought in the world; one may say, that to get anywhere near this standard, every critic should try and possess one great literature, at least, besides his own; and the more unlike his own, the better. But, after all, the criticism I am really concerned with,—the criticism which alone can much help us for the future, the criticism which, throughout Europe, is at the present day meant, when so much stress is laid on the importance of criticism and the critical spirit,—is a criticism which regards Europe as being, for intellectual and spiritual purposes, one great confederation, bound to a joint action and working to a common result; and whose members have, for their proper outfit, a knowledge of Greek, Roman, and Eastern antiquity, and of one another. Special, local, and temporary advantages being put out of account, that modern nation will in the intellectual and spiritual sphere make most progress, which most thoroughly carries out this programme. And what is that but saying that we too, all of us, as individuals, the more thoroughly we carry it out, shall make the more progress?

There is so much inviting us!—what are we to take? what will nourish us in growth towards perfection? That is the question which, with the immense field of life and of literature lying before him, the critic has to answer; for himself first, and afterwards for others. In this idea of the critic's business the essays brought together in the following pages have had their origin; in this idea, widely different as are their subjects, they have, perhaps, their unity.

I conclude with what I said at the beginning: to have the sense of creative activity is the great happiness and the great proof of being alive, and it is not denied to criticism to have it; but then criticism must be sincere, simple, flexible, ardent, ever widening its knowledge. Then it may have, in no contemptible measure, a joyful sense of creative activity; a sense which a man of insight and conscience will prefer to what he might derive from a poor, starved, fragmentary, inadequate creation. And at some epochs no other creation is possible.

Still, in full measure, the sense of creative activity belongs only to genuine creation; in literature we must never forget that. But what true man of letters ever can forget it? It is no such common matter for a gifted nature to come into possession of a current of true and living ideas, and to produce amidst the inspiration of them, that we are likely to underrate it. The epochs of Æschylus and Shakspeare make us feel their pre-eminence. In an epoch like those is, no doubt, the true life of literature; there is the promised land, towards which criticism can only beckon. That promised land it will not be ours to enter, and we shall die in the wilderness: but to have desired to enter it, to have saluted it from afar, is already, perhaps, the best distinction among contemporaries; it will certainly be the best title to esteem with posterity.

The Literary Influence of Academies

IT is impossible to put down a book like the history of the French Academy, by Pellisson and D'Olivet, which M. Charles Livet has lately re-edited, without being led to reflect upon the absence, in our own country, of any institution like the French Academy, upon the probable causes of this absence, and upon its results. A thousand voices will be ready to tell us that this absence is a signal mark of our national superiority; that it is in great part owing to this absence that the exhilarating words of Lord Macaulay, lately given to the world by his very clever nephew, Mr. Trevelyan, are so profoundly true: "It may safely be said that the literature now extant in the English language is of far greater value than all the literature which three hundred years ago was extant in all the languages of the world together." I daresay this is so; only, remembering Spinoza's maxim that the two great banes of humanity are self-conceit and the laziness coming from self-conceit, I think it may do us good, instead of resting in our pre-eminence with perfect security, to look a little more closely why this is so, and whether it is so without any limitations.

But first of all I must give a very few words to the outward history of the French Academy. About the year 1629, seven or eight persons in Paris, fond of literature, formed themselves into a sort of little club to meet at one another's houses and discuss literary matters. Their meetings got talked of, and Cardinal Richelieu, then minister and all-powerful, heard of them. He himself had a noble passion for letters, and for all fine culture; he was interested by what he heard of the nascent society. Himself a man in the grand style, if ever man was, he had the insight to perceive what a potent instrument of the grand style was here to his hand. It was the beginning of a great century for France, the seventeenth; men's minds were working, the French language was forming. Richelieu sent to ask the members of the new society whether they would be willing to become a body with a public character, holding regular meetings. Not without a little hesitation,—for apparently they found themselves very well as they were, and these seven or eight gentlemen of a social and literary turn were not perfectly at their ease as to what the great and terrible minister could want with them,—they consented. The favours of a man like Richelieu are not easily refused, whether they are honestly meant or no; but this favour of Richelieu's was meant quite honestly. The Parliament, however, had its doubts of this. The Parliament had none of Richelieu's enthusiasm about letters and culture; it was jealous of the apparition of a new public body in the State; above all, of a body called into existence by Richelieu. The King's letters-patent, establishing and authorising the new society, were granted early in 1635; but, by the old constitution of France, these letters-patent required the verification of the Parliament. It was two years and a half—towards the autumn of 1637—before the Parliament would give it; and it then gave it only after pressing solicitations, and earnest assurances of the innocent intentions of the young Academy. Jocose people said that this society, with its mission to purify and embellish the language, filled with terror a body of lawyers like the French Parliament, the stronghold of barbarous jargon and of chicane.

This improvement of the language was in truth the declared grand aim for the operations of the Academy. Its statutes of foundation, approved by Richelieu before the royal edict establishing it was issued, say expressly: "The Academy's principal function shall be to work with all the care and all the diligence possible at giving sure rules to our language, and rendering it pure, eloquent, and capable of treating the arts and sciences." This zeal for making a nation's great instrument of thought,—its language,—correct and worthy, is undoubtedly a sign full of promise,—a weighty earnest of future power. It is said that Richelieu had it in his mind that French should succeed Latin in its general ascendency, as Latin had succeeded Greek; if it was so, even this wish has to some extent been fulfilled. But, at any rate, the *ethical* influences of style in language,—its close relations, so often pointed out, with character,—are most important. Richelieu, a man of high culture, and, at the same time, of great character, felt them profoundly; and that he should have sought to regularise, strengthen, and perpetuate them by an institution for perfecting language, is alone a striking proof of his governing spirit and of his genius.

This was not all he had in his mind, however. The new Academy, now enlarged to a body of forty members, and meant to contain all the chief literary men of France, was to be a *literary tribunal*. The works of its members were to be brought before it previous to publication, were to be criticised by it, and finally, if it saw fit, to be published with its declared approbation. The works of other writers, not members of the Academy, might also, at the request of these writers themselves, be passed under the Academy's review. Besides this, in essays and discussions the Academy examined and judged works already published, whether by living or dead authors, and literary matters in general. The celebrated opinion on Corneille's *Cid*, delivered in 1637 by the Academy at Richelieu's urgent request, when this poem, which strongly occupied public attention, had been attacked by M. de Scudéry, shows how fully Richelieu designed his new creation to do duty as a supreme court of literature, and how early it in fact began to exercise this function. One [1] who had known Richelieu declared, after the Cardinal's death, that he had projected a yet greater institution than the Academy, a sort of grand European college of art, science, and literature, a Prytaneum, where the chief authors of all Europe should be gathered together in one central home, there to live in security, leisure, and honour;—that was a dream which will not bear to be pulled about too roughly. But the project of forming a high court of letters for France was no dream; Richelieu in great measure fulfilled it. This is what the Academy, by its idea, really is; that is what it has always tended to become; this is what it has, from time to time, really been; by being, or tending to be this, far more than even by what it has done for the language, it is of such importance in France. To give the law, the tone to literature, and that tone a high one, is its business. "Richelieu meant it," says M. Sainte-Beuve, "to be a *haut jury*,"—a jury the most choice and authoritative that could be found on all important literary matters in question before the public; to be, as it in fact became in the latter half of the eighteenth century, "a sovereign organ of opinion." "The duty of the Academy is," says M. Renan, "*maintenir la délicatesse de l'esprit français*"—to keep the fine quality of the French spirit unimpaired; it represents a kind of "*maîtrise en fait de bon ton*"—the authority of a recognised master in matters of tone and taste. "All ages," says M. Renan again, "have had their inferior literature; but the great danger of our time is that this

[1] La Mesnardière.

inferior literature tends more and more to get the upper place. No one has the same advantage as the Academy for fighting against this mischief;" the Academy, which, as he says elsewhere, has even special facilities for "creating a form of intellectual culture *which shall impose itself on all around.*" M. Sainte-Beuve and M. Renan are, both of them, very keen-sighted critics; and they show it signally by seizing and putting so prominently forward this character of the French Academy.

Such an effort to set up a recognised authority, imposing on us a high standard in matters of intellect and taste, has many enemies in human nature. We all of us like to go our own way, and not to be forced out of the atmosphere of commonplace habitual to most of us;—"*was uns alle bändigt,*" says Goethe, "*das Gemeine.*" We like to be suffered to lie comfortably in the old straw of our habits, especially of our intellectual habits, even though this straw may not be very clean and fine. But if the effort to limit this freedom of our lower nature finds, as it does and must find, enemies in human nature, it finds also auxiliaries in it. Out of the four great parts, says Cicero, of the *honestum*, or good, which forms the matter on which *officium*, or human duty, finds employment, one is the fixing of a *modus* and an *ordo*, a measure and an order, to fashion and wholesomely constrain our action, in order to lift it above the level it keeps if left to itself, and to bring it nearer to perfection. Man alone of living creatures, he says, goes feeling after "*quid sit* ordo, *quid sid quod* deceat, *in factis dictisque qui* modus—the discovery of an *order*, a law of *good taste*, a *measure* for his words and actions." Other creatures submissively follow the law of their nature; man alone has an impulse leading him to set up some other law to control the bent of his nature.

This holds good, of course, as to moral matters, as well as intellectual matters: and it is of moral matters that we are generally thinking when we affirm it. But it holds good as to intellectual matters too. Now, probably, M. Sainte-Beuve had not these words of Cicero in his mind when he made, about the French nation, the assertion I am going to quote; but, for all that, the assertion leans for support, one may say, upon the truth conveyed in those words of Cicero, and wonderfully illustrates and confirms them. "In France," says M. Sainte-Beuve, "the first consideration for us is not whether we are amused and pleased by a work of art or mind, nor is it whether we are touched by it. What we seek above all to learn is, whether *we were right* in being amused with it, and in applauding it, and in being moved by it." Those are very remarkable words, and they are, I believe, in the main quite true. A Frenchman has, to a considerable degree, what one may call a conscience in intellectual matters; he has an active belief that there is a right and a wrong in them, that he is bound to honour and obey the right, that he is disgraced by cleaving to the wrong. All the world has, or professes to have, this conscience in moral matters. The word *conscience* has become almost confined, in popular use, to the moral sphere, because this lively susceptibility of feeling is, in the moral sphere, so far more common than in the intellectual sphere; the livelier, in the moral sphere, this susceptibility is, the greater becomes a man's readiness to admit a high standard of action, an ideal authoritatively correcting his everyday moral habits; here, such willing admission of authority is due to sensitiveness of conscience. And a like deference to a standard higher than one's own habitual standard in intellectual matters, a like respectful recognition of a superior ideal, is caused, in the intellectual sphere, by sensitiveness of intelligence. Those whose intelligence is quickest, openest, most sensitive, are readiest with this deference; those who intelligence is less delicate and sensitive are less disposed to it. Well, now we are on the road to see why the French have their Academy and we have nothing of the kind.

What are the essential characteristics of the spirit of our nation? Not, certainly, an open and clear mind, not a quick and flexible intelligence. Our greatest admirers would not claim for us that we have these in a pre-eminent degree; they might say that we had more of them than our detractors gave us credit for; but they would not assert them to be our essential characteristics. They would rather allege, as our chief spiritual characteristics, energy and honesty; and, if we are judged favourably and positively, not invidiously and negatively, our chief characteristics are, no doubt, these:—energy and honesty, not an open and clear mind, not a quick and flexible intelligence. Openness of mind and flexibility of intelligence were very signal characteristics of the Athenian people in ancient times; everybody will feel that. Openness of mind and flexibility of intelligence are remarkable characteristics of the French people in modern times; at any rate, they strikingly characterise them as compared with us; I think everybody, or almost everybody, will feel that. I will not now ask what more the Athenian or the French spirit has than this, nor what shortcomings either of them may have as a set-off against this; all I want now to point out is that they have this, and that we have it in a much lesser degree.

Let me remark, however, that not only in the moral sphere, but also in the intellectual and spiritual sphere, energy and honesty are most important and fruitful qualities; that, for instance, of what we call genius energy is the most essential part. So, by assigning to a nation energy and honesty as its chief spiritual characteristics,—by refusing to it, as at all eminent characteristics, openness of mind and flexibility of intelligence,—we do not by any means, as some people might at first suppose, relegate its importance and its power of manifesting itself with effect from the intellectual to the moral sphere. We only indicate its probable special line of successful activity in the intellectual sphere, and, it is true, certain imperfections and failings to which, in this sphere, it will always be subject. Genius is mainly an affair of energy, and poetry is mainly an affair of genius; therefore, a nation whose spirit is characterised by energy may well be eminent in poetry;— and we have Shakspeare. Again, the highest reach of science is, one may say, an inventive power, a faculty of divination, akin to the highest power exercised in poetry; therefore, a nation whose spirit is characterised by energy may well be eminent in science;—and we have Newton. Shakspeare and Newton: in the intellectual sphere there can be no higher names. And what that energy, which is the life of genius, above everything demands and insists upon, is freedom; entire independence of all authority, prescription, and routine,—the fullest room to expand as it will. Therefore, a nation whose chief spiritual characteristic is energy, will not be very apt to set up, in intellectual matters, a fixed standard, an authority, like an academy. By this it certainly escapes certain real inconveniences and dangers, and it can, at the same time, as we have seen, reach undeniably splendid heights in poetry and science. On the other hand, some of the requisites of intellectual work are specially the affair of quickness of mind and flexibility of intelligence. The form, the method of evolution, the precision, the proportions, the relations of the parts to the whole, in an intellectual work, depend mainly upon them. And these are the elements of an intellectual work which are really most communicable from it, which can most be learned and adopted from it, which have, therefore, the greatest effect upon the intellectual performance of others. Even in poetry, these requisites are very important; and the poetry of a nation, not eminent for the gifts on which they depend, will, more or less, suffer by this shortcoming. In poetry, however, they are, after all, secondary, and energy is the first thing; but in prose they are of first-rate importance. In its prose literature, therefore, and in the routine of intellectual work generally, a nation with no particular gifts for these will not be so successful. These are what, as I have said, can to a certain degree be learned and appropriated, while the free activity of genius cannot. Academies consecrate and maintain them, and, therefore, a nation with an eminent turn for them naturally establishes academies. So far as routine and authority tend to embarrass energy and inventive genius, academies may be said to be obstructive to energy and inventive genius, and, to this extent, to the human spirit's general advance. But then this evil is so much compensated by the propagation, on a large scale, of the mental aptitudes and demands which an open mind and a flexible intelligence naturally engender, genius itself, in the long run, so greatly finds its account in this propagation, and bodies like the French Academy have such power for promoting it, that the general advance of the human spirit is perhaps, on the whole, rather furthered than impeded by their existence.

How much greater is our nation in poetry than prose! how much better, in general, do the productions of its spirit show in the qualities of genius than in the qualities of intelligence! One may constantly remark this in the work of individuals; how much more striking, in general, does any Englishman,—of some vigour of mind, but by no means a poet—seem in his verse than in his prose! His verse partly suffers from his not being really a poet, partly, no doubt, from the very same defects which impair his prose, and he cannot express himself with thorough success in it. But how much more powerful a personage does he appear in it, by dint of feeling, and of originality and movement of ideas, than when he is writing prose! With a Frenchman of like stamp, it is just the reverse: set him to write poetry, he is limited, artificial, and impotent; set him to write prose, he is free, natural, and effective. The power of French literature is in its prose-writers, the power of English literature is in its poets. Nay, many of the celebrated French poets depend wholly for their fame upon the qualities of intelligence which they exhibit,—qualities which are the distinctive support of prose; many of the celebrated English prose-writers depend wholly for their fame upon the qualities of genius and imagination which they exhibit,—qualities which are the distinctive support of poetry. But, as I have said, the qualities of genius are less transferable than the qualities of intelligence; less can be immediately learned and appropriated from their product; they are less direct and stringent intellectual agencies, though they may be more beautiful and divine. Shakspeare and our great Elizabethan group were certainly more gifted writers than Corneille and his group; but what was the sequel to this great literature, this literature of genius, as we may call it, stretching from Marlow to Milton? What did it lead up to in English literature? To our provincial and second-rate literature of the eighteenth century. What, on the other hand, was the sequel to the literature of the French "great century," to this literature of intelligence, as, by comparison with our Elizabethan literature, we may call it; what did it lead up to? To the French literature of the eighteenth century, one of the most powerful and pervasive intellectual agencies that have ever existed,—the greatest European force of the eighteenth century. In science, again, we had Newton, a genius of the very highest order, a type of genius in science, if ever there was one. On the continent, as a sort of counterpart to Newton, there was Leibnitz; a man, it seems to me (though on these matters I speak under correction), of much less creative energy of genius, much less power of divination than Newton, but rather a man of admirable intelligence, a type of intelligence in science, if ever there was one. Well, and what did they each directly lead up to in science? What was the intellectual generation that sprang from each of them? I only repeat what the men of science have themselves pointed out. The man of genius was continued by the English analysts of the eighteenth century, comparatively powerless and obscure followers of the renowned master. The man of intelligence was continued by successors like Bernouilli, Euler, Lagrange, and Laplace, the greatest names in modern mathematics.

What I want the reader to see is, that the question as to the utility of academies to the intellectual life of a nation is not settled when we say, for instance: "Oh, we have never had an academy, and yet we have, confessedly, a very great literature." It still remains to be asked: "What sort of a great literature? a literature great in the special qualities of genius, or great in the special qualities of intelligence?" If in the former, it is by no means sure that either our literature, or the general intellectual life of our nation, has got already, without academies, all that academies can give. Both the one and the other may very well be somewhat wanting in those qualities of intelligence out of a lively sense for which a body like the French Academy, as I have said, springs, and which such a body does a great deal to spread and confirm. Our literature, in spite of the genius manifested in it, may fall short in form, method, precision, proportions, arrangement,—all of them, I have said, things where intelligence proper comes in. It may be comparatively weak in prose, that branch of literature where intelligence proper is, so to speak, all in all. In this branch it may show many grave faults to which the want of a quick, flexible intelligence, and of the strict standard which such an intelligence tends to impose, makes it liable; it may be full of hap-hazard, crudeness, provincialism, eccentricity, violence, blundering.

It may be a less stringent and effective intellectual agency, both upon our own nation and upon the world at large, than other literatures which show less genius, perhaps, but more intelligence.

The right conclusion certainly is that we should try, so far as we can, to make up our shortcomings; and that to this end, instead of always fixing our thoughts upon the points in which our literature, and our intellectual life generally, are strong, we should, from time to time, fix them upon those in which they are weak, and so learn to perceive clearly what we have to amend. What is our second great spiritual characteristic,—our honesty,—good for, if it is not good for this? But it will,—I am sure it will,—more and more, as time goes on, be found good for this.

Well, then, an institution like the French Academy,—an institution owing its existence to a national bent towards the things of the mind, towards culture, towards clearness, correctness, and propriety in thinking and speaking, and, in its turn, promoting this bent,—sets standards in a number of directions, and creates, in all these directions, a force of educated opinion, checking and rebuking those who fall below these standards, or who set them at nought. Educated opinion exists here as in France; but in France the Academy serves as a sort of centre and rallying-point to it, and gives it a force which it has not got here. Why is all the *journeyman-work* of literature, as I may call it, so much worse done here than it is in France? I do not wish to hurt any one's feelings; but surely this is so. Think of the difference between our books of reference and those of the French, between our biographical dictionaries (to take a striking instance) and theirs; think of the difference between the translations of the classics turned out for Mr. Bohn's library and those turned out for M. Nisard's collection! As a general rule, hardly any one amongst us, who knows French and German well, would use an English book of reference when he could get a French or German one; or would look at an English prose translation of an ancient author when he could get a French or German one. It is not that there do not exist in England, as in France, a number of people perfectly well able to discern what is good, in these things, from what is bad, and preferring what is good; but they are isolated, they form no powerful body of opinion, they are not strong enough to set a standard, up to which even the journeyman-work of literature must be brought, if it is to be vendible. Ignorance and charlatanism in work of this kind are always trying to pass off their wares as excellent, and to cry down criticism as the voice of an insignificant, over-fastidious minority; they easily persuade the multitude that this is so when the minority is scattered about as it is here; not so easily when it is banded together as in the French Academy. So, again, with freaks in dealing with language; certainly all such freaks tend to impair the power and beauty of language; and how far more common they are with us than with the French! To take a very familiar instance. Every one has noticed the way in which the *Times* chooses to spell the word "diocese;" it always spells it dioce*ss*, deriving it, I suppose, from *Zeus* and *census*. The *Journal des Débats* might just as well write "diocess" instead of "diocèse," but imagine the *Journal des Débats* doing so! Imagine an educated Frenchman indulging himself in an orthographical antic of this sort, in face of the grave respect with which the Academy and its dictionary invest the French language! Some people will say these are little things; they are not; they are of bad example. They tend to spread the baneful notion that there is no such thing as a high, correct standard in intellectual matters; that every one may as well take his own way; they are at variance with the severe discipline necessary for all real culture; they confirm us in habits of wilfulness and eccentricity, which hurt our minds, and damage our credit with serious people. The late Mr. Donaldson was certainly a man of great ability, and I, who am not an Orientalist, do not pretend to judge his *Jashar*: but let the reader observe the form which a foreign Orientalist's judgment of it naturally takes. M. Renan calls it a *tentative malheureuse*, a failure, in short; this it may be, or it may not be; I am no judge. But he goes on: "It is astonishing that a recent article" (in a French periodical, he means) "should have brought forward as the last word of German exegesis a work like this, composed by a doctor of the University of Cambridge, and universally condemned by German critics." You see what he means to imply: an extravagance of this sort could never have come from Germany, where there is a great force of critical opinion controlling a learned man's vagaries, and keeping him straight; it comes from the native home óf intellectual eccentricity of all kinds,—from England, from a doctor of the University of Cambridge;—and I daresay he would not expect much better things from a doctor of the University of Oxford. Again, after speaking of what Germany and France have done for the history of Mahomet: "America and England," M. Renan goes on, "have also occupied themselves with Mahomet." He mentions Washington Irving's *Life of Mahomet*, which does not, he says, evince much of an historical sense, a *sentiment historique fort élevé*; "but," he proceeds, "this book shows a real progress, when one thinks that in 1829 Mr. Charles Forster published two thick volumes, which enchanted the English *reverends*, to make out that Mahomet was the little horn of the he-goat that figures in the eighth chapter of Daniel, and that the Pope was the great horn. Mr. Forster founded on this ingenious parallel a whole philosophy of history, according to which the Pope represented the Western corruption of Christianity, and Mahomet the Eastern; thence the striking resemblances between Mahometanism and Popery." And in a note M. Renan adds: "This is the same Mr. Charles Forster who is the author of a mystification about the Sinaitic inscriptions, in which he declares he finds the primitive language." As much as to say: "It is an Englishman, be surprised at no extravagance." If these innuendoes had no ground, and were made in hatred and malice, they would not be worth a moment's attention; but they come from a grave Orientalist, on his own subject, and they point to a real fact;— the absence, in this country, of any force of educated literary and scientific opinion, making aberrations like those of the author of *The One Primeval Language* out of the question. Not only the author of such aberrations, often a very clever man, suffers by the want of check, by the not being kept straight, and spends force in vain on a false road, which, under better discipline, he might have used with profit on a true one; but all his adherents, both "reverends" and others, suffer too, and the general rate of information and judgment is in this way kept low.

In a production which we have all been reading lately, a production stamped throughout with a literary quality very rare in this country, and of which I shall have a word to say presently —*urbanity*; in this production, the work of a man never to be named by any son of Oxford without sympathy, a man who alone in Oxford of his generation, alone of many generations, conveyed to us in his genius that same charm, that same ineffable sentiment which this exquisite place itself conveys,—I mean Dr. Newman,—an expression is frequently used which is more common in theological than in literary language, but which seems to me fitted to be of general service; the *note* of so and so, the note of catholicity, the note of antiquity, the note of sanctity, and so on. Adopting this expressive word, I say that in the bulk of the intellectual work of a nation which has no centre, no intellectual metropolis like an academy, like M. Sainte-Beuve's "sovereign organ of opinion," like M. Renan's "recognised authority in matters of tone and taste,"—there is observable a *note of provinciality*. Now to get rid of provinciality is a certain stage of culture; a stage the positive result of which we must not make of too much importance, but which is, nevertheless, indispensable, for it brings us on to the platform where alone the best and highest intellectual work can be said fairly to begin. Work done after men have reached this platform is *classical*; and that is the only work which, in the long run, can stand. All the *scoriæ* in the work of men of great genius who have not lived on this platform are due to their not having lived on it. Genius raises them to it by moments, and the portions of their work which are immortal are done at these moments; but more of it would have been immortal if they had not reached this platform at moments only, if they had had the culture which makes men live there.

The less a literature has felt the influence of a supposed centre of correct information, correct judgment, correct taste, the more we shall find in it this note of provinciality. I have shown the note of provinciality as caused by remoteness from a centre of correct information. Of course the note of provinciality from the want of a centre of correct taste is still more visible, and it is also still more common. For here great—even the greatest— powers of mind most fail a man. Great powers of mind will make him inform himself thoroughly, great powers of mind will make him think profoundly, even with ignorance and platitude all round him; but not even great powers of mind will keep his taste and style perfectly sound and sure, if he is left too much to himself, with no "sovereign organ of opinion" in these matters near him. Even men like Jeremy Taylor and Burke suffer here. Take this passage from Taylor's funeral sermon on Lady Carbery:—

"So have I seen a river, deep and smooth, passing with a still foot and a sober face, and paying to the *fiscus*, the great exchequer of the sea, a tribute large and full; and hard by it a little brook, skipping and making a noise upon its unequal and neighbour bottom; and after all its talking and bragged motion, it paid to its common audit no more than the revenues of a little cloud or a contemptible vessel: so have I sometimes compared the issues of her religion to the solemnities and famed outsides of another's piety."

That passage has been much admired, and, indeed, the genius in it is undeniable. I should say, for my part, that genius, the ruling divinity of poetry, had been too busy in it, and intelligence, the ruling divinity of prose, not busy enough. But can any one, with the best models of style in his head, help feeling the note of provinciality there, the want of simplicity, the want of measure, the want of just the qualities that make prose classical? If he does not feel what I mean, let him place beside

N

the passage of Taylor this passage from the Panegyric of St. Paul, by Taylor's contemporary, Bossuet:—

"Il ira, cet ignorant dans l'art de bien dire, avec cette locution rude, avec cette phrase qui sent l'étranger il ira en cette Grèce polie, la mère des philosophes et des orateurs; et malgré la résistance du monde, il y établira plus d'Eglises que Platon n'y a gagné de disciples par cette éloquence qu'on a crue divine."

There we have prose without the note of provinciality—classical prose, prose of the centre.

Or take Burke, our greatest English prose-writer, as I think; take expressions like this:—

"Blindfold themselves, like bulls that shut their eyes when they push, they drive, by the point of their bayonets, their slaves, blindfolded, indeed, no worse than their lords, to take their fictions for currencies, and to swallow down paper pills by thirty-four millions sterling at a dose."

Or this:—

"They used it" (the royal name) "as a sort of navel-string, to nourish their unnatural offspring from the bowels of royalty itself. Now that the monster can purvey for its own subsistence, it will only carry the mark about it, as a token of its having torn the womb it came from."

Or this:—

"Without one natural pang, he" (Rousseau) "casts away, as a sort of offal and excrement, the spawn of his disgustful amours, and sends his children to the hospital of foundlings."

Or this:—

"I confess I never liked this continual talk of resistance and revolution, or the practice of making the extreme medicine of the constitution its daily bread. It renders the habit of society dangerously valetudinary; it is taking periodical doses of mercury sublimate, and swallowing down repeated provocatives of cantharides to our love of liberty."

I say that is extravagant prose; prose too much suffered to indulge its caprices; prose at too great a distance from the centre of good taste; prose, in short, with the note of provinciality. People may reply, it is rich and imaginative; yes, that is just it, it is *Asiatic* prose, as the ancient critics would have said; prose somewhat barbarously rich and overloaded. But the true prose is Attic prose.

Well, but Addison's prose is Attic prose. Where, then, it may be asked, is the note of provinciality in Addison? I answer, in the commonplace of his ideas. This is a matter worth remarking. Addison claims to take leading rank as a moralist. To do that, you must have ideas of the first order on your subject—the best ideas, at any rate, attainable in your time—as well as be able to express them in a perfectly sound and sure style. Else you show your distance from the centre of ideas by your matter; you are provincial by your matter, though you may not be provincial by your style. It is comparatively a small matter to express oneself well, if one will be content with not expressing much, with expressing only trite ideas; the problem is to express new and profound ideas in a perfectly sound and classical style. He is the true classic, in every age, who does that. Now Addison has not, on his subject of morals, the force of ideas of the moralists of the first class—the classical moralists; he has not the best ideas attainable in or about his time, and which were, so to speak, in the air then, to be seized by the finest spirits; he is not to be compared for power, searchingness, or delicacy of thought to Pascal or La Bruyère or Vauvenargues; he is rather on a level, in this respect, with a man like Marmontel. Therefore, I say, he has the note of provinciality as a moralist; he is provincial by his matter, though not by his style.

To illustrate what I mean by an example. Addison, writing as a moralist on fixedness in religious faith, says:—

"Those who delight in reading books of controversy do very seldom arrive at a fixed and settled habit of faith. The doubt which was laid revives again, and shows itself in new difficulties; and that generally for this reason,—because the mind, which is perpetually tossed in controversies and disputes, is apt to forget the reasons which had once set it at rest, and to be disquieted with any former perplexity when it appears in a new shape, or is started by a different hand."

It may be said, that is classical English, perfect in lucidity, measure, and propriety. I make no objection; but, in my turn, I say that the idea expressed is perfectly trite and barren, and that it is a note of provinciality in Addison, in a man whom a nation puts forward as one of its great moralists, to have no profounder and more striking idea to produce on this great subject. Compare, on the same subject, these words of a moralist really of the first order, really at the centre by his ideas, —Joubert:—

"L'expérience de beaucoup d'opinions donne à l'esprit beaucoup de flexibilité et l'affermit dans celles qu'il croit les meilleures."

With what a flash of light that touches the subject! how it sets us thinking! what a genuine contribution to moral science it is!

In short, where there is no centre like an academy, if you have genius and powerful ideas, you are apt not to have the best style

going; if you have precision of style and not genius, you are apt
not to have the best ideas going.

The provincial spirit, again, exaggerates the value of its ideas
for want of a high standard at hand by which to try them.
Or rather, for want of such a standard, it gives one idea too much
prominence at the expense of others; it orders its ideas amiss;
it is hurried away by fancies; it likes and dislikes too passionately, too exclusively. Its admiration weeps hysterical tears,
and its disapprobation foams at the mouth. So we get the
eruptive and the *aggressive* manner in literature; the former prevails most in our criticism, the latter in our newspapers. For, not
having the lucidity of a large and centrally placed intelligence,
the provincial spirit has not its graciousness; it does not persuade, it makes war; it has not urbanity, the tone of the city,
of the centre, the tone which always aims at a spiritual and intellectual effect, and not excluding the use of banter, never disjoins banter itself from politeness, from felicity. But the
provincial tone is more violent, and seems to aim rather at an
effect upon the blood and senses than upon the spirit and intellect; it loves hard-hitting rather than persuading. The newspaper, with its party spirit, its thorough-goingness, its resolute
avoidance of shades and distinctions, its short, highly-charged,
heavy-shotted articles, its style so unlike that style *lenis mini-
mèque pertinax*—easy and not too violently insisting,—which
the ancients so much admired, is its true literature; the provincial spirit likes in the newspaper just what makes the newspaper such bad food for it,—just what made Goethe say, when
he was pressed hard about the immorality of Byron's poems,
that, after all, they were not so immoral as the newspapers.
The French talk of the *brutalité des journaux anglais.* What
strikes them comes from the necessary inherent tendencies of
newspaper-writing not being checked in England by any centre
of intelligent and urbane spirit, but rather stimulated by
coming in contact with a provincial spirit. Even a newspaper
like the *Saturday Review*, that old friend of all of us, a newspaper expressly aiming at an immunity from the common
newspaper-spirit, aiming at being a sort of organ of reason,—
and, by thus aiming, its merits great gratitude and has done great
good,—even the *Saturday Review*, replying to some foreign
criticism on our precautions against invasion, falls into a strain
of this kind:—

"To do this" (to take these precautions) "seems to us eminently worthy of a great nation, and to talk of it as unworthy of a
great nation, seems to us eminently worthy of a great fool."

There is what the French mean when they talk of the

brutalité des journaux anglais; there is a style certainly as far removed from urbanity as possible,—a style with what I call the note of provinciality. And the same note may not unfrequently be observed even in the ideas of this newspaper, full as it is of thought and cleverness: certain ideas allowed to become fixed ideas, to prevail too absolutely. I will not speak of the immediate present, but, to go a little while back, it had the critic who so disliked the Emperor of the French; it had the critic who so disliked the subject of my present remarks—academies; it had the critic who was so fond of the German element in our nation, and, indeed, everywhere; who ground his teeth if one said *Charlemagne* instead of *Charles the Great*, and, in short, saw all things in Teutonism, as Malebranche saw all things in God. Certainly any one may fairly find faults in the Emperor Napoleon or in academies, and merit in the German element; but it is a note of the provincial spirit not to hold ideas of this kind a little more easily, to be so devoured by them, to suffer them to become crotchets.

In England there needs a miracle of genius like Shakspeare's to produce balance of mind, and a miracle of intellectual delicacy like Dr. Newman's to produce urbanity of style. How prevalent all round us is the want of balance of mind and urbanity of style! How much, doubtless, it is to be found in ourselves, —in each of us! but, as human nature is constituted, every one can see it clearest in his contemporaries. There, above all, we should consider it, because they and we are exposed to the same influences; and it is in the best of one's contemporaries that it is most worth considering, because one then most feels the harm it does, when one sees what they would be without it. Think of the difference between Mr. Ruskin exercising his genius, and Mr. Ruskin exercising his intelligence; consider the truth and beauty of this:—

"Go out, in the spring-time, among the meadows that slope from the shores of the Swiss lakes to the roots of their lower mountains. There, mingled with the taller gentians and the white narcissus, the grass grows deep and free; and as you follow the winding mountain paths, beneath arching boughs all veiled and dim with blossom,—paths that for ever droop and rise over the green banks and mounds sweeping down in scented undulation, steep to the blue water studded here and there with new-mown heaps, filling all the air with fainter sweetness,—look up towards the higher hills, where the waves of everlasting green roll silently into their long inlets among the shadows of the pines. . . . . ."

There is what the genius, the feeling, the temperament in

Mr. Ruskin, the original and incommunicable part, has to do with; and how exquisite it is! All the critic could possibly suggest, in the way of objection, would be, perhaps, that Mr. Ruskin is there trying to make prose do more than it can perfectly do; that what he is there attempting he will never, except in poetry, be able to accomplish to his own entire satisfaction: but he accomplishes so much that the critic may well hesitate to suggest even this. Place beside this charming passage another,— a passage about Shakspeare's names, where the intelligence and judgment of Mr. Ruskin, the acquired, trained, communicable part in him, as brought into play,—and see the difference:—

"Of Shakspeare's names I will afterwards speak at more length; they are curiously—often barbarously—mixed out of various traditions and languages. Three of the clearest in meaning have been already noticed. Desdemona—'δυσδαιμονία,' *miserable fortune*—is also plain enough. Othello is, I believe, 'the careful;' all the calamity of the tragedy arising from the single flaw and error in his magnificently collected strength. Ophelia, 'serviceableness,' the true, lost wife of Hamlet, is marked as having a Greek name by that of her brother, Laertes; and its signification is once exquisitely alluded to in that brother's last word of her, where her gentle preciousness is opposed to the uselessness of the churlish clergy:—'A *ministering* angel shall my sister be, when thou liest howling.' Hamlet is, I believe, connected in some way with 'homely,' the entire event of the tragedy turning on betrayal of home duty. Hermione (ἕρμα), 'pillar-like' (ἡ εἶδος ἔχε χρυσῆς 'Αφροδίτης); Titania (τιτήνη), 'the queen;' Benedick and Beatrice, 'blessed and blessing;' Valentine and Proteus, 'enduring or strong' (*valens*), and 'changeful.' Iago and Iachimo have evidently the same root—probably the Spanish Iago, Jacob, 'the supplanter.'"

Now, really, what a piece of extravangance all that is! I will not say that the meaning of Shakspeare's names (I put aside the question as to the correctness of Mr. Ruskin's etymologies) has no effect at all, may be entirely lost sight of; but to give it that degree of prominence is to throw the reins to one's whim, to forget all moderation and proportion, to lose the balance of one's mind altogether. It is to show in one's criticism, to the highest excess, the note of provinciality.

Again, there is Mr. Palgrave, certainly endowed with a very fine critical tact: his *Golden Treasury* abundantly proves it. The plan of arrangement which he devised for that work, the mode in which he followed his plan out, nay, one might even say, merely the juxtaposition, in pursuance of it, of two such pieces as those of Wordsworth and Shelley which form the 285th and 286th in his collection, show a delicacy of feeling in these matters which is quite indisputable and very rare. And his notes are full of remarks which show it too. All the more striking, conjoined with so much justness of perception, are certain freaks and violences in Mr. Palgrave's criticism, mainly imputable, I think, to the critic's isolated position in this country, to his feeling himself too much left to take his own way, too much without any central authority representing high culture and sound judgment, by which he may be, on the one hand, confirmed as against the ignorant, on the other, held in respect when he himself is inclined to take liberties. I mean such things as this note on Milton's line,—

"The great Emathian conqueror bade spare" . . .

"When Thebes was destroyed, Alexander ordered the house of Pindar to be spared. *He was as incapable of appreciating the poet as Louis XIV. of appreciating Racine; but even the narrow and barbarian mind of Alexander could understand the advantage of a showy act of homage to poetry.*" A note like that I call a freak or a violence; if this disparaging view of Alexander and Louis XIV., so unlike the current view, is wrong,—if the current view is, after all, the truer one of them,—the note is a freak. But, even if its disparaging view is right, the note is a violence; for, abandoning the true mode of intellectual action—persuasion, the instilment of conviction,—it simply astounds and irritates the hearer by contradicting without a word of proof or preparation, his fixed and familiar notions; and this is mere violence. In either case, the fitness, the measure, the centrality, which is the soul of all good criticism, is lost, and the note of provinciality shows itself.

Thus, in the famous *Handbook*, marks of a fine power of perception are everywhere discernible, but so, too, are marks of the want of sure balance, of the check and support afforded by knowing one speaks before good and severe judges. When Mr. Palgrave dislikes a thing, he feels no pressure constraining him either to try his dislike closely or to express it moderately; he does not mince matters, he gives his dislike all its own way; both his judgment and his style would gain if he were under more restraint. "The style which has filled London with the dead monotony of Gower or Harley Streets, or the pale commonplace of Belgravia, Tyburnia, and Kensington; which has pierced Paris and Madrid with the feeble frivolities of the Rue Rivoli and the Strada de Toledo." He dislikes the architecture of the Rue Rivoli, and he puts it on a level with the architecture of Belgravia and Gower Street; he lumps them all together in one condemnation, he loses sight of the shade, the distinction, which is everything here; the distinction, namely, that the architecture of the Rue Rivoli expresses show, splendour, pleasure,—unworthy things, perhaps, to express alone and for their own sakes, but it expresses them; whereas the architecture of Gower Street and Belgravia merely expresses the impotence of the architect to express anything. Then, as to style: "sculpture which stands in a contrast with Woolner hardly more shameful than diverting." . . . "passing from Davy or Faraday to the art of the mountebank or the science of the spirit-rapper." . . . "it is the old, old story with Marochetti, the frog trying to blow himself out to bull dimensions. He may puff and be puffed, but he will never do it." We all remember that shower of amenities on poor M. Marochetti.[1] Now, here Mr. Palgrave himself enables us to form a contrast which lets us see just what the presence of an academy does for style; for he quotes a criticism by M. Gustave Planche on this very M. Marochetti. M. Gustave Planche was a critic of the very first order, a man of strong opinions, which he expressed with severity; he, too, condemns M. Marochetti's work, and Mr. Palgrave calls him as a witness to back what he has himself said; certainly Mr. Palgrave's translation will not exaggerate M. Planche's urbanity in dealing with M. Marochetti, but, even in this translation, see the difference in sobriety, in measure, between the critic writing in Paris and the critic writing in London:—

"These conditions are so elementary, that I am at a perfect loss to comprehend how M. Marochetti has neglected them. There are soldiers here like the leaden playthings of the nursery: it is almost impossible to guess whether there is a body beneath the dress. We have here no question of style, not even of grammar; it is nothing beyond mere matter of the alphabet of art. To break these conditions is the same as to be ignorant of spelling."

That is really more formidable criticism than Mr. Palgrave's, and yet in how perfectly temperate a style! M. Planche's advantage is, that he feels himself to be speaking before competent judges, that there is a force of cultivated opinion for him to appeal to. Therefore, he must not be extravagant, and he need not storm; he must satisfy the reason and taste,—that is his business. Mr. Palgrave, on the other hand, feels himself to be

[1] [Carlo Marochetti, sculptor (1805–1867). Favourite artist of Queen Victoria, and portrayer of many Victorian notabilities in marble or bronze. Responsible for, *inter alia*, the equestrian statue of Richard Cœur de Lion outside the House of Lords. It was originally exhibited at the Great Exhibition of 1851.]

speaking before a promiscuous multitude, with the few good judges so scattered through it as to be powerless; therefore, he has no calm confidence and no self-control; he relies on the strength of his lungs; he knows that big words impose on the mob, and that, even if he is outrageous, most of his audience are apt to be a great deal more so.

Again, the first two volumes of Mr. Kinglake's *Invasion of the Crimea* were certainly among the most successful and renowned English books of our time. Their style was one of the most renowned things about them, and yet how conspicuous a fault in Mr. Kinglake's style is this over-charge of which I have been speaking: Mr. James Gordon Bennett, of the *New York Herald*, says, I believe, that the highest achievement of the human intellect is what he calls "a good editorial." This is not quite so; but, if it were so, on what a height would these two volumes by Mr. Kinglake stand! I have already spoken of the Attic and the Asiatic styles; besides these, there is the Corinthian style. That is the style for "a good editorial," and Mr. Kinglake has really reached perfection in it. It has not the warm glow, blithe movement, and soft pliancy of life, as the Attic style has; it has not the over-heavy richness and encumbered gait of the Asiatic style; it has glitter without warmth, rapidity without ease, effectiveness without charm. Its characteristic is, that it has no *soul*; all it exists for, is to get its ends, to make its points, to damage its adversaries, to be admired, to triumph. A style so bent on effect at the expense of soul, simplicity and delicacy; a style so little studious of the charm of the great models; so far from classic truth and grace, must surely be said to have the note of provinciality. Yet Mr. Kinglake's talent is a really eminent one, and so in harmony with our intellectual habits and tendencies, that, to the great bulk of English people, the faults of his style seem its merits; all the more needful that criticism should not be dazzled by them.

We must not compare a man of Mr. Kinglake's literary talent with French writers like M. de Bazancourt.[1] We must compare him with M. Thiers. And what a superiority in style has M. Thiers from being formed in a good school, with severe traditions, wholesome restraining influences! Even in this age of Mr. James Gordon Bennett, his style has nothing Corinthian about it, its lightness and brightness make it almost Attic. It is not quite Attic, however; it has not the infallible sureness of Attic taste. Sometimes his head gets a little hot with the fumes of

[1] [Baron César de Bazancourt (1810–1865), French military historian: author of *L'Expédition de Crimée* (1857), *La Campagne de Italie de 1859* (1860).]

patriotism, and then he crosses the line, he loses perfect measure, he declaims, he raises a momentary smile. France condemned 'à être l'effroi du monde *dont elle pourrait être l'amour*,'— Cæsar, whose exquisite simplicity M. Thiers so much admires, would not have written like that. There is, if I may be allowed to say so, the slightest possible touch of fatuity in such language, —of that failure in good sense which comes from too warm a self-satisfaction. But compare this language with Mr. King-lake's Marshal St. Arnaud—"dismissed from the presence" of Lord Raglan or Lord Stratford, "cowed and pressed down" under their "stern reproofs," or under "the majesty of the great Elchi's Canning brow and tight, merciless lips!" The failure in good sense and good taste there reaches far beyond what the French mean by *fatuity*; they would call it by another word, a word expressing blank defect of intelligence, a word for which we have no exact equivalent in English,—*bête*. It is the differ-ence between a venial, momentary, good-tempered excess, in a man of the world, of an amiable and social weakness,—vanity; and a serious, settled, fierce, narrow, provincial misconception of the whole relative value of one's own things and the things of others. So baneful to the style of even the cleverest man may be the total want of checks.

In all I have said, I do not pretend that the examples given prove my rule as to the influence of academies; they only illu-strate it. Examples in plenty might very likely be found to set against them; the truth of the rule depends, no doubt, on whether the balance of all the examples is in its favour or not; but actually to strike this balance is always out of the question. Here, as everywhere else, the rule, the idea, if true, commends itself to the judicious, and then the examples make it clearer still to them. This is the real use of examples, and this alone is the purpose which I have meant mine to serve. There is also another side to the whole question,—as to the limiting and prejudicial operation which academies may have; but this side of the question it rather behoves the French, not us, to study.

The reader will ask for some practical conclusion about the establishment of an Academy in this country, and perhaps I shall hardly give him the one he expects. But nations have their own modes of acting, and these modes are not easily changed; they are even consecrated, when great things have been done in them. When a literature has produced Shakspeare and Milton, when it has even produced Barrow and Burke, it cannot well abandon its traditions; it can hardly begin, at this late time of day, with an institution like the French Academy. I think academies with a limited, special, scientific scope, in the various lines of intellectual work,—academies like that of Berlin, for instance,—we with time may, and probably shall, establish. And no doubt they will do good; no doubt the presence of such influential centres of correct information will tend to raise the standard amongst us for what I have called the *journeyman-work* of literature, and to free us from the scandal of such biographical dictionaries as Chalmers's, or such translations as a recent one of Spinoza, or perhaps, such philological freaks as Mr. Forster's about the one primeval language. But an academy quite like the French Academy, a sovereign organ of the highest literary opinion, a recognised authority in matters of intellectual tone and taste, we shall hardly have, and perhaps we ought not to wish to have it. But then every one amongst us with any turn for literature will do well to remember to what shortcomings and excesses, which such an academy tends to correct, we are liable; and the more liable, of course, for not having it. He will do well constantly to try himself in respect of these, steadily to widen his culture, severely to check in himself the provincial spirit; and he will do this the better the more he keeps in mind that all mere glorification by ourselves of ourselves or our literature, in the strain of what, at the beginning of these remarks, I quoted from Lord Macaulay, is both vulgar, and, besides being vulgar, retarding.

From *Heinrich Heine*

"I KNOW not if I deserve that a laurel-wreath should one day be laid on my coffin. Poetry, dearly as I have loved it, has always been to me but a divine plaything. I have never attached any great value to poetical fame; and I trouble myself very little whether people praise my verses or blame them. But lay on my coffin a *sword*; for I was a brave soldier in the Liberation War of humanity."

Heine had his full share of love of fame, and cared quite as much as his brethren of the *genus irritable* whether people praised his verses or blamed them. And he was very little of a hero. Posterity will certainly decorate his tomb with the emblem of the laurel rather than with the emblem of the sword. Still, for his contemporaries, for us, for the Europe of the present century, he is significant chiefly for the reason which he himself in the words just quoted assigns. He is significant because he was, if not pre-eminently a brave, yet a brilliant, most effective soldier in the Liberation War of humanity.

To ascertain the master-current in the literature of an epoch, and to distinguish this from all minor currents, is one of the critic's highest functions; in discharging it he shows how far he possesses the most indispensable quality of his office,—justness of spirit. The living writer who has done most to make England acquainted with German authors, a man of genius, but to whom precisely this one quality of justness of spirit is perhaps wanting, —I mean Mr. Carlyle,—seems to me in the result of his labours on German literature to afford a proof how very necessary to the critic this quality is. Mr. Carlyle has spoken admirably of Goethe; but then Goethe stands before all men's eyes, the manifest centre of German literature; and from this central source many rivers flow. Which of these rivers is the main stream? which of the courses of spirit which we see active in Goethe is the course which will most influence the future, and attract and be continued by the most powerful of Goethe's successors?—that is the question. Mr. Carlyle attaches, it seems to me, far too much importance to the romantic school of Germany,—Tieck, Novalis, Jean Paul Richter,—and gives to these writers, really gifted as two, at any rate, of them are, an undue prominence. These writers, and others with aims and a general tendency the same as theirs, are not the real inheritors and continuators of Goethe's power; the current of their activity is not the main current of German literature after Goethe. Far more in Heine's works flows this main current; Heine, far more than Tieck or Jean Paul Richter, is the continuator of that which, in Goethe's varied activity, is the most powerful and vital; on Heine, of all German authors who survived Goethe, incomparably the largest portion of Goethe's mantle fell. I do not forget that when Mr. Carlyle was dealing with German literature, Heine, though he was clearly risen above the horizon, had not shone forth with all his strength; I do not forget, too, that after ten or twenty years many things may come out plain before the critic which before were hard to be discerned by him; and assuredly no one would dream of imputing it as a fault to Mr. Carlyle that twenty years ago he mistook the central current in German literature, overlooked the rising Heine, and attached undue importance to that romantic school which Heine was to destroy; one may rather note it as a misfortune, sent perhaps as a delicate chastisement to a critic, who,—man of genius as he is, and no one recognises his genius more admirably than I do,— has, for the functions of the critic, a little too much of the self-will and eccentricity of a genuine son of Great Britain.

Heine is noteworthy, because he is the most important German successor and continuator of Goethe in Goethe's most important line of activity. And which of Goethe's lines of activity is this?—His line of activity as "a soldier in the war of liberation of humanity."

Heine himself would hardly have admitted this affiliation, though he was far too powerful-minded a man to decry, with some of the vulgar German liberals, Goethe's genius. "The wind of the Paris Revolution," he writes after the three days of 1830, "blew about the candles a little in the dark night of Germany, so that the red curtains of a German throne or two caught fire; but the old watchmen, who do the police of the German kingdoms, are already bringing out the fire engines, and will keep the candles closer snuffed for the future. Poor, fast-bound German people, lose not all heart in thy bonds! The fashionable coating of ice melts off from my heart, my soul quivers and my eyes burn, and that is a disadvantageous state of things for a writer, who should control his subject-matter and keep himself beautifully objective, as the artistic school would have us, and as Goethe has done; he has come to be eighty years old doing this, and minister, and in good condition:— poor German people! that is thy greatest man!"

But hear Goethe himself: "If I were to say what I had really been to the Germans in general, and to the young German poets in particular, I should say I had been their *liberator*."

Modern times find themselves with an immense system of institutions, established facts, accredited dogmas, customs, rules, which have come to them from times not modern. In this system their life has to be carried forward; yet they have a sense that this system is not of their own creation, that it by no means corresponds exactly with the wants of their actual life, that, for them, it is customary, not rational. The awakening of this sense is the awakening of the modern spirit. The modern spirit is now awake almost everywhere; the sense of want of correspondence between the forms of modern Europe and its spirit, between the new wine of the eighteenth and nineteenth centuries, and the old bottles of the eleventh and twelfth centuries, or even of the sixteenth and seventeenth, almost every one now perceives; it is no longer dangerous to affirm that this want of correspondence exists; people are even beginning to be shy of denying it. To remove this want of correspondence is beginning to be the settled endeavour of most persons of good sense. Dissolvents of the old European system of dominant ideas and facts we must all be, all of us who have any power of working; what we have to study is that we may not be acrid dissolvents of it.

And how did Goethe, that grand dissolvent in an age when there were fewer of them than at present, proceed in his task of dissolution, of liberation of the modern European from the old routine? He shall tell us himself. "Through me the German poets have become aware that, as man must live from within outwards, so the artist must work from within outwards, seeing that, make what contortions he will, he can only bring to light his own individuality. I can clearly mark where this influence of mine has made itself felt; there arises out of it a kind of poetry of nature, and only in this way is it possible to be original."

My voice shall never be joined to those which decry Goethe, and if it is said that the foregoing is a lame and impotent conclusion to Goethe's declaration that he had been the liberator of the Germans in general, and of the young German poets in particular, I say it is not. Goethe's profound, imperturbable naturalism is absolutely fatal to all routine thinking; he puts the standard, once for all, inside every man instead of outside him; when he is told, such a thing must be so, there is immense authority and custom in favour of its being so, it has been held to be so for a thousand years, he answers with Olympian politeness, "But *is* it so? is it so to *me*?" Nothing could be more really subversive of the foundations on which the old European order rested; and it may be remarked that no persons are so radically detached from this order, no persons so thoroughly modern, as those who have felt Goethe's influence most deeply. If it is said that Goethe professes to have in this way deeply influenced but a few persons, and those persons poets, one may answer that he could have taken no better way to secure, in the end, the ear of the world; for poetry is simply the most beautiful, impressive, and widely effective mode of saying things, and hence its importance. Nevertheless the process of liberation, as Goethe worked it, though sure, is undoubtedly slow; he came, as Heine says, to be eighty years old in thus working it, and at the end of that time the old Middle-Age machine was still creaking on, the thirty German courts and their chamberlains subsisted in all their glory; Goethe himself was a minister, and the visible triumph of the modern spirit over prescription and routine seemed as far off as ever. It was the year 1830; the German sovereigns had passed the preceding fifteen years in breaking the promises of freedom they had made to their subjects when they wanted their help in the final struggle with Napoleon. Great events were happening in France; the revolution, defeated in 1815, had arisen from its defeat, and was wresting from its adversaries the power. Heinrich Heine, a young man of genius, born at Hamburg, and with all the culture of Germany, but by race a Jew; with warm sympathies for France, whose revolution had given to his race the rights of citizenship, and whose rule had been, as is well known, popular in the Rhine provinces, where he passed his youth; with a passionate admiration for the great French Emperor, with a passionate contempt for the sovereigns who had overthrown him, for their agents, and for their policy,—Heinrich Heine was in 1830 in no humour for any such gradual process of liberation from the old order of things as that which Goethe had followed. His counsel was for open war. Taking that terrible modern weapon, the pen, in his hand, he passed the remainder of his life in one fierce battle. What was that battle? the reader will ask. It was a life and death battle with Philistinism.

Philistinism!—we have not the expression in English. Perhaps we have not the word because we have so much of the thing. At Soli, I imagine, they did not talk of solecisms; and here, at the very headquarters of Goliath, nobody talks of Philistinism. The French have adopted the term *épicier* (grocer), to designate the sort of being whom the Germans designate by the term Philistine; but the French term,—besides that it casts a slur upon a respectable class, composed of living and susceptible members, while the original Philistines are dead and buried long ago,—is really, I think, in itself much less apt and expressive than the German term. Efforts have been made to obtain in English some term equivalent to *Philister* or *épicier*; Mr. Carlyle has made several such efforts: "respectability with its thousand gigs," he says;—well, the occupant of every one of these gigs is, Mr. Carlyle means, a Philistine. However, the word *respectable* is far too valuable a word to be thus perverted from its proper meaning; if the English are ever to have a word for the thing we are speaking of,—and so prodigious are the changes which the modern spirit is introducing, that even we English shall perhaps one day come to want such a word,—I think we had much better take the term *Philistine* itself.

Philistine must have originally meant, in the mind of those who invented the nickname, a strong, dogged, unenlightened opponent of the chosen people, of the children of the light. The party of change, the would-be remodellers of the old traditional European order, the invokers of reason against custom, the representatives of the modern spirit in every sphere where it is applicable, regarded themselves, with the robust self-confidence natural to reformers as a chosen people, as children of the light. They regarded their adversaries as humdrum people, slaves to routine, enemies to light; stupid and oppressive, but at the same time very strong. This explains the love which Heine, that Paladin of the modern spirit, has for France; it explains the preference which he gives to France over Germany:

"the French," he says, "are the chosen people of the new religion, its first gospels and dogmas have been drawn up in their language; Paris is the new Jerusalem, and the Rhine is the Jordan which divides the consecrated land of freedom from the land of the Philistines." He means that the French, as a people, have shown more accessibility to ideas than any other people; that prescription and routine have had less hold upon them than upon any other people; that they have shown most readiness to move and to alter at the bidding (real or supposed) of reason. This explains, too, the detestation which Heine had for the English: "I might settle in England," he says, in his exile, "if it were not that I should find there two things, coal-smoke and Englishmen; I cannot abide either." What he hated in the English was the "ächtbrittische Beschränktheit," as he calls it,—the *genuine British narrowness*. In truth, the English, profoundly as they have modified the old Middle-Age order, great as is the liberty which they have secured for themselves, have in all their changes proceeded, to use a familiar expression, by the rule of thumb; what was intolerably inconvenient to them they have suppressed, and as they have suppressed it, not because it was irrational, but because it was practically inconvenient, they have seldom in suppressing it appealed to reason, but always, if possible, to some precedent, or form, or letter, which served as a convenient instrument for their purpose, and which saved them from the necessity of recurring to general principles. They have thus become, in a certain sense, of all people the most inaccessible to ideas and the most impatient of them; inaccessible to them, because of their want of familiarity with them; and impatient of them because they have got on so well without them, that they despise those who, not having got on as well as themselves, still make a fuss for what they themselves have done so well without. But there has certainly followed from hence, in this country, somewhat of a general depression of pure intelligence: Philistia has come to be thought by us the true Land of Promise, and it is anything but that; the born lover of ideas, the born hater of commonplaces, must feel in this country, that the sky over his head is of brass and iron. The enthusiast for the idea, for reason, values reason, the idea, in and for themselves; he values them, irrespectively of the practical conveniences which their triumph may obtain for him; and the man who regards the possession of these practical conveniences as something sufficient in itself, something which compensates for the absence or surrender of the idea, of reason, is, in his eyes, a Philistine. This is why Heine so often and so mercilessly attacks the liberals; much as he hates conservatism he hates Philistinism even more, and whoever attacks conservatism itself ignobly, not as a child of light, not in the name of the idea, is a Philistine. Our Cobbett is thus for him, much as he disliked our clergy and aristocracy whom Cobbett attacked, a Philistine with six fingers on every hand and on every foot six toes, four-and-twenty in number: a Philistine, the staff of whose spear is like a weaver's beam. Thus he speaks of him: `

"While I translate Cobbett's words, the man himself comes bodily before my mind's eye, as I saw him at that uproarious dinner at the Crown and Anchor Tavern, with his scolding red face and his radical laugh, in which venomous hate mingles with a mocking exultation at his enemies' surely approaching downfall. He is a chained cur, who falls with equal fury on every one whom he does not know, often bites the best friend of the house in his calves, barks incessantly, and just because of this incessantness of his barking cannot get listened to, even when he barks at a real thief. Therefore the distinguished thieves who plunder England do not think it necessary to throw the growling Cobbett a bone to stop his mouth. This makes the dog furiously savage, and he shows all his hungry teeth. Poor old Cobbett! England's dog! I have no love for thee, for every vulgar nature my soul abhors; but thou touchest me to the inmost soul with pity, as I see how thou strainest in vain to break loose and to get at those thieves, who make off with their booty before thy very eyes, and mock at thy fruitless springs and thine impotent howling."

There is balm in Philistia as well as in Gilead. A chosen circle of children of the modern spirit, perfectly emancipated from prejudice and commonplace, regarding the ideal side of things in all its efforts for change, passionately despising half-measures and condescension to human folly and obstinacy,—with a bewildered, timid, torpid multitude behind,—conducts a country to the government of Herr von Bismarck. A nation regarding the practical side of things in its efforts for change, attacking not what is irrational, but what is pressingly inconvenient, and attacking this as one body, "moving altogether if it move at all," and treating children of light like the very harshest of stepmothers, comes to the prosperity and liberty of modern England. For all that, however, Philistia (let me say it again) is not the true promised land, as we English commonly imagine it to be; and our excessive neglect of the idea, and consequent inaptitude for it, threatens us, at a moment when the idea is beginning to exercise a real power in human society, with serious future inconvenience, and, in the meanwhile, cuts us off from the sympathy of other nations, which feel its power more than we do.

But, in 1830, Heine very soon found that the fire-engines of the German governments were too much for his direct efforts at incendiarism. "What demon drove me," he cries, "to write my *Reisebilder*, to edit a newspaper, to plague myself with our time and its interests, to try and shake the poor German Hodge out of his thousand years' sleep in his hole? What good did I get by it? Hodge opened his eyes, only to shut them again immediately; he yawned, only to begin snoring again the next minute louder than ever; he stretched his stiff ungainly limbs, only to sink down again directly afterwards, and lie like a dead man in the old bed of his accustomed habits. I must have rest; but where am I to find a resting-place? In Germany I can no longer stay."

. . . .

I wish to mark Heine's place in modern European literature, the scope of his activity, and his value. I cannot attempt to give here a detailed account of his life, or a description of his separate works. In May 1831 he went over his Jordan, the Rhine, and fixed himself in his new Jerusalem, Paris. There, henceforward, he lived, going in general to some French watering-place in the summer, but making only one or two short visits to Germany during the rest of his life. His works, in verse and prose, succeeded each other without stopping; a collected edition of them, filling seven closely-printed octavo volumes, has been published in America; in the collected editions of few people's works is there so little to skip. Those who wish for a single good specimen of him should read his first important work, the work which made his reputation, the *Reisebilder*, or "Travelling Sketches:" prose and verse, wit and seriousness, are mingled in it, and the mingling of these is characteristic of Heine, and is nowhere to be seen practised more naturally and happily than in his *Reisebilder*. In 1847 his health, which till then had always been perfectly good, gave way. He had a kind of paralytic stroke. His malady proved to be a softening of the spinal marrow: it was incurable; it made rapid progress. In May 1848, not a year after his first attack, he went out of doors for the last time; but his disease took more than eight years to kill him. For nearly eight years he lay helpless on a couch, with the use of his limbs gone, wasted almost to the proportions of a child, wasted so that a woman could carry him about; the sight of one eye lost, that of the other greatly dimmed, and requiring, that it might be exercised, to have the palsied eyelid lifted and held up by the finger; all this, and, besides this, suffering at short intervals

paroxysms of nervous agony. I have said he was not pre-
eminently brave; but in the astonishing force of spirit with which
he restrained his activity of mind, even his gaiety, amid all his
suffering, and went on composing with undiminished fire to the
last, he was truly brave. Nothing could clog that aërial lightness.
"Pouvez-vous siffler?" his doctor asked him one day, when he
was almost at his last gasp;—"siffler," as every one knows, has
the double meaning of *to whistle* and *to hiss*:—"Hélas! non,"
was his whispered answer; "pas même une comédie de M.
Scribe!" M. Scribe is, or was, the favourite dramatist of the
French Philistine. "My nerves," he said to some one who asked
him about them in 1855, the year of the great Exhibition in
Paris, "my nerves are of that quite singularly remarkable
miserableness of nature, that I am convinced they would get at
the Exhibition the grand medal for pain and misery." He read
all the medical books which treated of his complaint. "But," said
he to some one who found him thus engaged, "what good this
reading is to do me I don't know, except that it will qualify me to
give lectures in heaven on the ignorance of doctors on earth
about diseases of the spinal marrow." What a matter of grim
seriousness are our own ailments to most of us! yet with this
gaiety Heine treated his to the end. That end, so long in coming,
came at last. Heine died on the 17th of February 1856, at the
age of fifty-eight. By his will he forbade that his remains should
be transported to Germany. He lies buried in the cemetery of
Montmartre, at Paris.

His direct political action was null, and this is neither to be
wondered at nor regretted; direct political action is not the true
function of literature, and Heine was a born man of letters.
Even in his favourite France the turn taken by public affairs
was not at all what he wished, though he read French politics
by no means as we in England, most of us, read them. He
thought things were tending there to the triumph of communism; and to a champion of the idea like Heine, what there is
gross and narrow in communism was very repulsive. "It is
all of no use," he cried on his death-bed, "the future belongs to
our enemies, the Communists, and Louis Napoleon is their John
the Baptist." "And yet,"—he added with all his old love for
that remarkable entity, so full of attraction for him, so profoundly unknown in England, the French people,—"do not
believe that God lets all this go forward merely as a grand
comedy. Even though the Communists deny him to-day, he
knows better than they do, that a time will come when they will
learn to believe in him." After 1831, his hopes of soon upsetting
the German Governments had died away, and his propagandism

took another, a more truly literary, character. It took the character of an intrepid application of the modern spirit to literature. To the ideas with which the burning questions of modern life filled him, he made all his subject-matter minister. He touched all the great points in the career of the human race, and here he but followed the tendency of the wide culture of Germany; but he touched them with a wand which brought them all under a light where the modern eye cares most to see them, and here he gave a lesson to the culture of Germany,— so wide, so impartial, that it is apt to become slack and powerless, and to lose itself in its materials for want of a strong central idea round which to group all its other ideas. So the mystic and romantic school of Germany lost itself in the Middle Ages, was overpowered by their influence, came to ruin by its vain dreams of renewing them. Heine, with a far profounder sense of the mystic and romantic charm of the Middle Age than Gœrres, or Brentano, or Arnim, Heine the chief romantic poet of Germany, is yet also much more than a romantic poet; he is a great modern poet, he is not conquered by the Middle Age, he has a talisman by which he can feel,—along with but above the power of the fascinating Middle Age itself,—the power of modern ideas.

A French critic of Heine thinks he has said enough in saying that Heine proclaimed in German countries, with beat of drum, the ideas of 1789, and that at the cheerful noise of his drum the ghosts of the Middle Age took to flight. But this is rather too French an account of the matter. Germany, that vast mine of ideas, had no need to import ideas, as such, from any foreign country; and if Heine had carried ideas, as such, from France into Germany, he would but have been carrying coals to New-castle. But that for which France, far less meditative than Germany, is eminent, is the prompt, ardent, and practical application of an idea, when she seizes it, in all departments of human activity which admit it. And that in which Germany most fails, and by failing in which she appears so helpless and impotent, is just the practical application of her innumerable ideas. "When Candide," says Heine himself, "came to Eldorado, he saw in the streets a number of boys who were playing with gold-nuggets instead of marbles. This degree of luxury made him imagine that they must be the king's children, and he was not a little astonished when he found that in Eldorado gold-nuggets are of no more value than marbles are with us, and that the schoolboys play with them. A similar thing happened to a friend of mine, a foreigner, when he came to Germany and first read German books. He was perfectly astounded at the wealth of ideas which he found in them; but he soon remarked that ideas in Germany are as plentiful as gold-nuggets in Eldorado, and that those writers whom he had taken for intellectual princes, were in reality only common schoolboys." Heine was, as he calls himself, a "Child of the French Revolution," an "Initiator," because he vigorously assured the Germans that ideas were not counters or marbles, to be played with for their own sake; because he exhibited in literature modern ideas applied with the utmost freedom, clearness, and originality. And therefore he declared that the great task of his life had been the endeavour to establish a cordial relation between France and Germany. It is because he thus operates a junction between the French spirit, and German ideas and German culture, that he found something new, opens a fresh period, and deserves the attention of criticism far more than the German poets his contemporaries, who merely continue an old period till it expires. It may be predicted that in the literature of other countries, too, the French spirit is destined to make its influence felt,—as an element, in alliance with the native spirit, of novelty and movement,—as it has made its influence felt in German literature; fifty years hence a critic will be demonstrating to our grandchildren how this phenomenon has come to pass.

We in England, in our great burst of literature during the first thirty years of the present century, had no manifestation of the modern spirit, as this spirit manifests itself in Goethe's works or Heine's. And the reason is not far to seek. We had neither the German wealth of ideas, nor the French enthusiasm for applying ideas. There reigned in the mass of the nation that inveterate inaccessibility to ideas, that Philistinism,—to use the German nickname,—which reacts even on the individual genius that is exempt from it. In our greatest literary epoch, that of the Elizabethan age, English society at large was accessible to ideas, was permeated by them, was vivified by them, to a degree which has never been reached in England since. Hence the unique greatness in English literature of Shakspeare and his contemporaries. They were powerfully upheld by the intellectual life of their nation; they applied freely in literature the then modern ideas,—the ideas of the Renascence and the Reformation. A few years afterwards the great English middle class, the kernel of the nation, the class whose intelligent sympathy had upheld a Shakspeare, entered the prison of Puritanism, and had the key turned on its spirit there for two hundred years. *He enlargeth a nation*, says Job, *and straiteneth it again.*

In the literary movement of the beginning of the nineteenth century the signal attempt to apply freely the modern spirit was made in England by two members of the aristocratic class, Byron and Shelley. Aristocracies are, as such, naturally impenetrable by ideas; but their individual members have a high courage and a turn for breaking bounds; and a man of genius, who is the born child of the idea, happening to be born in the aristocratic ranks, chafes against the obstacles which prevent him from freely developing it. But Byron and Shelley did not succeed in their attempt freely to apply the modern spirit in English literature; they could not succeed in it; the resistance to baffle them, the want of intelligent sympathy to guide and uphold them, were too great. Their literary creation, compared with the literary creation of Shakspeare and Spenser, compared with the literary creation of Goethe and Heine, is a failure. The best literary creation of that time in England proceeded from men who did not make the same bold attempt as Byron and Shelley. What, in fact, was the career of the chief English men of letters, their contemporaries? The gravest of them, Wordsworth, retired (in Middle-Age phrase) into a monastery. I mean, he plunged himself in the inward life, he voluntarily cut himself off from the modern spirit. Coleridge took to opium. Scott became the historiographer-royal of feudalism. Keats passionately gave himself up to a sensuous genius, to his faculty for interpreting nature; and he died of consumption at twenty-five. Wordsworth, Scott, and Keats have left admirable works; far more solid and complete works than those which Byron and Shelley have left. But their works have this defect,— they do not belong to that which is the main current of the literature of modern epochs, they do not apply modern ideas to life; they constitute, therefore, *minor currents*, and all other literary work of our day, however popular, which has the same defect, also constitutes but a minor current. Byron and Shelley will long be remembered, long after the inadequacy of their actual work is clearly recognised for their passionate, their Titanic effort to flow in the main stream of modern literature; their names will be greater than their writings; *stat magni nominis umbra*.

Heine's literary good fortune was superior to that of Byron and Shelley. His theatre of operations was Germany, whose Philistinism does not consist in her want of ideas, or in her inaccessibility to ideas, for she teems with them and loves them, but, as I have said, in her feeble and hesitating application of modern ideas to life. Heine's intense modernism, his absolute freedom, his utter rejection of stock classicism and stock romanticism, his bringing all things under the point of view of the nineteenth century, were understood and laid to heart by

Germany, through virtue of her immense, tolerant intellectualism, much as there was in all Heine said to affront and wound Germany. The wit and ardent modern spirit of France Heine joined to the culture, the sentiment, the thought of Germany. This is what makes him so remarkable; his wonderful clearness, lightness, and freedom, united with such power of feeling, and width of range. Is there anywhere keener wit than in his story of the French abbé who was his tutor, and who wanted to get from him that *la religion* is French for *der Glaube*: "Six times did he ask me the question: 'Henry, what is *der Glaube* in French?' and six times, and each time with a greater burst of tears, did I answer him—'It is *le crédit*.' And at the seventh time, his face purple with rage, the infuriated questioner screamed out: 'It is *la religion*;' and a rain of cuffs descended upon me, and all the other boys burst out laughing. Since that day I have never been able to hear *la religion* mentioned, without feeling a tremor run through my back, and my cheeks grow red with shame." Or in that comment on the fate of Professor Saalfeld, who had been addicted to writing furious pamphlets against Napoleon, and who was a professor at Göttingen, a great seat, according to Heine, of pedantry and Philistinism: "It is curious," says Heine, "the three greatest adversaries of Napoleon have all of them ended miserably. Castlereagh cut his own throat; Louis the Eighteenth rotted upon his throne; and Professor Saalfeld is still a professor at Göttingen." It is impossible to go beyond that.

What wit, again, in that saying which every one has heard: "The Englishman loves liberty like his lawful wife, the Frenchman loves her like his mistress, the German loves her like his old grandmother." But the turn Heine gives to this incomparable saying is not so well known; and it is by that turn he shows himself the born poet he is,—full of delicacy and tenderness, of inexhaustible resource, infinitely new and striking:—

"And yet, after all, no one can ever tell how things may turn out. The grumpy Englishman, in an ill-temper with his wife, is capable of some day putting a rope round her neck, and taking her to be sold at Smithfield. The inconstant Frenchman may become unfaithful to his adored mistress, and be seen fluttering about the Palais Royal after another. *But the German will never quite abandon his old grandmother*; he will always keep for her a nook by the chimney-corner, where she can tell her fairy stories to the listening children."

Is it possible to touch more delicately and happily both the weakness and the strength of Germany;—pedantic, simple, enslaved, free, ridiculous, admirable Germany?

And Heine's verse,—his *Lieder*? Oh, the comfort, after dealing with French people of genius, irresistibly impelled to try and express themselves in verse, launching out into a deep which destiny has sown with so many rocks for them,—the comfort of coming to a man of genius, who finds in verse his freest and most perfect expression, whose voyage over the deep of poetry destiny makes smooth! After the rhythm, to us, at any rate, with the German paste in our composition, so deeply unsatisfying, of—

> "Ah! que me dites-vous, et que vous dit mon âme?
> Que dit le ciel à l'aube et la flamme à la flamme?"

what a blessing to arrive at rhythms like—

> "Take, oh, take those lips away,
> That so sweetly were forsworn—"

or—

> "Siehst sehr sterbeblässlich aus,
> Doch getrost! du bist zu Haus—"

in which one's soul can take pleasure! The magic of Heine's poetical form is incomparable; he chiefly uses a form of old German popular poetry, a ballad-form which has more rapidity and grace than any ballad-form of ours; he employs this form with the most exquisite lightness and ease, and yet it has at the same time the inborn fulness, pathos, and old-world charm of all true forms of popular poetry. Thus in Heine's poetry, too, one perpetually blends the impression of French modernism and clearness, with that of German sentiment and fulness; and to give this blended impression is, as I have said, Heine's great characteristic. To feel it, one must read him; he gives it in his form as well as in his contents, and by translation I can only reproduce it so far as his contents give it. But even the contents of many of his poems are capable of giving a certain sense of it. Here, for instance, is a poem in which he makes his profession of faith to an innocent beautiful soul, a sort of Gretchen, the child of some simple mining people having their hut among the pines at the foot of the Hartz Mountains, who reproaches him with not holding the old articles of the Christian creed:—

"Ah, my child, while I was yet a little boy, while I yet sate upon my mother's knee, I believed in God the Father, who rules up there in Heaven, good and great;

"Who created the beautiful earth, and the beautiful men and women thereon; who ordained for sun, moon, and stars their courses.

"When I got bigger, my child, I comprehended yet a great deal more than this, and comprehended, and grew intelligent; and I believe on the Son also;

"On the beloved Son, who loved us, and revealed love to us; and, for his reward, as always happens, was crucified by the people.

"Now, when I am grown up, have read much, have travelled much, my heart swells within me, and with my whole heart I believe on the Holy Ghost.

"The greatest miracles were of his working, and still greater miracles doth he even now work; he burst in sunder the oppressor's stronghold, and he burst in sunder the bondsman's yoke.

"He heals old death-wounds, and renews the old right; all mankind are one race of noble equals before him.

"He chases away the evil clouds and the dark cobwebs of the brain, which have spoilt love and joy for us, which day and night have loured on us.

"A thousand knights, well harnessed, has the Holy Ghost chosen out to fulfil his will and he has put courage into their souls.

"Their good swords flash, their bright banners wave; what, thou wouldst give much, my child, to look upon such gallant knights?

"Well, on me, my child, look! kiss me, and look boldly upon me! one of those knights of the Holy Ghost am I."

. . . .

No account of Heine is complete which does not notice the Jewish element in him. His race he treated with the same freedom with which he treated everything else, but he derived a great force from it, and no one knew this better than he himself. He has excellently pointed out how in the sixteenth century there was a double renascence,—a Hellenic renascence and a Hebrew renascence,—and how both have been great powers ever since. He himself had in him both the spirit of Greece and the spirit of Judæa; both these spirits reach the infinite, which is the true goal of all poetry and all art,—the Greek spirit by beauty, the Hebrew spirit by sublimity. By his perfection of literary form, by his love of clearness, by his love of beauty, Heine is Greek; by his intensity, by his untamableness, by his "longing which cannot be uttered," he is Hebrew.

. . . .

He died, and has left a blemished name; with his crying faults,—his intemperate susceptibility, his unscrupulousness in passion, his inconceivable attacks on his enemies, his still more inconceivable attacks on his friends, his want of generosity, his sensuality, his incessant mocking,—how could it be otherwise? Not only was he not one of Mr. Carlyle's "respectable" people, he was profoundly *dis*respectable; and not even the merit of not being a Philistine can make up for a man's being that. To his intellectual deliverance there was an addition of something else wanting, and that something else was something immense; the old-fashioned, laborious, eternally needful moral deliverance. Goethe says that he was deficient in *love*; to me his weakness seems to be not so much a deficiency in love as a deficiency in self-respect, in true dignity of character. But on this negative side of one's criticism of a man of great genius, I for my part, when I have once clearly marked that this negative side is and must be there, have no pleasure in dwelling. I prefer to say of Heine something positive. He is not an adequate interpreter of the modern world. He is only a brilliant soldier in the Liberation War of humanity. But, such as he is, he is (and posterity too, I am quite sure, will say this), in the European poetry of that quarter of a century which follows the death of Goethe, incomparably the most important figure.

What a spendthrift, one is tempted to cry, is Nature! With what prodigality, in the march of generations, she employs human power, content to gather almost always little result from it, sometimes none! Look at Byron, that Byron whom the present generation of Englishmen are forgetting; Byron, the greatest natural force, the greatest elementary power, I cannot but think which has appeared in our literature since Shakspeare. And what became of this wonderful production of nature? He shattered himself, he inevitably shattered himself to pieces against the huge, black, cloud-topped, interminable precipice of British Philistinism. But Byron, it may be said, was eminent only by his genius, only by his inborn force and fire; he had not the intellectual equipment of a supreme modern poet; except for his genius he was an ordinary nineteenth-century English gentleman, with little culture and with no ideas. Well, then, look at Heine. Heine had all the culture of Germany; in his head fermented all the ideas of modern Europe. And what have we got from Heine? A half-result, for want of moral balance, and of nobleness of soul and character. That is what I say; there is so much power, so many seem able to run well, so many give promise of running well;—so few reach the goal, so few are chosen. *Many are called, few chosen.*

Pagan and Mediæval Religious Sentiment

I READ the other day in the *Dublin Review*:—"We Catholics are apt to be cowed and scared by the lordly oppression of public opinion, and not to bear ourselves as men in the face of the anti-Catholic society of England. It is good to have an habitual consciousness that the public opinion of Catholic Europe looks upon Protestant England with a mixture of impatience and compassion, which more than balances the arrogance of the English people towards the Catholic Church in these countries."

The Holy Catholic Church, Apostolic and Roman, can take very good care of herself, and I am not going to defend her against the scorns of Exeter Hall.[1] Catholicism is not a great visible force in this country, and the mass of mankind will always treat lightly even things the most venerable, if they do not present themselves as visible forces before its eyes. In Catholic countries, as the *Dublin Review* itself says with triumph, they make very little account of the greatness of Exeter Hall. The majority has eyes only for the things of the majority, and in England the immense majority is Protestant. And yet, in spite of all the shocks which the feeling of a good Catholic, like the writer in the *Dublin Review*, has in this Protestant country inevitably to undergo, in spite of the contemptuous insensibility to the grandeur of Rome which he finds so general and so hard to bear, how much has he to console him, how many acts of homage to the greatness of his religion may he see if he has his eyes open! I will tell him of one of them. Let him go in London to that delightful spot, that Happy Island in Bloomsbury, the reading-room of the British Museum. Let him visit its sacred quarter, the region where its theological books are placed. I am almost afraid to say what he will find there, for fear Mr. Spurgeon, like a second Caliph Omar, should give the library to the flames. He will find an immense Catholic work, the collection of the Abbé Migne, lording it over that whole region, reducing to insignificance the feeble Protestant forces which hang upon its skirts. Protestantism is duly represented, indeed: the librarian knows his business too well to suffer it to be otherwise; all the varieties of Protestantism are there; there is the Library of Anglo-Catholic Theology, learned, decorous, exemplary, but a little uninteresting; there are the

[1] [Exeter Hall in the Strand was opened in 1831 as a meeting place for religious and philanthropic bodies. Spurgeon, from 1856, held his immensely popular religious services there: and hence it is specially associated with Evangelicism.]

works of Calvin, rigid, militant, menacing; there are the works
of Dr. Chalmers, the Scotch thistle valiantly doing duty as the
rose of Sharon, but keeping something very Scotch about it
all the time; there are the works of Dr. Channing, the last word
of religious philosophy in a land where every one has some
culture, and where superiorities are discountenanced,—the
flower of moral and intelligent mediocrity. But how are all
these divided against one another, and how, though they were
all united, are they dwarfed by the Catholic Leviathan, their
neighbour! Majestic in its blue and gold unity, this fills shelf
after shelf and compartment after compartment, its right mounting up into heaven among the white folios of the *Acta Sanctorum*,
its left plunging down into hell among the yellow octavos of the
Law Digest. Everything is there, in that immense *Patrologiæ
Cursus Completus*, in that *Encyclopédie Théologique*, that *Nouvelle
Encyclopédie Théologique*, that *Troisième Encyclopédie Théologique*;
religion, philosophy, history, biography, arts, sciences, bibliography, gossip. The work embraces the whole range of human
interests; like one of the great Middle-Age Catholics, it is in
itself a study for a life. Like the net in Scripture, it drags everything to land, bad and good, lay and ecclesiastical, sacred and
profane, so that it be but matter of human concern. Wide-
embracing as the power whose product it is! a power, for history
at any rate, eminently *the Church*; not, perhaps, the Church of
the future, but indisputably the Church of the past and, in the
past, the Church of the multitude.

This is why the man of imagination—nay, and the philosopher too, in spite of her propensity to burn him—will always
have a weakness for the Catholic Church; because of the rich
treasures of human life which have been stored within her pale.
The mention of other religious bodies, or of their leaders, at
once calls up in our mind the thought of men of a definite
type as their adherents; the mention of Catholicism suggests
no such special following. Anglicanism suggests the English
episcopate; Calvin's name suggests Dr. Candlish; Chalmers's,
the Duke of Argyll; Channing's, Boston society;[1] but Catholicism
suggests,—what shall I say?—all the pell-mell of the men and
women of Shakspeare's plays. This abundance the Abbé
Migne's collection faithfully reflects. People talk of this or that
work which they would choose, if they were to pass their life

[1] [Chalmers and Candlish, Scottish theologians actively concerned
in the movement which led to the split in the Scottish Established
Church and the foundation of the Free Church in 1843. William
Ellery Channing (d. 1842) an influential Boston Congregational pastor,
apostle of Unitarianism and opponent of Calvinism.]

with only one; for my part I think I would choose the Abbé Migne's collection. *Quicquid agunt homines,*—everything, as I have said, is there. Do not seek in it splendour of form, perfection of editing; its paper is common, its type ugly, its editing indifferent, its printing careless. The greatest and most baffling crowd of misprints I ever met with in my life occurs in a very important page of the introduction to the *Dictionnaire des Apocryphes.* But this is just what you have in the world,—quantity rather than quality. Do not seek in it impartiality, the critical spirit; in reading it you must do the criticism for yourself; it loves criticism as little as the world loves it. Like the world, it chooses to have things all its own way, to abuse its adversary, to back its own notion through thick and thin, to put forward all the *pros* for its own notion to suppress all the *contras*; it does just all that the world does, and all that the critical shrinks from. Open the *Dictionnaire des Erreurs Sociales*: "The religious persecutions of Henry the Eighth's and Edward the Sixth's time abated a little in the reign of Mary, to break out again with new fury in the reign of Elizabeth." There is a summary of the history of religious persecution under the Tudors! But how unreasonable to reproach the Abbé Migne's work with wanting a criticism, which, by the very nature of things, it cannot have, and not rather to be grateful to it for its abundance, its variety, its infinite suggestiveness, its happy adoption, in many a delicate circumstance, of the urbane tone and temper of the man of the world, instead of the acrid tone and temper of the fanatic!

Still, in spite of their fascinations, the contents of this collection sometimes rouse the critical spirit within one. It happened that lately, after I had been thinking much of Marcus Aurelius and his times, I took down the *Dictionnaire des Origines du Christianisme*, to see what it had to say about paganism and pagans. I found much what I expected. I read the article, *Révélation Évangélique, sa Nécessité.* There I found what a sink of iniquity was the whole pagan world; how one Roman fed his oysters on his slaves, how another put a slave to death that a curious friend might see what dying was like; how Galen's mother tore and bit her waiting-women when she was in a passion with them. I found this account of the religion of paganism: "Paganism invented a mob of divinities with the most hateful character, and attributed to them the most monstrous and abominable crimes. It personified in them drunkenness, incest, kidnapping, adultery, sensuality, knavery, cruelty, and rage." And I found that from this religion there followed such practice as was to be expected: "What must naturally have been the state of morals under the influence of such a religion, which penetrated with its own spirit the public life, the family life, and the individual life of antiquity?"

The colours in this picture are laid on very thick, and I for my part cannot believe that any human societies, with a religion and practice such as those just described, could ever have endured as the societies of Greece and Rome endured, still less have done what the societies of Greece and Rome did. We are not brought far by descriptions of the vices of great cities, or even of individuals driven mad by unbounded means of self-indulgence. Feudal and aristocratic life in Christendom has produced horrors of selfishness and cruelty not surpassed by the grandee of pagan Rome; and then, again, in antiquity there is Marcus Aurelius's mother to set against Galen's. Eminent examples of vice and virtue in individuals prove little as to the state of societies. What, under the first emperors, was the condition of the Roman poor upon the Aventine compared with that of our poor in Spitalfields and Bethnal Green? What, in comfort, morals, and happiness, were the rural population of the Sabine country under Augustus's rule, compared with the rural population of Hertfordshire and Buckinghamshire under the rule of Queen Victoria?

But these great questions are not now for me. Without trying to answer them, I ask myself, when I read such declamation as the foregoing, if I can find anything that will give me a near, distinct sense of the real difference in spirit and sentiment between paganism and Christianity, and of the natural effect of this difference upon people in general. I take a representative religious poem of paganism—of the paganism which all the world has in its mind when it speaks of paganism. To be a representative poem, it must be one for popular use, one that the multitude listens to. Such a religious poem may be found at the end of one of the best and happiest of Theocritus's idylls, the fifteenth. In order that the reader may the better go along with me in the line of thought I am following, I will translate it; and, that he may see the medium in which religious poetry of this sort is found existing, the society out of which it grows, the people who form it and are formed by it, I will translate the whole, or nearly the whole, of the idyll (it is not long) in which the poem occurs.

The idyll is dramatic. Somewhere about two hundred and eighty years before the Christian era, a couple of Syracusan women, staying at Alexandria, agreed on the occasion of a great religious solemnity,—the feast of Adonis,—to go together to the palace of King Ptolemy Philadelphus, to see the image of Adonis, which the queen Arsinoe, Ptolemy's wife, had had decorated with peculiar magnificence. A hymn, by a celebrated performer, was to be recited over the image. The names of the two women are Gorgo and Praxinoe; their maids, who are mentioned in the poem, are called Eunoe and Eutychis. Gorgo comes by appointment to Praxinoe's house to fetch her, and there the dialogue begins:—

Gorgo.—Is Praxinoe at home?

Praxinoe.—My dear Gorgo, at last! Yes, here I am. Eunoe, find a chair,—get a cushion for it.

Gorgo.—It will do beautifully as it is.

Praxinoe.—Do sit down.

Gorgo.—Oh, this gad-about spirit: I could hardly get to you, Praxinoe, through all the crowd and all the carriages. Nothing but heavy boots, nothing but men in uniform. And what a journey it is! My dear child you really live *too* far off.

Praxinoe.—It is all that insane husband of mine. He has chosen to come out here to the end of the world and take a hole of a place,—for a house it is not,—on purpose that you and I might not be neighbours. He is always just the same;—anything to quarrel with one! anything for spite!

Gorgo.—My dear, don't talk so of your husband before the little fellow. Just see how astonished he looks at you. Never mind, Zopyrio, my pet, she is not talking about papa.

Praxinoe.—Good heavens! the child does really understand.

Gorgo.—Pretty papa!

Praxinoe.—That pretty papa of his the other day (though I told him beforehand to mind what he was about), when I sent him to a shop to buy soap and rouge, brought me home salt instead;—stupid, great, big, interminable animal!

Gorgo—Mine is just the fellow to him. . . . But never mind now, get on your things and let us be off to the palace to see the Adonis. I hear the Queen's decorations are something splendid.

Praxinoe.—In grand people's houses everything is grand. What things you have seen in Alexandria! What a deal you will have to tell to anybody who has never been here!

Gorgo.—Come, we ought to be going.

Praxinoe.—Every day is holiday to people who have nothing to do. Eunoe, pick up your work; and take care, lazy girl, how you leave it lying about again; the cats find it just the bed they like. Come, stir yourself, fetch me some water, quick! I wanted the water first, and the girl brings me the soap. Never mind; give it me. Not all that, extravagant! Now pour out the water; —stupid! why don't you take care of my dress? That will do. I have got my hands washed as it pleased God. Where is the key of the large wardrobe? Bring it here;—quick!

Gorgo.—Praxinoe, you can't think how well that dress, made full, as you have got it, suits you. Tell me, how much did it cost?—the dress by itself, I mean.

Praxinoe.—Don't talk of it, Gorgo: more than eight guineas of good hard money. And about the work on it I have almost worn my life out.

Gorgo.—Well, you couldn't have done better.

Praxinoe.—Thank you. Bring me my shawl, and put my hat properly on my head;—properly. No, child (*to her little boy*), I am not going to take you; there's a bogy on horseback, who bites. Cry as much as you like; I'm not going to have you lamed for life. Now we'll start. Nurse, take the little one and amuse him; call the dog in, and shut the street-door. (*They go out.*) Good heavens! what a crowd of people! How on earth are we ever to get through all this? They are like ants: you can't count them. My dearest Gorgo, what will become of us? here are the royal Horse Guards. My good man, don't ride over me! Look at that bay horse rearing bolt upright; what a vicious one! Eunoe, you mad girl, do take care!—that horse will certainly be the death of the men on his back. How glad I am now, that I left the child safe at home!

Gorgo.—All right, Praxinoe, we are safe behind them; and they have gone on to where they are stationed.

Praxinoe.—Well, yes, I begin to revive again. From the time I was a little girl I have had more horror of horses and snakes than of anything in the world. Let us get on; here's a great crowd coming this way upon us.

Gorgo (*to an old woman*).—Mother, are you from the palace?

Old Woman.—Yes, my dears.

Gorgo.—Has one a tolerable chance of getting there?

Old Woman.—My pretty young lady, the Greeks got to Troy by dint of trying hard; trying will do anything in this world.

Gorgo.—The old creature has delivered herself of an oracle and departed.

Praxinoe.—Women can tell you everything about everything, Jupiter's marriage with Juno not excepted.

Gorgo.—Look, Praxinoe, what a squeeze at the palace gates!

Praxinoe.—Tremendous! Take hold of me, Gorgo; and you, Eunoe, take hold of Eutychis!—tight hold, or you'll be lost. Here we go in all together. Hold tight to us, Eunoe! Oh, dear! oh, dear! Gorgo, there's my scarf torn right in two. For heaven's sake, my good man, as you hope to be saved, take care of my dress!

Stranger.—I'll do what I can, but it doesn't depend upon me.

Praxinoe.—What heaps of people! They push like a drove of pigs.

Stranger.—Don't be frightened, ma'am, we are all right.

Praxinoe.—May you be all right, my dear sir, to the last day you live, for the care you have taken of us! What a kind, considerate man! There is Eunoe jammed in a squeeze. Push, you goose, push! Capital! We are all of us the right side of the door, as the bridegroom said when he had locked himself in with the bride.

Gorgo.—Praxinoe, come this way. Do but look at that work, how delicate it is!—how exquisite! Why, they might wear it in heaven.

Praxinoe.—Heavenly patroness of needlewomen, what hands were hired to do that work? Who designed those beautiful patterns? They seem to stand up and move about, as if they were real;—as if they were living things, and not needlework. Well, man is a wonderful creature! And look, look, how charming he lies there on his silver couch, with just a soft down on his cheeks, that beloved Adonis,—Adonis, whom one loves even though he is dead!

Another Stranger.—You wretched women, do stop your incessant chatter! Like turtles, you go on for ever. They are enough to kill one with their broad lingo,—nothing but *a, a, a.*

Gorgo.—Lord, where does the man come from? What is it to you if we *are* chatterboxes? Order about your own servants! Do you give orders to Syracusan women? If you want to know, we came originally from Corinth, as Bellerophon did; we speak Peloponnesian. I suppose Dorian women may be allowed to have a Dorian accent.

Praxinoe.—Oh, honey-sweet Proserpine, let us have no more masters than the one we've got! We don't the least care for *you*; pray don't trouble yourself for nothing.

Gorgo.—Be quiet, Praxinoe! That first-rate singer, the Argive woman's daughter, is going to sing the *Adonis* hymn. She is the same who was chosen to sing the dirge last year. We are sure to have something first-rate from *her*. She is going through her airs and graces ready to begin.—

So far the dialogue; and, as it stands in the original, it can hardly be praised too highly. It is a page torn fresh out of the book of human life. What freedom! What animation! What gaiety! What naturalness! It is said that Theocritus, in composing this poem, borrowed from a work of Sophron, a poet of an earlier and better time; but, even if this is so, the form is still Theocritus's own, and how excellent is that form, how masterly! And this in a Greek poem of the decadence!—for Theocritus's

O

poetry, after all, is poetry of the decadence. When such is Greek poetry of the decadence, what must be Greek poetry of the prime?

Then the singer begins her hymn:—

"Mistress, who loveth the haunts of Golgi, and Idalium, and high-peaked Eryx, Aphrodite that playest with gold! how have the delicate-footed Hours, after twelve months, brought thy Adonis back to thee from the ever-flowing Acheron! Tardiest of the immortals are the boon Hours, but all mankind wait their approach with longing, for they ever bring something with them. O Cypris, Dione's child! thou didst change—so is the story among men—Berenice from mortal to immortal, by dropping ambrosia into her fair bosom; and in gratitude to thee for this, O thou of many names and many temples! Berenice's daughter, Arsinoe, lovely Helen's living counterpart, makes much of Adonis with all manner of graveries.

"All fruits that the tree bears are laid before him, all treasures of the garden in silver baskets, and alabaster boxes, gold-inlaid, of Syrian ointment; and all confectionery that cunning women make on their kneading-tray, kneading up every sort of flowers with white meal, and all that they make of sweet honey and delicate oil, and all winged and creeping things are here set before him. And there are built for him green bowers with wealth of tender anise, and little boy-loves flutter about over them, like young nightingales trying their new wings on the tree, from bough to bough. Oh, the ebony, the gold, the eagle of white ivory that bears aloft his cup-bearer to Cronos-born Zeus! And up there, see! a second couch strewn for lovely Adonis, scarlet coverlets softer than sleep itself (so Miletus and the Samian wool-grower will say); Cypris has hers, and the rosy-armed Adonis has his, that eighteen or nineteen-year-old bridegroom. His kisses will not wound, the hair on his lip is yet light.

"Now, Cypris, good-night, we leave thee with thy bridegroom; but to-morrow morning, with the earliest dew, we will one and all bear him forth to where the waves splash upon the sea-strand, and letting loose our locks, and letting fall our robes, with bosoms bare, we will set up this, our melodious strain:

" 'Beloved Adonis, alone of the demigods (so men say) thou art permitted to visit both us and Acheron! This lot had neither Agamemnon, nor the mighty moon-struck hero Ajax, nor Hector the first-born of Hecuba's twenty children, nor Patroclus, nor Pyrrhus who came home from Troy, nor those yet earlier Lapithæ and the sons of Deucalion, nor the Pelasgians, the root of Argos and of Pelop's isle. Be gracious to us now, loved

Adonis, and be favourable to us for the year to come! Dear to us hast thou been at this coming, dear to us shalt thou be when thou comest again!"

The poem concludes with a characteristic speech from Gorgo:—

"Praxinoe, certainly women are wonderful things. That lucky woman to know all that! and luckier still to have such a splendid voice! And now we must see about getting home. My husband has not had his dinner. That man is all vinegar, and nothing else; and if you keep him waiting for his dinner, he's dangerous to go near. Adieu, precious Adonis, and may you find us all well when you come next year!"

So, with the hymn still in her ears, says the incorrigible Gorgo.

But what a hymn that is! Of religious emotion, in our acceptation of the words, and of the comfort springing from religious emotion, not a particle. And yet many elements of religious emotion are contained in the beautiful story of Adonis. Symbolically treated, as the thoughtful man might treat it, as the Greek mysteries undoubtedly treat it, this story was capable of a noble and touching application, and could lead the soul to elevating and consoling thoughts. Adonis was the sun in his summer and in his winter course, in his time of triumph and his time of defeat; but in his time of triumph still moving towards his defeat, in his time of defeat still returning towards his triumph. Thus he became an emblem of the power of life and the bloom of beauty, the power of human life and the bloom of human beauty, hastening inevitably to diminution and decay, yet in that very decay finding

> "Hope, and a renovation without end."

But nothing of this appears in the story as prepared for popular religious use, as presented to the multitude in a popular religious ceremony. Its treatment is not devoid of a certain grace and beauty, but it has nothing whatever that is elevating, nothing that is consoling, nothing that is in our sense of the word religious. The religious ceremonies of Christendom, even on occasion of the most joyful and mundane matters, present the multitude with strains of profoundly religious character, such as the *Kyrie eleison* and the *Te Deum*. But this Greek hymn to Adonis adapts itself exactly to the tone and temper of a gay and pleasure-loving multitude,—of light-hearted people, like Gorgo and Praxinoe, whose moral nature is much of the same calibre as that of Phillina in Goethe's *Wilhelm Meister*, people who seem never made to be serious, never made to be sick or sorry. And, if they happen to be sick or sorry, what will they do then?

But that we have no right to ask. Phillina, within the enchanted bounds of Goethe's novel, Gorgo and Praxinoe, within the enchanted bounds of Theocritus's poem, never will be sick and sorry, never can be sick and sorry. The ideal, cheerful, sensuous, pagan life is not sick or sorry. No; yet its natural end is in the sort of life which Pompeii and Herculaneum bring so vividly before us,—a life which by no means in itself suggests the thought of horror and misery, which even, in many ways, gratifies the senses and the understanding; but by the very intensity and unremittingness of its appeal to the senses and the understanding, by its stimulating a single side of us too absolutely, ends by fatiguing and revolting us; ends by leaving us with a sense of confinement, of oppression,—with a desire for an utter change, for clouds, storms, effusion, and relief.

In the beginning of the thirteenth century, when the clouds and storms had come, when the gay sensuous pagan life was gone, when men were not living by the senses and understanding, when they were looking for the speedy coming of Antichrist, there appeared in Italy, to the north of Rome, in the beautiful Umbrian country at the foot of the Apennines, a figure of the most magical power and charm, St. Francis. His century is, I think, the most interesting in the history of Christianity after its primitive age, more interesting than even the century of the Reformation; and one of the chief figures, perhaps the very chief, to which this interest attaches itself, is St. Francis. And why? Because of the profound popular instinct which enabled him, more than any man since the primitive age, to fit religion for popular use. He brought religion to the people. He founded the most popular body of ministers of religion that has ever existed in the Church. He transformed monachism by uprooting the stationary monk, delivering him from the bondage of property, and sending him, as a mendicant friar, to be a stranger and sojourner, not in the wilderness, but in the most crowded haunts of men, to console them and to do them good. This popular instinct of his is at the bottom of his famous marriage with poverty. Poverty and suffering are the condition of the people, the multitude, the immense majority of mankind; and it was towards this *people* that his soul yearned. "He listens," it was said of him, "to those to whom God himself will not listen."

So in return, as no other man he was listened to. When an Umbrian town or village heard of his approach, the whole population went out in joyful procession to meet him, with green boughs, flags, music, and songs of gladness. The master, who began with two disciples, could in his own lifetime (and he died at forty-four) collect to keep Whitsuntide with him, in presence of an immense multitude, five thousand of his Minorites. And thus he found fulfilment of his prophetic cry: "I hear in my ears the sound of the tongues of all the nations who shall come unto us; Frenchmen, Spaniards, Germans, Englishmen. The Lord will make of us a great people, even unto the ends of the earth."

Prose could not satisfy this ardent soul, and he made poetry. Latin was too learned for this simple, popular nature, and he composed in his mother tongue, in Italian. The beginnings of the mundane poetry of the Italians are in Sicily, at the court of kings; the beginnings of their religious poetry are in Umbria, with St. Francis. His are the humble upper waters of a mighty stream; at the beginning of the thirteenth century it is St. Francis, at the end, Dante. Now it happens that St. Francis, too, like the Alexandrian songstress, has his hymn for the sun, for Adonis. *Canticle of the Sun, Canticle of the Creatures,*—the poem goes by both names. Like the Alexandrian hymn, it is designed for popular use, but not for use by King Ptolemy's people; artless in language, irregular in rhythm, it matches with the childlike genius that produced it, and the simple natures that loved and repeated it:—

"O most high, almighty, good Lord God, to thee belong praise, glory, honour, and all blessing!

"Praised be my Lord God with all his creatures; and specially our brother the sun, who brings us the day, and who brings us the light; fair is he, and shining with a very great splendour: O Lord, he signifies to us thee!

"Praised be my Lord for our sister the moon, and for the stars, the which he has set clear and lovely in heaven.

"Praised be my Lord for our brother the wind, and for air and cloud, calms and all weather, by the which thou upholdest in life all creatures.

"Praise be my Lord for our sister water, who is very serviceable unto us, and humble, and precious, and clean.

"Praised be my Lord for our brother fire, through whom thou givest us light in the darkness; and he is bright, and pleasant, and very mighty, and strong.

"Praised be my Lord for our mother the earth, the which doth sustain us and keep us, and bringeth forth divers fruits, and flowers of many colours, and grass.

"Praised be my Lord for all those who pardon one another for his love's sake, and who endure weakness and tribulation; blessed are they who peaceably shall endure, for thou, O most Highest, shalt give them a crown!

"Praised be my Lord for our sister, the death of the body,

from whom no man escapeth. Woe to him who dieth in mortal sin! Blessed are they who are found walking by thy most holy will, for the second death shall have no power to do them harm.

"Praise ye, and bless ye the Lord, and give thanks unto him, and serve him with great humility."

It is natural that man should take pleasure in his senses. But it is natural, also, that he should take refuge in his heart and imagination from his misery. And when one thinks what human life is for the vast majority of mankind, how little of a feast for their senses it can possibly be, one understands the charm for them of a refuge offered in the heart and imagination. Above all, when one thinks what human life was in the Middle Ages, one understands the charm of such a refuge.

Now, the poetry of Theocritus's hymn is poetry treating the world according to the demand of the senses; the poetry of St. Francis's hymn is poetry treating the world according to the demand of the heart and imagination. The first takes the world by its outward, sensible side; the second by its inward, symbolical side. The first admits as much of the world as is pleasure-giving; the second admits the whole world, rough and smooth, painful and pleasure-giving, all alike, but all transfigured by the power of a spiritual emotion, all brought under a law of super-sensual love, having its seat in the soul. It can thus even say: "Praised be my Lord for *our sister, the death of the body*."

But these very words are, perhaps, an indication that we are touching upon an extreme. When we see Pompeii, we can put our finger upon the pagan sentiment in its extreme. And when we read of Monte Alverno and the *stigmata*; when we read of the repulsive, because self-caused, sufferings of the end of St. Francis's life; when we find him even saying, "I have sinned against my brother the ass," meaning by these words that he had been too hard upon his own body; when we find him assailed, even himself, by the doubt "whether he who had destroyed himself by the severity of his penances could find mercy in eternity," we can put our finger on the mediæval Christian sentiment in its extreme. Human nature is neither all senses and understanding, nor all heart and imagination. Pompeii was a sign that for humanity at large the measure of sensualism had been overpassed; St. Francis's doubt was a sign that for humanity at large the measure of spiritualism had been overpassed. Humanity, in its violent rebound from one extreme, had swung from Pompeii to Monte Alverno ; but it was sure not to stay there.

The Renascence is, in part, a return towards the pagan spirit, in the special sense in which I have been using the word pagan ;

a return towards the life of the senses and the understanding.
The Reformation, on the other hand, is the very opposite to
this; in Luther there is nothing Greek or pagan; vehemently
as he attacked the adoration of St. Francis, Luther had himself
something of St. Francis in him; he was a thousand times more
akin to St. Francis than to Theocritus or to Voltaire. The
Reformation—I do not mean the inferior piece given under that
name, by Henry the Eighth and a second-rate company, in
this island, but the real Reformation, the German Reformation,
Luther's Reformation—was a reaction of the moral and spiritual
sense against the carnal and pagan sense; it was a religious
revival like St. Francis's, but this time against the Church of
Rome, not within her; for the carnal and pagan sense had now,
in the government of the Church of Rome herself, its prime
representative. But the grand reaction against the rule of the
heart and imagination, the strong return towards the rule of the
senses and understanding, is in the eighteenth century. And
this reaction has had no more brilliant champion than a man of
the nineteenth, of whom I have already spoken; a man who could
feel not only the pleasurableness but the poetry of the life of the
senses (and the life of the senses has its deep poetry); a man
who, in his very last poem, divided the whole world into
"barbarians and Greeks,"—Heinrich Heine. No man has
reproached the Monte Alverno extreme in sentiment, the
Christian extreme, the heart and imagination subjugating the
senses and understanding, more bitterly than Heine; no man has
extolled the Pompeii extreme, the pagan extreme, more
rapturously.

"All through the Middle Age these sufferings, this fever, this
over-tension lasted; and we moderns still feel in all our limbs
the pain and weakness from them. Even those of us who are
cured have still to live with a hospital-atmosphere all around us,
and find ourselves as wretched in it as a strong man among the
sick. Some day or other, when humanity shall have got quite
well again, when the body and soul shall have made their peace
together, the fictitious quarrel which Christianity has cooked up
between them will appear something hardly comprehensible.
The fairer and happier generations, offspring of unfettered
unions, that will rise up and bloom in the atmosphere of a
religion of pleasure, will smile sadly when they think of their
poor ancestors, whose life was passed in melancholy abstinence
from the joys of this beautiful earth, and who faded away into
spectres, from the mortal compression which they put upon the
warm and glowing emotions of sense. Yes, with assurance I
say it, our descendants will be fairer and happier than we are;

for I am a believer in progress, and I hold God to be a kind being who has intended man to be happy."

That is Heine's sentiment, in the prime of life, in the glow of activity, amid the brilliant whirl of Paris. I will no more blame it than I blamed the sentiment of the Greek hymn to Adonis. I wish to decide nothing as of my own authority; the great art of criticism is to get oneself out of the way and to let humanity decide. Well, the sentiment of the "religion of pleasure" has much that is natural in it; humanity will gladly accept it if it can live by it; to live by it one must never be sick or sorry, and the old, ideal, limited, pagan world never, I have said, *was* sick or sorry, never at least shows itself to us sick or sorry:—

"What pipes and timbrels! what wild ecstasy!"

For our imagination, Gorgo and Praxinoe cross the human stage chattering in their blithe Doric,—*like turtles*, as the cross stranger said,—and keep gaily chattering on till they disappear. But in the new, real, immense, post-pagan world,—in the barbarian world,—the shock of accident is unceasing, the serenity of existence is perpetually troubled, not even a Greek like Heine can get across the mortal stage without bitter calamity. How does the sentiment of the "religion of pleasure" serve then? does it help, does it console? Can a man live by it? Heine again shall answer; Heine just twenty years older, stricken with incurable disease, waiting for death:—

"The great pot stands smoking before me, but I have no spoon to help myself. What does it profit me that my health is drunk at banquets out of gold cups and in most exquisite wines, if I myself, while these ovations are going on, lonely and cut off from the pleasures of the world, can only just wet my lips with barley-water? What good does it do me that all the roses of Shiraz open their leaves and burn for me with passionate tenderness? Alas! Shiraz is some two thousand leagues from the Rue d'Amsterdam, where in the solitude of my sick chamber all the perfume I smell is that of hot towels. Alas! the mockery of God is heavy upon me! The great author of the universe, the Aristophanes of Heaven, has determined to make the petty earthly author, the so-called Aristophanes of Germany, feel to his heart's core what pitiful needle-pricks his cleverest sarcasms have been, compared with the thunderbolts which his divine humour can launch against feeble mortals! . . .

" In the year 1340, says the Chronicle of Limburg, all over Germany everybody was strumming and humming certain songs more lovely and delightful than any which had ever yet been known in German countries; and all people, old and young, the women particularly, were perfectly mad about them, so that from morning until night you heard nothing else. Only, the Chronicle adds, the author of these songs happened to be a young clerk, afflicted with leprosy, and living apart from all the world in a desolate place. The excellent reader does not require to be told how horrible a complaint was leprosy in the Middle Ages, and how the poor wretches who had this incurable plague were banished from society, and had to keep at a distance from every human being. Like living corpses, in a gray gown reaching down to the feet, and with the hood brought over their face, they went about, carrying in their hands an enormous rattle, called Saint Lazarus's rattle. With this rattle they gave notice of their approach, that every one might have time to get out of their way. This poor clerk, then, whose poetical gift the Limburg Chronicle extols, was a leper, and he sate moping in the dismal deserts of his misery, whilst all Germany, gay and tuneful, was praising his songs.

"Sometimes, in my sombre visions of the night, I imagine that I see before me the poor leprosy-stricken clerk of the Limburg Chronicle, and then from under his gay hood his distressed eyes look out upon me in a fixed and strange fashion; but the next instant he disappears, and I hear dying away in the distance, like the echo of a dream, the dull creak of Saint Lazarus's rattle."

We have come a long way from Theocritus there; the expression of that has nothing of the clear, positive, happy, pagan character; it has much more the character of one of the indeterminate grotesques of the suffering Middle Age. Profoundness and power it has, though at the same time it is not truly poetical; it is not natural enough for that, there is too much waywardness in it, too much bravado. But as a condition of sentiment to be popular,—to be a comfort for the mass of mankind, under the pressure of calamity, to live by,—what a manifest failure is this last word of the religion of pleasure! One man in many millions, a Heine, may console himself, and keep himself erect in suffering, by a colossal irony of this sort, by covering himself and the universe with the red fire of this sinister mockery; but the many millions cannot,—cannot if they would. That is where the sentiment of a religion of sorrow has such a vast advantage over the sentiment of a religion of pleasure; in its power to be a general, popular, religious sentiment, a stay for the mass of mankind, whose lives are full of hardship. It really succeeds in conveying far more joy, far more of what the mass of mankind are so much without, than its rival. I do not mean joy in prospect only, but joy in possession, actual enjoyment of the world. Mediæval Christianity is reproached with its gloom and austerities; it assigns the material world, says Heine, to the devil. But yet what a fulness of delight does St. Francis manage to draw from this material world itself, and from its commonest and most universally enjoyed elements,—sun, air, earth, water, plants! His hymn expresses a far more cordial sense of happiness, even in the material world, than the hymn of Theocritus. It is this which made the fortune of Christianity, —its gladness, not its sorrow; not its assigning the spiritual world to Christ, and the material world to the devil, but its drawing from the spiritual world a source of joy so abundant that it ran over upon the material world and transfigured it.

I have said a great deal of harm of paganism; and, taking paganism to mean a state of things which it is commonly taken to mean, and which did really exist, no more harm than it well deserved. Yet I must not end without reminding the reader, that before this state of things appeared, there was an epoch in Greek life,—in pagan life,—of the highest possible beauty and value. That epoch by itself goes far towards making Greece the Greece we mean when we speak of Greece,—a country hardly less important to mankind than Judæa. The poetry of later paganism lived by the senses and understanding; the poetry of mediæval Christianity lived by the heart and imagination. But the main element of the modern spirit's life is neither the senses and understanding, nor the heart and imagination; it is the imaginative reason. And there is a century in Greek life,—the century preceding the Peloponnesian war, from about the year 530 to the year 430 B.C.,—in which poetry made, it seems to me, the noblest, the most successful effort she has ever made as the priestess of the imaginative reason, of the element by which the modern spirit, if it would live right, has chiefly to live. Of this effort, of which the four great names are Simonides, Pindar, Æschylus, Sophocles, I must not now attempt more than the bare mention; but it is right, it is necessary, after all I have said, to indicate it. No doubt that effort was imperfect. Perhaps everything, take it at what point in its existence you will, carries within itself the fatal law of its own ulterior development. Perhaps, even of the life of Pindar's time, Pompeii was the inevitable bourne. Perhaps the life of their beautiful Greece could not afford to its poets all that fulness of varied experience, all that power of emotion, which

"... the heavy and the weary weight
　Of all this unintelligible world"

affords the poet of after-times. Perhaps in Sophocles the thinking-power a little overbalances the religious sense, as in

Dante the religious sense overbalances the thinking-power. The present has to make its own poetry, and not even Sophocles and his compeers, any more than Dante and Shakspeare, are enough for it. That I will not dispute; nor will I set up the Greek poets, from Pindar to Sophocles, as objects of blind worship. But no other poets so well show to the poetry of the present the way it must take; no other poets have lived so much by the imaginative reason; no other poets have made their work so well balanced; no other poets, who have so well satisfied the thinking-power, have so well satisfied the religious sense:—

"Oh! that my lot may lead me in the path of holy innocence of word and deed, the path which august laws ordain, laws that in the highest empyrean had their birth, of which Heaven is the father alone, neither did the race of mortal men beget them, nor shall oblivion ever put them to sleep. The power of God is mighty in them, and groweth not old."

Let St. Francis,—nay, or Luther either,—beat that!

From *Joubert*

WHY should we ever treat of any dead authors but the famous ones? Mainly for this reason: because, from these famous personages, home or foreign, whom we all know so well, and of whom so much has been said, the amount of stimulus which they contain for us has been in a great measure disengaged; people have formed their opinion about them, and do not readily change it. One may write of them afresh, combat received opinions about them, even interest one's readers in so doing; but the interest one's readers receive has to do, in general, rather with the treatment than with the subject; they are susceptible of a lively impression rather of the course of the discussion itself,— its turns, vivacity, and novelty,—than of the genius of the author who is the occasion of it. And yet what is really precious and inspiring, in all that we get from literature, except this sense of an immediate contact with genius itself, and the stimulus towards what is true and excellent which we derive from it? Now in literature, besides the eminent men of genius who have had their deserts in the way of fame, besides the eminent men of ability who have often had far more than their deserts in the way of fame, there are a certain number of personages who have been real men of genius,—by which I mean, that they have had a genuine gift for what is true and excellent, and are therefore capable of emitting a life-giving stimulus,—but who, for some reason or other, in most cases for very valid reasons, have remained obscure, nay, beyond a narrow circle in their own country, unknown. It is salutary from time to time to come across a genius of this kind, and to extract his honey. Often he has more of it for us, as I have already said, than greater men; for, though it is by no means true that from what is new to us there is most to be learnt, it is yet indisputably true that from what is new to us we in general learn most.

Of a genius of this kind, Joseph Joubert, I am now going to speak. His name is, I believe, almost unknown in England; and even in France, his native country, it is not famous. M. Sainte-Beuve has given of him one of his incomparable portraits; but,—besides that even M. Sainte-Beuve's writings are far less known amongst us than they deserve to be,—every country has its own point of view from which a remarkable author may most profitably be seen and studied.

Joseph Joubert was born (and his date should be remarked) in 1754, at Montignac, a little town in Périgord. His father was a doctor with small means and a large family; and Joseph, the eldest, had his own way to make in the world. He was for eight years, as pupil first, and afterwards as an assistant-master, in the public school of Toulouse, then managed by the Jesuits, who seem to have left in him a most favourable opinion, not only of their tact and address, but of their really good qualities as teachers and directors. Compelled by the weakness of his health to give up, at twenty-two, the profession of teaching, he passed two important years of his life in hard study, at home at Montignac; and came in 1778 to try his fortune in the literary world of Paris, then perhaps the most tempting field which has ever yet presented itself to a young man of letters. He knew Diderot, D'Alembert, Marmontel, Laharpe; he became intimate with one of the celebrities of the next literary generation, then, like himself, a young man,—Chateaubriand's friend, the future Grand Master of the University, Fontanes. But, even then, it began to be remarked of him, that M. Joubert, "*s'inquiétait de perfection bien plus que de gloire*—cared far more about perfecting himself than about making himself a reputation." His severity of morals may perhaps have been rendered easier to him by the delicacy of his health; but the delicacy of his health will not by itself account for his changeless preference of being to seeming, knowing to showing, studying to publishing; for what terrible public performers have some invalids been! This preference he retained all through his life, and it is by this that he is characterised. "He has chosen," Chateaubriand (adopting Epicurus's famous words) said of him, "*to hide his life.*" Of a life which its owner was bent on hiding there can be but little to tell. Yet the only two public incidents of Joubert's life, slight as they are, do all concerned in them so much credit that they deserve mention. In 1790 the Constituent Assembly made the office of justice of the peace elective throughout France. The people of Montignac retained such an impression of the character of their young townsman,—one of Plutarch's men of virtue, as he had lived amongst them, simple, studious, severe,—that, though he had left them for years, they elected him in his absence without his knowing anything about it. The appointment little suited Joubert's wishes or tastes; but at such a moment he thought it wrong to decline it. He held it for two years, the legal term, discharging its duties with a firmness and integrity which were long remembered; and then, when he went out of office, his fellow-townsmen re-elected him. But Joubert thought that he had now accomplished his duty towards them, and he went back to the retirement which he loved. That seems to me a little episode of the great French Revolution worth remembering. The sage who was asked by the king, why sages were seen at the doors of kings, but not kings at the doors of sages, replied, that it was because sages knew what was good for them, and kings did not. But at Montignac the king—for in 1790 the people in France was king with a vengeance—knew what was good for him, and came to the door of the sage.

The other incident was this. When Napoleon, in 1809, reorganised the public instruction of France, founded the University, and made M. de Fontanes its Grand Master, Fontanes had to submit to the Emperor a list of persons to form the council or governing body of the new University. Third on his list, after two distinguished names, Fontanes placed the unknown name of Joubert. "This name," he said in his accompanying memorandum to the Emperor, "is not known as the two first are; and yet this is the nomination to which I attach most importance. I have known M. Joubert all my life. His character and intelligence are of the very highest order. I shall rejoice if your Majesty will accept my guarantee for him." Napoleon trusted his Grand Master, and Joubert became a councillor of the University. It is something that a man, elevated to the highest posts of State, should not forget his obscure friends; or that, if he remembers and places them, he should regard in placing them their merit rather than their obscurity. It is more, in the eyes of those whom the necessities, real or supposed, of a political system have long familiarised with such cynical disregard of fitness in the distribution of office, to see a minister and his master alike zealous, in giving away places, to give them to the best men to be found.

Between 1792 and 1809 Joubert had married. His life was passed between Villeneuve-sur-Yonne, where his wife's family lived,—a pretty little Burgundian town, by which the Lyons railroad now passes,—and Paris. Here, in a house in the Rue St.-Honoré, in a room very high up, and admitting plenty of the light which he so loved,—a room from which he saw, in his own words, "a great deal of sky and very little earth,"—among the treasures of a library collected with infinite pains, taste, and skill, from which every book he thought ill of was rigidly excluded,—he never would possess either a complete Voltaire or a complete Rousseau,—the happiest hours of his life were passed. In the circle of one of those women who leave a sort of perfume in literary history, and who have the gift of inspiring successive generations of readers with an indescribable regret not to have known them,—Pauline de Montmorin, Madame de Beaumont,—he had become intimate with nearly all which at that time, in the Paris world of letters or of society, was most attractive and promising. Amongst his acquaintances one only misses the names of Madame de Staël and Benjamin Constant. Neither of them was to his taste, and with Madame de Staël he always refused to become acquainted; he thought she had more vehemence than truth, and more heat than light.

Years went on, and his friends became conspicuous authors or statesmen; but Joubert remained in the shade. His constitution was of such fragility that how he lived so long, or accomplished so much as he did, is a wonder: his soul had, for its basis of operations, hardly any body at all: both from his stomach and from his chest he seems to have had constant suffering, though he lived by rule, and was as abstemious as a Hindoo. Often, after overwork in thinking, reading, or talking, he remained for days together in a state of utter prostration,—condemned to absolute silence and inaction; too happy if the agitation of his mind would become quiet also, and let him have the repose of which he stood in so much need. With this weakness of health, these repeated suspensions of energy, he was incapable of the prolonged contention of spirit necessary for the creation of great works. But he read and thought immensely; he was an unwearied note-taker, a charming letter-writer; above all, an excellent and delightful talker. The gaiety and amenity of his natural disposition were inexhaustible; and his spirit, too, was of astonishing elasticity; he seemed to hold on to life by a single thread only, but that single thread was very tenacious. More and more, as his soul and knowledge ripened more and more, his friends pressed to his room in the Rue St.-Honoré; often he received them in bed, for he seldom rose before three o'clock in the afternoon; and at his bedroom-door, on his bad days, Madame Joubert stood sentry, trying, not always with success, to keep back the thirsty comers from the fountain which was forbidden to flow. Fontanes did nothing in the University without consulting him, and Joubert's ideas and pen were always at his friend's service.

When he was in the country, at Villeneuve, the young priests of his neighbourhood used to resort to him, in order to profit by his library and by his conversation. He, like our Coleridge, was particularly qualified to attract men of this kind and to benefit them: retaining perfect independence of mind, he was a religious philosopher. As age came on, his infirmities became more and more overwhelming; some of his friends, too, died; others became so immersed in politics, that Joubert, who hated politics, saw them seldomer than of old; but the moroseness of age and infirmity never touched him, and he never quarrelled with a friend or lost one. From these miseries he was preserved by that quality in him of which I have already spoken; a quality which is best expressed by a word, not of common use in English,—alas, we have too little in our national character of the quality which this word expresses,—his inborn, his constant amenity. He lived till the year 1824. On the 4th of May in that year he died, at the age of seventy. A day or two after his death M. de Chateaubriand inserted in the *Journal des Débats* a short notice of him, perfect for its feeling, grace, and propriety. *On ne vit dans la mémoire du monde*, he says and says truly, *que par des travaux pour le monde*,—"a man can live in the world's memory only by what he has done for the world." But Chateaubriand used the privilege which his great name gave him to assert, delicately but firmly, Joubert's real and rare merits, and to tell the world what manner of man had just left it.

Joubert's papers were accumulated in boxes and drawers. He had not meant them for publication; it was very difficult to sort them and to prepare them for it. Madame Joubert, his widow, had a scruple about giving them a publicity which her husband, she felt, would never have permitted. But, as her own end approached, the natural desire to leave of so remarkable a spirit some enduring memorial, some memorial to outlast the admiring recollection of the living who were so fast passing away, made her yield to the entreaties of his friends, and allow the printing, but for private circulation only, of a volume of his fragments. Chateaubriand edited it; it appeared in 1838, fourteen years after Joubert's death. The volume attracted the attention of those who were best fitted to appreciate it, and profoundly impressed them. M. Sainte-Beuve gave of it, in the

Revue des Deux Mondes, the admirable notice of which I have already spoken; and so much curiosity was excited about Joubert, that the collection of his fragments, enlarged by many additions, was at last published for the benefit of the world in general. It has since been twice reprinted. The first or preliminary chapter has some fancifulness and affectation in it; the reader should begin with the second.

I have likened Joubert to Coleridge; and indeed the points of resemblance between the two men are numerous. Both of them great and celebrated talkers, Joubert attracting pilgrims to his upper chamber in the Rue St.-Honoré, as Coleridge attracted pilgrims to Mr. Gilman's at Highgate; both of them desultory and incomplete writers,—here they had an outward likeness with one another. Both of them passionately devoted to reading in a class of books, and to thinking on a class of subjects, out of the beaten line of the reading and thought of their day; both of them ardent students and critics of old literature, poetry, and the metaphysics of religion; both of them curious explorers of words, and of the latent significance hidden under the popular use of them; both of them, in a certain sense, conservative in religion and politics, by antipathy to the narrow and shallow foolishness of vulgar modern liberalism;—here they had their inward and real likeness. But that in which the essence of their likeness consisted is this,—that they both had from nature an ardent impulse for seeking the genuine truth on all matters they thought about, and a gift for finding it and recognising it when it was found. To have the impulse for seeking this truth is much rarer than most people think; to have the gift for finding it is, I need not say, very rare indeed. By this they have a spiritual relationship of the closest kind with one another, and they become, each of them, a source of stimulus and progress for all of us.

Coleridge had less delicacy and penetration than Joubert, but more richness and power; his production, though far inferior to what his nature at first seemed to promise, was abundant and varied. Yet in all his production how much is there to dissatisfy us! How many reserves must be made in praising either his poetry, or his criticism, or his philosophy! How little either of his poetry, or of his criticism, or of his philosophy, can we expect permanently to stand! But that which will stand of Coleridge is this: the stimulus of his continual effort,—not a moral effort, for he had no morals—but of his continual instinctive effort, crowned often with rich success, to get at and to lay bare the real truth of his matter in hand, whether that matter were literary, or philosophical, or political, or religious; and this

in a country where at that moment such an effort was almost
unknown; where the most powerful minds threw themselves
upon poetry, which conveys truth, indeed, but conveys it indirectly; and where ordinary minds were so habituated to do
without thinking altogether, to regard considerations of established routine and practical convenience as paramount, that any
attempt to introduce within the domain of these the disturbing
element of thought, they were prompt to resent as an outrage.
Coleridge's great usefulness lay in his supplying in England, for
many years and under critical circumstances, by the spectacle
of this effort of his, a stimulus to all minds capable of profiting
by it; in the generation which grew up around him. His action
will still be felt as long as the need for it continues. When, with
the cessation of the need, the action too has ceased, Coleridge's
memory, in spite of the disesteem—nay, repugnance—which
his character may and must inspire, will yet for ever remain
invested with that interest and gratitude which invests the
memory of founders.

M. de Rémusat, indeed, reproaches Coleridge with his
jugements saugrenus; the criticism of a gifted truthfinder ought
not to be *saugrenu*, so on this reproach we must pause for a
moment. *Saugrenu* is a rather vulgar French word, but, like
many other vulgar words, very expressive; used as an epithet for
a judgment, it means something like *impudently absurd*. The
literary judgments of one nation about another are very apt to be
saugrenus. It is certainly true, as M. Sainte-Beuve remarks in
answer to Goethe's complaint against the French that they have
undervalued Du Bartas, that as to the estimate of its own authors
every nation is the best judge; the *positive* estimate of them, be it
understood, not, of course, the estimate of them in comparison
with the authors of other nations. Therefore a foreigner's
judgments about the intrinsic merit of a nation's authors will
generally, when at complete variance with that nation's own, be
wrong; but there is a permissible wrongness in these matters,
and to that permissible wrongness there is a limit. When that
limit is exceeded, the wrong judgment becomes more than
wrong, it becomes *saugrenu*, or impudently absurd. For instance,
the high estimate which the French have of Racine is probably
in great measure deserved; or, to take a yet stronger case, even
the high estimate which Joubert had of the Abbé Delille is
probably in great measure deserved; but the common disparaging judgment passed on Racine by English readers is not
saugrenu, still less is that passed by them on the Abbé Delille
saugrenu, because the beauty of Racine, and of Delille too, so
far as Delille's beauty goes, is eminently in their language, and

this is a beauty which a foreigner cannot perfectly seize;—this beauty of diction, *apicibus verborum ligata*, as M. Sainte-Beuve, quoting Quintilian, says of Chateaubriand's. As to Chateaubriand himself, again, the common English judgment, which stamps him as a mere shallow rhetorician, all froth and vanity, is certainly wrong; one may even wonder that we English should judge Chateaubriand so wrongly, for his power goes far beyond beauty of diction; it is a power, as well, of passion and sentiment, and this sort of power the English can perfectly well appreciate. One production of Chateaubriand's, *René*, is akin to the most popular productions of Byron,—to the *Childe Harold* or *Manfred*,—in spirit, equal to them in power, superior to them in form. But this work, I hardly know why, is almost unread in England. And only consider this criticism of Chateaubriand's on the true pathetic! "It is a dangerous mistake, sanctioned, like so many other dangerous mistakes, by Voltaire, to suppose that the best works of imagination are those which draw most tears. One could name this or that melodrama, which no one would like to own having written, and which yet harrows the feelings far more than the *Æneid*. The true tears are those which are called forth by the *beauty* of poetry; there must be as much admiration in them as sorrow. They are the tears which come to our eyes when Priam says to Achilles, ἔτλην δ', οἷ' οὔπω . . .—'And I have endured,—the like whereof no soul upon the earth hath yet endured,—to carry to my lips the hand of him who slew my child;' or when Joseph cries out: 'I am Joseph your brother, whom ye sold into Egypt.' " Who does not feel that the man who wrote that was no shallow rhetorician, but a born man of genius, with the true instinct of genius for what is really admirable? Nay, take these words of Chateaubriand, an old man of eighty, dying, amidst the noise and bustle of the ignoble revolution of February 1848: "Mon Dieu, mon Dieu, quand donc, quand donc serai-je délivré de tout ce monde, ce bruit; quand donc, quand donc cela finira-t-il?" Who, with any ear, does not feel that those are not the accents of a trumpery rhetorician, but of a rich and puissant nature,—the cry of the dying lion? I repeat it, Chateaubriand is most ignorantly underrated in England; and we English are capable of rating him far more correctly if we knew him better. Still Chateaubriand has such real and great faults, he falls so decidedly beneath the rank of the truly greatest authors, that the depreciatory judgment passed on him in England, though ignorant and wrong, can hardly be said to transgress the limits of permissible ignorance; it is not a *jugement saugrenu*. But when a critic denies genius to a literature which has produced Bossuet and Molière, he passes the bounds; and Coleridge's judgments on French literature and the French genius are undoubtedly, as M. de Rémusat calls them, *saugrenus*.

And yet, such is the impetuosity of our poor human nature, such its proneness to rush to a decision with imperfect knowledge, that his having delivered a *saugrenu* judgment or two in his life by no means proves a man not to have had, in comparison with his fellow-men in general, a remarkable gift for truth, or disqualifies him for being, by virtue of that gift, a source of vital stimulus for us. Joubert had far less smoke and turbid vehemence in him than Coleridge; he had also a far keener sense of what was absurd. But Joubert can write to M. Molé (the M. Molé who was afterwards Louis Philippe's well-known minister): "As to your Milton, whom the merit of the Abbé Delille" (the Abbé Delille translated *Paradise Lost*) "makes me admire, and with whom I have nevertheless still plenty of fault to find, why, I should like to know, are you scandalised that I have not enabled myself to read him? I don't understand the language in which he writes, and I don't much care to. If he is a poet one cannot put up with, even in the prose of the younger Racine, am I to blame for that? If by force you mean beauty manifesting itself with power, I maintain that the Abbé Delille has more force than Milton." That, to be sure, is a petulant outburst in a private letter; it is not, like Coleridge's, a deliberate proposition in a printed philosophical essay. But is it possible to imagine a more perfect specimen of a *saugrenu* judgment? It is even worse than Coleridge's, because it is *saugrenu* with reasons. That, however, does not prevent Joubert from having been really a man of extraordinary ardour in the search for truth, and of extraordinary fineness in the perception of it; and so was Coleridge.

Joubert had around him in France an atmosphere of literary, philosophical, and religious opinion as alien to him as that in England was to Coleridge. This is what makes Joubert, too, so remarkable, and it is on this account that I begged the reader to remark his date. He was born in 1754; he died in 1824. He was thus in the fulness of his powers at the beginning of the present century, at the epoch of Napoleon's consulate. The French criticism of that day—the criticism of Laharpe's successors, of Geoffroy and his colleagues in the *Journal des Débats*—had a dryness very unlike the telling vivacity of the early Edinburgh reviewers, their contemporaries, but a fundamental narrowness, a want of genuine insight, much on a par with theirs. Joubert, like Coleridge, has no respect for the dominant oracle; he treats his Geoffroy with about as little deference as Coleridge treats his

Jeffrey. "Geoffroy," he says in an article in the *Journal des Débats* criticising Chateaubriand's *Génie du Christianisme*—"Geoffroy in this article begins by holding out his paw prettily enough; but he ends by a volley of kicks, which lets the whole world see but too clearly the four iron shoes of the four-footed animal." There is, however, in France a sympathy with intellectual activity for its own sake, and for the sake of its inherent pleasurableness and beauty, keener than any which exists in England; and Joubert had more effect in Paris,—though his conversation was his only weapon, and Coleridge wielded besides his conversation his pen,—that Coleridge had or could have in London. I mean, a more immediate, appreciable effect; an effect not only upon the young and enthusiastic, to whom the future belongs, but upon formed and important personages to whom the present belongs, and who are actually moving society. He owed this partly to his real advantages over Coleridge. If he had, as I have already said, less power and richness than his English parallel, he had more tact and penetration. He was more *possible* than Coleridge; his doctrine was more intelligible than Coleridge's, more receivable. And yet with Joubert, the striving after a consummate and attractive clearness of expression came from no mere frivolous dislike of labour and inability for going deep, but was a part of his native love of truth and perfection. The delight of his life he found in truth, and in the satisfaction which the enjoying of truth gives to the spirit; and he thought the truth was never really and worthily said, so long as the least cloud, clumsiness, and repulsiveness hung about the expression of it.

Some of his best passages are those in which he upholds this doctrine. Even metaphysics he would not allow to remain difficult and abstract: so long as they spoke a professional jargon, the language of the schools, he maintained,—and who shall gainsay him?—that metaphysics were imperfect; or, at any rate, had not yet reached their ideal perfection.

"The true science of metaphysics," he says, "consists not in rendering abstract that which is sensible, but in rendering sensible that which is abstract; apparent that which is hidden; imaginable, if so it may be, that which is only intelligible; and intelligible, finally, that which an ordinary attention fails to seize."

And therefore:—

"Distrust, in books on metaphysics, words which have not been able to get currency in the world, and are only calculated to form a special language."

Nor would he suffer common words to be employed in a special sense by the schools:—

"Which is the best, if one wants to be useful and to be really understood, to get one's words in the world, or to get them in the schools. I maintain that the good plan is to employ words in their popular sense rather than in their philosophical sense; and the better plan still, to employ them in their natural sense rather than in their popular sense. By their natural sense, I mean the popular and universal acceptance of them brought to that which in this is essential and invariable. To prove a thing by definition proves nothing, if the definition is purely philosophical; for such definitions only bind him who makes them. To prove a thing by definition, when the definition expresses the necessary, inevitable, and clear idea which the world at large attaches to the object, is, on the contrary, all in all; because then what one does is simply to show people what they do really think, in spite of themselves and without knowing it. The rule that one is free to give to words what sense one will, and that the only thing needful is to be agreed upon the sense one gives them, is very well for the mere purposes of argumentation, and may be allowed in the schools where this sort of fencing is to be practised; but in the sphere of the true-born and noble science of metaphysics, and in the genuine world of literature, it is good for nothing. One must never quit sight of realities, and one must employ one's expressions simply as media,—as glasses, through which one's thoughts can be best made evident. I know, by my own experience, how hard this rule is to follow; but I judge of its importance by the failure of every system of metaphysics. Not one of them has succeeded; for the simple reason, that in every one ciphers have been constantly used instead of values, artificial ideas instead of native ideas, jargon instead of idiom."

I do not know whether the metaphysician will ever adopt Joubert's rules; but I am sure that the man of letters, whenever he has to speak of metaphysics, will do well to adopt them. He, at any rate, must remember:—

"It is by means of familiar words that style takes hold of the reader and gets possession of him. It is by means of these that great thoughts get currency and pass for true metal, like gold and silver which have had a recognised stamp put upon them. They beget confidence in the man who, in order to make his thoughts more clearly perceived, uses them; for people feel that such an employment of the language of common human life betokens a man who knows that life and its concerns, and who keeps himself in contact with them. Besides, these words make a style frank and easy. They show that an author has long made the thought or the feeling expressed his mental food; that he has so assimilated them and familiarised them, that the most common expressions suffice him in order to express ideas which have become every-day ideas to him by the length of time they have been in his mind. And lastly, what one says in such words looks more true; for, of all the words in use, none are so clear as those which we call common words; and clearness is so eminently one of the characteristics of truth, that often it even passes for truth itself."

These are not, in Joubert, mere counsels of rhetoric; they come from his accurate sense of perfection, from his having clearly seized the fine and just idea that beauty and light are properties of truth, and that truth is incompletely exhibited if it is exhibited without beauty and light:—

"Be profound with clear terms and not with obscure terms. What is difficult will at last become easy; but as one goes deep into things, one must still keep a charm, and one must carry into these dark depths of thought, into which speculation has only recently penetrated, the pure and antique clearness of centuries less learned than ours, but with more light in them."

And elsewhere he speaks of those "spirits, lovers of light, who, when they have an idea to put forth, brood long over it first, and wait patiently till it *shines*, as Buffon enjoined, when he defined genius to be the aptitude for patience; spirits who know by experience that the driest matter and the dullest words hide within them the germ and spark of some brightness, like those fairy nuts in which were found diamonds if one broke the shell and was the right person; spirits who maintain that, to see and exhibit things in beauty, is to see and show things as in their essence they really are, and not as they exist for the eye of the careless, who do not look beyond the outside; spirits hard to satisfy, because of a keen-sightedness in them, which makes them discern but too clearly both the models to be followed and those to be shunned; spirits active though meditative, who cannot rest except in solid truths, and whom only beauty can make happy; spirits far less concerned for glory than for perfection, who, because their art is long and life is short, often die without leaving a monument, having had their own inward sense of life and fruitfulness for their best reward."

No doubt there is something a little too ethereal in all this, something which reminds one of Joubert's physical want of body and substance; no doubt, if a man wishes to be a great author, it is to consider too curiously, to consider as Joubert did; it is a mistake to spend so much of one's time in setting up one's ideal standard of perfection, and in contemplating it. Joubert himself knew this very well: "I cannot build a house for my ideas," said he: "I have tried to do without words, and words take their revenge on me by their difficulty." "If there is a man upon earth tormented by the cursed desire to get a whole book into a page, a whole page into a phrase, and this phrase into one word,—that man is myself." "I can sow, but I cannot build." Joubert, however, makes no claim to be a great author; by renouncing all ambition to be this, by not trying to fit his ideas into a house, by making no compromise with words in spite of their difficulty, by being quite single-minded in his pursuit of perfection, perhaps he is enabled to get closer to the truth of the objects of his study, and to be of more service to us by setting before us ideals, than if he had composed a celebrated work. I doubt whether, in an elaborate work on the philosophy of religion, he would have got his ideas about religion to *shine*, to use his own expression, as they shine when he utters them in perfect freedom. Penetration in these matters is valueless without soul, and soul is valueless without penetration; both of these are delicate qualities, and, even in those who have them, easily lost; the charm of Joubert is, that he has and keeps both. Let us try and show that he does.

.   .   .   .

The most characteristic thoughts one can quote from any writer are always his thoughts on matters like these;[1] but the maxims of Joubert are purely literary subjects also, have the same purged and subtle delicacy; they show the same sedulousness in him to preserve perfectly true the balance of his soul. Let me begin with this, which contains a truth too many people fail to perceive:—

"Ignorance, which in matters of morals extenuates the crime, is itself, in matters of literature, a crime of the first order."

And here is another sentence, worthy of Goethe, to clear the air at one's entrance into the region of literature:—

"With the fever of the senses, the delirium of the passions, the weakness of the spirit; with the storms of the passing time and with the great scourges of human life,—hunger, thirst, dishonour, diseases, and death,—authors may as long as they like go on making novels which shall harrow our hearts; but the soul says all the while, 'You hurt me.' "

And again:—

"Fiction has no business to exist unless it is more beautiful than reality. Certainly the monstrosities of fiction may be found in the booksellers' shops; you buy them there for a certain number of francs, and you talk of them for a certain number of days; but they have no place in literature, because in literature the one

[1] [Arnold has been quoting from Joubert on matters of religion.]

aim of art is the beautiful. Once lose sight of that, and you have the mere frightful reality."

That is just the right criticism to pass on these "monstrosities:" *they have no place in literature*, and those who produce them are not really men of letters. One would think that this was enough to deter from such production any man of genuine ambition. But most of us, alas: are what we must be, not what we ought to be,—not even what we know we ought to be.

The following, of which the first part reminds one of Wordsworth's sonnet, "If thou indeed derive thy light from heaven," excellently defines the true salutary function of literature, and the limits of this function:—

"Whether one is an eagle or an ant, in the intellectual world, seems to me not to matter much; the essential thing is to have one's place marked there, one's station assigned, and to belong decidedly to a regular and wholesome order. A small talent, if it keeps within its limits and rightly fulfils its task, may reach the goal just as well as a greater one. To accustom mankind to pleasures which depend neither upon the bodily appetites nor upon money, by giving them a taste for the things of the mind, seems to me, in fact, the one proper fruit which nature has meant our literary productions to have. When they have other fruits, it is by accident, and, in general, not for good. Books which absorb our attention to such a degree that they rob us of all fancy for other books, are absolutely pernicious. In this way they only bring fresh crotchets and sects into the world; they multiply the great variety of weights, rules, and measures already existing; they are morally and politically a nuisance."

Who can read these words and not think of the limiting effect exercised by certain works in certain spheres and for certain periods; exercised even by the works of men of genius or virtue, —by the works of Rousseau, the works of Wesley, the works of Swedenborg? And what is it which makes the Bible so admirable a book, to be the one book of those who can have only one, but the miscellaneous character of the contents of the Bible?

Joubert was all his life a passionate lover of Plato; I hope other lovers of Plato will forgive me for saying that their adored object has never been more truly described than he is here:—

"Plato shows us nothing, but he brings brightness with him; he puts light into our eyes, and fills us with a clearness by which all objects afterwards become illuminated. He teaches us nothing; but he prepares us, fashions us, and makes us ready to know all. Somehow or other, the habit of reading him augments in us the capacity for discerning and entertaining whatever fine truths may afterwards present themselves. Like mountain-air, it sharpens our organs, and gives us an appetite for wholesome food."

"Plato loses himself in the void" (he says again); "but one sees the play of his wings, one hears their rustle." And the conclusion is: "It is good to breathe his air, but not to live upon him."

As a pendant to the criticism on Plato, this on the French moralist Nicole is excellent:—

"Nicole is a Pascal without style. It is not what he says which is sublime, but what he thinks; he rises, not by the natural elevation of his own spirit, but by that of his doctrines. One must not look to the form in him, but to the matter, which is exquisite. He ought to be read with a direct view of practice."

English people have hardly ears to hear the praises of Bossuet, and the Bossuet of Joubert is Bossuet at his very best; but this is a far truer Bossuet than the "declaimer" Bossuet of Lord Macaulay, himself a born rhetorician, if ever there was one:—

"Bossuet employs all our idioms, as Homer employed all the dialects. The language of kings, of statesmen, and of warriors; the language of the people and of the student, of the country and of the schools, of the sanctuary and of the courts of law; the old and the new, the trivial and the stately, the quiet and the resounding—he turns all to his use; and out of all this he makes a style, simple, grave, majestic. His ideas are, like his words, varied,—common and sublime together. Times and doctrines in all their multitude were ever before his spirit, as things and words in all their multitude were ever before it. He is not so much a man as a human nature, with the temperance of a saint, the justice of a bishop, the prudence of a doctor, and the might of a great spirit."

After this on Bossuet, I must quote a criticism on Racine, to show that Joubert did not indiscriminately worship all the French gods of the grand century:—

"Those who find Racine enough for them are poor souls and poor wits; they are souls and wits which have never got beyond the callow and boarding-school stage. Admirable, as no doubt he is, for his skill in having made poetical the most humdrum sentiments and the most middling sort of passions, he can yet stand us in stead of nobody but himself. He is a superior writer; and, in literature, that at once puts a man on a pinnacle. But he is not an inimitable writer."

And again: "The talent of Racine is in his works, but Racine himself is not there. That is why he himself became disgusted with them." "Of Racine, as of his ancients, the genius lay in taste. His elegance is perfect, but it is not supreme, like that of

Virgil." And, indeed, there is something *supreme* in an elegance which exercises such a fascination as Virgil's does; which makes one return to his poems again and again, long after one thinks one has done with them; which makes them one of those books that, to use Joubert's words, "lure the reader back to them, as the proverb says good wine lures back the wine-bibber." And the highest praise Joubert can at last find for Racine is this, that he is the Virgil of the ignorant:—"*Racine est le Virgile des ignorants.*"

Of Boileau, too, Joubert says: "Boileau is a powerful poet, but only in the world of half poetry." How true is that of Pope also! And he adds: "Neither Boileau's poetry nor Racine's flows from the fountainhead." No Englishman, controverting the exaggerated French estimate of these poets, could desire to use fitter words.

I will end with some remarks on Voltaire and Rousseau, remarks in which Joubert eminently shows his prime merit as a critic,—the soundness and completeness of his judgments. I mean that he has the faculty of judging with all the powers of his mind and soul at work together in due combination; and how rare is this faculty! how seldom is it exercised towards writers who so powerfully as Voltaire and Rousseau stimulate and call into activity a single side in us!

" Voltaire's wits came to their maturity twenty years sooner than the wits of other men, and remained in full vigour thirty years longer. The charm which our style in general gets from our ideas, his ideas get from his style. Voltaire is sometimes afflicted, sometimes strongly moved; but serious he never is. His very graces have an effrontery about them. He had correctness of judgment, liveliness of imagination, nimble wits, quick taste, and a moral sense in ruins. He is the most debauched of spirits, and the worst of him is that one gets debauched along with him. If he had been a wise man, and had had the self-discipline of wisdom, beyond a doubt half his wit would have been gone; it needed an atmosphere of *licence* in order to play freely. Those people who read him every day, create for themselves, by an invincible law, the necessity of liking him. But those people who, having given up reading him, gaze steadily down upon the influences which his spirit has shed abroad, find themselves in simple justice and duty compelled to detest him. It is impossible to be satisfied with him, and impossible not to be fascinated by him."

The literary sense in us is apt to rebel against so severe a judgment on such a charmer of the literary sense as Voltaire, and perhaps we English are not very liable to catch Voltaire's vices, while of some of his merits we have signal need; still, as the real definitive judgment on Voltaire, Joubert's is undoubtedly the true one. It is nearly identical with that of Goethe. Joubert's sentence on Rousseau is in some respects more favourable:—

"That weight in the speaker (*auctoritas*) which the ancients talk of, is to be found in Bossuet more than in any other French author; Pascal, too, has it, and La Bruyère; even Rousseau has something of it, but Voltaire not a particle. I can understand how a Rousseau—I mean a Rousseau cured of his faults—might at the present day do much good, and may even come to be greatly wanted; but under no circumstances can a Voltaire be of any use."

The peculiar power of Rousseau's style has never been better hit off than in the following passage:—

"Rosseau imparted, if I may so speak, *bowels of feeling* to the words he used (*donna des entrailles à tous les mots*), and poured into them such a charm, sweetness so penetrating, energy so puissant, that his writings have an effect upon the soul something like that of those illicit pleasures which steal away our taste and intoxicate our reason."

The final judgment, however, is severe, and justly severe:—

"Life without actions; life entirely resolved into affections and half-sensual thoughts; do-nothingness setting up for a virtue; cowardliness with voluptuousness; fierce pride with nullity underneath it; the strutting phrase of the most sensual of vagabonds, who has made his system of philosophy and can give it eloquently forth: there is Rousseau! A piety in which there is no religion; a severity which brings corruption with it; a dogmatism which serves to ruin all authority: there is Rousseau's philosophy! To all tender, ardent, and elevated natures, I say: Only Rousseau can detach you from religion, and only true religion can cure you of Rousseau."

I must yet find room, before I end, for one at least of Joubert's sayings on political matters; here, too, the whole man shows himself; and here, too, the affinity with Coleridge is very remarkable. How true, how true in France especially, is this remark on the contrasting direction taken by the aspirations of the community in ancient and in modern states:—

"The ancients were attached to their country by three things, —their temples, their tombs, and their forefathers. The two great bonds which united them to their government were the bonds of habit and antiquity. With the moderns, hope and the love of novelty have produced a total change. The ancients said *our forefathers*, we say *posterity*: we do not, like them, love our *patria*, that is to say, the country and the laws of our fathers, rather we love the laws and the country of our children; the charm we are most sensible to is the charm of the future, and not the charm of the past."

And how keen and true is this criticism on the changed sense of the word "liberty":—

"A great many words have changed their meaning. The word *liberty*, for example, had at bottom among the ancients the same meaning as the word *dominion*. *I would be free* meant, in the mouth of the ancient, *I would take part in governing or administering the State*; in the mouth of a modern it means, *I would be independent*. The word *liberty* has with us a moral sense; with them its sense was purely political."

Joubert had lived through the French Revolution, and to the modern cry for liberty he was prone to answer:—

"Let your cry be for free souls rather even than for free men. Moral liberty is the one vitally important liberty, the one liberty which is indispensable; the other liberty is good and salutary only so far as it favours this. Subordination is in itself a better thing than independence. The one implies order and arrangement; the other implies only self-sufficiency with isolation. The one means harmony, the other a single tone; the one is the whole, the other is but the part."

"Liberty! liberty!" he cries again; "in all things let us have *justice*, and then we shall have enough liberty."

Let us have justice, and then we shall have enough liberty! The wise man will never refuse to echo those words; but then, such is the imperfection of human governments, that almost always, in order to get justice, one has first to secure liberty.

I do not hold up Joubert as a very astonishing and powerful genius, but rather as a delightful and edifying genius. I have not cared to exhibit him as a sayer of brilliant epigrammatic things, such things as "Notre vie est du vent tissu . . . . les dettes abrégent la vie . . . . celui qui a de l'imagination sans érudition a des ailes et n'a pas de pieds (*Our life is woven wind . . . . debts take from life . . . . the man of imagination without learning has wings and no feet*)," though for such sayings he is famous. In the first place, the French language is in itself so favourable a vehicle for such sayings, that the making them in it has the less merit; at least half the merit ought to go, not to the maker of the saying, but to the French language. In the second place, the peculiar beauty of Joubert is not there; it is not in what is exclusively intellectual,—it is in the union of *soul* with intellect, and in the delightful, satisfying result which this union produces. "Vivre, c'est penser et sentir son âme . . . . le bonheur est de sentir son âme bonne . . . toute vérité nue et crue n'a pas assez passé par l 'âme . . . . les hommes ne sont justes qu'envers ceux qu'ils aiment (*The essence of life lies in thinking and being conscious of one's soul . . . . happiness is the sense of one's soul being good . . . if a truth is nude and crude, that is a proof it has not been steeped long enough in the soul, . . . man cannot even be just to his neighbour, unless he loves him*);" it is much rather in sayings like these that Joubert's best and inner-most nature manifests itself. He is the most prepossessing and convincing of witnesses to the good of loving light. Because he sincerely loved light, and did not prefer to it any little private darkness of his own, he found light; his eye was single, and therefore his whole body was full of light. And because he was full of light, he was also full of happiness. In spite of his infirmities, in spite of his sufferings, in spite of his obscurity, he was the happiest man alive; his life was as charming as his thoughts. For certainly it is natural that the love of light, which is already, in some measure, the possession of light, should irradiate and beatify the whole life of him who has it. There is something unnatural and shocking where, as in the case of Coleridge, it does not. Joubert pains us by no such contradic-tion; "the same penetration of spirit which made him such delightful company to his friends, served also to make him perfect in his own personal life, by enabling him always to perceive and do what was right;" he loved and sought light till he became so habituated to it, so accustomed to the joyful testimony of a good conscience, that, to use his own words, "he could no longer exist without this, and was obliged to live with-out reproach if he would live without misery."

Joubert was not famous while he lived, and he will not be famous now that he is dead. But, before we pity him for this, let us be sure what we mean, in literature, by *famous*. There are the famous men of genius in literature,—the Homers, Dantes, Shakspeares: of them we need not speak; their praise is for ever and ever. Then there are the famous men of ability in literature: their praise is in their own generation. And what makes this difference? The work of the two orders of men is at the bottom the same,—*a criticism of life*. The end and aim of all literature, if one considers it attentively, is, in truth, nothing but that. But the criticism which the men of genius pass upon human life is permanently acceptable to mankind; the criticism which the men of ability pass upon human life is transitorily acceptable. Between Shakspeare's criticism of human life and Scribe's the difference is there;—the one is permanently acceptable, the other transitorily. Whence then, I repeat, this difference?

It is that the acceptableness of Shakspeare's criticism depends upon its inherent truth: the acceptableness of Scribe's upon its suiting itself, by its subject-matter, ideas, mode of treatment, to the taste of the generation that hears it. But the taste and ideas of one generation are not those of the next. This next generation in its turn arrives;—first its sharpshooters, its quick-witted, audacious light troops; then the elephantine main body. The imposing array of its predecessor it confidently assails, riddles it with bullets, passes over its body. It goes hard then with many once popular reputations, with many authorities once oracular. Only two kinds of authors are safe in the general havoc. The first kind are the great abounding fountains of truth, whose criticism of life is a source of illumination and joy to the whole human race for ever,—the Homers, the Shakspeares. These are the sacred personages, whom all civilised warfare respects. The second are those whom the out-skirmishers of the new generation, its forerunners,—quick-witted soldiers, as I have said, the select of the army—recognise, though the bulk of their comrades behind might not, as of the same family and character with the sacred personages, exercising like them an immortal function, and like them inspiring a permanent interest. They snatch them up, and set them in a place of shelter, where the on-coming multitude may not overwhelm them. These are the Jouberts. They will never, like the Shakspeares, command the homage of the multitude; but they are safe; the multitude will not trample them down. Except these two kinds, no author is safe. Let us consider, for example, Joubert's famous contemporary, Lord Jeffrey. All his vivacity and accomplishment avail him nothing; of the true critic he had in an eminent degree no quality, except one,—curiosity. Curiosity he had, but he had no gift for truth; he cannot illuminate and rejoice us; no intelligent out-skirmisher of the new generation cares about him, cares to put him in safety; at this moment we are all passing over his body. Let us consider a greater than Jeffrey, a critic whose reputation still stands firm,—will stand, many people think, for ever,—the great apostle of the Philistines, Lord Macaulay. Lord Macaulay was, as I have already said, a born rhetorician; a splendid rhetorician doubtless, and, beyond that, an *English* rhetorician also, an *honest* rhetorician; still, beyond the apparent rhetorical truth of things he never could penetrate; for their vital truth, for what the French call the *vraie vérité*, he had absolutely no organ; therefore his reputation, brilliant as it is, is not secure. Rhetoric so good as his excites and gives pleasure; but by pleasure alone you cannot permanently bind men's spirits to you. Truth illuminates and gives joy, and it is by the bond of joy, not of pleasure, that men's spirits are indissolubly held. As Lord Macaulay's own generation dies out, as a new generation arrives, without those ideas and tendencies of its predecessor which Lord Macaulay so deeply shared and so happily satisfied, will he give the same pleasure? and, if he ceases to give this, has he enough of light in him to make him last? Pleasure the new generation will get from its own novel ideas and tendencies; but light is another and a rarer thing, and must be treasured wherever it can be found. Will Macaulay be saved, in the sweep and pressure of time, for his light's sake, as Johnson has already been saved by two generations, Joubert by one? I think it very doubtful. But for a spirit of any delicacy and dignity, what a fate, if he could foresee it! to be an oracle for one generation, and then of little or no account for ever. How far better, to pass with scant notice through one's own generation, but to be singled out and preserved by the very iconoclasts of the next, then in their turn by those of the next, and so, like the lamp of life itself, to be handed on from one generation to another in safety! This is Joubert's lot, and it is a very enviable one. The new men of the new generations, while they let the dust deepen on a thousand Laharpes, will say of him: "He lived in the Philistine's day, in a place and time when almost every idea current in literature had the mark of Dagon upon it, and not the mark of the children of light. Nay, the children of light were as yet hardly so much as heard of: the Canaanite was then in the land. Still, there were even then a few, who, nourished on some secret tradition, or illumined, perhaps, by a divine inspiration, kept aloof from the reigning superstitions, never bowed the knee to the gods of Canaan; and one of these few was called *Joubert*."

From *Marcus Aurelius*

MR. MILL says, in his book on Liberty, that "Christian morality is in great part merely a protest against paganism; its ideal is negative rather than positive, passive rather than active." He says, that, in certain most important respects, "it falls far below the best morality of the ancients." Now, the object of systems of morality is to take possession of human life, to save it from being abandoned to passion or allowed to drift at hazard, to give it happiness by establishing it in the practice of virtue; and this object they seek to attain by prescribing to human life fixed principles of action, fixed rules of conduct. In its uninspired as well as in its inspired moments, in its days of languor and gloom as well as in its days of sunshine and energy, human life has thus always a clue to follow, and may always be making way towards its goal. Christian morality has not failed to supply to human life aids of this sort. It has supplied them far more abundantly than many of its critics imagine. The most exquisite document, after those of the New Testament, of all the documents the Christian spirit has ever inspired,—the *Imitation*,—by no means contains the whole of Christian morality; nay, the disparagers of this morality would think themselves sure of triumphing if one agreed to look for it in the *Imitation* only. But even the *Imitation* is full of passages like these: "Vita sine proposito languida et vaga est;"—"Omni die renovare debemus propositum nostrum, dicentes: nunc hodie perfecte incipiamus, quia nihil est quod hactenus fecimus;"—"Secundum propositum nostrum est cursus profectus nostri;"—"Raro etiam unum vitium perfecte vincimus, et ad *quotidianum* profectum non accendimur;"—"Semper aliquid certi proponendum est;" —"Tibi ipsi violentiam frequenter fac:" (*A life without a purpose is a languid, drifting thing;—Every day we ought to renew our purpose, saying to ourselves: This day let us make a sound beginning, for what we have hitherto done is nought;—Our improvement is in proportion to our purpose;—We hardly ever manage to get completely rid even of one fault, and do not set our hearts on daily improvement;—Always place a definite purpose before thee;—Get the habit of mastering thine inclination.*) These are moral precepts, and moral precepts of the best kind. As rules to hold possession of our conduct, and to keep us in the right course through outward troubles and inward perplexity, they are equal to the best ever furnished by the great masters of morals— Epictetus or Marcus Aurelius.

But moral rules, apprehended as ideas first, and then rigorously followed as laws, are, and must be, for the sage only. The mass of mankind have neither force of intellect enough to apprehend them clearly as ideas, nor force of character enough to follow them strictly as laws. The mass of mankind can be carried along a course full of hardship for the natural man, can be borne over the thousand impediments of the narrow way, only by the tide of a joyful and bounding emotion. It is impossible to rise from reading Epictetus or Marcus Aurelius without a sense of constraint and melancholy, without feeling that the burden laid upon man is well-nigh greater than he can bear. Honour to the sages who have felt this, and yet have borne it! Yet, even for the sage, this sense of labour and sorrow in his march towards the goal constitutes a relative inferiority; the noblest souls of whatever creed, the pagan Empedocles as well as the Christian Paul, have insisted on the necessity of an inspiration, a joyful emotion, to make moral action perfect; an obscure indication of this necessity is the one drop of truth in the ocean of verbiage with which the controversy on justification by faith has flooded the world. But, for the ordinary man, this sense of labour and sorrow constitutes an absolute disqualification; it paralyses him; under the weight of it, he cannot make way towards the goal at all. The paramount virtue of religion is, that it has *lighted up* morality; that it has supplied the emotion and inspiration needful for carrying the sage along the narrow way perfectly, for carrying the ordinary man along it at all. Even the religions with most dross in them have had something of this virtue; but the Christian religion manifests it with unexampled splendour. "Lead me, Zeus and Destiny!" says the prayer of Epictetus, "whithersoever I am appointed to go; I will follow without wavering; even though I turn coward and shrink, I shall have to follow all the same." The fortitude of that is for the strong, for the few; even for them the spiritual atmosphere with which it surrounds them is bleak and gray. But, "Let thy loving spirit lead me forth into the land of righteousness;"—"The Lord shall be unto thee an everlasting light, and thy God thy glory;"—"Unto you that fear my name shall the sun of righteousness arise with healing in his wings," says the Old Testament; "Born, not of blood, nor of the will of the flesh, nor of the will of man, but of God;"—"Except a man be born again, he cannot see the kingdom of God;"—"Whatsoever is born of God, overcometh the world," says the New. The ray of sunshine is there, the glow of a divine warmth;—the austerity of the sage melts away under it, the paralysis of the weak is healed; he who is vivified by it renews his strength; "all things are possible to him;" "he is a new creature."

Epictetus says: "Every matter has two handles, one of which will bear taking hold of, the other not. If thy brother sin against thee, lay not hold of the matter by this, that he sins against thee; for by this handle the matter will not bear taking hold of. But rather lay hold of it by this, that he is thy brother, thy born mate; and thou wilt take hold of it by what will bear handling." Jesus, being asked whether a man is bound to forgive his brother as often as seven times, answers: "I say not unto thee, until seven times, but until seventy times seven." Epictetus here suggests to the reason grounds for forgiveness of injuries which Jesus does not; but it is vain to say that Epictetus is on that account a better moralist than Jesus, if the warmth, the emotion, of Jesus's answer fires his hearer to the practice of forgiveness of injuries, while the thought in Epictetus's leaves him cold. So with Christian morality in general: its distinction

P

is not that it propounds the maxim, "Thou shalt love God and thy neighbour," with more development, closer reasoning, truer sincerity, than other moral systems; it is that it propounds this maxim with an inspiration which wonderfully catches the hearer and makes him act upon it. It is because Mr. Mill has attained to the perception of truths of this nature, that he is,—instead of being, like the school from which he proceeds, doomed to sterility,—a writer of distinguished mark and influence, a writer deserving all attention and respect; it is (I must be pardoned for saying) because he is not sufficiently leavened with them, that he falls just short of being a great writer.

That which gives to the moral writings of the Emperor Marcus Aurelius their peculiar character and charm, is their being suffused and softened by something of this very sentiment whence Christian morality draws its best power. Mr. Long has recently published in a convenient form a translation of these writings, and has thus enabled English readers to judge Marcus Aurelius for themselves; he has rendered his countrymen a real service by so doing. Mr. Long's reputation as a scholar is a sufficient guarantee of the general fidelity and accuracy of his translation; on these matters, besides, I am hardly entitled to speak, and my praise is of no value. But that for which I and the rest of the unlearned may venture to praise Mr. Long is this; that he treats Marcus Aurelius's writings, as he treats all the other remains of Greek and Roman antiquity which he touches, not as a dead and dry matter of learning, but as documents with a side of modern applicability and living interest, and valuable mainly so far as this side in them can be made clear; that as in his notes on Plutarch's Roman Lives he deals with the modern epoch of Cæsar and Cicero, not as food for schoolboys, but as food for men, and men engaged in the current of contemporary life and action, so in his remarks and essays on Marcus Aurelius he treats this truly modern striver and thinker not as a Classical Dictionary hero, but as a present source from which to draw "example of life, and instruction of manners." Why may not a son of Dr. Arnold say, what might naturally here be said by any other critic, that in this lively and fruitful way of considering the men and affairs of ancient Greece and Rome, Mr. Long resembles Dr. Arnold?

. . . . . .

In general the substantiality, soundness, and precision of Mr. Long's rendering are (I will venture, after all, to give my opinion about them) as conspicuous as the living spirit with which he treats antiquity; and these qualities are particularly desirable in the translator of a work like that of Marcus Aurelius, of which the language is often corrupt, almost always hard and obscure. Any one who wants to appreciate Mr. Long's merits as a translator may read, in the original and in Mr. Long's translation, the seventh chapter of the tenth book; he will see how, through all the dubiousness and involved manner of the Greek, Mr. Long has firmly seized upon the clear thought which is certainly at the bottom of that troubled wording, and, in distinctly rendering this thought, has at the same time thrown round its expression a characteristic shade of painfulness and difficulty which just suits it. And Marcus Aurelius's book is one which, when it is rendered so accurately as Mr. Long renders it, even those who know Greek tolerably well may choose to read rather in the translation than in the original. For not only are the contents here incomparably more valuable than the external form, but this form, the Greek of a Roman, is not exactly one of those styles which have a physiognomy, which are an essential part of their author, which stamp an indelible impression of him on the reader's mind. An old Lyons commentator finds, indeed, in Marcus Aurelius's Greek, something characteristic, something specially firm and imperial; but I think an ordinary mortal will hardly find this: he will find crabbed Greek, without any great charm of distinct physiognomy. The Greek of Thucydides and Plato has this charm, and he who reads them in a translation, however accurate, loses it, and loses much in losing it; but the Greek of Marcus Aurelius, like the Greek of the New Testament, and even more than the Greek of the New Testament, is wanting in it. If one could be assured that the English Testament were made perfectly accurate, one might be almost content never to open a Greek Testament again; and, Mr. Long's version of Marcus Aurelius being what it is, an Englishman who reads to live, and does not live to read, may henceforth let the Greek original repose upon its shelf.

The man whose thoughts Mr. Long has thus faithfully reproduced, is perhaps the most beautiful figure in history. He is one of those consoling and hope-inspiring marks, which stand for ever to remind our weak and easily discouraged race how high human goodness and perseverance have once been carried, and may be carried again. The interest of mankind is peculiarly attracted by examples of signal goodness in high places; for that testimony to the worth of goodness is the most striking which is borne by those to whom all the means of pleasure and self-indulgence lay open, by those who had at their command the kingdoms of the world and the glory of them. Marcus Aurelius was the ruler of the grandest of empires; and he was one of the best of men. Besides him, history presents one or two sovereigns eminent for their goodness, such as Saint Louis or Alfred. But Marcus Aurelius has, for us moderns, this great superiority in interest over Saint Louis or Alfred, that he lived and acted in a state of society modern by its essential characteristics, in an epoch akin to our own, in a brilliant centre of civilisation. Trajan talks of "our enlightened age" just as glibly as the *Times* talks of it. Marcus Aurelius thus becomes for us a man like ourselves, a man in all things tempted as we are. Saint Louis inhabits an atmosphere of mediæval Catholicism, which the man of the nineteenth century may admire, indeed, may even passionately wish to inhabit, but which, strive as he will, he cannot really inhabit. Alfred belongs to a state of society (I say it with all deference to the *Saturday Review* critic who keeps such jealous watch over the honour of our Saxon ancestors) half barbarous. Neither Alfred nor Saint Louis can be morally and intellectually as near to us as Marcus Aurelius.

The record of the outward life of this admirable man has in it little of striking incident. He was born at Rome on the 26th of April, in the year 121 of the Christian era. He was nephew and son-in-law to his predecessor on the throne, Antoninus Pius. When Antoninus died, he was forty years old, but from the time of his earliest manhood he had assisted in administering public affairs. Then, after his uncle's death in 161, for nineteen years he reigned as emperor. The barbarians were pressing on the Roman frontier, and a great part of Marcus Aurelius's nineteen years of reign was passed in campaigning. His absences from Rome were numerous and long. We hear of him in Asia Minor, Syria, Egypt, Greece; but, above all, in the countries on the Danube, where the war with the barbarians was going on,— in Austria, Moravia, Hungary. In these countries much of his Journal seems to have been written; parts of it are dated from them; and there, a few weeks before his fifty-ninth birthday, he fell sick and died.[1] The record of him on which his fame chiefly rests is the record of his inward life,—his *Journal*, or *Commentaries*, or *Meditations*, or *Thoughts* for by all these names has the work been called. Perhaps the most interesting of the records of his outward life is that which the first book of this work supplies, where he gives an account of his education, recites the names of those to whom he is indebted for it, and enumerates his obligations to each of them. It is a refreshing and consoling picture, a priceless treasure for those, who, sick of the "wild and dreamlike trade of blood and guile," which seems to be nearly the whole of what history has to offer to our view, seek eagerly

[1] He died on the 17th of March, A.D. 180.

for that substratum of right thinking and well-doing which in all ages must surely have somewhere existed, for without it the continued life of humanity would have been impossible. "From my mother I learnt piety and beneficence, and abstinence not only from evil deeds but even from evil thoughts; and further, simplicity in my way of living, far removed from the habits of the rich." Let us remember that, the next time we are reading the sixth satire of Juvenal. "From my tutor I learnt" (hear it, ye tutors of princes!) "endurance of labour, and to want little, and to work with my own hands, and not to meddle with other people's affairs, and not be ready to listen to slander." The vices and foibles of the Greek sophist or rhetorician—the *Græculus esuriens*—are in everybody's mind; but he who reads Marcus Aurelius's account of his Greek teachers and masters, will understand how it is that, in spite of the vices and foibles of individual *Græculi*, the education of the human race owes to Greece a debt which can never be overrated. The vague and colourless praise of history leaves on the mind hardly any impression of Antoninus Pius: it is only from the private memoranda of his nephew that we learn what a disciplined, hard-working, gentle, wise, virtuous man he was; a man who, perhaps, interests mankind less than his immortal nephew only because he has left in writing no record of his inner life,—*caret quia vate sacro.*

Of the outward life and circumstances of Marcus Aurelius, beyond these notices which he has himself supplied, there are few of much interest and importance. There is the fine anecdote of his speech when he heard of the assassination of the revolted Avidius Cassius, against whom he was marching; *he was sorry*, he said, *to be deprived of the pleasure of pardoning him.* And there are one or two more anecdotes of him which show the same spirit. But the great record for the outward life of a man who has left such a record of his lofty inward aspirations as that which Marcus Aurelius has left, is the clear consenting voice of all his contemporaries,—high and low, friend and enemy, pagan and Christian,—in praise of his sincerity, justice, and goodness. The world's charity does not err on the side of excess, and here was a man occupying the most conspicuous station in the world, and professing the highest possible standard of conduct;—yet the world was obliged to declare that he walked worthily of his profession. Long after his death, his bust was to be seen in the houses of private men through the wide Roman empire. It may be the vulgar part of human nature which busies itself with the semblance and doings of living sovereigns, it is its nobler part which busies itself with those of the dead; these busts of Marcus Aurelius, in the homes of Gaul, Britain, and Italy, bare witness, not to the inmates' frivolous curiosity about princes and palaces, but to their reverential memory of the passage of a great man upon the earth.

Two things, however, before one turns from the outward to the inward life of Marcus Aurelius, force themselves upon one's notice, and demand a word of comment; he persecuted the Christians, and he had for his son the vicious and brutal Commodus. The persecution at Lyons, in which Attalus and Pothinus suffered, the persecution at Smyrna, in which Polycarp suffered, took place in his reign. Of his humanity, of his tolerance, of his horror of cruelty and violence, of his wish to refrain from severe measures against the Christians, of his anxiety to temper the severity of these measures when they appeared to him indispensable, there is no doubt: but, on the one hand, it is certain that the letter, attributed to him, directing that no Christian should be punished for being a Christian, is spurious; it is almost certain that his alleged answer to the authorities of Lyons, in which he directs that Christians persisting in their profession shall be dealt with according to law, is genuine. Mr. Long seems inclined to try and throw doubt over the persecution at Lyons, by pointing out that the letter of the Lyons Christians relating it, alleges it to have been attended by miraculous and incredible incidents. "A man," he says, "can only act consistently by accepting all this letter or rejecting it all, and we cannot blame him for either." But it is contrary to all experience to say that because a fact is related with incorrect additions, and embellishments, therefore it probably never happened at all; or that it is not, in general, easy for an impartial mind to distinguish between the fact and the embellishments. I cannot doubt that the Lyons persecution took place, and that the punishment of Christians for being Christians was sanctioned by Marcus Aurelius. But then I must add that nine modern readers out of ten, when they read this, will, I believe, have a perfectly false notion of what the moral action of Marcus Aurelius, in sanctioning that punishment, really was. They imagine Trajan, or Antoninus Pius, or Marcus Aurelius, fresh from the perusal of the Gospel, fully aware of the spirit and holiness of the Christian saints ordering their extermination because he loved darkness rather than light. Far from this, the Christianity which these emperors aimed at repressing was, in their conception of it, something philosophically contemptible, politically subversive, and morally abominable. As men, they sincerely regarded it much as well-conditioned people, with us, regard Mormonism; as rulers, they regarded it much as Liberal statesmen, with us, regard the Jesuits. A kind of Mormonism,

constituted as a vast secret society, with obscure aims of political
and social subversion, was what Antoninus Pius and Marcus
Aurelius believed themselves to be repressing when they
punished Christians. The early Christian apologists again and
again declare to us under what odious imputations the Christians
lay, how general was the belief that these imputations were well-
grounded, how sincere was the horror which the belief inspired.
The multitude, convinced that the Christians were atheists who
ate human flesh and thought incest no crime, displayed against
them a fury so passionate as to embarrass and alarm their rulers.
The severe expressions of Tacitus, *exitiabilis superstitio—odio
humani generis convicti*, show how deeply the prejudices of the
multitude imbued the educated class also. One asks oneself
with astonishment how a doctrine so benign as that of Jesus
Christ can have incurred misrepresentation so monstrous.
The inner and moving cause of the misrepresentation lay, no
doubt, in this,—that Christianity was a new spirit in the Roman
world, destined to act in that world as its dissolvent; and it was
inevitable that Christianity in the Roman world, like democracy
in the modern world, like every new spirit with a similar
mission assigned to it, should at its first appearance occasion
an instinctive shrinking and repugnance in the world which it
was to dissolve. The outer and palpable causes of the misrepresentation were, for the Roman public at large, the confounding of the Christians with the Jews, that isolated, fierce,
and stubborn race, whose stubbornness, fierceness, and isolation, real as they were, the fancy of a civilised Roman yet
further exaggerated; the atmosphere of mystery and novelty
which surrounded the Christian rites; the very simplicity of
Christian theism. For the Roman statesman, the cause of mistake lay in that character of secret assemblages which the meetings of the Christian community wore, under a State-system as
jealous of unauthorised associations as is the State-system of
modern France.

A Roman of Marcus Aurelius's time and position could not
well see the Christians except through the mist of these prejudices. Seen through such a mist, the Christians appeared with
a thousand faults not their own; but it has not been sufficiently
remarked that faults really their own many of them assuredly
appeared with besides, faults especially likely to strike such an
observer as Marcus Aurelius, and to confirm him in the prejudices of his race, station, and rearing. We look back upon
Christianity after it has proved what a future it bore within it,
and for us the sole representatives of its early struggles are the
pure and devoted spirits through whom it proved this; Marcus

Aurelius saw it with its future yet unshown, and with the tares among its professed progeny not less conspicuous than the wheat. Who can doubt that among the professing Christians of the second century, as among the professing Christians of the nineteenth, there was plenty of folly, plenty of rabid nonsense, plenty of gross fanaticism? who will even venture to affirm that, separated in great measure from the intellect and civilisation of the world for one or two centuries, Christianity, wonderful as have been its fruits, had the development perfectly worthy of its inestimable germ? Who will venture to affirm that, by the alliance of Christianity with the virtue and intelligence of men like the Antonines,—of the best product of Greek and Roman civilisation, while Greek and Roman civilisation had yet life and power,—Christianity and the world, as well as the Antonines themselves, would not have been gainers? That alliance was not to be. The Antonines lived and died with an utter misconception of Christianity; Christianity grew up in the Catacombs, not on the Palatine. And Marcus Aurelius incurs no moral reproach by having authorised the punishment of the Christians; he does not thereby become in the least what we mean by a *persecutor*. One may concede that is was impossible for him to see Christianity as it really was;—as impossible as for even the moderate and sensible Fleury to see the Antonines as they really were;— one may concede that the point of view from which Christianity appeared something anti-civil and anti-social, which the State had the faculty to judge and the duty to suppress, was inevitably his. Still, however, it remains true that this sage, who made perfection his aim and reason his law, did Christianity an immense injustice and rested in an idea of State-attributes which was illusive. And this is, in truth, characteristic of Marcus Aurelius, that he is blameless, yet, in a certain sense, unfortunate; in his character, beautiful as it is, there is something melancholy, circumscribed, and ineffectual.

For of his having such a son as Commodus, too, one must say that he is not to be blamed on that account, but that he is unfortunate. Disposition and temperament are inexplicable things; there are natures on which the best education and example are thrown away; excellent fathers may have, without any fault of theirs, incurably vicious sons. It is to be remembered, also, that Commodus was left, at the perilous age of nineteen, master of the world; while his father, at that age, was but beginning a twenty years' apprenticeship to wisdom, labour, and self-command, under the sheltering teachership of his uncle Antoninus. Commodus was a prince apt to be led by favourites; and if the story is true which says that he left, all through his reign, the Christians untroubled, and ascribes this lenity to the influence of his mistress Marcia, it shows that he could be led to good as well as to evil. But for such a nature to be left at a critical age with absolute power, and wholly without good counsel and direction, was the more fatal. Still one cannot help wishing that the example of Marcus Aurelius could have availed more with his own only son. One cannot but think that with such virtue as his there should go, too, the ardour which removes mountains, and that the ardour which removes mountains might have even won Commodus. The word *ineffectual* again rises to one's mind; Marcus Aurelius saved his own soul by his righteousness, and he could do no more. Happy they who can do this! but still happier, who can do more!

Yet, when one passes from his outward to his inward life, when one turns over the pages of his *Meditations*,—entries jotted down from day to day, amid the business of the city or the fatigues of the camp, for his own guidance and support, meant for no eye but his own, without the slightest attempt at style, with no care, even, for correct writing, not to be surpassed for naturalness and sincerity,—all disposition to carp and cavil dies away, and one is overpowered by the charm of a character of such purity, delicacy, and virtue. He fails neither in small things nor in great; he keeps watch over himself both that the great springs of action may be right in him, and that the minute details of action may be right also. How admirable in a hard-tasked ruler, and a ruler, too, with a passion for thinking and reading, is such a memorandum as the following:—

"Not frequently nor without necessity to say to any one, or to write in a letter, that I have no leisure; nor continually to excuse the neglect of duties required by our relation to those with whom we live, by alleging urgent occupation."

And, when that ruler is a Roman emperor, what an "idea" is this to be written down and meditated by him:—

"The idea of a polity in which there is the same law for all, a polity administered with regard to equal rights and equal freedom of speech, and the idea of a kingly government which respects most of all the freedom of the governed."

And, for all men who "drive at practice," what practical rules may not one accumulate out of these *Meditations*:—

"The greatest part of what we say or do being unnecessary, if a man takes this away, he will have more leisure and less uneasiness. Accordingly, on every occasion a man should ask himself: 'Is this one of the unnecessary things?' Now a man should take away not only unnecessary acts, but also unnecessary thoughts, for thus superfluous acts will not follow after."

And again:—

"We ought to check in the series of our thoughts everything that is without a purpose and useless, but most of all the over-curious feeling and the malignant; and a man should use himself to think of those things only about which if one should suddenly ask, 'What hast thou now in thy thoughts?' with perfect openness thou mightest immediately answer, 'This or That;' so that from thy words it should be plain that everything in thee is simple and benevolent, and such as befits a social animal, and one that cares not for thoughts about sensual enjoyments, or any rivalry or envy and suspicion, or anything else for which thou wouldst blush if thou shouldst say thou hadst it in thy mind."

So, with a stringent practicalness worthy of Franklin, he discourses on his favourite text, *Let nothing be done without a purpose*. But it is when he enters the region where Franklin cannot follow him, when he utters his thoughts on the ground-motives of human action, that he is most interesting; that he becomes the unique, the incomparable Marcus Aurelius. Christianity uses language very liable to be misunderstood when it seems to tell men to do good, not, certainly, from the vulgar motives of worldly interest, or vanity, or love of human praise, but "that their Father which seeth in secret may reward them openly." The motives of reward and punishment have come, from the misconception of language of this kind, to be strangely overpressed by many Christian moralists, to the deterioration and disfigurement of Christianity. Marcus Aurelius says, truly and nobly:—

"One man, when he has done a service to another, is ready to set it down to his account as a favour conferred. Another is not ready to do this, but still in his own mind he thinks of the man as his debtor, and he knows what he has done. A third in a manner does not even know what he has done, *but he is like a vine which has produced grapes, and seeks for nothing more after it has once produced its proper fruit*. As a horse when he has run, a dog when he has caught the game, a bee when it has made its honey, so a man when he has done a good act, does not call out for others to come and see, but he goes on to another act, as a vine goes on to produce again the grapes in season. Must a man, then, be one of these, who in a manner acts thus without observing it? Yes."

And again:—

"What more dost thou want when thou hast done a man a service? Art thou not content that thou hast done something conformable to thy nature, and dost thou seek to be paid for it, *just as if the eye demanded a recompense for seeing, or the feet for walking?*"

Christianity, in order to match morality of this strain, has to
correct its apparent offers of external reward, and to say: *The
kingdom of God is within you.*

I have said that it is by its accent of emotion that the morality
of Marcus Aurelius acquires a special character, and reminds
one of Christian morality. The sentences of Seneca are stimulating to the intellect; the sentences of Epictetus are fortifying
to the character; the sentences of Marcus Aurelius find their way
to the soul. I have said that religious emotion has the power to
light up morality: the emotion of Marcus Aurelius does not
quite light up his morality, but it suffuses it; it has not power
to melt the clouds of effort and austerity quite away, but it
shines through them and glorifies them; it is a spirit, not so
much of gladness and elation, as of gentleness and sweetness;
a delicate and tender sentiment, which is less than joy and more
than resignation. He says that in his youth he learned from
Maximus, one of his teachers, "cheerfulness in all circumstances
as well as in illness; *and a just admixture in the moral character of
sweetness and dignity:*" and it is this very admixture of sweetness
with his dignity which makes him so beautiful a moralist. It
enables him to carry even into his observation of nature, a
delicate penetration, a sympathetic tenderness, worthy of
Wordsworth; the spirit of such a remark as the following has
hardly a parallel, so far as my knowledge goes, in the whole
range of Greek and Roman literature:—

"Figs, when they are quite ripe, gape open; and in the ripe
olives the very circumstance of their being near to rottenness
adds a peculiar beauty to the fruit. And the ears of corn bending
down, and the lion's eyebrows, and the foam which flows from
the mouth of wild boars, and many other things,—though they
are far from being beautiful, in a certain sense,—still, because
they come in the course of nature, have a beauty in them, and
they please the mind; so that if a man should have a feeling and
a deeper insight with respect to the things which are produced
in the universe, there is hardly anything which comes in the
course of nature which will not seem to him to be in a manner
disposed so as to give pleasure."

But it is when his strain passes to directly moral subjects that
his delicacy and sweetness lend to it the greatest charm. Let
those who can feel the beauty of spiritual refinement read this,
the reflection of an emperor who prized mental superiority
highly:—

"Thou sayest, 'Men cannot admire the sharpness of thy wits.'
Be it so; but there are many other things of which thou canst
not say, 'I am not formed for them by nature.' Show those

qualities, then, which are altogether in thy power,—sincerity, gravity, endurance of labour, aversion to pleasure, contentment with thy portion and with few things, benevolence, frankness, no lover of superfluity, freedom from trifling, magnanimity. Dost thou not see how many qualities thou art at once able to exhibit, as to which there is no excuse of natural incapacity and unfitness, and yet thou still remainest voluntarily below the mark? Or art thou compelled, through being defectively furnished by nature, to murmur, and to be mean, and to flatter, and to find fault with thy poor body, and to try to please men, and to make great display, and to be so restless in thy mind? No, indeed; but thou mightest have been delivered from these things long ago. Only, if in truth thou canst be charged with being rather slow and dull of comprehension, thou must exert thyself about this also, not neglecting nor yet taking pleasure in thy dulness."

The same sweetness enables him to fix his mind, when he sees the isolation and moral death caused by sin, not on the cheerless thought of the misery of this condition, but on the inspiriting thought that man is blest with the power to escape from it:—

"Suppose that thou hast detached thyself from the natural unity,—for thou wast made by nature a part, but now thou hast cut thyself off—yet here is this beautiful provision, that it is in thy power again to unite thyself. God has allowed this to no other part,—after it has been separated and cut asunder, to come together again. But consider the goodness with which he has privileged man; for he has put it in his power, when he has been separated, to return and to be united and to resume his place."

It enables him to control even the passion for retreat and solitude, so strong in a soul like his, to which the world could offer no abiding city:—

"Men seek retreat for themselves, houses in the country, seashores, and mountains; and thou, too, art wont to desire such things very much. But this is altogether a mark of the most common sort of men, for it is in thy power whenever thou shalt choose to retire into thyself. For nowhere either with more quiet or more freedom from trouble does a man retire than into his own soul, particularly when he has within him such thoughts that by looking into them he is immediately in perfect tranquillity. Constantly, then, give to thyself this retreat, and renew thyself; and let thy principles be brief and fundamental, which, as soon as thou shalt recur to them, will be sufficient to cleanse the soul completely, and to send thee back free from all discontent with the things to which thou returnest."

Against this feeling of discontent and weariness, so natural to the great for whom there seems nothing left to desire or to strive after, but so enfeebling to them, so deteriorating, Marcus Aurelius never ceased to struggle. With resolute thankfulness he kept in remembrance the blessings of his lot; the true blessings of it, not the false:—

"I have to thank Heaven that I was subjected to a ruler and a father (Antoninus Pius) who was able to take away all pride from me, and to bring me to the knowledge that it is possible for a man to live in a palace without either guards, or embroidered dresses, or any show of this kind; but that it is in such a man's power to bring himself very near to the fashion of a private person, without being for this reason either meaner in thought or more remiss in action with respect to the things which must be done for public interest. . . . I have to be thankful that my children have not been stupid nor deformed in body; that I did not make more proficiency in rhetoric, poetry, and the other studies, by which I should perhaps have been completely engrossed, if I had seen that I was making great progress in them; . . . that I knew Apollonius, Rusticus, Maximus; . . . that I received clear and frequent impressions about living according to nature, and what kind of a life that is, so that, so far as depended on Heaven, and its gifts, help, and inspiration, nothing hindered me from forthwith living according to nature, though I still fall short of it through my own fault, and through not observing the admonitions of Heaven, and, I may almost say, its direct instructions; that my body has held out so long in such a kind of life as mine; that though it was my mother's lot to die young, she spent the last years of her life with me; that whenever I wished to help any man in his need, I was never told that I had not the means of doing it; that, when I had an inclination to philosophy, I did not fall into the hands of a sophist."

And, as he dwelt with gratitude on these helps and blessings vouchsafed to him, his mind (so, at least, it seems to me) would sometimes revert with awe to the perils and temptations of the lonely height where he stood, to the lives of Tiberius, Caligula, Nero, Domitian, in their hideous blackness and ruin; and then he wrote down for himself such a warning entry as this, significant and terrible in its abruptness:—

"A black character, a womanish character, a stubborn character, bestial, childish, animal, stupid, counterfeit, scurrilous, fraudulent, tyrannical!"

Or this:—

"About what am I now employing my soul? On every occasion I must ask myself this question, and enquire, What have I now in this part of me which they call the ruling principle, and whose soul have I now?—that of a child, or of a young man, or of a weak woman, or of a tyrant, or of one of the lower animals in the service of man, or of a wild beast?"

The character he wished to attain he knew well, and beautifully he has marked it, and marked, too, his sense of shortcoming:—

"When thou hast assumed these names,—good, modest, true, rational, equal-minded, magnanimous,—take care that thou dost not change these names; and, if thou shouldst lose them, quickly return to them. If thou maintainest thyself in possession of these names without desiring that others should call thee by them, thou wilt be another being, and wilt enter on another life. For to continue to be such as thou hast hitherto been, and to be torn in pieces and defiled in such a life, is the character of a very stupid man, and one overfond of his life, and like those half-devoured fighters with wild beasts, who though covered with wounds and gore still entreat to be kept to the following day, though they will be exposed in the same state to the same claws and bites. Therefore fix thyself in the possession of these few names: and if thou art able to abide in them, abide as if thou wast removed to the Happy Islands."

For all his sweetness and serenity, however, man's point of life "between two infinities" (of that expression Marcus Aurelius is the real owner) was to him anything but a Happy Island, and the performances on it he saw through no veils of illusion. Nothing is in general more gloomy and monotonous than declamations on the hollowness and transitoriness of human life and grandeur: but here, too, the great charm of Marcus Aurelius, his emotion, comes in to relieve the monotony and to break through the gloom; and even on this eternally used topic he is imaginative, fresh, and striking:—

"Consider, for example, the times of Vespasian. Thou wilt see all these things, people marrying, bringing up children, sick, dying, warring, feasting, trafficking, cultivating the ground, flattering, obstinately arrogant, suspecting, plotting, wishing for somebody to die, grumbling about the present, loving, heaping up treasure, desiring to be consuls or kings. Well then that life of these people no longer exists at all. Again, go to the times of Trajan. All is again the same. Their life too is gone. But chiefly thou shouldst think of those whom thou hast thyself known distracting themselves about idle things, neglecting to do what was in accordance with their proper constitution, and to hold firmly to this and to be content with it."

Again:—

"The things which are much valued in life are empty, and

rotten, and trifling; and people are like little dogs, biting one
another, and little children quarrelling, crying, and then straightway laughing. But fidelity, and modesty, and justice, and truth,
are fled

'Up to Olympus from the wide-spread earth.'

What then is there which still detains thee here?"

And once more:—

"Look down from above on the countless herds of men, and
their countless solemnities, and the infinitely varied voyagings
in storms and calms, and the differences among those who are
born, who live together, and die. And consider too the life lived
by others in olden time, and the life now lived among barbarous
nations, and how many know not even thy name, and how
many will soon forget it, and how they who perhaps now are
praising thee will very soon blame thee, and that neither a
posthumous name is of any value, nor reputation, nor anything
else."

He recognised, indeed, that (to use his own words) "the prime
principle in man's constitution is the social;" and he laboured
sincerely to make not only his acts towards his fellow-men, but
his thoughts also, suitable to his conviction:—

"When thou wishest to delight thyself, think of the virtues
of those who live with thee; for instance, the activity of one, and
the modesty of another, and the liberality of a third, and some
other good quality of a fourth."

Still, it is hard for a pure and thoughtful man to live in a state
of rapture at the spectacle afforded to him by his fellow-
creatures; above all it is hard, when such a man is placed as
Marcus Aurelius was placed, and has had the meanness and
perversity of his fellow-creatures thrust, in no common measure,
upon his notice,—has had, time after time, to experience how
"within ten days thou wilt seem a god to those to whom thou
art now a beast and an ape." His true strain of thought as to his
relations with his fellow-men is rather the following. He has
been enumerating the higher consolations which may support a
man at the approach of death, and he goes on:—

"But if thou requirest also a vulgar kind of comfort which
shall reach thy heart, thou wilt be made best reconciled to death
by observing the objects from which thou art going to be
removed, and the morals of those with whom thy soul will no
longer be mingled. For it is no way right to be offended with
men, but it is thy duty to care for them and to bear with them
gently; and yet to remember that thy departure will not be from
men who have the same principles as thyself. For this is the

only thing, if there be any, which could draw us the contrary way and attach us to life, to be permitted to live with those who have the same principles as ourselves. But now thou seest how great is the distress caused by the difference of those who live together, so that thou mayest say: 'Come quick, O death, lest perchance I too should forget myself.' "

O faithless and perverse generation! how long shall I be with you? how long shall I suffer you? Sometimes this strain rises even to passion:—

"Short is the little which remains to thee of life. Live as on a mountain. Let men see, let them know, a real man, who lives as he was meant to live. If they cannot endure him, let them kill him. For that is better than to live as men do."

It is remarkable how little of a merely local and temporary character, how little of those *scoriæ* which a reader has to clear away before he gets to the precious ore, how little that even admits of doubt or question, the morality of Marcus Aurelius exhibits. Perhaps as to one point we must make an exception. Marcus Aurelius is fond of urging as a motive for man's cheerful acquiescence in whatever befalls him, that "whatever happens to every man *is for the interest of the universal*;" that the whole contains nothing *which is not for its advantage*; that everything which happens to a man is to be accepted, "even if it seems disagreeable, *because it leads to the health of the universe*." And the whole course of the universe, he adds, has a providential reference to man's welfare: "*all other things have been made for the sake of rational beings*." Religion has in all ages freely used this language, and it is not religion which will object to Marcus Aurelius's use of it; but science can hardly accept as severely accurate this employment of the terms *interest* and *advantage*. To a sound nature and a clear reason the proposition that things happen "for the interest of the universal," as men conceive of interest, may seem to have no meaning at all, and the proposition that "all things have been made for the sake of rational beings" may seem to be false. Yet even to this language, not irresistibly cogent when it is thus absolutely used, Marcus Aurelius gives a turn which makes it true and useful, when he says: "The ruling part of man can make a material for itself out of that which opposes it, as fire lays hold of what falls into it, and rises higher by means of this very material;"—when he says: "What else are all things except exercises for the reason? Persevere then until thou shalt have made all things thine own, as the stomach which is strengthened makes all things its own, as the blazing fire makes flame and brightness out of everything that is thrown into it;"—when he says: "Thou wilt not cease to be miserable till thy mind is in such a condition, that, what luxury is to those who enjoy pleasure, such shall be to thee, in every matter which presents itself, the doing of the things which are conformable to man's constitution; for a man ought to consider as an enjoyment everything which it is in his power to do according to his own nature,—and it is in his power everywhere." In this sense it is, indeed, most true that "all things have been made for the sake of rational beings;" that "all things work together for good."

In general, however, the action Marcus Aurelius prescribes is action which every sound nature must recognise as right, and the motives he assigns are motives which every clear reason must recognise as valid. And so he remains the especial friend and comforter of all clear-headed and scrupulous, yet pure-hearted and upward striving men, in those ages most especially that walk by sight, not by faith, but yet have no open vision. He cannot give such souls, perhaps, all they yearn for, but he gives them much; and what he gives them, they can receive.

Yet no, it is not for what he thus gives them that such souls love him most: it is rather because of the emotion which lends to his voice so touching an accent, it is because he too yearns as they do for something unattained by him. What an affinity for Christianity had this persecutor of the Christians! The effusion of Christianity, its relieving tears, its happy self-sacrifice, were the very element, one feels, for which his soul longed; they were near him, they brushed him, he touched them, he passed them by. One feels, too, that the Marcus Aurelius one reads must still have remained, even had Christianity been fully known to him, in a great measure himself; he would have been no Justin;—but how would Christianity have affected him? in what measure would it have changed him? Granted that he might have found, like the *Alogi* of modern times, in the most beautiful of the Gospels, the Gospel which has leavened Christendom most powerfully, the Gospel of St. John, too much Greek metaphysics, too much *gnosis*; granted that this Gospel might have looked too like what he knew already to be a total surprise to him: what, then, would he have said to the Sermon on the Mount, to the twenty-sixth chapter of St. Matthew? What would have become of his notions of the *exitiabilis superstitio*, of the "obstinacy of the Christians"? Vain question! yet the greatest charm of Marcus Aurelius is that he makes us ask it. We see him wise, just, self-governed, tender thankful, blameless; yet, with all this, agitated, stretching out his arms for something beyond,—*tendentemque manus ripæ ulterioris amore.*

ON THE STUDY OF CELTIC LITERATURE

1867

On the Study of Celtic Literature. By Matthew Arnold, Professor of Poetry in the University of Oxford. London.
Smith, Elder & Co., 65 Cornhill. 1867.

ORIGINALLY delivered as lectures from the Chair of Poetry at Oxford,
1865–1866, and published separately in four numbers of the *Cornhill
Magazine*, 1866. Arnold hoped that as a result of these lectures a Professorship of Celtic might be founded at Oxford. He wrote to his
mother that when he had delivered the final lecture Dr. Williams, the
aged Principal of Jesus College, said audibly after a pause, "The Angel
ended . . ."

The professorship was founded and attached to Jesus College in
1876.

THE STUDY OF CELTIC
LITERATURE

"They went forth to the war, but they always fell."

OSSIAN.

I. *Introduction*

THE summer before last I spent some weeks at Llandudno, on
the Welsh coast. The best lodging-houses at Llandudno look
eastward, towards Liverpool; and from that Saxon hive swarms
are incessantly issuing, crossing the bay, and taking possession
of the beach and the lodging-houses. Guarded by the Great
and Little Orme's Head, and alive with the Saxon invaders
from Liverpool, the eastern bay is an attractive point of interest,
and many visitors to Llandudno never contemplate anything
else. But, putting aside the charm of the Liverpool steamboats,
perhaps the view, on this side, a little dissatisfies one after a
while; the horizon wants mystery, the sea wants beauty, the
coast wants verdure, and has a too bare austereness and aridity.
At last one turns round and looks westward. Everything is
changed. Over the mouth of the Conway and its sands is the
eternal softness and mild light of the west; the low line of the
mystic Anglesey, and the precipitous Penmaenmawr, and the
great group of Carnedd Llewelyn and Carnedd David and their
brethren fading away, hill behind hill, in an aërial haze, make the
horizon; between the foot of Penmaenmawr and the bending
coast of Anglesey, the sea, a silver stream, disappears one knows
not whither. On this side, Wales,—Wales, where the past still
lives, where every place has its tradition, every name its poetry,
and where the people, the genuine people, still knows this past,
this tradition, this poetry, and lives with it, and clings to it;
while, alas, the prosperous Saxon on the other side, the invader
from Liverpool and Birkenhead, has long ago forgotten his.
And the promontory where Llandudno stands is the very centre
of this tradition; it is Creuddyn, *the bloody city*, where every
stone has its story; there, opposite its decaying rival, Conway
Castle, is Diganwy, not decaying but long since utterly decayed,
some crumbling foundations on a crag top and nothing more;

Diganwy, where Mael-gwyn shut up Elphin, and where Taliesin
came to free him. Below, in a fold of the hill, is Llan-rhos, the
church of the marsh, where the same Mael-gwyn, a British
prince of real history, a bold and licentious chief, the original,
it is said, of Arthur's Lancelot, shut himself up in the church to
avoid the Yellow Plague, and peeped out through a hole in the
door, and saw the monster and died. Behind among the woods,
is Gloddaeth, *the place of feasting*, where the bards were entertained; and farther away, up the valley of the Conway towards
Llanrwst, is the Lake of Ceirio-nydd and Taliesin's grave. Or,
again, looking seawards and Anglesey-wards, you have Pen-
mon, Seiriol's isle and priory, where Mael-gwyn lies buried;
you have the *Sands of Lamentation* and Llys Helig, *Heilig's
Mansion*, a mansion under the waves, a sea-buried palace and
realm. *Hac ibat Simois; hic est Sigeia tellus.*

As I walked up and down, looking at the waves as they washed
this Sigeian land which has never had its Homer, and listening
with curiosity to the strange, unfamiliar speech of its old
possessors' obscure descendants,—bathing people, vegetable-
sellers, and donkey-boys,—who were all about me, suddenly I
heard, through the stream of unknown Welsh, words, not
English, indeed, but still familiar. They came from a French
nursery-maid, with some children. Profoundly ignorant of her
relationship, this Gaulish Celt moved among her British cousins,
speaking her polite neo-Latin tongue, and full of compassionate
contempt, probably, for the Welsh barbarians and their jargon.
What a revolution was here! How had the star of this daughter
of Gomer waxed, while the star of these Cymry, his sons, had
waned! What a difference of fortune in the two, since the days
when, speaking the same language, they left their common
dwelling-place in the heart of Asia; since the Cimmerians of the
Euxine came in upon their western kinsmen, the sons of the
giant Galates; since the sisters, Gaul and Britain, cut the mistletoe in their forests, and saw the coming of Cæsar! *Blanc, rouge,
rocher, champ, église, seigneur,*—these words, by which the Gallo-
Roman Celt now names white, and red, and rock, and field, and
church, and lord, are no part of the speech of his true ancestors,
they are words he has learnt; but since he learned them they have
had a world-wide success, and we all teach them to our children,
and armies speaking them have domineered in every city of that
Germany by which the British Celt was broken, and in the train
of these armies, Saxon auxiliaries, a humbled contingent, have
been fain to follow;—the poor Welshman still says, in the
genuine tongue of his ancestors, *gwyn, goch, craig, maes, llan,
arglwydd*; but his land is a province, and his history petty, and

his Saxon subduers scout his speech as an obstacle to civilisation; and the echo of all its kindred in other lands is growing every day fainter and more feeble; gone in Cornwall, going in Brittany and the Scotch Highlands, going, too, in Ireland;—and there, above all, the badge of the beaten race, the property of the vanquished.

II. *The English Spirit*

Let me repeat what I have often said of the characteristics which mark the English spirit, the English genius. This spirit, this genius, judged, to be sure, rather from a friend's than an enemy's point of view, yet judged on the whole fairly, is characterised, I have repeatedly said, by *energy with honesty*. Take away some of the energy which comes to us, as I believe, in part from Celtic and Roman sources; instead of energy, say rather *steadiness*; and you have the Germanic genius: *steadiness with honesty*. It is evident how nearly the two characterisations approach one another; and yet they leave, as we shall see, a great deal of room for difference. Steadiness with honesty; the danger for a national spirit thus composed is the humdrum, the plain and ugly, the ignoble: in a word, *das Gemeine, die Gemeinheit*, that curse of Germany, against which Goethe was all his life fighting. The excellence of a national spirit thus composed is freedom from whim, flightiness, perverseness; patient fidelity to Nature,—in a word, *science*,—leading it at last, though slowly, and not by the most brilliant road, out of the bondage of the humdrum and common, into the better life. The universal dead-level of plainness and homeliness, the lack of all beauty and distinction in form and feature, the slowness and clumsiness of the language, the eternal beer, sausages, and bad tobacco, the blank commonness everywhere, pressing at last like a weight on the spirits of the traveller in Northern Germany, and making him impatient to be gone—this is the weak side; the industry, the well-doing, the patient steady elaboration of things, the idea of science governing all departments of human activity,—this is the strong side; and through this side of her genius, Germany has already obtained excellent results, and is destined, we may depend upon it, however her pedantry, her slowness, her fumbling, her ineffectiveness, her bad government, may at times make us cry out, to an immense development.

III. *The Celtic Spirit*

Sentimental,—*always ready to react against the despotism of fact*; that is the description of a great friend of the Celt gives of him; and it is not a bad description of the sentimental temperament; it lets us into the secret of its dangers and of its habitual want of success. Balance, measure, and patience, these are the eternal conditions, even supposing the happiest temperament to start with, of high success; and balance, measure, and patience are just what the Celt has never had. Even in the world of spiritual creation, he has never, in spite of his admirable gifts of quick perception and warm emotion, succeeded perfectly, because he never has had steadiness, patience, sanity enough to comply with the conditions under which alone can expression be perfectly given to the finest perceptions and emotions. The Greek has the same perceptive, emotional temperament as the Celt; but he adds to this temperament the sense of *measure*; hence his admirable success in the plastic arts, in which the Celtic genius, with its chafing against the despotism of fact, its perpetual straining after mere emotion, has accomplished nothing. In the comparatively petty art of ornamentation, in rings, brooches, crosiers, relic-cases, and so on, he has done just enough to show his delicacy of taste, his happy temperament; but the grand difficulties of painting and sculpture, the prolonged dealings of spirit with matter, he has never had patience for. Take the more spiritual arts of music and poetry. All that emotion alone can do in music the Celt has done; the very soul of emotion breathes in the Scotch and Irish airs; but with all this power of musical feeling, what has the Celt, so eager for emotion that he has not patience for science, effected in music, to be compared with what the less emotional German, steadily developing his musical feeling with the science of a Sebastian Bach or a Beethoven, has effected? In poetry, again,—poetry which the Celt has so passionately, so nobly loved; poetry where emotion counts for so much, but where reason, too, reason, measure, sanity, also count for so much,— the Celt has shown genius, indeed, splendid genius; but even here his faults have clung to him, and hindered him from producing great works, such as other nations with a genius for poetry,—the Greeks, say, or the Italians,—have produced. The Celt has not produced great poetical works, he has only produced poetry with an air of greatness investing it all, and sometimes giving, moreover, to short pieces, or to passages, lines, and snatches of long pieces, singular beauty and power.

And yet he loved poetry so much that he grudged no pains to it; but the true art, the *architectonicé* which shapes great works, such as the *Agamemnon* or the *Divine Comedy*, comes only after a steady, deep-searching survey, a firm conception of the facts of human life, which the Celt has not patience for. So he runs off into technic, where he employs the utmost elaboration, and attains astonishing skill; but in the contents of his poetry you have only so much interpretation of the world as the first dash of a quick, strong perception, and then sentiment, infinite sentiment, can bring you. Here, too, his want of sanity and steadfastness has kept the Celt back from the highest success.

IV. *Celtic Sensibility*

And as in material civilisation he has been ineffectual, so has the Celt been ineffectual in politics. This colossal, impetuous, adventurous wanderer, the Titan of the early world, who in primitive times fills so large a place on earth's scene, dwindles and dwindles as history goes on, and at last is shrunk to what we now see him. For ages and ages the world has been constantly slipping, ever more and more out of the Celt's grasp. "They went forth to the war," Ossian says most truly, "*but they always fell.*"

And yet, if one sets about constituting an ideal genius, what a great deal of the Celt does one find oneself drawn to put into it! Of an ideal genius one does not want the elements, any of them, to be in a state of weakness; on the contrary, one wants all of them to be in the highest state of power; but with a law of measure, of harmony, presiding over the whole. So the sensibility of the Celt, if everything else were not sacrificed to it, is a beautiful and admirable force. For sensibility, the power of quick and strong perception and emotion, is one of the very prime constituents of genius, perhaps its most positive constituent; it is to the soul what good senses are to the body, the grand natural condition of successful activity. Sensibility gives genius its materials; one cannot have too much of it, if one can but keep its master and not be its slave. Do not let us wish that the Celt had had less sensibility, but that he had been more master of it. Even as it is, if his sensibility has been a source of weakness to him, it has been a source of power too, and a source of happiness. Some people have found in the Celtic nature and its sensibility the main root out of which chivalry and romance and the glorification of a feminine ideal spring; this is a great question, with which I cannot deal here. Let me notice in passing, however, that there is, in truth, a Celtic air about the extravagance of chivalry, its reaction against the despotism of fact, its straining human nature further than it will stand. But putting all this question of chivalry and its origin on one side, no doubt the sensibility of the Celtic nature, its nervous exaltation, have something feminine in them, and the Celt is thus peculiarly disposed to feel the spell of the feminine idiosyncrasy; he has an affinity to it; he is not far from its secret. Again, his sensibility gives him a peculiarly near and intimate feeling of nature and the life of nature; here, too, he seems in a special way attracted by the secret before him, the secret of natural beauty and natural magic, and to be close to it, to half-divine it. In the productions of the Celtic genius, nothing, perhaps, is so interesting as the evidences of this power: I shall have occasion to give specimens of them by-and-by. The same sensibility made the Celts full of reverence and enthusiasm for genius, learning, and the things of the mind; *to be a bard, freed a man,*—that is a characteristic stroke of this generous and ennobling ardour of theirs, which no race has ever shown more strongly. Even the extravagance and exaggeration of the sentimental Celtic nature has often something romantic and attractive about it, something which has a sort of smack of misdirected good. The Celt, undisciplinable, anarchical, and turbulent by nature, but out of affection and admiration giving himself body and soul to some leader, that is not a promising political temperament, it is just the opposite of the Anglo-Saxon temperament, disciplinable and steadily obedient within certain limits, but retaining an inalienable part of freedom and self-dependence; but it is a temperament for which one has a kind of sympathy notwithstanding. And very often, for the gay defiant reaction against fact of the lively Celtic nature one has more than sympathy; one feels, in spite of the extravagance, in spite of good sense disapproving, magnetised and exhilarated by it. The Gauls had a rule inflicting a fine on every warrior who, when he appeared on parade, was found to stick out too much in front,—to be corpulent, in short. Such a rule is surely the maddest article of war ever framed, and to people to whom nature has assigned a large volume of intestines, must appear, no doubt, horrible; but yet has it not an audacious, sparkling, immaterial manner with it, which lifts one out of routine. and sets one's spirits in a glow?

All tendencies of human nature are in themselves vital and profitable; when they are blamed, they are only to be blamed relatively, not absolutely. This holds true of the Saxon's phlegm as well as of the Celt's sentiment. Out of the steady

humdrum habit of the creeping Saxon, as the Celt calls him,—
out of his way of going near the ground,—has come, no doubt,
Philistinism, that plant of essentially Germanic growth, flourishing with its genuine marks only in the German fatherland,
Great Britain and her colonies, and the United States of
America; but what a soul of goodness there is in Philistinism
itself! and this soul of goodness I, who am often supposed to be
Philistinism's mortal enemy merely because I do not wish it to
have things all its own way, cherish as much as anybody.
This steady-going habit leads at last, as I have said, up to science,
up to the comprehension and interpretation of the world. With
us in Great Britain, it is true, it does not seem to lead so far as
that; it is in Germany, where the habit is more unmixed, that
it can lead to science. Here with us it seems at a certain point
to meet with a conflicting force, which checks it and prevents its
pushing on to science; but before reaching this point what conquests has it not won! and all the more, perhaps, for stopping
short at this point, for spending its exertions within a bounded
field, the field of plain sense, of direct practical utility. How it
has augmented the comforts and conveniences of life for us!
Doors that open, windows that shut, locks that turn, razors that
shave, coats that wear, watches that go, and a thousand more
such good things, are the invention of the Philistines.

V. *Style*

If I were asked where English poetry got these three things, its
turn for style, its turn for melancholy, and its turn for natural
magic, for catching and rendering the charm of nature in a
wonderfully near and vivid way,—I should answer, with some
doubt, that it got much of its turn for style from a Celtic source;
with less doubt, that it got much of its melancholy from a Celtic
source; with no doubt at all, that from a Celtic source it got
nearly all its natural magic.

Any German with penetration and tact in matters of literary
criticism will own that the principal deficiency of German
poetry is in style; that for style, in the highest sense, it shows but
little feeling. Take the eminent masters of style, the poets who
best give the idea of what the peculiar power which lies in style
is,—Pindar, Virgil, Dante, Milton. An example of the peculiar
effect which these poets produce, you can hardly give from
German poetry. Examples enough you can give from German
poetry of the effect produced by genius, thought, and feeling
expressing themselves in clear language, simple language,

passionate language, eloquent language, with harmony and melody; but not of the peculiar effect exercised by eminent power of style. Every reader of Dante can at once call to mind what the peculiar effect I mean is; I spoke of it in my lectures on translating Homer, and there I took an example of it from Dante, who perhaps manifests it more eminently than any other poet. But from Milton, too, one may take examples of it abundantly; compare this from Milton:—

> . . . . nor sometimes forget
> Those other two equal with me in fate,
> So were I equall'd with them in renown,
> Blind Thamyris and blind Mæonides—

with this from Goethe:—

> Es bildet ein Talent sich in der Stille,
> Sich ein Character in dem Strom der Welt.

Nothing can be better in its way than the style in which Goethe there presents his thought, but it is the style of prose as much as of poetry; it is lucid, harmonious, earnest, eloquent, but it has not received that peculiar kneading, heightening, and re-casting which is observable in the style of the passage from Milton,— a style which seems to have for its cause a certain pressure of emotion, and an ever-surging, yet bridled, excitement in the poet, giving a special intensity to his way of delivering himself. In poetical races and epochs this turn for style is peculiarly observable; and perhaps it is only on condition of having this somewhat heightened and difficult manner, so different from the plain manner of prose, that poetry gets the privilege of being loosed, at its best moments, into that perfectly simple, limpid style, which is the supreme style of all, but the simplicity of which is still not the simplicity of prose. The simplicity of Menander's style is the simplicity of prose, and is the same kind of simplicity as that which Goethe's style, in the passage I have quoted, exhibits; but Menander does not belong to a great poetical moment, he comes too late for it; it is the simple passages in poets like Pindar or Dante which are perfect, being masterpieces of *poetical* simplicity. One may say the same of the simple passages in Shakspeare; they are perfect, their simplicity being a *poetical* simplicity. They are the golden, easeful, crowning moments of a manner which is always pitched in another key from that of prose, a manner changed and heightened; the Elizabethan style, regnant in most of our dramatic poetry to this day, is mainly the continuation of this manner of Shakspeare's. It was a manner much more turbid and strewn with blemishes than the manner of Pindar, Dante, or Milton; often it was detestable; but it owed its existence to Shakspeare's instinctive impulse towards *style* in poetry, to his native sense of the necessity for it; and without the basis of style everywhere, faulty though it may in some places be, we should not have had the beauty of expression, unsurpassable for effectiveness and charm, which is reached in Shakspeare's best passages. The turn for style is perceptible all through English poetry, proving, to my mind, the genuine poetical gift of the race; this turn imparts to our poetry a stamp of high distinction, and sometimes it doubles the force of a poet not by nature of the very highest order, such as Gray, and raises him to a rank beyond what his natural richness and power seem to promise. Goethe, with his fine critical perception, saw clearly enough both the power of style in itself, and the lack of style in the literature of his own country; and perhaps if we regard him solely as a German, not as a European, his great work was that he laboured all his life to impart style into German literature, and firmly to establish it there. Hence the immense importance to him of the world of classical art, and of the productions of Greek or Latin genius, where style so eminently manifests its power. Had he found in the German genius and literature an element of style existing by nature and ready to his hand, half his work, one may say, would have been saved him, and he might have done much more in poetry. But as it was, he had to try and create out of his own powers, a style for German poetry, as well as to provide contents for this style to carry; and thus his labour as a poet was doubled.

It is to be observed that power of style, in the sense in which I am here speaking of style, is something quite different from the power of idiomatic, simple, nervous, racy expression, such as the expression of healthy, robust natures so often is, such as Luther's was in a striking degree. Style, in my sense of the word, is a peculiar re-casting and heightening, under a certain condition of spiritual excitement, of what a man has to say, in such a manner as to add dignity and distinction to it; and dignity and distinction are not terms which suit many acts or words of Luther. Deeply touched with the *Gemeinheit* which is the bane of his nation, as he is at the same time a grand example of the honesty which is his nation's excellence, he can seldom even show himself brave, resolute and truthful, without showing a strong dash of coarseness and commonness all the while; the right definition of Luther, as of our own Bunyan, is that he is a Philistine of genius. So Luther's sincere idiomatic German,— such language is this: "Hilf lieber Gott, wie manchen Jammer habe ich gesehen, dass der gemeine Mann doch so gar nichts weiss von der christlichen Lehre!"—no more proves a power of style in German literature, than Cobbett's sinewy idiomatic English proves it in English literature. Power of style, properly so-called, as manifested in masters of style like Dante or Milton in poetry, Cicero, Bossuet or Bolingbroke in prose, is something quite different, and has, as I have said, for its characteristic effect, this: to add dignity and distinction.

Style, then, the Germans are singularly without, and it is strange that the power of style should show itself so strongly as it does in the Icelandic poetry, if the Scandinavians are such genuine Teutons as is commonly supposed. Fauriel used to talk of the Scandinavian Teutons and the German Teutons, as if they were two divisions of the same people, and the common notion about them, no doubt, is very much this. Since the war in Schleswig-Holstein, however, all one's German friends are exceedingly anxious to insist on the difference of nature between themselves and the Scandinavians; when one expresses surprise that the German sense of nationality should be so deeply affronted by the rule over Germans, not of Latins or Celts, but of brother Teutons or next door to it, a German will give you I know not how long a catalogue of the radical points of unlikeness, in genius and disposition, between himself and a Dane. This emboldens me to remark that there is a fire, a sense of style, a distinction, in Icelandic poetry, which German poetry has not. Icelandic poetry, too, shows a powerful and developed technic; and I wish to throw out, for examination by those who are competent to sift the matter, the suggestion that this power of style and development of technic in the Norse poetry seems to point towards an early Celtic influence or intermixture. It is curious that Zeuss, in his grammar, quotes a text which gives countenance to this notion; as late as the ninth century, he says, there were Irish Celts in Iceland; and the text he quotes to show this, is as follows:—"In 870 A.D., when the Norwegians came to Iceland, there were Christians there, who departed, and left behind them Irish books, bells, and other things; from whence it may be inferred that these Christians were Irish." I speak, and ought to speak, with the utmost diffidence on all these questions of ethnology; but I must say that when I read this text in Zeuss, I caught eagerly at the clue it seemed to offer; for I had been hearing the *Nibelungen* read and commented on in German schools (German schools have the good habit of reading and commenting on German poetry, as we read and comment on Homer and Virgil, but do *not* read and comment on Chaucer and Shakspeare), and it struck me how

the fatal humdrum and want of style of the Germans had marred
their way of telling this magnificent tradition of the *Nibelungen*,
and taken half its grandeur and power out of it; while in the
Icelandic poems which deal with this tradition, its grandeur and
power are much more fully visible, and everywhere in the
poetry of the Edda there is a force of style and a distinction as
unlike as possible to the want of both in the German *Nibelungen*.
At the same time the Scandinavians have a realism, as it is
called, in their genius, which abundantly proves their relationship with the Germans; any one whom Mr. Dasent's delightful
books have made acquainted with the prose tales of the Norse-
men, will be struck with the stamp of a Teutonic nature in
them; but the Norse poetry seems to have something which
from Teutonic sources alone it could not have derived; which
the Germans have not, and which the Celts have.

This something is *style*, and the Celts certainly have it in a
wonderful measure. Style is the most striking quality of their
poetry. Celtic poetry seems to make up to itself for being unable to master the world and give an adequate interpretation of
it, by throwing all its force into style, by bending language at
any rate to its will, and expressing the ideas it has with unsurpassable intensity, elevation, and effect. It has all through it
a sort of intoxication of style,—a *Pindarism*, to use a word
formed from the name of the poet, on whom, above all other
poets, the power of style seems to have exercised an inspiring
and intoxicating effect; and not in its great poets only, in
Taliesin, or Llywarch Hen, or Ossian, does the Celtic genius
show this Pindarism, but in all its productions.

VI. *Melancholy*

Its chord of penetrating passion and melancholy, again, its
Titanism as we see it in Byron,—what other European poetry
possesses that like the English, and where do we get it from?
The Celts, with their vehement reaction against the despotism
of fact, with their sensuous nature, their manifold striving, their
adverse destiny, their immense calamities, the Celts are the
prime authors of this vein of piercing regret and passion,—of
this Titanism in poetry. A famous book, Macpherson's *Ossian*,
carried in the last century this vein like a flood of lava through
Europe. I am not going to criticise Macpherson's *Ossian* here.
Make the part of what is forged, modern, tawdry, spurious, in
the book, as large as you please; strip Scotland, if you like, of
every feather of borrowed plumes which on the strength of

Macpherson's *Ossian* she may have stolen from that *vetus et major Scotia*, the true home of the Ossianic poetry, Ireland; I make no objection. But there will still be left in the book a residue with the very soul of the Celtic genius in it, and which has the proud distinction of having brought this soul of the Celtic genius into contact with the genius of the nations of modern Europe, and enriched all our poetry by it. Woody Morven, and echoing Sora, and Selma with its silent halls!— we all owe them a debt of gratitude, and when we are unjust enough to forget it, may the Muse forget us! Choose any one of the better passages in Macpherson's *Ossian* and you can see even at this time of day what an apparition of newness and power such a strain must have been to the eighteenth century:—

"I have seen the walls of Balclutha, but they were desolate. The fox looked out from the windows, the rank grass of the wall waved round her head. Raise the song of mourning, O bards, over the land of strangers. They have but fallen before us, for one day we must fall. Why dost thou build the hall, son of the winged days? Thou lookest from thy towers to-day; yet a few years, and the blast of the desert comes; it howls in thy empty court, and whistles round thy half-worn shield. Let the blast of the desert come! we shall be renowned in our day."

All Europe felt the power of that melancholy; but what I wish to point out is, that no nation of Europe so caught in its poetry the passionate penetrating accent of the Celtic genius, its strain of Titanism, as the English. Goethe, like Napoleon, felt the spell of Ossian very powerfully, and he quotes a long passage from him in his *Werther*. But what is there Celtic, turbulent, and Titanic about the German Werther, that amiable, cultivated, and melancholy young man, having for his sorrow and suicide the perfectly definite motive that Lotte cannot be his? Faust, again, has nothing unaccountable, defiant and Titanic in him; his knowledge does not bring him the satisfaction he expected from it, and meanwhile he finds himself poor and growing old, and baulked of the palpable enjoyment of life; and here is the motive for Faust's discontent. In the most energetic and impetuous of Goethe's creations,—his *Prometheus*,—it is not Celtic self-will and passion, it is rather the Germanic sense of justice and reason, which revolts against the despotism of Zeus. The German *Sehnsucht* itself is a wistful, soft, tearful longing, rather than a struggling, fierce, passionate one. But the Celtic melancholy is struggling, fierce, passionate; to catch its note, listen to Llywarch Hen in old age, addressing his crutch:—

O my crutch! is it not autumn, when the fern is red, the water-flag yellow? Have I not hated that which I love?

O my crutch! is it not winter-time now, when men talk together after that they have drunken? Is not the side of my bed left desolate?

O my crutch! is it not spring, when the cuckoo passes through the air, when the foam sparkles on the sea? The young maidens no longer love me.

O my crutch! is it not the first day of May? The furrows, are they not shining; the young corn, is it not springing? Ah! the sight of thy handle makes me wroth.

O my crutch! stand straight, thou wilt support me the better; it is very long since I was Llywarch.

Behold old age, which makes sport of me, from the hair of my head to my teeth, to my eyes, which women loved.

The four things I have all my life most hated fall upon me together,—coughing and old age, sickness and sorrow.

I am old, I am alone, shapeliness and warmth are gone from me; the couch of honour shall be no more mine; I am miserable, I am bent on my crutch.

How evil was the lot allotted to Llywarch, the night when he was brought forth! sorrows without end, and no deliverance from his burden.

There is the Titanism of the Celt, his passionate, turbulent, indomitable reaction against the despotism of fact; and of whom does it remind us so much as of Byron?

> The fire which on my bosom preys
> Is lone as some volcanic isle;
> No torch is kindled at its blaze;
>   A funeral pile!

Or, again:—

> Count o'er the joys thine hours have seen,
> Count o'er thy days from anguish free,
> And know, whatever thou hast been,
> 'Tis something better not to be.

One has only to let one's memory begin to fetch passages from Byron striking the same note as that passage from Llywarch Hen, and she will not soon stop. And all Byron's heroes, not so much in collision with outward things, as breaking on some rock of revolt and misery in the depths of their own nature; Manfred, self-consumed, fighting blindly and passionately with I know not what, having nothing of the consistent development and intelligible motive of Faust,—Manfred, Lara, Cain, what are they but Titanic? Where in European poetry are we to find this Celtic passion of revolt so warm-breathing, puissant and sincere; except perhaps in the creation of a yet greater poet

Q

than Byron, but an English poet, too, like Byron,—in the Satan
of Milton?

> .... What though the field be lost?
> All is not lost; the unconquerable will,
> And study of revenge, immortal hate,
> And courage never to submit or yield,
> And what is else not to be overcome.

There, surely, speaks a genius to whose composition the Celtic
fibre was not wholly a stranger!

And as, after noting the Celtic Pindarism or power of style
present in our poetry, we noted the German flatness coming in
in our hymns, and found here a proof of our compositeness of
nature; so, after noting the Celtic Titanism or power of rebel-
lious passion in our poetry, we may also note the Germanic
patience and reasonableness in it, and get in this way a second
proof how mixed a spirit we have. After Llywarch Hen's:—

> How evil was the lot allotted to Llywarch, the night when he
> was brought forth—

after Byron's:—

> Count o'er the joys thine hours have seen—

take this of Southey's, in answer to the question whether he
would like to have his youth over again:—

> Do I regret the past?
> Would I live o'er again
> The morning hours of life?
> Nay, William, nay, not so!
> Praise be to God who made me what I am,
> Other I would not be.

There we have the other side of our being; the Germanic
goodness, docility, and fidelity to nature, in place of the Celtic
Titanism.

The Celt's quick feeling for what is noble and distinguished
gave his poetry style; his indomitable personality gave it pride
and passion; his sensibility and nervous exaltation gave it a
better gift still, the gift of rendering with wonderful felicity
the magical charm of nature. The forest solitude, the bubbling
spring, the wild flowers, are everywhere in romance. They have
a mysterious life and grace there; they are nature's own children,
and utter her secret in a way which makes them something quite
different from the woods, waters, and plants of Greek and Latin
poetry. Now of this delicate magic, Celtic romance is so pre-
eminent a mistress, that it seems impossible to believe the power

did not come into romance from the Celts.[1] Magic is just the word for it,—the magic of nature; not merely the beauty of nature,—that the Greeks and Latins had; not merely an honest smack of the soil, a faithful realism,—that the Germans had; but the intimate life of nature, her weird power and her fairy charm.

VII. *Natural Magic*

There are many ways of handling nature, and we are here only concerned with one of them; but a rough-and-ready critic imagines that it is all the same so long as nature is handled at all, and fails to draw the needful distinction between modes of handling her. But these modes are many; I will mention four of them now: there is the conventional way of handling nature, there is the faithful way of handling nature, there is the Greek way of handling nature, there is the magical way of handling nature. In all these three last the eye is on the object, but with a difference; in the faithful way of handling nature, the eye is on the object, and that is all you can say; in the Greek, the eye is on the object, but lightness and brightness are added; in the magical, the eye is on the object, but charm and magic are added. In the conventional way of handling nature, the eye is not on the object; what that means we all know, we have only to think of our eighteenth-century poetry:—

> As when the moon, refulgent lamp of night—

to call up any number of instances. Latin poetry supplies plenty of instances too; if we put this from Propertius's *Hylas*:—

> . . . manus heroum . . . .
> Mollia composita litora fronde tegit—

side by side with the line of Theocritus by which it was suggested:—

> λειμὼν γάρ σφιν ἔκειτο μέγας, στιβάδεσσιω ὄνειαρ—

we get at the same moment a good specimen both of the conventional and of the Greek way of handling nature. But from our own poetry we may get specimens of the Greek way of

---

[1] Rhyme,—the most striking characteristic of our modern poetry as distinguished from that of the ancients, and a main source, to our poetry, of its magic and charm, of what we call its *romantic element*,—rhyme itself, all the weight of evidence tends to show, comes into our poetry from the Celts.

handling nature, as well as of the conventional: for instance, Keats's:—

> What little town by river or seashore,
> Or mountain-built with quiet citadel,
> Is emptied of its folk, this pious morn?

is Greek, as Greek as a thing from Homer or Theocritus; it is composed with the eye on the object, a radiancy and light clearness being added. German poetry abounds in specimens of the faithful way of handling nature; an excellent example is to be found in the stanzas called *Zueignung*, prefixed to Goethe's poems; the morning walk, the mist, the dew, the sun, are as faithful as they can be, they are given with the eye on the object, but there the merit of the work, as a handling of nature, stops; neither Greek radiance nor Celtic magic is added; the power of these is not what gives the poem in question its merit, but a power of quite another kind, a power of moral and spiritual emotion. But the power of Greek radiance Goethe could give to his handling of nature, and nobly too, as any one who will read his *Wanderer*,—the poem in which a wanderer falls in with a peasant woman and her child by their hut, built out of the ruins of a temple near Cuma,—may see. Only the power of natural magic Goethe does not, I think, give; whereas Keats passes at will from the Greek power to that power which is, as I say, Celtic; from his:—

> What little town by river or seashore—

to his:—

> White hawthorn and the pastoral eglantine,
> Fast-fading violets cover'd up in leaves—

or his:—

> . . . magic casements, opening on the foam
> Of perilous seas, in fairy lands forlorn—

in which the very same note is struck as in those extracts which I quoted from Celtic romance, and struck with authentic and unmistakeable power.

Shakspeare, in handling nature, touches this Celtic note so exquisitely, that perhaps one is inclined to be always looking for the Celtic note in him, and not to recognise his Greek note when it comes. But if one attends well to the difference between the two notes, and bears in mind, to guide one, such things as Virgil's "moss-grown springs and grass softer than sleep":—

> Muscosi fontes et somno mollior herba—

as his charming flower-gatherer, who—

> Pallentes violas et summa papavera carpens
> Narcissum et florem jungit bene olentis anethi—

as his quinces and chestnuts:—

> . . . cana legam tenera lanugine mala
> Castaneasque nuces . . . .

then, I think, we shall be disposed to say that in Shakspeare's—

> I know a bank where the wild thyme blows,
> Where oxlips and the nodding violet grows,
> Quite over-canopied with luscious woodbine,
> With sweet musk-roses and with eglantine—

it is mainly a Greek note which is struck. Then, again in his:—

> . . . . look how the floor of heaven
> Is thick inlaid with patines of bright gold!

we are at the very point of transition from the Greek note to the Celtic; there is the Greek clearness and brightness, with the Celtic aërialness and magic coming in. Then we have the sheer, inimitable Celtic note in passages like this:—

> Met we on hill, in dale, forest or mead,
> By paved fountain or by rushy brook,
> Or in the beached margent of the sea—

or this, the last I will quote:—

> The moon shines bright. In such a night as this,
> When the sweet wind did gently kiss the trees,
> And they did make no noise, in such a night
> Troilus, methinks, mounted the Trojan walls—

> . . . . in such a night
> Did Thisbe fearfully o'ertrip the dew—

> . . . . in such a night
> *Stood Dido, with a willow in her hand,*
> *Upon the wild sea-banks, and waved her love*
> *To come again to Carthage.*

And those last lines of all are so drenched and intoxicated with the fairy-dew of that natural magic which is our theme, that I cannot do better than end with them.

And now, with the pieces of evidence in our hand, let us go to those who say it is vain to look for Celtic elements in any Englishman, and let us ask them, first, if they seize what we mean by the power of natural magic in Celtic poetry; secondly, if English poetry does not eminently exhibit this power; and thirdly, where they suppose English poetry got it from?

CULTURE AND ANARCHY
1869

Culture and Anarchy. An Essay in Political and Social Criticism.
By Matthew Arnold. London. Smith, Elder and Co., 15
Waterloo Place. 1869.

ARNOLD'S final lecture as Professor of Poetry, delivered in June 1867, was on *Culture and its Enemies*, and this was published in the July *Cornhill* of that year. It provoked *Culture, A Dialogue* from Frederic Harrison in the *Fortnightly Review* for November. Arnold replied with five articles on *Anarchy and Authority* in the *Cornhill* from January to August 1868.

In 1869 he published the original lecture along with the *Cornhill* articles, somewhat revised, under the title *Culture and Anarchy* and added a Preface, Introduction and Conclusion.

The text is that of the second edition, 1875. This was revised and abridged by the author, and the chapter headings were added. A reprint of the 1869 edition incorporating the alterations made in 1875 has been edited by J. Dover Wilson (Cambridge University Press, 1932).

CULTURE AND ANARCHY

AN ESSAY IN POLITICAL AND SOCIAL CRITICISM

From *Sweetness and Light*

But the point of view of culture, keeping the mark of human perfection simply and broadly in view, and not assigning to this perfection, as religion or utilitarianism assign to it, a special and limited character,—this point of view, I say, of culture, is best given by these words of Epictetus:—"It is a sign of ἀφυΐα," says he,—that is, of a nature not finely tempered,—"to give yourselves up to things which relate to the body; to make, for instance, a great fuss about exercise, a great fuss about eating, a great fuss about drinking, a great fuss about walking, a great fuss about riding. All these things ought to be done merely by the way: the formation of the spirit and character must be our real concern." This is admirable; and, indeed, the Greek word εὐφυΐα, a finely tempered nature, gives exactly the notion of perfection as culture brings us to conceive it: a harmonious perfection, a perfection in which the characters of beauty and intelligence are both present, which unites "the two noblest of things,"—as Swift, who of one of the two, at any rate, had himself all too little, most happily calls them in his *Battle of the Books*,—"the two noblest of things, *sweetness and light*." The εὐφυής is the man who tends towards sweetness and light; the ἀφυής, on the other hand, is our Philistine. The immense spiritual significance of the Greeks is due to their having been inspired with this central and happy idea of the essential character of human perfection; and Mr. Bright's misconception of culture, as a smattering of Greek and Latin, comes itself, after all, from this wonderful significance of the Greeks having affected the very machinery of our education, and is in itself a kind of homage to it.

In thus making sweetness and light to be characters of perfection, culture is of like spirit with poetry, follows one law with poetry. Far more than on our freedom, our population, and our industrialism, many amongst us rely upon our religious organisations to save us. I have called religion a yet more important manifestation of human nature than poetry, because it has worked on a broader scale for perfection, and with greater masses of men. But the idea of beauty and of a human nature perfect on

489

all its sides, which is the dominant idea of poetry, is a true and invaluable idea, though it has not yet had the success that the idea of conquering the obvious faults of our animality, and of a human nature perfect on the moral side,—which is the dominant idea of religion,—has been enabled to have; and it is destined, adding to itself the religious idea of a devout energy, to transform and govern the other.

The best art and poetry of the Greeks, in which religion and poetry are one, in which the idea of beauty and of a human nature perfect on all sides adds to itself a religious and devout energy, and works in the strength of that, is on this account of such surpassing interest and instructiveness for us, though it was, —as, having regard to the human race in general, and, indeed, having regard to the Greeks themselves, we must own,—a premature attempt, an attempt which for success needed the moral and religious fibre in humanity to be more braced and developed than it had yet been. But Greece did not err in having the idea of beauty, harmony, and complete human perfection, so present and paramount. It is impossible to have this idea too present and paramount; only, the moral fibre must be braced too. And we, because we have braced the moral fibre, are not on that account in the right way, if at the same time the idea of beauty, harmony, and complete human perfection, is wanting or misapprehended amongst us; and evidently it *is* wanting or misapprehended at present. And when we rely as we do on our religious organisations, which in themselves do not and cannot give us this idea, and think we have done enough if we make them spread and prevail, then, I say, we fall into our common fault of over-valuing machinery.

Culture, however, shows its single-minded love of perfection, its desire simply to make reason and the will of God prevail, its freedom from fanaticism, by its attitude towards all this machinery, even while it insists that it *is* machinery. Fanatics, seeing the mischief men do themselves by their blind belief in some machinery or other,—whether it is wealth and industrialism, or whether it is the cultivation of bodily strength, and activity, or whether it is a political organisation,—or whether it is a religious organisation,—oppose with might and main the tendency to this or that political and religious organisation, or to games and athletic exercises, or to wealth and industrialism, and try violently to stop it. But the flexibility which sweetness and light give, and which is one of the rewards of culture pursued in good faith, enables a man to see that a tendency may be necessary, and even, as a preparation for something in the future, salutary, and yet that the generations or individuals who obey this tendency are sacrificed to it, that they fall short of the hope of perfection by following it; and that its mischiefs are to be criticised, lest it should take too firm a hold and last after it has served its purpose.

. . . .

Oxford, the Oxford of the past, has many faults; and she has heavily paid for them in defeat, in isolation, in want of hold upon the modern world. Yet we in Oxford, brought up amidst the beauty and sweetness of that beautiful place, have not failed to seize one truth:—the truth that beauty and sweetness are essential characters of a complete human perfection. When I insist on this, I am all in the faith and tradition of Oxford. I say boldly that this our sentiment for beauty and sweetness, our sentiment against hideousness and rawness, has been at the bottom of our attachment to so many beaten causes, of our opposition to so many triumphant movements. And the sentiment is true, and has never been wholly defeated, and has shown its power even in its defeat. We have not won our political battles, we have not carried our main points, we have not stopped our adversaries' advance, we have not marched victoriously with the modern world; but we have told silently upon the mind of the country, we have prepared currents of feeling which sap our adversaries' position when it seems gained, we have kept up our own communications with the future. Look at the course of the great movement which shook Oxford to its centre some thirty years ago! It was directed, as anyone who reads Dr. Newman's *Apology* may see, against what in one word may be called "Liberalism." Liberalism prevailed; it was the appointed force to do the work of the hour; it was necessary, it was inevitable that it should prevail. The Oxford movement was broken, it failed; our wrecks are scattered on every shore:—

Quæ regio in terris nostri non plena laboris?

But what was it, this liberalism, as Dr. Newman saw it, and as it really broke the Oxford movement? It was the great middle-class liberalism, which had for the cardinal points of its belief the Reform Bill of 1832, and local self-government, in politics; in the social sphere, free-trade, unrestricted competition, and the making of large industrial fortunes; in the religious sphere, the Dissidence of Dissent and the Protestantism of the Protestant religion. I do not say that other and more intelligent forces than this were not opposed to the Oxford movement: but this was the force which really beat it; this was the force which Dr. Newman felt himself fighting with; this was the force which till only the other day seemed to be the paramount force in this country, and to be in possession of the future; this was the force whose achievements fill Mr. Lowe [1] with such inexpressible admiration, and whose rule he was so horror-struck to see threatened. And where is this great force of Philistinism now? It is thrust into the second rank, it is become a power of yesterday, it has lost the future. A new power has suddenly appeared, a power which it is impossible yet to judge fully, but which is certainly a wholly different force from middle-class liberalism; different in its cardinal points of belief, different in its tendencies in every sphere. It loves and admires neither the legislation of middle-class Parliaments, nor the local self-government of middle-class vestries, nor the unrestricted competition of middle-class industrialists, nor the dissidence of middle-class Dissent and the Protestantism of middle-class Protestant religion. I am not now praising this new force, or saying that its own ideals are better; all I say is, that they are wholly different. And who will estimate how much the currents of feeling created by Dr. Newman's movements, the keen desire for beauty and sweetness which it nourished, the deep aversion it manifested to the hardness and vulgarity of middle-class liberalism, the strong light it turned on the hideous and grotesque illusions of middle-class Protestantism,—who will estimate how much all these contributed to swell the tide of secret dissatisfaction which has mined the ground under the self-confident liberalism of the last thirty years, and has prepared the way for its sudden collapse and supersession? It is in this manner that the sentiment of Oxford for beauty and sweetness conquers, and in this manner long may it continue to conquer!

.   .   .   .

The pursuit of perfection, then, is the pursuit of sweetness and light. He who works for sweetness and light, works to make reason and the will of God prevail. He who works for machinery, he who works for hatred, works only for confusion. Culture looks beyond machinery, culture hates hatred; culture has one great passion, the passion for sweetness and light. It has one even yet greater!—the passion for making them *prevail*. It is not satisfied till we *all* come to a perfect man; it knows that the sweetness and light of the few must be imperfect until the raw and unkindled masses of humanity are touched with sweetness and light. If I have not shrunk from saying that we must work for

---

[1] [Robert Lowe (1811–1892), distinguished Liberal politician. Opposed Newman and Ward in the Tractarian dispute at Oxford. Vice-president of the Committee of Council on Education 1859, and took an important part in the Reform debates of 1866–67. He held various government offices and was created Viscount Sherbrooke in 1880.]

sweetness and light, so neither have I shrunk from saying that we must have a broad basis, must have sweetness and light for as many as possible. Again and again I have insisted how those are the happy moments of humanity, how those are the marking epochs of a people's life, how those are the flowering times for literature and art and all the creative power of genius, when there is a *national* glow of life and thought, when the whole of society is in the fullest measure permeated by thought, sensible to beauty, intelligent and alive. Only it must be *real* thought and *real* beauty; *real* sweetness and *real* light. Plenty of people will try to give the masses, as they call them, an intellectual food prepared and adapted in the way they think proper for the actual condition of the masses. The ordinary popular literature is an example of this way of working on the masses. Plenty of people will try to indoctrinate the masses with the set of ideas and judgments constituting the creed of their own profession or party. Our religious and political organisations give an example of this way of working on the masses. I condemn neither way; but culture works differently. It does not try to teach down to the level of inferior classes; it does not try to win them for this or that sect of its own, with ready-made judgments and watchwords. It seeks to do away with classes; to make the best that has been thought and known in the world current everywhere; to make all men live in an atmosphere of sweetness and light, where they may use ideas, as it uses them itself, freely,—nourished, and not bound by them.

This is the *social idea*; and the men of culture are the true apostles of equality. The great men of culture are those who have had a passion for diffusing, for making prevail, for carrying from one end of society to the other, the best knowledge, the best ideas of their time; who have laboured to divest knowledge of all that was harsh, uncouth, difficult, abstract, professional, exclusive; to humanise it, to make it efficient outside the clique of the cultivated and learned, yet still remaining the *best* knowledge and thought of the time, and a true source, therefore, of sweetness and light. Such a man was Abelard in the Middle Ages, in spite of all his imperfections; and thence the boundless emotion and enthusiasm which Abelard excited. Such were Lessing and Herder in Germany, at the end of the last century; and their services to Germany were in this way inestimably precious. Generations will pass, and literary monuments will accumulate, and works far more perfect than the works of Lessing and Herder will be produced in Germany; and yet the names of these two men will fill a German with a reverence and enthusiasm such as the names of the most gifted masters will hardly awaken. And why?

Because they *humanised* knowledge; because they broadened the basis of life and intelligence; because they worked powerfully to diffuse sweetness and light, to make reason and the will of God prevail. With Saint Augustine they said; "Let us not leave Thee alone to make in the secret of thy knowledge, as thou didst before the creation of the firmament, the division of light from darkness; let the children of thy spirit, placed in their firmament, make their light shine upon the earth, mark the division of night and day, and announce the revolution of the times; for the old order is passed, and the new arises; the night is spent, the day is come forth; and thou shalt crown the year with thy blessing, when thou shalt send forth labourers into thy harvest sown by other hands than theirs; when thou shalt send forth new labourers to new seed-times, whereof the harvest shall be not yet."

From *Doing as one Likes*

I HAVE been trying to show that culture is, or ought to be, the study and pursuit of perfection; and that of perfection, as pursued by culture, beauty and intelligence, or, in other words, sweetness and light, are the main characters. But hitherto I have been insisting chiefly on beauty, or sweetness, as a character of perfection. To complete rightly my design, it evidently remains to speak also of intelligence, or light, as a character of perfection.

. . . .

One has often wondered whether upon the whole earth there is anything so unintelligent, so unapt to perceive how the world is really going, as an ordinary young Englishman of our upper class. Ideas he has not, and neither has he that seriousness of our middle class which is, as I have often said, the great strength of this class, and may become its salvation. Why, a man may hear a young Dives of the aristocratic class, when the whim takes him to sing the praises of wealth and material comfort, sing them with a cynicism from which the conscience of the veriest Philistine of our industrial middle class would recoil in affright. And when, with the natural sympathy of aristocracies for firm dealing with the multitude, and his uneasiness at our feeble dealing with it at home, an unvarnished young Englishman of our aristocratic class applauds the absolute rulers on the Continent, he in general manages completely to miss the grounds of reason and intelligence which alone can give any colour of justification, any possibility of existence, to those rulers, and applauds them on grounds which it would make their own hair stand on end to listen to.

. . . .

I must remark that the culture of which I talked was an endeavour to come at reason and the will of God by means of reading, observing, and thinking; and that whoever calls anything else culture, may, indeed, call it so if he likes, but then he talks of something quite different from what I talked of. And, again, as culture's way of working for reason and the will of God is by directly trying to know more about them, while the Dissidence of Dissent is evidently in itself no effort of this kind, nor is its Free Church, in fact, a church with worthier conceptions of God and the ordering of the world than the State Church professes, but with mainly the same conceptions of these as the State Church has, only that every man is to comport himself as he likes in professing them,—this being so, I cannot at once accept the Nonconformity any more than the industrialism and the other great works of our Liberal middle class as proof positive that this class is in possession of light, and that here is the true seat of authority for which we are in search; but I must try a little further, and seek for other indications which may enable me to make up my mind.

From *Barbarians, Philistines, Populace*

THE same desire for clearness, which has led me thus to extend a little my first analysis of the three great classes of English society, prompts me also to improve my nomenclature for them a little, with a view to making it thereby more manageable. It is awkward and tiresome to be always saying the aristocratic class, the middle class, the working class. For the middle class, for that great body which, as we know, "has done all the great things that have been done in all departments," and which is to be conceived as moving between its two cardinal points of our commercial member of Parliament and our fanatical Protestant Dissenter,— for this class we have a designation which now has become pretty well known, and which we may as well still keep for them, the designation of Philistines. What this term means I have so often explained that I need not repeat it here. For the aristocratic class, conceived mainly as a body moving between the two cardinal points of our chivalrous lord and our defiant baronet, we have as yet got no special designation. Almost all my attention has naturally been concentrated on my own class, the middle class, with which I am in closest sympathy, and which has been, besides, the great power of our day, and has had its praises sung by all speakers and newspapers.

Still the aristocratic class is so important in itself, and the weighty functions which Mr. Carlyle proposes at the present critical time to commit to it must add so much to its importance, that it seems neglectful, and a strong instance of that want of coherent philosophic method for which Mr. Frederic Harrison blames me, to leave the aristocratic class so much without notice and denomination. It may be thought that the characteristic which I have occasionally mentioned as proper to aristocracies,—their natural inaccessibility, as children of the established fact, to ideas,—points to our extending to this class also the designation of Philistines; the Philistine being, as is well known, the enemy of the children of light or servants of the idea. Nevertheless, there seems to be an inconvenience in thus giving one and the same designation to two very different classes; and besides, if we look into the thing closely, we shall find that the term Philistine conveys a sense which makes it more peculiarly appropriate to our middle class than to our aristocratic. For *Philistine* gives the notion of something particularly stiff-necked and perverse in the resistance to light and its children; and therein it specially suits our middle class, who not only do not pursue sweetness and light, but who even prefer to them that sort of machinery of business, chapels, tea-meetings, and addresses from Mr. Murphy, which makes up the dismal and illiberal life on which I have so often touched. But the aristocratic class has actually, as we have seen, in its well-known politeness, a kind of image or shadow of sweetness; and as for light, if it does not pursue light, it is not that it perversely cherishes some dismal and illiberal existence in preference to light, but it is lured off from following light by those mighty and eternal seducers of our race which weave for this class their most irresistible charms,—by worldly splendour, security, power and pleasure. These seducers are exterior goods, but in a way they are goods; and he who is hindered by them from caring for light and ideas, is not so much doing what is perverse as what is too natural.

Keeping this in view, I have in my own mind often indulged myself with the fancy of employing, in order to designate our aristocratic class, the name of *The Barbarians*. The Barbarians, to whom we all owe so much, and who reinvigorated and renewed our worn-out Europe, had, as is well known, eminent merits; and in this country, where we are for the most part sprung from the Barbarians, we have never had the prejudice against them which prevails among the races of Latin origin. The Barbarians brought with them that staunch individualism, as the modern phrase is, and that passion for doing as one likes, for the assertion of personal liberty, which appears to Mr. Bright the central idea of English life, and of which we have, at any rate, a very rich supply. The stronghold and natural seat of this passion was in the nobles of whom our aristocratic class are the inheritors; and this class, accordingly, have signally manifested it, and have done much by their example to recommend it to the body of the nation, who already, indeed, had it in their blood. The Barbarians, again, had the passion for field-sports; and they have handed it on to our aristocratic class, who of this passion too, as of the passion for asserting one's personal liberty, are the great natural stronghold. The care of the Barbarians for the body, and for all manly exercises; the vigour, good looks, and fine complexion which they acquired and perpetuated in their families by these means,—all this may be observed still in our aristocratic class. The chivalry of the Barbarians, with its characteristics of high spirit, choice manners, and distinguished bearing,—what is this but the attractive commencement of the politeness of our aristocratic class? In some Barbarian noble, no doubt, one would have admired, if one could have been then alive to see it, the rudiments of our politest peer. Only, all this culture (to call it by that name) of the Barbarians was an exterior culture mainly. It consisted principally in outward gifts and graces, in looks, manners, accomplishments, prowess. The chief inward gifts which had part in it were the most exterior, so to speak, of inward gifts, those which come nearest to outward ones; they were courage, a high spirit, self-confidence. Far within, and unawakened, lay a whole range of powers of thought and feeling, to which these interesting productions of nature had, from the circumstances of their life, no access. Making allowances for the difference of the times, surely we can observe precisely the same thing now in our aristocratic class. In general its culture is exterior chiefly; all the exterior graces and accomplishments, and the more external of the inward virtues, seem to be principally its portion. It now, of course, cannot but be often in contact with those studies by which, from the world of thought and feeling, true culture teaches us to fetch sweetness and light; but its hold upon these very studies appears remarkably external, and unable to exert any deep power upon its spirit. Therefore the one insufficiency which we noted in the perfect mean of this class was an insufficiency of light. And owing to the same causes, does not a subtle criticism lead us to make, even on the good looks and politeness of our aristocratic class, and of even the most fascinating half of that class, the feminine half, the one qualifying remark, that in these charming gifts there should perhaps be, for ideal perfection, a shade more *soul*?

I often, therefore, when I want to distinguish clearly the aristocratic class from the Philistines proper, or middle class, name the former, in my own mind, *the Barbarians*. And when I go through the country, and see this and that beautiful and imposing seat of theirs crowning the landscape, "There," I say to myself, "is a great fortified post of the Barbarians."

It is obvious that that part of the working class which, working diligently by the light of Mrs. Gooch's Golden Rule, looks forward to the happy day when it will sit on thrones with commercial members of Parliament and other middle-class potentates, to survey, as Mr. Bright beautifully says, "the cities it has built, the railroads it has made, the manufactures it has produced, the cargoes which freight the ships of the greatest mercantile navy the world has ever seen,"—it is obvious, I say, that this part of the working class is, or is in a fair way to be, one in spirit with the industrial middle class. It is notorious that our middle-class Liberals have long looked forward to this consummation, when the working class shall join forces with them, aid them heartily to carry forward their great works, go in a body to their tea-meetings, and, in short, enable them to bring about their millennium. That part of the working class, therefore, which does really seem to lend itself to these great aims, may, with propriety, be numbered by us among the Philistines. That part of it, again, which so much occupies the attention of philanthropists at present,— the part which gives all its energies to organising itself, through trades' unions and other means, so as to constitute, first, a great working-class power independent of the middle and aristocratic classes, and then, by dint of numbers, give the law to them and itself reign absolutely,—this lively and promising part must also, according to our definition, go with the Philistines; because it is its class and its class instinct which it seeks to affirm, its ordinary self, not its best self; and it is a machinery, an industrial machinery, and power and pre-eminence and other external goods, which fill its thoughts, and not an inward perfection. It is wholly occupied, according to Plato's subtle expression, with the things of itself and not its real self, with the things of the State and not the real State. But that vast portion, lastly, of the working class which, raw and half-developed, has long lain half-hidden amidst its poverty and squalor, and is now issuing from its hiding-place to assert an Englishman's heaven-born privilege of doing as he likes, and is beginning to perplex us by marching where it likes, meeting where it likes, bawling what it likes, breaking what it likes,—to this vast residuum we may with great propriety give the name of *Populace*.

Thus we have got three district terms, *Barbarians*, *Philistines*, *Populace*, to denote roughly the three great classes into which our society is divided; and though this humble attempt at a scientific nomenclature falls, no doubt, very far short in precision of what might be required from a writer equipped with a complete and coherent philosophy, yet, from a notoriously unsystematic and unpretending writer, it will, I trust, be accepted as sufficient.

But in using this new, and, I hope, convenient division of English society, two things are to be borne in mind. The first is, that since, under all our class divisions, there is a common basis of human nature, therefore, in every one of us, whether we be properly Barbarians, Philistines, or Populace, there exists, sometimes only in germ and potentially, sometimes more or less developed, the same tendencies and passions which have made our fellow-citizens of other classes what they are. This consideration is very important, because it has great influence in begetting that spirit of indulgence which is a necessary part of sweetness, and which, indeed, when our culture is complete, is, as I have said, inexhaustible. Thus, an English Barbarian who examines himself will, in general, find himself to be not so entirely a Barbarian but that he has in him, also, something of the Philistine, and even something of the Populace as well. And the same with Englishmen of the two other classes.

This is an experience which we may all verify every day. For instance, I myself (I again take myself as a sort of *corpus vile* to serve for illustration in a matter where serving for illustration may not by every one be thought agreeable), I myself am properly a Philistine,—Mr. Swinburne would add, the son of a Philistine. And although, through circumstances which will perhaps one day be known if ever the affecting history of my conversion comes to be written, I have, for the most part, broken with the ideas and the tea-meetings of my own class, yet I have not, on that account, been brought much the nearer to the ideas and works of the Barbarians or of the Populace. Nevertheless, I never take a gun or a fishing-rod in my hands without feeling that I have in the ground of my nature the self-same seeds which, fostered by circumstances, do so much to make the Barbarian; and that, with the Barbarian's advantages, I might have rivalled him. Place me in one of his great fortified posts, with these seeds of a love for field-sports sown in my nature, with all the means of developing them, with all pleasures at my command, with most whom I met deferring to me, every one I met smiling on me, and with every appearance of permanence and security before me and behind me,—then I too might have grown, I feel, into a very passable child of the established fact, of commendable spirit and politeness, and, at the same time, a little inaccessible to ideas and light; not, of course, with either the eminent fine spirit of our type of aristocratic perfection, or the eminent turn for resistance of our type of aristocratic excess, but, according to the measure of the common run of mankind, something between the two. And as to the Populace, who, whether he be Barbarian or Philistine, can look at them without sympathy, when he remembers how often,—every time that we snatch up a vehement opinion in ignorance and passion, every time that we long to crush an adversary by sheer violence, every time that we are envious, every time that we are brutal, every time that we adore mere power or success, every time that we add our voice to swell a blind clamour against some unpopular personage, every time that we trample savagely on the fallen,—he has found in his own bosom the eternal spirit of the Populace, and that there needs only a little help from circumstances to make it triumph in him untameably.

The second thing to be borne in mind I have indicated several times already. It is this. All of us, so far as we are Barbarians, Philistines, or Populace, imagine happiness to consist in doing what one's ordinary self likes. What one's ordinary self likes differs according to the class to which one belongs, and has its severer and its lighter side; always, however, remaining machinery, and nothing more. The graver self of the Barbarian likes honours and consideration; his more relaxed self, field-sports and pleasure. The graver self of one kind of Philistine likes fanaticism, business, and money-making; his more relaxed self, comfort and tea-meetings. Of another kind of Philistine, the graver self likes rattening; the relaxed self, deputations, or hearing Mr. Odger[1] speak. The sterner self of the Populace likes bawling, hustling, and smashing; the lighter self, beer. But in each class there are born a certain number of natures with a curiosity about their best self, with a bent for seeing things as they are, for disentangling themselves from machinery, for simply concerning themselves with reason and the will of God, and doing their best to make these prevail;—for the pursuit, in a word, of perfection. To certain manifestations of this love for perfection mankind have accustomed themselves to give the name of genius; implying, by this name, something original and heaven-bestowed in the passion. But the passion is to be found far beyond those manifestations of it to which the world usually gives the name of genius, and in which there is, for the most part, a *talent* of some kind or other, a special and striking faculty of execution, informed by the heaven-bestowed ardour, or genius. It is to be found in many manifestations besides these, and may best be called, as we have called it, the love and pursuit of perfection; culture being the true

[1] [George Odger (1820–1877), trade-unionist, who made five unsuccessful attempts to enter Parliament. President of the International Association of Working-men.]

nurse of the pursuing love, and sweetness and light the true character of the pursued perfection. Natures with this bent emerge in all classes,—among the Barbarians, among the Philistines, among the Populace. And this bent always tends to take them out of their class, and to make their distinguishing characteristic not their Barbarianism or their Philistinism, but their *humanity*. They have, in general, a rough time of it in their lives; but they are sown more abundantly than one might think, they appear where and when one least expects it, they set up a fire which enfilades, so to speak, the class with which they are ranked; and, in general, by the extrication of their best self as the self to develope, and by the simplicity of the ends fixed by them as paramount, they hinder the unchecked predominance of that class-life which is the affirmation of our ordinary self, and seasonably disconcert mankind in their worship of machinery.

Hebraism and Hellenism

This fundamental ground is our preference of doing to thinking. Now this preference is a main element in our nature, and as we study it we find ourselves opening up a number of large questions on every side.

Let me go back for a moment to Bishop Wilson,[1] who says;—"First, never go against the best light you have; secondly, take care that your light be not darkness." We show, as a nation, laudable energy and persistence in walking according to the best light we have, but are not quite careful enough, perhaps, to see that our light be not darkness. This is only another version of the old story that energy is our strong point and favourable characteristic rather than intelligence. But we may give to this idea a more general form still, in which it will have a yet larger range of application. We may regard this energy driving at practice, this paramount sense of the obligation of duty, self-control, and work, this earnestness in going manfully with the best light we have, as one force. And we may regard the intelligence driving at those ideas which are, after all, the basis of right practice, the ardent sense for all the new and changing combinations of them which man's development brings with it, the indomitable impulse to know and adjust them perfectly, as another force. And these two

[1] [Thomas Wilson (1663–1755), Bishop of Sodor and Man, who was responsible for the translation of the Gospels into Manx. Author of numerous devotional works admired by Newman and Keble. He was one of Arnold's favourite religious writers. The *Maxims of Piety and Christianity* are praised in the Preface to *Culture and Anarchy*, and his *Sacra Privata* are frequently quoted in Arnold's Note-Books.]

forces we may regard as in some sense rivals,—rivals not by the
necessity of their own nature, but as exhibited in man and his
history,—and rivals dividing the empire of the world between
them. And to give these forces names from the two races of men
who have supplied the most signal and splendid manifestations
of them, we may call them respectively the forces of Hebraism
and Hellenism. Hebraism and Hellenism,—between these two
points of influence moves our world. At one time it feels more
powerfully the attraction of one of them, at another time of the
other; and it ought to be, though it never is, evenly and happily
balanced between them.

The final aim of both Hellenism and Hebraism, as of all great
spiritual disciplines, is no doubt the same: man's perfection or
salvation. The very language which they both of them use in
schooling us to reach this aim is often identical. Even when their
language indicates by variation,—sometimes a broad variation,
often a but slight and subtle variation,—the different courses of
thought which are uppermost in each discipline, even then the
unity of the final end and aim is still apparent. To employ the
actual words of that discipline with which we ourselves are all
of us most familiar, and the words of which, therefore, come most
home to us, that final end and aim is "that we might be partakers
of the divine nature." These are the words of a Hebrew apostle,
but of Hellenism and Hebraism alike this is, I say, the aim. When
the two are confronted, as they very often are confronted, it is
nearly always with what I may call a rhetorical purpose; the
speaker's whole design is to exalt and enthrone one of the two,
and he uses the other only as a foil and to enable him the better
to give effect to his purpose. Obviously, with us, it is usually
Hellenism which is thus reduced to minister to the triumph of
Hebraism. There is a sermon on Greece and the Greek spirit by
a man never to be mentioned without interest and respect,
Frederick Robertson,[1] in which this rhetorical use of Greece and
the Greek spirit, and the inadequate exhibition of them necessarily consequent upon this, is almost ludicrous, and would be
censurable if it were not to be explained by the exigencies of a
sermon. On the other hand, Heinrich Heine, and other writers
of his sort, give us the spectacle of the tables completely turned,
and of Hebraism brought in just as a foil and contrast to Hellenism, and to make the superiority of Hellenism more manifest. In

---

[1] [F. W. Robertson, incumbent of Trinity Chapel, Brighton, from
1847 till his death in 1853. The integrity of his character, the zeal and
eloquence of his sermons, and his interest in the working classes
gained him an outstanding reputation in his time. Among his friends
was Lady Byron.]

both these cases there is injustice and misrepresentation. The aim and end of both Hebraism and Hellenism is, as I have said, one and the same, and this aim and end is august and admirable.

Still, they pursue this aim by very different courses. The uppermost idea with Hellenism is to see things as they really are; the uppermost idea with Hebraism is conduct and obedience. Nothing can do away with this ineffaceable difference. The Greek quarrel with the body and its desires is, that they hinder right thinking, the Hebrew quarrel with them is, that they hinder right acting. "He that keepeth the law, happy is he;" "Blessed is the man that feareth the Eternal, that delighteth greatly in his commandments;"—that is the Hebrew notion of felicity; and, pursued with passion and tenacity, this notion would not let the Hebrew rest till, as is well known, he had at last got out of the law a network of prescriptions to enwrap his whole life, to govern every moment of it, every impulse, every action. The Greek notion of felicity, on the other hand, is perfectly conveyed in these words of a great French moralist: '*C'est le bonheur des hommes*,'—when? when they abhor that which is evil?—no; when they exercise themselves in the law of the Lord day and night?—no; when they die daily?—no; when they walk about the New Jerusalem with palms in their hands?—no; but when they think aright, when their thought hits: "*quand ils pensent juste*." At the bottom of both the Greek and the Hebrew notion is the desire, native in man, for reason, and the will of God, the feeling after the universal order,—in a word, the love of God. But, while Hebraism seizes upon certain plain, capital intimations of the universal order, and rivets itself, one may say, with unequalled grandeur of earnestness and intensity on the study and observance of them, the bent of Hellenism is to follow, with flexible activity, the whole play of the universal order, to be apprehensive of missing any part of it, of sacrificing one part to another, to slip away from resting in this or that intimation of it, however capital. An unclouded clearness of mind, an unimpeded play of thought, is what this bent drives at. The governing idea of Hellenism is *spontaneity of consciousness*; that of Hebraism, *strictness of conscience*.

Christianity changed nothing in this essential bent of Hebraism to set doing above knowing. Self-conquest, self-devotion, the following not our own individual will, but the will of God, *obedience*, is the fundamental idea of this form, also, of the discipline to which we have attached the general name of Hebraism. Only, as the old law and the network of prescriptions with which it enveloped human life were evidently a motive-power not driving and searching enough to produce the result aimed at,—patient continuance in well doing, self-conquest,—Christianity substituted for them boundless devotion to that inspiring and affecting pattern of self-conquest offered by Jesus Christ; and by the new motive-power, of which the essence was this, though the love and admiration of Christian churches have for centuries been employed in varying, amplifying, and adorning the plain description of it, Christianity, as St. Paul truly says, "establishes the law," and in the strength of the ampler power which she has thus supplied to fulfil it, has accomplished the miracles, which we all see, of her history.

So long as we do not forget that both Hellenism and Hebraism are profound and admirable manifestations of man's life, tendencies, and powers, and that both of them aim at a like final result, we can hardly insist too strongly on the divergence of line and of operation with which they proceed. It is a divergence so great that it most truly, as the prophet Zechariah says, "has raised up thy sons, O Zion, against thy sons, O Greece!" The difference whether it is by doing or by knowing that we set most store, and the practical consequences which follow from this difference, leave their mark on all the history of our race and of its development. Language may be abundantly quoted from both Hellenism and Hebraism to make it seem that one follows the same current as the other towards the same goal. They are, truly, borne towards the same goal; but the currents which bear them are infinitely different. It is true, Solomon will praise knowing: "Understanding is a well-spring of life unto him that hath it." And in the New Testament, again, Jesus Christ is a "light," and "truth makes us free." It is true, Aristotle will undervalue knowing: "In what concerns virtue," says he, "three things are necessary—knowledge, deliberate will, and perseverance; but, whereas the two last are all-important, the first is a matter of little importance." It is true that with the same impatience with which St. James enjoins a man to be not a forgetful hearer, but a *doer of the work*,[1] Epictetus exhorts us to *do* what we have demonstrated to ourselves we ought to do; or he taunts us with futility, for being armed at all points to prove that lying is wrong, yet all the time continuing to lie. It is true, Plato, in words which are almost the words of the New Testament or the Imitation, calls life a learning to die. But underneath the superficial agreement the fundamental divergence still subsists. The understanding of Solomon is "the walking in the way of the commandments;" this is "the way of peace," and it is of this that blessedness comes. In the New Testament, the truth which gives us the peace of God and makes us free, is the love of Christ constraining us to

---

[1] [Sic, in all editions. James I. 22. "But be ye doers of the word, and not hearers only . . . "]

crucify, as he did, and with a like purpose of moral regeneration, the flesh with its affections and lusts, and thus establishing, as we have seen, the law. The moral virtues, on the other hand, are with Aristotle but the porch and access to the intellectual, and with these last is blessedness. That partaking of the divine life, which both Hellenism and Hebraism, as we have said, fix as their crowning aim, Plato expressly denies to the man of practical virtue merely, of self-conquest with any other motive than that of perfect intellectual vision. He reserves it for the lover of pure knowledge, of seeing things as they really are,—the φιλομαθής.

Both Hellenism and Hebraism arise out of the wants of human nature, and address themselves to satisfying those wants. But their methods are so different, they lay stress on such different points, and call into being by their respective disciplines such different activities, that the face which human nature presents when it passes from the hands of one of them to those of the other, is no longer the same. To get rid of one's ignorance, to see things as they are, and by seeing them as they are to see them in their beauty, is the simple and attractive ideal which Hellenism holds out before human nature; and from the simplicity and charm of this ideal, Hellenism, and human life in the hands of Hellenism, is invested with a kind of aërial ease, clearness, and radiancy; they are full of what we call sweetness and light. Difficulties are kept out of view, and the beauty and rationalness of the ideal have all our thoughts. "The best man is he who most tries to perfect himself, and the happiest man is he who most feels that he *is* perfecting himself,"—this account of the matter by Socrates, the true Socrates of the *Memorabilia*, has something so simple, spontaneous, and unsophisticated about it, that it seems to fill us with clearness and hope when we hear it. But there is a saying which I have heard attributed to Mr. Carlyle about Socrates,—a very happy saying, whether it is really Mr. Carlyle's or not,—which excellently marks the essential point in which Hebraism differs from Hellenism. "Socrates," this saying goes, "is terribly *at ease in Zion*." Hebraism,—and here is the source of its wonderful strength,—has always been severely pre-occupied with an awful sense of the impossibility of being at ease in Zion; of the difficulties which oppose themselves to man's pursuit or attainment of that perfection of which Socrates talks so hopefully, and, as from this point of view one might almost say, so glibly. It is all very well to talk of getting rid of one's ignorance, of seeing things in their reality, seeing them in their beauty; but how is this to be done when there is something which thwarts and spoils all our efforts?

This something is *sin*; and the space which sin fills in Hebraism, as compared with Hellenism, is indeed prodigious. This obstacle to perfection fills the whole scene, and perfection appears remote and rising away from earth, in the background. Under the name of sin, the difficulties of knowing oneself and conquering oneself which impede man's passage to perfection, become, for Hebraism, a positive, active entity hostile to man, a mysterious power which I heard Dr. Pusey the other day, in one of his impressive sermons, compare to a hideous hunchback seated on our shoulders, and which it is the main business of our lives to hate and oppose. The discipline of the Old Testament may be summed up as a discipline teaching us to abhor and flee from sin; the discipline of the New Testament, as a discipline teaching us to die to it. As Hellenism speaks of thinking clearly, seeing things in their essence and beauty, as a grand and precious feat for man to achieve, so Hebraism speaks of becoming conscious of sin, of awakening to a sense of sin, as a feat of this kind. It is obvious to what wide divergence these differing tendencies, actively followed, must lead. As one passes and repasses from Hellenism to Hebraism, from Plato to St. Paul, one feels inclined to rub one's eyes and ask oneself whether man is indeed a gentle and simple being, showing the traces of a noble and divine nature; or an unhappy chained captive, labouring with groanings that cannot be uttered to free himself from the body of this death.

Apparently it was the Hellenic conception of human nature which was unsound, for the world could not live by it. Absolutely to call it unsound, however, is to fall into the common error of its Hebraising enemies; but it was unsound at that particular moment of man's development, it was premature. The indispensable basis of conduct and self-control, the platform upon which alone the perfection aimed at by Greece can come into bloom, was not to be reached by our race so easily; centuries of probation and discipline were needed to bring us to it. Therefore the bright promise of Hellenism faded, and Hebraism ruled the world. Then was seen that astonishing spectacle, so well marked by the often-quoted words of the prophet Zechariah, when men of all languages and nations took hold of the skirt of him that was a Jew, saying:—"*We will go with you, for we have heard that God is with you.*" And the Hebraism which thus received and ruled a world all gone out of the way and altogether become unprofitable, was, and could not but be, the later, the more spiritual, the more attractive development of Hebraism. It was Christianity; that is to say, Hebraism aiming at self-conquest and rescue from the thrall of vile affections, not by obedience to the letter of a law, but by conformity to the image of a self-sacrificing example. To a world stricken with moral enervation Christianity offered its spectacle of an inspired self-sacrifice; to men who refused themselves nothing, it showed one who refused himself everything;— "*my Saviour banished joy!*" says George Herbert. When the *alma Venus*, the life-giving and joy-giving power of nature, so fondly cherished by the pagan world, could not save her followers from self-dissatisfaction and ennui, the severe words of the apostle came bracingly and refreshingly: "Let no man deceive you with vain words, for because of these things cometh the wrath of God upon the children of disobedience." Through age after age and generation after generation, our race, or all that part of our race which was most living and progressive, was *baptized into a death*; and endeavoured, by suffering in the flesh, to cease from sin. Of this endeavour, the animating labours and afflictions of early Christianity, the touching asceticism of mediæval Christianity, are the great historical manifestations. Literary monuments of it, each in its own way incomparable, remain in the Epistles of St. Paul, in St. Augustine's Confessions, and in the two original and simplest books of the Imitation.

Of two disciplines laying their main stress, the one, on clear intelligence, the other, on firm obedience; the one, on comprehensively knowing the grounds of one's duty, the other, on diligently practising it; the one, on taking all possible care (to use Bishop Wilson's words again) that the light we have be not darkness, the other, that according to the best light we have we diligently walk,—the priority naturally belongs to that discipline which braces all man's moral powers, and founds for him an indispensable basis of character. And, therefore, it is justly said of the Jewish people, who were charged with setting powerfully forth that side of the divine order to which the words *conscience* and *self-conquest* point, that they were "entrusted with the oracles of God;" as it is justly said of Christianity, which followed Judaism and which set forth this side with a much deeper effectiveness and a much wider influence, that the wisdom of the old Pagan world was foolishness compared to it. No words of devotion and admiration can be too strong to render thanks to these beneficent forces which have so borne forward humanity in its appointed work of coming to the knowledge and possession of itself; above all, in those great moments when their action was the wholesomest and the most necessary.

But the evolution of these forces, separately and in themselves, is not the whole evolution of humanity,—their single history is not the whole history of man; whereas their admirers are always apt to make it stand for the whole history. Hebraism and Hellenism are, neither of them, the *law* of human development, as their admirers are prone to make them; they are, each of them, *contributions* to human development,—august contributions, invaluable contributions; and each showing itself to us more august, more invaluable, more preponderant over the other, according to the moment in which we take them, and the relation in which we stand to them. The nations of our modern world, children of that immense and salutary movement which broke up the Pagan world, inevitably stand to Hellenism in a relation which dwarfs it, and to Hebraism in a relation which magnifies it. They are inevitably prone to take Hebraism as the law of human development, and not as simply a contribution to it, however precious. And yet the lesson must perforce be learned, that the human spirit is wider than the most priceless of the forces which bear it onward, and that to the whole development of man Hebraism itself, is, like Hellenism, but a contribution.

Perhaps we may help ourselves to see this clearer by an illustration drawn from the treatment of a single great idea which has profoundly engaged the human spirit, and has given it eminent opportunities for showing its nobleness and energy. It surely must be perceived that the idea of immortality, as this idea rises in its generality before the human spirit, is something grander, truer, and more satisfying, than it is in the particular forms by which St. Paul, in the famous fifteenth chapter of the Epistle to the Corinthians, and Plato, in the *Phædo*, endeavour to develop and establish it. Surely we cannot but feel, that the argumentation with which the Hebrew apostle goes about to expound this great idea is, after all, confused and inconclusive; and that the reasoning, drawn from analogies of likeness and equality, which is employed upon it by the Greek philosopher, is over-subtle and sterile. Above and beyond the inadequate solutions which Hebraism and Hellenism here attempt, extends the immense and august problem itself, and the human spirit which gave birth to it. And this single illustration may suggest to us how the same thing happens in other cases also.

But meanwhile, by alternations of Hebraism and Hellenism, of a man's intellectual and moral impulses, of the effort to see things as they really are, and the effort to win peace by self-conquest, the human spirit proceeds; and each of these two forces has its appointed hours of culmination and seasons of rule. As the great movement of Christianity was a triumph of Hebraism and man's moral impulses, so the great movement which goes by the name of the Renascence [1] was an uprising and re-instate-

---

[1] I have ventured to give to the foreign word *Renaissance*,—destined to become of more common use amongst us as the movement which it denotes comes, as it will come, increasingly to interest us,—an English form.

ment of man's intellectual impulses and of Hellenism. We in England, the devoted children of Protestantism, chiefly know the Renascence by its subordinate and secondary side of the Reformation. The Reformation has been often called a Hebraising revival, a return to the ardour and sincereness of primitive Christianity. No one, however, can study the development of Protestantism and of Protestant churches without feeling that into the Reformation too,—Hebraising child of the Renascence and offspring of its fervour, rather than its intelligence, as it undoubtedly was,—the subtle Hellenic leaven of the Renascence found its way, and that the exact respective parts, in the Reformation, of Hebraism and of Hellenism, are not easy to separate. But what we may with truth say is, that all which Protestantism was to itself clearly conscious of, all which it succeeded in clearly setting forth in words, had the characters of Hebraism rather than of Hellenism. The Reformation was strong, in that it was an earnest return to the Bible and to doing from the heart the will of God as there written. It was weak, in that it never consciously grasped or applied the central idea of the Renascence,—the Hellenic idea of pursuing, in all lines of activity, the law and science, to use Plato's words, of things as they really are. Whatever direct superiority, therefore, Protestantism had over Catholicism was a moral superiority, a superiority arising out of its greater sincerity and earnestness,—at the moment of its apparition at any rate,—in dealing with the heart and conscience. Its pretensions to an intellectual superiority are in general quite illusory. For Hellenism, for the thinking side in man as distinguished from the acting side, the attitude of mind of Protestantism towards the Bible in no respect differs from the attitude of mind of Catholicism towards the Church. The mental habit of him who imagines that Balaam's ass spoke, in no respect differs from the mental habit of him who imagines that a Madonna of wood or stone winked; and the one, who says that God's Church makes him believe what he believes, and the other, who says that God's Word makes him believe what he believes, are for the philosopher perfectly alike in not really and truly knowing, when they say *God's Church* and *God's Word*, what it is they say, or whereof they affirm.

In the sixteenth century, therefore, Hellenism re-entered the world, and again stood in presence of Hebraism,—a Hebraism renewed and purged. Now, it has not been enough observed, how, in the seventeenth century, a fate befell Hellenism in some respects analogous to that which befell it at the commencement of our era. The Renascence, that great re-awakening of Hellenism, that irresistible return of humanity to nature and to seeing

things as they are, which in art, in literature, and in physics, produced such splendid fruits, had, like the anterior Hellenism of
the Pagan world, a side of moral weakness, and of relaxation or
insensibility of the moral fibre, which in Italy showed itself with
the most startling plainness, but which in France, England, and
other countries, was very apparent too. Again this loss of spiritual balance, this exclusive preponderance given to man's perceiving and knowing side, this unnatural defect of his feeling and
acting side, provoked a reaction. Let us trace that reaction where
it most nearly concerns us.

Science has now made visible to everybody the great and pregnant elements of difference which lie in race, and in how signal a
manner they make the genius and history of an Indo-European
people vary from those of a Semitic people. Hellenism is of
Indo-European growth, Hebraism is of Semitic growth; and we
English, a nation of Indo-European stock, seem to belong naturally to the movement of Hellenism. But nothing more strongly
marks the essential unity of man, than the affinities we can perceive, in this point or that, between members of one family of
peoples and members of another. And no affinity of this kind is
more strongly marked than that likeness in the strength and prominence of the moral fibre, which, notwithstanding immense elements of difference, knits in some special sort the genius and
history of us English, and our American descendants across the
Atlantic, to the genius and history of the Hebrew people. Puritanism, which has been so great a power in the English nation,
and in the strongest part of the English nation, was originally the
reaction in the seventeenth century of the conscience and moral
sense of our race, against the moral indifference and lax rule of
conduct which in the sixteenth century came in with the Renascence. It was a reaction of Hebraism against Hellenism; and it
powerfully manifested itself, as was natural, in a people with
much of what we call a Hebraising turn, with a signal affinity for
the bent which was the master-bent of Hebrew life. Eminently
Indo-European by its *humour*, by the power it shows, through
this gift, of imaginatively acknowledging the multiform aspects
of the problem of life, and of thus getting itself unfixed from its
own over-certainty, of smiling at its own over-tenacity, our race
has yet (and a great part of its strength lies here), in matters of
practical life and moral conduct, a strong share of the assured-
ness, the tenacity, the intensity of the Hebrews. This turn manifested itself in Puritanism, and has had a great part in shaping
our history for the last two hundred years. Undoubtedly it
checked and changed amongst us that movement of the Renascence which we see producing in the reign of Elizabeth such

wonderful fruits. Undoubtedly it stopped the prominent rule and direct development of that order of ideas which we call by the name of Hellenism, and gave the first rank to a different order of ideas. Apparently, too, as we said of the former defeat of Hellenism, if Hellenism was defeated, this shows that Hellenism was imperfect, and that its ascendancy at that moment would not have been for the world's good.

Yet there is a very important difference between the defeat inflicted on Hellenism by Christianity eighteen hundred years ago, and the check given to the Renascence by Puritanism. The greatness of the difference is well measured by the difference in force, beauty, significance and usefulness, between primitive Christianity and Protestantism. Eighteen hundred years ago it was altogether the hour of Hebraism. Primitive Christianity was legitimately and truly the ascendant force in the world at that time, and the way of mankind's progress lay through its full development. Another hour in man's development began in the fifteenth century, and the main road of his progress then lay for a time through Hellenism. Puritanism was no longer the central current of the world's progress, it was a side stream crossing the central current and checking it. The cross and the check may have been necessary and salutary, but that does not do away with the essential difference between the main stream of man's advance and a cross or side stream. For more than two hundred years the main stream of man's advance has moved towards knowing himself and the world, seeing things as they are, spontaneity of consciousness; the main impulse of a great part, and that the strongest part, of our nation has been towards strictness of conscience. They have made the secondary the principal at the wrong moment, and the principal they have at the wrong moment treated as secondary. This contravention of the natural order has produced, as such contravention always must produce, a certain confusion and false movement, of which we are now beginning to feel, in almost every direction, the inconvenience. In all directions our habitual courses [1] of action seem to be losing efficaciousness, credit, and control, both with others and even with ourselves. Everywhere we see the beginnings of confusion, and we want a clue to some sound order and authority. This we can only get by going back upon the actual instincts and forces which rule our life, seeing them as they really are, connecting them with other instincts and forces, and enlarging our whole view and rule of life.

[1] [Original text, "causes."]

From *Porro Unum est Necessarium*

THE Puritan's great danger is that he imagines himself in possession of a rule telling him the *unum necessarium*, or one thing needful, and that he then remains satisfied with a very crude conception of what this rule really is and what it tells him, thinks he has
now knowledge and henceforth needs only to act, and, in this
dangerous state of assurance and self-satisfaction, proceeds to
give full swing to a number of the instincts of his ordinary self.
Some of the instincts of his ordinary self he has, by the help of
his rule of life, conquered; but others which he has not conquered
by this help he is so far from perceiving to need subjugation, and
to be instincts of an inferior self, that he even fancies it to be his
right and duty, in virtue of having conquered a limited part of
himself, to give unchecked swing to the remainder. He is, I say,
a victim of Hebraism, of the tendency to cultivate strictness of
conscience rather than spontaneity of consciousness. And what
he wants is a larger conception of human nature, showing him
the number of other points at which his nature must come to its
best, besides the points which he himself knows and thinks of.
There is no *unum necessarium*, or one thing needful, which can
free human nature from the obligation of trying to come to its
best at all these points. The real *unum necessarium* for us is to
come to our best at all points. Instead of our "one thing needful," justifying in us vulgarity, hideousness, ignorance, violence,
—our vulgarity, hideousness, ignorance, violence, are really so
many touchstones which try our one thing needful, and which
prove that in the state, at any rate, in which we ourselves have it,
it is not all we want. And as the force which encourages us to
stand staunch and fast by the rule and ground we have is Hebraism, so the force which encourages us to go back upon this rule,
and to try the very ground on which we appear to stand, is Hellenism,—a turn for giving our consciousness free play and enlarging
its range. And what I say is, not that Hellenism is always for
everybody more wanted than Hebraism, but that for Mr.
Murphy [1] at this particular moment, and for the great majority of
us his fellow-countrymen, it is more wanted.

Nothing is more striking than to observe in how many ways a
limited conception of human nature, the notion of a one thing
needful, a one side in us to be made uppermost, the disregard of a
full and harmonious development of ourselves, tells injuriously
on our thinking and acting. In the first place, our hold upon the

[1] [Arnold's example of the dangerous demagogue: Murphy had
made abusive and inflammatory speeches at Birmingham against the
Catholic element in the city.]

rule or standard, to which we look for our one thing needful, tends to become less and less near and vital, our conception of it more and more mechanical, and more and more unlike the thing itself as it was conceived in the mind where it originated. The dealings of Puritanism with the writings of St. Paul afford a noteworthy illustration of this. Nowhere so much as in the writings of St. Paul, and in that great apostle's greatest work, the Epistle to the Romans, has Puritanism found what seemed to furnish it with the one thing needful, and to give it canons of truth absolute and final. Now all writings, as has been already said, even the most precious writings and the most fruitful, must inevitably, from the very nature of things, be but contributions to human thought and human development, which extend wider than they do. Indeed, St. Paul, in the very Epistle of which we are speaking, shows, when he asks, "Who hath known the mind of the Lord?"—who hath known, that is, the true and divine order of things in its entirety,—that he himself acknowledges this fully. And we have already pointed out in another Epistle of St. Paul a great and vital idea of the human spirit,—the idea of immortality,—transcending and overlapping, so to speak, the expositor's power to give it adequate definition and expression.

But quite distinct from the question whether St. Paul's expression, or any man's expression, can be a perfect and final expression of truth, comes the question whether we rightly seize and understand his expression as it exists. Now, perfectly to seize another man's meaning, as it stood in his own mind, is not easy; especially when the man is separated from us by such differences of race, training, time, and circumstances as St. Paul. But there are degrees of nearness in getting at a man's meaning; and though we cannot arrive quite at what St. Paul had in his mind, yet we may come near it. And who, that comes thus near it, must not feel how terms which St. Paul employs, in trying to follow with his analysis of such profound power and originality some of the most delicate, intricate, obscure, and contradictory workings and states of the human spirit, are detached and employed by Puritanism, not in the connected and fluid way in which St. Paul employs them, and for which alone words are really meant, but in an isolated, fixed, mechanical way, as if they were talismans; and how all trace and sense of St. Paul's true movement of ideas, and sustained masterly analysis, is thus lost? Who, I say, that has watched Puritanism,—the force which so strongly Hebraises, which so takes St. Paul's writings as something absolute and final, containing the one thing needful,—handle such terms as *grace, faith, election, righteousness*, but must feel, not only that these terms have for the mind of Puritanism a sense false and

R

misleading, but also that this sense is the most monstrous and grotesque caricature of the sense of St. Paul, and that his true meaning is by these worshippers of his words altogether lost?

Or to take another eminent example, in which not Puritanism only, but, one may say, the whole religious world, by their mechanical use of St. Paul's writings, can be shown to miss or change his real meaning. The whole religious world, one may say, use now the word *resurrection*,—a word which is so often in their thoughts and on their lips, and which they find so often in St. Paul's writings,—in one sense only. They use it to mean a rising again after the physical death of the body. Now it is quite true that St. Paul speaks of resurrection in this sense, that he tries to describe and explain it, and that he condemns those who doubt and deny it. But it is true, that in nine cases out of ten where St. Paul thinks and speaks of resurrection, he thinks and speaks of it in a sense different from this;—in the sense of a rising to a new life before the physical death of the body, and not after it. The idea on which we have already touched, the profound idea of being baptized into the death of the great exemplar of self-devotion and self-annulment, of repeating in our own person, by virtue of identification with our exemplar, his course of self-devotion and self-annulment, and of thus coming, within the limits of our present life, to a new life, in which, as in the death going before it, we are identified with our exemplar,—this is the fruitful and original conception of being *risen with Christ* which possesses the mind of St. Paul, and this is the central point round which, with such incomparable emotion and eloquence, all his teaching moves. For him, the life after our physical death is really in the main but a consequence and continuation of the inexhaustible energy of the new life thus originated on this side the grave. This grand Pauline idea of Christian resurrection is worthily rehearsed in one of the noblest collects of the Prayer-Book, and is destined, no doubt, to fill a more and more important place in the Christianity of the future. But meanwhile, almost as signal as the essentialness of this characteristic idea in St. Paul's teaching, is the completeness with which the worshippers of St. Paul's words as an absolute final expression of saving truth have lost it, and have substituted for the apostle's living and near conception of a resurrection now, their mechanical and remote conception of a resurrection hereafter.

In short, so fatal is the notion of possessing, even in the most precious words or standards, the one thing needful, of having in them, once for all, a full and sufficient measure of light to guide us, and of there being no duty left for us except to make our practice square exactly with them,—so fatal, I say, is this notion to the right knowledge and comprehension of the very words or standards we thus adopt, and to such strange distortions and perversions of them does it inevitably lead, that whenever we hear that commonplace which Hebraism, if we venture to inquire what a man knows, is so apt to bring out against us, in disparagement of what we call culture, and in praise of a man's sticking to the one thing needful,—*he knows*, says Hebraism, *his Bible!*— whenever we hear this said, we may, without any elaborate defence of culture, content ourselves with answering simply: "No man, who knows nothing else, knows even his Bible."

Now the force which we have so much neglected, Hellenism, may be liable to fail in moral strength and earnestness, but by the law of its nature,—the very same law which makes it sometimes deficient in intensity when intensity is required,—it opposes itself to the notion of cutting our being in two, of attributing to one part the dignity of dealing with the one thing needful, and leaving the other part to take its chance, which is the bane of Hebraism. Essential in Hellenism is the impulse to the development of the whole man, to connecting and harmonising all parts of him, perfecting all, leaving none to take their chance.

The characteristic bent of Hellenism, as has been said, is to find the intelligible law of things, to see them in their true nature and as they really are. But many things are not seen in their true nature and as they really are, unless they are seen as beautiful. Behaviour is not intelligible, does not account for itself to the mind and show the reason for its existing, unless it is beautiful. The same with discourse, the same with song, the same with worship, all of them modes in which man proves his activity and expresses himself. To think that when one produces in these what is mean, or vulgar, or hideous, one can be permitted to plead that one has that within which passes show; to suppose that the possession of what benefits and satisfies one part of our being can make allowable either discourse like Mr. Murphy's or poetry like the hymns we all hear, or places of worship like the chapels we all see,—this it is abhorrent to the nature of Hellenism to concede. And to be, like our honoured and justly honoured Faraday, a great natural philosopher with one side of his being and a Sandemanian with the other, would to Archimedes have been impossible.

It is evident to what a many-sided perfecting of man's powers and activities this demand of Hellenism for satisfaction to be given to the mind by everything which we do, is calculated to impel our race. It has its dangers, as has been fully granted. The notion of this sort of equipollency in man's modes of activity may lead to moral relaxation; what we do not make our one thing needful, we may come to treat not enough as if it were needful, though it is indeed very needful and at the same time very hard. Still, what side in us has not its dangers, and which of our impulses can be a talisman to give us perfection outright, and not merely a help to bring us towards it? Has not Hebraism, as we have shown, its dangers as well as Hellenism? or have we used so excessively the tendencies in ourselves to which Hellenism makes appeal, that we are now suffering from it? Are we not, on the contrary, now suffering because we have not enough used these tendencies as a help towards perfection?

For we see whither it has brought us, the long exclusive predominance of Hebraism,—the insisting on perfection in one part of our nature and not in all; the singling out the moral side, the side of obedience and action, for such intent regard; making strictness of the moral conscience so far the principal thing, and putting off for hereafter and for another world the care for being complete at all points, the full and harmonious development of our humanity. Instead of watching and following on its ways the desire which, as Plato says, "for ever through all the universe tends towards that which is lovely," we think that the world has settled its accounts with this desire, knows what this desire wants of it, and that all the impulses of our ordinary self which do not conflict with the terms of this settlement, in our narrow view of it, we may follow unrestrainedly, under the sanction of some such text as "Not slothful in business," or, "Whatsoever thy hand findeth to do, do it with all thy might," or something else of the same kind. And to any of these impulses we soon come to give that same character of a mechanical, absolute law, which we give to our religion; we regard it, as we do our religion, as an object for strictness of conscience, not for spontaneity of consciousness; for unremitting adherence on its own account, not for going back upon, viewing in its connexion with other things, and adjusting to a number of changing circumstances. We treat it, in short, just as we treat our religion,—as machinery. It is in this way that the Barbarians treat their bodily exercises, the Philistines their business, Mr. Spurgeon his voluntaryism, Mr. Bright the assertion of personal liberty, Mr. Beales [1] the right of meeting in Hyde Park. In all those cases what is needed is a freer play of consciousness upon the object of pursuit; and in all of them Hebraism, the valuing staunchness and earnestness more than this free play, the entire subordination of thinking to doing, has led to a mistaken and misleading treatment of things. . . . .

[1] [Edmond Beales (1803–1881), lawyer and political agitator. President of the Reform League at the time of the Hyde Park riots, 1866.]

From *Conclusion*

EVERYONE is now boasting of what he has done to educate men's minds and to give things the course they are taking. Mr. Disraeli educates, Mr. Bright educates, Mr. Beales educates. We, indeed, pretend to educate no one, for we are still engaged in trying to clear and educate ourselves. But we are sure that the endeavour to reach, through culture, the firm intelligible law of things—we are sure that the detaching ourselves from our stock notions and habits—that a more free play of consciousness, an increased desire for sweetness and light, and all the bent which we call Hellenising, is the master-impulse even now of the life of our nation and of humanity,—somewhat obscurely perhaps for this actual moment, but decisively and certainly for the immediate future; and that those who work for this are the sovereign educators.

Docile echoes of the eternal voice, pliant organs of the infinite will, such workers are going along with the essential movement of the world; and this is their strength, and their happy and divine fortune. For if the believers in action, who are so impatient with us and call us effeminate, had had the same good fortune, they would, no doubt, have surpassed us in this sphere of vital influence by all the superiority of their genius and energy over ours. But now we go the way the human race is going, while they abolish the Irish Church by the power of the Nonconformists' antipathy to establishments, or they enable a man to marry his deceased wife's sister.

FRIENDSHIP'S GARLAND

1871

Friendship's Garland. Being the Conversations, Letters and Opinions of the late Arminius, Baron von Thunder-ten-Tronckh. Collected and Edited with a Dedicatory Letter to Adolescens Leo, Esq. of the Daily Telegraph, by Matthew Arnold. . . . . *manibus date lilia plenis*. London. Smith, Elder & Co., 15 Waterloo Place. 1871.

DURING 1866–7 Arnold wrote several letters to the *Pall Mall Gazette* purporting to give the views of Arminius von Thunder-ten-Tronckh, a visiting German, on the English way of life. They were resumed in 1869 and the whole series collected as *Friendship's Garland* in 1871. To Arnold's lecture on *Culture and its Enemies* (*Cornhill*, July 1867) Frederic Harrison replied with a parody of the Arminius conversations called *Culture, A Dialogue* (Fortnightly Review, November 1867). It is reprinted in Harrison's *The Choice of Books*, 1886.

FRIENDSHIP'S GARLAND

BEING THE CONVERSATIONS, LETTERS AND OPINIONS
OF THE LATE ARMINIUS,
BARON VON THUNDER-TEN-TRONCKH.
COLLECTED AND EDITED WITH A DEDICATORY LETTER
TO ADOLESCENS LEO, ESQ. OF THE DAILY TELEGRAPH

From *Dedicatory Letter*

(THE acquaintance of the ever-to-be-lamented Arminius was
made by the present Editor on the Continent in the year 1865.
The early history of the noble family of von Thunder-ten-
Tronckh, to which Arminius belonged, their establishment in
Westphalia, the sack of their castle in the middle of the last century by the Bulgarians, the fate of their principal dependents
(among whom was the famous optimist philosopher, Dr. Pan-
gloss), the adventures of Arminius's grandfather and his deporta-
tion to the Jesuits at Rome, are recorded in a well-known treatise
of Voltaire. Additional information is supplied in several of the
following letters.

Arminius came to England in 1866, and the correspondence
now given in a collected form to the public commenced in the
summer of that year, at the outbreak of the war between Prussia
and Austria. Many will yet remember the thrill with which they
originally received, through the unworthy ministry of the present
Editor, the communication of the great doctrine of "Geist."
What then, must it have been to hear that doctrine in its first
newness from the lips of Arminius himself! Yet it will, I hope,
be admitted, that even in this position of exceptional privilege,
the present Editor succeeded in preserving his coolness, his independent judgment, and his proper feelings as a Briton.)—ED.

From *Letter V*

Arminius's Appearance

I DON'T know that I have ever described Arminius's personal appearance. He has the true square Teutonic head, a blond and
disorderly mass of tow-like hair, a podgy and sanguine countenance, shaven cheeks, and a whity-brown moustache. He wears a

rough pilot-coat, and generally smokes away with his hands in the pockets of it, and his light blue eyes fixed on his interlocutor's face. When he takes his hands out of his pockets, his pipe out of his mouth, and his eyes off his friend's face, it is a sign that he is deeply moved.

Letter VI

I become intrusted with the Views of Arminius on Compulsory Education

Grub Street, April 20, 1867.

SIR,—

It is a long while since you have heard anything of Arminius and me, though I do hope you have sometimes given a thought to us both. The truth is we have been in the country. You may imagine how horribly disagreeable Arminius made himself during the famous snow in London at the beginning of this year. About the state of the streets he was bad enough, but about the poor frozen-out working men who went singing without let or hindrance before our houses, he quite made my blood creep. "The dirge of a society *qui s'en va,*" he used to call their pathetic songs. It is true I had always an answer for him—"Thank God, we are not Hausmannised yet!" and if that was not enough, and he wanted the philosophy of the thing, why I turned to a sort of constitutional commonplace book, or true Englishman's *vade mecum,* which I have been these many years forming for my own use by potting extracts from the *Times* and which I hope one day to give to the world, and I read him this golden aphorism: "Administrative, military, and clerical tyranny are unknown in this country, because the educated class discharges all the corresponding functions through committees of its own body." "Well, then," Arminius would answer, "show me your administrative committee for ridding us of these cursed frozen-out impostors." "My dear Arminius," was my quiet reply, "voluntary organisations are not to be dealt with in this peremptory manner. The administrative committee you ask for will develop itself in good time; its future members are probably now at nurse. In England we like our improvements to *grow,* not to be manufactured."

However the mental strain, day after day, of this line of high constitutional argument was so wearing, that I gladly acceded to a proposal made by Arminius in one of his fits of grumbling to go with him for a little while into the country. So into the country we went, and there, under his able guidance, I have been assiduously pursuing the study of German philosophy. As a rule, I

attend to nothing else just now; but when we were taking one of
our walks abroad the other morning, an incident happened which
led us to discuss the subject of compulsory education, and, as this
subject is beginning to awaken deep interest in the public mind,
I think you may be glad to have an account of the incident, and
of the valuable remarks on compulsory education which were
drawn from Arminius by it.

We were going out the other morning on one of our walks, as
I said, when we saw a crowd before the inn of the country town
where we have been staying. It was the magistrates' day for sitting, and I was glad of an opportunity to show off our local self-
government to a bureaucracy-ridden Prussian like Arminius. So
I stopped in the crowd, and there we saw an old fellow in a
smock-frock, with a white head, a low forehead, a red nose, and
a foxy expression of countenance, being taken along to the
justice-room. Seeing among the bystanders a contributor to the
Daily Telegraph, whom I formerly knew well enough,—for he
had the drawing-room floor underneath me in Grub Street, but
the magnificent circulation of that journal has long since carried
him, like the course of empire, westward,—I asked him if he
could tell me what the prisoner was charged with. I found it was
a hardened old poacher, called Diggs,—Zephaniah Diggs,—and
that he was had up for snaring a hare,—probably his ten-thou-
sandth. The worst of the story, to my mind, was that the old
rogue had a heap of young children by a second wife whom he
had married late in life, and that not one of these children would
he send to school, but persisted in letting them all run wild, and
grow up in utter barbarism.

I hastened to tell Arminius that it was a poaching case; and I
added that it was not always, perhaps, in poaching cases that our
local self-government appeared to the best advantage. "In the
present case, however, there is," said I, "no danger; for a representative of the *Daily Telegraph* is down here, to be on the look-
out for justices' justice, and to prevent oppression." Immediately afterwards I was sorry I had said this, for there are unfortunately several things which operate on Arminius like scarlet on
a bull, making him vicious the moment he comes across them;
and the *Daily Telegraph* is one of these things. He declares it
foments our worst faults; and he is fond of applying to it Dryden's dictum on Elkanah Settle, that its style is boisterous and its
prose incorrigibly lewd. Though I do certainly think its prose
a little full-bodied, yet I cannot bear to hear Arminius apply such
a term to it as "incorrigibly lewd;" and I always remonstrate
with him. "No, Arminius," I always say, "I hope not *incorrigibly*; I should be sorry to think that of a publication which is

forming the imagination and taste of millions of Englishmen."
"Pleasant news," was Arminius's answer, the last time I urged
this to him, "pleasant news; the next batch of you, then, will be
even more charming than the present!"

I trouble you with all this, Sir, to account for the acerbity of
tone in some of Arminius's subsequent conversation; an acerbity he too often manifests, and which tends, as I tell him, to
detract from the influence which his talents and acquirements
would otherwise give him. On the present occasion he took no
direct notice of my mention of the *Daily Telegraph*, but seemed
quite taken up with scrutinising old Diggs. "Such a peasant as
that wretched old creature," he said at last, "is peculiar, my dear
friend, to your country. Only look at that countenance! Centuries of feudalism have effaced in it every gleam of humane life."
... "Centuries of fiddlesticks!" interrupted I (for I assure you,
Sir, I can stand up to Arminius well enough on a proper occasion). "My dear Arminius, how can you allow yourself to talk
such rubbish? Gleam of humane life, indeed! do but look at the
twinkle in the old rogue's eye. He has plenty of life and wits
about him, has old Diggs, I can assure you; you just try and
come round him about a pot of beer!" "The mere cunning of an
animal!" retorted Arminius. "For my part," pursued I, "it is his
children I think most about; I am told not one of them has ever
seen the inside of a school. Do you know, Arminius, I begin to
think, and many people in this country begin to think, that the
time has almost come for taking a leaf out of your Prussian book,
and applying, in the education of children of this class, what the
great Kant calls the categorical imperative. The gap between
them and our educated and intelligent classes is really too frightful." "Your educated and intelligent classes!" sneered Arminius, in his very most offensive manner; "where are they? I should
like to see them."

I was not going to stand and hear our aristocracy and middle-
class set down in this way; so, treating Arminius's ebullition of
spite as beneath my notice, I pushed my way through the crowd
to the inn-door. I asked the policeman there what magistrates
were on the bench to-day. "Viscount Lumpington," says the
man, "Reverend Esau Hittall, and Bottles Esquire." "Good
heavens!" I exclaimed, turning round to Arminius, who had followed me, and forgetting, in my excitement, my just cause of
offence with him,—"Good heavens, Arminius, if Bottles hasn't
got himself made a county magistrate! *Sic itur ad astra.*" "Yes,"
says Arminius, with a smile, "one of your educated and intelligent classes, I suppose. And I dare say the other two are to
match. Your magistrates are a sort of judges, I know; just the

people who are drawn from the educated and intelligent classes. Now, what's sauce for the goose is sauce for the gander; if you put a pressure on one class to make it train itself properly, you must put a pressure on others to the same end. That is what we do in Prussia, if you are going to take a leaf out of our book. I want to hear what steps you take to put this pressure on people above old Diggs there, and then I will talk to you about putting it on old Diggs. Take his judges who are going to try him to-day; how about them? What training have you made them give themselves, and what are their qualifications?"

I luckily happen to know Lord Lumpington and Hittall pretty well, having been at college with them in former days, when I little thought the Philistines would have brought my grey hairs to a garret in Grub Street; and I have made the acquaintance of Mr. Bottles since, and know all about him. So I was able to satisfy Arminius's curiosity, and I had great pleasure in making him remark, as I did so, the rich diversity of our English life, the healthy natural play of our free institutions, and the happy blending of classes and characters which this promotes. "The three magistrates in that inn," said I, "are not three Government functionaries all cut out of one block; they embody our whole national life;—the land, religion, commerce, are all represented by them. Lord Lumpington is a peer of old family and great estate; Esau Hittall is a clergyman; Mr. Bottles is one of our self-made middle-class men. Their politics are not all of one colour, and that colour the Government's. Lumpington is a Constitutional Whig; Hittall is a benighted old Tory. As for Mr. Bottles, he is a Radical of the purest water; quite one of the Manchester school. He was one of the earliest free-traders; he has always gone as straight as an arrow about Reform; he is an ardent voluntary in every possible line, opposed the Ten Hours' Bill, was one of the leaders of the Dissenting opposition out of Parliament which smashed up the education clauses of Sir James Graham's Factory Act; and he paid the whole expenses of a most important church-rate contest out of his own pocket. And, finally, he looks forward to marrying his deceased wife's sister. Table, as my friend Mr. Grant Duff says, the whole Liberal creed, and in not a single point of it will you find Bottles tripping!"

"That is all very well as to their politics," said Arminius, "but I want to hear about their education and intelligence." "There, too, I can satisfy you," I answered. "Lumpington was at Eton. Hittall was on the foundation at Charterhouse, placed there by his uncle, a distinguished prelate, who was one of the trustees. You know we English have no notion of your bureaucratic tyranny of treating the appointments to these great foundations as public patronage, and vesting them in a responsible minister; we vest them in independent magnates, who relieve the State of all work and responsibility, and never take a shilling of salary for their trouble. Hittall was the last of six nephews nominated to the Charterhouse by his uncle, this good prelate, who had thoroughly learnt the divine lesson that charity begins at home." "But I want to know what his nephew learnt," interrupted Arminius, "and what Lord Lumpington learnt at Eton." "They followed," said I, "the grand, old, fortifying, classical curriculum." "Did they know anything when they left?" asked Arminius. "I have seen some longs and shorts of Hittall's," said I, "about the Calydonian Boar, which were not bad. But you surely don't need me to tell you, Arminius, that it is rather in training and bracing the mind for future acquisition,—a course of mental gymnastics we call it,—than in teaching any set thing, that the classical curriculum is so valuable." "Were the minds of Lord Lumpington and Mr. Hittall much braced by their mental gymnastics?" inquired Arminius. "Well," I answered, "during their three years at Oxford they were so much occupied with Bullingdon and hunting that there was no great opportunity to judge. But for my part I have always thought that their both getting their degree at last with flying colours, after three weeks of a famous coach for fast men, four nights without going to bed, and an incredible consumption of wet towels, strong cigars, and brandy-and-water, was one of the most astonishing feats of mental gymnastics I ever heard of."

"That will do for the land and the Church," said Arminius. "And now let us hear about commerce." "You mean how was Bottles educated?" answered I. "Here we get into another line altogether, but a very good line in its way, too. Mr. Bottles was brought up at the Lycurgus House Academy, Peckham. You are not to suppose from the name of Lycurgus that any Latin and Greek was taught in the establishment; the name only indicates the moral discipline, and the strenuous earnest character, imparted there. As to the instruction, the thoughtful educator who was principal of the Lycurgus House Academy,—Archimedes Silverpump, Ph.D., you must have heard of him in Germany?— had modern views. 'We must be men of our age,' he used to say. 'Useful knowledge, living languages, and the forming of the mind through observation and experiment, these are the fundamental articles of my educational creed.' Or, as I have heard his pupil Bottles put it in his expansive moments after dinner (Bottles used to ask me to dinner till that affair of yours with him in the Reigate train): 'Original man, Silverpump! fine mind! fine system! None of your antiquated rubbish—all practical work—

latest discoveries in science—mind constantly kept excited—lots of interesting experiments—lights of all colours—fizz! fizz! bang! bang! That's what I call forming a man.' "

"And pray," cried Arminius, impatiently, "what sort of man do you suppose this infernal quack really formed in your precious friend Mr. Bottles?" "Well," I replied, "I hardly know how to answer that question. Bottles has certainly made an immense fortune; but as to Silverpump's effect on his mind, whether it was from any fault in the Lycurgus House system, whether it was that with a sturdy self-reliance thoroughly English, Bottles, ever since he quitted Silverpump, left his mind wholly to itself, his daily newspaper, and the Particular Baptist minister under whom he sate, or from whatever cause it was, certainly his mind, *quâ* mind——" "You need not go on," interrupted Arminius, with a magnificent wave of his hand, "I know what that man's mind, *quâ* mind, is, well enough."

But, Sir, the midnight oil is beginning to run very low; I hope, therefore, you will permit me to postpone the rest of Arminius's discourse till to-morrow. And meanwhile, Sir, I am, with all respect,

Your humble servant,
MATTHEW ARNOLD.

To

The EDITOR *of the* PALL MALL GAZETTE.

Letter VII

More about Compulsory Education

Grub Street, April 21, 1867.

SIR,—

I take up the thread of the interesting and important discussion on compulsory education between Arminius and me where I left it last night.

"But," continued Arminius, "you were talking of compulsory education, and your common people's want of it. Now, my dear friend, I want you to understand what this principle of compulsory education really means. It means that to ensure, as far as you can, every man's being fit for his business in life, you put education as a bar, or condition, between him and what he aims at. The principle is just as good for one class as another, and it is only by applying it impartially that you save its application from being insolent and invidious. Our Prussian peasant stands our compelling him to instruct himself before he may go about his calling, because he sees we believe in instruction, and compel our own class, too, in a way to make it really feel the pressure, to instruct itself before it may go about its calling. Now, you propose to make old Diggs's boys instruct themselves before they may go bird-scaring or sheep-tending. I want to know what you do to make those three worthies in that justice-room instruct themselves before they may go acting as magistrates and judges." "Do?" said I; "why, just look what they have done all of themselves. Lumpington and Hittall have had a public-school and university education; Bottles has had Dr. Silverpump's, and the practical training of business. What on earth would you have us make them do more?" "Qualify themselves for administrative or judicial functions, if they exercise them," said Arminius. "That is what really answers, in their case, to the compulsion you propose to apply to Diggs's boys. Sending Lord Lumpington and Mr. Hittall to school is nothing; the natural course of things takes them there. Don't suppose that, by doing this, you are applying the principle of compulsory education fairly, and as you apply it to Diggs's boys. You are not interposing, for the rich, education as a bar or condition between them and that which they aim at. But interpose it, as we do, between the rich and things they aim at, and I will say something to you. I should like to know what has made Lord Lumpington a magistrate?" "Made Lord Lumpington a magistrate?" said I; "why, the Lumpington estate, to be sure." "And the Reverend Esau Hittall?" continued Arminius. "Why, the Lumpington living, of course," said I. "And that man Bottles?" he went on. "His English energy and self-reliance," I answered very stiffly, for Arminius's incessant carping began to put me in a huff; "those same incomparable and truly British qualities which have just triumphed over every obstacle and given us the Atlantic telegraph!—and let me tell you, Von T., in my opinion it will be a long time before the 'Geist' of any pedant of a Prussian professor gives us anything half so valuable as that." "Pshaw!" replied Arminius, contemptuously; "that great rope, with a Philistine at each end of it talking inutilities!

"But in my country," he went on, "we should have begun to put a pressure on these future magistrates at school. Before we allowed Lord Lumpington and Mr. Hittall to go to the university at all, we should have examined them, and we should not have trusted the keepers of that absurd cockpit you took me down to see, to examine them as they chose, and send them jogging comfortably off to the university on their lame longs and shorts. No; there would have been some Mr. Grote as School Board Commissary, pitching into them questions about history, and some Mr. Lowe, as Crown Patronage Commissary, pitching into them questions about English literature; and these young men would have been kept from the university, as Diggs's boys are kept from their bird-scaring, till they had instructed themselves. Then, if, after three years of their university, they wanted to be magistrates, another pressure!—a great Civil Service examination before a board of experts, an examination in English law, Roman law, English history, history of jurisprudence——" "A most abominable liberty to take with Lumpington and Hittall!" exclaimed I. "Then your compulsory education is a most abominable liberty to take with Diggs's boys," retorted Arminius. "But good gracious! my dear Arminius," expostulated I, "do you really mean to maintain that a man can't put old Diggs in quod for snaring a hare without all this elaborate apparatus of Roman law and history of jurisprudence?" " And do you really mean to maintain," returned Arminius, "that a man can't go bird-scaring or sheep-tending without all this elaborate apparatus of a compulsory school?" "Oh, but," I answered, "to live at all, even at the lowest stage of human life, a man needs instruction." "Well," returned Arminius, "and to administer at all, even at the lowest stage of public administration, a man needs instruction." "We have never found it so," said I.

Arminius shrugged his shoulders and was silent. By this time the proceedings in the justice-room were drawn to an end, the majesty of the law had been vindicated against old Diggs, and the magistrates were coming out. I never saw a finer spectacle than my friend Arminius presented, as he stood by to gaze on the august trio as they passed. His pilot-coat was tightly buttoned round his stout form, his light blue eye shone, his sanguine cheeks were ruddier than ever with the cold morning and the excitement of discourse, his fell of tow was blown about by the March wind, and volumes of tobacco-smoke issued from his lips. So in old days stood, I imagine, his great namesake by the banks of the Lippe, glaring on the Roman legions before their destruction.

Lord Lumpington was the first who came out. His lordship good-naturedly recognised me with a nod, and then eyeing Arminius with surprise and curiosity: "Whom on earth have you got there?" he whispered. "A very distinguished young Prussian *savant*," replied I; and then dropping my voice, in my most impressive undertones I added: "And a young man of very good family, besides, my lord." Lord Lumpington looked at Arminius again; smiled, shook his head, and then, turning away, and half aloud: "Can't compliment you on your friend," says he.

As for that centaur Hittall, who thinks of nothing on earth but field-sports, and in the performance of his sacred duties never warms up except when he lights on some passage about hunting or fowling, he always, whenever he meets me, remembers that in my unregenerate days, before Arminius inoculated me with a passion for intellect, I was rather fond of shooting, and not quite such a successful shot as Hittall himself. So, the moment he catches sight of me: "How d'ye do, old fellow?" he blurts out; "well, been shooting any straighter this year than you used to, eh?"

I turned from him in pity, and then I noticed Arminius, who had unluckily heard Lord Lumpington's unfavourable comment on him, absolutely purple with rage and blowing like a turkey-cock. "Never mind, Arminius," said I soothingly; "run after Lumpington, and ask him the square root of thirty-six." But now it was my turn to be a little annoyed, for at the same instant Mr. Bottles stepped into his brougham, which was waiting for him, and observing Arminius, his old enemy of the Reigate train, he took no notice whatever of me who stood there, with my hat in my hand, practising all the airs and graces I have learnt on the Continent; but, with that want of amenity I so often have to deplore in my countrymen, he pulled up the glass on our side with a grunt and a jerk, and drove off like the wind, leaving Arminius in a very bad temper indeed, and me, I confess, a good deal shocked and mortified.

However, both Arminius and I got over it, and have now returned to London, where I hope we shall before long have another good talk about educational matters. Whatever Arminius may say, I am still for going straight, with all our heart and soul, at compulsory education for the lower orders. Why, good heavens! Sir, with our present squeezable Ministry, we are evidently drifting fast to household suffrage, pure and simple; and I observe, moreover, a Jacobinical spirit growing up in some quarters which gives me more alarm than even household suffrage. My elevated position in Grub Street, Sir, where I sit commercing with the stars, commands a view of a certain spacious and secluded back yard; and in that back yard, Sir, I tell you confidentially that I saw the other day with my own eyes that powerful young publicist, Mr. Frederic Harrison, in full evening costume, furbishing up a guillotine. These things are very serious; and I say, if the masses are to have power, let them be instructed, and don't swamp with ignorance and unreason the education and intelligence which now bear rule amongst us. For my part, when I think of Lumpington's estate, family, and connections, when I think of Hittall's shooting, and of the energy and self-reliance of Bottles, and when I see the unexampled pitch of splendour and security to which these have conducted us, I am bent, I own, on trying to make the new elements of our political system worthy of the old; and I say kindly, but firmly, to the compound householder in the French poet's beautiful words,[1] slightly altered: "Be great, O working class, for the middle and upper class are great!"

I am, Sir,
Your humble servant,
Matthew Arnold.

To

The Editor *of the* Pall Mall Gazette.

---

[1] "Et tâchez d'être grand, car le peuple grandit."

LITERATURE AND DOGMA
1873

Literature and Dogma. An Essay towards a Better Apprehension of the Bible by Matthew Arnold, D.C.L., formerly Professor of Poetry in the University of Oxford and Fellow of Oriel College. London. Smith, Elder and Co., 15 Waterloo Place. 1873.

THE text is that of the abbreviated "popular edition" prepared by the author in 1883.

LITERATURE AND DOGMA

AN ESSAY TOWARDS A BETTER APPREHENSION OF THE BIBLE

From *Preface*

THOSE who "ask for the *reason* and *authority* for the things they have been taught to believe," as the people, we are told, are now doing will begin at the beginning. Rude and hard reasoners as they are, they will never consent to admit, as a self-evident axiom, the preliminary assumption with which the churches start. So, if the people are to receive a religion of the Bible, we must find for the Bible some other basis than that which the churches assign to it, a verifiable basis and not an assumption. This new religion of the Bible the people may receive; the version now current of the religion of the Bible they will not receive.

Here, then, is the problem: to find, for the Bible, for Christianity, for our religion, a basis in something which can be verified, instead of in something which has to be assumed. So true and prophetic are Vinet's words: "We *must*," he said, "make it our business to bring forward the rational side of Christianity, and to show that for thinkers, too, it has a right to be an authority." Yes, and the problem we have stated must be the first stage in the business. With this problem unsolved, all other religious discussion is idle trifling.

This is why Dissent, as a religious movement of our day, would be almost droll, if it were not, from the tempers and actions it excites, so extremely irreligious. But what is to be said for men, aspiring to deal with the cause of religion, who either cannot see that what the people now require is a religion of the Bible quite different from that which *any* of the churches or sects supply; or who, seeing this, spend their energies in fiercely battling as to whether the Church should be a national institution or no? The question, at the present juncture, is in itself so absolutely unimportant! The thing is, to recast religion. If this is done, the new religion will be the national one; if it is not done, the separating the nation, in its collective and corporate character, from religion, will not do it. It is as if men's minds were much unsettled about mineralogy, and the teachers of it were at variance, and no teacher was convincing, and many

535

people, therefore, were disposed to throw the study of mineralogy overboard altogether. What would naturally be the first business for every friend of the study? Surely, to establish on safe grounds the value of the study, and to put its claims in a new light where they could no longer be denied. But if he acted as our Dissenters act in religion, what would he do? Give himself, heart and soul, to a furious crusade against keeping the Government School of Mines!

Meanwhile, however, there is now an end to all fear of doing harm by gainsaying the received theology of the churches and sects. For this theology is itself now a hindrance to the Bible rather than a help. Nay, to abandon it, to put some other construction on the Bible than this theology puts, to find some other basis for the Bible than this theology finds, is indispensable, if we would have the Bible reach the people. And this is the aim of the following essay: to show that, when we come to put the right construction on the Bible, we give to the Bible a real experimental basis, and keep on this basis throughout; instead of any basis of unverifiable assumption to start with, followed by a string of other unverifiable assumptions of the like kind, such as the received theology necessitates.

And this aim we cannot seek without coming in sight of another aim too, which we have often and often pointed out, and tried to recommend: *culture*, the acquainting ourselves with the best that has been known and said in the world, and thus with the history of the human spirit. One cannot go far in the attempt to bring in, for the Bible, a right construction, without seeing how necessary is something of culture to its being admitted and used. The correspondent whom we have above quoted notices how the lack of culture disposes the masses to conclude at once, from any imperfection or fallibility in the Bible, that it is a priestly imposture. To a certain extent this is the fault, not of the people's want of culture, but of the priests and theologians themselves, who for centuries have kept assuring men that perfect and infallible the Bible is. Still, even without this confusion added by his theological instructors, the *homo unius libri*, the man of no range in his reading, must almost inevitably misunderstand the Bible, cannot treat it largely enough, must be inclined to treat it all alike, and to press every word.

To understand that the language of the Bible is fluid, passing, and literary, not rigid, fixed, and scientific, is the first step towards a right understanding of the Bible. But to take this very first step, some experience of how men have thought and expressed themselves, and some flexibility of spirit, are necessary; and this is culture. After all, the Bible is *not* a talisman, to be

taken and used literally; neither is any existing Church a talisman, whatever pretensions of the sort it may make, for giving the
right interpretation of the Bible. But only true culture can give
us this interpretation; so that if conduct is, as it is, inextricably
bound up with the Bible and the right interpretation of it, then
the importance of culture becomes unspeakable. For if conduct
is necessary (and there is nothing so necessary), culture is
necessary.

And the poor require it as much as the rich; and at present
their education, even when they get education, gives them hardly
anything of it. Yet hardly less of it, perhaps, than the education
of the rich gives to the rich. For when we say that culture is, *To
know the best that has been thought and said in the world*, we imply
that, for culture, a system directly tending to this end is necessary
in our reading. Now, there is no such system yet present to guide
the reading of the rich, any more than of the poor. Such a system
is hardly even thought of; a man who wants it must make it for
himself. And our reading being so without purpose as it is, nothing can be truer than what Butler says, that really, in general, no
part of our time is more idly spent than the time spent in reading.

Still, culture is indispensably necessary, and culture is *reading*;
but reading with a purpose to guide it, and with system. He does
a good work who does anything to help this; indeed, it is the one
essential service now to be rendered to education. And the plea,
that this or that man has no time for culture, will vanish as soon
as we desire culture so much that we begin to examine seriously
our present use of our time. It has often been said, and cannot
be said too often: Give to any man all the time that he now
wastes, not only on his vices (when he has them), but on useless
business, wearisome or deteriorating amusements, trivial letter-
writing, random reading; and he will have plenty of time for culture. *"Die Zeit ist unendlich lang,"* says Goethe; and so it really
is. Some of us waste all of it, most of us waste much, but all of
us waste some.

Conclusion

1.

But now, after all we have been saying of the pre-eminency of
righteousness, we remember what we have said formerly in praise
of culture and of Hellenism, and against too much Hebraism, too
exclusive a pursuit of the "one thing needful," as people call it.
And we cannot help wondering whether we shall not be reproached with inconsistency, and told that we ought at least to

sing, as the Greeks said, a *palinode*; and whether it may not really be so, and we ought. And, certainly, if we had ever said that Hellenism was three-fourths of human life, and conduct or righteousness but one-fourth, a palinode, as well as an un-musical man may, we would sing. But we have never said it. In praising culture, we have never denied that conduct, not culture, is three-fourths of human life.

Only it certainly appears, when the thing is examined, that conduct comes to have relations of a very close kind with culture. And the reason seems to be given by some words of our Bible, which, though they may not be exactly the right rendering of the original in that place, yet in themselves they explain the con-nexion of culture with conduct very well. "I have seen the travail," says the Preacher, "which God hath given to the sons of men to be exercised in it; he hath made everything beautiful in his time; also, he hath set the world in their heart." *He hath set the world in their heart!*—that is why art and science, and what we call culture, are necessary. They may be only one-fourth of man's life, but they are *there*, as well as the three-fourths which conduct occupies. "He hath set *the world* in their heart." And, really, the reason which we hence gather for the close connexion between culture and conduct, is so simple and natural that we are almost ashamed to give it; but we have offered so many simple and natural explanations in place of the abstruse ones which are current, that our hesitation is foolish.

Let us suggest, then, that, having this one-fourth of their nature concerned with art and science, men cannot but somehow employ it. If they think that the three-fourths of their nature concerned with conduct are the whole of their nature, and that this is all they have to attend to, still the neglected one-fourth is there, it ferments, it breaks wildly out, it employs itself all at random and amiss. And hence, no doubt, our hymns and our dogmatic theology. What is our dogmatic theology, except the mis-attribution to the Bible,—the Book of *conduct*,—of a science and an abstruse metaphysic which is not there, because our theologians have in themselves a faculty for science, for it makes one-eighth of them? But they do not employ it on its proper objects; so it invades the Bible, and tries to make the Bible what it is not, and to put into it what is not there. And this prevents their attending enough to what *is* in the Bible, and makes them battle for what is *not* in the Bible, but they have put it there!— battle for it in a manner clean contrary, often, to the teaching of the Bible. So has arisen, for instance, all religious persecution. And thus, we say, has conduct itself become impaired.

So that conduct is impaired by the want of science and culture;

and our theologians really suffer, not from having too much science, but from having too little. Whereas, if they had turned their faculty for abstruse reasoning towards the proper objects, and had given themselves, in addition, a wide and large acquaintance with the productions of the human spirit and with men's way of thinking and of using words, then, on the one hand, they would not have been tempted to misemploy on the Bible their faculty for abstruse reasoning, for they would have had plenty of other exercise for it; and, on the other hand, they would have escaped that literary inexperience which now makes them fancy that the Bible-language is scientific, and fit matter for the application of their powers of abstruse reasoning to it, when it is no such thing. Then they would have seen the fallacy of confounding the obscurity attaching to the idea of God,—that vast *not ourselves* which transcends us,—with the obscurity attaching to the idea of their Trinity, a confused metaphysical speculation which puzzles us. The one, they would have perceived, is the obscurity of the immeasurable depth of air, the other is the obscurity of a fog. And fog, they would have known, has no proper place in our conceptions of God; since whatever our minds *can* possess of God they know clearly, for no man, as Goethe says, possesses what he does not understand; but they can possess of Him but a very little. All this our dogmatic theologians would have known, if they had had more science and more literature. And therefore, simple as the Bible and conduct are, still culture seems to be required for them,—required to prevent our mishandling and sophisticating them.

2.

Culture, then, and science and literature are requisite, in the interest of religion itself, even when, taking nothing but *conduct* into account, we rightly make the God of the Bible, as Israel made him, to be simply and solely "the Eternal Power, not ourselves, that makes for *righteousness*." For we are not to forget, that, grand as this conception of God is, and well as it meets the wants of far the largest part of our being, of three-fourths of it, yet there is one-fourth of our being of which it does not strictly meet the wants, the part which is concerned with art and science; or, in other words, with beauty and exact knowledge.

For the total man, therefore, the truer conception of God is as "the Eternal Power, not ourselves, by which all things fulfil the law of their being;" by which, therefore, we fulfil the law of our being so far as our being is æsthetic and intellective, as well as so far as it is moral. And it is evident, as we have before now remarked, that in this wider sense God is displeased and disserved by many things which cannot be said, except by putting a strain upon words, to displease and disserve him as the God of righteousness. He is displeased and disserved by men uttering such doggerel hymns as: *Sing glory, glory, glory to the great God Triune!* and: *Out of my stony griefs Bethels I'll raise!* and: *My Jesus to know, and feel his blood flow, 'tis life everlasting, 'tis heaven below!*—or by theologians uttering such pseudo-science as their *blessed truth that the God of the universe is a* PERSON. But it would be harsh to give, at present, this turn to our employment of the phrases, *pleasing God, displeasing God.*

And yet, as man makes progress, we shall surely come to doing this. For, the clearer our conceptions in science and art become, the more will they assimilate themselves to the conceptions of duty in conduct, will become practically stringent like rules of conduct, and will invite the same sort of language in dealing with them. And so far let us venture to poach on M. Emile Burnouf's manor, and to talk about the Aryan genius, as to say, that the love of art and science, and the energy and honesty in the pursuit of art and science, in the best of the Aryan races, do seem to correspond in a remarkable way to the love of conduct, and the energy and honesty in the pursuit of conduct, in the best of the Semitic. To treat science and art with the same kind of seriousness as conduct, does seem, therefore, to be a not impossible thing for the Aryan genius to come to.

But for all this, however, man is hardly yet ripe. For our race, as we see it now and as ourselves we form a part of it, the true God is and must be pre-eminently the God of the Bible, *the Eternal who makes for righteousness*, from whom Jesus came forth, and whose Spirit governs the course of humanity. Only, we see that even for apprehending this God of the Bible rightly and not wrongly, science, and what so many people now disparage, letters, and what we call, in general, *culture*, seem to be necessary.

And meanwhile, to prevent our at all pluming ourselves on having apprehended what so much baffles our dogmatic friends (although indeed it is not so much we who apprehend it as the "Zeit-Geist" who discovers it to us), what a chastening and wholesome reflexion for us it is, that it is only our natural inferiority to these ingenious men that we are indebted for our advantage over them! For while *they* were born with talents for metaphysical speculation and abstruse reasoning, we are so notoriously deficient in everything of that kind, that our adversaries often taunt us with our weakness, and have held us up to public ridicule as being "without a system of philosophy based on principles interdependent, subordinate, and coherent." And so we were thrown on letters; thrown upon reading this and that,

—which anybody can do,—and thus gradually getting a notion of the human mind, which enables us (the "Zeit-Geist" favouring) to correct, in reading the Bible, some of the mistakes into which men of more metaphysical talents than literary experience have fallen. Cripples in like manner have been known, now and then, to be cast by their very infirmity upon some mental pursuit which has turned out happily for them; and a good fortune of this kind has perhaps been ours.

But we do not forget that this good fortune we owe to our weakness, and that the natural superiority remains with our adversaries. And some day, perhaps, the nature of God may be as well known as the nature of a cone or a triangle; and then our two bishops may deduce its properties with success, and make their brilliant logical play about it,—rightly, instead of as now, wrongly; and will resume all their advantage. But this will hardly be in our time. So that the superiority of this pair of distinguished metaphysicians will never perhaps, after all, be of any real advantage to them, but they will be deluded and bemocked by it until they die.

MIXED ESSAYS
1879

Mixed Essays. By Matthew Arnold. London. Smith, Elder & Co., 15 Waterloo Place. 1879.

Of these essays *Democracy* had been previously published as the Preface to *The Popular Education of France, etc.* 1861; and the others had already appeared in various periodicals.

The following essays are omitted from the present selection: *Irish Catholicism and British Liberalism, 'Porro Unum est Necessarium', A Guide to English Literature, A French Critic on Goethe.*

MIXED ESSAYS

From *Preface*

WHOEVER seriously occupies himself with literature, will soon perceive its vital connexion with other agencies. Suppose a man to be ever so much convinced that literature is, as indisputably it is, a powerful agency for benefiting the world and for civilising it, such a man cannot but see that there are many obstacles preventing what is salutary in literature from gaining general admission, and from producing due effect. Undoubtedly, literature can of itself do something towards removing those obstacles, and towards making straight its own way. But it cannot do all. In other words, literature is a part of civilisation; it is not the whole. What then is civilisation, which some people seem to conceive of as if it meant railroads and the penny post, and little more, but which is really so complex and vast a matter that a great spiritual power, like literature, is a part of it, and a part only? Civilisation is the humanisation of man in society. Man is civilised, when the whole body of society comes to live with a life worthy to be called *human*, and corresponding to man's true aspirations and powers.

The means by which man is brought towards this goal of his endeavour are various. It is of great importance to us to attain an adequate notion of them, and to keep it present before our minds. They may be conceived quite plainly, and enounced without any parade of hard and abstruse expression.

First and foremost of the necessary means towards man's civilisation we must name *expansion*. The need of expansion is as genuine an instinct in man as the need in plants for the light, or the need in man himself for going upright. All the conveniences of life by which man has enlarged and secured his existence—railroads and the penny post among the number—are due to the working in man of this force or instinct of expansion. But the manifestation of it which we English know best, and prize most, is the love of liberty.

The love of liberty is simply the instinct in man for expansion. Not only to find oneself tyrannised over and outraged is a defeat to this instinct; but in general, to feel oneself over-tutored, over-governed, *sate upon* (as the popular phrase is) by authority, is a defeat to it. Prince Bismarck: says "After all, a benevolent rational absolutism is the best form of government." Plenty of arguments may be adduced in support of such a thesis. The one fatal objection to it is that it is against nature, that it contradicts a vital instinct in man—the instinct of expansion. And man is not to be civilised or humanised, call it which you will, by thwarting his vital instincts. In fact, the benevolent rational absolutism always breaks down. It is found that the ruler cannot in the long run be trusted; it is found that the ruled deteriorate. Why? Because the proceeding is against nature.

The other great manifestation of the instinct of expansion is the love of equality. Of the love of equality we English have little; but, undoubtedly, it is no more a false tendency than the love of liberty. Undoubtedly, immense inequality of conditions and property is a defeat to the instinct of expansion; it depresses and degrades the inferior masses. The common people is and must be, as Tocqueville said, more uncivilised in aristocratic countries than in any others. A thousand arguments may be discovered in favour of inequality, just as a thousand arguments may be discovered in favour of absolutism. And the one insuperable objection to inequality is the same as the one insuperable objection to absolutism: namely, that inequality, like absolutism, thwarts a vital instinct, and being thus against nature, is against our humanisation. On the one side, in fact, inequality harms by pampering; on the other, by vulgarising and depressing. A system founded on it is against nature, and in the long run breaks down.

I put first among the elements in human civilisation the instinct of expansion, because it is the basis which man's whole effort to civilise himself presupposes. General civilisation presupposes this instinct, which is inseparable from human nature; presupposes its being satisfied, not defeated. The basis being given, we may rapidly enumerate the powers which, upon this basis, contribute to build up human civilisation. They are the power of conduct, the power of intellect and knowledge, the power of beauty, the power of social life and manners. Expansion, conduct, science, beauty, manners,—here are the conditions of civilisation, the claimants which man must satisfy before he can be humanised.

That the aim for all of us is to make civilisation pervasive and general; that the requisites for civilisation are substantially what have been here enumerated; that they all of them hang together, that they must all have their development, that the development of one does not compensate for the failure of others; that one nation suffers by failing in this requisite, and another by failing in that: such is the line of thought which the essays in the present

volume follow and represent. They represent it in their variety
of subject, their so frequent insistence on defects in the present
actual life of our nation, their unity of final aim. Undoubtedly,
that aim is not given by the life which we now see around us.
Undoubtedly, it is given by "a sentiment of the ideal life." But
then the ideal life is, in sober and practical truth, "none other
than man's normal life, as we shall one day know it."

Democracy

In giving an account of education in certain countries of the Continent, I have often spoken of the State and its action in such a
way as to offend, I fear, some of my readers, and to surprise
others. With many Englishmen, perhaps with the majority, it is
a maxim that the State, the executive power, ought to be entrusted with no more means of action than those which it is impossible to withhold from it; that the State neither would nor
could make a safe use of any more extended liberty; would not,
because it has in itself a natural instinct of despotism, which, if
not jealously checked, would become outrageous; could not, because it is, in truth, not at all more enlightened, or fit to assume
a lead, than the mass of this enlightened community.

No sensible man will lightly go counter to an opinion firmly
held by a great body of his countrymen. He will take for granted,
that for any opinion which has struck deep root among a people
so powerful, so successful, and so well worthy of respect as the
people of this country, there certainly either are, or have been,
good and sound reasons. He will venture to impugn such an
opinion with real hesitation, and only when he thinks he perceives that the reasons which once supported it exist no longer,
or at any rate seem about to disappear very soon. For undoubtedly there arrive periods, when, the circumstances and
conditions of government having changed, the guiding maxims
of government ought to change also. *J'ai dit souvent*, says Mirabeau,[1] admonishing the Court of France in 1790, *qu'on devait
changer de manière de gouverner, lorsque le gouvernement n'est plus
le même*. And these decisive changes in the political situation
of a people happen gradually as well as violently. "In the silent
lapse of events," says Burke,[2] writing in England twenty years
before the French Revolution, "as material alterations have
been insensibly brought about in the policy and character of

---

[1] *Correspondance entre le Comte de Mirabeau et le Comte de la Marck*,
publiée par M. de Bacourt; Paris, 1851; vol. ii, p. 143.
[2] Burke's *Works* (edit. of 1852); vol. iii, p. 115.

governments and nations, as those which have been marked by the tumult of public revolutions."

I propose to submit to those who have been accustomed to regard all State-action with jealousy, some reasons for thinking that the circumstances which once made that jealousy prudent and natural have undergone an essential change. I desire to lead them to consider with me, whether, in the present altered conjuncture, that State-action, which was once dangerous, may not become, not only without danger in itself, but the means of helping us against dangers from another quarter. To combine and present the considerations upon which these two propositions are based, is a task of some difficulty and delicacy. My aim is to invite impartial reflexion upon the subject, not to make a hostile attack against old opinions, still less to set on foot and fully equip a new theory. In offering, therefore, the thoughts which have suggested themselves to me, I shall studiously avoid all particular applications of them likely to give offence, and shall use no more illustration and development than may be indispensable to enable the reader to seize and appreciate them.

The dissolution of the old political parties which have governed this country since the Revolution of 1688 has long been remarked. It was repeatedly declared to be happening long before it actually took place, while the vital energy of these parties still subsisted in full vigour, and was threatened only by some temporary obstruction. It has been eagerly deprecated long after it had actually begun to take place, when it was in full progress, and inevitable. These parties, differing in so much else, were yet alike in this, that they were both, in a certain broad sense, *aristocratical* parties. They were combinations of persons considerable, either by great family and estate, or by Court favour, or, lastly, by eminent abilities and popularity: this last body, however, attaining participation in public affairs only through a conjunction with one or other of the former. These connexions, though they contained men of very various degrees of birth and property, were still wholly leavened with the feelings and habits of the upper class of the nation. They had the bond of a common culture; and, however their political opinions and acts might differ, what they said and did had the stamp and style imparted by this culture, and by a common and elevated social condition.

Aristocratical bodies have no taste for a very imposing executive, or for a very active and penetrating domestic administration. They have a sense of equality among themselves, and of constituting in themselves what is greatest and most dignified in the realm, which makes their pride revolt against the overshadowing greatness and dignity of a commanding executive.

They have a temper of independence, and a habit of uncontrolled action, which makes them impatient of encountering, in the management of the interior concerns of the country, the machinery and regulations of a superior and peremptory power. The different parties amongst them, as they successively get possession of the government, respect this jealous disposition in their opponents, because they share it themselves. It is a disposition proper to them as great personages, not as ministers; and as they are great personages for their whole life, while they may probably be ministers but for a very short time, the instinct of their social condition avails more with them than the instinct of their official function. To administer as little as possible, to make its weight felt in foreign affairs rather than in domestic, to see in ministerial station rather the means of power and dignity than a means of searching and useful administrative activity, is the natural tendency of an aristocratic executive. It is a tendency which is creditable to the good sense of aristocracies, honourable to their moderation, and at the same time fortunate for their country, of whose internal development they are not fitted to have the full direction.

One strong and beneficial influence, however, the administration of a vigorous and high-minded aristocracy is calculated to exert upon a robust and sound people. I have had occasion, in speaking of Homer, to say very often, and with much emphasis, that he is *in the grand style*. It is the chief virtue of a healthy and uncorrupted aristocracy, that it is, in general, in this grand style. That elevation of character, that noble way of thinking and behaving, which is an eminent gift of nature to some individuals, is also often generated in whole classes of men (at least when these come of a strong and good race) by the possession of power, by the importance and responsibility of high station, by habitual dealing with great things, by being placed above the necessity of constantly struggling for little things. And it is the source of great virtues. It may go along with a not very quick or open intelligence; but it cannot well go along with a conduct vulgar and ignoble. A governing class imbued with it may not be capable of intelligently leading the masses of a people to the highest pitch of welfare for them; but it sets them an invaluable example of qualities without which no really high welfare can exist. This has been done for their nation by the best aristocracies. The Roman aristocracy did it; the English aristocracy has done it. They each fostered in the mass of the peoples they governed,—peoples of sturdy moral constitution and apt to learn such lessons,—a greatness of spirit, the natural growth of the condition of magnates and rulers, but not the natural growth of the condition of the common people. They made, the one of the Roman, the other of the English people, in spite of all the shortcomings of each, great peoples, peoples *in the grand style*. And this they did, while wielding the people according to their own notions, and in the direction which seemed good to them; not as servants and instruments of the people, but as its commanders and heads; solicitous for the good of their country, indeed, but taking for granted that of that good they themselves were the supreme judges, and were to fix the conditions.

The time has arrived, however, when it is becoming impossible for the aristocracy of England to conduct and wield the English nation any longer. It still, indeed, administers public affairs; and it is a great error to suppose, as many persons in England suppose, that it administers but does not govern. He who administers, governs,[1] because he infixes his own mark and stamps his own character on all public affairs as they pass through his hands; and, therefore, so long as the English aristocracy administers the commonwealth, it still governs it. But signs not to be mistaken show that its headship and leadership of the nation, by virtue of the substantial acquiescence of the body of the nation in its predominance and right to lead, is nearly over. That acquiescence was the tenure by which it held its power; and it is fast giving way. The superiority of the upper class over all others is no longer so great; the willingness of the others to recognise that superiority is no longer so ready.

This change has been brought about by natural and inevitable causes, and neither the great nor the multitude are to be blamed for it. The growing demands and audaciousness of the latter, the encroaching spirit of democracy, are, indeed, matters of loud complaint with some persons. But these persons are complaining of human nature itself, when they thus complain of a manifestation of its native and ineradicable impulse. Life itself consists, say the philosophers, in the effort *to affirm one's own essence*; meaning by this, to develop one's own existence fully and freely, to have ample light and air, to be neither cramped nor overshadowed. Democracy is trying *to affirm its own essence*; to live, to enjoy, to possess the world, as aristocracy has tried, and successfully tried, before it. Ever since Europe emerged from barbarism, ever since the condition of the common people began a little to improve, ever since their minds began to stir, this effort of democracy has been gaining strength; and the more their condition improves, the more strength this effort gains. So potent is the charm of life and expansion upon the living; the moment men

---

[1] *Administrer, c'est gouverner*, says Mirabeau; *gouverner, c'est régner; tout se réduit là.*

are aware of them, they begin to desire them, and the more they
have of them, the more they crave.

This movement of democracy, like other operations of nature,
merits properly neither blame nor praise. Its partisans are apt
to give it credit which it does not deserve, while its enemies are
apt to upbraid it unjustly. Its friends celebrate it as the author
of all freedom. But political freedom may very well be established by aristocratic founders; and, certainly, the political freedom of England owes more to the grasping English barons than
to democracy. Social freedom,—equality,—that is rather the
field of the conquests of democracy. And here what I must call
the injustice of its enemies comes in. For its seeking after equality, democracy is often, in this country above all, vehemently and
scornfully blamed; its temper contrasted with that worthier
temper which can magnanimously endure social distinctions; its
operations all referred, as of course, to the stirrings of a base and
malignant envy. No doubt there is a gross and vulgar spirit of
envy, prompting the hearts of many of those who cry for equality. No doubt there are ignoble natures which prefer equality to
liberty. But what we have to ask is, when the life of democracy
is admitted as something natural and inevitable, whether this or
that product of democracy is a necessary growth from its parent
stock, or merely an excrescence upon it. If it be the latter, certainly it may be due to the meanest and most culpable passions.
But if it be the former, then this product, however base and
blameworthy the passions which it may sometimes be made to
serve, can in itself be no more reprehensible than the vital impulse of democracy is in itself reprehensible; and this impulse is,
as has been shown, identical with the ceaseless vital effort of
human nature itself.

Now, can it be denied, that a certain approach to equality, at
any rate a certain reduction of signal inequalities, is a natural,
instinctive demand of that impulse which drives society as a
whole,—no longer individuals and limited classes only, but the
mass of a community,—to develop itself with the utmost possible
fulness and freedom? Can it be denied, that to live in a society
of equals tends in general to make a man's spirits expand, and his
faculties work easily and actively; while, to live in a society of
superiors, although it may occasionally be a very good discipline,
yet in general tends to tame the spirits and to make the play of
the faculties less secure and active? Can it be denied, that to be
heavily overshadowed, to be profoundly insignificant, has, on the
whole, a depressing and benumbing effect on the character? I
know that some individuals react against the strongest impediments, and owe success and greatness to the efforts which they

are thus forced to make. But the question is not about individuals. The question is about the common bulk of mankind, persons without extraordinary gifts or exceptional energy, and who will ever require, in order to make the best of themselves, encouragement and directly favouring circumstances. Can any one deny, that for these the spectacle, when they would rise, of a condition of splendour, grandeur, and culture, which they cannot possibly reach, has the effect of making them flag in spirit, and of disposing them to sink despondingly back into their own condition? Can any one deny, that the knowledge how poor and insignificant the best condition of improvement and culture attainable by them must be esteemed by a class incomparably richer-endowed, tends to cheapen this modest possible amelioration in the account of those classes also for whom it would be relatively a real progress, and to disenchant their imaginations with it? It seems to me impossible to deny this. And therefore a philosophic observer,[1] with no love for democracy, but rather with a terror of it, has been constrained to remark, that "the common people is more uncivilised in aristocratic countries than in any others;" because there "the lowly and the poor feel themselves, as it were, overwhelmed with the weight of their own inferiority." He has been constrained to remark,[2] that "there is such a thing as a manly and legitimate passion for equality, prompting men to desire to be, *all* of them, in the enjoyment of power and consideration." And, in France, that very equality, which is by us so impetuously decried, while it has by no means improved (it is said) the upper classes of French society, has undoubtedly given to the lower classes, to the body of the common people, a self-respect, an enlargement of spirit, a consciousness of counting for something in their country's action, which has raised them in the scale of humanity. The common people, in France, seems to me the soundest part of the French nation. They seem to me more free from the two opposite degradations of multitudes, brutality and servility, to have a more developed human life, more of what distinguishes elsewhere the cultured classes from the vulgar, than the common people in any other country with which I am acquainted.

I do not say that grandeur and prosperity may not be attained

[1] M. de Tocqueville. See his *Démocratie en Amérique* (edit. of 1835); vol. i, p. 11. "Le peuple est plus grossier dans les pays aristocratiques que partout ailleurs. Dans ces lieux, où se rencontrent des hommes si forts et si riches, les faibles et les pauvres se sentent comme accablés de leur bassesse; ne découvrant aucun point par lequel ils puissent regagner l'égalité, ils désespèrent entièrement d'eux-mêmes, et se laissent tomber au-dessous de la dignité humaine."

[2] *Démocratie en Amérique;* vol. i, p. 60.

by a nation divided into the most widely distinct classes, and presenting the most signal inequalities of rank and fortune. I do not say that great national virtues may not be developed in it. I do not even say that a popular order, accepting this demarcation of classes as an eternal providential arrangement, not questioning the natural right of a superior order to lead it, content within its own sphere, admiring the grandeur and highmindedness of its ruling class, and catching on its own spirit some reflex of what it thus admires, may not be a happier body, as to the eye of the imagination it is certainly a more beautiful body, than a popular order, pushing, excited, and presumptuous; a popular order, jealous of recognising fixed superiorities, petulantly claiming to be as good as its betters, and tastelessly attiring itself with the fashions and designations which have become unalterably associated with a wealthy and refined class, and which, tricking out those who have neither wealth nor refinement, are ridiculous. But a popular order of that old-fashioned stamp exists now only for the imagination. It is not the force with which modern society has to reckon. Such a body may be a sturdy, honest, and sound-hearted lower class; but it is not a democratic people. It is not that power, which at the present day in all nations is to be found existing; in some, has obtained the mastery; in others, is yet in a state of expectation and preparation.

The power of France in Europe is at this day mainly owing to the completeness with which she has organised democratic institutions. The action of the French State is excessive; but it is too little understood in England that the French people has adopted this action for its own purposes, has in great measure attained those purposes by it, and owes to its having done so the chief part of its influence in Europe. The growing power in Europe is democracy; and France has organised democracy with a certain indisputable grandeur and success. The ideas of 1789 were working everywhere in the eighteenth century; but it was because in France the State adopted them that the French Revolution became an historic epoch for the world, and France the lode-star of Continental democracy. Her airs of superiority and her overweening pretensions come from her sense of the power which she derives from this cause. Every one knows how Frenchmen proclaim France to be at the head of civilisation, the French army to be the soldier of God, Paris to be the brain of Europe, and so on. All this is, no doubt, in a vein of sufficient fatuity and bad taste; but it means, at bottom, that France believes she has so organised herself as to facilitate for all members of her society full and free expansion; that she believes herself to have remodelled her institutions with an eye to reason rather than custom, and to right rather than fact; it means, that she believes the other peoples of Europe to be preparing themselves, more or less rapidly, for a like achievement, and that she is conscious of her power and influence upon them as an initiatress and example. In this belief there is a part of truth and a part of delusion. I think it is more profitable for a Frenchman to consider the part of delusion contained in it; for an Englishman, the part of truth.

It is because aristocracies almost inevitably fail to appreciate justly, or even to take into their mind, the instinct pushing the masses towards expansion and fuller life, that they lose their hold over them. It is the old story of the incapacity of aristocracies for ideas; the secret of their want of success in modern epochs. The people treats them with flagrant injustice, when it denies all obligation to them. They can, and often do, impart a high spirit, a fine ideal of grandeur, to the people; thus they lay the foundations of a great nation. But they leave the people still the multitude, the crowd; they have small belief in the power of the ideas which are its life. Themselves a power reposing on all which is most solid, material, and visible, they are slow to attach any great importance to influences impalpable, spiritual, and viewless. Although, therefore, a disinterested looker-on might often be disposed, seeing what has actually been achieved by aristocracies, to wish to retain or replace them in their preponderance, rather than commit a nation to the hazards of a new and untried future; yet the masses instinctively feel that they can never consent to this without renouncing the inmost impulse of their being; and that they should make such a renunciation cannot seriously be expected of them. Except on conditions which make its expansion, in the sense understood by itself, fully possible, democracy will never frankly ally itself with aristocracy; and on these conditions perhaps no aristocracy will ever frankly ally itself with it. Even the English aristocracy, so politic, so capable of compromises, has shown no signs of being able so to transform itself as to render such an alliance possible. The reception given by the Peers to the bill for establishing life-peerages was, in this respect, of ill omen. The separation between aristocracy and democracy will probably, therefore, go on still widening.

And it must in fairness be added, that as in one most important part of general human culture,—openness to ideas and ardour for them,—aristocracy is less advanced than democracy, to replace or keep the latter under the tutelage of the former would in some respects be actually unfavourable to the progress of the world. At epochs when new ideas are powerfully fermenting in a society, and profoundly changing its spirit, aristocracies, as they are in

general not long suffered to guide it without question, so are they
by nature not well fitted to guide it intelligently.

In England, democracy has been slow in developing itself,
having met with much to withstand it, not only in the worth of
the aristocracy, but also in the fine qualities of the common
people. The aristocracy has been more in sympathy with the
common people than perhaps any other aristocracy. It has rarely
given them great umbrage; it has neither been frivolous, so as to
provoke their contempt, nor impertinent, so as to provoke their
irritation. Above all, it has in general meant to act with justice,
according to its own notions of justice. Therefore the feeling of
admiring deference to such a class was more deep-rooted in the
people of this country, more cordial, and more persistent, than
in any people of the Continent. But, besides this, the vigour and
high spirit of the English common people bred in them a self-
reliance which disposed each man to act individually and independently; and so long as this disposition prevails through a
nation divided into classes, the predominance of an aristocracy,
of the class containing the greatest and strongest individuals of
the nation, is secure. Democracy is a force in which the concert
of a great number of men makes up for the weakness of each man
taken by himself; democracy accepts a certain relative rise in
their condition, obtainable by this concert for a great number, as
something desirable in itself, because though this is undoubtedly
far below grandeur, it is yet a good deal above insignificance. A
very strong, self-reliant people neither easily learns to act in concert, nor easily brings itself to regard any middling good, any
good short of the best, as an object ardently to be coveted and
striven for. It keeps its eye on the grand prizes, and these are to
be won only by distancing competitors, by getting before one's
comrades, by succeeding all by one's self; and so long as a people
works thus individually, it does not work democratically. The
English people has all the qualities which dispose a people to
work individually; may it never lose them! A people without the
salt of these qualities, relying wholly on mutual co-operation, and
proposing to itself second-rate ideals, would arrive at the pettiness
and stationariness of China. But the English people is no longer
so entirely ruled by them as not to show visible beginnings of
democratic action; it becomes more and more sensible to the
irresistible seduction of democratic ideas, promising to each individual of the multitude increased self-respect and expansion
with the increased importance and authority of the multitude to
which he belongs, with the diminished preponderance of the
aristocratic class above him.

While the habit and disposition of deference are thus dying out among the lower classes of the English nation, it seems to me indisputable that the advantages which command deference, that eminent superiority in high feeling, dignity, and culture, tend to diminish among the highest class. I shall not be suspected of any inclination to underrate the aristocracy of this country. I regard it as the worthiest, as it certainly has been the most successful, aristocracy of which history makes record. If it has not been able to develop excellences which do not belong to the nature of an aristocracy, yet it has been able to avoid defects to which the nature of an aristocracy is peculiarly prone. But I cannot read the history of the flowering time of the English aristocracy, the eighteenth century, and then look at this aristocracy in our own century, without feeling that there has been a change. I am not now thinking of private and domestic virtues, of morality, of decorum. Perhaps with respect to these there has in this class, as in society at large, been a change for the better. I am thinking of those public and conspicuous virtues by which the multitude is captivated and led,—lofty spirit, commanding character, exquisite culture. It is true that the advance of all classes in culture and refinement may make the culture of one class, which, isolated, appeared remarkable, appear so no longer; but exquisite culture and great dignity are always something rare and striking, and it is the distinction of the English aristocracy, in the eighteenth century, that not only was their culture something rare by comparison with the rawness of the masses, it was something rare and admirable in itself. It is rather that this rare culture of the highest class has actually somewhat declined,[1] than that it has come to look less by juxtaposition with the augmented culture of other classes.

Probably democracy has something to answer for in this falling off of her rival. To feel itself raised on high; venerated, followed, no doubt stimulates a fine nature to keep itself worthy to be followed, venerated, raised on high; hence that lofty maxim, *noblesse oblige*. To feel its culture something precious and singular, makes such a nature zealous to retain and extend it. The elation and energy thus fostered by the sense of its advantages, certainly enhances the worth, strengthens the behaviour, and quickens all the active powers of the class enjoying it. *Possunt quia posse videntur*. The removal of the stimulus a little relaxes their energy. It

---

[1] This will appear doubtful to no one well acquainted with the literature and memoirs of the last century. To give but two illustrations out of a thousand. Let the reader refer to the anecdote told by Robert Wood in his *Essay on the Genius of Homer* (London, 1775), p. vii, and to Lord Chesterfield's *Letters* (edit. of 1845), vol. i, pp. 115, 143, vol. ii, p. 54; and then say, whether the culture there indicated as the culture of a *class* has maintained itself at that level.

is not so much that they sink to be somewhat less than themselves, as that they cease to be somewhat more than themselves. But, however this may be, whencesoever the change may proceed, I cannot doubt that in the aristocratic virtue, in the intrinsic commanding force of the English upper class, there is a diminution. Relics of a great generation are still, perhaps, to be seen amongst them, surviving exemplars of noble manners and consummate culture; but they disappear one after the other, and no one of their kind takes their place. At the very moment when democracy becomes less and less disposed to follow and to admire, aristocracy becomes less and less qualified to command and to captivate.

On the one hand, then, the masses of the people in this country are preparing to take a much more active part than formerly in controlling its destinies; on the other hand, the aristocracy (using this word in the widest sense, to include not only the nobility and landed gentry, but also those reinforcements from the classes bordering upon itself, which this class constantly attracts and assimilates), while it is threatened with losing its hold on the rudder of government, its power to give to public affairs its own bias and direction, is losing also that influence on the spirit and character of the people which it long exercised.

I know that this will be warmly denied by some persons. Those who have grown up amidst a certain state of things, those whose habits, and interests, and affections, are closely concerned with its continuance, are slow to believe that it is not a part of the order of nature, or that it can ever come to an end. But I think that what I have here laid down will not appear doubtful either to the most competent and friendly foreign observers of this country, or to those Englishmen who, clear of all influences of class or party, have applied themselves steadily to see the tendencies of their nation as they really are. Assuming it to be true, a great number of considerations are suggested by it; but it is my purpose here to insist upon one only.

That one consideration is: On what action may we rely to replace, for some time at any rate, that action of the aristocracy upon the people of this country, which we have seen exercise an influence in many respects elevating and beneficial, but which is rapidly, and from inevitable causes, ceasing? In other words, and to use a short and significant modern expression which every one understands, what influence may help us to prevent the English people from becoming, with the growth of democracy, *Americanised?* I confess I am disposed to answer: On the action of the State.

I know what a chorus of objectors will be ready. One will say:

Rather repair and restore the influence of aristocracy. Another will say: It is not a bad thing, but a good thing, that the English people should be Americanised. But the most formidable and the most widely entertained objection, by far, will be that which founds itself upon the present actual state of things in another country; which says: Look at France! there you have a signal example of the alliance of democracy with a powerful State-action, and see how it works.

This last and principal objection I will notice at once. I have had occasion to touch upon the first already, and upon the second I shall touch presently. It seems to me, then, that one may save one's self from much idle terror at names and shadows if one will be at the pains to remember what different conditions the different character of two nations must necessarily impose on the operation of any principle. That which operates noxiously in one, may operate wholesomely in the other; because the unsound part of the one's character may be yet further inflamed and enlarged by it, the unsound part of the other's may find in it a corrective and an abatement. This is the great use which two unlike characters may find in observing each other. Neither is likely to have the other's faults, so each may safely adopt as much as suits him of the other's qualities. If I were a Frenchman I should never be weary of admiring the independent, individual, local habits of action in England, of directing attention to the evils occasioned in France by the excessive action of the State; for I should be very sure that, say what I might, the part of the State would never be too small in France, nor that of the individual too large. Being an Englishman, I see nothing but good in freely recognising the coherence, rationality, and efficaciousness which characterise the strong State-action of France, of acknowledging the want of method, reason, and result which attend the feeble State-action of England; because I am very sure that, strengthen in England the action of the State as one may, it will always find itself sufficiently controlled. But when either the *Constitutional* sneers at the do-little talkativeness of parliamentary government, or when the *Morning Star* inveighs against the despotism of a centralised administration, it seems to me that they lose their labour, because they are hardening themselves against dangers to which they are neither of them liable. Both the one and the other, in plain truth,

> Compound for sins they are inclined to,
> By damning those they have no mind to.

They should rather exchange doctrines one with the other, and each might thus, perhaps, be profited.

So that the exaggeration of the action of the State, in France, furnishes no reason for absolutely refusing to enlarge the action of the State in England; because the genius and temper of the people of this country are such as to render impossible that exaggeration which the genius and temper of the French rendered easy. There is no danger at all that the native independence and individualism of the English character will ever belie itself, and become either weakly prone to lean on others, or blindly confiding in them.

English democracy runs no risk of being over-mastered by the State; it is almost certain that it will throw off the tutelage of aristocracy. Its real danger is, that it will have far too much its own way, and be left far too much to itself. "What harm will there be in that?" say some; "are we not a self-governing people?" I answer: "We have never yet been a *self-governing democracy*, or anything like it." The difficulty for democracy is, how to find and keep high ideals. The individuals who compose it are, the bulk of them, persons who need to follow an ideal, not to set one; and one ideal of greatness, high feeling, and fine culture, which an aristocracy once supplied to them, they lose by the very fact of ceasing to be a lower order and becoming a democracy. Nations are not truly great solely because the individuals composing them are numerous, free, and active; but they are great when these numbers, this freedom, and this activity are employed in the service of an ideal higher than that of an ordinary man, taken by himself. Our society is probably destined to become much more democratic; who or what will give a high tone to the nation then? That is the grave question.

The greatest men of America, her Washingtons, Hamiltons, Madisons, well understanding that aristocratical institutions are not in all times and places possible; well perceiving that in their Republic there was no place for these; comprehending, therefore, that from these that security for national dignity and greatness, an ideal commanding popular reverence, was not to be obtained, but knowing that this ideal was indispensable, would have been rejoiced to found a substitute for it in the dignity and authority of the State. They deplored the weakness and insignificance of the executive power as a calamity. When the inevitable course of events has made our self-government something really like that of America, when it has removed or weakened that security for national dignity, which we possessed in *aristocracy*, will the substitute of the *State* be equally wanting to us? If it is, then the dangers of America will really be ours; the dangers which come from the multitude being in power, with no adequate ideal to elevate or guide the multitude.

It would really be wasting time to contend at length, that to give more prominence to the idea of the State is now possible in this country, without endangering liberty. In other countries the habits and dispositions of the people may be such that the State, if once it acts, may be easily suffered to usurp exorbitantly; here they certainly are not. Here the people will always sufficiently keep in mind that any public authority is a trust delegated by themselves, for certain purposes, and with certain limits; and if that authority pretends to an absolute, independent character, they will soon enough (and very rightly) remind it of its error. Here there can be no question of a paternal government, of an irresponsible executive power, professing to act for the people's good, but without the people's consent, and, if necessary, against the people's wishes; here no one dreams of removing a single constitutional control, of abolishing a single safe-guard for securing a correspondence between the acts of government and the will of the nation. The question is, whether, retaining all its power of control over a government which should abuse its trust, the nation may not now find advantage in voluntarily allowing to it purposes somewhat ampler, and limits somewhat wider within which to execute them, than formerly; whether the nation may not thus acquire in the State an ideal of high reason and right feeling, representing its best self, commanding general respect, and forming a rallying-point for the intelligence and for the worthiest instincts of the community, which will herein find a true bond of union.

I am convinced that if the worst mischiefs of democracy ever happen in England, it will be, not because a new condition of things has come upon us unforeseen, but because, though we all foresaw it, our efforts to deal with it were in the wrong direction. At the present time, almost every one believes in the growth of democracy, almost every one talks of it, almost every one laments it; but the last thing people can be brought to do is to make timely preparation for it. Many of those who, if they would, could do most to forward this work of preparation, are made slack and hesitating by the belief that, after all, in England, things may probably never go very far; that it will be possible to keep much more of the past than speculators say. Others, with a more robust faith, think that all democracy wants is vigorous putting-down; and that, with a good will and strong hand, it is perfectly possible to retain or restore the whole system of the Middle Ages. Others, free from the prejudices of class and position which warp the judgment of these, and who would, I believe, be the first and greatest gainers by strengthening the hands of the State, are averse from doing so by reason of suspicions and fears, once perfectly well-grounded, but, in this age and in the present circumstances, well-grounded no longer.

I speak of the middle classes. I have already shown how it is the natural disposition of an aristocratical class to view with jealousy the development of a considerable State-power. But this disposition has in England found extraordinary favour and support in regions not aristocratical,—from the middle classes; and, above all, from the kernel of these classes, the Protestant Dissenters. And for a very good reason. In times when passions ran high, even an aristocratical executive was easily stimulated into using, for the gratification of its friends and the abasement of its enemies, those administrative engines which, the moment it chose to stretch its hand forth, stood ready for its grasp. Matters of domestic concern, matters of religious profession and religious exercise, offered a peculiar field for an intervention gainful and agreeable to friends, injurious and irritating to enemies. Such an intervention was attempted and practised. Government lent its machinery and authority to the aristocratical and ecclesiastical party, which it regarded as its best support. The party which suffered comprised the flower and strength of that middle class of society, always very flourishing and robust in this country. That powerful class, from this specimen of the administrative activity of government, conceived a strong antipathy against all intervention of the State in certain spheres. An active, stringent administration in those spheres, meant at that time a High Church and Prelatic administration in them, an administration galling to the Puritan party and to the middle class; and this aggrieved class had naturally no proneness to draw nice philosophical distinctions between State-action in these spheres, as a thing for abstract consideration, and State-action in them as they practically felt it and supposed themselves likely long to feel it, guided by their adversaries. In the minds of the English middle class, therefore, State-action in social and domestic concerns became inextricably associated with the idea of a Conventicle Act, a Five-Mile Act, an Act of Uniformity. Their abhorrence of such a State-action as this they extended to State-action in general; and, having never known a beneficent and just State-power, they enlarged their hatred of a cruel and partial State-power, the only one they had ever known, into a maxim that no State-power was to be trusted, that the least action, in certain provinces, was rigorously to be denied to the State, whenever this denial was possible.

Thus that jealousy of an important, sedulous, energetic executive, natural to grandees unwilling to suffer their personal authority to be circumscribed, their individual grandeur to be eclipsed, by the authority and grandeur of the State, became re-inforced in this country by a like sentiment among the middle classes, who had no such authority or grandeur to lose, but who, by a hasty reasoning, had theoretically condemned for ever an agency which they had practically found at times oppressive. *Leave us to ourselves!* magnates and middle classes alike cried to the State. Not only from those who were full and abounded went up this prayer, but also from those whose condition admitted of great amelioration. Not only did the whole repudiate the physician, but also those who were sick.

For it is evident, that the action of a diligent, an impartial, and a national government, while it can do little to better the condition, already fortunate enough, of the highest and richest class of its people, can really do much, by institution and regulation, to better that of the middle and lower classes. The State can bestow certain broad collective benefits, which are indeed not much if compared with the advantages already possessed by individual grandeur, but which are rich and valuable if compared with the make-shifts of mediocrity and poverty. A good thing meant for the many cannot well be so exquisite as the good things of the few; but it can easily, if it comes from a donor of great resources and wide power, be incomparably better than what the many could, unaided, provide for themselves.

In all the remarks which I have been making, I have hitherto abstained from any attempt to suggest a positive application of them. I have limited myself to simply pointing out in how changed a world of ideas we are living; I have not sought to go further, and to discuss in what particular manner the world of facts is to adapt itself to this changed world of ideas. This has been my rule so far; but from this rule I shall here venture to depart, in order to dwell for a moment on a matter of practical institution, designed to meet new social exigencies: on the intervention of the State in public education.

The public secondary schools of France, decreed by the Revolution and established under the Consulate, are said by many good judges to be inferior to the old colleges. By means of the old colleges and of private tutors, the French aristocracy could procure for its children (so it is said, and very likely with truth) a better training than that which is now given in the lyceums. Yes; but the boon conferred by the State, when it founded the lyceums, was not for the aristocracy; it was for the vast middle class of Frenchmen. This class, certainly, had not already the means of a better training for its children, before the State interfered. This class, certainly, would not have succeeded in procuring by its own efforts a better training for its children, if the

State had not interfered. Through the intervention of the State this class enjoys better schools for its children, not than the great and rich enjoy (that is not the question), but than the same class enjoys in any country where the State has not interfered to found them. The lyceums may not be so good as Eton or Harrow; but they are a great deal better than a *Classical and Commercial Academy.*

The aristocratic classes in England may, perhaps, be well content to rest satisfied with their Eton and Harrow. The State is not likely to do better for them. Nay, the superior confidence, spirit, and style, engendered by a training in the great public schools, constitute for these classes a real privilege, a real engine of command, which they might, if they were selfish, be sorry to lose by the establishment of schools great enough to beget a like spirit in the classes below them. But the middle classes in England have every reason not to rest content with their private schools; the State can do a great deal better for them. By giving to schools for these classes a public character, it can bring the instruction in them under a criticism which the stock of knowledge and judgment in our middle classes is not of itself at present able to supply. By giving to them a national character, it can confer on them a greatness and a noble spirit, which the tone of these classes is not of itself at present adequate to impart. Such schools would soon prove notable competitors with the existing public schools; they would do these a great service by stimulating them, and making them look into their own weak points more closely. Economical, because with charges uniform and under severe revision, they would do a great service to that large body of persons who, at present, seeing that on the whole the best secondary instruction to be found is that of the existing public schools, obtain it for their children from a sense of duty, although they can ill afford it, and although its cost is certainly exorbitant. Thus the middle classes might, by the aid of the State, better their instruction, while still keeping its cost moderate. This in itself would be a gain; but this gain would be slight in comparison with that of acquiring the sense of belonging to great and honourable seats of learning, and of breathing in their youth the air of the best culture of their nation. This sense would be an educational influence for them of the highest value. It would really augment their self-respect and moral force; it would truly fuse them with the class above, and tend to bring about for them the equality which they are entitled to desire.

So it is not State-action in itself which the middle and lower classes of a nation ought to deprecate; it is State-action exercised by a hostile class, and for their oppression. From a State-action reasonably, equitably, and nationally exercised, they may derive great benefit; greater, by the very nature and necessity of things, than can be derived from this source by the class above them. For the middle or lower classes to obstruct such a State-action, to repel its benefits, is to play the game of their enemies, and to prolong for themselves a condition of real inferiority.

This, I know, is rather dangerous ground to tread upon. The great middle classes of this country are conscious of no weakness, no inferiority; they do not want any one to provide anything for them. Such as they are, they believe that the freedom and prosperity of England are their work, and that the future belongs to them. No one esteems them more than I do; but those who esteem them most, and who most believe in their capabilities, can render them no better service than by pointing out in what they underrate their deficiencies, and how their deficiencies, if unremedied, may impair their future. They want culture and dignity; they want ideas. Aristocracy has culture and dignity; democracy has readiness for new ideas, and ardour for what ideas it possesses. Of these, our middle class has the last only: ardour for the ideas it already possesses. It believes ardently in liberty, it believes ardently in industry; and, by its zealous belief in these two ideas, it has accomplished great things. What it has accomplished by its belief in industry is patent to all the world. The liberties of England are less its exclusive work than it supposes; for these, aristocracy has achieved nearly as much. Still, of one inestimable part of liberty, liberty of thought, the middle class has been (without precisely intending it) the principal champion. The intellectual action of the Church of England upon the nation has been insignificant; its social action has been great. The social action of Protestant Dissent, that genuine product of the English middle class, has not been civilising; its positive intellectual action has been insignificant; its negative intellectual action,—in so far as by strenuously maintaining for itself, against persecution, liberty of conscience and the right of free opinion, it at the same time maintained and established this right as a universal principle,—has been invaluable. But the actual results of this negative intellectual service rendered by Protestant Dissent,—by the middle class,—to the whole community, great as they undoubtedly are, must not be taken for something which they are not. It is a very great thing to be able to think as you like; but, after all, an important question remains: *what* you think. It is a fine thing to secure a free stage and no favour; but, after all, the part which you play on that stage will have to be criticised. Now, all the liberty and industry in the world will not ensure these two things: a high reason and a fine culture. They may favour them, but they will not of themselves produce them; they may exist without them. But it is by the appearance of these two things, in some shape or other, in the life of a nation, that it becomes something more than an independent, an energetic, a successful nation,—that it becomes a *great* nation.

In modern epochs the part of a high reason, of ideas, acquires constantly increasing importance in the conduct of the world's affairs. A fine culture is the complement of a high reason, and it is in the conjunction of both with character, with energy, that the ideal for men and nations is to be placed. It is common to hear remarks on the frequent divorce between culture and character, and to infer from this that culture is a mere varnish, and that character only deserves any serious attention. No error can be more fatal. Culture without character is, no doubt, something frivolous, vain, and weak; but character without culture is, on the other hand, something raw, blind, and dangerous. The most interesting, the most truly glorious peoples, are those in which the alliance of the two has been effected most successfully, and its result spread most widely. This is why the spectacle of ancient Athens has such profound interest for a rational man; that it is the spectacle of the culture of a *people*. It is not an aristocracy, leavening with its own high spirit the multitude which it wields, but leaving it the unformed multitude still; it is not a democracy, acute and energetic, but tasteless, narrow-minded, and ignoble; it is the middle and lower classes in the highest development of their humanity that these classes have yet reached. It was the *many* who relished those arts, who were not satisfied with less than those monuments. In the conversations recorded by Plato, or even by the matter-of-fact Xenophon, which for the free yet refined discussion of ideas have set the tone for the whole cultivated world, shopkeepers and tradesmen of Athens mingle as speakers. For any one but a pedant, this is why a handful of Athenians of two thousand years ago are more interesting than the millions of most nations our contemporaries. Surely, if they knew this, those friends of progress, who have confidently pronounced the remains of the ancient world to be so much lumber, and a classical education an aristocratic impertinence, might be inclined to reconsider their sentence.

The course taken in the next fifty years by the middle classes of this nation will probably give a decisive turn to its history. If they will not seek the alliance of the State for their own elevation, if they go on exaggerating their spirit of individualism, if they persist in their jealousy of all governmental action, if they cannot learn that the antipathies and the Shibboleths of a past age are now an anachronism for them,—that will not prevent them, probably, from getting the rule of their country for a season, but they will certainly *Americanise* it. They will rule it by their energy, but they will deteriorate it by their low ideals and want of culture. In the decline of the aristocratical element, which in some sort supplied an ideal to ennoble the spirit of the nation and to keep it together, there will be no other element present to perform this service. It is of itself a serious calamity for a nation that its tone of feeling and grandeur of spirit should be lowered or dulled. But the calamity appears far more serious still, when we consider that the middle classes, remaining as they are now, with their narrow, harsh, unintelligent, and unattractive spirit and culture, will almost certainly fail to mould or assimilate the masses below them, whose sympathies are at the present moment actually wider and more liberal than theirs. They arrive, these masses, eager to enter into possession of the world, to gain a more vivid sense of their own life and activity. In this their irrepressible development, their natural educators and initiators are those immediately above them, the middle classes. If these classes cannot win their sympathy or give them their direction, society is in danger of falling into anarchy.

Therefore, with all the force I can, I wish to urge upon the middle classes of this country, both that they might be very greatly profited by the action of the State, and also that they are continuing their opposition to such action out of an unfounded fear. But at the same time I say that the middle classes have the right, in admitting the action of government, to make the condition that this government shall be one of their own adoption, one that they can trust. To ensure this is now in their own power. If they do not as yet ensure this, they ought to do so, they have the means of doing so. Two centuries ago they had not; now they have. Having this security, let them now show themselves jealous to keep the action of the State equitable and rational, rather than to exclude the action of the State altogether. If the State acts amiss, let them check it; but let them no longer take it for granted that the State cannot possibly act usefully.

The State,—but what is *the State?* cry many. Speculations on the idea of a State abound, but these do not satisfy them; of that which is to have practical effect and power they require a plain account. The full force of the term, *the State*, as the full force of any other important term, no one will master without going a little deeply, without resolutely entering the world of ideas; but it is possible to give in very plain language an account of it sufficient for all practical purposes. The State is properly just what Burke called it: *the nation in its collective and corporate character*. The State is the representative acting-power of the nation; the action of the State is the representative action of the nation. Nominally emanating from the Crown, as the ideal unity in which the nation concentrates itself, this action, by the constitution of our country, really emanates from the Ministers of the Crown. It is common to hear the depreciators of State-action run through a string of Ministers' names, and then say: "Here is really your *State*; would you accept the action of these men as your own representative action? in what respect is their judgment on national affairs likely to be any better than that of the rest of the world?" In the first place I answer: Even supposing them to be originally no better or wiser than the rest of the world, they have two great advantages from their position: access to almost boundless means of information, and the enlargement of mind which the habit of dealing with great affairs tends to produce. Their position itself, therefore, if they are men of only average honesty and capacity, tends to give them a fitness for acting on behalf of the nation superior to that of other men of equal honesty and capacity who are not in the same position. This fitness may be yet further increased by treating them as persons on whom, indeed, a very grave responsibility has fallen, and from whom very much will be expected;—nothing less than the representing, each of them in his own department, under the control of Parliament, and aided by the suggestions of public opinion, the collective energy and intelligence of his nation. By treating them as men on whom all this devolves to do, to their honour if they do it well, to their shame if they do it ill, one probably augments their faculty of well-doing; as it is excellently said: "To treat men as if they were better than they are, is the surest way to *make* them better than they are." But to treat them as if they had been shuffled into their places by a lucky accident, were most likely soon to be shuffled out of them again, and meanwhile ought to magnify themselves and their office as little as possible; to treat them as if they and their functions could without much inconvenience be quite dispensed with, and they ought perpetually to be admiring their own inconceivable good fortune in being permitted to discharge them;—this is the way to paralyse all high effort in the executive government, to extinguish all lofty sense of responsibility; to make its members either merely solicitous for the gross advantages, the emolument and self-importance, which they derive from their offices, or else timid, apologetic, and self-mistrustful in filling them; in either case, formal and inefficient.

But in the second place I answer: If the executive government is really in the hands of men no wiser than the bulk of mankind, of men whose action an intelligent man would be unwilling to accept as representative of his own action, whose fault is that? It is the fault of the nation itself, which, not being in the hands of a despot or an oligarchy, being free to control the choice of those who are to sum up and concentrate its action, controls it in such a manner that it allows to be chosen agents so little in its confidence, or so mediocre, or so incompetent, that it thinks the best thing to be done with them is to reduce their action as near as possible to a nullity. Hesitating, blundering, unintelligent, inefficacious, the action of the State may be; but, such as it is, it is the collective action of the nation itself, and the nation is responsible for it. It is our own action which we suffer to be thus unsatisfactory. Nothing can free us from this responsibility. The conduct of our affairs is in our own power. To carry on into its executive proceedings the indecision, conflict, and discordance of its parliamentary debates, may be a natural defect of a free nation, but it is certainly a defect; it is a dangerous error to call it, as some do, a perfection. The want of concert, reason, and organisation in the State, is the want of concert, reason, and organisation in the collective nation.

Inasmuch, therefore, as collective action is more efficacious than isolated individual efforts, a nation having great and complicated matters to deal with must greatly gain by employing the action of the State. Only, the State-power which it employs should be a power which really represents its best self, and whose action its intelligence and justice can heartily avow and adopt; not a power which reflects its inferior self, and of whose action, as of its own second-rate action, it has perpetually to be ashamed. To offer a worthy initiative, and to set a standard of rational and equitable action,—this is what the nation should expect of the State; and the more the State fulfils this expectation, the more will it be accepted in practice for what in idea it must always be. People will not then ask the State, what title it has to commend or reward genius and merit, since commendation and reward imply an attitude of superiority, for it will then be felt that the State truly acts for the English nation; and the genius of the English nation is greater than the genius of any individual, greater even than Shakspeare's genius, for it includes the genius of Newton also.

I will not deny that to give a more prominent part to the State would be a considerable change in this country; that maxims once very sound, and habits once very salutary, may be appealed to against it. The sole question is, whether those maxims and habits are sound and salutary at this moment. A yet graver and more difficult change,—to reduce the all-effacing prominence of the State, to give a more prominent part to the individual,—is imperiously presenting itself to other countries. Both are the suggestions of one irresistible force, which is gradually making its way everywhere, removing old conditions and imposing new, altering long-fixed habits, undermining venerable institutions, even modifying national character: *the modern spirit.*

Undoubtedly we are drawing on towards great changes; and for every nation the thing most needful is to discern clearly its own condition, in order to know in what particular way it may best meet them. Openness and flexibility of mind are at such a time the first of virtues. *Be ye perfect,* said the Founder of Christianity; *I count not myself to have apprehended,* said its greatest Apostle. Perfection will never be reached; but to recognise a period of transformation when it comes, and to adapt themselves honestly and rationally to its laws, is perhaps the nearest approach to perfection of which men and nations are capable. No habits or attachments should prevent their trying to do this; nor indeed, in the long run, can they. Human thought, which made all institutions, inevitably saps them, resting only in that which is absolute and eternal.

Equality [1]

THERE is a maxim which we all know, which occurs in our copy-books, which occurs in that solemn and beautiful formulary against which the Nonconformist genius is just now so angrily chafing,—the Burial Service. The maxim is this: "Evil communications corrupt good manners." It is taken from a chapter of the First Epistle to the Corinthians; but originally it is a line of poetry, of Greek poetry. *Quid Athenis et Hierosolymis?* asks a Father; what have Athens and Jerusalem to do with one another? Well, at any rate, the Jerusalemite Paul, exhorting his converts, enforces what he is saying by a verse of Athenian comedy,—a verse, probably, from the great master of that comedy, a man unsurpassed for fine and just observation of human life, Menander. Φθείρουσιν ἤθη χρήσθ' ὁμιλίαι κακαί—"Evil communications corrupt good manners."

In that collection of single, sententious lines, printed at the end of Menander's fragments, where we now find the maxim quoted by St. Paul, there is another striking maxim, not alien certainly to the language of the Christian religion, but which has not passed into our copy-books: "Choose equality and flee greed." The same profound observer, who laid down the maxim so universally accepted by us that it has become commonplace,

[1] Address delivered at the Royal Institution.

the maxim that evil communications corrupt good manners, laid down also, as a no less sure result of the accurate study of human life, this other maxim as well: "Choose equality and flee greed" —'Ἰσότητα δ' αἱροῦ καὶ πλεονεξίαν φύγε.

Pleonexia, or greed, the wishing and trying for the bigger share, we know under the name of covetousness. We understand by covetousness something different from what *pleonexia* really means: we understand by it the longing for other people's goods: and covetousness, so understood, it is a commonplace of morals and of religion with us that we should shun. As to the duty of pursuing equality, there is no such consent amongst us. Indeed, the consent is the other way, the consent is against equality. Equality before the law we all take as a matter of course; that is not the equality which we mean when we talk of equality. When we talk of equality, we understand social equality; and for equality in this Frenchified sense of the term almost everybody in England has a hard word. About four years ago Lord Beaconsfield held it up to reprobation in a speech to the students at Glasgow;—a speech so interesting, that being asked soon afterwards to hold a discourse at Glasgow, I said that if one spoke there at all at that time it would be impossible to speak on any other subject but equality. However, it is a great way to Glasgow, and I never yet have been able to go and speak there.

But the testimonies against equality have been steadily accumulating from the date of Lord Beaconsfield's Glasgow speech down to the present hour. Sir Erskine May [1] winds up his new and important *History of Democracy* by saying: "France has aimed at social equality. The fearful troubles through which she has passed have checked her prosperity, demoralised her society, and arrested the intellectual growth of her people." Mr. Froude, again, who is more his own master than I am, has been able to go to Edinburgh and to speak there upon equality. Mr. Froude told his hearers that equality splits a nation into "a multitude of disconnected units," that "the masses require leaders whom they can trust," and that "the natural leaders in a healthy country are the gentry." And only just before the *History of Democracy* came out, we had that exciting passage of arms between Mr. Lowe and Mr. Gladstone, where equality, poor thing, received blows from them both. Mr. Lowe declared that "no concession should be made to the cry for equality, unless it appears that the State is menaced with more danger by its refusal than by its admission. No such case exists now or ever has existed in this country."

---

[1] [Sir Thomas Erskine May (1815–1886), constitutional lawyer, and author of works on parliamentary procedure. Created Baron Farnborough, 1886.]

And Mr. Gladstone replied that equality was so utterly unattractive to the people of this country, inequality was so dear to their hearts, that to talk of concessions being made to the cry for equality was absurd. "There is no broad political idea," says Mr. Gladstone quite truly, "which has entered less into the formation of the political system of this country than the love of equality." And he adds: "It is not the love of equality which has carried into every corner of the country the distinct undeniable popular preference, wherever other things are equal, for a man who is a lord over a man who is not. The love of freedom itself is hardly stronger in England than the love of aristocracy." Mr. Gladstone goes on to quote a saying of Sir William Molesworth,[1] that with our people the love of aristocracy "is a religion." And he concludes in his copious and eloquent way: "Call this love of inequality by what name you please,—the complement of the love of freedom, or its negative pole, or the shadow which the love of freedom casts, or the reverberation of its voice in the halls of the constitution,—it is an active, living, and life-giving power, which forms an inseparable essential element in our political habits of mind, and asserts itself at every step in the processes of our system."

And yet, on the other side, we have a consummate critic of life like Menander, delivering, as if there were no doubt at all about the matter, the maxim: "Choose equality!" An Englishman with any curiosity must surely be inclined to ask himself how such a maxim can ever have got established, and taken rank along with "Evil communications corrupt good manners." Moreover, we see that among the French, who have suffered so grievously, as we hear, from choosing equality, the most gifted spirits continue to believe passionately in it nevertheless. "The human ideal, as well as the social ideal, is," says George Sand, "to achieve equality." She calls equality "the goal of man and the law of the future." She asserts that France is the most civilised of nations, and that its pre-eminence in civilisation it owes to equality.

But Menander lived a long while ago, and George Sand was an enthusiast. Perhaps their differing from us about equality need not trouble us much. France, too, counts for but one nation, as England counts for one also. Equality may be a religion with the people of France, as inequality, we are told, is a religion with the people of England. But what do other nations seem to think about the matter?

---

[1] [Sir William Molesworth (1810–1855), politician. Sent down from Trinity College, Cambridge, for challenging his tutor to a duel. Started the *London Review* with John Stuart Mill in 1835. He was responsible for the opening of Kew Gardens to the public on Sundays.]

Now, my discourse to-night is most certainly not meant to be a disquisition on law, and on the rules of bequest. But it is evident that in the societies of Europe, with a constitution of property such as that which the feudal Middle Age left them with,— a constitution of property full of inequality,—the state of the law of bequest shows us how far each society wishes the inequality to continue. The families in possession of great estates will not break them up if they can help it. Such owners will do all they can, by entail and settlement, to prevent their successors from breaking them up. They will preserve inequality. Freedom of bequest, then, the power of making entails and settlements, is sure, in an old European country like ours, to maintain inequality. And with us, who have the religion of inequality, the power of entailing and settling, and of willing property as one likes, exists, as is well known, in singular fulness,—greater fulness than in any country of the Continent. The proposal of a measure such as the Real Estates Intestacy Bill is, in a country like ours, perfectly puerile. A European country like ours, wishing not to preserve inequality but to abate it, can only do so by interfering with the freedom of bequest. This is what Turgot, the wisest of French statesmen, pronounced before the Revolution to be necessary, and what was done in France at the great Revolution. The *Code Napoléon*, the actual law of France, forbids entails altogether, and leaves a man free to dispose of but one-fourth of his property, of whatever kind, if he have three children or more, of one-third if he have two children, of one-half if he have but one child. Only in the rare case, therefore, of a man's having but one child, can that child take the whole of his father's property. If there are two children, two-thirds of the property must be equally divided between them; if there are more than two, three-fourths. In this way has France, desiring equality, sought to bring equality about.

Now the interesting point for us is, I say, to know how far other European communities, left in the same situation with us and with France, having immense inequalities of class and property created for them by the Middle Age, have dealt with these inequalities by means of the law of bequest. Do they leave bequest free, as we do? then, like us, they are for inequality. Do they interfere with the freedom of bequest, as France does? then, like France, they are for equality. And we shall be most interested, surely, by what the most civilised European communities do in this matter,—communities such as those of Germany, Italy, Belgium, Holland, Switzerland. And among those communities we are most concerned, I think, with such as, in the conditions of freedom and of self-government which they demand for their life, are most like ourselves. Germany, for instance, we shall less regard, because the conditions which the Germans seem to accept for their life are so unlike what we demand for ours; there is so much personal government there, so much *junkerism*, militarism, officialism; the community is so much more trained to submission than we could bear, so much more used to be, as the popular phrase is, sat upon. Countries where the community has more a will of its own, or can more show it, are the most important for our present purpose,—such countries as Belgium, Holland, Italy, Switzerland. Well, Belgium adopts purely and simply, as to bequest and inheritance, the provisions of the *Code Napoléon*. Holland adopts them purely and simply. Italy has adopted them substantially. Switzerland is a republic, where the general feeling against inequality is strong, and where it might seem less necessary, therefore, to guard against inequality by interfering with the power of bequest. Each Swiss canton has its own law of bequest. In Geneva, Vaud, and Zurich,—perhaps the three most distinguished cantons,—the law is identical with that of France. In Berne, one-third is the fixed proportion which a man is free to dispose of by will; the rest of his property must go among his children equally. In all the other cantons there are regulations of a like kind. Germany, I was saying, will interest us less than these freer countries. In Germany,—though there is not the English freedom of bequest, but the rule of the Roman law prevails, the rule obliging the parent to assign a certain portion to each child,—in Germany entails and settlements in favour of an eldest son are generally permitted. But there is a remarkable exception. The Rhine countries, which in the early part of this century were under French rule, and which then received the *Code Napoléon*, these countries refused to part with it when they were restored to Germany; and to this day Rhenish Prussia, Rhenish Hesse, and Baden, have the French law of bequest, forbidding entails, and dividing property in the way we have seen.

The United States of America have the English liberty of bequest. But the United States are, like Switzerland, a republic, with the republican sentiment for equality. Theirs is, besides, a new society; it did not inherit the system of classes and of property which feudalism established in Europe. The class by which the United States were settled was not a class with feudal habits and ideas. It is notorious that to acquire great landed estates and to entail them upon an eldest son, is neither the practice nor the desire of any class in America. I remember hearing it said to an American in England: "But, after all, you have the same freedom of bequest and inheritance as we have, and if a man to-morrow chose in your country to entail a great landed estate rigorously, what could you do?" The American answered: "Set aside the will on the ground of insanity."

You see we are in a manner taking the votes for and against equality. We ought not to leave out our own colonies. In general they are, of course, like the United States of America, new societies. They have the English liberty of bequest. But they have no feudal past, and were not settled by a class with feudal habits and ideas. Nevertheless it happens that there have arisen, in Australia, exceedingly large estates, and that the proprietors seek to keep them together. And what have we seen happen lately? An Act has been passed which in effect inflicts a fine upon every proprietor who holds a landed estate of more than a certain value. The measure has been severely blamed in England; to Mr. Lowe such a "concession to the cry for equality" appears, as we might expect, pregnant with warnings. At present I neither praise it nor blame it; I simply count it as one of the votes for equality. And is it not a singular thing, I ask you, that while we have the religion of inequality, and can hardly bear to hear equality spoken of, there should be, among the nations of Europe which have politically most in common with us, and in the United States of America, and in our own colonies, this diseased appetite, as we must think it, for equality? Perhaps Lord Beaconsfield may not have turned your minds to this subject as he turned mine, and what Menander or George Sand happen to have said may not interest you much; yet surely, when you think of it, when you see what a practical revolt against inequality there is amongst so many people not so very unlike to ourselves, you must feel some curiosity to sift the matter a little further, and may be not ill-disposed to follow me while I try to do so.

I have received a letter from Clerkenwell, in which the writer reproaches me for lecturing about equality at this which he calls "the most aristocratic and exclusive place out." I am here because your secretary invited me. But I am glad to treat the subject of equality before such an audience as this. Some of you may remember that I have roughly divided our English society into Barbarians, Philistines, Populace, each of them with their prepossessions, and loving to hear what gratifies them. But I remarked at the same time, that scattered throughout all these three classes were a certain number of generous and humane souls, lovers of man's perfection, detached from the prepossessions of the class to which they might naturally belong, and desirous that he who speaks to them should, as Plato says, not try to please his fellow-servants, but his true and legitimate masters, the heavenly Gods. I feel sure that among the members and frequenters of an institution like this, such humane souls are apt to congregate in numbers. Even from the reproach which my Clerkenwell friend brings against you of being too aristocratic, I derive some comfort. Only I give to the term *aristocratic* a rather wide extension. An accomplished American, much known and much esteemed in this country, the late Mr Charles Sumner,[1] says that what particularly struck him in England was the large class of gentlemen as distinct from the nobility, and the abundance amongst them of serious knowledge, high accomplishment, and refined taste,— taste fastidious perhaps, says Mr. Sumner, to excess, but erring on virtue's side. And he goes on: "I do not know that there is much difference between the manners and social observances of the highest classes of England and those of the corresponding classes of France and Germany; but in the rank immediately below the highest,—as among the professions, or military men, or literary men,—there you will find that the Englishmen have the advantage. They are better educated and better bred, more careful in their personal habits and in social conventions, more refined." Mr. Sumner's remark is just and important; this large class of gentlemen in the professions, the services, literature, politics,—and a good contingent is now added from business also, —this large class, not of the nobility, but with the accomplishments and taste of an upper class, is something peculiar to England. Of this class I may probably assume that my present audience is in large measure composed. It is aristocratic in this sense, that it has the tastes of a cultivated class, a certain high standard of civilisation. Well, it is in its effects upon *civilisation* that equality interests me. And I speak to an audience with a high standard of civilisation. If I say that certain things in certain classes do not come up to a high standard of civilisation, I need not prove how and why they do not; you will feel instinctively whether they do or no. If they do not, I need not prove that this is a bad thing, that a high standard of civilisation is desirable; you will instinctively feel that it is. Instead of calling this "the most aristocratic and exclusive place out," I conceive of it as a *civilised* place; and in speaking about civilisation half one's labour is saved when one speaks about it among those who are civilised.

Politics are forbidden here; but equality is not a question of English politics. The abstract right to equality may, indeed, be a question of speculative politics. French equality appeals to this abstract natural right as its support. It goes back to a state of nature where all were equal, and supposes that "the poor consented," as Rousseau says, "to the existence of rich people,"

---

[1] [Charles Sumner (1811–1874), Boston lawyer and leading Republican. Supporter of emancipation and equal civil rights for negroes.]

reserving always a natural right to return to the state of nature. It supposes that a child has a natural right to his equal share in his father's goods. The principle of abstract right, says Mr. Lowe, has never been admitted in England, and is false. I so entirely agree with him, that I run no risk of offending by discussing equality upon the basis of this principle. So far as I can sound human consciousness, I cannot, as I have often said, perceive that man is really conscious of any abstract natural rights at all. The natural right to have work found for one to do, the natural right to have food found for one to eat, rights sometimes so confidently and so indignantly asserted, seem to me quite baseless. It cannot be too often repeated: peasants and workmen have no natural rights, not one. Only we ought instantly to add, that kings and nobles have none either. If it is the sound English doctrine that all rights are created by law and are based on expediency, and are alterable as the public advantage may require, certainly that orthodox doctrine is mine. Property is created and maintained by law. It would disappear in that state of private war and scramble which legal society supersedes. Legal society creates, for the common good, the right of property, and for the common good that right is by legal society limitable. That property should exist, and that it should be held with a sense of security and with a power of disposal, may be taken, by us here at any rate, as a settled matter of expediency. With these conditions a good deal of inequality is inevitable. But that the power of disposal should be practically *unlimited*, that the inequality should be *enormous*, or that the degree of inequality admitted at one time should be admitted *always*,—this is by no means so certain. The right of bequest was in early times, as Sir Henry Maine [1] and Mr. Mill have pointed out, seldom recognised. In later times it has been limited in many countries in the way that we have seen; even in England itself it is not formally quite unlimited. The question is one of expediency. It is assumed, I grant, with great unanimity amongst us, that our signal inequality of classes and property is expedient for our civilisation and welfare. But this assumption, of which the distinguished personages who adopt it seem so sure that they think it needless to produce grounds for it, is just what we have to examine.

Now, there is a sentence of Sir Erskine May, whom I have already quoted, which will bring us straight to the very point

[1] [Sir Henry James Sumner Maine (1822–1888), Corpus professor of Jurisprudence at Oxford, and later professor of International Law at Cambridge. Author of important works on the history of political institutions.]

that I wish to raise. Sir Erskine May, after saying, as you have heard, that France has pursued social equality, and has come to fearful troubles, demoralisation, and intellectual stoppage by doing so, continues thus: "Yet is she high, if not the first, in the scale of civilised nations." Why, here is a curious thing, surely! A nation pursues social equality, supposed to be an utterly false and baneful ideal; it arrives, as might have been expected, at fearful misery and deterioration by doing so; and yet, at the same time, it is high, if not the first, in the scale of civilised nations. What do we mean by *civilised?* Sir Erskine May does not seem to have asked himself the question, so we will try to answer it for ourselves. Civilisation is the humanisation of man in society. To be humanised is to comply with the true law of our human nature: *servare modum, finemque tenere, Naturamque sequi*, says Lucan; "to keep our measure, and to hold fast our end, and to follow Nature." To be humanised is to make progress towards this, our true and full humanity. And to be civilised is to make progress towards this in civil society; in that civil society "without which," says Burke, "man could not by any possibility arrive at the perfection of which his nature is capable, nor even make a remote and faint approach to it." To be the most civilised of nations, therefore, is to be the nation which comes nearest to human perfection, in the state which that perfection essentially demands. And a nation which has been brought by the pursuit of social equality to moral deterioration, intellectual stoppage, and fearful troubles, is perhaps the nation which has come nearest to human perfection in that state which such perfection essentially demands! Michelet himself, who would deny the demoralisation and the stoppage, and call the fearful troubles a sublime expiation for the sins of the whole world, could hardly say more for France than this. Certainly Sir Erskine May never intended to say so much. But into what a difficulty has he somehow run himself, and what a good action would it be to extricate him from it! Let us see whether the performance of that good action may not also be a way of clearing our minds as to the uses of equality.

When we talk of man's advance towards his full humanity, we think of an advance, not along one line only, but several. Certain races and nations, as we know, are on certain lines pre-eminent and representative. The Hebrew nation was pre-eminent on one great line. "What nation," it was justly asked by their lawgiver, "hath statutes and judgments so righteous as the law which I set before you this day? Keep therefore and do them; for this is your wisdom and your understanding in the sight of the nations which shall hear all these statutes and say: Surely this great nation is a wise and understanding people!"

T

The Hellenic race was pre-eminent on other lines. Isocrates could say of Athens: "Our city has left the rest of the world so far behind in philosophy and eloquence, that those educated by Athens have become the teachers of the rest of mankind; and so well has she done her part, that the name of Greeks seems no longer to stand for a race but to stand for intelligence itself, and they who share in our culture are called Greeks even before those who are merely of our own blood." The power of intellect and science, the power of beauty, the power of social life and manners,—these are what Greece so felt and fixed, and may stand for. They are great elements in our humanisation. The power of conduct is another great element; and this was so felt and fixed by Israel that we can never with justice refuse to permit Israel, in spite of all his shortcomings, to stand for it.

So you see that in being humanised we have to move along several lines, and that on certain lines certain nations find their strength and take a lead. We may elucidate the thing yet further. Nations now existing may be said to feel or to have felt the power of this or that element in our humanisation so signally that they are characterised by it. No one who knows this country would deny that it is characterised, in a remarkable degree, by a sense of the power of conduct. Our feeling for religion is one part of this; our industry is another. What foreigners so much remark in us, —our public spirit, our love, amidst all our liberty, for public order and for stability,—are parts of it too. Then the power of beauty was so felt by the Italians that their art revived, as we know, the almost lost idea of beauty, and the serious and successful pursuit of it. Cardinal Antonelli,[1] speaking to me about the education of the common people in Rome, said that they were illiterate indeed, but whoever mingled with them at any public show, and heard them pass judgment on the beauty or ugliness of what came before them,—"è brutto," "è bello,"—would find that their judgment agreed admirably, in general, with just what the most cultivated people would say. Even at the present time, then, the Italians are pre-eminent in feeling the power of beauty. The power of knowledge, in the same way, is eminently an influence with the Germans. This by no means implies, as is sometimes supposed, a high and fine general culture. What it implies is a strong sense of the necessity of knowing *scientifically*, as the expression is, the things which have to be known by us; of knowing them systematically, by the regular and right process, and in the

---

[1] [Giacomo Antonelli (1806–1876), Cardinal and Secretary of State. The dominating figure at the Vatican during the reign of Pius IX. In 1867 secured French aid against Garibaldi, and devoted his energies to the struggle between the Papacy and the *Risorgimento*.]

only real way. And this sense the Germans especially have.
Finally, there is the power of social life and manners. And even
the Athenians themselves, perhaps, have hardly felt this power so
much as the French.

Voltaire, in a famous passage where he extols the age of Louis
the Fourteenth and ranks it with the chief epochs in the civilisation of our race, has to specify the gift bestowed on us by the age
of Louis the Fourteenth, as the age of Pericles, for instance, bestowed on us its art and literature, and the Italian Renascence its
revival of art and literature. And Voltaire shows all his acuteness
in fixing on the gift to name. It is not the sort of gift which we
expect to see named. The great gift of the age of Louis the
Fourteenth to the world, says Voltaire, was this: *l'esprit de société*,
the spirit of society, the social spirit. And another French writer,
looking for the good points in the old French nobility, remarks
that this at any rate is to be said in their favour: they established
a high and charming ideal of social intercourse and manners, for
a nation formed to profit by such an ideal, and which has profited
by it ever since. And in America, perhaps, we see the disadvantages of having social equality before there has been any such
high standard of social life and manners formed.

We are not disposed in England, most of us, to attach all this
importance to social intercourse and manners. Yet Burke says:
"There ought to be a system of manners in every nation which a
well-formed mind would be disposed to relish." And the power
of social life and manners is truly, as we have seen, one of the
great elements in our humanisation. Unless we have cultivated
it, we are incomplete. The impulse for cultivating it is not, indeed, a moral impulse. It is by no means identical with the moral
impulse to help our neighbour and to do him good. Yet in many
ways it works to a like end. It brings men together, makes them
feel the need of one another, be considerate of one another,
understand one another. But, above all things, it is a promoter
of equality. It is by the humanity of their manners that men are
made equal. "A man thinks to show himself my equal," says
Goethe, "by being *grob*,—that is to say, coarse and rude; he does
not show himself my equal, he shows himself *grob*." But a community having humane manners is a community of equals, and
in such a community great social inequalities have really no
meaning, while they are at the same time a menace and an em-
barrassment to perfect ease of social intercourse. A community
with the spirit of society is eminently, therefore, a community
with the spirit of equality. A nation with a genius for society,
like the French or the Athenians, is irresistibly drawn towards
equality. From the first moment when the French people, with

its congenital sense for the power of social intercourse and manners, came into existence, it was on the road to equality. When it
had once got a high standard of social manners abundantly established, and at the same time the natural, material necessity for the
feudal inequality of classes and property pressed upon it no
longer, the French people introduced equality and made the
French Revolution. It was not the spirit of philanthropy which
mainly impelled the French to that Revolution, neither was it the
spirit of envy, neither was it the love of abstract ideas, though all
these did something towards it; but what did most was the spirit
of society.

The well-being of the many comes out more and more distinctly, in proportion as time goes on, as the object we must pursue. An individual or a class, concentrating their efforts upon
their own well-being exclusively, do but beget troubles both for
others and for themselves also. No individual life can be truly
prosperous, passed, as Obermann says, in the midst of men who
suffer; *passée au milieu des générations qui souffrent.* To the noble
soul, it cannot be happy; to the ignoble, it cannot be secure.
Socialistic and communistic schemes have generally, however, a
fatal defect; they are content with too low and material a standard of well-being. That instinct of perfection, which is the
master-power in humanity, always rebels at this, and frustrates
the work. Many are to be made partakers of well-being, true;
but the ideal of well-being is not to be, on that account, lowered
and coarsened. M. de Laveleye,[1] the political economist, who is
a Belgian and a Protestant, and whose testimony therefore we
may the more readily take about France, says that France, being
the country of Europe where the soil is more divided than anywhere except in Switzerland and Norway, is at the same time the
country where material well-being is most widely spread, where
wealth has of late years increased most, and where population is
least outrunning the limits which, for the comfort and progress
of the working classes themselves, seem necessary. This may go
for a good deal. It supplies an answer to what Sir Erskine May
says about the bad effects of equality upon French prosperity.
But I will quote to you from Mr. Hamerton[2] what goes, I think,
for yet more. Mr. Hamerton is an excellent observer and reporter, and has lived for many years in France. He says of the
French peasantry that they are exceedingly ignorant. So they

[1] [Emile de Laveleye (1822–1892), Belgian political economist and
political writer. Contributed to English newspapers and reviews.]
[2] [Philip Gilbert Hamerton (1834–1894), artist, etcher and essayist.
Founded and edited the art periodical *The Portfolio.* Resided in
France, and wrote with distinction on aspects of French life and
thought.]

are. But he adds: "They are at the same time full of intelligence; their manners are excellent, they have delicate perceptions, they have tact, they have a certain refinement which a brutalised peasantry could not possibly have. If you talk to one of them at his own home, or in his field, he will enter into conversation with you quite easily, and sustain his part in a perfectly becoming way, with a pleasant combination of dignity and quiet humour. The interval between him and a Kentish labourer is enormous."

This is indeed worth your attention. Of course all mankind are, as Mr. Gladstone says, of our own flesh and blood. But you know how often it happens in England that a cultivated person, a person of the sort that Mr. Charles Sumner describes, talking to one of the lower class, or even of the middle class, feels, and cannot but feel, that there is somehow a wall of partition between himself and the other, that they seem to belong to two different worlds. Thoughts, feelings, perceptions, susceptibilities, language, manners,—everything is different. Whereas, with a French peasant, the most cultivated man may find himself in sympathy, may feel that he is talking to an equal. This is an experience which has been made a thousand times, and which may be made again any day. And it may be carried beyond the range of mere conversation, it may be extended to things like pleasures, recreations, eating and drinking, and so on. In general the pleasures, recreations, eating and drinking of English people, when once you get below that class which Mr. Charles Sumner calls the class of gentlemen, are to one of that class unpalatable and impossible. In France there is not this incompatibility. Whether he mix with high or low, the gentleman feels himself in a world not alien or repulsive, but a world where people make the same sort of demands upon life, in things of this sort, which he himself does. In all these respects France is the country where the people, as distinguished from a wealthy refined class, most lives what we call a humane life, the life of civilised man.

Of course, fastidious persons can and do pick holes in it. There is just now, in France, a *noblesse* newly revived, full of pretension, full of airs and graces and disdains; but its sphere is narrow, and out of its own sphere no one cares very much for it. There is a general equality in a humane kind of life. This is the secret of the passionate attachment with which France inspires all Frenchmen, in spite of her fearful troubles, her checked prosperity, her disconnected units, and the rest of it. There is so much of the goodness and agreeableness of life there, and for so many. It is the secret of her having been able to attach so ardently to her the German and Protestant people of Alsace, while we have been so little able to attach the Celtic and Catholic people of Ireland.

France brings the Alsatians into a social system so full of the goodness and agreeableness of life; we offer to the Irish no such attraction. It is the secret, finally, of the prevalence which we have remarked in other continental countries of a legislation tending, like that of France, to social equality. The social system which equality creates in France is, in the eyes of others, such a giver of the goodness and agreeableness of life, that they seek to get the goodness by getting the equality.

Yet France has had her fearful troubles, as Sir Erskine May justly says. She suffers too, he adds, from demoralisation and intellectual stoppage. Let us admit, if he likes, this to be true also. His error is that he attributes all this to equality. Equality, as we have seen, has brought France to a really admirable and enviable pitch of humanisation in one important line. And this, the work of equality, is so much a good in Sir Erskine May's eyes, that he has mistaken it for the whole of which it is a part, frankly identifies it with civilisation, and is inclined to pronounce France the most civilised of nations.

But we have seen how much goes to full humanisation, to true civilisation, besides the power of social life and manners. There is the power of conduct, the power of intellect and knowledge, the power of beauty. The power of conduct is the greatest of all. And without in the least wishing to preach, I must observe, as a mere matter of natural fact and experience, that for the power of conduct France has never had anything like the same sense which she has had for the power of social life and manners. Michelet, himself a Frenchman, gives us the reason why the Reformation did not succeed in France. It did not succeed, he says, because *la France ne voulait pas de réforme morale*—moral reform France would not have; and the Reformation was above all a moral movement. The sense in France for the power of conduct has not greatly deepened, I think, since. The sense for the power of intellect and knowledge has not been adequate either. The sense for beauty has not been adequate. Intelligence and beauty have been, in general, but so far reached, as they can be and are reached by men who, of the elements of perfect humanisation, lay thorough hold upon one only,—the power of social intercourse and manners. I speak of France in general; she has had, and she has, individuals who stand out and who form exceptions. Well then, if a nation laying no sufficient hold upon the powers of beauty and knowledge, and a most failing and feeble hold upon the power of conduct, comes to demoralisation and intellectual stoppage and fearful troubles, we need not be inordinately surprised. What we should rather marvel at is the healing and bountiful operation of Nature, whereby the laying firm hold on one real element in our humanisation has had for France results so beneficent.

And thus, when Sir Erskine May gets bewildered between France's equality and fearful troubles on the one hand, and the civilisation of France on the other, let us suggest to him that perhaps he is bewildered by his data because he combines them ill. France has not exemplary disaster and ruin as the fruits of equality, and at the same time, and independently of this, an exemplary civilisation. She has a large measure of happiness and success as the fruits of equality, and she has a very large measure of dangers and troubles as the fruits of something else.

We have more to do, however, than to help Sir Erskine May out of his scrape about France. We have to see whether the considerations which we have been employing may not be of use to us about England.

We shall not have much difficulty in admitting whatever good is to be said of ourselves, and we will try not to be unfair by excluding all that is not so favourable. Indeed, our less favourable side is the one which we should be the most anxious to note, in order that we may mend it. But we will begin with the good. Our people has energy and honesty as its good characteristics. We have a strong sense for the chief power in the life and progress of man,—the power of conduct. So far we speak of the English people as a whole. Then we have a rich, refined, and splendid aristocracy. And we have, according to Mr. Charles Sumner's acute and true remark, a class of gentlemen, not of the nobility, but well-bred, cultivated, and refined, larger than is to be found in any other country. For these last we have Mr. Sumner's testimony. As to the splendour of our aristocracy, all the world is agreed. Then we have a middle class and a lower class; and they, after all, are the immense bulk of the nation.

Let us see how the civilisation of these classes appears to a Frenchman, who has witnessed, in his own country, the considerable humanisation of these classes by equality. To such an observer our middle class divides itself into a serious portion and a gay or rowdy portion; both are a marvel to him. With the gay or rowdy portion we need not much concern ourselves; we shall figure it to our minds sufficiently if we conceive it as the source of that war-song produced in these recent days of excitement:

> We don't want to fight, but by jingo, if we do,
> We've got the ships, we've got the men, and we've got
> the money too.

We may also partly judge its standard of life, and the needs of its nature, by the modern English theatre, perhaps the most contemptible in Europe. But the real strength of the English middle class is in its serious portion. And of this a Frenchman, who was here some little time ago as the correspondent, I think, of the *Siècle* newspaper, and whose letters were afterwards published in a volume, writes as follows. He had been attending some of the Moody and Sankey[1] meetings, and he says: "To understand the success of Messrs. Moody and Sankey, one must be familiar with English manners, one must know the mind-deadening influence of a narrow Biblism, one must have experienced the sense of acute ennui which the aspect and the frequentation of this great division of English society produce in others, the want of elasticity and the chronic ennui which characterise this class itself, petrified in a narrow Protestantism and in a perpetual reading of the Bible."

You know the French;—a little more Biblism, one may take leave to say, would do them no harm. But an audience like this, —and here, as I said, is the advantage of an audience like this,— will have no difficulty in admitting the amount of truth which there is in the Frenchman's picture. It is the picture of a class which, driven by its sense for the power of conduct, in the beginning of the seventeenth century entered,—as I have more than once said, and as I may more than once have occasion in future to say,—*entered the prison of Puritanism, and had the key turned upon its spirit there for two hundred years.* They did not know, good and earnest people as they were, that to the building up of human life there belong all those other powers also,—the power of intellect and knowledge, the power of beauty, the power of social life and manners. And something, by what they became, they gained, and the whole nation with them; they deepened and fixed for this nation the sense of conduct. But they created a type of life and manners, of which they themselves indeed are slow to recognise the faults, but which is fatally condemned by its hideousness, its immense ennui and against which the instinct of self-preservation in humanity rebels.

Partisans fight against facts in vain. Mr. Goldwin Smith, a writer of eloquence and power, although too prone to acerbity, is a partisan of the Puritans, and of the Nonconformists who are the special inheritors of the Puritan tradition. He angrily resents the imputation upon that Puritan type of life, by which the life of our serious middle class has been formed, that it was doomed

[1] [Dwight Lyman Moody (1837–1899) and Ira David Sankey (1840–1908), the American evangelists carried on a great revivalist campaign throughout the United States and Great Britain. Its special feature was their once well-known and popular Gospel Hymns. Sankey was organist and singer.]

to hideousness, to immense ennui. He protests that it had beauty, amenity, accomplishment. Let us go to facts. Charles the First, who, with all his faults, had the just idea that art and letters are great civilisers, made, as you know, a famous collection of pictures,—our first National Gallery. It was, I suppose, the best collection at that time north of the Alps. It contained nine Raphaels, eleven Corregios, twenty-eight Titians. What became of that collection? The journals of the House of Commons will tell you. There you may see the Puritan Parliament disposing of this Whitehall or York House collection as follows: "Ordered, that all such pictures and statues there as are without any superstition, shall be forthwith sold. . . . Ordered, that all such pictures there as have the representation of the Second Person in Trinity upon them, shall be forthwith burnt. Ordered, that all such pictures there as have the representation of the Virgin Mary upon them, shall be forthwith burnt." There we have the weak side of our parliamentary government and our serious middle class. We are incapable of sending Mr. Gladstone to be tried at the Old Bailey because he proclaims his antipathy to Lord Beaconsfield. A majority in our House of Commons is incapable of hailing, with frantic laughter and applause, a string of indecent jests against Christianity and its Founder. But we are not, or were not, incapable of producing a Parliament which burns or sells the masterpieces of Italian art. And one may surely say of such a Puritan Parliament, and of those who determine its line for it, that they had not the spirit of beauty.

What shall we say of amenity? Milton was born a humanist, but the Puritan temper, as we know, mastered him. There is nothing more unlovely and unamiable than Milton the Puritan disputant. Some one answers his *Doctrine and Discipline of Divorce*. "I mean not," rejoins Milton, "to dispute philosophy with this pork, who never read any." However, he does reply to him, and throughout the reply Milton's great joke is, that his adversary, who was anonymous, is a serving-man. "Finally, he winds up his text with much doubt and trepidation; for it may be his trenchers were not scraped, and that which never yet afforded corn of favour to his noddle,—the salt-cellar,—was not rubbed; and therefore, in this haste, easily granting that his answers fall foul upon each other, and praying you would not think he writes as a prophet, but as a man, he runs to the black jack, fills his flagon, spreads the table, and serves up dinner." There you have the same spirit of urbanity and amenity, as much of it and as little, as generally informs the religious controversies of our Puritan middle class to this day.

But Mr. Goldwin Smith insists, and picks out his own exemplar of the Puritan type of life and manners; and even here let us follow him. He picks out the most favourable specimen he can find,—Colonel Hutchinson, whose well-known memoirs, written by his widow, we have all read with interest. "Lucy Hutchinson," says Mr. Goldwin Smith, "is painting what she thought a perfect Puritan would be; and her picture presents to us not a coarse, crop-eared, and snuffling fanatic, but a highly accomplished, refined, gallant, and most amiable, though religious and seriously minded, gentleman." Let us, I say, in this example of Mr. Goldwin Smith's own choosing, lay our finger upon the points where this type deflects from the truly humane ideal.

Mrs. Hutchinson relates a story which gives us a good notion of what the amiable and accomplished social intercourse, even of a picked Puritan family, was. Her husband was governor of Nottingham. He had occasion, she says, "to go and break up a private meeting in the cannoneer's chamber;" and in the cannoneer's chamber "were found some notes concerning pædobaptism, which, being brought into the governor's lodgings, his wife having perused them and compared them with the Scriptures, found not what to say against the truths they asserted concerning the misapplication of that ordinance to infants." Soon afterwards she expects her confinement, and communicates the cannoneer's doubts about pædobaptism to her husband. The fatal cannoneer makes a breach in him too. "Then he bought and read all the eminent treatises on both sides, which at that time came thick from the presses, and still was cleared in the error of the pædobaptists." Finally, Mrs. Hutchinson is confined. Then the governor "invited all the ministers to dinner, and propounded his doubt and the ground thereof to them. None of them could defend their practice with any satisfactory reason, but the tradition of the Church from the primitive times, and their main buckler of federal holiness, which Tombs and Denne had excellently overthrown. He and his wife then, professing themselves unsatisfied, desired their opinions." With the opinions I will not trouble you, but hasten to the result: "Whereupon that infant was not baptised."

No doubt to a large division of English society at this very day, that sort of dinner and discussion, and, indeed, the whole manner of life and conversation here suggested by Mrs. Hutchinson's narrative, will seem both natural and amiable, and such as to meet the needs of man as a religious and social creature. You know the conversation which reigns in thousands of middle-class families at this hour, about nunneries, teetotalism, the confessional, eternal punishment, ritualism, disestablishment. It goes wherever the class goes which is moulded on the Puritan type of life. In the long winter evenings of Toronto Mr. Goldwin Smith has had, probably, abundant experience of it. What is its enemy? The instinct of self-preservation in humanity. Men make crude types and try to impose them, but to no purpose. *"L'homme s'agite, Dieu le mène,"* says Bossuet. "There are many devices in a man's heart; nevertheless the counsel of the Eternal, that shall stand." Those who offer us the Puritan type of life offer us a religion not true, the claims of intellect and knowledge not satisfied, the claim of beauty not satisfied, the claim of manners not satisfied. In its strong sense for conduct that life touches truth; but its other imperfections hinder it from employing even this sense aright. The type mastered our nation for a time. Then came the reaction. The nation said: "This type, at any rate, is amiss; we are not going to be all like *that!*" The type retired into our middle class, and fortified itself there. It seeks to endure, to emerge, to deny its own imperfections, to impose itself again;— impossible! If we continue to live, we must outgrow it. The very class in which it is rooted, our middle class, will have to acknowledge the type's inadequacy, will have to acknowledge the hideousness, the immense ennui of the life which this type has created, will have to transform itself thoroughly. It will have to admit the large part of truth which there is in the criticisms of our Frenchman, whom we have too long forgotten.

After our middle class he turns his attention to our lower class. And of the lower and larger portion of this, the portion not bordering on the middle class and sharing its faults, he says: "I consider this multitude to be absolutely devoid, not only of political principles, but even of the most simple notions of good and evil. Certainly it does not appeal, this mob, to the principles of '89, which you English make game of; it does not insist on the rights of man; what it wants is beer, gin, and *fun.*" [1]

That is a description of what Mr. Bright would call the residuum, only our author seems to think the residuum a very large body. And its condition strikes him with amazement and horror. And surely well it may. Let us recall Mr. Hamerton's account of the most illiterate class in France; what an amount of civilisation they have notwithstanding! And this is always to be understood, in hearing or reading a Frenchman's praise of England. He envies our liberty, our public spirit, our trade, our stability. But there is always a reserve in his mind. He never means for a moment that he would like to change with us. Life seems to him so much better a thing in France for so many more people, that, in spite of the fearful troubles of France, it is best to be a Frenchman. A Frenchman might agree with Mr. Cobden, that

[1] So in the original.

life is good in England for those people who have at least 5,000*l*. a year. But the civilisation of that immense majority who have not 5,000*l*. a year, or 500*l*., or even 100*l*.,—of our middle and lower class,—seems to him too deplorable.

And now what has this condition of our middle and lower class to tell us about equality? How is it, must we not ask, how is it that, being without fearful troubles, having so many achievements to show and so much success, having as a nation a deep sense for conduct, having signal energy and honesty, having a splendid aristocracy, having an exceptionally large class of gentlemen, we are yet so little civilised? How is it that our middle and lower classes, in spite of the individuals among them who are raised by happy gifts of nature to a more humane life, in spite of the seriousness of the middle class, in spite of the honesty and power of true work, the *virtus verusque labor*, which are to be found in abundance throughout the lower, do yet present, as a whole, the characters which we have seen?

And really it seems as if the current of our discourse carried us of itself to but one conclusion. It seems as if we could not avoid concluding, that just as France owes her fearful troubles to other things and her civilisedness to equality, so we owe our immunity from fearful troubles to other things, and our uncivilisedness to inequality. "Knowledge is easy," says the wise man, "to him that understandeth;" easy, he means, to him who will use his mind simply and rationally, and not to make him think he can know what he cannot, or to maintain, *per fas et nefas*, a false thesis with which he fancies his interests to be bound up. And to him who will use his mind as the wise man recommends, surely it is easy to see that our shortcomings in civilisation are due to our inequality; or in other words, that the great inequality of classes and property, which came to us from the Middle Age and which we maintain because we have the religion of inequality, that this constitution of things, I say, has the natural and necessary effect, under present circumstances, of materialising our upper class, vulgarising our middle class, and brutalising our lower class. And this is to fail in civilisation.

For only just look how the facts combine themselves. I have said little as yet about our aristocratic class, except that it is splendid. Yet these, "our often very unhappy brethren," as Burke calls them, are by no means matter for nothing but ecstasy. Our charity ought certainly, Burke says, to "extend a due and anxious sensation of pity to the distresses of the miserable great." Burke's extremely strong language about their miseries and defects I will not quote. For my part, I am always disposed to marvel that human beings, in a position so false, should be so good as these are. Their reason for existing was to serve as a number of centres in a world disintegrated after the ruin of the Roman Empire, and slowly re-constituting itself. Numerous centres of material force were needed, and these a feudal aristocracy supplied. Their large and hereditary estates served this public end. The owners had a positive function, for which their estates were essential. In our modern world the function is gone; and the great estates, with an infinitely multiplied power of ministering to mere pleasure and indulgence, remain. The energy and honesty of our race does not leave itself without witness in this class, and nowhere are there more conspicuous examples of individuals raised by happy gifts of nature far above their fellows and their circumstances. For distinction of all kinds this class has an esteem. Everything which succeeds they tend to welcome, to win over, to put on their side; genius may generally make, if it will, not bad terms for itself with them. But the total result of the class, its effect on society at large and on national progress, are what we must regard. And on the whole, with no necessary function to fulfil, never conversant with life as it really is, tempted, flattered, and spoiled from childhood to old age, our aristocratic class is inevitably materialised, and the more so the more the development of industry and ingenuity augments the means of luxury. Every one can see how bad is the action of such an aristocracy upon the class of newly enriched people, whose great danger is a materialistic ideal, just because it is the ideal they can easiest comprehend. Nor is the mischief of this action now compensated by signal services of a public kind. Turn even to that sphere which aristocracies think specially their own, and where they have under other circumstances been really effective, —the sphere of politics. When there is need, as now, for any large forecast of the course of human affairs, for an acqaintance with the ideas which in the end sway mankind, and for an estimate of their power, aristocracies are out of their element, and materialised aristocracies most of all. In the immense spiritual movement of our day, the English aristocracy, as I have elsewhere said, always reminds me of Pilate confronting the phenomenon of Christianity. Nor can a materialised class have any serious and fruitful sense for the power of beauty. They may imagine themselves to be in pursuit of beauty; but how often, alas, does the pursuit come to little more than dabbling a little in what they are pleased to call art, and making a great deal of what they are pleased to call love!

Let us return to their merits. For the power of manners an aristocratic class, whether materialised or not, will always, from its circumstances, have a strong sense. And although for this power of social life and manners, so important to civilisation, our English race has no special natural turn, in our aristocracy this power emerges, and marks them. When the day of general humanisation comes, they will have fixed the standard of manners. The English simplicity, too, makes the best of the English aristocracy more frank and natural than the best of the like class anywhere else, and even the worst of them it makes free from the incredible fatuities and absurdities of the worst. Then the sense of conduct they share with their countrymen at large. In no class has it such trials to undergo; in none is it more often and more grievously overborne. But really the right comment on this is the comment of Pepys upon the evil courses of Charles the Second and the Duke of York and the court of that day: "At all which I am sorry; but it is the effect of idleness, and having nothing else to employ their great spirits upon."

Heaven forbid that I should speak in dispraise of that unique and most English class which Mr. Charles Sumner extols,—the large class of gentlemen, not of the landed class or of the nobility, but cultivated and refined. They are a seemly product of the energy and of the power to rise in our race. Without, in general, rank and splendour and wealth and luxury to polish them, they have made their own the high standard of life and manners of an aristocratic and refined class. Not having all the dissipations and distractions of this class, they are much more seriously alive to the power of intellect and knowledge, to the power of beauty. The sense of conduct, too, meets with fewer trials in this class. To some extent, however, their contiguousness to the aristocratic class has now the effect of materialising them, as it does the class of newly enriched people. The most palpable action is on the young amongst them, and on their standard of life and enjoyment. But in general, for this whole class, established facts, the materialism which they see regnant, too much block their mental horizon, and limit the possibilities of things to them. They are deficient in openness and flexibility of mind, in free play of ideas, in faith and ardour. Civilised they are, but they are not much of a civilising force; they are somehow bounded and ineffective.

So on the middle class they produce singularly little effect. What the middle class sees is that splendid piece of materialism, the aristocratic class, with a wealth and luxury utterly out of their reach, with a standard of social life and manners, the offspring of that wealth and luxury, seeming utterly out of their reach also. And thus they are thrown back upon themselves,—upon a defective type of religion, a narrow range of intellect and knowledge, a stunted sense of beauty, a low standard of manners. And the lower class see before them the aristocratic class, and its civilisation, such as it is, even infinitely more out of *their* reach than out of that of the middle class ; while the life of the middle class, with its unlovely types of religion, thought, beauty, and manners, has naturally, in general, no great attractions for them either. And so they too are thrown back upon themselves ; upon their beer, their gin, and their *fun*. Now, then, you will understand what I meant by saying that our inequality materialises our upper class, vulgarises our middle class, brutalises our lower.

And the greater the inequality the more marked is its bad action upon the middle and lower classes. In Scotland the landed aristocracy fills the scene, as is well known, still more than in England ; the other classes are more squeezed back and effaced. And the social civilisation of the lower middle class and of the poorest class, in Scotland, is an example of the consequences. Compared with the same class even in England, the Scottish lower middle class is most visibly, to vary Mr. Charles Sumner's phrase, *less* well-bred, *less* careful in personal habits and in social conventions, *less* refined. Let any one who doubts it go, after issuing from the aristocratic solitudes which possess Loch Lomond, let him go and observe the shopkeepers and the middle class in Dumbarton, and Greenock, and Gourock, and the places along the mouth of the Clyde. And for the poorest class, who that has seen it can ever forget the hardly human horror, the abjection and uncivilisedness of Glasgow?

What a strange religion, then, is our religion of inequality! Romance often helps a religion to hold its ground, and romance is good in its way ; but ours is not even a romantic religion. No doubt our aristocracy is an object of very strong public interest. The *Times* itself bestows a leading article by way of epithalamium on the Duke of Norfolk's marriage. And those journals of a new type, full of talent, and which interest me particularly because they seem as if they were written by the young lion of our youth,—the young lion grown mellow and, as the French say, *viveur*, arrived at his full and ripe knowledge of the world, and minded to enjoy the smooth evening of his days,—those journals, in the main a sort of social gazette of the aristocracy, are apparently not read by that class only which they most concern, but are read with great avidity by other classes also. And the common people too have undoubtedly, as Mr. Gladstone says, a wonderful preference for a lord. Yet our aristocracy, from the action upon it of the Wars of the Roses, the Tudors, and the political necessities of George the Third, is for the imagination a singularly modern and uninteresting one. Its splendour of station, its wealth, show, and luxury, is then what the other classes really admire in it ; and this is not an elevating admiration.

Such an admiration will never lift us out of our vulgarity and brutality, if we chance to be vulgar and brutal to start with; it will rather feed them and be fed by them. So that when Mr. Gladstone invites us to call our love of inequality "the complement of the love of freedom or its negative pole, or the shadow which the love of freedom casts, or the reverberation of its voice in the halls of the constitution," we must surely answer that all this mystical eloquence is not in the least necessary to explain so simple a matter; that our love of inequality is really the vulgarity in us, and the brutality, admiring and worshipping the splendid materiality.

Our present social organisation, however, will and must endure until our middle class is provided with some better ideal of life than it has now. Our present organisation has been an appointed stage in our growth; it has been of good use, and has enabled us to do great things. But the use is at an end, and the stage is over. Ask yourselves if you do not sometimes feel in yourselves a sense, that in spite of the strenuous efforts for good of so many excellent persons amongst us, we begin somehow to flounder and to beat the air; that we seem to be finding ourselves stopped on this line of advance and on that, and to be threatened with a sort of standstill. It is that we are trying to live on with a social organisation of which the day is over. Certainly equality will never of itself alone give us a perfect civilisation. But, with such inequality as ours, a perfect civilisation is impossible.

To that conclusion, facts, and the stream itself of this discourse, do seem, I think, to carry us irresistibly. We arrive at it because they so choose, not because we so choose. Our tendencies are all the other way. We are all of us politicians, and in one of two camps, the Liberal or the Conservative. Liberals tend to accept the middle class as it is, and to praise the nonconformists; while Conservatives tend to accept the upper class as it is, and to praise the aristocracy. And yet here we are at the conclusion, that whereas one of the great obstacles to our civilisation is, as I have often said, British nonconformity, another main obstacle to our civilisation is British aristocracy! And this while we are yet forced to recognise excellent special qualities as well as the general English energy and honesty, and a number of emergent humane individuals, in both nonconformists and aristocracy. Clearly such a conclusion can be none of our own seeking.

Then again, to remedy our inequality, there must be a change in the law of bequest, as there has been in France; and the faults and inconveniences of the present French law of bequest are obvious. It tends to over-divide property; it is unequal in operation, and can be eluded by people limiting their families; it makes the children, however ill they may behave, independent of the parent. To be sure, Mr. Mill and others have shown that a law of bequest fixing the maximum, whether of land or money, which any one individual may take by bequest or inheritance, but in other respects leaving the testator quite free, has none of the inconveniences of the French law, and is in every way preferable. But evidently these are not questions of practical politics. Just imagine Lord Hartington going down to Glasgow, and meeting his Scotch Liberals there, and saying to them: "You are ill at ease, and you are calling for change, and very justly. But the cause of your being ill at ease is not what you suppose. The cause of your being ill at ease is the profound imperfectness of your social civilisation. Your social civilisation is indeed such as I forbear to characterise. But the remedy is not disestablishment. The remedy is social equality. Let me direct your attention to a reform in the law of bequest and entail." One can hardly speak of such a thing without laughing. No, the matter is at present one for the thoughts of those who think. It is a thing to be turned over in the minds of those who, on the one hand, have the spirit of scientific inquirers, bent on seeing things as they really are; and, on the other hand, the spirit of friends of the humane life, lovers of perfection. To your thoughts I commit it. And perhaps, the more you think of it, the more you will be persuaded that Menander showed his wisdom quite as much when he said *Choose equality*, as when he assured us that *Evil communications corrupt good manners*.

Falkland

SHALL we blame him for his lucidity of mind and largeness of temper? Shall we even pity him? By no means. They are his great title to our veneration. They are what make him ours; what link him with the nineteenth century. He and his friends, by their heroic and hopeless stand against the inadequate ideals dominant in their time, kept open their communications with the future, lived with the future. Their battle is ours too; and that we pursue it with fairer hopes of success than they did, we owe to their having waged it and fallen. To our English race, with its insularity, its profound faith in action, its contempt for dreamers and failers, inadequate ideals in life, manners, government, thought, religion, will always be a source of danger. Energetic action makes up, we think, for imperfect knowledge. We think that all is well, that a man is following "a moral impulse," if he pursues an end which he "deems of supreme importance." We impose neither on him nor on ourselves the duty of discerning whether he is *right* in deeming it so.

Hence our causes are often as small as our noise about them is great. To see people busy themselves about Ritualism, that question of not the most strong-minded portion of the clergy and laity, or to see them busy themselves about that "burning question" of the fierce and acrimonious political Dissenters, the Burials Bill, leading up to the other "burning question" of disestablishment,—to see people so eager about these things, one might sometimes fancy that the whole English nation, as in Chillingworth's time it was divided into two great hosts of publicans and sinners on the one side, scribes and Pharisees on the other, so in ours it was going to divide itself into two vast camps of Simpletons here, under the command, suppose, of Mr. Beresford Hope,[1] and of Savages there, under the command of Mr. Henry Richard.[2] And it is so notorious that great movements are always led by aliens to the sort of people who make the mass of the movement,—by gifted outsiders,—that I shall not, I hope, be suspected of implying that Mr. Beresford Hope is a simpleton or Mr. Henry Richard a savage. But what we have to do is to raise and multiply in this country a third host, with the conviction that the ideals both of Simpletons and Savages are profoundly inadequate and profoundly unedifying, and with the resolve to win victory for a better ideal than that of either of them.

Falkland and his friends had in their day a like task. On the one hand was the Royalist party, with its vices, its incurable delusions ; on the other, the Puritans, with their temper, their false, old-Jewish mixture of politics with an ill-understood religion. I should have been glad to say not one word against Hampden in his honourable grave. But the lovers of Hampden cannot forbear to extol him at Falkland's expense. Alas! yet with what benign disdain might not Jesus have whispered to that exemplary but somewhat Philistine Buckinghamshire squire, *seeking the Lord* about militia or ship-money: "Man, who made me a judge or a divider over you?"

---

[1] [Alexander James Beresford-Hope (1820–1887), politician and art-patron. Fervent supporter of the Church of England, whose form of worship he wished to bring into line with the traditions of the historic Catholic church. Built at his own expense All Saints, Margaret St., London. Opposed the Deceased Wife's Sister Bill, 1859, and the Reform Bill of 1867. Founded the *Saturday Review*.]

[2] [Henry Richard (1812–1888), Congregational pastor. Secretary of the Peace Society, and ardent advocate of arbitration as a means of settling international disputes.]

No, the true martyr was not Hampden. If we are to find a martyr in the history of the Great Civil War, let it be Falkland. He was the martyr of lucidity of mind and largeness of temper, in a strife of imperfect intelligences and tempers illiberal. Like his friend Hales of Eton, who in our century will again, he too, emerge, after having been long obscured by the Lauds and the Sheldons, by the Owens and the Baxters,—like Hales, Falkland in that age of harsh and rancorous tempers was "of a nature so kind, so sweet, that it was near as easy a task for anyone to become so knowing as so obliging." Like Hales, too, Falkland could say: "The pursuit of truth hath been my only care ever since I fully understood the meaning of the word. For this I have forsaken all hopes, all friends, all desires which might bias me, and hinder me from driving right at what I aimed." Like Hales, and unlike our nation in general, Falkland concerned himself with the *why* of things as well as the *what.* "I comprise it all," says Hales, in two words: "*what* and *wherefore.* That part of your burden which contains *what,* you willingly take up. But that other, which comprehends *why,* that is either too hot or too heavy; you dare not meddle with it. But I must add that also to your burden, or else I must leave you for idle persons; for without the knowledge of why, of the grounds or reasons of things, there is no possibility of not being deceived." How countless are the deceived and deceiving from this cause! Nay, and the fanatics of the *what,* the neglecters of the *why,* are not unfrequently men of genius; they have the temperament which influences, which prevails, which acts magnetically upon men. So we have the Philistine of genius in religion,—Luther; the Philistine of genius in politics,—Cromwell; the Philistine of genius in literature,—Bunyan. All three of them, let us remark, are Germanic, and two of them are English. Mr. Freeman must be enchanted.

But let us return to Falkland,—to our martyr of sweetness and light, of lucidity of mind and largeness of temper. Let us bid him farewell, not with compassion for him and not with excuses, but in confidence and pride. Slowly, very slowly, his ideal of lucidity of mind and largeness of temper conquers; but it conquers. In the end it will prevail; only we must have patience. The day will come when this nation shall be renewed by it. But, O lime-trees of Tew, and quiet Oxfordshire field-banks where the first violets are even now raising their heads!—how often, ere that day arrive for Englishmen, shall your renewal be seen!

From *A French Critic on Milton*

BUT in his last sentences M. Scherer comes upon what is undoubtedly Milton's true distinction as a poet, his "unfailing level
of style." Milton has always the sure, strong touch of the master.
His power both of diction and of rhythm is unsurpassable, and it
is characterised by being always present—not depending on an
access of emotion, not intermittent, but, like the grace of Raphael,
working in its possessor as a constant gift of nature. Milton's
style, moreover, has the same propriety and soundness in presenting plain matters, as in the comparatively smooth task for a
poet of presenting grand ones. His rhythm is as admirable where,
as in the line

> And Tiresias and Phineus, prophets old——

it is unusual, as in such lines as—

> With dreadful faces throng'd and fiery arms——

where it is simplest. And what high praise this is, we may best
appreciate by considering the ever-recurring failure, both in
rhythm and in diction, which we find in the so-called Miltonic
blank verse of Thomson, Cowper, Wordsworth. What leagues
of lumbering movement! what desperate endeavours, as in
Wordsworth's

> And at the "Hoop" alighted, famous inn,

to render a platitude endurable by making it pompous! Shakspeare himself, divine as are his gifts, has not, of the marks of the
master, this one: perfect sureness of hand in his style. Alone of
English poets, alone in English art, Milton has it; he is our great
artist in style, our one first-rate master in the grand style. He is
as truly a master in this style as the great Greeks are, or Virgil,
or Dante. The number of such masters is so limited that a man
acquires a world-rank in poetry and art, instead of a mere local
rank, by being counted among them. But Milton's importance
to us Englishmen, by virtue of this distinction of his, is incalcul-
able. The charm of a master's unfailing touch in diction and in
rhythm, no one, after all, can feel so intimately, so profoundly,
as his own countrymen. Invention, plan, wit, pathos, thought,
all of them are in great measure capable of being detached from
the original work itself, and of being exported for admiration
abroad. Diction and rhythm are not. Even when a foreigner can
read the work in its own language, they are not, perhaps, easily
appreciable by him. It shows M. Scherer's thorough knowledge

of English, and his critical sagacity also, that he has felt the force
of them in Milton. We natives must naturally feel it yet more
powerfully. Be it remembered, too, that English literature, full
of vigour and genius as it is, is peculiarly impaired by gropings
and inadequacies in form. And the same with English art. Therefore for the English artist in any line, if he is a true artist, the
study of Milton may well have an indescribable attraction. It
gives him lessons which nowhere else from an Englishman's
work can he obtain, and feeds a sense which English work, in
general, seems bent on disappointing and baffling. And this
sense is yet so deep-seated in human nature,—this sense of style,
—that probably not for artists alone, but for all intelligent Englishmen who read him, its gratification by Milton's poetry is a
large though often not fully recognised part of his charm, and a
very wholesome and fruitful one.

As a man, too, not less than as a poet, Milton has a side of unsurpassable grandeur. A master's touch is the gift of nature.
Moral qualities, it is commonly thought, are in our own power.
Perhaps the germs of such qualities are in their greater or less
strength as much a part of our natural constitution as the sense
for style. The range open to our own will and power, however,
in developing and establishing them, is evidently much larger.
Certain high moral dispositions Milton had from nature, and he
sedulously trained and developed them until they became habits
of great power.

Some moral qualities seem to be connected in a man with his
power of style. Milton's power of style, for instance, has for its
great character *elevation*; and Milton's elevation clearly comes,
in the main, from a moral quality in him,—his pureness. "By
pureness, by kindness!" says St. Paul. These two, pureness and
kindness, are, in very truth, the two signal Christian virtues, the
two mighty wings of Christianity, with which it winnowed and
renewed, and still winnows and renews, the world. In kindness,
and in all which that word conveys or suggests, Milton does not
shine. He had the temper of his Puritan party. We often hear
the boast, on behalf of the Puritans, that they produced "our
great epic poet." Alas! one might not unjustly retort that they
spoiled him. However, let Milton bear his own burden; in his
temper he had natural affinities with the Puritans. He has paid
for it by limitations as a poet. But, on the other hand, how high,
clear, and splendid is his pureness; and how intimately does its
might enter into the voice of his poetry!

From *George Sand*

The months go round, and anniversaries return ; on the ninth of June [1] George Sand will have been dead just one year. She was born in 1804 ; she was almost seventy-two years old when she died. She came to Paris after the revolution of 1830, with her *Indiana* written, and began her life of independence, her life of authorship, her life as *George Sand*. She continued at work till she died. For forty-five years she was writing and publishing, and filled Europe with her name.

It seems to me but the other day that I saw her, yet it was in the August of 1846, more than thirty years ago. I saw her in her own Berry, at Nohant, where her childhood and youth were passed, where she returned to live after she became famous, where she died and has now her grave. There must be many who, after reading her books, have felt the same desire which in those days of my youth, in 1846, took me to Nohant,—the desire to see the country and the places of which the books that so charmed us were full. Those old provinces of the centre of France, primitive and slumbering,—Berry, La Marche, Bourbonnais ; those sites and streams in them, of name once so indifferent to us, but to which George Sand gave such a music for our ear,—La Châtre, Ste. Sévère, the *Vallée Noire*, the Indre, the Creuse ; how many a reader of George Sand must have desired, as I did, after frequenting them so much in thought, fairly to set eyes upon them!

I had been reading *Jeanne*. I made up my mind to go and see Toulx Ste. Croix and Boussac, and the Druidical stones on Mont Barlot, the *Pierres Jaunâtres*. I remember looking out Toulx in Cassini's great map at the Bodleian Library. The railway through the centre of France went in those days no farther than Vierzon. From Vierzon to Châteauroux one travelled by an ordinary diligence, from Châteauroux to La Châtre by a humbler diligence, from La Châtre to Boussac by the humblest diligence of all. At Boussac diligence ended, and *patache* began. Between Châteauroux and La Châtre, a mile or two before reaching the latter place, the road passes by the village of Nohant. The Château of Nohant, in which Madame Sand lived, is a plain house by the road-side, with a walled garden. Down in the meadows, not far off, flows the Indre, bordered by trees. I passed Nohant without stopping, at La Châtre I dined and changed diligence, and went on by night up the valley of the Indre, the *Vallée Noire*, past Ste. Sévère to Boussac. At Ste.

[1] 1877.

Sévère the Indre is quite a small stream. In the darkness we quitted its valley, and when day broke we were in the wilder and barer country of La Marche, with Boussac before us, and its high castle on a precipitous rock over the Little Creuse.

That day and the next I wandered through a silent country of heathy and ferny *landes*, a region of granite boulders, holly, and broom, of copsewood and great chestnut trees ; a region of broad light, and fresh breezes, and wide horizons. I visited the *Pierres Jaunâtres*. I stood at sunset on the platform of Toulx Ste. Croix, by the scrawled and almost effaced stone lions,—a relic, it is said, of the English rule,—and gazed on the blue mountains of Auvergne filling the distance, and, south-eastward of them, in a still further and fainter distance, on what seemed to be the mountains over Le Puy and the high valley of the Loire.

From Boussac I addressed to Madame Sand the sort of letter of which she must in her lifetime have had scores, a letter conveying to her, in bad French, the homage of a youthful and enthusiastic foreigner who had read her works with delight. She received the infliction good-naturedly, for on my return to La Châtre I found a message left at the inn by a servant from Nohant that Madame Sand would be glad to see me if I called. The midday breakfast at Nohant was not yet over when I reached the house, and I found a large party assembled. I entered with some trepidation, as well I might, considering how I had got there ; but the simplicity of Madame Sand's manner put me at ease in a moment. She named some of those present ; amongst them were her son and daughter, the Maurice and Solange so familiar to us from her books, and Chopin with his wonderful eyes. There was at that time nothing astonishing in Madame Sand's appearance. She was not in man's clothes, she wore a sort of costume not impossible, I should think (although on these matters I speak with hesitation), to members of the fair sex at this hour amongst ourselves, as an out-door dress for the country or for Scotland. She made me sit by her and poured out for me the insipid and depressing beverage, *boisson fade et mélancolique*, as Balzac called it, for which English people are thought abroad to be always thirsting,—tea. She conversed of the country through which I had been wandering, of the Berry peasants and their mode of life, of Switzerland whither I was going ; she touched politely, by a few questions and remarks, upon England and things and persons English,—upon Oxford and Cambridge, Byron, Bulwer. As she spoke, her eyes, head, bearing, were all of them striking ; but the main impression she made was an impression of what I have already mentioned,—of *simplicity*, frank, cordial simplicity. After breakfast she led the way into the garden, asked me a few kind questions about myself and my plans, gathered a flower or two and gave them to me, shook hands heartily at the gate, and I saw her no more. In 1859 M. Michelet gave me a letter to her, which would have enabled me to present myself in more regular fashion. Madame Sand was then in Paris. But a day or two passed before I could call, and when I called, Madame Sand had left Paris and had gone back to Nohant. The impression of 1846 has remained my single impression of her.

. . . .

Whether or not the number of George Sand's works,—always fresh, always attractive, but poured out too lavishly and rapidly,— is likely to prove a hindrance to her fame, I do not care to consider. Posterity, alarmed at the way in which its literary baggage grows upon it, always seeks to leave behind it as much as it can, as much as it dares,—everything but masterpieces. But the immense vibration of George Sand's voice upon the ear of Europe will not soon die away. Her passions and her errors have been abundantly talked of. She left them behind her, and men's memory of her will leave them behind also. There will remain of her to mankind the sense of benefit and stimulus from the passage upon earth of that large and frank nature, of that large and pure utterance,—the *large utterance of the early gods*. There will remain an admiring and ever widening report of that great and ingenuous soul, simple, affectionate, without vanity, without pedantry, human, equitable, patient, kind. She believed herself, she said, "to be in sympathy, across time and space, with a multitude of honest wills which interrogate their conscience and try to put themselves in accord with it." This chain of sympathy will extend more and more.

It is silent, that eloquent voice! it is sunk, that noble, that speaking head! we sum up, as we best can, what she said to us, and we bid her adieu. From many hearts in many lands a troop of tender and grateful regrets converge towards her humble churchyard in Berry. Let them be joined by these words of sad homage from one of a nation which she esteemed, and which knew her very little and very ill. Her guiding thought, the guiding thought which she did her best to make ours too, "the sentiment of the ideal life, which is none other than man's normal life as we shall one day know it," is in harmony with words and promises familiar to that sacred place where she lies. *Exspectat resurrectionem mortuorum, et vitam venturi sæculi.*

IRISH ESSAYS AND OTHERS
1882

Irish Essays and Others. By Matthew Arnold. London. Smith, Elder & Co., 15 Waterloo Place. 1882.

IN this collection Arnold reprinted the Preface to the First Edition of *Poems*, 1853, and also that to the Second Edition, 1854. *The French Play in London* had already appeared in *The Nineteenth Century*, August 1879.

The following essays are omitted from the present selection: *The Incompatibles, An Unregarded Irish Grievance, Ecce, Convertimur ad Gentes, The Future of Liberalism, A Speech at Eton, Copyright, Preface to Second Edition of Poems*, 1854.

Arnold's interest in the contemporary theatre is further illustrated by five pieces of dramatic criticism over the signature "An Old Playgoer" which he contributed to the *Pall Mall Gazette* (under the editorship of John Morley) between December 1882 and October 1884. These he did not reprint. Four of them were printed by C. K. Shorter in *Matthew Arnold as Dramatic Critic* (London, 1903), and they have been edited with an introduction by Brander Matthews, *Letters of an Old Playgoer* (Columbia University 1919). They are also to be found in the *édition de luxe* of the Collected Works, Macmillan & Co. (1903–4).

IRISH ESSAYS AND OTHERS

From *The French Play in London*

THE nice sense of measure is certainly not one of Nature's gifts to her English children. But then we all of us fail in it, we natives of Great Britain; we have all of us yielded to infatuation at some moment of our lives; we are all in the same boat, and one of us has no right to laugh at the other. I am sure I have not. I remember how in my youth, after a first sight of the divine Rachel at the Edinburgh Theatre, in the part of Hermione, I followed her to Paris, and for two months never missed one of her representations. I, at least, will not cast a stone at the London public for running eagerly after the charming company of actors which has just left us; or at the great ladies who are seeking for soul and have found it in Mdlle. Sarah Bernhardt. I will not quarrel with our newspapers for their unremitting attention to these French performances, their copious criticism of them; particularly when the criticism is so interesting and so good as that which the *Times* and the *Daily News* and the *Pall Mall Gazette* have given us. Copious, indeed!—why should not our newspapers be copious on the French play, when they are copious on the Clewer case, and the Mackonochie case, and so many other matters besides, a great deal less important and interesting, all of them, than the *Maison de Molière*?

So I am not going to join the cynics, and to find fault with the *enjouement*, the infatuation, shown by the English public in its passion for the French plays and players. A passion of this kind may be salutary, if we will learn the lessons for us with which it is charged. Unfortunately, few people who feel a passion think of learning anything from it. A man feels a passion, he passes through it, and he goes his way and straightway forgets, as the Apostle says, what manner of man he was. Above all, this is apt to happen with us English, who have, as an eminent German professor is good enough to tell us, "so much genius, so little method." The much genius hurries us into infatuations; the little method prevents our learning the right and wholesome lesson from them. Let us join, then, devoutly and with contrition, in the prayer of the German professor's great countryman, Goethe, a prayer which is more needful, one may surely say, for us than for him: "God help us, and enlighten us for the time to come! that we may not stand in our own way so much, but may have clear notions of the consequences of things!"

To get a clear notion of the consequences which do in reason follow from what we have been seeing and admiring at the Gaiety Theatre, to get a clear notion of them, and frankly to draw them, is the object which I propose to myself here. I am not going to criticise one by one the French actors and actresses who have been giving us so much pleasure. For a foreigner this must always be a task, as it seems to me, of some peril. Perilous or not, it has been abundantly attempted; and to attempt it yet again, now that the performances are over and the performers gone back to Paris, would be neither timely nor interesting. One remark I will make, a remark suggested by the inevitable comparison of Mdlle. Sarah Bernhardt with Rachel. One talks vaguely of genius, but I had never till now comprehended how much of Rachel's superiority was purely in intellectual power, how eminently this power counts in the actor's art as in all art, how just is the instinct which led the Greeks to mark with a high and severe stamp the Muses. Temperament and quick intelligence, passion, nervous mobility, grace, smile, voice, charm, poetry,—Mdlle. Sarah Bernhardt has them all. One watches her with pleasure, with admiration,—and yet not without a secret disquietude. Something is wanting, or, at least, not present in sufficient force; something which alone can secure and fix her administration of all the charming gifts which she has, can alone keep them fresh, keep them sincere, save them from perils by caprice, perils by mannerism. That something is high intellectual power. It was here that Rachel was so great: she began, one says to oneself as one recalls her image and dwells upon it,—she began almost where Mdlle. Sarah Bernhardt ends.

. . . .

The case of the great Molière himself will illustrate the truth of what I say. Molière is by far the chief name in French poetry; he is one of the very greatest names in all literature. He has admirable and delightful power, penetrativeness, insight; a masterly criticism of life. But he is a comic poet. Why? Had he no seriousness and depth of nature? He had profound seriousness. And would not a dramatic poet with this depth of nature be a tragedian if he could? Of course he would. For only by breasting in full the storm and cloud of life, breasting it and passing through it and above it, can the dramatist who feels the weight of mortal things liberate himself from the pressure, and rise, as we all seek to rise, to content and joy. Tragedy breasts the pressure of life. Comedy eludes it, half liberates itself from it by irony. But the tragedian, if he has the sterner labour, has also the higher prize. Shakespeare has more joy than Molière, more assurance and peace. *Othello*, with all its passion and terror, is on the whole a work animating and fortifying; more so a thousand times than *George Dandin*, which is mournfully depressing. Molière, if he could, would have given us Othellos instead of George Dandins; let us not doubt it. If he did not give Othellos to us, it was because the highest sort of poetic power was wanting to him. And if the highest sort of poetic power had been not wanting to him but present, he would have found no adequate form of dramatic verse for conveying it, he would have had to create one. For such tasks Molière had not power; and this is only another way of saying that for the highest tasks in poetry the genius of his nation appears to have not power. But serious spirit and great poet that he was, Molière had far too sound an instinct to attempt so earnest a matter as tragic drama with inadequate means. It would have been a heart-breaking business for him. He did not attempt it, therefore, but confined himself to comedy.

The *Misanthrope* and the *Tartuffe* are comedy, but they are comedy in verse, poetic comedy. They employ the established verse of French dramatic poetry, the Alexandrine. Immense power has gone to the making of them; a world of vigorous sense, piercing observation, pathetic meditation, profound criticism of life. Molière had also one great advantage as a dramatist over Shakespeare; he wrote for a more developed theatre, a more developed society. Moreover he was at the same time, probably, by nature a better *theatre-poet* than Shakespeare; he had a keener sense for theatrical situation. Shakespeare is not rightly to be called, as Goethe calls him, an epitomator rather than a dramatist; but he may rightly be called rather a dramatist than a theatre-poet. Molière,—and here his French nature stood him in good stead,—was a theatre-poet of the very first order. Comedy, too, escapes, as has been already said, the test of entire seriousness; it remains, by the law of its being, in a region of comparative lightness and of irony. What is artificial can pass in comedy more easily. In spite of all these advantages, the *Misanthrope* and the *Tartuffe* have, and have by reason of their poetic form, an artificiality which makes itself too much felt, and which provokes weariness. The freshness and power of Molière are best felt when he uses prose, in pieces such as the *Avare*, or the *Fourberies de Scapin*, or *George Dandin*. How entirely the contrary is the case with Shakespeare; how undoubtedly is it his verse which shows his power most! But so inadequate a vehicle for dramatic poetry is the French Alexandrine, that its sway hindered Molière, one may think, from being a tragic poet at all, in spite of his having gifts for this highest form of dramatic poetry which are immeasurably superior to those of any other French poet. And in comedy, where Molière thought he could use the Alexandrine, and where he did use it with splendid power, it yet in a considerable degree hampered and lamed him, so that this true and great poet is actually most satisfactory in his prose.

If Molière cannot make us insensible to the inherent defects of French dramatic poetry, still less can Corneille and Racine. Corneille has energy and nobility, Racine an often Virgilian sweetness and pathos. But while Molière in depth, penetrativeness, and powerful criticism of life, belongs to the same family as Sophocles and Shakespeare, Corneille and Racine are quite of another order. We must not be misled by the excessive estimate of them among their own countrymen. I remember an answer of M. Sainte-Beuve, who always treated me with great kindness, and to whom I once ventured to say that I could not think Lamartine a poet of very high importance. "He was important to *us*," answered M. Sainte-Beuve. In a far higher degree can a Frenchman say of Corneille and Racine: "They were important to *us*." Voltaire pronounces of them: "These men taught our nation to think, to feel, and to express itself." *Ces hommes enseignèrent à la nation à penser, à sentir et à s'exprimer.* They were thus the instructors and formers of a society in many respects the most civilised and consummate that the world has ever seen, and which certainly has not been inclined to underrate its own advantages. How natural, then, that it should feel grateful to its formers, and should extol them! "Tell your brother Rodolphe," writes Joseph de Maistre from Russia to his daughter at home, "to get on with his French poets; let him have them by heart,— the inimitable Racine above all; never mind whether he understands him or not. I did not understand him, when my mother used to come and sit on my bed, and repeat from him, and put me to sleep with her beautiful voice to the sound of this incomparable music. I knew hundreds of lines of him before I could read ; and that is why my ears, having drunk in this ambrosia betimes, have never been able to endure common stuff since." What a spell must such early use have had for riveting the affections ; and how civilising are such affections, how honourable to the society which can be imbued with them, to the literature which can inspire them! Pope was in a similar way, though not at all in the same degree, a forming and civilising influence to our grandfathers, and limited their literary taste while he stimulated and formed it. So, too, the Greek boy was fed by his mother and nurse with Homer: but then in this case it was Homer!

We English had Shakespeare waiting to open our eyes, whensoever a favourable moment came, to the insufficiencies of Pope. But the French had no Shakespeare to open their eyes to the insufficiencies of Corneille and Racine. Great artists like Talma and Rachel, whose power, as actors, was far superior to the power, as poets, of the dramatists whose work they were rendering, filled out with their own life and warmth the parts into which they threw themselves, gave body to what was meagre, fire to what was cold, and themselves supported the poetry of the French classic drama rather than were supported by it. It was easier to think the poetry of Racine inimitable, when Talma or Rachel were seen producing in it such inimitable effects. Indeed French acting is so good, that there are few pieces, excepting always those of Molière, in the repertory of a company such as that which we have just seen, where the actors do not show themselves to be superior to the pieces they render, and to be worthy of pieces which are better. *Phèdre* is a work of much beauty, yet certainly one felt this in seeing Rachel in the part of Phèdre. I am not sure that one feels it in seeing Mdlle. Sarah Bernhardt as Phèdre, but I am sure that one feels it in seeing her as Doña Sol.[1]

.   .   .   .

The Society of the French Theatre dates from Louis the Fourteenth and from France's great century. It has, therefore, traditions, effect, consistency, and a place in the public esteem, which are not to be won in a day. But its organisation is such as a judicious man, desiring the results which in France have been by this time won, would naturally have devised; and it is such as a judicious man, desiring in another country to secure like results, would naturally imitate.

We have in England everything to make us dissatisfied with the chaotic and ineffective condition into which our theatre has fallen. We have the remembrance of better things in the past, and the elements for better things in the future. We have a splendid national drama of the Elizabethan age, and a later drama of 'the town' which has no lack of pieces conspicuous by their stage-qualities, their vivacity and their talent, and interesting by their pictures of manners. We have had great actors. We have good actors not a few at the present moment. But we have been unlucky, as we so often are, in the work of organisation. In the essay at organisation which in the patent theatres, with their exclusive privilege of acting Shakespeare, we formerly had, we find by no means an example, such as we have in the constitution of the French Theatre, of what a judicious man, seeking the good

[1] [In Victor Hugo's *Hernani*.]

of the drama and of the public, would naturally devise. We find rather such a machinery as might be devised by a man prone to stand in his own way, a man devoid of clear notions of the consequences of things. It was inevitable that the patent theatres should provoke discontent and attack. They were attacked, and their privilege fell. Still, to this essay, however imperfect, of a public organisation for the English theatre, our stage owes the days of power and greatness which it has enjoyed. So far as we have had a school of great actors, so far as our stage has had tradition, effect, consistency, and a hold on public esteem, it had them under the system of the privileged theatres. The system had its faults, and was abandoned; but then, instead of devising a better plan of public organisation for the English theatre, we gladly took refuge in our favourite doctrines of the mischief of State interference, of the blessedness of leaving every man free to do as he likes, of the impertinence of presuming to check any man's natural taste for the bathos and pressing him to relish the sublime. We left the English theatre to take its chance. Its present impotence is the result.

It seems to me that every one of us is concerned to find a remedy for this melancholy state of things; and that the pleasure we have had in the visit of the French company is barren, unless it leaves us with the impulse to mend the condition of our theatre, and with the lesson how alone it can be rationally attempted. "Forget",—can we not hear these fine artists saying in an undertone to us, amidst their graceful compliments of adieu?—"forget your clap-trap, and believe that the State, the nation in its collective and corporate character, does well to concern itself about an influence so important to national life and manners as the theatre. Form a company out of the materials ready to your hand in your many good actors or actors of promise. Give them a theatre at the West End. Let them have a grant from your Science and Art Department; let some intelligent and accomplished man, like our friend Mr. Pigott, your present Examiner of Plays, be joined to them as Commissioner from the Department, to see that the conditions of the grant are observed. Let the conditions of the grant be that a repertory is agreed upon, taken out of the works of Shakespeare and out of the volumes of the *Modern British Drama*, and that pieces from this repertory are played a certain number of times in each season; as to new pieces, let your company use its discretion. Let a school of dramatic elocution and declamation be instituted in connexion with your company. It may surprise you to hear that elocution and declamation are things to be taught and learnt, and do not come by nature; but it is so. Your best and most serious actors" (this is added with a smile) "would have been better, if in their youth they had learnt elocution. These recommendations, you may think, are not very much; but, as your divine William says, they are enough; they will serve. Try them. When your institution in the West of London has become a success, plant a second of like kind in the East. The people *will* have the theatre; then make it a good one. Let your two or three chief provincial towns institute, with municipal subsidy and co-operation, theatres such as you institute in the metropolis with State subsidy and co-operation. So you will restore the English theatre. And then a modern drama of your own will also, probably, spring up amongst you, and you will not have to come to us for pieces like *Pink Dominoes*."

No, and we will hope, too, that the modern English drama, when it comes, may be something different from even the *Sphinx* and the *Demi-Monde*. For my part, I have all confidence, that if it ever does come, it will be different and better. But let us not say a word to wound the feelings of those who have given us so much pleasure, and who leave to us as a parting legacy such excellent advice. For excellent advice it is, and everything we saw these artists say and do upon the Gaiety stage inculcates it for us, whether they exactly formulated it in words or no. And still, even now that they are gone, when I pass along the Strand and come opposite to the Gaiety Theatre, I see a fugitive vision of delicate features under a shower of hair and a cloud of lace, and hear the voice of Mdlle. Sarah Bernhardt saying in its most caressing tones to the Londoners: "The theatre is irresistible; *organise the theatre*!"

Preface to First Edition of Poems

1853

IN two small volumes of Poems, published anonymously, one in 1849, the other in 1852, many of the poems which compose the present volume have already appeared. The rest are now published for the first time.

I have, in the present collection, omitted the poem from which the volume published in 1852 took its title. I have done so, not because the subject of it was a Sicilian Greek born between two and three thousand years ago, although many persons would think this a sufficient reason. Neither have I done so because I had, in my own opinion, failed in the delineation which I intended to effect. I intended to delineate the feelings of one of the last of the Greek religious philosophers, one of the family of Orpheus and Musæus, having survived his fellows, living on into

U

a time when the habits of Greek thought and feeling had begun fast to change, character to dwindle, the influence of the Sophists to prevail. Into the feelings of a man so situated there entered much that we are accustomed to consider as exclusively modern; how much, the fragments of Empedocles himself which remain to us are sufficient at least to indicate. What those who are familiar only with the great monuments of early Greek genius suppose to be its exclusive characteristics, have disappeared; the calm, the cheerfulness, the disinterested objectivity have disappeared; the dialogue of the mind itself has commenced; modern problems have presented themselves; we hear already the doubts, we witness the discouragement, of Hamlet and of Faust.

The representation of such a man's feelings must be interesting, if consistently drawn. We all naturally take pleasure, says Aristotle, in any imitation or representation whatever; this is the basis of our love of poetry; and we take pleasure in them, he adds, because all knowledge is naturally agreeable to us; not to the philosopher only, but to mankind at large. Every representation, therefore, which is consistently drawn may be supposed to be interesting, inasmuch as it gratifies this natural interest in knowledge of all kinds. What is *not* interesting, is that which does not add to our knowledge of any kind; that which is vaguely conceived and loosely drawn; a representation which is general, indeterminate, and faint, instead of being particular, precise, and firm.

Any accurate representation may therefore be expected to be interesting; but, if the representation be a poetical one, more than this is demanded. It is demanded, not only that it shall interest, but also that it shall inspirit and rejoice the reader; that it shall convey a charm, and infuse delight. For the Muses, as Hesiod says, were born that they might be "a forgetfulness of evils, and a truce from cares:" and it is not enough that the poet should add to the knowledge of men, it is required of him also that he should add to their happiness. "All art," says Schiller, "is dedicated to Joy, and there is no higher and no more serious problem, than how to make men happy. The right art is that alone, which creates the highest enjoyment."

A poetical work, therefore, is not yet justified when it has been shown to be an accurate, and therefore interesting representation; it has to be shown also that it is a representation from which men can derive enjoyment. In presence of the most tragic circumstances, represented in a work of art, the feeling of enjoyment, as is well known, may still subsist: the representation of the most utter calamity, of the liveliest anguish, is not sufficient to destroy it; the more tragic the situation, the deeper becomes the enjoyment; and the situation is more tragic in proportion as it becomes more terrible.

What then are the situations, from the representation of which, though accurate, no poetical enjoyment can be derived? They are those in which the suffering finds no vent in action; in which a continuous state of mental distress is prolonged, unrelieved by incident, hope, or resistance; in which there is everything to be endured, nothing to be done. In such situations there is inevitably something morbid, in the description of them something monotonous. When they occur in actual life, they are painful, not tragic; the representation of them in poetry is painful also.

To this class of situations, poetically faulty as it appears to me, that of Empedocles, as I have endeavoured to represent him, belongs; and I have therefore excluded the poem from the present collection.

And why, it may be asked, have I entered into this explanation respecting a matter so unimportant as the admission or exclusion of the poem in question? I have done so, because I was anxious to avow that the sole reason for its exclusion was that which has been stated above; and that it has not been excluded in deference to the opinion which many critics of the present day appear to entertain against subjects chosen from distant times and countries: against the choice, in short, of any subjects but modern ones.

"The poet," it is said,[1] and by an intelligent critic, "the poet who would really fix the public attention must leave the exhausted past, and draw his subjects from matters of present import, and *therefore* both of interest and novelty."

Now this view I believe to be completely false. It is worth examining, inasmuch as it is a fair sample of a class of critical dicta everywhere current at the present day, having a philosophical form and air, but no real basis in fact; and which are calculated to vitiate the judgment of readers of poetry, while they exert, so far as they are adopted, a misleading influence on the practice of those who make it.

What are the eternal objects of poetry, among all nations, and at all times? They are actions; human actions; possessing an inherent interest in themselves, and which are to be communicated in an interesting manner by the art of the poet. Vainly will the latter imagine that he has everything in his own power; that he can make an intrinsically inferior action equally delightful with a more excellent one by his treatment of it. He may indeed compel

[1] In the *Spectator* of April 2, 1853. The words quoted were not used with reference to poems of mine.

us to admire his skill, but his work will possess, within itself, an incurable defect.

The poet, then, has in the first place to select an excellent action; and what actions are the most excellent? Those, certainly, which most powerfully appeal to the great primary human affections; to those elementary feelings which subsist permanently in the race, and which are independent of time. These feelings are permanent and the same; that which interests them is permanent and the same also. The modernness or antiquity of an action, therefore, has nothing to do with its fitness for poetical representation; this depends upon its inherent qualities. To the elementary part of our nature, to our passions, that which is great and passionate is eternally interesting; and interesting solely in proportion to its greatness and to its passion. A great human action of a thousand years ago is more interesting to it than a smaller human action of to-day, even though upon the representation of this last the most consummate skill may have been expended, and though it has the advantage of appealing by its modern language, familiar manners, and contemporary allusions, to all our transient feelings and interests. These, however, have no right to demand of a poetical work that it shall satisfy them; their claims are to be directed elsewhere. Poetical works belong to the domain of our permanent passions; let them interest these, and the voice of all subordinate claims upon them is at once silenced.

Achilles, Prometheus, Clytemnestra, Dido,—what modern poem presents personages as interesting, even to us moderns, as these personages of an "exhausted past?" We have the domestic epic dealing with the details of modern life which pass daily under our eyes; we have poems representing modern personages in contact with the problems of modern life, moral, intellectual, and social; these works have been produced by poets the most distinguished of their nation and time; yet I fearlessly assert that Hermann and Dorothea, Childe Harold, Jocelyn, the Excursion, leave the reader cold in comparison with the effect produced upon him by the latter books of the Iliad, by the Oresteia, or by the episode of Dido. And why is this? Simply because in the three last-named cases the action is greater, the personages nobler, the situations more intense: and this is the true basis of the interest in a poetical work, and this alone.

It may be urged, however, that past actions may be interesting in themselves, but that they are not to be adopted by the modern poet, because it is impossible for him to have them clearly present to his own mind, and he cannot therefore feel them deeply, nor represent them forcibly. But this is not necessarily the case.

The externals of a past action, indeed, he cannot know with the precision of a contemporary; but his business is with its essentials. The outward man of Œdipus or of Macbeth, the houses in which they lived, the ceremonies of their courts, he cannot accurately figure to himself; but neither do they essentially concern him. His business is with their inward man; with their feelings and behaviour in certain tragic situations, which engage their passions as men; these have in them nothing local and casual; they are as accessible to the modern poet as to a contemporary.

The date of an action, then, signifies nothing; the action itself, its selection and construction, this is what is all-important. This the Greeks understood far more clearly than we do. The radical difference between their poetical theory and ours consists, as it appears to me, in this: that, with them, the poetical character of the action in itself, and the conduct of it, was the first consideration; with us, attention is fixed mainly on the value of the separate thoughts and images which occur in the treatment of an action. They regarded the whole; we regard the parts. With them, the action predominated over the expression of it; with us, the expression predominates over the action. Not that they failed in expression, or were inattentive to it; on the contrary, they are the highest models of expression, the unapproached masters of the *grand style*. But their expression is so excellent because it is so admirably kept in its right degree of prominence; because it is so simple and so well subordinated; because it draws its force directly from the pregnancy of the matter which it conveys. For what reason was the Greek tragic poet confined to so limited a range of subjects? Because there are so few actions which unite in themselves, in the highest degree, the conditions of excellence; and it was not thought that on any but an excellent subject could an excellent poem be constructed. A few actions, therefore, eminently adapted for tragedy, maintained almost exclusive possession of the Greek tragic stage. Their significance appeared inexhaustible: they were as permanent problems, perpetually offered to the genius of every fresh poet. This too is the reason of what appears to us moderns a certain baldness of expression in Greek tragedy; of the triviality with which we often reproach the remarks of the chorus, where it takes part in the dialogue: that the action itself, the situation of Orestes, or Merope, or Alcmæon, was to stand the central point of interest, unforgotten, absorbing, principal; that no accessories were for a moment to distract the spectator's attention from this; that the tone of the parts was to be perpetually kept down, in order not to impair the grandiose effect of the whole. The terrible old mythic story on which the drama was founded stood, before he entered the theatre, traced in its bare outlines upon the spectator's mind; it stood in his memory, as a group of statuary, faintly seen, at the end of a long and dark vista: then came the poet, embodying outlines, developing situations, not a word wasted, not a sentiment capriciously thrown in: stroke upon stroke, the drama proceeded: the light deepened upon the group; more and more it revealed itself to the riveted gaze of the spectator: until at last, when the final words were spoken, it stood before him in broad sunlight, a model of immortal beauty.

This was what a Greek critic demanded; this was what a Greek poet endeavoured to effect. It signified nothing to what time an action belonged. We do not find that the Persæ occupied a particularly high rank among the dramas of Æschylus, because it represented a matter of contemporary interest; this was not what a cultivated Athenian required. He required that the permanent elements of his nature should be moved; and dramas of which the action, though taken from a long-distant mythic time, yet was calculated to accomplish this in a higher degree than that of the Persæ, stood higher in his estimation accordingly. The Greeks felt, no doubt, with their exquisite sagacity of taste, that an action of present times was too near them, too much mixed up with what was accidental and passing, to form a sufficiently grand, detached, and self-subsistent object for a tragic poem. Such objects belonged to the domain of the comic poet, and of the lighter kinds of poetry. For the more serious kinds, for *pragmatic* poetry, to use an excellent expression of Polybius, they were more difficult and severe in the range of subjects which they permitted. Their theory and practice alike, the admirable treatise of Aristotle, and the unrivalled works of their poets, exclaim with a thousand tongues—"All depends upon the subject; choose a fitting action, penetrate yourself with the feeling of its situations; this done, everything else will follow."

But for all kinds of poetry alike there was one point on which they were rigidly exacting; the adaptability of the subject to the kind of poetry selected, and the careful construction of the poem.

How different a way of thinking from this is ours! We can hardly at the present day understand what Menander meant, when he told a man who enquired as to the progress of his comedy that he had finished it, not having yet written a single line, because he had constructed the action of it in his mind. A modern critic would have assured him that the merit of his piece depended on the brilliant things which arose under his pen as he went along. We have poems which seem to exist merely for the sake of single lines and passages; not for the sake of producing any total impression. We have critics who seem to direct their attention merely to detached expressions, to the language about the action, not to the action itself. I verily think that the majority of them do not in their hearts believe that there is such a thing as a total impression to be derived from a poem at all, or to be demanded from a poet; they think the term a commonplace of metaphysical criticism. They will permit the poet to select any action he pleases, and to suffer that action to go as it will, provided he gratifies them with occasional bursts of fine writing, and with a shower of isolated thoughts and images. That is, they permit him to leave their poetical sense ungratified, provided that he gratifies their rhetorical sense and their curiosity. Of his neglecting to gratify these, there is little danger. He needs rather to be warned against the danger of attempting to gratify these alone; he needs rather to be perpetually reminded to prefer his action to everything else; so to treat this, as to permit its inherent excellences to develope themselves, without interruption from the intrusion of his personal peculiarities; most fortunate, when he most entirely succeeds in effacing himself, and in enabling a noble action to subsist as it did in nature.

But the modern critic not only permits a false practice; he absolutely prescribes false aims.—"A true allegory of the state of one's own mind in a representative history," the poet is told, "is perhaps the highest thing that one can attempt in the way of poetry." And accordingly he attempts it. An allegory of the state of one's own mind, the highest problem of an art which imitates actions! No assuredly, it is not, it never can be so: no great poetical work has ever been produced with such an aim. Faust itself, in which something of the kind is attempted, wonderful passages as it contains, and in spite of the unsurpassed beauty of the scenes which relate to Margaret, Faust itself, judged as a whole, and judged strictly as a poetical work, is defective: its illustrious author, the greatest poet of modern times, the greatest critic of all times, would have been the first to acknowledge it; he only defended his work, indeed, by asserting it to be "something incommensurable."

The confusion of the present times is great, the multitude of voices counselling different things bewildering, the number of existing works capable of attracting a young writer's attention and of becoming his models, immense. What he wants is a hand to guide him through the confusion, a voice to prescribe to him the aim which he should keep in view, and to explain to him that the value of the literary works which offer themselves to his attention is relative to their power of helping him forward on his road towards this aim. Such a guide the English writer at the present day will nowhere find. Failing this, all that can be looked for, all indeed that can be desired, is, that his attention should be fixed on excellent models; that he may reproduce, at any rate, something of their excellence, by penetrating himself with their works and by catching their spirit, if he cannot be taught to produce what is excellent independently.

Foremost among these models for the English writer stands Shakespeare: a name the greatest perhaps of all poetical names; a name never to be mentioned without reverence. I will venture, however, to express a doubt, whether the influence of his works, excellent and fruitful for the readers of poetry, for the great majority, has been of unmixed advantage to the writers of it. Shakespeare indeed chose excellent subjects; the world could afford no better than Macbeth, or Romeo and Juliet, or Othello; he had no theory respecting the necessity of choosing subjects of present import, or the paramount interest attaching to allegories of the state of one's own mind; like all great poets, he knew well what constituted a poetical action; like them, wherever he found such an action, he took it; like them, too, he found his best in past times. But to these general characteristics of all great poets he added a special one of his own; a gift, namely, of happy, abundant, and ingenious expression, eminent and unrivalled: so eminent as irresistibly to strike the attention first in him, and even to throw into comparative shade his other excellences as a poet. Here has been the mischief. These other excellences were his fundamental excellences *as a poet*; what distinguishes the artist from the mere amateur, says Goethe, is *Architectonicè* in the highest sense; that power of execution, which creates, forms, and constitutes: not the profoundness of single thoughts, not the richness of imagery, not the abundance of illustration. But these attractive accessories of a poetical work being more easily seized than the spirit of the whole, and these accessories being possessed by Shakespeare in an unequalled degree, a young writer having recourse to Shakespeare as his model runs great risk of being vanquished and absorbed by them, and, in consequence, of reproducing, according to the measure of his power, these, and these alone. Of this preponderating quality of Shakespeare's genius, accordingly, almost the whole of modern English poetry has, it appears to me, felt the influence. To the exclusive attention on the part of his imitators to this it is in a great degree owing, that of the majority of modern poetical works the details alone are valuable, the composition worthless. In reading them one is perpetually reminded of that terrible sentence on a modern French poet:—*Il dit tout ce qu'il veut, mais malheureusement il n'a rien à dire*.

Let me give an instance of what I mean. I will take it from the

works of the very chief among those who seem to have been
formed in the school of Shakespeare: of one whose exquisite
genius and pathetic death render him for ever interesting. I will
take the poem of Isabella, or the Pot of Basil, by Keats. I choose
this rather than the Endymion, because the latter work, (which
a modern critic has classed with the Fairy Queen!) although undoubtedly there blows through it the breath of genius, is yet as a
whole so utterly incoherent, as not strictly to merit the name of
a poem at all. The poem of Isabella, then, is a perfect treasure-
house of graceful and felicitous words and images: almost in
every stanza there occurs one of those vivid and picturesque
turns of expression, by which the object is made to flash upon the
eye of the mind, and which thrill the reader with a sudden delight.
This one short poem contains, perhaps, a greater number of
happy single expressions which one could quote than all the extant tragedies of Sophocles. But the action, the story? The
action in itself is an excellent one; but so feebly is it conceived by
the poet, so loosely constructed, that the effect produced by it,
in and for itself, is absolutely null. Let the reader, after he has
finished the poem of Keats, turn to the same story in the Deca-
meron: he will then feel how pregnant and interesting the same
action has become in the hands of a great artist, who above all
things delineates his object; who subordinates expression to that
which it is designed to express.

I have said that the imitators of Shakespeare, fixing their attention on his wonderful gift of expression, have directed their
imitation to this, neglecting his other excellences. These excellences, the fundamental excellences of poetical art, Shakespeare
no doubt possessed them,—possessed many of them in a splendid
degree; but it may perhaps be doubted whether even he himself
did not sometimes give scope to his faculty of expression to the
prejudice of a higher poetical duty. For we must never forget
that Shakespeare is the great poet he is from his skill in discerning and firmly conceiving an excellent action, from his power of
intensely feeling a situation, of intimately associating himself
with a character; not from his gift of expression, which rather
even leads him astray, degenerating sometimes into a fondness
for curiosity of expression, into an irritability of fancy, which
seems to make it impossible for him to say a thing plainly, even
when the press of the action demands the very directest language, or its level character the very simplest. Mr. Hallam, than
whom it is impossible to find a saner and more judicious critic,
has had the courage (for at the present day it needs courage) to
remark, how extremely and faultily difficult Shakespeare's language often is. It is so: you may find main scenes in some of his

greatest tragedies, King Lear for instance, where the language is so artificial, so curiously tortured, and so difficult, that every speech has to be read two or three times before its meaning can be comprehended. This over-curiousness of expression is indeed but the excessive employment of a wonderful gift,—of the power of saying a thing in a happier way than any other man; nevertheless, it is carried so far that one understands what M. Guizot meant, when he said that Shakespeare appears in his language to have tried all styles except that of simplicity. He has not the severe and scrupulous self-restraint of the ancients, partly no doubt, because he had a far less cultivated and exacting audience. He has indeed a far wider range than they had, a far richer fertility of thought; in this respect he rises above them. In his strong conception of his subject, in the genuine way in which he is penetrated with it, he resembles them, and is unlike the moderns. But in the accurate limitation of it, the conscientious rejection of superfluities, the simple and rigorous development of it from the first line of his work to the last, he falls below them, and comes nearer to the moderns. In his chief works, besides what he has of his own, he has the elementary soundness of the ancients; he has their important action and their large and broad manner; but he has not their purity of method. He is therefore a less safe model; for what he has of his own is personal, and inseparable from his own rich nature; it may be imitated and exaggerated, it cannot be learned or applied as an art. He is above all suggestive; more valuable, therefore, to young writers as men than as artists. But clearness of arrangement, rigour of development, simplicity of style,—these may to a certain extent be learned; and these may, I am convinced, be learned best from the ancients, who, although infinitely less suggestive than Shakespeare, are thus, to the artist, more instructive.

What then, it will be asked, are the ancients to be our sole models? the ancients with their comparatively narrow range of experience, and their widely different circumstances? Not, certainly, that which is narrow in the ancients, nor that in which we can no longer sympathise. An action like the action of the Antigone of Sophocles, which turns upon the conflict between the heroine's duty to her brother's corpse and that to the laws of her country, is no longer one in which it is possible that we should feel a deep interest. I am speaking too, it will be remembered, not of the best sources of intellectual stimulus for the general reader, but of the best models of instruction for the individual writer. This last may certainly learn of the ancients, better than anywhere else, three things which it is vitally important for him to know:—the all-importance of the choice of a subject; the necessity of accurate construction; and the subordinate character of expression. He will learn from them how unspeakably superior is the effect of the one moral impression left by a great action treated as a whole, to the effect produced by the most striking single thought or by the happiest image. As he penetrates into the spirit of the great classical works, as he becomes gradually aware of their intense significance, their noble simplicity, and their calm pathos, he will be convinced that it is this effect, unity and profoundness of moral impression, at which the ancient poets aimed; that it is this which constitutes the grandeur of their works, and which makes them immortal. He will desire to direct his own efforts towards producing the same effect. Above all, he will deliver himself from the jargon of modern criticism, and escape the danger of producing poetical works conceived in the spirit of the passing time, and which partake of its transitoriness.

The present age makes great claims upon us; we owe its service, it will not be satisfied without our admiration. I know not how it is, but their commerce with the ancients appears to me to produce, in those who constantly practise it, a steadying and composing effect upon their judgment, not of literary works only, but of men and events in general. They are like persons who have had a very weighty and impressive experience; they are more truly than others under the empire of facts, and more independent of the language current among those with whom they live. They wish neither to applaud nor to revile their age; they wish to know what it is, what it can give them, and whether this is what they want. What they want, they know very well; they want to educe and cultivate what is best and noblest in themselves; they know, too, that this is no easy task—χαλεπὸν, as Pittacus said, χαλεπὸν ἐσθλὸν ἔμμεναι—and they ask themselves sincerely whether their age and its literature can assist them in the attempt. If they are endeavouring to practise any art, they remember the plain and simple proceedings of the old artists, who attained their grand results by penetrating themselves with some noble and significant action, not by inflating themselves with a belief in the preeminent importance and greatness of their own times. They do not talk of their mission, nor of interpreting their age, nor of the coming poet; all this, they know, is the mere delirium of vanity; their business is not to praise their age, but to afford to the men who live in it the highest pleasure which they are capable of feeling. If asked to afford this by means of subjects drawn from the age itself, they ask what special fitness the present age has for supplying them. They are told that it is an era of progress, an age commissioned to carry out the great ideas of industrial development and social amelioration. They reply that with all this they can do nothing; that the elements they need for the exercise of their art are great actions, calculated powerfully and delightfully to affect what is permanent in the human soul; that so far as the present age can supply such actions, they will gladly make use of them; but that an age wanting in moral grandeur can with difficulty supply such, and an age of spiritual discomfort with difficulty be powerfully and delightfully affected by them.

A host of voices will indignantly rejoin that the present age is inferior to the past neither in moral grandeur nor in spiritual health. He who possesses the discipline I speak of will content himself with remembering the judgments passed upon the present age, in this respect, by the men of strongest head and widest culture whom it has produced; by Goethe and by Niebuhr. It will be sufficient for him that he knows the opinions held by these two great men respecting the present age and its literature; and that he feels assured in his own mind that their aims and demands upon life were such as he would wish, at any rate, his own to be; and their judgment as to what is impeding and disabling such as he may safely follow. He will not, however, maintain a hostile attitude towards the false pretensions of his age; he will content himself with not being overwhelmed by them. He will esteem himself fortunate if he can succeed in banishing from his mind all feelings of contradiction, and irritation, and impatience; in order to delight himself with the contemplation of some noble action of a heroic time, and to enable others, through his representation of it, to delight in it also.

I am far indeed from making any claim, for myself, that I possess this discipline; or for the following poems, that they breathe its spirit. But I say, that in the sincere endeavour to learn and practise, amid the bewildering confusion of our times, what is sound and true in poetical art, I seemed to myself to find the only sure guidance, the only solid footing, among the ancients. They, at any rate, knew what they wanted in art, and we do not. It is this uncertainty which is disheartening, and not hostile criticism. How often have I felt this when reading words of disparagement or of cavil: that it is the uncertainty as to what is really to be aimed at which makes our difficulty, not the dissatisfaction of the critic, who himself suffers from the same uncertainty! *Non me tua fervida terrent Dicta; . . . Dii me terrent, et Jupiter hostis.*

Two kinds of *dilettanti*, says Goethe, there are in poetry: he who neglects the indispensable mechanical part, and thinks he has done enough if he shows spirituality and feeling; and he who seeks to arrive at poetry merely by mechanism, in which he can acquire an artisan's readiness, and is without soul and matter. And he adds, that the first does most harm to art, and the last to himself. If we must be *dilettanti*: if it is impossible for us, under the circumstances amidst which we live, to think clearly, to feel nobly, and to delineate firmly: if we cannot attain to the mastery of the great artists;—let us, at least, have so much respect for our art as to prefer it to ourselves. Let us not bewilder our successors; let us transmit to them the practice of poetry, with its boundaries and wholesome regulative laws, under which excellent works may again, perhaps, at some future time, be produced, not yet fallen into oblivion through our neglect, not yet condemned and cancelled by the influence of their eternal enemy, caprice.

DISCOURSES IN AMERICA

1885

Discourses in America. By Matthew Arnold. London. Macmillan and Co. 1885.

Numbers appeared in *The Nineteenth Century*, April 1884: *Literature and Science* (originally the Rede Lecture at Cambridge) was published in *The Nineteenth Century*, August 1882, and later revised for this volume: *Emerson* appeared in *Macmillan's Magazine*, May 1884.

Arnold twice visited America; on an extended lecture tour in 1883-4, and after his retirement from the Education Office for a short visit in 1886. The three essays which make up this volume were delivered as lectures during the first visit. Arnold said that of all his prose-writings this was the book by which he would most wish to be remembered.

A Chicago newspaper reporter gave his impression of Arnold's appearance as lecturer during the first tour: "He has harsh features, supercilious manners, parts his hair down the middle, wears a single eye-glass and ill-fitting clothes."

DISCOURSES IN AMERICA

Numbers
or, the Majority and the Remnant

THERE is a characteristic saying of Dr. Johnson: "Patriotism is the last refuge of a scoundrel." The saying is cynical, many will even call it brutal; yet it has in it something of plain, robust sense and truth. We do often see men passing themselves off as patriots, who are in truth scoundrels; we meet with talk and proceedings laying claim to patriotism, which are these gentlemen's last refuge. We may all of us agree in praying to be delivered from patriots and patriotism of this sort. Short of such, there is undoubtedly, sheltering itself under the fine name of patriotism, a good deal of self-flattery and self-delusion which is mischievous. "Things are what they are, and the consequences of them will be what they will be; why, then, should we desire to be deceived?" In that uncompromising sentence of Bishop Butler's is surely the right and salutary maxim for both individuals and nations.

Yet there is an honourable patriotism which we should satisfy if we can, and should seek to have on our side. At home I have said so much of the characters of our society and the prospects of our civilisation, that I can hardly escape the like topic elsewhere. Speaking in America, I cannot well avoid saying something about the prospects of society in the United States. It is a topic where one is apt to touch people's patriotic feelings. No one will accuse me of having flattered the patriotism of that great country of English people on the other side of the Atlantic, amongst whom I was born. Here, so many miles from home, I begin to reflect with tender contrition, that perhaps I have not,—I will not say flattered the patriotism of my own countrymen enough, but regarded it enough. Perhaps that is one reason why I have produced so very little effect upon them. It was a fault of youth and inexperience. But it would be unpardonable to come in advanced life and repeat the same error here. You will not expect impossibilities of me. You will not expect me to say that things are not what, in my judgment, they are, and that the consequences of them will not be what they will be. I should make nothing of it; I should be a too palpable failure. But I confess that I should be glad if in what I say here I could engage American patriotism on my side, instead of rousing it against me. And it so happens that the paramount thoughts which your great country raises in my mind are really and truly of a kind to please, I think, any true American patriot, rather than to offend him.

The vast scale of things here, the extent of your country, your numbers, the rapidity of your increase, strike the imagination, and are a common topic for admiring remark. Our great orator, Mr. Bright, is never weary of telling us how many acres of land you have at your disposal, how many bushels of grain you produce, how many millions you are, how many more millions you will be presently, and what a capital thing this is for you. Now, though I do not always agree with Mr. Bright, I find myself agreeing with him here. I think your numbers afford a very real and important ground for satisfaction.

Not that your great numbers, or indeed great numbers of men anywhere, are likely to be all good, or even to have the majority good. "The majority are bad," said one of the wise men of Greece; but he was a pagan. Much to the same effect, however, is the famous sentence of the New Testament: "Many are called, few chosen." This appears a hard saying; frequent are the endeavours to elude it, to attenuate its severity. But turn it how you will, manipulate it as you will, the few, as Cardinal Newman well says, can never mean the many. Perhaps you will say that the majority *is*, sometimes, good; that its impulses are good generally, and its action is good occasionally. Yes, but it lacks principle, it lacks persistence; if to-day its good impulses prevail, they succumb to-morrow; sometimes it goes right, but it is very apt to go wrong. Even a popular orator, or a popular journalist, will hardly say that the multitude may be trusted to have its judgment generally just, and its action generally virtuous. It may be better, it is better, that the body of the people, with all its faults, should act for itself, and control its own affairs, than that it should be set aside as ignorant and incapable, and have its affairs managed for it by a so-called superior class, possessing property and intelligence. Property and intelligence cannot be trusted to show a sound majority themselves; the exercise of power by the people tends to educate the people. But still, the world being what it is, we must surely expect the aims and doings of the majority of men to be at present very faulty, and this in a numerous community no less than in a small one. So much we must certainly, I think, concede to the sages and to the saints.

Sages and saints are apt to be severe, it is true; apt to take a gloomy view of the society in which they live, and to prognosticate evil to it. But then it must be added that their prognostications are very apt to turn out right. Plato's account of the most gifted and brilliant community of the ancient world, of that Athens of his to which we all owe so much, is despondent enough. "There is but a very small remnant," he says, "of honest followers of wisdom, and they who are of these few, and who have tasted how sweet and blessed a possession is wisdom, and who can fully see, moreover, the madness of the multitude, and that there is no one, we may say, whose action in public matters is sound, and no ally for whosoever would help the just, what," asks Plato, "are they to do? They may be compared," says Plato, "to a man who has fallen among wild beasts; he will not be one of them, but he is too unaided to make head against them; and before he can do any good to society or his friends, he will be overwhelmed and perish uselessly. When he considers this, he will resolve to keep still, and to mind his own business; as it were standing aside under a wall in a storm of dust and hurricane of driving wind; and he will endure to behold the rest filled with iniquity, if only he himself may live his life clear of injustice and of impiety, and depart, when his time comes, in mild and gracious mood, with fair hope."

Plato's picture here of democratic Athens is certainly gloomy enough. We may be sure the mass of his contemporaries would have pronounced it to be monstrously overcharged. We ourselves, if we had been living then, should most of us have by no means seen things as Plato saw them. No, if we had seen Athens even nearer its end than when Plato wrote the strong words which I have been quoting, Athens in the very last days of Plato's life, we should most of us probably have considered that things were not going badly with Athens. There is a long sixteen years' administration,—the administration of Eubulus,—which fills the last years of Plato's life, and the middle years of the fourth century before Christ. A temperate German historian thus describes Athens during this ministry of Eubulus: "The grandeur and loftiness of Attic democracy had vanished, while all the pernicious germs contained in it were fully developed. A life of comfort and a craving for amusement were encouraged in every way, and the interest of the citizens was withdrawn from serious things. Conversation became more and more superficial and frivolous. Famous courtesans formed the chief topic of talk; the new inventions of Thearion, the leading pastry-cook in Athens, were hailed with loud applause; and the witty sayings which had been uttered in gay circles were repeated about town as matters of prime importance."

No doubt, if we had been living then to witness this, we should from time to time have shaken our heads gravely, and said how sad it all was. But most of us would not, I think, have been very seriously disquieted by it. On the other hand, we should have found many things in the Athens of Eubulus to gratify us. "The democrats," says the same historian whom I have just quoted, "saw in Eubulus one of their own set at the head of affairs;" and I suppose no good democrat would see that without pleasure. Moreover, Eubulus was of popular character. In one respect he seems to have resembled your own "heathen Chinee;" he had "guileless ways," says our historian, "in which the citizens took pleasure." He was also a good speaker, a thorough man of business; and, above all, he was very skilful in matters of finance. His administration was both popular and prosperous. We should certainly have said, most of us, if we had encountered somebody announcing his resolve to stand aside under a wall during such an administration, that he was a goose for his pains; and if he had called it "a falling among wild beasts" to have to live with his fellow-citizens who had confidence in Eubulus, their country, and themselves, we should have esteemed him very impertinent.

Yes;—and yet at the close of that administration of Eubulus came the collapse, and the end of Athens as an independent State. And it was to the fault of Athens herself that the collapse was owing. Plato was right after all; the majority were bad, and the remnant were impotent.

So fared it with that famous Athenian State, with the brilliant people of art and intellect. Now let us turn to the people of religion. We have heard Plato speaking of the very small remnant which honestly sought wisdom. *The remnant!*—it is the word of the Hebrew prophets also, and especially is it the word of the greatest of them all, Isaiah. Not used with the despondency of Plato, used with far other power informing it, and with a far other future awaiting it, filled with fire, filled with hope, filled with faith, filled with joy, this term itself, *the remnant*, is yet Isaiah's term as well as Plato's. The texts are familiar to all Christendom. "Though thy people Israel be as the sand of the sea, only a remnant of them shall return." Even this remnant, a tenth of the whole, if so it may be, shall have to come back into the purging fire, and be again cleared and further reduced there. But nevertheless, "as a terebinth tree, and as an oak, whose substance is in them, though they be cut down, so the stock of that burned tenth shall be a holy seed."

Yes, the small remnant should be a holy seed; but the great majority, as in democratic Athens, so in the kingdoms of the Hebrew nation, were unsound, and their State was doomed. This was Isaiah's point. The actual commonwealth of the "drunkards" and the "blind," as he calls them, in Israel and Judah, of the dissolute grandees and gross and foolish common people, of the great majority, must perish; its perishing was the necessary stage towards a happier future. And Isaiah was right, as Plato was right. No doubt to most of us, if we had been there to see it, the kingdom of Ephraim or of Judah, the society of Samaria and Jerusalem, would have seemed to contain a great deal else besides dissolute grandees and foolish common people. No doubt we should have thought parts of their policy serious, and some of their alliances promising. No doubt, when we read the Hebrew prophets now, with the larger and more patient temper of a different race and an augmented experience, we often feel the blame and invective to be too absolute. Nevertheless, as to his grand point, Isaiah, I say, was right. The majority in the Jewish State, whatever they might think or say, whatever their guides and flatterers might think or say, the majority were unsound, and their unsoundness must be their ruin.

Isaiah, however, does not make his remnant confine itself, like Plato's, to standing aside under a wall during this life and then departing in mild temper and good hope when the time for departure comes; Isaiah's remnant saves the State. Undoubtedly he means to represent it as doing so. Undoubtedly he imagines his Prince of the house of David who is to be born within a year's time, his royal and victorious Immanuel, he imagines him witnessing as a child the chastisement of Ephraim and the extirpation of the bad majority there; then witnessing as a youth the chastisement of Judah and the extirpation of the bad majority there also; but finally, in mature life, reigning over a State renewed, preserved, and enlarged, a greater and happier kingdom of the chosen people.

Undoubtedly Isaiah conceives his remnant in this wise; undoubtedly he imagined for it a part which, in strict truth, it did not play, and could not play. So manifest was the non-fulfilment of his prophecy, taken strictly, that ardent souls feeding upon his words had to wrest them from their natural meaning, and to say that Isaiah directly meant something which he did not directly mean. Isaiah, like Plato, with inspired insight foresaw that the world before his eyes, the world of actual life, the State and city of the unsound majority, could not stand. Unlike Plato, Isaiah announced with faith and joy a leader and a remnant certain to supersede them. But he put the leader's coming, and he put the success of the leader's and the remnant's work, far, far too soon; and his conception, in this respect, is fantastic. Plato betook himself for the bringing in of righteousness to a visionary republic in the clouds; Isaiah,—and it is the immortal glory of him and of his race to have done so,—brought it in upon earth. But Immanuel and his reign, for the eighth century before Christ, were fantastic. For the kingdom of Judah they were fantastic. Immanuel and the remnant could not come to reign under the conditions there and then offered to them; the thing was impossible.

The reason of the impossibility is quite simple. The scale of things, in petty States like Judah and Athens, is too small; the numbers are too scanty. Admit that for the world, as we hitherto know it, what the philosophers and prophets say is true: that the majority are unsound. Even in communities with exceptional gifts, even in the Jewish State, the Athenian State, the majority are unsound. But there is "the remnant." Now the important thing, as regards States such as Judah and Athens, is not that the remnant bears but a small proportion to the majority; the remnant always bears a small proportion to the majority. The grave thing for States like Judah and Athens is, that the remnant must in positive bulk be so small, and therefore so powerless for reform. To be a voice outside the State, speaking to mankind or to the future, perhaps shaking the actual State to pieces in doing so, one man will suffice. But to reform the State in order to save it, to preserve it by changing it, a body of workers is needed as well as a leader;—a considerable body of workers, placed at many points, and operating in many directions. This considerable body of workers for good is what is wanting in petty States such as were Athens and Judah. It is said that the Athenian State had in all but 350,000 inhabitants. It is calculated that the population of the kingdom of Judah did not exceed a million and a quarter. The scale of things, I say, is here too small, the numbers are too scanty, to give us a remnant capable of saving and perpetuating the community. The remnant, in these cases, may influence the world and the future, may transcend the State and survive it; but it cannot possibly transform the State and perpetuate the State: for such a work it is numerically too feeble.

Plato saw the impossibility. Isaiah refused to accept it, but facts were too strong for him. The Jewish State could not be renewed and saved, and he was wrong in thinking that it could. And therefore I call his grand point this other, where he was altogether right: that the actual world of the unsound majority, though it fancied itself solid, and though most men might call it solid, could not stand. Let us read him again and again, until we fix in our minds this true conviction of his, to edify us whenever we see such a world existing: his indestructible conviction that such a world, with its prosperities, idolatries, oppression, luxury, pleasures, drunkards, careless women, governing classes, systems of policy, strong alliances, shall come to nought and pass away; that nothing can save it. Let us do homage, also, to his indestructible conviction that States are saved by their righteous remnant, however clearly we may at the same time recognise that his own building on this conviction was premature.

That, however, matters to us little. For how different is the scale of things in the modern States to which we belong, how far greater are the numbers! It is impossible to over-rate the importance of the new element introduced into our calculations by increasing the size of the remnant. And in our great modern States, where the scale of things is so large, it does seem as if the remnant might be so increased as to become an actual power, even though the majority be unsound. Then the lover of wisdom may come out from under his wall, the lover of goodness will not be alone among the wild beasts. To enable the remnant to succeed, a large strengthening of its numbers is everything.

Here is good hope for us, not only, as for Plato's recluse, in departing this life, but while we live and work in it. Only, before we dwell too much on this hope, it is advisable to make sure that we have earned the right to entertain it. We have earned the right to entertain it, only when we are at one with the philosophers and prophets in their conviction respecting the world which now is, the world of the unsound majority; when we feel what they mean, and when we go thoroughly along with them in it. Most of us, as I have said already, would by no means have been with them when they were here in life, and most of us are not really with them now. What is saving? Our institutions, says an American; the British Constitution, says an Englishman; the civilising mission of France, says a Frenchman. But Plato and the sages, when they are asked what is saving, answer: "To love righteousness, and to be convinced of the unprofitableness of iniquity." And Isaiah and the prophets, when they are asked the same question, answer to just the same effect: that what is saving is to "order one's conversation right"; to "cease to do evil"; to "delight in the law of the Eternal"; and to "make one's study in it all day long."

The worst of it is, that this loving of righteousness and this delighting in the law of the Eternal sound rather vague to us. Not that they are vague really; indeed, they are less vague than American institutions, or the British Constitution, or the civilising mission of France. But the phrases sound vague because of the quantity of matters they cover. The thing is to have a brief but adequate enumeration of these matters. The New Testament tells us how righteousness is composed. In England and America we have been brought up in familiarity with the New

Testament. And so, before Mr. Bradlaugh[1] on our side of the water, and the Congress of American Freethinkers on yours, banish it from our education and memory, let us take from the New Testament a text showing what it is that both Plato and the prophets mean when they tell us that we ought to love righteousness and to make our study in the law of the Eternal, but that the unsound majority do nothing of the kind. A score of texts offer themselves in a moment. Here is one which will serve very well: "Whatsoever things are true, whatsoever things are elevated, whatsoever things are just, whatsoever things are pure, whatsoever things are amiable, whatsoever things are of good report; if there be any virtue, and if there be any praise; have these in your mind, let your thoughts run upon these."[2] That is what both Plato and the prophets mean by loving righteousness, and making one's study in the law of the Eternal.

Now the matters just enumerated do not come much into the heads of most of us, I suppose, when we are thinking of politics. But the philosophers and prophets maintain that these matters, and not those of which the heads of politicians are full, do really govern politics and save or destroy States. They save or destroy them by a silent, inexorable fatality; while the politicians are making believe, plausibly and noisily, with their American institutions, British Constitution, and civilising mission of France. And because these matters are what do really govern politics and save or destroy States, Socrates maintained that in his time he and a few philosophers, who alone kept insisting on the good of righteousness and the unprofitableness of iniquity, were the only real politicians then living.

I say, if we are to derive comfort from the doctrine of *the remnant* (and there is great comfort to be derived from it), we must also hold fast to the austere but true doctrine as to what really governs politics, overrides with an inexorable fatality the combinations of the so-called politicians, and saves or destroys States. Having in mind things true, things elevated, things just, things pure, things amiable, things of good report; having these in mind, studying and loving these, is what saves States.

There is nothing like positive instances to illustrate general propositions of this kind, and to make them believed. I hesitate to take an instance from America. Possibly there are some people who think that already, on a former occasion, I have said enough

---

[1] [Charles Bradlaugh (1833–1891), politician and advocate of free-thought. On election to Parliament in 1880 he refused to swear on the Bible asserting his right to affirm, which was refused: he was ultimately allowed to take his seat in 1886. He supported Mrs. Annie Besant's work in liberal causes.]

[2] *Philippians*, iv, 8.

about America without duly seeing and knowing it. So I will take my instances from England, and from England's neighbour and old co-mate in history, France. The instance from England I will take first. I will take it from the grave topic of England's relations with Ireland. I am not going to reproach either England or Ireland. To reproach Ireland here would probably be indiscreet. As to England, anything I may have to say against my own countrymen I prefer to say at home; America is the last place where I should care to say it. However, I have no wish or intention now to reproach either the English or the Irish. But I want to show you from England's relations with Ireland how right the philosophers and prophets are. Every one knows that there has been conquest and confiscation in Ireland. So there has elsewhere. Every one knows that the conquest and the confiscation have been attended with cupidity, oppression, and ill-usage. So they have elsewhere. "Whatsoever things are just" are not exactly the study, so far as I know, of conquerors and confiscators anywhere; certainly they were not the study of the English conquerors of Ireland. A failure in justice is a source of danger to States. But it may be made up for and got over; it has been made up for and got over in many communities. England's confiscations in Ireland are a thing of the past; the penal laws against Catholics are a thing of the past; much has been done to make up for the old failure in justice; Englishmen generally think that it has been pretty well made up for, and that Irishmen ought to think so too. And politicians invent Land Acts for curing the last results of the old failure in justice, for insuring the contentment of the Irish with us, and for consolidating the Union: and are surprised and plaintive if it is not consolidated. But now see how much more serious people are the philosophers and prophets than the politicians. *Whatsoever things are amiable!*—the failure in amiability, too, is a source of danger and insecurity to States, as well as the failure in justice. And we English are not amiable, or at any rate, what in this case comes to the same thing, do not appear so. The politicians never thought of that! Quite outside their combinations lies this hindrance, tending to make their most elaborate combinations ineffectual. Thus the joint operation of two moral causes together,—the sort of causes which politicians do not seriously regard,—tells against the designs of the politicians with what seems to be an almost inexorable fatality. If there were not the failure in amiability, perhaps the original failure in justice might by this time have been got over; if there had not been the failure in justice, perhaps the failure in amiability might not have mattered much. The two failures together create a difficulty almost insurmountable. Public men in

England keep saying that it will be got over. I hope that it will be got over, and that the union between England and Ireland may become as solid as that between England and Scotland. But it will not become solid by means of the contrivances of the mere politician, or without the intervention of moral causes of concord to heal the mischief wrought by moral causes of division. Everything, in this case, depends upon the "remnant," its numbers, and its powers of action.

My second instance is even more important. It is so important, and its reach is so wide, that I must go into it with some little fulness. The instance is taken from France. To France I have always felt myself powerfully drawn. People in England often accuse me of liking France and things French far too well. At all events I have paid special regard to them, and am always glad to confess how much I owe to them. M. Sainte-Beuve wrote to me in the last years of his life: "You have passed through our life and literature by a deep inner line, which confers initiation, and which you will never lose." *Vous avez traversé notre vie et notre littérature par une ligne intérieure, profonde, qui fait les initiés, et que vous ne perdrez jamais.* I wish I could think that this friendly testimony of that accomplished and charming man, one of my chief benefactors, were fully deserved. But I have pride and pleasure in quoting it; and I quote it to bear me out in saying, that whatever opinion I may express about France, I have at least been a not inattentive observer of that great country, and anything but a hostile one.

The question was once asked by the town clerk of Ephesus: "What man is there that knoweth not how that the city of the Ephesians is a worshipper of the great goddess Diana?" Now really, when one looks at the popular literature of the French at this moment,—their popular novels, popular stage-plays, popular newspapers,—and at the life of which this literature of theirs is the index, one is tempted to make a goddess out of a word of their own, and then, like the town clerk of Ephesus, to ask: "What man is there that knoweth not how that the city of the French is a worshipper of the great goddess Lubricity?" Or rather, as Greek is the classic and euphonious language for names of gods and goddesses, let us take her name from the Greek Testament, and call her the goddess Aselgeia. That goddess has always been a sufficient power amongst mankind, and her worship was generally supposed to need restraining rather than encouraging. But here is now a whole popular literature, nay, and art too, in France at her service! stimulations and suggestions by her and to her meet one in it at every turn. She is becoming the great recognised power there; never was anything like it. M. Renan himself seems half inclined to apologise for not having paid her more attention. "Nature cares nothing for chastity," says he; *Les frivoles ont peut-être raison;* "The gay people are perhaps in the right." Men even of this force salute her; but the allegiance now paid to her, in France, by the popular novel, the popular newspaper, the popular play, is, one may say, boundless.

I have no wish at all to preach to the French; no intention whatever, in what I now say, to upbraid or wound them. I simply lay my finger on a fact in their present condition; a fact insufficiently noticed, as it seems to me, and yet extremely potent for mischief. It is well worth while to trace the manner of its growth and action.

The French have always had a leaning to the goddess of whom we speak, and have been willing enough to let the world know of their leaning, to pride themselves on their Gaulish salt, their gallantry, and so on. But things have come to their present head gradually. Catholicism was an obstacle; the serious element in the nation was another obstacle. But now just see the course which things have taken, and how they all, one may say, have worked together for this goddess. First, there was the original Gaul, the basis of the French nation; the Gaul, gay, sociable, quick of sentiment, quick of perception; apt, however, very apt, to be presumptuous and puffed up. Then came the Roman conquest, and from this we get a new personage, the Gallo-Latin; with the Gaulish qualities for a basis, but with Latin order, reason, lucidity, added, and also Latin sensuality. Finally, we have the Frankish conquest and the Frenchman. The Frenchman proper is the Gallo-Latin, with Frankish or Germanic qualities added and infused. No mixture could be better. The Germans have plenty of faults, but in this combination they seem not to have taken hold; the Germans seem to have given of their seriousness and honesty to the conquered Gallo-Latin, and not of their brutality. And mediæval France, which exhibits the combination and balance, under the influence then exercised by Catholicism, of Gaulish quickness and gaiety with Latin rationality and German seriousness, offers to our view the soundest and the most attractive stage, perhaps, in all French history.

But the balance could not be maintained; at any rate, it was not maintained. Mediæval Catholicism lost its virtue. The serious Germanic races made the Reformation, feeling that without it there was no safety and continuance for those moral ideas which they loved and which were the ground of their being. France did not go with the Reformation; the Germanic qualities in her were not strong enough to make her go with it. "France did not want a reformation which was a moral one," is Michelet's account of the matter: *La France ne voulait pas de réforme morale.* Let us put the case more favourably for her, and say that perhaps, with her quick perception, France caught sense, from the very outset, of that intellectual unsoundness and incompleteness in the Reformation, which is now so visible. But, at any rate, the Reformation did not carry France with it; and the Germanic side in the Frenchman, his Germanic qualities, thus received a check. They subsisted, however, in good force still; the new knowledge and new ideas, brought by the revival of letters, gave an animating stimulus; and in the seventeenth century the Gaulish gaiety and quickness of France, the Latin rationality, and the still subsisting German seriousness, all combining under the puissant breath of the Renascence, produced a literature, the strongest, the most substantial and the most serious which the French have ever succeeded in producing, and which has, indeed, consummate and splendid excellences.

Still, the Germanic side in the Frenchman had received a check, and in the next century this side became quite attenuated. The Germanic steadiness and seriousness gave way more and more; the Gaulish salt, the Gaulish gaiety, quickness, sentiment, and sociability, the Latin rationality, prevailed more and more, and had the field nearly to themselves. They produced a brilliant and most efficacious literature,—the French literature of the eighteenth century. The goddess Aselgeia had her part in it; it was a literature to be praised with reserves; it was, above all, a revolutionary literature. But European institutions were then in such a superannuated condition, straightforward and just perception, free thought and rationality, were at such a discount, that the brilliant French literature in which these qualities predominated, and which by their predominance was made revolutionary, had in the eighteenth century a great mission to fulfil, and fulfilled it victoriously.

The mission is fulfilled, but meanwhile the Germanic quality in the Frenchman seems pretty nearly to have died out, and the Gallo-Latin in him has quite got the upper hand. Of course there are individuals and groups who are to be excepted; I will allow any number of exceptions you please; and in the mass of the French people, which works and is silent, there may be treasures of resource. But taking the Frenchman who is commonly in view—the usual type of speaking, doing, vocal, visible Frenchman—we may say, and he will probably be not at all displeased at our saying, that the German in him has nearly died out, and the Gallo-Latin has quite got the upper hand. For us, however, this means that the chief source of seriousness and of moral ideas is failing and drying up in him, and that what remains are the sources of Gaulish salt, and quickness, and sentiment, and sociability, and sensuality, and rationality. And, of course, the play and working of these qualities is altered by their being no longer in combination with a dose of German seriousness, but left to work by themselves. Left to work by themselves, they give us what we call the *homme sensuel moyen*, the average sensual man. The highest art, the art which by its height, depth, and gravity possesses religiousness,—such as the Greeks had, the art of Pindar and Phidias; such as the Italians had, the art of Dante and Michael Angelo,—this art, with the training which it gives and the standard which it sets up, the French have never had. On the other hand, they had a dose of German seriousness, a Germanic bent for ideas of moral duty, which neither the Greeks had, nor the Italians. But if this dies out, what is left is the *homme sensuel moyen*. This average sensual man has his very advantageous qualities. He has his gaiety, quickness, sentiment, sociability, rationality. He has his horror of sour strictness, false restraint, hypocrisy, obscurantism, cretinism, and the rest of it. And this is very well; but on the serious, moral side he is almost ludicrously insufficient. Fine sentiments about his dignity and his honour and his heart, about the dignity and the honour and the heart of France, and his adoration of her, do duty for him here; grandiose phrases about the spectacle offered in France and in the French Republic of the ideal for our race, of the *épanouissement de l'élite de l'humanité*, "the coming into blow of the choice flower of humanity." In M. Victor Hugo we have (his worshippers must forgive me for saying so) the average sensual man impassioned and grandiloquent; in M. Zola we have the average sensual man going near the ground. "Happy the son," cries M. Victor Hugo, "of whom one can say, 'He has consoled his mother!' Happy the poet of whom one can say, 'He has consoled his country!' " The French themselves, even when they are severest, call this kind of thing by only the mild name of emphasis, "*emphase*,"—other people call it fustian. And a surly Johnson will growl out in answer, at one time, that "Patriotism is the last refuge of a scoundrel"; at another time, that fine sentiments about *ma mère* are the last refuge of a scoundrel. But what they really are is the creed which in France the average sensual man rehearses, to do duty for serious moral ideas. And, as the result, we have a popular literature and a popular art serving, as has been already said, the goddess Aselgeia.

Such an art and literature easily make their way everywhere. In England and America the French literature of the seventeenth century is peculiarly fitted to do great good, and nothing but good; it can hardly be too much studied by us. And it is studied by us very little. The French literature of the eighteenth century, also, has qualities to do us much good, and we are not likely to take harm from its other qualities; we may study it to our great profit and advantage. And it is studied by us very little. The higher French literature of the present day has more knowledge and a wider range than its great predecessors, but less soundness and perfection, and it exerts much less influence than they did. Action and influence are now with the lower literature of France, with the popular literature in the service of the goddess Aselgeia. And this popular modern French literature, and the art which corresponds to it, bid fair to make their way in England and America far better than their predecessors. They appeal to instincts so universal and accessible; they appeal, people are beginning boldly to say, to Nature herself. Few things have lately struck me more than M. Renan's dictum, which I have already quoted, about what used to be called the virtue of chastity. The dictum occurs in his very interesting autobiography, published but the other day. M. Renan, whose genius I unfeignedly admire, is, I need hardly say, a man of the most perfect propriety of life; he has told us so himself. He was brought up for a priest, and he thinks it would not have been in good taste for him to become a free liver. But this abstinence is a mere matter of personal delicacy, a display of good and correct taste on his own part in his own very special circumstances. "Nature," he cries, "cares nothing about chastity." What a slap in the face to the sticklers for "Whatsoever things are pure"!

I have had to take a long sweep to arrive at the point which I wished to reach. If we are to enjoy the benefit, I said, of the comfortable doctrine of the remnant, we must be capable of receiving also, and of holding fast, the hard doctrine of the unsoundness of the majority, and of the certainty that the unsoundness of the majority, if it is not withstood and remedied, must be their ruin. And therefore, even though a gifted man like M. Renan may be so carried away by the tide of opinion in France where he lives, as to say that Nature cares nothing about chastity, and to see with amused indulgence the worship of the great goddess Lubricity, let us stand fast, and say that her worship is against nature, human nature, and that it is ruin. For this is the test of its being against human nature, that for human societies it is ruin. And the test is one from which there is no escape, as from the old tests in such matters there may be. For if you allege that it is the will of God that we should be pure, the sceptical Gallo-Latins will tell you that they do not know any such person. And in like manner, if it is said that those who serve the goddess Aselgeia shall not inherit the kingdom of God, the Gallo-Latin may tell you that he does not believe in any such place. But that the sure tendency and upshot of things establishes that the service of the goddess Aselgeia is ruin, that her followers are marred and stunted by it and disqualified for the ideal society of the future, is an infallible test to employ.

The saints admonish us to let our thoughts run upon whatsoever things are pure, if we would inherit the kingdom of God; and the divine Plato tells us that we have within us a many-headed beast and a man, and that by dissoluteness we feed and strengthen the beast in us, and starve the man; and finally, following the divine Plato among the sages at a humble distance, comes the prosaic and unfashionable Paley, and says in his precise way that "this vice has a tendency, which other species of vice have not so directly, to unsettle and weaken the powers of the understanding; as well as, I think, in a greater degree than other vices, to render the heart thoroughly corrupt." True; and once admitted and fostered, it eats like a canker, and with difficulty can ever be brought to let go its hold again, but for ever tightens it. Hardness and insolence come in its train; an insolence which grows until it ends by exasperating and alienating everybody; a hardness which grows until the man can at last scarcely take pleasure in anything, outside the service of his goddess, except cupidity and greed, and cannot be touched with emotion by any language except fustian. Such are the fruits of the worship of the great goddess Aselgeia.

So, instead of saying that Nature cares nothing about chastity, let us say that human nature, *our* nature, cares about it a great deal. Let us say that, by her present popular literature, France gives proof that she is suffering from a dangerous and perhaps fatal disease; and that it is not clericalism which is the real enemy to the French so much as their goddess; and if they can none of them see this themselves, it is only a sign of how far the disease has gone, and the case is so much the worse. The case is so much the worse; and for men in such case to be so vehemently busy about clerical and dynastic intrigues at home, and about alliances and colonial acquisitions and purifications of the flag abroad, might well make one borrow of the prophets and exclaim, "Surely ye are perverse"! perverse to neglect your really pressing matters for those secondary ones. And when the ingenious and inexhaustible M. Blowitz,[1] of our great London *Times*, who sees everybody and knows everything, when he

---

[1] [Henri G. S. A. de Blowitz (1825–1903), journalist of international reputation; Paris representative of *The Times*. Retired in 1901: his *Memoirs* published 1903.]

expounds the springs of politics and the causes of the fall and success of ministries, and the combinations which have not been tried but should be, and takes upon him the mystery of things in the way with which we are so familiar,—to this wise man himself one is often tempted, again, to say with the prophets: "Yet the Eternal also is wise, and will not call back his words." M. Blowitz is not the only wise one; the Eternal has his wisdom also, and somehow or other it is always the Eternal's wisdom which at last carries the day. The Eternal has attached to certain moral causes the safety or the ruin of States, and the present popular literature of France is a sign that she has a most dangerous moral disease.

Now if the disease goes on and increases, then, whatever sagacious advice M. Blowitz may give, and whatever political combinations may be tried, and whether France gets colonies or not and whether she allies herself with this nation or with that, things will only go from bad to worse with her; she will more and more lose her powers of soul and spirit, her intellectual productiveness, her skill in counsel, her might for war, her formidableness as a foe, her value as an ally, and the life of that famous State will be more and more impaired, until it perish. And this is that hard but true doctrine of the sages and prophets, of the inexorable fatality of operation, in moral failure of the unsound majority, to impair and destroy States. But we will not talk or think of destruction for a State with such gifts and graces as France, and which has had such a place in history, and to which we, many of us, owe so much delight and so much good. And yet if France had no greater numbers than the Athens of Plato or the Judah of Isaiah, I do not see how she could well escape out of the throttling arms of her goddess and recover. She must recover through a powerful and profound renewal, a great inward change, brought about by "the remnant" amongst her people; and, for this, a remnant small in numbers would not suffice. But in a France of thirty-five millions, who shall set bounds to the numbers of the remnant, or to its effectualness and power of victory?

In these United States (for I come round to the United States at last) you are fifty millions and more. I suppose that, as in England, as in France, as everywhere, so likewise here, the majority of people doubt very much whether the majority is unsound; or, rather, they have no doubt at all about the matter, they are sure that it is not unsound. But let us consent to-night to remain to the end in the ideas of the sages and prophets whom we have been following all along; and let us suppose that in the present actual stage of the world, as in all the stages through which the world has passed hitherto, the majority is and must be in general unsound everywhere,—even in the United States, even here in New York itself. Where is the failure? I have already, in the past, speculated in the abstract about you, perhaps, too much. But I suppose that in a democratic community like this, with its newness, its magnitude, its strength, its life of business, its sheer freedom and equality, the danger is in the absence of the discipline of respect; in hardness and materialism, exaggeration and boastfulness; in a false smartness, a false audacity, a want of soul and delicacy. "Whatsoever things are *elevated*,"—whatsoever things are nobly serious, have true elevation,[1]—that perhaps, in our catalogue of maxims which are to possess the mind, is the maxim which points to where the failure of the unsound majority, in a great democracy like yours, will probably lie. At any rate let us for the moment agree to suppose so. And the philosophers and the prophets, whom I at any rate am disposed to believe, and who say that moral causes govern the standing and the falling of States, will tell us that the failure to mind whatsoever things are elevated must impair with an inexorable fatality the life of a nation, just as the failure to mind whatsoever things are just, or whatsoever things are amiable, or whatsoever things are pure, will impair it; and that if the failure to mind whatsoever things are elevated should be real in your American democracy, and should grow into a disease, and take firm hold on you, then the life of even these great United States must inevitably suffer and be impaired more and more, until it perish.

Then from this hard doctrine we will betake ourselves to the more comfortable doctrine of *the remnant*. "The remnant shall return;" shall "convert and be healed" itself first, and shall then recover the unsound majority. And you are fifty millions and growing apace. What a remnant yours may be, surely! A remnant of how great numbers, how mighty strength, how irresistible efficacy! Yet we must not go too fast, either, nor make too sure of our efficacious remnant. Mere multitude will not give us a saving remnant with certainty. The Assyrian Empire had multitude, the Roman Empire had multitude; yet neither the one nor the other could produce a sufficing remnant any more than Athens or Judah could produce it, and both Assyria and Rome perished like Athens and Judah.

But you are something more than a people of fifty millions. You are fifty millions mainly sprung, as we in England are mainly sprung, from that German stock which has faults indeed, —faults which have diminished the extent of its influence, diminished its power of attraction and the interest of its history, and which seems moreover just now, from all I can see and hear, to

[1] Ὅσα σεμνά.

x

be passing, through a not very happy moment, morally, in Germany proper. Yet of the German stock it is, I think, true, as my father said more than fifty years ago, that it has been a stock "of the most moral races of men that the world has yet seen, with the soundest laws, the least violent passions, the fairest domestic and civil virtues." You come, therefore, of about the best parentage which a modern nation can have. Then you have had, as we in England have also had, but more entirely than we and more exclusively, the Puritan discipline. Certainly I am not blind to the faults of that discipline. Certainly I do not wish it to remain in possession of the field for ever, or too long. But as a stage and a discipline, and as means for enabling that poor inattentive and immoral creature, man, to love and appropriate and make part of his being divine ideas, on which he could not otherwise have laid or kept hold, the discipline of Puritanism has been invaluable; and the more I read history, the more I see of mankind, the more I recognise its value. Well, then, you are not merely a multitude of fifty millions; you are fifty millions sprung from this excellent Germanic stock, having passed through this excellent Puritan discipline, and set in this enviable and unbounded country. Even supposing, therefore, that by the necessity of things your majority must in the present stage of the world probably be unsound, what a remnant, I say,—what an incomparable, all-transforming remnant,—you may fairly hope with your numbers, if things go happily, to have!

From *Literature and Science*

I AM going to ask whether the present movement for ousting letters from their old predominance in education, and for transferring the predominance in education to the natural sciences, whether this brisk and flourishing movement ought to prevail, and whether it is likely that in the end it really will prevail. An objection may be raised which I will anticipate. My own studies have been almost wholly in letters, and my visits to the field of the natural sciences have been very slight and inadequate, although those sciences have always strongly moved my curiosity. A man of letters, it will perhaps be said, is not competent to discuss the comparative merits of letters and natural science as means of education. To this objection I reply, first of all, that his incompetence, if he attempts the discussion but is really incompetent for it, will be abundantly visible; nobody will be taken in; he will have plenty of sharp observers and critics to save mankind from that danger. But the line I am going to follow is, as you will soon discover, so extremely simple, that perhaps it may be followed without failure even by one who for a more ambitious line of discussion would be quite incompetent.

Some of you may possibly remember a phrase of mine which has been the object of a good deal of comment; an observation to the effect that in our culture, the aim being *to know ourselves and the world*, we have, as the means to this end, *to know the best which has been thought and said in the world*. A man of science, who is also an excellent writer and the very prince of debaters, Professor Huxley, in a discourse at the opening of Sir Josiah Mason's college at Birmingham, laying hold of this phrase, expanded it by quoting some more words of mine, which are these: "The civilised world is to be regarded as now being, for intellectual and spiritual purposes, one great confederation, bound to a joint action and working to a common result; and whose members have for their proper outfit a knowledge of Greek, Roman, and Eastern antiquity, and of one another. Special local and temporary advantages being put out of account, that modern nation will in the intellectual and spiritual sphere make most progress, which most thoroughly carries out this programme."

Now on my phrase, thus enlarged, Professor Huxley remarks that when I speak of the above-mentioned knowledge as enabling us to know ourselves and the world, I assert *literature* to contain the materials which suffice for thus making us know ourselves and the world. But it is not by any means clear, says he, that after having learnt all which ancient and modern literatures have to tell us, we have laid a sufficiently broad and deep foundation for that criticism of life, that knowledge of ourselves and the world, which constitutes culture. On the contrary, Professor Huxley declares that he finds himself "wholly unable to admit that either nations or individuals will really advance, if their outfit draws nothing from the stores of physical science. An army without weapons of precision, and with no particular base of operations, might more hopefully enter upon a campaign on the Rhine, than a man, devoid of a knowledge of what physical science has done in the last century, upon a criticism of life."

This shows how needful it is for those who are to discuss any matter together, to have a common understanding as to the sense of the terms they employ,—how needful, and how difficult. What Professor Huxley says, implies just the reproach which is so often brought against the study of *belles lettres*, as they are called: that the study is an elegant one, but slight and ineffectual; a smattering of Greek and Latin and other ornamental things, of little use for any one whose object is to get at truth, and to be a practical man. So, too, M. Renan talks of the "superficial humanism" of a school-course which treats us as if we were all going to be poets, writers, preachers, orators, and he opposes this humanism to positive science, or the critical search after truth. And there is always a tendency in those who are remonstrating against the predominance of letters in education, to understand by letters *belles lettres*, and by *belles lettres* a superficial humanism, the opposite of science or true knowledge.

But when we talk of knowing Greek and Roman antiquity, for instance, which is the knowledge people have called the humanities, I for my part mean a knowledge which is something more than a superficial humanism, mainly decorative. "I call all teaching *scientific*," says Wolf, the critic of Homer, "which is systematically laid out and followed up to its original sources. For example: a knowledge of classical antiquity is scientific when the remains of classical antiquity are correctly studied in the original languages." There can be no doubt that Wolf is perfectly right; that all learning is scientific which is systematically laid out and followed up to its original sources, and that a genuine humanism is scientific.

When I speak of knowing Greek and Roman antiquity, therefore, as a help to knowing ourselves and the world, I mean more than a knowledge of so much vocabulary, so much grammar, so many portions of authors in the Greek and Latin languages. I mean knowing the Greeks and Romans, and their life and genius, and what they were and did in the world; what we get from them, and what is its value. That, at least, is the ideal; and when we talk of endeavouring to know Greek and Roman antiquity, as a help to knowing ourselves and the world, we mean endeavouring so to know them as to satisfy this ideal, however much we may still fall short of it.

The same also as to knowing our own and other modern nations, with the like aim of getting to understand ourselves and the world. To know the best that has been thought and said by the modern nations, is to know, says Professor Huxley, "only what modern *literatures* have to tell us; it is the criticism of life contained in modern literature." And yet "the distinctive character of our times," he urges, "lies in the vast and constantly increasing part which is played by natural knowledge." And how, therefore, can a man, devoid of knowledge of what physical science has done in the last century, enter hopefully upon a criticism of modern life?

Let us, I say, be agreed about the meaning of the terms we are using. I talk of knowing the best which has been thought and uttered in the world; Professor Huxley says this means knowing *literature*. Literature is a large word; it may mean everything written with letters or printed in a book. Euclid's *Elements* and Newton's *Principia* are thus literature. All knowledge that reaches us through books is literature. But by literature Professor Huxley means *belles lettres*. He means to make me say, that knowing the best which has been thought and said by the modern nations is knowing their *belles lettres* and no more. And this is no sufficient equipment, he argues, for a criticism of modern life. But as I do not mean, by knowing ancient Rome, knowing merely more or less of Latin *belles lettres*, and taking no account of Rome's military, and political, and legal, and administrative work in the world; and as, by knowing ancient Greece, I understand knowing her as the giver of Greek art, and the guide to a free and right use of reason and to scientific method, and the founder of our mathematics and physics and astronomy and biology,—I understand knowing her as all this, and not merely knowing certain Greek poems, and histories, and treatises, and speeches,—so as to the knowledge of modern nations also. By knowing modern nations, I mean not merely knowing their *belles lettres*, but knowing also what has been done by such men as Copernicus, Galileo, Newton, Darwin. "Our ancestors learned," say Professor Huxley, "that the earth is the centre of the visible universe, and that man is the cynosure of things terrestrial; and more especially was it inculcated that the course of nature had no fixed order, but that it could be, and constantly was, altered." But for us now, continues Professor Huxley, "the notions of the beginning and the end of the world entertained by our forefathers are no longer credible. It is very certain that the earth is not the chief body in the material universe, and that the world is not subordinated to man's use. It is even more certain that nature is the expression of a definite order, with which nothing interferes." "And yet," he cries, "the purely classical education advocated by the representatives of the humanists in our day gives no inkling of all this!"

In due place and time I will just touch upon that vexed question of classical education; but at present the question is as to what is meant by knowing the best which modern nations have thought and said. It is not knowing their *belles lettres* merely which is meant. To know Italian *belles lettres* is not to know Italy, and to know English *belles lettres* is not to know England. Into knowing Italy and England there comes a great deal more, Galileo and Newton, amongst it. The reproach of being a superficial humanism, a tincture of *belles lettres*, may attach rightly enough to some other disciplines; but to the particular discipline recommended when I proposed knowing the best that has been thought and said in the world, it does not apply. In that best I certainly include what in modern times has been thought and said by the great observers and knowers of nature.

There is, therefore, really no question between Professor Huxley and me as to whether knowing the great results of the modern scientific study of nature is not required as a part of our culture, as well as knowing the products of literature and art. But to follow the processes by which those results are reached, ought, say the friends of physical science, to be made the staple of education for the bulk of mankind. And here there does arise a question between those whom Professor Huxley calls with playful sarcasm "the Levites of culture," and those whom the poor humanist is sometimes apt to regard as its Nebuchadnezzars.

The great results of the scientific investigation of nature we are agreed upon knowing, but how much of our study are we bound to give to the processes by which those results are reached? The results have their visible bearing on human life. But all the processes, too, all the items of fact, by which those results are reached and established, are interesting. All knowledge is interesting to a wise man, and the knowledge of nature is interesting to all men. It is very interesting to know, that, from the albuminous white of the egg, the chick in the egg gets the materials for its flesh, bones, blood, and feathers; while, from the fatty yolk of the egg, it gets the heat and energy which enable it at length to break its shell and begin the world. It is less interesting, perhaps, but still it is interesting, to know that when a taper burns, the wax is converted into carbonic acid and water. Moreover, it is quite true that the habit of dealing with facts, which is given by the study of nature is, as the friends of physical science praise it for being, an excellent discipline. The appeal, in the study of nature, is constantly to observation and experiment; not only is it said that the thing is so, but we can be made to see that it is so. Not only does a man tell us that when a taper burns the wax is converted into carbonic acid and water, as a man may tell us, if he likes, that Charon is punting his ferry-boat on the river Styx, or that Victor Hugo is a sublime poet, or Mr. Gladstone the most admirable of statesmen; but we are made to see that the conversion into carbonic acid and water does actually happen. This reality of natural knowledge it is, which makes the friends of physical science contrast it, as a knowledge of things, with the humanist's knowledge, which is, say they, a knowledge of words. And hence Professor Huxley is moved to lay it down that, "for the purpose of attaining real culture, an exclusively scientific education is at least as effectual as an exclusively literary education." And a certain President of the Section for Mechanical Science in the British Association is, in Scripture phrase, "very bold," and declares that if a man, in his mental training, "has substituted literature and history for natural science, he has chosen the less useful alternative." But whether we go these lengths or not, we must all admit that in natural science the habit gained of dealing with facts is a most valuable discipline, and that every one should have some experience of it.

More than this, however, is demanded by the reformers. It is proposed to make the training in natural science the main part of education, for the great majority of mankind at any rate. And here, I confess, I part company with the friends of physical science, with whom up to this point I have been agreeing. In differing from them, however, I wish to proceed with the utmost caution and diffidence. The smallness of my own acquaintance with the disciplines of natural science is ever before my mind, and I am fearful of doing these disciplines an injustice. The ability and pugnacity of the partisans of natural science makes them formidable persons to contradict. The tone of tentative inquiry, which befits a being of dim faculties and bounded knowledge, is the tone I would wish to take and not to depart from. At present it seems to me, that those who are for giving to natural knowledge, as they call it, the chief place in the education of the majority of mankind, leave one important thing out of their account: the constitution of human nature. But I put this forward on the strength of some facts not at all recondite, very far from it; facts capable of being stated in the simplest possible fashion, and to which, if I so state them, the man of science will, I am sure, be willing to allow their due weight.

Deny the facts altogether, I think, he hardly can. He can hardly deny, that when we set ourselves to enumerate the powers which go to the building up of human life, and say that they are the power of conduct, the power of intellect and knowledge, the power of beauty, and the power of social life and manners,—he can hardly deny that this scheme, though drawn in rough and plain lines enough, and not pretending to scientific exactness, does yet give a fairly true representation of the matter. Human nature is built up by these powers; we have the need for them all. When we have rightly met and adjusted the claims of them all, we shall then be in a fair way for getting soberness and righteousness, with wisdom. This is evident enough, and the friends of physical science would admit it.

But perhaps they may not have sufficiently observed another thing: namely, that the several powers just mentioned are not isolated, but there is, in the generality of mankind, a perpetual tendency to relate them one to another in divers ways. With one such way of relating them I am particularly concerned now. Following our instinct for intellect and knowledge, we acquire pieces of knowledge; and presently, in the generality of men, there arises the desire to relate these pieces of knowledge to our sense for conduct, to our sense for beauty,—and there is weariness and dissatisfaction if the desire is baulked. Now in this desire lies, I think, the strength of that hold which letters have upon us.

All knowledge is, as I said just now, interesting; and even items of knowledge which from the nature of the case cannot well be related, but must stand isolated in our thoughts, have their interest. Even lists of exceptions have their interest. If we are studying Greek accents, it is interesting to know that *pais* and *pas*, and some other monosyllables of the same form of declension, do not take the circumflex upon the last syllable of the genitive plural, but vary, in this respect, from the common rule. If we are studying physiology, it is interesting to know that the pulmonary artery carries dark blood and the pulmonary vein carries bright blood, departing in this respect from the common rule for the division of labour between the veins and the arteries. But every one knows how we seek naturally to combine the pieces of our knowledge together, to bring them under general rules, to relate them to principles; and how unsatisfactory and tiresome it would be to go on for ever learning lists of exceptions, or accumulating items of fact which must stand isolated.

Well, that same need of relating our knowledge, which operates here within the sphere of our knowledge itself, we shall find operating, also, outside that sphere. We experience, as we go on learning and knowing,—the vast majority of us experience,—the need of relating what we have learnt and known to the sense which we have in us for conduct, to the sense which we have in us for beauty.

A certain Greek prophetess of Mantineia in Arcadia, Diotima by name, once explained to the philosopher Socrates that love, and impulse, and bent of all kinds, is, in fact, nothing else but the desire in men that good should for ever be present to them. This desire for good, Diotima assured Socrates, is our fundamental desire, of which fundamental desire every impulse in us is only some one particular form. And therefore this fundamental desire it is, I suppose,—this desire in men that good should be for ever present to them,—which acts in us when we feel the impulse for relating our knowledge to our sense for conduct and to our sense for beauty. At any rate, with men in general the instinct exists. Such is human nature. And the instinct, it will be admitted, is innocent, and human nature is preserved by our following the lead of its innocent instincts. Therefore, in seeking to gratify this instinct in question, we are following the instinct of self-preservation in humanity.

But, no doubt, some kinds of knowledge cannot be made to directly serve the instinct in question, cannot be directly related to the sense for beauty, to the sense for conduct. These are instrument-knowledges; they lead on to other knowledges, which can. A man who passes his life in instrument-knowledges is a specialist. They may be invaluable as instruments to something beyond, for those who have the gift thus to employ them; and they may be disciplines in themselves wherein it is useful for every one to have some schooling. But it is inconceivable that the generality of men should pass all their mental life with Greek accents or with formal logic. My friend Professor Sylvester,[1] who is one of the first mathematicians in the world, holds transcendental doctrines as to the virtue of mathematics, but those doctrines are not for common men. In the very Senate House and heart of our English Cambridge I once ventured, though not without an apology for my profaneness, to hazard the opinion that for the majority of mankind a little of mathematics, even, goes a long way. Of course this is quite consistent with their being of immense importance as an instrument to something else; but it is the few who have the aptitude for thus using them not the bulk of mankind.

The natural sciences do not, however, stand on the same footing with these instrument-knowledges. Experience shows us that the generality of men will find more interest in learning that, when a taper burns, the wax is converted into carbonic acid and water, or in learning the explanation of the phenomenon of dew, or in learning how the circulation of the blood is carried on, than they find in learning that the genitive plural of *pais* and *pas* does not take the circumflex on the termination. And one piece of natural knowledge is added to another, and others are added to that, and at last we come to propositions so interesting as Mr. Darwin's famous proposition that "our ancestor was a hairy quadruped furnished with a tail and pointed ears, probably arboreal in his habits." Or we come to propositions of such reach and magnitude as those which Professor Huxley delivers, when he says that the notions of our forefathers about the beginning

[1] [James Joseph Sylvester (1814–1897), mathematician: professor of natural philosophy at University College, London, and later Savilian professor of geometry at Oxford.]

and the end of the world were all wrong, and that nature is the expression of a definite order with which nothing interferes.

Interesting, indeed, these results of science are, important they are, and we should all of us be acquainted with them. But what I now wish you to mark is, that we are still, when they are propounded to us and we receive them, we are still in the sphere of intellect and knowledge. And for the generality of men there will be found, I say, to arise, when they have duly taken in the proposition that their ancestor was "a hairy quadruped furnished with a tail and pointed ears, probably arboreal in his habits," there will be found to arise an invincible desire to relate this proposition to the sense in us for conduct, and to the sense in us for beauty. But this the men of science will not do for us, and will hardly even profess to do. They will give us other pieces of knowledge, other facts, about other animals and their ancestors, or about plants, or about stones, or about stars; and they may finally bring us to those great "general conceptions of the universe which are forced upon us all," says Professor Huxley, "by the progress of physical science." But still it will be *knowledge* only which they give us; knowledge not put for us into relation with our sense for conduct, our sense for beauty, and touched with emotion by being so put; not thus put for us, and therefore, to the majority of mankind, after a certain while, unsatisfying, wearying.

Not to the born naturalist, I admit. But what do we mean by a born naturalist? We mean a man in whom the zeal for observing nature is so uncommonly strong and eminent, that it marks him off from the bulk of mankind. Such a man will pass his life happily in collecting natural knowledge and reasoning upon it, and will ask for nothing, or hardly anything, more. I have heard it said that the sagacious and admirable naturalist whom we lost not very long ago, Mr. Darwin, once owned to a friend that for his part he did not experience the necessity for two things which most men find so necessary to them,—religion and poetry; science and the domestic affections, he thought, were enough. To a born naturalist, I can well understand that this should seem so. So absorbing is his occupation with nature, so strong his love for his occupation, that he goes on acquiring natural knowledge and reasoning upon it, and has little time or inclination for thinking about getting it related to the desire in man for conduct, the desire in man for beauty. He relates it to them for himself as he goes along, so far as he feels the need; and he draws from the domestic affections all the additional solace necessary. But then Darwins are extremely rare. Another great and admirable master of natural knowledge, Faraday, was a Sandemanian. That is to say, he related his knowledge to his instinct for conduct and to his instinct for beauty, by the aid of that respectable Scottish sectary, Robert Sandeman.[1] And so strong, in general, is the demand of religion and poetry to have their share in a man, to associate themselves with his knowing, and to relieve and rejoice it, that, probably, for one man amongst us with the disposition to do as Darwin did in this respect, there are at least fifty with the disposition to do as Faraday.

Education lays hold upon us, in fact, by satisfying this demand. Professor Huxley holds up to scorn mediæval education, with its neglect of the knowledge of nature, its poverty even of literary studies, its formal logic devoted to " showing how and why that which the Church said was true must be true." But the great mediæval Universities were not brought into being, we may be sure, by the zeal for giving a jejune and contemptible education. Kings have been their nursing fathers, and queens have been their nursing mothers, but not for this. The mediæval Universities came into being, because the supposed knowledge, delivered by Scripture and the Church, so deeply engaged men's hearts, by so simply, easily, and powerfully relating itself to their desire for conduct, their desire for beauty. All other knowledge was dominated by this supposed knowledge and was subordinated to it, because of the surpassing strength of the hold which it gained upon the affections of men, by allying itself profoundly with their sense for conduct, their sense for beauty.

But now, says Professor Huxley, conceptions of the universe fatal to the notions held by our forefathers have been forced upon us by physical science. Grant to him that they are thus fatal, that the new conceptions must and will soon become current everywhere, and that every one will finally perceive them to be fatal to the beliefs of our forefathers. The need of humane letters, as they are truly called, because they serve the paramount desire in men that good should be for ever present to them,—the need of humane letters, to establish a relation between the new conceptions, and our instinct for beauty, our instinct for conduct, is only the more visible. The Middle Age could do without humane letters, as it could do without the study of nature, because its supposed knowledge was made to engage its emotions so powerfully. Grant that the supposed knowledge disappears, its power of being made to engage the emotions will of course

[1] [Robert Sandeman (1718–1771), founder of the strict Calvinistic sect which bears his name. He was associated with John Glas (1695–1773) another Scottish sectary, founder of the Glassite community. A few Sandemanians still exist and have a church at Highbury, London, and others in Scotland.]

disappear along with it,—but the emotions themselves, and their claim to be engaged and satisfied, will remain. Now if we find by experience that humane letters have an undeniable power of engaging the emotions, the importance of humane letters in a man's training becomes not less, but greater, in proportion to the success of modern science in extirpating what it calls "mediæval thinking."

Have humane letters, then, have poetry and eloquence, the power here attributed to them of engaging the emotions, and do they exercise it? And if they have it and exercise it, *how* do they exercise it, so as to exert an influence upon man's sense for conduct, his sense for beauty? Finally, even if they both can and do exert an influence upon the senses in question, how are they to relate to them the results,—the modern results,—of natural science? All these questions may be asked. First, have poetry and eloquence the power of calling out the emotions? The appeal is to experience. Experience shows that for the vast majority of men, for mankind in general, they have the power. Next do they exercise it? They do. But then, *how* do they exercise it so as to affect man's sense for conduct, his sense for beauty? And this is perhaps a case for applying the Preacher's words: "Though a man labour to seek it out, yet he shall not find it; yea, farther, though a wise man think to know it, yet shall he not be able to find it."[1] Why should it be one thing, in its effect upon the emotions, to say, "Patience is a virtue," and quite another thing, in its effect upon the emotions, to say with Homer,

τλητὸν γὰρ Μοῖραι θυμὸν θέσαν ἀνθρώποισιν—[2]

"for an enduring heart have the destinies appointed to the children of men?" Why should it be one thing, in its effect upon the emotions, to say with the philosopher Spinoza, *Felicitas in eo consistit quod homo suum esse conservare potest*—"Man's happiness consists in his being able to preserve his own essence," and quite another thing, in its effect upon the emotions, to say with the Gospel, "What is a man advantaged, if he gain the whole world, and lose himself, forfeit himself?" How does this difference of effect arise? I cannot tell, and I am not much concerned to know; the important thing is that it does arise, and that we can profit by it. But how, finally, are poetry and eloquence to exercise the power of relating the modern results of natural science to man's instinct for conduct, his instinct for beauty? And here again I answer that I do not know *how* they will exercise it, but that they can and will exercise it I am sure. I do not

---

[1] *Ecclesiastes*, viii. 17.   [2] *Iliad*, xxiv. 49.

mean that modern philosophical poets and modern philosophical moralists are to come and relate for us, in express terms, the results of modern scientific research to our instinct for conduct, our instinct for beauty. But I mean that we shall find, as a matter of experience, if we know the best that has been thought and uttered in the world, we shall find that the art and poetry and eloquence of men who lived, perhaps, long ago, who had the most limited natural knowledge, who had the most erroneous conceptions about many important matters, we shall find that this art, and poetry, and eloquence, have in fact not only the power of refreshing and delighting us, they have also the power, —such is the strength and worth, in essentials, of their authors' criticism of life,—they have a fortifying, and elevating, and quickening, and suggestive power, capable of wonderfully helping us to relate the results of modern science to our need for conduct, our need for beauty. Homer's conceptions of the physical universe were, I imagine, grotesque; but really, under the shock of hearing from modern science that "the world is not subordinated to man's use, and that man is not the cynosure of things terrestrial," I could, for my own part, desire no better comfort than Homer's line which I quoted just now,

τλητὸν γὰρ Μοῖραι θυμὸν θέσαν ἀνθρώποισιν—

"for an enduring heart have the destinies appointed to the children of men!"

And the more that men's minds are cleared, the more that the results of science are frankly accepted, the more that poetry and eloquence come to be received and studied as what in truth they really are,—the criticism of life by gifted men, alive and active with extraordinary power at an unusual number of points;—so much the more will the value of humane letters, and of art also, which is an utterance having a like kind of power with theirs, be felt and acknowledged, and their place in education be secured.

Let us therefore, all of us, avoid indeed as much as possible any invidious comparison between the merits of humane letters, as means of education, and the merits of the natural sciences. But when some President of a Section for Mechanical Science insists on making the comparison, and tells us that "he who in his training has substituted literature and history for natural science has chosen the less useful alternative," let us make answer to him that the student of humane letters only, will, at least, know also the great general conceptions brought in by modern physical science; for science, as Professor Huxley says, forces them upon us all. But the student of the natural sciences only, will, by our very hypothesis, know nothing of humane letters;

not to mention that in setting himself to be perpetually accumulating natural knowledge, he sets himself to do what only specialists have in general the gift for doing genially. And so he will probably be unsatisfied, or at any rate incomplete, and even more incomplete than the student of humane letters only.

I once mentioned in a school-report, how a young man in one of our English training colleges having to paraphrase the passage in *Macbeth* beginning,

> "Can'st thou not minister to a mind diseased?"

turned this line into, "Can you not wait upon the lunatic?" And I remarked what a curious state of things it would be, if every pupil of our national schools knew, let us say, that the moon is two thousand one hundred and sixty miles in diameter, and thought at the same time that a good paraphrase for

> "Can'st thou not minister to a mind diseased?"

was, "Can you not wait upon the lunatic?" If one is driven to choose, I think I would rather have a young person ignorant about the moon's diameter, but aware that "Can you not wait upon the lunatic" is bad, than a young person whose education had been such as to manage things the other way.

Or to go higher than the pupils of our national schools. I have in my mind's eye a member of our British Parliament who comes to travel here in America, who afterwards relates his travels, and who shows a really masterly knowledge of the geology of this great country and of its mining capabilities, but who ends by gravely suggesting that the United States should borrow a prince from our Royal Family, and should make him their king, and should create a House of Lords of great landed proprietors after the pattern of ours; and then America, he thinks, would have her future happily and perfectly secured. Surely, in this case, the President of the Section for Mechanical Science would himself hardly say that our member of Parliament, by concentrating himself upon geology and mineralogy, and so on, and not attending to literature and history, had "chosen the more useful alternative."

If then there is to be separation and option between humane letters on the one hand, and the natural sciences on the other, the great majority of mankind, all who have not exceptional and overpowering aptitudes for the study of nature, would do well, I cannot but think, to choose to be educated in humane letters rather than in the natural sciences. Letters will call out their being at more points, will make them live more.

I said that before I ended I would just touch on the question of classical education, and I will keep my word. Even if literature is to retain a large place in our education, yet Latin and Greek, say the friends of progress, will certainly have to go. Greek is the grand offender in the eyes of these gentlemen. The attackers of the established course of study think that against Greek, at any rate, they have irresistible arguments. Literature may perhaps be needed in education, they say; but why on earth should it be Greek literature? Why not French or German? Nay, "has not an Englishman models in his own literature of every kind of excellence?" As before, it is not on any weak pleadings of my own that I rely for convincing the gainsayers; it is on the constitution of human nature itself, and on the instinct of self-preservation in humanity. The instinct for beauty is set in human nature, as surely as the instinct for knowledge is set there, or the instinct for conduct. If the instinct for beauty is served by Greek literature and art as it is served by no other literature and art, we may trust to the instinct of self-preservation in humanity for keeping Greek as part of our culture. We may trust to it for even making the study of Greek more prevalent than it is now. Greek will come, I hope, some day to be studied more rationally than at present; but it will be increasingly studied as men increasingly feel the need in them for beauty, and how powerfully Greek art and Greek literature can serve this need. Women will again study Greek, as Lady Jane Grey did; I believe that in that chain of forts, with which the fair host of the Amazons are now engirdling our English universities, I find that here in America, in colleges like Smith College in Massachusetts, and Vassar College in the State of New York, and in the happy families of the mixed universities out West, they are studying it already.

Defuit una mihi symmetria prisca,—"The antique symmetry was the one thing wanting to me," said Leonardo da Vinci; and he was an Italian. I will not presume to speak for the Americans, but I am sure that, in the Englishman, the want of this admirable symmetry of the Greeks is a thousand times more great and crying than in any Italian. The results of the want show themselves most glaringly, perhaps, in our architecture, but they show themselves, also, in all our art. *Fit details strictly combined, in view of a large general result nobly conceived;* that is just the beautiful *symmetria prisca* of the Greeks, and it is just where we English fail, where all our art fails. Striking ideas we have, and well-executed details we have; but that high symmetry which, with satisfying and delightful effect, combines them, we seldom or never have. The glorious beauty of the Acropolis at Athens did not come from single fine things stuck about on that hill, a statue here, a gateway there;—no, it arose from all things being perfectly combined for a supreme total effect. What must not an Englishman feel about our deficiencies in this respect, as the sense for beauty, whereof this symmetry is an essential element, awakens and strengthens within him! what will not one day be his respect and desire for Greece and its *symmetria prisca*, when the scales drop from his eyes as he walks the London streets, and he sees such a lesson in meanness as the Strand, for instance, in its true deformity! But here we are coming to our friend Mr. Ruskin's province, and I will not intrude upon it, for he is its very sufficient guardian.

And so we at last find, it seems, we find flowing in favour of the humanities the natural and necessary stream of things, which seemed against them when we started. The "hairy quadruped furnished with a tail and pointed ears, probably arboreal in his habits," this good fellow carried hidden in his nature, apparently, something destined to develop into a necessity for humane letters. Nay, more; we seem finally to be even led to the further conclusion that our hairy ancestor carried in his nature, also, a necessity for Greek.

And therefore, to say the truth, I cannot really think that humane letters are in much actual danger of being thrust out from their leading place in education, in spite of the array of authorities against them at this moment. So long as human nature is what it is, their attractions will remain irresistible. As with Greek, so with letters generally: they will some day come, we may hope, to be studied more rationally, but they will not lose their place. What will happen will rather be that there will be crowded into education other matters besides, far too many; there will be, perhaps, a period of unsettlement and confusion and false tendency; but letters will not in the end lose their leading place. If they lose it for a time, they will get it back again. We shall be brought back to them by our wants and aspirations. And a poor humanist may possess his soul in patience, neither strive nor cry, admit the energy and brilliancy of the partisans of physical science, and their present favour with the public, to be far greater than his own, and still have a happy faith that the nature of things works silently on behalf of the studies which he loves, and that, while we shall all have to acquaint ourselves with the great results reached by modern science, and to give ourselves as much training in its disciplines as we can conveniently carry, yet the majority of men will always require humane letters; and so much the more, as they have the more and the greater results of science to relate to the need in man for conduct, and to the need in him for beauty.

From *Emerson*

FORTY years ago, when I was an undergraduate at Oxford, voices were in the air there which haunt my memory still. Happy the man who in that susceptible season of youth hears such voices! they are a possession to him for ever. No such voices as those which we heard in our youth at Oxford are sounding there now. Oxford has more criticism now, more knowledge, more light; but such voices as those of our youth it has no longer. The name of Cardinal Newman [1] is a great name to the imagination still; his genius and his style are still things of power. But he is over eighty years old; he is in the Oratory at Birmingham; he has adopted, for the doubts and difficulties which beset men's minds to-day, a solution which, to speak frankly, is impossible. Forty years ago he was in the very prime of life; he was close at hand to us at Oxford; he was preaching in St. Mary's pulpit every Sunday; he seemed about to transform and to renew what was for us the most national and natural institution in the world, the Church of England. Who could resist the charm of that spiritual apparition, gliding in the dim afternoon light through the aisles of St. Mary's, rising into the pulpit, and then, in the most entrancing of voices, breaking the silence with words and thoughts which were a religious music,—subtle, sweet, mournful? I seem to hear him still, saying: "After the fever of life, after weariness and sicknesses, fightings and despondings, languor and fretfulness, struggling and succeeding; after all the changes and chances of this troubled, unhealthy state,—at length comes death, at length the white throne of God, at length the beatific vision." Or, if we followed him back to his seclusion at Littlemore, that dreary village by the London road, and to the house of retreat and the church which he built there,—a mean house such as Paul might have lived in when he was tent-making at Ephesus, a church plain and thinly sown with worshippers,—who could resist him there either, welcoming back to the severe joys of church-fellowship, and of daily worship and prayer, the firstlings of a generation which had well-nigh forgotten them? Again I seem to hear him: "The season is chill and dark, and the breath of the morning is damp, and worshippers are few; but all this befits those who are by their profession penitents and mourners, watchers and pilgrims. More dear to them that loneliness, more cheerful that severity, and more bright that gloom, than all those aids and appliances

[1] [For other expression of Arnold's veneration for Newman, and for an account of their meeting, see selection from the Letters, pp. 768 and 775.]

of luxury by which men nowadays attempt to make prayer less disagreeable to them. True faith does not covet comforts; they who realise that awful day, when they shall see Him face to face whose eyes are as a flame of fire, will as little bargain to pray pleasantly now as they will think of doing so then.''

Somewhere or other I have spoken of those "last enchantments of the Middle Age" which Oxford sheds around us, and here they were! But there were other voices sounding in our ear besides Newman's. There was the puissant voice of Carlyle; so sorely strained, over-used, and mis-used since, but then fresh, comparatively sound, and reaching our hearts with true, pathetic eloquence. Who can forget the emotion of receiving in its first freshness such a sentence as that sentence of Carlyle upon Edward Irving, then just dead: "Scotland sent him forth a herculean man; our mad Babylon wore and wasted him with all her engines,—and it took her twelve years!" A greater voice still,—the greatest voice of the century,—came to us in those youthful years through Carlyle: the voice of Goethe. To this day,—such is the force of youthful associations,—I read the *Wilhelm Meister* with more pleasure in Carlyle's translation than in the original. The large, liberal view of human life in *Wilhelm Meister*, how novel it was to the Englishman in those days! and it was salutary, too, and educative for him, doubtless, as well as novel. But what moved us most in *Wilhelm Meister* was that which, after all, will always move the young most,—the poetry, the eloquence. Never, surely, was Carlyle's prose so beautiful and pure as in his rendering of the Youths' dirge over Mignon!— "Well is our treasure now laid up, the fair image of the past. Here sleeps it in the marble, undecaying; in your hearts, also, it lives, it works. Travel, travel, back into life! Take along with you this holy earnestness, for earnestness alone makes life eternity." Here we had the voice of the great Goethe;—not the stiff, and hindered, and frigid, and factitious Goethe who speaks to us too often from those sixty volumes of his, but of the great Goethe, and the true one.

And besides those voices, there came to us in that old Oxford time a voice also from this side of the Atlantic,—a clear and pure voice, which for my ear, at any rate, brought a strain as new, and moving, and unforgettable, as the strain of Newman, or Carlyle, or Goethe. Mr. Lowell has well described the apparition of Emerson to your young generation here, in that distant time of which I am speaking, and of his workings upon them. He was your Newman, your man of soul and genius visible to you in the flesh, speaking to your bodily ears, a present object for your heart and imagination. That is surely the most potent

of all influences! nothing can come up to it. To us at Oxford
Emerson was but a voice speaking from three thousand miles
away.   But so well he spoke, that from that time forth Boston
Bay and Concord were names invested to my ear with a sentiment akin to that which invests for me the names of Oxford and
of Weimar; and snatches of Emerson's strain fixed themselves
in my mind as imperishably as any of the eloquent words which
I have been just now quoting.   "Then dies the man in you;
then once more perish the buds of art, poetry, and science, as
they have died already in a thousand thousand men."   "What
Plato has thought, he may think; what a saint has felt, he may
feel; what at any time has befallen any man, he can understand."
"Trust thyself! every heart vibrates to that iron string.   Accept
the place the Divine Providence has found for you, the society
of your contemporaries, the connexion of events.   Great men have
always done so, and confided themselves childlike to the genius
of their age; betraying their perception that the Eternal was
stirring at their heart, working through their hands, predominating in all their being.   And we are now men, and must accept in
the highest spirit the same transcendent destiny; and not
pinched in a corner, not cowards fleeing before a revolution,
but redeemers and benefactors, pious aspirants to be noble clay
plastic under the Almighty effort, let us advance and advance on
chaos and the dark!"   These lofty sentences of Emerson, and a
hundred others of my memory, I never have lost out of my
memory; I never *can* lose them.

ESSAYS IN CRITICISM

SECOND SERIES

1888

Essays in Criticism, Second Series by Matthew Arnold.   London.   Macmillan and Co., and New York.   1888.

The Study of Poetry had been previously published as the General Introduction to *The English Poets*: edited by T. H. Ward, 1880. *Milton*, in *The Century Magazine*, May 1888; *Thomas Gray*, in Ward's *English Poets*, Vol. IV, 1880; *Wordsworth*, in *Macmillan's Magazine*, July 1879 and as Preface to *The Poems of Wordsworth*, 1879; *Byron*, in *Macmillan's Magazine*, March 1881 and as Preface to *Poetry of Byron*, 1881; *Shelley*, as a review of Stopford Brooke's *Life of Shelley*, in *The Nineteenth Century*, January 1888.

Two essays are omitted from the present selection: *Count Leo Tolstoy, Amiel*.

Arnold died suddenly from heart failure at Liverpool on 15 April 1888, as he was hurrying to meet his daughter, Mrs. Whitridge, on her arrival from America.   He had been preparing a Second Series of *Essays in Criticism* consisting of his recent writings ; this was published posthumously with a brief prefatory note by Lord Coleridge.

ESSAYS IN CRITICISM
SECOND SERIES

The Study of Poetry

"THE future of poetry is immense, because in poetry, where it is worthy of its high destinies, our race, as time goes on, will find an ever surer and surer stay. There is not a creed which is not shaken, not an accredited dogma which is not shown to be questionable, not a received tradition which does not threaten to dissolve. Our religion has materialised itself in the fact, in the supposed fact; it has attached its emotion to the fact, and now the fact is failing it. But for poetry the idea is everything; the rest is a world of illusion, of divine illusion. Poetry attaches its emotion to the idea; the idea *is* the fact. The strongest part of our religion to-day is its unconscious poetry."

Let me be permitted to quote these words of my own, as uttering the thought which should, in my opinion, go with us and govern us in all our study of poetry. In the present work it is the course of one great contributory stream to the world-river of poetry that we are invited to follow. We are here invited to trace the stream of English poetry. But whether we set ourselves, as here, to follow only one of the several streams that make the mighty river of poetry, or whether we seek to know them all, our governing thought should be the same. We should conceive of poetry worthily, and more highly than it has been the custom to conceive of it. We should conceive of it as capable of higher uses, and called to higher destinies, than those which in general men have assigned to it hitherto. More and more mankind will discover that we have to turn to poetry to interpret life for us, to console us, to sustain us. Without poetry, our science will appear incomplete; and most of what now passes with us for religion and philosophy will be replaced by poetry. Science, I say, will appear incomplete without it. For finely and truly does Wordsworth call poetry "the impassioned expression which is in the countenance of all science"; and what is a countenance without its expression? Again, Wordsworth finely and truly calls poetry "the breath and finer spirit of all knowledge": our religion, parading evidences such as those on which the popular mind relies now; our philosophy, pluming itself on its reasonings about causation and finite and infinite being; what are they but the shadows and dreams and false shows of knowledge? The day will come when we shall wonder at ourselves for having trusted to them, for having taken them seriously; and the more we perceive their hollowness, the more we shall prize "the breath and finer spirit of knowledge" offered to us by poetry.

But if we conceive thus highly of the destinies of poetry, we must also set our standard for poetry high, since poetry, to be capable of fulfilling such high destinies, must be poetry of a high order of excellence. We must accustom ourselves to a high standard and to a strict judgment. Sainte-Beuve relates that Napoleon one day said, when somebody was spoken of in his presence as a charlatan: "Charlatan as much as you please; but where is there *not* charlatanism;"—"Yes," answers Sainte-Beuve, "in politics, in the art of governing mankind, that is perhaps true. But in the order of thought, in art, the glory, the eternal honour is that charlatanism shall find no entrance; herein lies the inviolableness of that noble portion of man's being." It is admirably said, and let us hold fast to it. In poetry, which is thought and art in one, it is the glory, the eternal honour, that charlatanism shall find no entrance; that this noble sphere be kept inviolate and inviolable. Charlatanism is for confusing or obliterating the distinctions between excellent and inferior, sound and unsound or only half-sound, true and untrue or only half-true. It is charlatanism, conscious or unconscious, whenever we confuse or obliterate these. And in poetry, more than anywhere else, it is unpermissible to confuse or obliterate them. For in poetry the distinction between excellent and inferior, sound and unsound or only half-sound, true and untrue or only half-true, is of paramount importance. It is of paramount importance because of the high destinies of poetry. In poetry, as a criticism of life under the conditions fixed for such a criticism by the laws of poetic truth and poetic beauty, the spirit of our race will find, we have said, as time goes on and as other helps fail, its consolation and stay. But the consolation and stay will be of power in proportion to the power of the criticism of life. And the criticism of life will be of power in proportion as the poetry conveying it is excellent rather than inferior, sound rather than unsound or half-sound, true rather than untrue or half-true.

The best poetry is what we want; the best poetry will be found to have a power of forming, sustaining, and delighting us, as nothing else can. A clearer, deeper sense of the best in poetry, and of the strength and joy to be drawn from it, is the most precious benefit which we can gather from a poetical collection such as the present. And yet in the very nature and conduct of such a collection there is inevitably something which tends to obscure in us the consciousness of what our benefit should be, and to distract us from the pursuit of it. We should therefore steadily set it before our minds at the outset, and should compel ourselves to revert constantly to the thought of it as we proceed.

Yes; constantly in reading poetry, a sense for the best, the really excellent, and of the strength and joy to be drawn from it, should be present in our minds and should govern our estimate of what we read. But this real estimate, the only true one, is liable to be superseded, if we are not watchful, by two other kinds of estimate, the historic estimate and the personal estimate, both of which are fallacious. A poet or a poem may count to us historically, they may count to us on grounds personal to ourselves, and they may count to us really. They may count to us historically. The course of development of a nation's language, thought, and poetry, is profoundly interesting; and by regarding a poet's work as a stage in this course of development we may easily bring ourselves to make it of more importance as poetry than in itself it really is, we may come to use a language of quite exaggerated praise in criticising it; in short, to over-rate it. So arises in our poetic judgments the fallacy caused by the estimate which we may call historic. Then, again, a poet or a poem may count to us on grounds personal to ourselves. Our personal affinities, likings, and circumstances, have great power to sway our estimate of this or that poet's work, and to make us attach more importance to it as poetry than in itself it really possesses, because to us it is, or has been, of high importance. Here also we over-rate the object of our interest, and apply to it a language of praise which is quite exaggerated. And thus we get the source of a second fallacy in our poetic judgments—the fallacy caused by an estimate which we may call personal.

Both fallacies are natural. It is evident how naturally the study of the history and development of a poetry may incline a man to pause over reputations and works once conspicuous but now obscure, and to quarrel with a careless public for skipping, in obedience to mere tradition and habit, from one famous name or work in its national poetry to another, ignorant of what it misses, and of the reason for keeping what it keeps, and of the whole process of growth in its poetry. The French have become diligent students of their own early poetry, which they long neglected; the study makes many of them dissatisfied with their so-called classical poetry, the court-tragedy of the seventeenth century, a poetry which Pellisson long ago reproached with its want of the true poetic stamp, with its *politesse stérile et rampante*, but which nevertheless has reigned in France as absolutely as if it had been the perfection of classical poetry indeed. The dissatisfaction is natural; yet a lively and accomplished critic, M. Charles d'Héricault, the editor of Clément Marot, goes too far when he says that "the cloud of glory playing round a classic is a mist as dangerous to the future of a literature as it is intolerable for the purposes of history." "It hinders," he goes on, "it hinders us from seeing more than one single point, the culminating and exceptional point; the summary, fictitious and arbitrary, of a thought and of a work. It substitutes a halo for a physiognomy, it puts a statue where there was once a man, and hiding from us all trace of the labour, the attempts, the weaknesses, the failures, it claims not study but veneration; it does not show us how the thing is done, it imposes upon us a model. Above all, for the historian this creation of classic personages is inadmissible; for it withdraws the poet from his time, from his proper life, it breaks historical relationships, it blinds criticism by conventional admiration, and renders the investigation of literary origins unacceptable. It gives us a human personage no longer, but a God seated immovable amidst His perfect work, like Jupiter on Olympus; and hardly will it be possible for the young student, to whom such work is exhibited at such a distance from him, to believe that it did not issue ready made from that divine head."

All this is brilliantly and tellingly said, but we must plead for a distinction. Everything depends on the reality of a poet's classic character. If he is a dubious classic, let us sift him; if he is a false classic, let us explode him. But if he is a real classic, if his work belongs to the class of the very best (for this is the true and right meaning of the word *classic, classical*), then the great thing for us is to feel and enjoy his work as deeply as ever we can, and to appreciate the wide difference between it and all work which has not the same high character. This is what is salutary, this is what is formative; this is the great benefit to be got from the study of poetry. Everything which interferes with it, which hinders it, is injurious. True, we must read our classic with open eyes, and not with eyes blinded with superstition; we must perceive when his work comes short, when it drops out of the class of the very best, and we must rate it, in such cases, at its proper value. But the use of this negative criticism is not in itself, it is entirely in its enabling us to have a clearer sense and a deeper enjoyment of what is truly excellent. To trace the labour, the attempts, the weaknesses, the failures of a genuine classic, to acquaint oneself with his time and his life and his historical relationships, is mere literary dilettantism unless it has that clear sense and deeper enjoyment for its end. It may be said that the more we know about a classic the better we shall enjoy him; and, if we live as long as Methuselah and had all of us heads of perfect clearness and wills of perfect steadfastness, this might be true in fact as it is plausible in theory. But the case here is much the same as the case with the Greek and Latin studies of our schoolboys. The elaborate philological groundwork which we require them to lay is in theory an admirable preparation for appreciating the Greek and Latin authors worthily. The more thoroughly we lay the groundwork, the better we shall be able, it may be said, to enjoy the authors. True, if time were not so short, and schoolboys' wits not so soon tired and their power of attention exhausted; only, as it is, the elaborate philological preparation goes on, but the authors are little known and less enjoyed. So with the investigator of "historic origins" in poetry. He ought to enjoy the true classic all the better for his investigations; he often is distracted from the enjoyment of the best, and with the less good he overbusies himself and is prone to over-rate it in proportion to the trouble which it has cost him.

The idea of tracing historic origins and historical relationships cannot be absent from a compilation like the present. And naturally the poets to be exhibited in it will be assigned to those persons for exhibition who are known to prize them highly, rather than to those who have no special inclination towards them. Moreover the very occupation with an author, and the business of exhibiting him, disposes us to affirm and amplify his importance. In the present work, therefore, we are sure of frequent temptation to adopt the historic estimate, or the personal estimate, and to forget the real estimate; which latter, nevertheless, we must employ if we are to make poetry yield us its full benefit. So high is that benefit, the benefit of clearly feeling and of deeply enjoying the really excellent, the truly classic in poetry, that we do well, I say, to set it fixedly before our minds as our object in studying poets and poetry, and to make the desire of attaining it the one principle to which, as the *Imitation* says, whatever we may read or come to know, we always return. *Cum multa legeris et cognoveris, ad unum semper oportet redire principium.*

The historic estimate is likely in especial to affect our judgment and our language when we are dealing with ancient poets; the personal estimate when we are dealing with poets our contemporaries, or at any rate modern. The exaggerations due to the historic estimate are not in themselves, perhaps, of very much gravity. Their report hardly enters the general ear;

probably they do not always impose even on the literary men who adopt them. But they lead to a dangerous abuse of language. So we hear Cædmon, amongst our own poets, compared to Milton. I have already noticed the enthusiasm of one accomplished French critic for "historic origins." Another eminent French critic, M. Vitet, comments upon that famous document of the early poetry of his nation, the *Chanson de Roland*. It is indeed a most interesting document. The *joculator* or *jongleur* Taillefer, who was with William the Conqueror's army at Hastings, marched before the Norman troops, so said the tradition, singing "of Charlemagne and of Roland and of Oliver, and of the vassals who died at Roncevaux"; and it is suggested that in the *Chanson de Roland* by one Turoldus or Théroulde, a poem preserved in a manuscript of the twelfth century in the Bodleian Library at Oxford, we have certainly the matter, perhaps even some of the words, of the chant which Taillefer sang. The poem has vigour and freshness; it is not without pathos. But M. Vitet is not satisfied with seeing it in a document of some poetic value, and of very high historic and linguistic value; he sees in it a grand and beautiful work, a monument of epic genius. In its general design he finds the grandiose conception, in its details he finds the constant union of simplicity with greatness, which are the marks, he truly says, of the genuine epic, and distinguish it from the artificial epic of literary ages. One thinks of Homer; this is the sort of praise which is given to Homer, and justly given. Higher praise there cannot well be, and it is the praise due to epic poetry of the highest order only, and to no other. Let us try, then, the *Chanson de Roland* at its best. Roland, mortally wounded, lays himself down under a pine-tree, with his face turned towards Spain and the enemy—

> "De plusurs choses à remembrer li prist,
> De tantes teres cume lie bers cunquist,
> De dulce France, des humes de sun lign,
> De Carlemagne sun seignor ki l'nurrit." [1]

That is primitive work, I repeat, with an undeniable poetic quality of its own. It deserves such praise, and such praise is sufficient for it. But now turn to Homer—

> Ὣς φάτο· τοὺς δ ἤδη κατέχεν φυσίζοος αἶα
> ἐν Λακεδαίμονι αὖθι, φίλῃ ἐν πατρίδι γαίῃ. [2]

---

[1] "Then began he to call many things to remembrance,—all the lands which his valour conquered, and pleasant France, and the men of his lineage, and Charlemagne his liege lord who nourished him."— *Chanson de Roland*, iii. 939–942.

[2] "So said she; they long since in Earth's soft arms were reposing, There, in their own dear land, their fatherland, Lacedæmon." —*Iliad*, iii. 243, 244 (translated by Dr. Hawtrey).

We are here in another world, another order of poetry altogether; here is rightly due such supreme praise as that which M. Vitet gives to the *Chanson de Roland*. If our words are to have any meaning, if our judgments are to have any solidity, we must not heap that supreme praise upon poetry of an order immeasurably inferior.

Indeed there can be no more useful help for discovering what poetry belongs to the class of the truly excellent, and can therefore do us most good, than to have always in one's mind lines and expressions of the great masters, and to apply them as a touchstone to other poetry. Of course we are not to require this other poetry to resemble them; it may be very dissimilar. But if we have any tact we shall find them, when we have lodged them well in our minds, an infallible touchstone for detecting the presence or absence of high poetic quality, and also the degree of this quality, in all other poetry which we may place beside them. Short passages, even single lines, will serve our turn quite sufficiently. Take the two lines which I have just quoted from Homer, the poet's comment on Helen's mention of her brothers; —or take his

> Ἀ δειλώ, τί σφῶϊ δόμεν Πηλῆϊ ἄνακτι
> θνητᾷ; ὑμεῖς δ' ἐστὸν ἀγήρω τ' ἀθανάτω τε.
> ἦ ἵνα δυστήνοισι μετ' ἀνδράσιν ἄλγε' ἔχητον;[1]

the address of Zeus to the horses of Peleus;—or take finally his

> Καὶ σέ, γέρον, τὸ πρὶν μὲν ἀκούομεν ὄλβιον εἶναι·[2]

the words of Achilles to Priam, a suppliant before him. Take that incomparable line and a half of Dante, Ugolino's tremendous words—

> "Io no piangeva; sì dentro impietrai.
> Piangevan elli . . ."[3]

take the lovely words of Beatrice to Virgil—

> "Io son fatta da Dio, sua mercè, tale,
> Che la vostra miseria non mi tange,
> Nè fiamma d'esto incendio non m'assale . . ."[4]

[1] "Ah, unhappy pair, why gave we you to King Peleus, to a mortal? but ye are without old age, and immortal. Was it that with men born to misery ye might have sorrow?"—*Iliad*, xvii. 443–445.

[2] "Nay, and thou too, old man, in former days wast, as we hear, happy."—*Iliad*, xxiv. 543.

[3] "I wailed not, so of stone grew I within;—*they* wailed."—*Inferno*, xxxiii. 39, 40.

[4] "Of such sort hath God, thanked be His mercy, made me, that your misery toucheth me not, neither doth the flame of this fire strike me."—*Inferno*, ii. 91–93.

take the simple, but perfect, single line—

> "In la sua volontade è nostra pace."[1]

Take of Shakespeare a line or two of Henry the Fourth's expostulation with sleep—

> "Wilt thou upon the high and giddy mast
> Seal up the ship-boy's eyes, and rock his brains
> In cradle of the rude imperious surge . . ."

and take, as well, Hamlet's dying request to Horatio—

> "If thou didst ever hold me in thy heart,
> Absent thee from felicity awhile,
> And in this harsh world draw thy breath in pain
> To tell my story . . ."

Take of Milton that Miltonic passage—

> "Darken'd so, yet shone
> Above them all the archangel; but his face
> Deep scars of thunder had intrench'd, and care
> Sat on his faded cheek . . ."

add two such lines as—

> "And courage never to submit or yield
> And what is else not to be overcome . . ."

and finish with the exquisite close to the loss of Proserpine, the loss

> ". . . . which cost Ceres all that pain
> To seek her through the world."

These few lines, if we have tact and can use them, are enough even of themselves to keep clear and sound our judgments about poetry, to save us from fallacious estimates of it, to conduct us to a real estimate.

The specimens I have quoted differ widely from one another, but they have in common this: the possession of the very highest poetical quality. If we are thoroughly penetrated by their power, we shall find that we have acquired a sense enabling us, whatever poetry may be laid before us, to feel the degree in which a high poetical quality is present or wanting there. Critics give themselves great labour to draw out what in the abstract constitutes the characters of a high quality of poetry. It is much better simply to have recourse to concrete examples;—to take specimens of poetry of the high, the very highest quality, and to say: The characters of a high quality of poetry are what is expressed *there*. They are far better recognised by being felt in the verse of the master, than by being perused in the prose of the critic.

---

[1] "In His will is our peace."—*Paradiso*, iii. 85.

Nevertheless if we are urgently pressed to give some critical account of them, we may safely, perhaps, venture on laying down, not indeed how and why the characters arise, but where and in what they arise. They are in the matter and substance of the poetry, and they are in its manner and style. Both of these, the substance and matter on the one hand, the style and manner on the other, have a mark, an accent, of high beauty, worth, and power. But if we are asked to define this mark and accent in the abstract, our answer must be: No, for we should thereby be darkening the question, not clearing it. The mark and accent are as given by the substance and matter of that poetry, by the style and manner of that poetry, and of all other poetry which is akin to it in quality.

Only one thing we may add as to the substance and matter of poetry, guiding ourselves by Aristotle's profound observation that the superiority of poetry over history consists in its possessing a higher truth and a higher seriousness ($\phi\iota\lambda o\sigma o\phi\omega\tau\epsilon\rho o\nu$ $\kappa\alpha\iota$ $\sigma\pi o\upsilon\delta\alpha\iota o\tau\epsilon\rho o\nu$). Let us add, therefore, to what we have said, this: that the substance and matter of the best poetry acquire their special character from possessing, in an eminent degree, truth and seriousness. We may add yet further, what is in itself evident, that to the style and manner of the best poetry their special character, their accent, is given by their diction, and, even yet more, by their movement. And though we distinguish between the two characters, the two accents, of superiority, yet they are nevertheless vitally connected one with the other. The superior character of truth and seriousness, in the matter and substance of the best poetry, is inseparable from the superiority of diction and movement marking its style and manner. The two superiorities are closely related, and are in steadfast proportion one to the other. So far as high poetic truth and seriousness are wanting to a poet's matter and substance, so far also, we may be sure, will a high poetic stamp of diction and movement be wanting to his style and manner. In proportion as this high stamp of diction and movement, again, is absent from a poet's style and manner, we shall find, also, that high poetic truth and seriousness are absent from his substance and matter.

So stated, these are but dry general ties; their whole force lies in their application. And I could wish every student of poetry to make the application of them for himself. Made by himself, the application would impress itself upon his mind far more deeply than made by me. Neither will my limits allow me to make any full application of the generalities above propounded; but in the hope of bringing out, at any rate, some significance in them, and of establishing an important principle more firmly by their means,

I will, in the space which remains to me, follow rapidly from the commencement the course of our English poetry with them in my view.

Once more I return to the early poetry of France, with which our own poetry, in its origins, is indissolubly connected. In the twelfth and thirteenth centuries, that seed-time of all modern language and literature, the poetry of France had a clear predominance in Europe. Of the two divisions of that poetry, its productions in the *langue d'oïl* and its productions in the *langue d'oc*, the poetry of the *langue d'oc*, of southern France, of the troubadours, is of importance because of its effect on Italian literature;—the first literature of modern Europe to strike the true and grand note, and to bring forth, as in Dante and Petrarch it brought forth, classics. But the predominance of French poetry in Europe, during the twelfth and thirteenth centuries, is due to its poetry of the *langue d'oïl*, the poetry of northern France and of the tongue which is now the French language. In the twelfth century the bloom of this romance-poetry was earlier and stronger in England, at the court of our Anglo-Norman kings, than in France itself. But it was a bloom of French poetry; and as our native poetry formed itself, it formed itself out of this. The romance-poems which took possession of the heart and imagination of Europe in the twelfth and thirteenth centuries are French; "they are," as Southey justly says, "the pride of French literature, nor have we anything which can be placed in competition with them." Themes were supplied from all quarters; but the romance-setting which was common to them all, and which gained the ear of Europe, was French. This constituted for the French poetry, literature, and language, at the height of the Middle Age, an unchallenged predominance. The Italian Brunetto Latini, the master of Dante, wrote his *Treasure* in French because, he says, "la parleure en est plus délitable et plus commune à toutes gens." In the same century, the thirteenth, the French romance-writer, Christian of Troyes, formulates the claims, in chivalry and letters, of France, his native country, as follows:—

"Or vous ert par ce livre apris,
Que Gresse ot de chevalerie
Le premier los et de clergie;
Puis vint chevalerie à Rome,
Et de la clergie la some,
Qui ore est en France venue.
Diex doinst qu'ele i soit retenue,
Et aue li lius li abelisse
Tant que de France n'isse
L'onor qui s'i est arestée!"

"Now by this book you will learn that first Greece had the renown for chivalry and letters; then chivalry and the primacy in letters passed to Rome, and now it is come to France. God grant it may be kept there; and that the place may please it so well, that the honour which has come to make stay in France may never depart thence!"

Yet it is now all gone, this French romance-poetry, of which the weight of substance and the power of style are not unfairly represented by this extract from Christian of Troyes. Only by means of the historic estimate can we persuade ourselves now to think that any of it is of poetical importance.

But in the fourteenth century there comes an Englishman nourished on this poetry, taught his trade by this poetry, getting words, rhyme, metre from this poetry; for even of that stanza which the Italians used, and which Chaucer derived immediately from the Italians, the basis and suggestion was probably given in France. Chaucer (I have already named him) fascinated his contemporaries, but so too did Christian of Troyes and Wolfram of Eschenbach. Chaucer's power of fascination, however, is enduring; his poetical importance does not need the assistance of the historic estimate; it is real. He is a genuine source of joy and strength, which is flowing still for us and will flow always. He will be read, as time goes on, far more generally than he is read now. His language is a cause of difficulty for us; but so also, and I think in quite as great a degree, is the language of Burns. In Chaucer's case, as in that of Burns, it is a difficulty to be unhesitatingly accepted and overcome.

If we ask ourselves wherein consists the immense superiority of Chaucer's poetry over the romance-poetry—why it is that in passing from this to Chaucer we suddenly feel ourselves to be in another world we shall find that his superiority is both in the substance of his poetry and in the style of his poetry. His superiority in substance is given by his large, free, simple, clear yet kindly view of human life,—so unlike the total want, in the romance-poets, of all intelligent command of it. Chaucer has not their helplessness; he has gained the power to survey the world from a central, a truly human point of view. We have only to call to mind the Prologue to *The Canterbury Tales*. The right comment upon it is Dryden's: "It is sufficient to say, according to the proverb, that *here is God's plenty*." And again: "He is a perpetual fountain of good sense." It is by a large, free, sound representation of things, that poetry, this high criticism of life, has truth of substance; and Chaucer's poetry has truth of substance.

Of his style and manner, if we think first of the romance-poetry
Y

and then of Chaucer's divine liquidness of diction, his divine
fluidity of movement, it is difficult to speak temperately. They
are irresistible, and justify all the rapture with which his successors speak of his "gold dew-drops of speech." Johnson misses
the point entirely when he finds fault with Dryden for ascribing
to Chaucer the first refinement of our numbers, and says that
Gower also can show smooth numbers and easy rhymes. The
refinement of our numbers means something far more than this.
A nation may have versifiers with smooth numbers and easy
rhymes, and yet may have no real poetry at all. Chaucer is the
father of our splendid English poetry; he is our "well of English
undefiled," because by the lovely charm of his diction, the lovely
charm of his movement, he makes an epoch and founds a tradition. In Spenser, Shakespeare, Milton, Keats, we can follow the
tradition of the liquid diction, the fluid movement, of Chaucer;
at one time it is his liquid diction of which in these poets we feel
the virtue, and at another time it is his fluid movement. And
the virtue is irresistible.

Bounded as is my space, I must yet find room for an example
of Chaucer's virtue, as I have given examples to show the virtue
of the great classics. I feel disposed to say that a single line is
enough to show the charm of Chaucer's verse; that merely one
line like this—

> "O martyr souded[1] in virginitee!"

has a virtue of manner and movement such as we shall not find
in all the verse of romance-poetry;—but this is saying nothing.
The virtue is such as we shall not find, perhaps, in all English
poetry, outside the poets whom I have named as the special
inheritors of Chaucer's tradition. A single line, however, is too
little if we have not the strain of Chaucer's verse well in our
memory; let us take a stanza. It is from *The Prioress's Tale*, the
story of the Christian child murdered in a Jewry—

> "My throte is cut unto my nekke-bone
> Saidè this child, and as by way of kinde
> I should have deyd, yea, longè time agone;
> But Jesu Christ, as ye in bookès finde,
> Will that his glory last and be in minde,
> And for the worship of his mother dere
> Yet may I sing *O Alma* loud and clere."

Wordsworth has modernised this Tale, and to feel how delicate
and evanescent is the charm of verse, we have only to read
Wordsworth's first three lines of this stanza after Chaucer's—

---

[1] The French *soudé*; soldered, fixed fast.

"My throat is cut unto the bone, I trow,
    Said this young child, and by the law of kind
    I should have died, yea, many hours ago."

The charm is departed. It is often said that the power of
liquidness and fluidity in Chaucer's verse was dependent upon a
free, a licentious dealing with language, such as is now impossible; upon a liberty, such as Burns too enjoyed, of making
words like *neck*, *bird*, into a dissyllable by adding to them, and
words like *cause*, *rhyme*, into a dissyllable by sounding the *e*
mute. It is true that Chaucer's fluidity is conjoined with this
liberty, and is admirably served by it; but we ought not to say
that it was dependent upon it. It was dependent upon his
talent. Other poets with a like liberty do not attain to the
fluidity of Chaucer; Burns himself does not attain to it. Poets,
again, who have a talent akin to Chaucer's, such as Shakespeare
or Keats, have known how to attain to his fluidity without the
like liberty.

And yet Chaucer is not one of the great classics. His poetry
transcends and effaces, easily and without effort, all the romance-
poetry of Catholic Christendom; it transcends and effaces all the
English poetry contemporary with it, it transcends and effaces
all the English poetry subsequent to it down to the age of
Elizabeth. Of such avail is poetic truth of substance, in its natural
and necessary union with poetic truth of style. And yet, I say,
Chaucer is not one of the great classics. He has not their accent.
What is wanting to him is suggested by the mere mention of the
name of the first great classic of Christendom, the immortal poet
who died eighty years before Chaucer,—Dante. The accent of
such verse as

"In la sua volontade è nostra pace . . ."

is altogether beyond Chaucer's reach; we praise him, but we feel
that this accent is out of the question for him. It may be said
that it was necessarily out of the reach of any poet in the England
of that stage of growth. Possibly; but we are to adopt a real, not
a historic, estimate of poetry. However we may account for its
absence, something is wanting, then, to the poetry of Chaucer,
which poetry must have before it can be placed in the glorious
class of the best. And there is no doubt what that something is.
It is the σπουδαιότης, the high and excellent seriousness, which
Aristotle assigns as one of the grand virtues of poetry. The substance of Chaucer's poetry, his view of things and his criticism
of life, has largeness, freedom, shrewdness, benignity; but it has
not this high seriousness. Homer's criticism of life has it,
Dante's has it, Shakespeare's has it. It is this chiefly which gives

to our spirits what they can rest upon; and with the increasing demands of our modern ages upon poetry, this virtue of giving us what we can rest upon will be more and more highly esteemed. A voice from the slums of Paris, fifty or sixty years after Chaucer, the voice of poor Villon out of his life of riot and crime, has at its happy moments (as, for instance, in the last stanza of *La Belle Heaulmière*[1]) more of this important poetic virtue of seriousness than all the productions of Chaucer. But its apparition in Villon, and in men like Villon, is fitful; the greatness of the great poets, the power of their criticism of life, is that their virtue is sustained.

To our praise, therefore, of Chaucer as a poet there must be this limitation; he lacks the high seriousness of the great classics, and therewith an important part of their virtue. Still, the main fact for us to bear in mind about Chaucer is his sterling value according to that real estimate which we firmly adopt for all poets. He has poetic truth of substance, though he has not high poetic seriousness, and corresponding to his truth of substance he has an exquisite virtue of style and manner. With him is born our real poetry.

For my present purpose I need not dwell on our Elizabethan poetry, or on the continuation and close of this poetry in Milton. We all of us profess to be agreed in the estimate of this poetry; we all of us recognise it as great poetry, our greatest, and Shakespeare and Milton as our poetical classics. The real estimate, here, has universal currency. With the next age of our poetry divergency and difficulty begin. An historic estimate of that poetry has established itself; and the question is, whether it will be found to coincide with the real estimate.

The age of Dryden, together with our whole eighteenth century which followed it, sincerely believed itself to have pro-

---

[1] The name *Heaulmière* is said to be derived from a headdress (helm) worn as a mark by courtesans. In Villon's ballad, a poor old creature of this class laments her days of youth and beauty. This last stanza of the ballad runs thus—

> "Ainsi le bon temps regretons
> Entre nous, pauvres vieilles sottes,
> Assises bas, à croppetons,
> Tout en ung tas comme pelottes;
> A petit feu de chenevottes
> Tost allumées, tost estainctes.
> Et jadis fusmes si mignottes !
> Ainsi en prend à maintz et maintes."

"Thus amongst ourselves we regret the good time, poor silly old things, low-seated on our heels, all in a heap like so many balls; by a little fire of hemp-stalks, soon lighted, soon spent. And once we were such darlings ! So fares it with many and many a one."

duced poetical classics of its own, and even to have made advance, in poetry, beyond all its predecessors. Dryden regards as not seriously disputable the opinion "that the sweetness of English verse was never understood or practised by our fathers." Cowley could see nothing at all in Chaucer's poetry. Dryden heartily admired it, and, as we have seen, praised its matter admirably; but of its exquisite manner and movement all he can find to say is that "there is the rude sweetness of a Scotch tune in it, which is natural and pleasing, though not perfect." Addison, wishing to praise Chaucer's numbers, compares them with Dryden's own. And all through the eighteenth century, and down even into our own times, the stereotyped phrase of approbation for good verse found in our early poetry has been, that it even approached the verse of Dryden, Addison, Pope, and Johnson.

Are Dryden and Pope poetical classics? Is the historic estimate, which represents them as such, and which has been so long established that it cannot easily give way, the real estimate? Wordsworth and Coleridge, as is well known, denied it; but the authority of Wordsworth and Coleridge does not weigh much with the young generation, and there are many signs to show that the eighteenth century and its judgments are coming into favour again. Are the favourite poets of the eighteenth century classics?

It is impossible within my present limits to discuss the question fully. And what man of letters would not shrink from seeming to dispose dictatorially of the claims of two men who are, at any rate, such masters in letters as Dryden and Pope; two men of such admirable talent, both of them, and one of them, Dryden, a man, on all sides, of such energetic and genial power? And yet, if we are to gain the full benefit from poetry, we must have the real estimate of it. I cast about for some mode of arriving, in the present case, at such an estimate without offence. And perhaps the best way is to begin, as it is easy to begin, with cordial praise.

When we find Chapman, the Elizabethan translator of Homer, expressing himself in his preface thus: "Though truth in her very nakedness sits in so deep a pit, that from Gades to Aurora and Ganges few eyes can sound her, I hope yet those few here will so discover and confirm that, the date being out of her darkness in this morning of our poet, he shall now gird his temples with the sun,"—we pronounce that such a prose is intolerable. When we find Milton writing: "And long it was not after, when I was confirmed in this opinion, that he, who would not be frustrate of his hope to write well hereafter in laudable things, ought himself to be a true poem,"—we pronounce that such a prose has its own grandeur, but that it is obsolete and inconvenient. But when we find Dryden telling us: "What Virgil wrote in the vigour of his age, in plenty and at ease, I have undertaken to translate in my declining years; struggling with wants, oppressed with sickness, curbed in my genius, liable to be misconstrued in all I write,"—then we exclaim that here at last we have the true English prose, a prose such as we would all gladly use if we only knew how. Yet Dryden was Milton's contemporary.

But after the Restoration the time had come when our nation felt the imperious need of a fit prose. So, too, the time had likewise come when our nation felt the imperious need of freeing itself from the absorbing preoccupation which religion in the Puritan age had exercised. It was impossible that this freedom should be brought about without some negative excess, without some neglect and impairment of the religious life of the soul; and the spiritual history of the eighteenth century shows us that the freedom was not achieved without them. Still, the freedom was achieved; the preoccupation, an undoubtedly baneful and retarding one if it had continued, was got rid of. And as with religion amongst us at that period, so it was also with letters. A fit prose was a necessity; but it was impossible that a fit prose should establish itself amongst us without some touch of frost to the imaginative life of the soul. The needful qualities for a fit prose are regularity, uniformity, precision, balance. The men of letters, whose destiny it may be to bring their nation to the attainment of a fit prose, must of necessity, whether they work in prose or in verse, give a predominating, an almost exclusive attention to the qualities of regularity, uniformity, precision, balance. But an almost exclusive attention to these qualities involves some repression and silencing of poetry.

We are to regard Dryden as the puissant and glorious founder, Pope as the splendid high priest, of our age of prose and reason, of our excellent and indispensable eighteenth century. For the purpose of their mission and destiny their poetry, like their prose, is admirable. Do you ask me whether Dryden's verse, take it almost where you will, is not good?

> "A milk-white Hind, immortal and unchanged,
>   Fed on the lawns and in the forest ranged."

I answer: Admirable for the purposes of the inaugurator of an age of prose and reason. Do you ask me whether Pope's verse, take it almost where you will, is not good?

> "To Hounslow Heath I point, and Banstead Down;
>   Thence comes your mutton, and these chicks my own."

I answer: Admirable for the purposes of the high priest of an age of prose and reason. But do you ask me whether such verse proceeds from men with an adequate poetic criticism of life, from men whose criticism of life has a high seriousness, or even, without that high seriousness, has poetic largeness, freedom, insight, benignity? Do you ask me whether the application of ideas to life in the verse of these men, often a powerful application, no doubt, is a powerful *poetic* application? Do you ask me whether the poetry of these men has either the matter or the inseparable manner of such an adequate poetic criticism; whether it has the accent of

"Absent thee from felicity awhile . . ."

or of

"And what is else not to be overcome . . ."

or of

"O martyr souded in virginitee!"

I answer: It has not and cannot have them; it is the poetry of the builders of an age of prose and reason. Though they may write in verse, though they may in a certain sense be masters of the art of versification, Dryden and Pope are not classics of our poetry, they are classics of our prose.

Gray is our poetical classic of that literature and age; the position of Gray is singular, and demands a word of notice here. He has not the volume or the power of poets who, coming in times more favourable, have attained to an independent criticism of life. But he lived with the great poets, he lived, above all, with the Greeks, through perpetually studying and enjoying them; and he caught their poetic point of view for regarding life, caught their poetic manner. The point of view and the manner are not self-sprung in him, he caught them of others; and he had not the free and abundant use of them. But whereas Addison and Pope never had the use of them, Gray had the use of them at times. He is the scantiest and frailest of classics in our poetry, but he is a classic.

And now, after Gray, we are met, as we draw towards the end of the eighteenth century, we are met by the great name of Burns. We enter now on times where the personal estimate of poets begins to be rife, and where the real estimate of them is not reached without difficulty. But in spite of the disturbing pressures of personal partiality, of national partiality, let us try to reach a real estimate of the poetry of Burns.

By his English poetry Burns in general belongs to the eighteenth century, and has little importance for us.

> "Mark ruffian Violence, distain'd with crimes,
> Rousing elate in these degenerate times;
> View unsuspecting Innocence a prey,
> As guileful Fraud points out the erring way;
> While subtle Litigation's pliant tongue
> The life-blood equal sucks of Right and Wrong!"

Evidently this is not the real Burns, or his name and fame would have disappeared long ago. Nor is Clarinda's love-poet, Sylvander, the real Burns either. But he tells us himself: "These English songs gravel me to death. I have not the command of the language that I have of my native tongue. In fact, I think that my ideas are more barren in English than in Scotch. I have been at *Duncan Gray* to dress it in English, but all I can do is desperately stupid." We English turn naturally, in Burns, to the poems in our own language, because we can read them easily; but in those poems we have not the real Burns.

The real Burns is of course in his Scotch poems. Let us boldly say that of much of this poetry, a poetry dealing perpetually with Scotch drink, Scotch religion, and Scotch manners, a Scotchman's estimate is apt to be personal. A Scotchman is used to this world of Scotch drink, Scotch religion, and Scotch manners; he has a tenderness for it; he meets its poet half way. In this tender mood he reads pieces like the *Holy Fair* or *Halloween*. But this world of Scotch drink, Scotch religion, and Scotch manners is against a poet, not for him, when it is not a partial countryman who reads him; for in itself it is not a beautiful world, and no one can deny that it is of advantage to a poet to deal with a beautiful world. Burns's world of Scotch drink, Scotch religion, and Scotch manners, is often a harsh, a sordid, a repulsive world; even the world of his *Cotter's Saturday Night* is not a beautiful world. No doubt a poet's criticism of life may have such truth and power that it triumphs over its world and delights us. Burns may triumph over his world, often he does triumph over his world, but let us observe how and where. Burns is the first case we have had where the bias of the personal estimate tends to mislead; let us look at him closely, he can bear it.

Many of his admirers will tell us that we have Burns, convivial, genuine, delightful, here—

> "Leeze me on drink! it gies us mair
> Than either school or college;
> It kindles wit, it waukens lair,
> It pangs us fou o' knowledge.
> Be 't whisky gill or penny wheep
> Or ony stronger potion,
> It never fails, on drinking deep,
> To kittle up our notion
> By night or day."

There is a great deal of that sort of thing in Burns, and it is unsatisfactory, not because it is bacchanalian poetry, but because it has not that accent of sincerity which bacchanalian poetry, to do it justice, very often has. There is something in it of bravado, something which makes us feel that we have not the man speaking to us with his real voice; something, therefore, poetically unsound.

With still more confidence will his admirers tell us that we have the genuine Burns, the great poet, when his strain asserts the independence, equality, dignity, of men, as in the famous song *For a' that and a' that*—

> "A prince can mak' a belted knight,
>   A marquis, duke, and a' that;
> But an honest man's aboon his might,
>   Guid faith he manna fa' that!
>   For a' that, and a' that,
>   Their dignities, and a' that,
>   The pith o' sense, and pride o' worth,
>   Are higher rank than a' that."

Here they find his grand, genuine touches; and still more, when this puissant genius, who so often set morality at defiance, falls moralising—

> "The sacred lowe o' weel-placed love
>   Luxuriantly indulge it;
> But never tempt th' illicit rove,
>   Tho' naething should divulge it.
>   I waive the quantum o' the sin,
>   The hazard o' concealing,
>   But och! it hardens a' within,
>   And petrifies the feeling."

Or in a higher strain—

> "Who made the heart, 'tis He alone
>   Decidedly can try us;
> He knows each chord, its various tone;
>   Each spring, its various bias.
>   Then at the balance let's be mute,
>   We never can adjust it;
>   What's *done* we partly may compute,
>   But know not what's resisted."

Or in a better strain yet, a strain, his admirers will say, unsurpassable—

> "To make a happy fire-side clime
>   To weans and wife,
>   That's the true pathos and sublime
>   Of human life."

There is criticism of life for you, the admirers of Burns will say to us; there is the application of ideas to life! There is, undoubtedly. The doctrine of the last-quoted lines coincides almost exactly with what was the aim and end, Xenophon tells us, of all the teaching of Socrates. And the application is a powerful one; made by a man of vigorous understanding, and (need I say?) a master of language.

But for supreme poetical success more is required than the powerful application of ideas to life; it must be an application under the conditions fixed by the laws of poetic truth and poetic beauty. Those laws fix as an essential condition, in the poet's treatment of such matters as are here in question, high seriousness;—the high seriousness which comes from absolute sincerity. The accent of high seriousness, born of absolute sincerity, is what gives to such verse as

> "In la sua volontade è nostra pace . . ."

to such criticism of life as Dante's, its power. Is this accent felt in the passages which I have been quoting from Burns? Surely not; surely, if our sense is quick, we must perceive that we have not in those passages a voice from the very inmost soul of the genuine Burns; he is not speaking to us from these depths, he is more or less preaching. And the compensation for admiring such passages less, from missing the perfect poetic accent in them, will be that we shall admire more the poetry where that accent is found.

No; Burns, like Chaucer, comes short of the high seriousness of the great classics, and the virtue of matter and manner which goes with that high seriousness is wanting to his work. At moments he touches it in a profound and passionate melancholy, as in those four immortal lines taken by Byron as a motto for *The Bride of Abydos*, but which have in them a depth of poetic quality such as resides in no verse of Byron's own—

> "Had we never loved sae kindly,
> Had we never loved sae blindly,
> Never met, or never parted,
> We had ne'er been broken-hearted."

But a whole poem of that quality Burns cannot make; the rest, in the *Farewell to Nancy*, is verbiage.

We arrive best at the real estimate of Burns, I think, by conceiving his work as having truth of matter and truth of manner, but not the accent or the poetic virtue of the highest masters. His genuine criticism of life, when the sheer poet in him speaks, is ironic; it is not—

"Thou Power Supreme, whose mighty scheme
        These woes of mine fulfil,
    Here firm I rest, they must be best
        Because they are Thy will! "

It is far rather: *Whistle owre the lave o't!* Yet we may say of
him as of Chaucer, that of life and the world, as they come
before him, his view is large, free, shrewd, benignant,—truly
poetic, therefore; and his manner of rendering what he sees is
to match. But we must note, at the same time, his great difference from Chaucer. The freedom of Chaucer is heightened, in
Burns, by a fiery, reckless energy; the benignity of Chaucer
deepens, in Burns, into an overwhelming sense of the pathos of
things;—of the pathos of human nature, the pathos, also, of
non-human nature. Instead of the fluidity of Chaucer's manner,
the manner of Burns has spring, bounding swiftness. Burns is
by far the greater force, though he has perhaps less charm. The
world of Chaucer is fairer, richer, more significant than that of
Burns; but when the largeness and freedom of Burns get full
sweep, as in *Tam o' Shanter*, or still more in that puissant and
splendid production, *The Jolly Beggars*, his world may be what
it will, his poetic genius triumphs over it. In the world of *The
Jolly Beggars* there is more than hideousness and squalor, there
is bestiality; yet the piece is a superb poetic success. It has a
breadth, truth, and power which make the famous scene in Auer-
bach's Cellar, of Goethe's *Faust*, seem artificial and tame beside
it, and which are only matched by Shakespeare and Aristophanes.

Here, where his largeness and freedom serve him so admirably,
and also in those poems and songs where to shrewdness he adds
infinite archness and wit, and to benignity infinite pathos, where
his manner is flawless, and a perfect poetic whole is the result,—
in things like the address to the mouse whose home he had
ruined, in things like *Duncan Gray, Tam Glen, Whistle and I'll
come to you my Lad, Auld Lang Syne* (this list might be made
much longer),—here we have the genuine Burns, of whom the
real estimate must be high indeed. Not a classic, nor with the
excellent σπουδαιότης of the great classics, nor with a verse
rising to a criticism of life and a virtue like theirs; but a poet
with thorough truth of substance and an answering truth of
style, giving us a poetry sound to the core. We all of us have a
leaning towards the pathetic, and may be inclined perhaps to
prize Burns most for his touches of piercing, sometimes almost
intolerable, pathos; for verse like—

"We twa hae paidl't i' the burn
        From mornin' sun till dine;
    But seas between us braid hae roar'd
        Sin auld lang syne . . ."

where he is as lovely as he is sound. But perhaps it is by the perfection of soundness of his lighter and archer masterpieces that he is poetically most wholesome for us. For the votary misled by a personal estimate of Shelley, as so many of us have been, are, and will be,—of that beautiful spirit building his many-coloured haze of words and images

> "Pinnacled dim in the intense inane"—

no contact can be wholesomer than the contact with Burns at his archest and soundest. Side by side with the

> "On the brink of the night and the morning
> My coursers are wont to respire,
> But the Earth has just whispered a warning
> That their flight must be swifter than fire . . ."

of *Prometheus Unbound*, how salutary, how very salutary, to place this from *Tam Glen*—

> "My minnie does constantly deave me
> And bids me beware o' young men;
> They flatter, she says, to deceive me;
> But wha can think sae o' Tam Glen?"

But we enter on burning ground as we approach the poetry of times so near to us—poetry like that of Byron, Shelley, and Wordsworth—of which the estimates are so often not only personal, but personal with passion. For my purpose, it is enough to have taken the single case of Burns, the first poet we come to of whose work the estimate formed is evidently apt to be personal, and to have suggested how we may proceed, using the poetry of the great classics as a sort of touchstone, to correct this estimate, as we had previously corrected by the same means the historic estimate where we met with it. A collection like the present, with its succession of celebrated names and celebrated poems, offers a good opportunity to us for resolutely endeavouring to make our estimates of poetry real. I have sought to point out a method which will help us in making them so, and to exhibit it in use so far as to put any one who likes in a way of applying it for himself.

At any rate the end to which the method and the estimate are designed to lead, and from leading to which, if they do lead to it, they get their whole value,—the benefit of being able clearly to feel and deeply to enjoy the best, the truly classic, in poetry,—is an end, let me say it once more at parting, of supreme importance. We are often told that an era is opening in which we are to see multitudes of a common sort of readers, and masses of a common sort of literature; that such readers do not want and could not relish anything better than such literature, and that to provide it is becoming a vast and profitable industry. Even if good literature entirely lost currency with the world, it would still be abundantly worth while to continue to enjoy it by oneself. But it never will lose currency with the world, in spite of mommentary appearances; it never will lose supremacy. Currency and supremacy are insured to it, not indeed by the world's deliberate and conscious choice, but by something far deeper,—by the instinct of self-preservation in humanity.

From *Milton*

THE most eloquent voice of our century uttered, shortly before leaving the world, a warning cry against "the Anglo-Saxon contagion." The tendencies and aims, the view of life and the social economy of the ever-multiplying and spreading Anglo-Saxon race, would be found congenial, this prophet feared, by all the prose, all the vulgarity amongst mankind, and would invade and overpower all nations. The true ideal would be lost, a general sterility of mind and heart would set in.

The prophet had in view, no doubt, in the warning thus given, us and our colonies, but the United States still more. There the Anglo-Saxon race is already most numerous, there it increases fastest; there material interests are most absorbing and pursued with most energy; there the ideal, the saving ideal, of a high and rare excellence, seems perhaps to suffer most danger of being obscured and lost. Whatever one may think of the general danger to the world from the Anglo-Saxon contagion, it appears to me difficult to deny that the growing greatness and influence of the United States does bring with it some danger to the ideal of a high and rare excellence. The *average man* is too much a religion there; his performance is unduly magnified, his shortcomings are not duly seen and admitted. A lady in the State of Ohio sent to me only the other day a volume on American authors; the praise given throughout was of such high pitch that in thanking her I could not forbear saying that for only one or two of the authors named was such a strain of praise admissible, and that we lost all real standard of excellence by praising so uniformly and immoderately. She answered me with charming good temper, that very likely I was quite right, but it was pleasant to her to think that excellence was common and abundant. But excellence is not common and abundant; on the contrary, as the Greek poet long ago said, excellence dwells among rocks hardly accessible, and a man must almost wear his heart out before he can reach her. Whoever talks of excellence as common and abundant, is on the way to lose all right standard of excellence. And when the right standard of excellence is lost, it is not likely that much which is excellent will be produced.

To habituate ourselves, therefore, to approve, as the Bible says, things that are really excellent, is of the highest importance. And some apprehension may justly be caused by a tendency in Americans to take, or, at any rate, attempt to take, profess to take, the average man and his performances too seriously, to over-rate and over-praise what is not really superior.

Thomas Gray

JAMES BROWN, Master of Pembroke Hall at Cambridge, Gray's friend and executor, in a letter written a fortnight after Gray's death to another of his friends, Dr. Wharton of Old Park, Durham, has the following passage:—

"Everything is now dark and melancholy in Mr. Gray's room, not a trace of him remains there; it looks as if it had been for some time uninhabited, and the room bespoke for another inhabitant. The thoughts I have of him will last, and will be useful to me the few years I can expect to live. He never spoke out, but I believe from some little expressions I now remember to have dropped from him, that for some time past he thought himself nearer his end than those about him apprehended."

He never spoke out. In these four words is contained the whole history of Gray, both as a man and as a poet. The words fell naturally, and as it were by chance, from their writer's pen; but let us dwell upon them, and press into their meaning, for in following it we shall come to understand Gray.

He was in his fifty-fifth year when he died, and he lived in ease and leisure, yet a few pages hold all his poetry; *he never spoke out* in poetry. Still, the reputation which he has achieved by his few pages is extremely high. True, Johnson speaks of him with coldness and disparagement. Gray disliked Johnson, and refused to make his acquaintance; one might fancy that Johnson wrote with some irritation from this cause. But Johnson was not by nature fitted to do justice to Gray and to his poetry; this by itself is a sufficient explanation of the deficiencies of his criticism of Gray. We may add a further explanation of them which is supplied by Mr. Cole's papers. "When Johnson was publishing his Life of Gray," says Mr. Cole, "I gave him several anecdotes, *but he was very anxious as soon as possible to get to the end of his labours.*" Johnson was not naturally in sympathy with Gray, whose life he had to write, and when he wrote it he was in a hurry besides. He did Gray injustice, but even Johnson's authority failed to make injustice, in this case, prevail. Lord Macaulay calls the Life of Gray the worst of Johnson's Lives, and it had found many censurers before Macaulay. Gray's poetical reputation grew and flourished in spite of it. The poet Mason, his first biographer, in his epitaph equalled him with Pindar. Britain has known, says Mason,

> ". . . a Homer's fire in Milton's strains,
> A Pindar's rapture in the lyre of Gray."

The immense vogue of Pope and of his style of versification had at first prevented the frank reception of Gray by the readers of poetry. The *Elegy* pleased; it could not but please: but Gray's poetry, on the whole, astonished his contemporaries at first more than it pleased them; it was so unfamiliar, so unlike the sort of poetry in vogue. It made its way, however, after his death, with the public as well as with the few; and Gray's second biographer, Mitford, remarks that "the works which were either neglected or ridiculed by their contemporaries have now raised Gray and Collins to the rank of our two greatest lyric poets." Their reputation was established, at any rate, and stood extremely high, even if they were not popularly read. Johnson's disparagement of Gray was called "petulant," and severely blamed. Beattie, at the end of the eighteenth century, writing to Sir William Forbes, says: "Of all the English poets of this age Mr. Gray is most admired, and I think with justice." Cowper writes: "I have been reading Gray's works, and think him the only poet since Shakespeare entitled to the character of sublime. Perhaps you will remember that I once had a different opinion of him. I was prejudiced." Adam Smith says: "Gray joins to the sublimity of Milton the elegance and harmony of Pope; and nothing is wanting to render him, perhaps, the first poet in the English language, but to have written a little more." And, to come nearer to our own times, Sir James Mackintosh speaks of Gray thus: "Of all English poets he was the most finished artist. He attained the highest degree of splendour of which poetical style seemed to be capable."

In a poet of such magnitude, how shall we explain his scantiness of production? Shall we explain it by saying that to make of Gray a poet of this magnitude is absurd; that his genius and resources were small, and that his production, therefore, was small also, but that the popularity of a single piece, the *Elegy*,— a popularity due in great measure to the subject,—created for Gray a reputation to which he has really no right? He himself was not deceived by the favour shown to the *Elegy*. "Gray told me with a good deal of acrimony," writes Dr. Gregory, "that the *Elegy* owed its popularity entirely to the subject, and that the public would have received it as well if it had been written in prose." This is too much to say; the *Elegy* is a beautiful poem, and in admiring it the public showed a true feeling for poetry. But it is true that the *Elegy* owed much of its success to its subject, and that it has received a too unmeasured and unbounded praise.

Gray himself, however, maintained that the *Elegy* was not his best work in poetry, and he was right. High as is the praise due to the *Elegy*, it is yet true that in other productions of Gray he exhibits poetical qualities even higher than those exhibited in the *Elegy*. He deserves, therefore, his extremely high reputation as a poet, although his critics and the public may not always have praised him with perfect judgment. We are brought back, then, to the question: How, in a poet so really considerable, are we to explain his scantiness of production?

Scanty Gray's production, indeed, is; so scanty that to supplement our knowledge of it by a knowledge of the man is in this case of peculiar interest and service. Gray's letters and the records of him by his friends have happily made it possible for us thus to know him, and to appreciate his high qualities of mind and soul. Let us see these in the man first, and then observe how they appear in his poetry; and why they cannot enter into it more freely and inspire it with more strength, render it more abundant.

We will begin with his acquirements. "Mr. Gray was," writes his friend Temple, "perhaps the most learned man in Europe. He knew every branch of history both natural and civil; had read all the original historians of England, France, and Italy; and was a great antiquarian. Criticism, metaphysics, morals, politics, made a principal part of his study. Voyages and travels of all sorts were his favourite amusements; and he had a fine taste in painting, prints, architecture, and gardening." The notes in his interleaved copy of Linnæus remained to show the extent and accuracy of his knowledge in the natural sciences, particularly in botany, zoology, and entomology. Entomologists testified that his account of English insects was more perfect than any that had then appeared. His notes and papers, of which some have been published, others remain still in manuscript, give evidence, besides, of his knowledge of literature, ancient and modern, geography and topography, painting, architecture and antiquities, and of his curious researches in heraldry. He was an excellent musician. Sir James Mackintosh reminds us, moreover, that to all the other accomplishments and merits of Gray we are to add this: "That he was the first discoverer of the beauties of nature in England, and has marked out the course of every picturesque journey that can be made in it."

Acquirements take all their value and character from the power of the individual storing them. Let us take, from amongst Gray's observations on what he read, enough to show us his power. Here are criticisms on three very different authors, criticisms without any study or pretension, but just thrown out in chance letters to his friends. First, on Aristotle:—

"In the first place he is the hardest author by far I ever meddled with. Then he has a dry conciseness that makes one imagine one is perusing a table of contents rather than a book; it tastes for all the world like chopped hay, or rather like chopped logic; for he has a violent affection to that art, being in some sort his own invention; so that he often loses himself in little trifling distinctions and verbal niceties, and what is worse, leaves you to extricate yourself as you can. Thirdly, he has suffered vastly by his transcribers, as all authors of great brevity necessarily must. Fourthly and lastly, he has abundance of fine, uncommon things, which make him well worth the pains he gives one. You see what you have to expect."

Next, on Isocrates:—

"It would be strange if I should find fault with you for reading Isocrates; I did so myself twenty years ago, and in an edition at least as bad as yours. The Panegyric, the De Pace, Areopagitic, and Advice to Philip, are by far the noblest remains we have of this writer, and equal to most things extant in the Greek tongue; but it depends on your judgment to distinguish between his real and occasional opinion of things, as he directly contradicts in one place what he has advanced in another; for example, in the Panathenaic and the De Pace, on the naval power of Athens; the latter of the two is undoubtedly his own undisguised sentiment."

After hearing Gray on Isocrates and Aristotle, let us hear him on Froissart:—

"I rejoice you have met with Froissart, he is the Herodotus of a barbarous age; had he but had the luck of writing in as good a language, he might have been immortal. His locomotive disposition (for then there was no other way of learning things), his simple curiosity, his religious credulity, were much like those of the old Grecian. When you have *tant chevauché* as to get to the end of him, there is Monstrelet waits to take you up, and will set you down at Philip de Commines; but previous to all these, you should have read Villehardouin and Joinville."

Those judgments, with their true and clear ring, evince the high quality of Gray's mind, his power to command and use his learning. But Gray was a poet; let us hear him on a poet, on Shakespeare. We must place ourselves in the full midst of the eighteenth century and of its criticism; Gray's friend, West, had praised Racine for using in his dramas "the language of the times and that of the purest sort"; and he had added: "I will not decide what style is fit for our English stage, but I should rather choose one that bordered upon Cato, than upon Shakespeare." Gray replies:—

"As to matter of style, I have this to say: The language of the age is never the language of poetry; except among the French, whose verse, where the thought does not support it, differs in nothing from prose. Our poetry, on the contrary, has a language peculiar to itself, to which almost every one that has written has added something. In truth, Shakespeare's language is one of his principal beauties; and he has no less advantage over your Addisons and Rowes in this, than in those other great excellences you mention. Every word in him is a picture. Pray put me the following lines into the tongue of our modern dramatics—

' "But I, that am not shaped for sportive tricks,
    Nor made to court an amorous looking-glass"—

and what follows? To me they appear untranslatable; and if this be the case, our language is greatly degenerated."

It is impossible for a poet to lay down the rules of his own art with more insight, soundness, and certainty. Yet at that moment in England there was perhaps not one other man, besides Gray, capable of writing the passage just quoted.

Gray's quality of mind, then, we see; his quality of soul will no less bear inspection. His reserve, his delicacy, his distaste for many of the persons and things surrounding him in the Cambridge of that day,—"this silly, dirty place," as he calls it,—have produced an impression of Gray as being a man falsely fastidious, finical, effeminate. But we have already had that grave testimony to him from the Master of Pembroke Hall: "The thoughts I have of him will last, and will be useful to me the few years I can expect to live." And here is another to the same effect from a younger man, from Gray's friend Nicholls:—

"You know," he writes to his mother, from abroad, when he heard of Gray's death, "that I considered Mr. Gray as a second parent, that I thought only of him, built all my happiness on him, talked of him for ever, wished him with me whenever I partook of any pleasure, and flew to him for refuge whenever I felt any uneasiness. To whom now shall I talk of all I have seen here? Who will teach me to read, to think, to feel? I protest to you, that whatever I did or thought had a reference to him. If I met with any chagrins, I comforted myself that I had a treasure at home; if all the world had despised and hated me, I should have thought myself perfectly recompensed in his friendship. There remains only one loss more; if I lose you, I am left alone in the world. At present I feel that I have lost half of myself."

Testimonies such as these are not called forth by a fastidious effeminate weakling; they are not called forth, even, by mere qualities of mind; they are called forth by qualities of soul. And of Gray's high qualities of soul, of his σπουδαιότης, his excellent seriousness, we may gather abundant proof from his letters. Writing to Mason who had just lost his father, he says:—

"I have seen the scene you describe, and know how dreadful it is; I know too I am the better for it. We are all idle and thoughtless things, and have no sense, no use in the world any longer than that sad impression lasts; the deeper it is engraved the better."

And again, on a like occasion to another friend:—

"He who best knows our nature (for he made us what we are) by such afflictions recalls us from our wandering thoughts and idle merriment, from the insolence of youth and prosperity, to serious reflection, to our duty, and to himself; nor need we hasten to get rid of these impressions. Time (by appointment of the same Power) will cure the smart and in some hearts soon blot out all the traces of sorrow; but such as preserve them longest (for it is partly left in our own power) do perhaps best acquiesce in the will of the chastiser."

And once more to Mason, in the very hour of his wife's death; Gray was not sure whether or not his letter would reach Mason before the end:—

"If the worst be not yet past, you will neglect and pardon me; but if the last struggle be over, if the poor object of your long anxieties be no longer sensible to your kindness or to her own sufferings, allow me, at least an idea (for what could I do, were I present, more than this?) to sit by you in silence and pity from my heart not her, who is at rest, but you, who lose her. May he, who made us, the Master of our pleasures and of our pains, support you! Adieu."

Seriousness, character, was the foundation of things with him; where this was lacking he was always severe, whatever might be offered to him in its stead. Voltaire's literary genius charmed him, but the faults of Voltaire's nature he felt so strongly that when his young friend Nicholls was going abroad in 1771, just before Gray's death, he said to him: "I have one thing to beg of you which you must not refuse." Nicholls answered: "You know you have only to command; what is it?"— "Do not go to see Voltaire," said Gray; and then added: "No one knows the mischief that man will do." Nicholls promised compliance with Gray's injunction; "But what," he asked, "could a visit from me signify?"—"Every tribute to such a man signifies," Gray answered. He admired Dryden, admired him, even, too much; had too much felt his influence as a poet. He told Beattie "that if there was any excellence in his own numbers he had learned it wholly from that great poet"; and writing to Beattie afterwards he recurs to Dryden, whom Beattie, he thought, did not honour enough as a poet: "Remember Dryden," he writes, "and be blind to all his faults." Yes, his faults as a poet; but on the man Dryden, nevertheless, his sentence is stern. Speaking of the Poet-Laureateship, "Dryden," he writes to Mason, "was as disgraceful to the office from his character, as the poorest scribbler could have been from his verses. Even where crying blemishes were absent, the want of weight and depth of character in a man deprived him, in Gray's judgment, of serious significance. He says of Hume: "Is not that *naïveté* and good-humour, which his admirers celebrate in him, owing to this, that he has continued all his days an infant, but one that has unhappily been taught to read and write?"

And with all this strenuous seriousness, a pathetic sentiment, and an element, likewise, of sportive and charming humour. At Keswick, by the lakeside on an autumn evening, he has the accent of the *Rêveries*, or of Obermann, or Wordsworth:—

"In the evening walked down alone to the lake by the side of Crow Park after sunset and saw the solemn colouring of light draw on, the last gleam of sunshine fading away on the hill-tops, the deep serene of the waters, and the long shadows of the mountains thrown across them, till they nearly touched the hithermost shore. At distance heard the murmur of many waterfalls, not audible in the daytime. Wished for the Moon, but she was *dark to me and silent, hid in her vacant interlunar cave*."

Of his humour and sportiveness his delightful letters are full; his humour appears in his poetry too, and is by no means to be passed over there. Horace Walpole said that "Gray never wrote anything easily but things of humour; humour was his natural and original turn."

Knowledge, penetration, seriousness, sentiment, humour, Gray had them all; he had the equipment and endowment for the office of poet. But very soon in his life appear traces of something obstructing, something disabling; of spirits failing,

and health not sound; and the evil increases with years. He
writes to West in 1737:—

"Low spirits are my true and faithful companions; they get
up with me, go to bed with me, make journeys and returns as I
do; nay, and pay visits and will even affect to be jocose and force
a feeble laugh with me; but most commonly we sit alone together,
and are the prettiest insipid company in the world."

The tone is playful, Gray was not yet twenty-one. "Mine," he
tells West four or five years later, "mine, you are to know, is a
white Melancholy, or rather *Leucocholy*, for the most part; which,
though it seldom laughs or dances, nor ever amounts to what one
calls joy or pleasure, yet is a good easy sort of a state." But, he
adds in this same letter:—

"But there is another sort, black indeed, which I have now
and then felt, that has something in it like Tertullian's rule of
faith, *Credo quia impossibile est*; for it believes, nay, is sure of
everything that is unlikely, so it be but frightful; and on the
other hand excludes and shuts its eyes to the most possible hopes,
and everything that is pleasurable; from this the Lord deliver us!
for none but he and sunshiny weather can do it."

Six or seven years pass, and we find him writing to Wharton
from Cambridge thus:—

"The spirit of laziness (the spirit of this place) begins to possess
even me, that have so long declaimed against it. Yet has it not
so prevailed, but that I feel that discontent with myself, that
ennui, that ever accompanies it in its beginnings. Time will settle
my conscience, time will reconcile my languid companion to me;
we shall smoke, we shall tipple, we shall doze together, we shall
have our little jokes, like other people, and our long stories.
Brandy will finish what port began; and, a month after the time,
you will see in some corner of a London Evening Post, "Yesterday died the Rev. Mr. John Gray, Senior-Fellow of Clare Hall, a
facetious companion, and well-respected by all who knew him." '

The humorous advertisement ends, in the original letter, with
a Hogarthian touch which I must not quote. Is it Leucocholy
or is it Melancholy which predominates here? at any rate, this
entry in his diary, six years later, is black enough:—

"*Insomnia crebra, atque expergiscenti surdus quidam doloris
sensus; frequens etiam in regione sterni oppressio, et cardialgia
gravis, fere sempiterna.*"

And in 1757 he writes to Hurd:—

"To be employed is to be happy. This principle of mine (and
I am convinced of its truth) has, as usual, no influence on my
practice. I am alone, and *ennuyé* to the last degree, yet do nothing. Indeed I have one excuse; my health (which you have so

kindly inquired after) is not extraordinary. It is no great malady, but several little ones, that seem brewing no good to me."

From thence to the end his languor and depression, though still often relieved by occupation and travel, keep fatally gaining on him. At last the depression became constant, became mechanical. "Travel I must," he writes to Dr. Wharton, "or cease to exist. Till this year I hardly knew what *mechanical* low spirits were; but now I even tremble at an east wind." Two months afterwards he died.

What wonder, that with this troublous cloud, throughout the whole term of his manhood, brooding over him and weighing him down, Gray, finely endowed though he was, richly stored with knowledge though he was, yet produced so little, found no full and sufficient utterance, "*never*," as the Master of Pembroke Hall said, "*spoke out.*" He knew well enough, himself, how it was with him.

"My *verve* is at best, you know" (he writes to Mason), "of so delicate a constitution, and has such weak nerves, as not to stir out of its chamber above three days in a year." And to Horace Walpole he says: "As to what you say to me civilly, that I ought to write more, I will be candid, and avow to you, that till four-score and upward, whenever the humour takes me, I will write; because I like it, and because I like myself better when I do so. If I do not write much, it is because I cannot." How simply said, and how truly also! Fain would a man like Gray speak out if he could, he "likes himself better" when he speaks out; if he does not speak out, "it is because I cannot."

Bonstetten, that mercurial Swiss who died in 1832 at the age of eighty-seven, having been younger and livelier from his sixtieth year to his eightieth than at any other time in his life, paid a visit in his early days to Cambridge, and saw much of Gray, to whom he attached himself with devotion. Gray, on his part, was charmed with his young friend; "I never saw such a boy," he writes; "our breed is not made on this model." Long afterwards Bonstetten published his reminiscences of Gray. "I used to tell Gray," he says, "about my life and my native country, but *his* life was a sealed book to me; he never would talk of himself, never would allow me to speak to him of his poetry. If I quoted lines of his to him, he kept silence like an obstinate child. I said to him sometimes: 'Will you have the goodness to give me an answer?' But not a word issued from his lips." *He never spoke out.* Bonstetten thinks that Gray's life was poisoned by an unsatisfied sensibility, was withered by his having never loved; by his days being passed in the dismal cloisters of Cambridge, in the company of a set of monastic book-

worms, "whose existence no honest woman ever came to cheer."
Sainte-Beuve, who was much attracted and interested by Gray,
doubts whether Bonstetten's explanation of him is admissible;
the secret of Gray's melancholy he finds rather in the sterility
of his poetic talent, "so distinguished, so rare, but so stinted";
in the poet's despair at his own unproductiveness.

But to explain Gray, we must do more than allege his sterility,
as we must look further than to his reclusion at Cambridge.
What caused his sterility? Was it his ill-health, his hereditary
gout? Certainly we will pay all respect to the powers of hereditary gout for afflicting us poor mortals. But Goethe, after pointing out that Schiller, who was so productive, was "almost constantly ill," adds the true remark that it is incredible how much
the spirit can do, in these cases, to keep up the body. Pope's
animation and activity through all the course of what he pathe-
tically calls "that long disease, my life," is an example presenting
itself signally, in Gray's own country and time, to confirm what
Goethe here says. What gave the power to Gray's reclusion and
ill-health to induce his sterility?

The reason, the indubitable reason as I cannot but think it, I
have already given elsewhere. Gray, a born poet, fell upon an
age of prose. He fell upon an age whose task was such as to call
forth in general men's powers of understanding, wit and cleverness, rather than their deepest powers of mind and soul. As
regards literary production, the task of the eighteenth century in
England was not the poetic interpretation of the world, its task
was to create a plain, clear, straightforward, efficient prose.
Poetry obeyed the bent of mind requisite for the due fulfilment
of this task of the century. It was intellectual, argumentative,
ingenious; not seeing things in their truth and beauty, not interpretative. Gray, with the qualities of mind and soul of a genuine
poet, was isolated in his century. Maintaining and fortifying
them by lofty studies, he yet could not fully educe and enjoy
them; the want of a genial atmosphere, the failure of sympathy
in his contemporaries, were too great. Born in the same year
with Milton, Gray would have been another man; born in the
same year with Burns, he would have been another man. A man
born in 1608 could profit by the larger and more poetic scope of
the English spirit in the Elizabethan age; a man born in 1750
could profit by that European renewing of men's minds of which
the great historical manifestation is the French Revolution.
Gray's alert and brilliant young friend, Bonstetten, who would
explain the void in the life of Gray by his having never loved,
Bonstetten himself loved, married, and had children. Yet at the
age of fifty he was bidding fair to grow old, dismal and torpid

like the rest of us, when he was roused and made young again for some thirty years, says M. Sainte-Beuve, by the events of 1789. If Gray, like Burns, had been just thirty years old when the French Revolution broke out, he would have shown, probably, productiveness and animation in plenty. Coming when he did, and endowed as he was, he was a man born out of date, a man whose full spiritual flowering was impossible. The same thing is to be said of his great contemporary, Butler, the author of the *Analogy*. In the sphere of religion, which touches that of poetry, Butler was impelled by the endowment of his nature to strive for a profound and adequate conception of religious things, which was not pursued by his contemporaries, and which at that time, and in that atmosphere of mind, was not fully attainable. Hence, in Butler too, a dissatisfaction, a weariness, as in Gray; "great labour and weariness, great disappointment, pain and even vexation of mind." A sort of spiritual east wind was at that time blowing; neither Butler nor Gray could flower. They *never spoke out*.

Gray's poetry was not only stinted in quantity by reason of the age wherein he lived, it suffered somewhat in quality also. We have seen under what obligation to Dryden Gray professed himself to be—"if there was any excellence in his numbers, he had learned it wholly from that great poet." It was not for nothing that he came when Dryden had lately "embellished," as Johnson says, English poetry; had "found it brick and left it marble." It was not for nothing that he came just when "the English ear," to quote Johnson again, "had been accustomed to the mellifluence of Pope's numbers, and the diction of poetry had grown more splendid." Of the intellectualities, ingenuities, personifications, of the movement and diction of Dryden and Pope, Gray caught something, caught too much. We have little of Gray's poetry, and that little is not free from the faults of his age. Therefore it was important to go for aid, as we did, to Gray's life and letters, to see his mind and soul there, and to corroborate from thence that high estimate of his quality which his poetry indeed calls forth, but does not establish so amply and irresistibly as one could desire.

For a just criticism it does, however, clearly establish it. The difference between genuine poetry and the poetry of Dryden, Pope, and all their school, is briefly this: their poetry is conceived and composed in their wits, genuine poetry is conceived and composed in the soul. The difference between the two kinds of poetry is immense. They differ profoundly in their modes of language, they differ profoundly in their modes of evolution. The poetic language of our eighteenth century in general is the

language of men composing *without their eye on the object*, as
Wordsworth excellently said of Dryden; language merely recall-
ing the object, as the common language of prose does, and then
dressing it out with a certain smartness and brilliancy for the
fancy and understanding. This is called "splendid diction."
The evolution of the poetry of our eighteenth century is likewise
intellectual; it proceeds by ratiocination, antithesis, ingenious
turns and conceits. This poetry is often eloquent, and always,
in the hands of such masters as Dryden and Pope, clever; but it
does not take us much below the surface of things, it does not
give us the emotion of seeing things in their truth and beauty.
The language of genuine poetry, on the other hand, is the
language of one composing with his eye on the object; its evolution is that of a thing which has been plunged in the poet's soul
until it comes forth naturally and necessarily. This sort of
evolution is infinitely simpler than the other, and infinitely more
satisfying; the same thing is true of the genuine poetic language
likewise. But they are both of them also infinitely harder of
attainment; they come only from those who, as Emerson says,
"live from a great depth of being."

Goldsmith disparaged Gray who had praised his *Traveller*,
and indeed in the poem on the *Alliance of Education and Government* had given him hints which he used for it. In retaliation let
us take from Goldsmith himself a specimen of the poetic language of the eighteenth century.

> "No cheerful murmurs fluctuate in the gale"—

there is exactly the poetic diction of our prose century! rhetorical,
ornate,—and, poetically, quite false. Place beside it a line of
genuine poetry, such as the

> "In cradle of the rude, imperious surge"

of Shakespeare; and all its falseness instantly becomes apparent.

Dryden's poem on the death of Mrs. Killigrew is, says Johnson, "undoubtedly the noblest ode that our language ever has
produced." In this vigorous performance Dryden has to say,
what is interesting enough, that not only in poetry did Mrs.
Killigrew excel, but she excelled in painting also. And thus he
says it—

> "To the next realm she stretch'd her sway,
>   For Painture near adjoining lay—
> A plenteous province and alluring prey.
> A Chamber of Dependencies was framed
> (As conquerors will never want pretence
>   When arm'd, to justify the offence),
> And the whole fief, in right of Poetry, she claim'd."

The intellectual, ingenious, superficial evolution of poetry of
this school could not be better illustrated. Place beside it
Pindar's

$$αἰὼν ἀσφαλὴς$$
$$οὐκ ἔγεντ' ουτ' Αἰακίδᾳ παρὰ Πηλεῖ,$$
$$οὔτε παρ̀ ἀντιθέῳ Κάδμῳ . . .$$

"A secure time fell to the lot neither of Peleus the son of Æacus,
nor of the godlike Cadmus; howbeit these are said to have had,
of all mortals, the supreme of happiness, who heard the golden-
snooded Muses sing,—on the mountain the one heard them, the
other in seven-gated Thebes."

There is the evolution of genuine poetry, and such poetry kills
Dryden's the moment it is put near it.

Gray's production was scanty, and scanty, as we have seen, it
could not but be. Even what he produced is not always pure in
diction, true in evolution. Still, with whatever drawbacks, he is
alone, or almost alone (for Collins has something of the like
merit) in his age. Gray said himself that "the style he aimed at
was extreme conciseness of expression, yet pure, perspicuous,
and musical." Compared, not with the work of the great
masters of the golden ages of poetry, but with the poetry of his
own contemporaries in general, Gray's may be said to have
reached, in style, the excellence at which he aimed; while the
evolution also of such a piece as his *Progress of Poesy* must be
accounted not less noble and sound than its style.

Wordsworth

I REMEMBER hearing Lord Macaulay say, after Wordsworth's
death, when subscriptions were being collected to found a
memorial of him, that ten years earlier more money could have
been raised in Cambridge alone, to do honour to Wordsworth,
than was now raised all through the country. Lord Macaulay
had, as we know, his own heightened and telling way of putting
things, and we must always make allowance for it. But probably
it is true that Wordsworth has never, either before or since, been
so accepted and popular, so established in possession of the
minds of all who profess to care for poetry, as he was between
the years 1830 and 1840, and at Cambridge. From the very
first, no doubt, he had his believers and witnesses. But I have
myself heard him declare that, for he knew not how many years,
his poetry had never brought him in enough to buy his shoe-
strings. The poetry-reading public was very slow to recognise

him, and was very easily drawn away from him. Scott effaced him with this public, Byron effaced him.

The death of Byron, seemed, however, to make an opening for Wordsworth. Scott, who had for some time ceased to produce poetry himself, and stood before the public as a great novelist; Scott, too genuine himself not to feel the profound genuineness of Wordsworth, and with an instinctive recognition of his firm hold on nature and of his local truth, always admired him sincerely, and praised him generously. The influence of Coleridge upon young men of ability was then powerful, and was still gathering strength; this influence told entirely in favour of Wordsworth's poetry. Cambridge was a place where Coleridge's influence had great action, and where Wordsworth's poetry, therefore, flourished especially. But even amongst the general public its sale grew large, the eminence of its author was widely recognised, and Rydal Mount became an object of pilgrimage. I remember Wordsworth relating how one of the pilgrims, a clergyman, asked him if he had ever written anything besides the *Guide to the Lakes.* Yes, he answered modestly, he had written verses. Not every pilgrim was a reader, but the vogue was established, and the stream of pilgrims came.

Mr. Tennyson's decisive appearance dates from 1842.[1] One cannot say that he effaced Wordsworth as Scott and Byron had effaced him. The poetry of Wordsworth had been so long before the public, the suffrage of good judges were so steady and so strong in its favour, that by 1842 the verdict of posterity, one may almost say, had been already pronounced, and Wordsworth's English fame was secure. But the vogue, the ear and applause of the great body of poetry-readers, never quite thoroughly perhaps his, he gradually lost more and more, and Mr. Tennyson gained them. Mr. Tennyson drew to himself, and away from Wordsworth, the poetry-reading public, and the new generations. Even in 1850, when Wordsworth died, this diminution of popularity was visible, and occasioned the remark of Lord Macaulay which I quoted at starting.

The diminution has continued. The influence of Coleridge has waned, and Wordsworth's poetry can no longer draw succour from this ally. The poetry has not, however, wanted eulogists; and it may be said to have brought its eulogists luck, for almost every one who has praised Wordsworth's poetry has praised it well. But the public has remained cold, or, at least, undetermined. Even the abundance of Mr. Palgrave's fine and skilfully chosen specimens of Wordsworth, in the *Golden Treasury*, surprised many readers, and gave offence to not a few. To tenth-

[1] [*Poems by Alfred Tennyson.* In two volumes, 1842.]

rate critics and compilers, for whom any violent shock to the public taste would be a temerity not to be risked, it is still quite permissible to speak of Wordsworth's poetry, not only with ignorance, but with impertinence. On the Continent he is almost unknown.

I cannot think, then, that Wordsworth has, up to this time, at all obtained his deserts. "Glory," said M. Renan the other day, "glory after all is the thing which has the best chance of not being altogether vanity." Wordsworth was a homely man, and himself would certainly never have thought of talking of glory as that which, after all, has the best chance of not being altogether vanity. Yet we may well allow that few things are less vain than *real* glory. Let us conceive of the whole group of civilised nations as being, for intellectual and spiritual purposes, one great confederation, bound to a joint action and working towards a common result; a confederation whose members have a due knowledge both of the past, out of which they all proceed, and of one another. This was the ideal of Goethe, and it is an ideal which will impose itself upon the thoughts of our modern societies more and more. Then to be recognised by the verdict of such a confederation as a master, or even as a seriously and eminently worthy workman, in one's own line of intellectual or spiritual activity, is indeed glory; a glory which it would be difficult to rate too highly. For what could be more beneficent, more salutary? The world is forwarded by having its attention fixed on the best things; and here is a tribunal, free from all suspicion of national and provincial partiality, putting a stamp on the best things, and recommending them for general honour and acceptance. A nation, again, is furthered by recognition of its real gifts and successes; it is encouraged to develop them further. And here is an honest verdict, telling us which of our supposed successes are really, in the judgment of the great impartial world, and not in our own private judgment only, successes, and which are not.

It is so easy to feel pride and satisfaction in one's own things, so hard to make sure that one is right in feeling it! We have a great empire. But so had Nebuchadnezzar. We extol the "unrivalled happiness" of our national civilisation. But then comes a candid friend, and remarks that our upper class is materialised, our middle class vulgarised, and our lower class brutalised. We are proud of our painting, our music. But we find that in the judgment of other people our painting is questionable, and our music non-existent. We are proud of our men of science. And here it turns out that the world is with us; we find that in the judgment of other people, too, Newton among the dead, and Mr.

Darwin among the living, hold as high a place as they hold in our national opinion.

Finally, we are proud of our poets and poetry. Now poetry is nothing less than the most perfect speech of man, that in which he comes nearest to being able to utter the truth. It is no small thing, therefore, to succeed eminently in poetry. And so much is required for duly estimating success here, that about poetry it is perhaps hardest to arrive at a sure general verdict, and takes longest. Meanwhile, our own conviction of the superiority of our national poets is not decisive, is almost certain to be mingled, as we see constantly in English eulogy of Shakespeare, with much of provincial infatuation. And we know what was the opinion current amongst our neighbours the French—people of taste, acuteness, and quick literary tact—not a hundred years ago, about our great poets. The old *Biographie Universelle* notices the pretension of the English to a place for their poets among the chief poets of the world, and says that this is a pretension which to no one but an Englishman can ever seem admissible. And the scornful, disparaging things said by foreigners about Shakespeare and Milton, and about our national over-estimate of them, have been often quoted, and will be in every one's remembrance.

A great change has taken place, and Shakespeare is now generally recognized, even in France, as one of the greatest of poets. Yes, some anti-Gallican cynic will say, the French rank him with Corneille and with Victor Hugo! But let me have the pleasure of quoting a sentence about Shakespeare, which I met with by accident not long ago in the *Correspondant*, a French review which not a dozen English people, I suppose, look at. The writer is praising Shakespeare's prose. With Shakespeare, he says, "prose comes in whenever the subject, being more familiar, is unsuited to the majestic English iambic." And he goes on: "Shakespeare is the king of poetic rhythm and style, as well as the king of the realm of thought; along with his dazzling prose, Shakespeare has succeeded in giving us the most varied, the most harmonious verse which has ever sounded upon the human ear since the verse of the Greeks." M. Henry Cochin, the writer of this sentence deserves our gratitude for it; it would not be easy to praise Shakespeare, in a single sentence, more justly. And when a foreigner and a Frenchman writes thus of Shakespeare, and when Goethe says of Milton, in whom there was so much to repel Goethe rather than to attract him, that "nothing has been ever done so entirely in the sense of the Greeks as *Samson Agonistes*," and that "Milton is in very truth a poet whom we must treat with all reverence," then we understand what constitutes a European recognition of poets and poetry as contradistinguished from a merely national recognition, and that in favour both of Milton and of Shakespeare the judgment of the high court of appeal has finally gone.

I come back to M. Renan's praise of glory, from which I started. Yes, real glory is a most serious thing, glory authenticated by the Amphictyonic Court of final appeal, definitive glory. And even for poets and poetry, long and difficult as may be the process of arriving at the right award, the right award comes at last, the definitive glory rests where it is deserved. Every establishment of such a real glory is good and wholesome for mankind at large, good and wholesome for the nation which produced the poet crowned with it. To the poet himself it can seldom do harm; for he, poor man, is in his grave, probably, long before his glory crowns him.

Wordsworth has been in his grave for some thirty years, and certainly his lovers and admirers cannot flatter themselves that this great and steady light of glory as yet shines over him. He is not fully recognised at home; he is not recognised at all abroad. Yet I firmly believe that the poetical performance of Wordsworth is, after that of Shakespeare and Milton, of which all the world now recognises the worth, undoubtedly the most considerable in our language from the Elizabethan age to the present time. Chaucer is anterior; and on other grounds, too, he cannot well be brought into the comparison. But taking the roll of our chief poetical names, besides Shakespeare and Milton, from the age of Elizabeth downwards, and going through it,— Spenser, Dryden, Pope, Gray, Goldsmith, Cowper, Burns, Coleridge, Scott, Campbell, Moore, Byron, Shelley, Keats (I mention those only who are dead),—I think it certain that Wordsworth's name deserves to stand, and will finally stand, above them all. Several of the poets named have gifts and excellences which Wordsworth has not. But taking the performance of each as a whole, I say that Wordsworth seems to me to have left a body of poetical work superior in power, in interest, in the qualities which give enduring freshness, to that which any one of the others has left.

But this is not enough to say. I think it certain, further, that if we take the chief poetical names of the Continent since the death of Molière, and, omitting Goethe, confront the remaining names with that of Wordsworth, the result is the same. Let us take Klopstock, Lessing, Schiller, Uhland, Rückert, and Heine for Germany; Filicaia, Alfieri, Manzoni, and Leopardi for Italy; Racine, Boileau, Voltaire, André Chenier, Béranger, Lamartine, Musset, M. Victor Hugo (he has been so long celebrated that although he still lives I may be permitted to name him) for France. Several of these, again, have evidently gifts and excellences to which Wordsworth can make no pretension. But in real poetical achievement it seems to me indubitable that to Wordsworth, here again, belongs the palm. It seems to me that Wordsworth has left behind him a body of poetical work which wears, and will wear, better on the whole than the performance of any one of these personages, so far more brilliant and celebrated, most of them, than the homely poet of Rydal. Wordsworth's performance in poetry is on the whole, in power, in interest, in the qualities which give enduring freshness, superior to theirs.

This is a high claim to make for Wordsworth. But if it is a just claim, if Wordsworth's place among the poets who have appeared in the last two or three centuries is after Shakespeare, Molière, Milton, Goethe, indeed, but before all the rest, then in time Wordsworth will have his due. We shall recognise him in his place, as we recognise Shakespeare and Milton; and not only we ourselves shall recognise him, but he will be recognised by Europe also. Meanwhile, those who recognise him already may do well, perhaps, to ask themselves whether there are not in the case of Wordsworth certain special obstacles which hinder or delay his due recognition by others, and whether these obstacles are not in some measure removable.

The *Excursion* and the *Prelude*, his poems of greatest bulk, are by no means Wordsworth's best work. His best work is in his shorter pieces, and many indeed are there of these which are of first-rate excellence. But in his seven volumes the pieces of high merit are mingled with a mass of pieces very inferior to them; so inferior to them that it seems wonderful how the same poet should have produced both. Shakespeare frequently has lines and passages in a strain quite false, and which are entirely unworthy of him. But one can imagine his smiling if one could meet him in the Elysian Fields and tell him so; smiling and replying that he knew it perfectly well himself, and what did it matter? But with Wordsworth the case is different. Work altogether inferior, work quite uninspired, flat and dull, is produced by him with evident unconsciousness of its defects, and he presents it to us with the same faith and seriousness as his best work. Now a drama or an epic fill the mind, and one does not look beyond them; but in a collection of short pieces the impression made by one piece requires to be continued and sustained by the piece following. In reading Wordsworth the impression made by one of his fine pieces is too often dulled and spoiled by a very inferior piece coming after it.

Wordsworth composed verses during a space of some sixty years; and it is no exaggeration to say that within one single decade of those years, between 1798 and 1808, almost all his really first-rate work was produced. A mass of inferior work remains, work done before and after this golden prime, imbedding the first-rate work and clogging it, obstructing our approach to it, chilling, not unfrequently, the high-wrought mood with which we leave it. To be recognised far and wide as a great poet, to be possible and receivable as a classic, Wordsworth needs to be relieved of a great deal of the poetical baggage which now encumbers him. To administer this relief is indispensable, unless he is to continue to be a poet for the few only,— a poet valued far below his real worth by the world.

There is another thing. Wordsworth classified his poems not according to any commonly received plan of arrangement, but according to a scheme of mental physiology. He has poems of the fancy, poems of the imagination, poems of sentiment and reflection, and so on. His categories are ingenious but far-fetched, and the result of his employment of them is unsatisfactory. Poems are separated one from another which possess a kinship of subject or of treatment far more vital and deep than the supposed unity of mental origin, which was Wordsworth's reason for joining them with others.

The tact of the Greeks in matters of this kind was infallible. We may rely upon it that we shall not improve upon the classification adopted by the Greeks for kinds of poetry; that their categories of epic, dramatic, lyric, and so forth, have a natural propriety, and should be adhered to. It may sometimes seem doubtful to which of two categories a poem belongs; whether this or that poem is to be called, for instance, narrative or lyric, lyric or elegiac. But there is to be found in every good poem a strain, a predominant note, which determines the poem as belonging to one of these kinds rather than the other; and here is the best proof of the value of the classification, and of the advantage of adhering to it. Wordsworth's poems will never produce their due effect until they are freed from their present artificial arrangement, and grouped more naturally.

Disengaged from the quantity of inferior work which now obscures them, the best poems of Wordsworth, I hear many people say, would indeed stand out in great beauty, but they would prove to be very few in number, scarcely more than half a dozen. I maintain, on the other hand, that what strikes me with admiration, what establishes in my opinion Wordsworth's superiority, is the great and ample body of powerful work which remains to him, even after all his inferior work has been cleared away. He gives us so much to rest upon, so much which communicates his spirit and engages ours!

This is of very great importance. If it were a comparison of single pieces, or of three or four pieces, by each poet, I do not say that Wordsworth would stand decisively above Gray, or Burns, or Coleridge, or Keats, or Manzoni, or Heine. It is in his ampler body of powerful work that I find his superiority. His good work itself, his work which counts, is not all of it, of course, of equal value. Some kinds of poetry are in themselves lower kinds than others. The ballad kind is a lower kind; the didactic kind, still more, is a lower kind. Poetry of this latter sort counts, too, sometimes, by its biographical interest partly, not by its poetical interest pure and simple; but then this can only be when the poet producing it has the power and importance of Wordsworth, a power and importance which he assuredly did not establish by such didactic poetry alone. Altogether, it is, I say, by the great body of powerful and significant work which remains to him, after every reduction and deduction has been made, that Wordsworth's superiority is proved.

To exhibit this body of Wordsworth's best work, to clear away obstructions from around it, and to let it speak for itself, is what every lover of Wordsworth should desire. Until this has been done, Wordsworth, whom we, to whom he is dear, all of us know and feel to be so great a poet, has not had a fair chance before the world. When once it has been done, he will make his way best, not by our advocacy of him, but by his own worth and power. We may safely leave him to make his way thus, we who believe that a superior worth and power in poetry finds in mankind a sense responsive to it and disposed at last to recognise it. Yet at the outset, before he has been duly known and recognised, we may do Wordsworth a service, perhaps, by indicating in what his superior power and worth will be found to consist, and in what it will not.

Long ago, in speaking of Homer, I said that the noble and profound application of ideas to life is the most essential part of poetic greatness. I said that a great poet receives his distinctive character of superiority from his application, under the conditions immutably fixed by the laws of poetic beauty and poetic truth, from his application, I say, to his subject, whatever it may be, of the ideas

"On man, on nature, and on human life,"

which he has acquired for himself. The line quoted is Words-worth's own; and his superiority arises from his powerful use, in his best pieces, his powerful application to his subject, of ideas "on man, on nature, and on human life."

Voltaire, with his signal acuteness, most truly remarked that
z

"no nation has treated in poetry moral ideas with more energy and depth than the English nation." And he adds: "There, it seems to me, is the great merit of the English poets." Voltaire does not mean, by "treating in poetry moral ideas," the composing moral and didactic poems;—that brings us but a very little way in poetry. He means just the same thing as was meant when I spoke above "of the noble and profound application of ideas to life"; and he means the application of these ideas under the conditions fixed for us by the laws of poetic beauty and poetic truth. If it is said that to call these ideas *moral* ideas is to introduce a strong and injurious limitation, I answer that it is to do nothing of the kind, because moral ideas are really so main a part of human life. The question, *how to live*, is itself a moral idea; and it is the question which most interests every man, and with which, in some way or other, he is perpetually occupied. A large sense is of course to be given to the term *moral*. Whatever bears upon the question, "how to live," comes under it.

> "Nor love thy life, nor hate; but, what thou liv'st,
>   Live well; how long or short, permit to heaven."

In those fine lines Milton utters, as every one at once perceives, a moral idea. Yes, but so too, when Keats consoles the forward-bending lover on the Grecian Urn, the lover arrested and presented in immortal relief by the sculptor's hand before he can kiss, with the line,

> "For ever wilt thou love, and she be fair"—

he utters a moral idea. When Shakespeare says, that

> "We are such stuff
> As dreams are made of, and our little life
> Is rounded with a sleep,"

he utters a moral idea.

Voltaire was right in thinking that the energetic and profound treatment of moral ideas, in this large sense, is what distinguishes the English poetry. He sincerely meant praise, not dispraise or hint of limitation; and they err who suppose that poetic limitation is a necessary consequence of the fact, the fact being granted as Voltaire states it. If what distinguishes the greatest poets is their powerful and profound application of ideas to life, which surely no good critic will deny, then to prefix to the term ideas here the term moral makes hardly any difference, because human life itself is in so preponderating a degree moral.

It is important, therefore, to hold fast to this: that poetry is at bottom a criticism of life; that the greatness of a poet lies in his powerful and beautiful application of ideas to life,—to the question: How to live. Morals are often treated in a narrow and false fashion; they are bound up with systems of thought and belief which have had their day; they are fallen into the hands of pedants and professional dealers; they grow tiresome to some of us. We find attraction, at times, even in a poetry of revolt against them; in a poetry which might take for its motto Omar Kheyam's words: "Let us make up in the tavern for the time which we have wasted in the mosque." Or we find attractions in a poetry indifferent to them; in a poetry where the contents may be what they will, but where the form is studied and exquisite. We delude ourselves in either case; and the best cure for our delusion is to let our minds rest upon that great and inexhaustible word *life*, until we learn to enter into its meaning. A poetry of revolt against moral ideas is a poetry of revolt against *life*; a poetry of indifference towards moral ideas is a poetry of indifference towards *life*.

Epictetus had a happy figure for things like the play of the senses, or literary form and finish, or argumentative ingenuity, in comparison with "the best and master thing" for us, as he called it, the concern, how to live. Some people were afraid of them, he said, or they disliked and undervalued them. Such people were wrong; they were unthankful or cowardly. But the things might also be over-prized, and treated as final when they are not. They bear to life the relation which inns bear to home. "As if a man, journeying home, and finding a nice inn on the road, and liking it, were to stay for ever at the inn! Man, thou hast forgotten thine object; thy journey was not *to* this, but *through* this. 'But this inn is taking.' And how many other inns, too, are taking, and how many fields and meadows! but as places of passage merely. You have an object, which is this: to get home, to do your duty to your family, friends, and fellow-countrymen, to attain inward freedom, serenity, happiness, contentment. Style takes your fancy, arguing takes your fancy, and you forget your home and want to make your abode with them and to stay with them, on the plea that they are taking. Who denies that they are taking? but as places of passage, as inns. And when I say this, you suppose me to be attacking the care for style, the care for argument. I am not; I attack the resting in them, the not looking to the end which is beyond them."

Now, when we come across a poet like Théophile Gautier, we have a poet who has taken up his abode at an inn, and never got farther. There may be inducements to this or that one of us, at this or that moment, to find delight in him, to cleave to him; but after all, we do not change the truth about him,—we only stay ourselves in his inn along with him. And when we come across a poet like Wordsworth, who sings

> "Of truth, of grandeur, beauty, love and hope.
> And melancholy fear subdued by faith,
> Of blessed consolations in distress,
> Of moral strength and intellectual power,
> Of joy in widest commonalty spread"—

then we have a poet intent on "the best and master thing," and who prosecutes his journey home. We say, for brevity's sake, that he deals with *life*, because he deals with that in which life really consists. This is what Voltaire means to praise in the English poets,—this dealing with what is really life. But always it is the mark of the greatest poets that they deal with it; and to say that the English poets are remarkable for dealing with it, is only another way of saying, what is true, that in poetry the English genius has especially shown its power.

Wordsworth deals with it, and his greatness lies in his dealing with it so powerfully. I have named a number of celebrated poets above all of whom he, in my opinion, deserves to be placed. He is to be placed above poets like Voltaire, Dryden, Pope, Lessing, Schiller, because these famous personages, with a thousand gifts, and merits, never, or scarcely ever, attain the distinctive accent and utterance of the high and genuine poets—

> "Quique pii vates et Phœbo digna locuti."

at all. Burns, Keats, Heine, not to speak of others in our list, have this accent;—who can doubt it? And at the same time they have treasures of humour, felicity, passion, for which in Wordsworth we shall look in vain. Where, then, is Wordsworth's superiority? It is here; he deals with more of *life* than they do; he deals with *life*, as a whole, more powerfully.

No Wordsworthian will doubt this. Nay, the fervent Wordsworthian will add, as Mr. Leslie Stephen does, that Wordsworth's poetry is precious because his philosophy is sound; that his "ethical system is as distinctive and capable of exposition as Bishop Butler's; that his poetry is informed by ideas which "fall spontaneously into a scientific system of thought." But we must be on our guard against the Wordsworthians, if we want to secure for Wordsworth his due rank as a poet. The Wordsworthians are apt to praise him for the wrong things, and to lay far too much stress upon what they call his philosophy. His poetry is the reality, his philosophy,—so far, at least, as it may put on the form and habit of "a scientific system of thought," and the more that it puts them on,—is the illusion. Perhaps we shall one day learn to make this proposition general, and to say: Poetry is the reality, philosophy the illusion. But in Wordsworth's case, at any rate, we cannot do him justice until we dismiss his formal philosophy.

The *Excursion* abounds with philosophy, and therefore the *Excursion* is to the Wordsworthian what it never can be to the disinterested lover of poetry,—a satisfactory work. "Duty exists," says Wordsworth, in the *Excursion*; and then he proceeds thus—

> ". . . Immutably survive,
> For our support, the measures and the forms,
> Which an abstract Intelligence supplies,
> Whose kingdom is, where time and space are not."

And the Wordsworthian is delighted, and thinks that here is a sweet union of philosophy and poetry. But the disinterested lover of poetry will feel that the lines carry us really not a step farther than the proposition which they would interpret; that they are a tissue of elevated but abstract verbiage, alien to the very nature of poetry.

Or let us come direct to the centre of Wordsworth's philosophy, as "an ethical system, as distinctive and capable of systematical exposition as Bishop Butler's"—

> ". . . One adequate support
> For the calamities of mortal life
> Exists, one only;—an assured belief
> That the procession of our fate, howe'er
> Sad or disturbed, is ordered by a Being
> Of infinite benevolence and power;
> Whose everlasting purposes embrace
> All accidents, converting them to good."

That is doctrine such as we hear in church too, religious and philosophic doctrine; and the attached Wordsworthian loves passages of such doctrine, and brings them forward in proof of his poet's excellence. But however true the doctrine may be, it has, as here presented, none of the characters of *poetic* truth, the kind of truth which we require from a poet, and in which Wordsworth is really strong.

Even the "intimations" of the famous Ode, those cornerstones of the supposed philosophic system of Wordsworth,—the idea of the high instincts and affections coming out in childhood, testifying of a divine home recently left, and fading away as our life proceeds,—this idea, of undeniable beauty as a play of fancy, has itself not the character of poetic truth of the best kind; it has no real solidity. The instinct of delight in Nature and her beauty had no doubt extraordinary strength in Wordsworth himself as a child. But to say that universally this instinct is mighty in childhood, and tends to die away afterwards, is to say what is extremely doubtful. In many people, perhaps with the majority of educated persons, the love of nature is nearly imperceptible at ten years old, but strong and operative at thirty. In general we may say of these high instincts of early childhood, the base of the alleged systematic philosophy of Wordsworth, what Thucydides says of the early achievements of the Greek race: "It is impossible to speak with certainty of what is so remote; but from all that we can really investigate, I should say that they were no very great things."

Finally, the "scientific system of thought" in Wordsworth gives us at last such poetry as this, which the devout Words-worthian accepts—

> "O for the coming of that glorious time
> When, prizing knowledge as her noblest wealth
> And best protection, this Imperial Realm,
> While she exacts allegiance, shall admit
> An obligation, on her part, to *teach*
> Them who are born to serve her and obey;
> Binding herself by statute to secure,
> For all the children whom her soil maintains,
> The rudiments of letters, and inform
> The mind with moral and religious truth."

Wordsworth calls Voltaire dull, and surely the production of these un-Voltairian lines must have been imposed on him as a judgment! One can hear them being quoted at a Social Science Congress; one can call up the whole scene. A great room in one of our dismal provincial towns; dusty air and jaded afternoon daylight; benches full of men with bald heads and women in spectacles; an orator lifting up his face from a manuscript written within and without to declaim these lines of Wordsworth; and in the soul of any poor child of nature who may have wandered in thither, an unutterable sense of lamentation, and mourning, and woe!

"But turn we," as Wordsworth says, "from these bold, bad men," the haunters of Social Science Congresses. And let us be on our guard, too, against the exhibitors and extollers of a "scientific system of thought" in Wordsworth's poetry. The poetry will never be seen aright while they thus exhibit it. The cause of its greatness is simple, and may be told quite simply. Wordsworth's poetry is great because of the extraordinary power with which Wordsworth feels the joy offered to us in nature, the joy offered to us in the simple primary affections and duties;

and because of the extraordinary power with which, in case after case, he shows us this joy, and renders it so as to make us share it.

The source of joy from which he thus draws is the truest and most unfailing source of joy accessible to man. It is also accessible universally. Wordsworth brings us word, therefore, according to his own strong and characteristic line, he brings us word

"Of joy in widest commonalty spread."

Here is an immense advantage for a poet. Wordsworth tells of what all seek, and tells of it at its truest and best source, and yet a source where all may go and draw for it.

Nevertheless, we are not to suppose that everything is precious which Wordsworth, standing even at this perennial and beautiful source, may give us. Wordsworthians are apt to talk as if it must be. They will speak with the same reverence of *The Sailor's Mother*, for example, as of *Lucy Gray*. They do their master harm by such lack of discrimination. *Lucy Gray* is a beautiful success; *The Sailor's Mother* is a failure. To give aright what he wishes to give, to interpret and render successfully, is not always within Wordsworth's own command. It is within no poet's command; here is the part of the Muse, the inspiration, the God, the "not ourselves." In Wordsworth's case, the accident, for so it may almost be called, of inspiration, is of peculiar importance. No poet, perhaps, is so evidently filled with a new and sacred energy when the inspiration is upon him; no poet, when it fails him, is so left "weak as is a breaking wave." I remember hearing him say that "Goethe's poetry was not inevitable enough." The remark is striking and true; no line in Goethe, as Goethe said himself, but its maker knew well how it came there. Wordsworth is right, Goethe's poetry is not inevitable; not inevitable enough. But Wordsworth's poetry, when he is at his best, is inevitable, as inevitable as Nature herself. It might seem that Nature not only gave him the matter for his poem, but wrote his poem for him. He has no style. He was too conversant with Milton not to catch at times his master's manner, and he has fine Miltonic lines; but he has no assured poetic style of his own, like Milton. When he seeks to have a style he falls into ponderosity and pomposity. In the *Excursion* we have his style, as an artistic product of his own creation; and although Jeffrey completely failed to recognise Wordsworth's real greatness, he was yet not wrong in saying of the *Excursion*, as a work of poetic style: "This will never do." And yet magical as is that power, which Wordsworth has not, of assured and possessed poetic style, he has something which is an equivalent for it.

Every one who has any sense for these things feels the subtle turn, the heightening, which is given to a poet's verse by his genius for style. We can feel it in the

"After life's fitful fever, he sleeps well"—

of Shakespeare; in the

". . . though fall'n on evil days,
On evil days though fall'n, and evil tongues"—

of Milton. It is the incomparable charm of Milton's power of poetic style which gives such worth to *Paradise Regained*, and makes a great poem of a work in which Milton's imagination does not soar high. Wordsworth has in constant possession, and at command, no style of this kind; but he had too poetic a nature, and had read the great poets too well, not to catch, as I have already remarked, something of it occasionally. We find it not only in his Miltonic lines; we find it in such a phrase as this, where the manner is his own, not Milton's—

". . . the fierce confederate storm
Of sorrow barricadoed evermore
Within the walls of cities;"

although even here, perhaps, the power of style, which is undeniable, is more properly that of eloquent prose than the subtle heightening and change wrought by genuine poetic style. It is style, again, and the elevation given by style, which chiefly makes the effectiveness of *Laodameia*. Still the right sort of verse to choose from Wordsworth, if we are to seize his true and most characteristic form of expression, is a line like this from *Michael*—

"And never lifted up a single stone."

There is nothing subtle in it, no heightening, no study of poetic style, strictly so called, at all; yet it is expression of the highest and most truly expressive kind.

Wordsworth owed much to Burns, and a style of perfect plainness, relying for effect solely on the weight and force of that which with entire fidelity it utters, Burns could show him.

"The poor inhabitant below
Was quick to learn and wise to know,
And keenly felt the friendly glow
    And softer flame;
But thoughtless follies laid him low
    And stain'd his name."

Every one will be conscious of a likeness here to Wordsworth; and if Wordsworth did great things with this nobly plain manner, we must remember, what indeed he himself would always have been forward to acknowledge, that Burns used it before him.

Still Wordsworth's use of it has something unique and unmatchable. Nature herself seems, I say, to take the pen out of his hand, and to write for him with her own bare, sheer, penetrating power. This arises from two causes; from the profound sincereness with which Wordsworth feels his subject, and also from the profoundly sincere and natural character of his subject itself. He can and will treat such a subject with nothing but the most plain, first-hand, almost austere naturalness. His expression may often be called bald, as, for instance, in the poem of *Resolution and Independence;* but it is bald as the bare mountain tops are bald, with a baldness which is full of grandeur.

Wherever we meet with the successful balance, in Wordsworth, of profound truth of subject with profound truth of execution, he is unique. His best poems are those which most perfectly exhibit this balance. I have a warm admiration for *Laodameia* and for the great *Ode;* but if I am to tell the very truth, I find *Laodameia* not wholly free from something artificial, and the great *Ode* not wholly free from something declamatory. If I had to pick out poems of a kind most perfectly to show Wordsworth's unique power, I should rather choose poems such as *Michael, The Fountain, The Highland Reaper.* And poems with the peculiar and unique beauty which distinguishes these, Wordsworth produced in considerable number; besides very many other poems of which the worth, although not so rare as the worth of these, is still exceedingly high.

On the whole, then, as I said at the beginning, not only is Wordsworth eminent by reason of the goodness of his best work, but he is eminent also by reason of the great body of good work which he has left to us. With the ancients I will not compare him. In many respects the ancients are far above us, and yet there is something that we demand which they can never give. Leaving the ancients, let us come to the poets and poetry of Christendom. Dante, Shakespeare, Molière, Milton, Goethe, are altogether larger and more splendid luminaries in the poetical heaven than Wordsworth. But I know not where else, among the moderns, we are to find his superiors.

To disengage the poems which show his power, and to present them to the English-speaking public and to the world, is the object of this volume. I by no means say that it contains all which in Wordsworth's poems is interesting. Except in the case of *Margaret,* a story composed separately from the rest of the *Excursion,* and which belongs to a different part of England, I have not ventured on detaching portions of poems, or on giving any piece otherwise than as Wordsworth himself gave it. But under the conditions imposed by this reserve, the volume contains, I think, everything, or nearly everything, which may best serve him with the majority of lovers of poetry, nothing which may disserve him.

I have spoken lightly of Wordsworthians; and if we are to get Wordsworth recognised by the public and by the world, we must recommend him not in the spirit of a clique, but in the spirit of disinterested lovers of poetry. But I am a Wordsworthian myself. I can read with pleasure and edification *Peter Bell*, and the whole series of *Ecclesiastical Sonnets*, and the address to Mr. Wilkinson's spade, and even the *Thanksgiving Ode;*—everything of Wordsworth, I think, except *Vaudracour and Julia*. It is not for nothing that one has been brought up in the veneration of a man so truly worthy of homage; that one has seen him and heard him, lived in his neighbourhood, and been familiar with his country. No Wordsworthian has a tenderer affection for this pure and sage master than I, or is less really offended by his defects. But Wordsworth is something more than the pure and safe master of a small band of devoted followers, and we ought not to rest satisfied until he is seen to be what he is. He is one of the very chief glories of English Poetry; and by nothing is England so glorious as by her poetry. Let us lay aside every weight which hinders our getting him recognised as this, and let our one study be to bring to pass, as widely as possible and as truly as possible, his own word concerning his poems: "They will co-operate with the benign tendencies in human nature and society, and will, in their degree, be efficacious in making men wiser, better, and happier."

Byron

WHEN at last I held in my hand the volume of poems which I had chosen from Wordsworth, and began to turn over its pages, there arose in me almost immediately the desire to see beside it, as a companion volume, a like collection of the best poetry of Byron. Alone amongst our poets of the earlier part of this century, Byron and Wordsworth not only furnish material enough for a volume of this kind, but also, as it seems to me, they both of them gain considerably by being thus exhibited. There are poems of Coleridge and of Keats equal, if not superior, to anything of Byron or Wordsworth; but a dozen pages or two will contain them, and the remaining poetry is of a quality much inferior. Scott never, I think, rises as a poet to the level of Byron and Wordsworth at all. On the other hand, he never falls below his own usual level very far; and by a volume of selections from him, therefore, his effectiveness is not increased. As to Shelley there will be more question; and indeed Mr. Stopford Brooke, whose accomplishments, eloquence, and love of poetry we must all recognise and admire, has actually given us Shelley in such a volume. But for my own part I cannot think that Shelley's poetry, except by snatches and fragments, has the value of the good work of Wordsworth and Byron; or that it is possible for even Mr. Stopford Brooke to make up a volume of selections from him which, for real substance, power, and worth, can at all take rank with a like volume from Byron or Wordsworth.

Shelley knew quite well the difference between the achievement of such a poet as Byron and his own. He praises Byron too unreservedly, but he sincerely felt, and he was right in feeling, that Byron was a greater poetical power than himself. As a man, Shelley is at a number of points immeasurably Byron's superior; he is a beautiful and enchanting spirit, whose vision, when we call it up, has far more loveliness, more charm for our soul, than the vision of Byron. But all the personal charm of Shelley cannot hinder us from at last discovering in his poetry the incurable want, in general, of a sound subject-matter, and the incurable fault, in consequence, of unsubstantiality. Those who extol him as the poet of clouds, the poet of sunsets, are only saying that he did not, in fact, lay hold upon the poet's right subject-matter; and in honest truth, with all his charm of soul and spirit, and with all his gift of musical diction and movement, he never, or hardly ever, did. Except, as I have said, for a few short things and single stanzas, his original poetry is less satisfactory than his translations, for in these the subject-matter was found for him. Nay, I doubt whether his delightful Essays and Letters, which deserve to be far more read than they are now, will not resist the wear and tear of time better, and finally come to stand higher, than his poetry.

There remain to be considered Byron and Wordsworth. That Wordsworth affords good material for a volume of selections, and that he gains by having his poetry thus presented, is an old belief of mine which led me lately to make up a volume of poems chosen out of Wordsworth, and to bring it before the public. By its kind reception of the volume, the public seems to show itself a partaker in my belief. Now Byron also supplies plenty of material for a like volume, and he too gains, I think, by being so presented. Mr. Swinburne urges, indeed, that "Byron, who rarely wrote anything either worthless or faultless, can only be judged or appreciated in the mass; the greatest of his works was his whole work taken together." It is quite true that Byron rarely wrote anything either worthless or faultless; it is quite true also that in the appreciation of Byron's power a sense of the amount and variety of his work, defective though much of his work is, enters justly into our estimate. But although there may be little in Byron's poetry which can be pronounced either worthless or faultless, there are portions of it which are far higher in worth and far more free from fault than others. And although, again, the abundance and variety of his production is undoubtedly a proof of his power, yet I question whether by reading everything which he gives us we are so likely to acquire an admiring sense even of his variety and abundance, as by reading what he gives us at his happier moments. Varied and abundant he amply proves himself even by this taken alone. Receive him absolutely without omission or compression, follow his whole outpouring stanza by stanza and line by line from the very commencement to the very end, and he is capable of being tiresome.

Byron has told us himself that the *Giaour* "is but a string of passages." He has made full confession of his own negligence. "No one," says he, "has done more through negligence to corrupt the language." This accusation brought by himself against his poems is not just; but when he goes on to say of them, that "their faults, whatever they may be, are those of negligence and not of labour," he says what is perfectly true. "*Lara*," he declares, "I wrote while undressing after coming home from balls and masquerades, in the year of revelry, 1814. The *Bride* was written in four, the *Corsair* in ten days." He calls this "a humiliating confession, as it proves my own want of judgment in publishing, and the public's in reading, things which cannot have stamina for permanence." Again he does his poems injustice; the producer of such poems could not but publish them, the public could not but read them. Nor could Byron have produced his work in any other fashion; his poetic work could not have first grown and matured in his own mind, and then come forth as an organic whole; Byron had not enough of the artist in him for this, nor enough of self-command. He wrote, as he truly tells us, to relieve himself, and he went on writing because he found the relief become indispensable. But it was inevitable that works so produced should be, in general, "a string of passages," poured out, as he describes them, with rapidity and excitement, and with new passages constantly suggesting themselves, and added while his work was going through the press. It is evident that we have here neither deliberate scientific construction, nor yet the instinctive artistic creation of poetic wholes; and that to take passages from work produced as Byron's was is a very different thing from taking passages out of the *Œdipus* or the *Tempest*, and deprives the poetry far less of its advantage.

Nay, it gives advantage to the poetry, instead of depriving it of any. Byron, I said, has not a great artist's profound and patient skill in combining an action or in developing a character, —a skill which we must watch and follow if we are to do justice to it. But he has a wonderful power of vividly conceiving a single incident, a single situation; of throwing himself upon it, grasping it as if it were real and he saw and felt it, and of making us see and feel it too. The *Giaour* is, as he truly called it, "a string of passages," not a work moving by a deep internal law of development to a necessary end; and our total impression from it cannot but receive from this, its inherent defect, a certain dimness and indistinctness. But the incidents of the journey and death of Hassan, in that poem, are conceived and presented with a vividness not to be surpassed; and our impression from them is correspondingly clear and powerful. In *Lara*, again, there is no adequate development either of the character of the chief personage or of the action of the poem; our total impression from the work is a confused one. Yet such an incident as the disposal of the slain Ezzelin's body passes before our eyes as if we actually saw it. And in the same way as these bursts of incident, bursts of sentiment also, living and vigorous, often occur in the midst of poems which must be admitted to be but weakly-conceived and loosely-combined wholes. Byron cannot but be a gainer by having attention concentrated upon what is vivid, powerful, effective in his work, and withdrawn from what is not so.

Byron, I say, cannot but be a gainer by this, just as Wordsworth is a gainer by a like proceeding. I esteem Wordsworth's poetry so highly, and the world, in my opinion, has done it such scant justice, that I could not rest satisfied until I had fulfilled, on Wordsworth's behalf, a long-cherished desire;—had disengaged, to the best of my power, his good work from the inferior work joined with it, and had placed before the public the body of his good work by itself. To the poetry of Byron the world has ardently paid homage; full justice from his contemporaries, perhaps even more than justice, his torrent of poetry received. His poetry was admired, adored, "with all its imperfections on its head,"—in spite of negligence, in spite of diffuseness, in spite of repetitions, in spite of whatever faults it possessed. His name is still great and brilliant. Nevertheless the hour of irresistible vogue has passed away for him; even for Byron it could not but pass away. The time has come for him, as it comes for all poets, when he must take his real and permanent place, no longer depending upon the vogue of his own day and upon the enthusiasm of his contemporaries. Whatever we may think of him, we shall not be subjugated by him as they were; for, as he cannot be for us what he was for them, we cannot admire him so hotly and indiscriminately as they. His faults of negligence, of diffuseness, of repetition, his faults of whatever kind, we shall abundantly feel and unsparingly criticise; the more interval of time between us and him makes disillusion of this kind inevitable. But how then will Byron stand, if we relieve him too, so far as we can, of the encumbrance of his inferior and weakest work, and if we bring before us his best and strongest work in one body together? That is the question which I, who can even remember the latter years of Byron's vogue, and have myself felt the expiring wave of that mighty influence, but who certainly also regard him, and have long regarded him, without illusion, cannot but ask myself, cannot but seek to answer. The present volume is an attempt to provide adequate data for answering it.

Byron has been over-praised, no doubt. "Byron is one of our French superstitions," says M. Edmond Scherer; but where has Byron not been a superstition? He pays now the penalty of this exaggerated worship. "Alone among the English poets his contemporaries, Byron," said M. Taine, "*atteint à la cîme*,—gets to the top of the poetic mountain." But the idol that M. Taine had thus adored M. Scherer is almost for burning. "In Byron," he declares,"there is a remarkable inability ever to lift himself into the region of real poetic art,—art impersonal and disinterested,—at all. He has fecundity, eloquence, wit, but even these qualities themselves are confined within somewhat narrow limits. He has treated hardly any subject but one,—himself; now the man, in Byron, is of a nature even less sincere than the poet. This beautiful and blighted being is at bottom a coxcomb. He posed all his life long."

Our poet could not well meet with more severe and unsympathetic criticism. However, the praise often given to Byron has been so exaggerated as to provoke, perhaps, a reaction in which he is unduly disparaged. "As various in composition as Shakespeare himself, Lord Byron has embraced," says Sir Walter Scott, "every topic of human life, and sounded every string on the divine harp, from its slightest to its most powerful and heart-astounding tones." It is not surprising that some one with a cool head should retaliate, on such provocation as this, by saying: "He has treated hardly any subject but one, *himself*." "In the very grand and tremendous drama of *Cain*," says Scott, "Lord

Byron has certainly matched Milton on his own ground." And
Lord Byron has done all this, Scott adds, "while managing his
pen with the careless and negligent ease of a man of quality."
Alas, "managing his pen with the careless and negligent ease of
a man of quality," Byron wrote in his *Cain*—

> "Souls that dare look the Omnipotent tyrant in
> His everlasting face, and tell him that
> His evil is not good;"

or he wrote—

> ". . . And *thou* would'st go on aspiring
> To the great double Mysteries! the *two Principles!*" [1]

One has only to repeat to oneself a line from *Paradise Lost* in
order to feel the difference.

Sainte-Beuve, speaking of that exquisite master of language,
the Italian poet Leopardi, remarks how often we see the alliance,
singular though it may at first sight appear, of the poetical genius
with the genius for scholarship and philology.[2] Dante and Milton
are instances which will occur to every one's mind. Byron is so
negligent in his poetical style, he is often, to say the truth, so
slovenly, slipshod, and infelicitous, he is so little haunted by
the true artist's fine passion for the correct use and consummate
management of words, that he may be described as having for
this artistic gift the insensibility of the barbarian;—which is
perhaps only another and a less flattering way of saying, with
Scott, that he " manages his pen with the careless and negligent
ease of a man of quality." Just of a piece with the rhythm of

> "Dare you await the event of a few minutes'
> Deliberation?"

or of

> "All shall be void—
> Destroy'd!"

is the diction of

> "Which now is painful to these eyes,
> Which have not seen the sun to rise;"

or of

> ". . . there let him lay!"

or of the famous passage beginning

> "He who hath bent him o'er the dead;"

---

[1] The italics are in the original.

[2] [Sainte-Beuve, *Portraits Contemporains*, vol. IV. (Paris, n.d.
[1876]). The essay was first published in 1844, and it was this, no
doubt, which first introduced Arnold to Leopardi.]

with those trailing relatives, that crying grammatical solecism, that inextricable anacolouthon! To class the work of the author of such things with the work of the authors of such verse as

> "In the dark backward and abysm of time"—

or as

> "Presenting Thebes, or Pelops' line,
> Or the tale of Troy divine"—

is ridiculous. Shakespeare and Milton, with their secret of consummate felicity in diction and movement, are of another and an altogether higher order from Byron, nay, for that matter, from Wordsworth also; from the author of such verse as

> "Sol hath dropt into his harbour"—

or (if Mr. Ruskin pleases) as

> "Parching summer hath no warrant"—

as from the author of

> "All shall be void—
> Destroy'd!"

With a poetical gift and a poetical performance of the very highest order, the slovenliness and tunelessness of much of Byron's production, the pompousness and ponderousness of much of Wordsworth's are incompatible. Let us admit this to the full.

Moreover, while we are hearkening to M. Scherer, and going along with him in his fault-finding, let us admit, too, that the man in Byron is in many respects as unsatisfactory as the poet. And, putting aside all direct moral criticism of him,—with which we need not concern ourselves here,—we shall find that he is unsatisfactory in the same way. Some of Byron's most crying faults as a man,—his vulgarity, his affectation,—are really akin to the faults of commonness, of want of art, in his workmanship as a poet. The ideal nature for the poet and artist is that of the finely touched and finely gifted man, the εὐφνής of the Greeks; now, Byron's nature was in substance not that of the εὐφνής at all, but rather, as I have said, of the barbarian. The want of fine perception which made it possible for him to formulate either the comparison between himself and Rousseau, or his reason for getting Lord Delawarr excused from a "licking" at Harrow, is exactly what made possible for him also his terrible dealings in, *An ye wool; I have redde thee; Sunburn me; Oons, and it is excellent well.* It is exactly, again, what made possible for him his precious dictum that Pope is a Greek temple, and a string of other criticisms of the like force; it is exactly, in fine, what deteriorated the quality of his poetic production. If we think of a good representative of that finely touched and exquisitely gifted nature which is the ideal nature for the poet and artist,—if we think of Raphael, for instance, who truly is εὐφυής just as Byron is not,—we shall bring into clearer light the connection in Byron between the faults of the man and the faults of the poet. With Raphael's character Byron's sins of vulgarity and false criticism would have been impossible, just as with Raphael's art Byron's sins of common and bad workmanship.

Yes, all this is true, but it is not the whole truth about Byron nevertheless; very far from it. The severe criticism of M. Scherer by no means gives us the whole truth about Byron, and we have not yet got it in what has been added to that criticism here. The negative part of the true criticism of him we perhaps have; the positive part, by far the more important, we have not. Byron's admirers appeal eagerly to foreign testimonies in his favour. Some of these testimonies do not much move me; but one testimony there is among them which will always carry, with me at any rate, very great weight,—the testimony of Goethe. Goethe's sayings about Byron were uttered, it must however be remembered, at the height of Byron's vogue, when that puissant and splendid personality was exercising its full power of attraction. In Goethe's own household there was an atmosphere of glowing Byron-worship; his daughter-in-law was a passionate admirer of Byron, nay, she enjoyed and prized his poetry, as did Tieck and so many others in Germany at that time, much above the poetry of Goethe himself. Instead of being irritated and rendered jealous by this, a nature like Goethe's was inevitably led by it to heighten, not lower, the note of his praise. The Time-Spirit, or *Zeit-Geist*, he would himself have said, was working just then for Byron. This working of the *Zeit-Geist* in his favour was an advantage added to Byron's other advantages, an advantage of which he had a right to get the benefit. This is what Goethe would have thought and said to himself; and so he would have been led even to heighten somewhat his estimate of Byron, and to accentuate the emphasis of praise. Goethe speaking of Byron at that moment was not and could not be quite the same cool critic as Goethe speaking of Dante, or Molière, or Milton. This, I say, we ought to remember in reading Goethe's judgments on Byron and his poetry. Still, if we are careful to bear this in mind, and if we quote Goethe's praise correctly,—which is not always done by those who in this country quote it,—and if we add to it that great and due qualification added to it by Goethe himself,—which so far as I have seen has never yet been done by his quoters in this country at all,—then we shall have a judgment on Byron, which comes, I think, very near to the truth, and which may well command our adherence.

In his judicious and interesting Life of Byron, Professor Nichol quotes Goethe as saying that Byron "is undoubtedly to be regarded as the greatest genius of our century." What Goethe did really say was "the greatest *talent*," not "the greatest *genius*." The difference is important, because, while talent gives the notion of power in a man's performance, genius gives rather the notion of felicity and perfection in it; and this divine gift of consummate felicity by no means, as we have seen, belongs to Byron and to his poetry. Goethe said that Byron "must unquestionably be regarded as the greatest talent of the century."[1] He said of him moreover: "The English may think of Byron what they please, but it is certain that they can point to no poet who is his like. He is different from all the rest, and in the main greater." Here, again, Professor Nichol translates: "They can show no (living) poet who is to be compared to him;"—inserting the word *living*, I suppose, to prevent its being thought that Goethe would have ranked Byron, as a poet, above Shakespeare and Milton. But Goethe did not use, or, I think, mean to imply, any limitation such as is added by Professor Nichol. Goethe said simply, and he meant to say, "*no* poet." Only the words which follow [2] ought not, I think, to be rendered, "who is to be compared to him," that is to say, "*who is his equal as a poet*." They mean rather, "who may properly be compared with him," "*who is his parallel*." And when Goethe said that Byron was "in the main greater" than all the rest of the English poets, he was not so much thinking of the strict rank, as poetry, of Byron's production; he was thinking of that wonderful personality of Byron which so enters into his poetry, and which Goethe called "a personality such, for its eminence, as has never been yet, and such as is not likely to come again." He was thinking of that "daring, dash, and grandiosity," [3] of Byron, which are indeed so splendid; and which were, so Goethe maintained, of a character to do good, because "everything great is formative," and what is thus formative does us good.

The faults which went with this greatness, and which impaired Byron's poetical work, Goethe saw very well. He saw the constant state of warfare and combat, the "negative and polemical

[1] "Der ohne Frage als das grösste Talent des Jahrhunderts anzusehen ist."
[2] "Der ihm su vergleichen wäre."
[3] "Byron's Kühnheit, Keckheit und Grandiositat, ist das nicht alles bildend?—Alles Grosse bildet, sobald wir es gewahr werden."

working," which makes Byron's poetry a poetry in which we can so little find rest; he saw the *Hang zum Unbegrenzten*, the straining after the unlimited, which made it impossible for Byron to produce poetic wholes such as the *Tempest* or *Lear;* he saw the *zu viel Empirie*, the promiscuous adoption of all the matter offered to the poet by life, just as it was offered, without thought or patience for the mysterious transmutation to be operated on this matter by poetic form. But in a sentence which I cannot, as I say, remember to have yet seen quoted in any English criticism of Byron, Goethe lays his finger on the cause of all these defects in Byron, and on his real source of weakness both as a man and as a poet. "The moment he reflects, he is a child," says Goethe;—"*sobald er reflectirt ist er ein Kind.*"

Now if we take the two parts of Goethe's criticism of Byron, the favourable and the unfavourable, and put them together, we shall have, I think, the truth. On the one hand, a splendid and puissant personality—a personality "in eminence such as has never been yet, and is not likely to come again"; of which the like, therefore, is not to be found among the poets of our nation, by which Byron "is different from all the rest, and in the main greater." Byron is, moreover, "the greatest talent of our century." On the other hand, this splendid personality and unmatched talent, this unique Byron, "is quite too much in the dark about himself;" [1] nay, "the moment he begins to reflect, he is a child." There we have, I think, Byron complete; and in estimating him and ranking him we have to strike a balance between the gain which accrues to his poetry, as compared with the productions of other poets, from his superiority, and the loss which accrues to it from his defects.

A balance of this kind has to be struck in the case of all poets except the few supreme masters in whom a profound criticism of life exhibits itself in indissoluble connection with the laws of poetic truth and beauty. I have seen it said that I allege poetry to have for its characteristic this: that it is a criticism of life; and that I make it to be thereby distinguished from prose, which is something else. So far from it, that when I first used this expression, *a criticism of life*, now many years ago, it was to literature in general that I applied it, and not to poetry in especial. "The end and aim of all literature," I said, "is, if one considers it attentively, nothing but that: *a criticism of life.*" And so it surely is; the main end and aim of all our utterance, whether in prose or in verse, is surely a criticism of life. We are not brought much on our way, I admit, towards an adequate definition of poetry as distinguished from prose by that truth; still a truth it is, and

[1] "Gar zu dunkel über sich selbst."

poetry can never prosper if it is forgotten. In poetry, however, the criticism of life has to be made conformably to the laws of poetic truth and poetic beauty. Truth and seriousness of sub-stance and matter, felicity and perfection of diction and manner, as these are exhibited in the best poets, are what constitute a criticism of life made in conformity with the laws of poetic truth and poetic beauty; and it is by knowing and feeling the work of those poets, that we learn to recognise the fulfilment and non-fulfilment of such conditions.

The moment, however, that we leave the small band of the very best poets, the true classics, and deal with poets of the next rank, we shall find that perfect truth and seriousness of matter, in close alliance with perfect truth and felicity of manner, is the rule no longer. We have now to take what we can get, to forego something here, to admit compensation for it there; to strike a balance, and to see how our poets stand in respect to one another when that balance has been struck. Let us observe how this is so.

We will take three poets, among the most considerable of our century: Leopardi, Byron, Wordsworth. Giacomo Leopardi was ten years younger than Byron, and he died thirteen years after him; both of them, therefore, died young—Byron at the age of thirty-six, Leopardi at the age of thirty-nine. Both of them were of noble birth, both of them suffered from physical defect, both of them were in revolt against the established facts and beliefs of their age; but here the likeness between them ends. The stricken poet of Recanati had no country, for an Italy in his day did not exist; he had no audience, no celebrity. The volume of his poems, published in the very year of Byron's death, hardly sold, I suppose, its tens, while the volumes of Byron's poetry were selling their tens of thousands. And yet Leopardi has the very qualities which we have found wanting to Byron; he has the sense for form and style, the passion for just expression, the sure and firm touch of the true artist. Nay, more, he has a grave fulness of knowledge, an insight into the real bearings of the questions which as a sceptical poet he raises, a power of seizing the real point, a lucidity, with which the author of *Cain* has nothing to compare. I can hardly imagine Leopardi reading the

"... And *thou* would'st go on aspiring
To the great double Mysteries! the *two Principles!*"

or following Byron in his theological controversy with Dr. Kennedy, without having his features overspread by a calm and fine smile, and remarking of his brilliant contemporary, as Goethe did, that "the moment he begins to reflect, he is a child." But indeed whoever wishes to feel the full superiority of Leopardi over Byron in philosophic thought, and in the expression of it, has only to read one paragraph of one poem, the paragraph of *La Ginestra*, beginning

'Sovente in queste piagge,"

and ending

"Non so se il riso o la pietà prevale."

In like manner, Leopardi is at many points the poetic superior of Wordsworth too. He has a far wider culture than Wordsworth, more mental lucidity, more freedom from illusions as to the real character of the established fact and of reigning conventions; above all, this Italian, with his pure and sure touch, with his fineness of perception, is far more of the artist. Such a piece of pompous dulness as

"O for the coming of that glorious time."

and all the rest of it, or such lumbering verse as Mr. Ruskin's enemy,

"Parching summer hath no warrant"—

would have been as impossible to Leopardi as to Dante. Where, then, is Wordsworth's superiority? for the worth of what he has given us in poetry I hold to be greater, on the whole, than the worth of what Leopardi has given us. It is in Wordworth's sound and profound sense

"Of joy in widest commonalty spread;"

whereas Leopardi remains with his thoughts ever fixed upon the *essenza insanabile*, upon the *acerbo, indegno mistero delle cose*. It is in the power with which Wordsworth feels the resources of joy offered to us in nature, offered to us in the primary human affections and duties, and in the power with which, in his moments of inspiration, he renders this joy, and makes us, too, feel it; a force greater than himself seeming to lift him and to prompt his tongue, so that he speaks in a style far above any style of which he has the constant command, and with a truth far beyond any philosophic truth of which he has the conscious and assured possession. Neither Leopardi nor Wordsworth are of the same order with the great poets who made such verse as

Τλητὸν γὰρ Μοῖραι θυμὸν θέσαν ἀνθρώποισιν·

or as

"In la sua volontade è nostra pace;"

or as

". . . Men must endure
Their going hence, even as their coming hither;
Ripeness is all."

But as compared with Leopardi, Wordsworth, though at many points less lucid, though far less a master of style, far less of an artist, gains so much by his criticism of life being, in certain matters of profound importance, healthful and true, whereas Leopardi's pessimism is not, that the value of Wordsworth's poetry, on the whole, stands higher for us than that of Leopardi's, as it stands higher for us, I think, than that of any modern poetry except Goethe's.

Byron's poetic value is also greater, on the whole, than Leopardi's; and his superiority turns in the same way upon the surpassing worth of something which he had and was, after all deduction has been made for his shortcomings. We talk of Byron's *personality*, "a personality in eminence such as has never been yet, and is not likely to come again;" and we say that by this personality Byron is "different from all the rest of English poets, and in the main greater." But can we not be a little more circumstantial, and name that in which the wonderful power of this personality consisted? We can; with the instinct of a poet Mr. Swinburne has seized upon it and named it for us. The power of Byron's personality lies in "the splendid and imperishable excellence which covers all his offences and outweighs all his defects: *the excellence of sincerity and strength*."

Byron found our nation, after its long and victorious struggle with revolutionary France, fixed in a system of established facts and dominant ideas which revolted him. The mental bondage of the most powerful part of our nation, of its strong middle-class, to a narrow and false system of this kind, is what we call British Philistinism. That bondage is unbroken to this hour, but in Byron's time it was even far more deep and dark than it is now. Byron was an aristocrat, and it is not difficult for an aristocrat to look on the prejudices and habits of the British Philistine with scepticism and disdain. Plenty of young men of his own class Byron met at Almack's or at Lady Jersey's, who regarded the established facts and reigning beliefs of the England of that day with as little reverence as he did. But these men, disbelievers in British Philistinism in private, entered English public life, the most conventional in the world, and at once they saluted with respect the habits and ideas of British Philistinism as if they were a part of the order of creation, and as if in public no sane man would think of warring against them. With Byron it was different. What he called the *cant* of the great middle part of the English nation, what we call its Philistinism, revolted him; but the cant of his own class, deferring to this Philistinism and profiting by it, while they disbelieved in it, revolted him even more. "Come what may," are his own words, "I will never flatter the million's canting in any shape." His class in general, on the other hand, shrugged their shoulders at this cant, laughed at it, pandered to it, and ruled by it. The falsehood, cynicism, insolence, misgovernment, oppression, with their consequent unfailing crop of human misery, which were produced by this state of things, roused Byron to irreconcilable revolt and battle. They made him indignant, they infuriated him; they were so strong, so defiant, so maleficent,—and yet he felt that they were doomed. "You have seen every trampler down in turn," he comforts himself with saying, "from Buonaparte to the simplest individuals." The old order, as after 1815 it stood victorious, with its ignorance and misery below, its cant, selfishness, and cynicism above, was at home and abroad equally hateful to him. " I have simplified my politics," he writes, "into an utter detestation of all existing governments." And again: "Give me a republic. The king-times are fast finishing; there will be blood shed like water and tears like mist, but the peoples will conquer in the end. I shall not live to see it, but I foresee it."

Byron himself gave the preference, he tells us, to politicians and doers, far above writers and singers. But the politics of his own day and of his own class,—even of the Liberals of his own class,—were impossible for him. Nature had not formed him for a Liberal peer, proper to move the Address in the House of Lords, to pay compliments to the energy and self-reliance of British middle-class Liberalism, and to adapt his politics to suit it. Unfitted for such politics, he threw himself upon poetry as his organ; and in poetry his topics were not Queen Mab, and the Witch of Atlas, and the Sensitive Plant—they were the upholders of the old order, George the Third and Lord Castlereagh and the Duke of Wellington and Southey, and they were the canters and tramplers of the great world, and they were his enemies and himself.

Such was Byron's personality, by which "he is different from all the rest of English poets, and in the main greater." But he posed all his life, says M. Scherer. Let us distinguish. There is the Byron who posed, there is the Byron with his affectations and silliness, the Byron whose weakness Lady Blessington, with a woman's acuteness, so admirably seized: "His great defect is flippancy and a total want of self-possession." But when this theatrical and easily criticised personage betook himself to poetry, and when he had fairly warmed to his work, then he became another man; then the theatrical personage passed away; then a higher power took possession of him and filled him; then at last came forth into light that true and puissant personality, with its direct strokes, its ever-welling force, its satire, its energy, and its agony. This is the real Byron; whoever stops at the theatrical preludings does not know him. And this real Byron may well be superior to the stricken Leopardi, he may well be declared "different from all the rest of English poets, and in the main greater," in so far as it is true of him, as M. Taine well says, that "all other souls, in comparison with his, seem inert"; in so far as it is true of him that with superb, exhaustless energy, he maintained, as Professor Nichol well says, "the struggle that keeps alive, if it does not save, the soul"; in so far, finally, as he deserves (and he does deserve) the noble praise of him which I have already quoted from Mr. Swinburne; the praise for "the splendid and imperishable excellence which covers all his offences and outweighs all his defects: *the excellence of sincerity and strength.*"

True, as a man, Byron could not manage himself, could not guide his ways aright, but was all astray. True, he has no light, cannot lead us from the past to the future; "the moment he reflects, he is a child." The way out of the false state of things which enraged him he did not see,—the slow and laborious way upward; he had not the patience, knowledge, self-discipline, virtue, requisite for seeing it. True, also, as a poet, he has no fine and exact sense for word and structure and rhythm; he has not the artist's nature and gifts. Yet a personality of Byron's force counts for so much in life, and a rhetorician of Byron's force counts for so much in literature! But it would be most unjust to label Byron, as M. Scherer is disposed to label him, as a rhetorician only. Along with his astounding power and passion he had a strong and deep sense for what is beautiful in nature, and for what is beautiful in human action and suffering. When he warms to his work, when he is inspired, Nature herself seems to take the pen from him as she took it from Wordsworth, and to write for him as she wrote for Wordsworth, though in a different fashion, with her own penetrating simplicity. Goethe has well observed of Byron, that when he is at his happiest his representation of things is as easy and real as if he were improvising. It is so; and his verse then exhibits quite another and a higher quality from the rhetorical quality,—admirable as this also in its own kind of merit is,—of such verse as

"Minions of splendour shrinking from distress,"

and of so much more verse of Byron's of that stamp. Nature, I say, takes the pen for him; and then, assured master of a true poetic style though he is not, any more than Wordsworth, yet as from Wordsworth at his best there will come such verse as

"Will no one tell me what she sings?"

so from Byron, too, at his best, there will come such verse as

> "He heard it, but he heeded not; his eyes
> Were with his heart, and that was far away."

Of verse of this high quality, Byron has much; of verse of a quality lower than this, of a quality rather rhetorical than truly poetic, yet still of extraordinary power and merit, he has still more. To separate, from the mass of poetry which Byron poured forth, all this higher portion, so superior to the mass, and still so considerable in quantity, and to present it in one body by itself, is to do a service, I believe, to Byron's reputation, and to the poetic glory of our country.

Such a service I have in the present volume attempted to perform. To Byron, after all the tributes which have been paid to him, here is yet one tribute more—

> "Among thy mightier offerings here are mine!"

not a tribute of boundless homage certainly, but sincere; a tribute which consists not in covering the poet with eloquent eulogy of our own, but in letting him, at his best and greatest, speak for himself. Surely the critic who does most for his author is the critic who gains readers for his author himself, not for any lucubrations on his author;—gains more readers for him, and enables those readers to read him with more admiration.

And in spite of his prodigious vogue, Byron has never yet, perhaps, had the serious admiration which he deserves. Society read him and talked about him, as it reads and talks about *Endymion* today; and with the same sort of result. It looked in Byron's glass as it looks in Lord Beaconsfield's, and sees, or fancies that it sees, its own face there; and then it goes its way, and straightway forgets what manner of man it saw. Even of his passionate admirers, how many never got beyond the theatrical Byron, from whom they caught the fashion of deranging their hair, or of knotting their neck-handkerchief, or of leaving their shirt-collar unbuttoned; how few profoundly felt his vital influence, the influence of his splendid and imperishable excellence of sincerity and strength!

His own aristocratic class, whose cynical make-believe drove him to fury; the great middle-class, on whose impregnable Philistinism he shattered himself to pieces,—how little have either of these felt Byron's vital influence! As the inevitable break-up of the old order comes, as the English middle-class slowly awakens from its intellectual sleep of two centuries, as our actual present world, to which this sleep has condemned us, shows itself more clearly,—our world of an aristocracy materialised and null, a middle-class purblind and hideous, a lower class crude and brutal,—we shall turn our eyes again, and to more purpose, upon this passionate and dauntless soldier of a forlorn hope, who, ignorant of the future and unconsoled by its promises, nevertheless waged against the conservation of the old impossible world so fiery battle; waged it till he fell,—waged it with such splendid and imperishable excellence of sincerity and strength.

Wordsworth's value is of another kind. Wordsworth has an insight into permanent sources of joy and consolation for mankind which Byron has not; his poetry gives us more which we may rest upon than Byron's—more which we can rest upon now, and which men may rest upon always. I place Wordsworth's poetry, therefore, above Byron's on the whole, although in some points he was greatly Byron's inferior, and although Byron's poetry will always, probably, find more readers than Wordsworth's, and will give pleasure more easily. But these two, Wordsworth and Byron, stand, it seems to me, first and pre-eminent in actual performance, a glorious pair, among the English poets of this century. Keats had probably, indeed, a more consummate poetic gift than either of them; but he died having produced too little and being as yet too immature to rival them. I for my part can never even think of equalling with them any other of their contemporaries;—either Coleridge, poet and philosopher wrecked in a mist of opium; or Shelley, beautiful and ineffectual angel, beating in the void his luminous wings in vain. Wordsworth and Byron stand out by themselves. When the year 1900 is turned, and our nation comes to recount her poetic glories in the century which has then just ended, the first names with her will be these.

From *Shelley*

To all this we have to add the charm of the man's writings—of Shelley's poetry. It is his poetry, above everything else, which for many people establishes that he is an angel. Of his poetry I have not space now to speak. But let no one suppose that a want of humour and a self-delusion such as Shelley's have no effect upon a man's poetry. The man Shelley, in very truth, is not entirely sane, and Shelley's poetry is not entirely sane either. The Shelley of actual life is a vision of beauty and radiance, indeed, but availing nothing, effecting nothing. And in poetry, no less than in life, he is "a beautiful *and ineffectual* angel, beating in the void his luminous wings in vain."

LETTERS

Letters of Matthew Arnold 1848–1888. Collected and arranged by George W. E. Russell. 2 vols. London. Macmillan and Co. 1895.

The Letters of Matthew Arnold to Arthur Hugh Clough. Edited with an introductory study by Howard Forster Lowry. London and New York. Oxford University Press. 1932.

Unpublished Letters of Matthew Arnold. Edited by Arnold Whitridge. New Haven. Yale University Press.
MDCCCCXXIII.

A NUMBER of other letters have appeared in periodicals and books about Arnold. *Letters from Matthew Arnold to John Churton Collins* (London: privately printed, 1910) contains three letters on the subject of English studies at the Universities. A series of six friendly letters to Swinburne in the T. J. Wise collection, ranging from 1867 to 1882, were printed by Edmund Gosse in *The Times Literary Supplement*, 12 August 1920.

For details of Arnold's uncollected correspondence see *A Check-List of Matthew Arnold's Letters* by T. H. Vail Motter (*Studies in Philology*, Vol. 31, 1934); appendix to *Matthew Arnold, poète: Essai de biographie psychologique* by Louis Bonnerot (Paris, 1947); and *Notes Toward a Matthew Arnold Bibliography* by Marion Mainwaring (*Modern Philology*, Vol. 49, 1952).

It was Arnold's wish that no official biography should be written. To a certain extent the Letters published after his death can take its place. A selection from them gives a more intimate picture of Arnold the man than is gained from his formal writing, and illustrates his long and wearisome task as Inspector of Schools. The letters also make valuable comments on his own poetry and on the work of his contemporaries. Two letters to Clough contain all that is not guess-work about the Marguerite episode.

Relevant passages have been chosen: the text of a letter is not necessarily given in full. The letters collected by G. W. E. Russell in 1895 were considerably censored and edited by the family before being handed over to him.

LETTERS

To A. H. Clough

London, Tuesday. [December 1847; or early part of 1848.]

My dearest Clough

. . . One does not always remember that one of the signs of the Decadence of a literature, one of the factors of its decadent condition indeed, is this—that new authors attach themselves to the poetic expression the founders of a literature have flowered into, which may be *learned* by a sensitive person, to the neglect of an inward poetic life. The strength of the German literature consists in this—that having no national models from whence to get an idea of *style* as half the work, they were thrown upon themselves, and driven to make the fulness of the content of a work atone for deficiencies of form. Even Goethe at the end of his life has not the inversions, the taking tourmenté style we admire in the Latins, in some of the Greeks, and in the great French and English authors. And had Shakspeare and Milton lived in the atmosphere of modern feeling, had they had the multitude of new thoughts and feelings to deal with a modern has, I think it likely the style of each would have been far less *curious* and exquisite. For in a *man* style is the saying in the best way *what you have to say*. The *what you have to say* depends on your age. In the 17th century it was *a smaller harvest than now*, and sooner to be reaped! and therefore to its reaper was left time to stow it more finely and curiously. Still more was this the case in the ancient world. The poet's matter being *the hitherto experience of the world, and his own*, increases with every century.

. . . .

A growing sense of the deficiency of the *beautiful* in your poems, and of this alone being properly *poetical* as distinguished from rhetorical, devotional or metaphysical, made me speak as I did. But your line is a line: and you have most of the promising English verse-writers with you now: Festus[1] for instance. Still, problem as the production of the beautiful remains still to

[1] *Festus*, a poem by Philip James Bailey, father of the 'Spasmodic' school, appeared in 1839. Its subject resembles the Faust story. It grew in successive editions till it ran finally to over 40,000 lines.

me, I will die protesting against the world that the other is false and JARRING.

No—I doubt your being an *artist*: but have you read Novalis? He certainly is not one either: but in the way of direct communication, insight, and report, his tendency has often reminded me of yours, though tenderer and less systematic than you. And there are the sciences: in which I think the passion for truth, not special curiosities about birds and beasts, makes the great professor . . .

To the Same

Baths of Leuk, Sept^{ber} 29, 1848.

My dear Clough

A woodfire is burning in the grate and I have been forced to drink champagne to guard against the cold and the café noir is about to arrive, to enable me to write a little. For I am all alone in this vast hotel: and the weather having been furious rain for the last few days, has tonight turned itself towards frost. Tomorrow I repass the Gemmi and get to Thun: linger one day at the Hotel Bellevue for the sake of the blue eyes of one of its inmates: and then proceed by slow stages down the Rhine to Cologne, thence to Amiens and Boulogne and England.

The day before yesterday I passed the Simplon—and yesterday I repassed it. The day before yesterday I lay at Domo d'Ossola and yesterday morning the old man within me and the guide were strong for proceeding to the Lago Maggiore: but no, I said, first impressions must not be trifled with: I have but 3 days and they, according to the public voice will be days of rain: coupons court à notre voyage—revenons en Suisse—So I ordered a char yesterday to remount the Simplon. It rained still . . . here and there was something unblurred by rain. Précisons: I have noticed in Italy—the chestnuts: the vines: the courtliness and kingliness of buildings and people as opposed to this land of a republican peasantry: and one or two things more: but d—n description. My guide assures me he saw one or two "superbes filles" in Domo d'Ossola (nothing improper): but I rose late and disheartened by the furious rain, and saw nothing but what I saw from the carriage. So Italy remains for a second entry. From Isella to Simplon the road is glory to God. In these rains maps and guides have suffered more or less: but your Keller very little: I travel with a live guide as well as Murray: an expensive luxury: but if he is a good Xtian and a family man like mine, a true comfort. I gave him today a foulard for his daughter who is learning French at Neufchatel to qualify her first for the place of fille de chambre in a hotel and afterwards for that of soubrette in a private family. I love gossip and the smallwood of humanity generally among these raw mammoth-belched half-delightful objects the Swiss Alps. The limestone is terribly gingerbready: the pines terribly larchy: and above all the grand views being ungifted with self-controul almost invariably desinunt in piscem. And the curse of the dirty water—the real pain it occasions to one who looks upon water as the Mediator between the inanimate and man is not to be described. —I have seen clean water in parts of the lake of Geneva (which whole locality is spoiled by the omnipresence there of that furiously flaring bethiefed rushlight, the vulgar Byron): in the Aar at the exit of the Lac de Thoune: and in the little stream's beginnings on the Italian side of the Simplon. I have however done very little, having been baffled in two main wishes—the Tschingel Glacier and the Monte Moro, by the weather. My golies, how jealous you would have been of the first: 'we fools accounted his calves meagre, and his legs to be without honor'. All I have done however is to ascend the Faulhorn—8300 above the sea, my duck.

This people, the Swiss, are on the whole what they should be; so I am satisfied.—L'homme sage ne cherche point le sentiment parmi les habitans des montagnes: ils ont quelque chose de mieux—le bonheur. That is but indifferent French though. For their extortion, it is all right I think—as the wise man pumpeth the fool, who is made for to be pumped.

I have with me only Béranger and Epictetus: the latter tho: familiar to me, yet being Greek, when tired I am, is not much read by me: of the former I am getting tired. Horace whom he resembles had to write only for a circle of highly cultivated désillusionés roués, in a sceptical age: we have the sceptical age, but a far different and wider audience: voilà pourquoi, with all his genius, there is something "fade" about Béranger's Epicureanism. Perhaps you don't see the pourquoi, but I think my love does and the paper draws to an end. In the reste, I am glad to be tired of an author: one link in the immense series of cognoscenda et indigenda despatched. More particularly is this my feeling with regard to (I hate the word) women. We know beforehand all they can teach us: yet we are obliged to learn it directly from them. Why here is a marvellous thing. The following is curious—

> "Say this of her:
> The day was, thou wert not: the day will be
> Thou wilt be most unlovely: shall I chuse
> Thy little moment life of loveliness

Betwixt blank nothing and abhorred decay
To glue my fruitless gaze on, and to pine,
Sooner than those twin reaches of great time,
When thou art either nought, and so not loved,
Or somewhat, but that most unloveable,
That preface and post-scribe thee?"—

Farewell, my love, to meet I hope at Oxford: not alas in Heaven: tho: thus much I cannot but think: that our spirits retain their conquests: that from the height they succeed in raising themselves to, they can never fall. Tho: this uti possedetes principle may be compatible with entire loss of individuality and of the power to recognize one another. Therefore, my well-known love, accept my heartiest greeting and farewell, while it is called today.

Yours,
M. Arnold.

To Mrs. Forster [1]

London, Monday 1849.

My dearest K,—
. . . More and more I think ill of the great people here: that is their two capital faults, stupidity & hardness of heart become more and more clear to me. Their faults of character seem to me, as I watch the people in the park, to be the grand impairers of English beauty. In the men certainly; for the faces of the handsomest express either a stupid pride, or the stupidity without the pride, & the half alive look of many pretty faces among the women, so different from the southern langour, points to something very like stupidity. And a proud looking Englishwoman is the hardest looking thing I know in the world. So I should not be sorry to get away; but I still accustom myself to feel that we should pity these people rather than be angry with them.

I do not think any fruitful revolution can come in my time; and meanwhile, thank God, there are many honest people on earth, and the month of May comes every year.

To the Same

London, Wednesday [probably 1849].

I have not heard from you my darling since you got my book,[2] which I hoped to have done, seeing your intimacy with it and

---

[1] Jane, the poet's favourite sister, known in the family as 'K'. She married W. E. Forster in 1850.
[2] *The Strayed Reveller*, 1849.

me. I will say a little about it. I hear from Fellowes that it is selling very well; and from a good many quarters I hear interest expressed about it, though every one likes something different (except that everyone likes the Merman) and most people would have this & and would have that which they do not find. At Oxford particularly many complain that the subjects treated do not interest them. But as I feel rather as a reformer in poetical matters, I am glad of this opposition. If I have health & opportunity to go on, I will shake the present methods until they go down, see if I don't. More and more I feel bent against the modern English habit (too much encouraged by Wordsworth) of using poetry as a channel for thinking aloud, instead of making anything.

To A. H. Clough

[1848–9.]

My dearest Clough

What a brute you were to tell me to read Keats' Letters. However it is over now: and reflexion resumes her power over agitation.

What harm he has done in English Poetry. As Browning is a man with a moderate gift passionately desiring movement and fulness, and obtaining but a confused multitudinousness, so Keats with a very high gift, is yet also consumed by this desire: and cannot produce the truly living and moving, as his conscience keeps telling him. They will not be patient neither understand that they must begin with an Idea of the world in order not to be prevailed over by the world's multitudinousness: or if they cannot get that, at least with isolated ideas: and all other things shall (perhaps) be added unto them.

—I recommend you to follow up these letters with the Laocoön of Lessing: it is not quite satisfactory, and a little mare's nesty—but very searching.

—I have had that desire of fulness without respect of the means, which may become almost maniacal: but nature had placed a bar thereto not only in the conscience (as with all men) but a great numbness in that direction. But what perplexity Keats, Tennyson et id genus omne must occasion to young writers of the ὁπλίτης sort: yes and those d—d Elizabethan poets generally. Those who cannot read Greek should read nothing but Milton and parts of Wordsworth: the state should see to it: for the failures of the σταθμοί may leave them good⸴ citizens enough, as Trench: but the others go to the dogs failing or succeeding . . .

A A

To the Same

[February 1849.]

. . . Many persons with far lower gifts than yours yet seem to find their natural mode of expression in poetry, and tho: the contents may not be very valuable they appeal with justice from the judgement of the mere thinker to the world's general appreciation of naturalness—i.e.—an absolute propriety—of form, as the sole *necessary* of Poetry as such: whereas the greatest wealth and depth of matter is merely a superfluity in the Poet *as such*.

—Form of Conception comes by nature certainly, but is generally developed late: but this lower form, of expression, is found from the beginning amongst all born poets, even feeble thinkers, and in an unpoetical age: as Collins, Greene and fifty more, in England only.

The question is not of congruity between conception and expression: which when both are poetical, is the poet's highest result:—you say what you mean to say: but in such a way as to leave it doubtful whether your mode of expression is not quite arbitrarily adopted.

I often think that even a slight gift of poetical expression which in a common person might have developed itself easily and naturally, is overlaid and crushed in a profound thinker so as to be of no use to him to help him to express himself.—The trying to go into and to the bottom of an object instead of grouping *objects* is as fatal to the sensuousness of poetry as the mere painting, (for, *in Poetry*, this is not *grouping*) is to its airy and rapidly moving life.

"Not deep the Poet sees, but wide":—think of this as you gaze from the Cumner Hill toward Cirencester and Cheltenham.

To the Same

[March 1849.]

. . . It is true about form: something of the same sort is in my letter which crossed yours on the road. On the other hand, there are two offices of Poetry—one to add to one's store of thoughts and feelings—another to compose and elevate the mind by a sustained tone, numerous allusions, and a grand style. What other process is Milton's than this last, in Comus for instance. There is no fruitful analysis of character: but a great effect is produced. What is Keats? A style and form seeker, and this with an impetuosity that heightens the effect of his style almost painfully. Nay in Sophocles what is valuable is not so

much his contributions to psychology and the anatomy of sentiment, as the grand moral effects produced by *style*. For the
style is the expression of the nobility of the poet's character, as
the matter is the expression of the richness of his mind: but on
men character produces as great an effect as mind.

This however does not save Burbridge [1] who planes and polishes
to the forgetting of matter without ever arriving at style. But my
Antigone supports me and in some degree subjugates destiny . . .

To the Same

Thun, Sunday, Sept^ber 23 [1849].

My dear Clough

I wrote to you from this place last year. It is long since I have
communicated with you and I often think of you among the
untoward generation with whom I live and of whom all I read
testifies. With me it is curious at present: I am getting to feel
more independent and unaffectible as to all intellectual and
poetical performance the impatience at being faussé in which
drove me some time since so strongly into myself, and more
snuffing after a moral atmosphere to respire in than ever before
in my life. Marvel not that I say unto you, ye must be born again.
While I will not much talk of these things, yet the considering
of them has led me constantly to you the only living one almost
that I know of of

> The children of the second birth
> Whom the world could not tame— [2]

for my dear Tom has not sufficient besonnenheit for it to be any
rest to think of him any more than it is a *rest* to think of mystics
and such cattle—not that Tom is in any sense cattle or even a
mystic but he has not a "still, considerate mind".

What I must tell you is that I have never yet succeeded in any
one great occasion in consciously mastering myself: I can go
thro: the imaginary process of mastering myself and see the
whole affair as it would then stand, but at the critical point I
am too apt to hoist up the mainsail to the wind and let her drive.
However as I get more awake to this it will I hope mend for I
find that with me a clear almost palpable intuition (damn the
logical senses of the word) is necessary before I get into prayer:
unlike many people who set to work at their duty self-denial
etc. like furies in the dark hoping to be gradually illuminated as

[1] Thomas Burbridge, friend of Arnold and Clough. Joint-author
with Clough of *Ambarvalia* (1849).
[2] From *Stanzas in Memory of the Author of Obermann*.

they persist in this course. Who also perhaps may be sheep but not of my fold, whose one natural craving is not for profound thoughts, mighty spiritual workings etc. etc. but a distinct seeing of my way as far as my own nature is concerned: which I believe to be the reason why the mathematics were ever foolishness to me.

—I am here in a curious and not altogether comfortable state: however tomorrow I carry my aching head to the mountains and to my cousin the Blumlis Alp.

> Fast, fast by my window
> The rushing winds go
> Towards the ice-cumber'd gorges,
> The vast fields of snow.
> There the torrents drive upward
> Their rock strangled hum,
> And the avalanche thunders
> The hoarse torrent dumb.
> I come, O ye mountains—
> Ye torrents, I come,[1]

Yes, I come, but in three or four days I shall be back here, and then I must try how soon I can ferociously turn towards England.

My dearest Clough these are damned times—everything is against one—the height to which knowledge is come, the spread of luxury, our physical enervation, the absence of great *natures*, the unavoidable contact with millions of small ones, newspapers, cities, light profligate friends, moral desperadoes like Carlyle, our own selves, and the sickening consciousness of our difficulties: but for God's sake let us neither be fanatics nor yet chaff blown by the wind but let us be ὡς ὁ φρονιμος διαρισειεν and not as any one else διαρισειεν. When I come to town I tell you beforehand I will have a real effort at managing myself as to newspapers and the talk of the day. Why the devil do I read about Ld. Grey's sending convicts to the Cape, and excite myself thereby, when I can thereby produce no possible good. But public opinion consists in a multitude of such excitements. Thou fool—that which is morally worthless remains so, and undesired by Heaven, whatever results flow from it. And which of the units which has felt the excitement caused by reading of Lord Grey's conduct has been made one iota a better man thereby, or can honestly call his excitement a *moral* feeling.

You will not I know forget me. You cannot answer this letter for I know not how I come home.

Yours faithfully,
M. A.

[1] These lines became part (ll. 25–35) of the lyric "Parting," the second poem of the "Switzerland" group. See note to that poem.

To Miss Wightman

Fox How, December 21, 1850.

At seven came Miss Martineau and Miss Brontë (Jane Eyre); talked to Miss Martineau (who blasphemes frightfully) about the prospects of the Church of England, and, wretched man that I am, promised to go and see her cow-keeping miracles to-morrow—I, who hardly know a cow from a sheep. I talked to Miss Brontë (past thirty and plain, with expressive gray eyes, though) of her curates, of French novels, and her education in a school at Brussels, and sent the lions roaring to their dens at half-past nine, and came to talk to you . . .

To Mrs. Forster

London, January 25, 1851.

. . . How strong the tendency is, though, as characters take their bent, and lives their separate course, to submit oneself gradually to the silent influence that attaches us more and more to those whose characters are like ours, and whose lives are running the same way with our own, and that detaches us from everything besides, as if we could only acquire any solidity of shape and power of acting by narrowing and narrowing our sphere, and diminishing the number of affections and interests which continually distract us while young, and hold us unfixed and without energy to mark our place in the world; which we thus succeed in marking only by making it a very confined and joyless one. The aimless and unsettled, but also open and liberal state of our youth we *must* perhaps all leave and take refuge in our morality and character; but with most of us it is a melancholy passage from which we emerge shorn of so many beams that we are almost tempted to quarrel with the law of nature which imposes it on us . . .

To the Same

Queen's Hotel. Birmingham, December 2, 1851.

I have had a hard day. Thirty pupil teachers to examine in an inconvenient room, and nothing to eat except a biscuit, which a charitable lady gave me. I was asked to dinner, this time at five, but excused myself on the ground of work. However, one's only difficulty will be not to know the whole of schismatical Birmingham. The schools are mostly in the hands of very intelligent wealthy Unitarians, who abound here, and belong to the class of what we call ladies and gentlemen. This is next to Liverpool the finest of the manufacturing towns: the situation high and good, the principal street capital, the shops good, cabs splendid, and the Music Hall [1] unequalled by any Greek building in England that I have seen.

To A. H. Clough

[October 28, 1852.]

. . . More and more I feel that the difference between a mature and a youthful age of the world compels the poetry of the former to use great plainess of speech as compared with that of the latter: and that Keats and Shelley were on a false track when they set themselves to reproduce the exuberance of expression, the charm, the richness of images, and the felicity, of the Elizabethan poets. Yet critics cannot get to learn this, because the Elizabethan poets are our greatest, and our canons of poetry are founded on their works. They still think that the object of poetry is to produce exquisite bits and images—such as Shelley's *clouds shepherded by the slow unwilling wind*, and Keats passim: whereas modern poetry can only subsist by its *contents*; by becoming a complete magister vitae as the poetry of the ancients did; by including, as theirs did, religion with poetry, instead of existing as poetry only, and leaving religious wants to be supplied by the Christian religion, as a power existing independent of the poetical power. But the language, style and general proceedings of a poetry which has such an immense task to perform, must be very plain direct and severe: and it must not lose itself in parts and episodes and ornamental work, but must press forwards to the whole . . .

To his Mother

Cambridge, March 2, 1853.

. . . The two things I wanted to see in Cambridge were, the statue of Newton and King's College Chapel; the former is hardly as effective as I expected, because the chapel, or rather ante-chapel, where it stands, is so poor; yet it is noble for all that. King's College Chapel deserves all that can be said of it. Yet I feel that the Middle Ages and all their poetry and impressiveness are in Oxford and not here. I want you sadly to go about with me; everything would be just doubly as interesting.

[1] Birmingham Town Hall—designed and begun by Joseph Aloysius Hansom in 1832, finished by John Foster of Liverpool in 1834. Hansom was the inventor of the cab which bears his name.

To Mrs. Forster

London, April 14, 1853.

. . . Why is *Villette* disagreeable? Because the writer's mind contains nothing but hunger, rebellion, and rage, and therefore that is all she can, in fact, put into her book. No fine writing can hide this thoroughly, and it will be fatal to her in the long run. *My Novel* I have just finished. I have read it with great pleasure, though Bulwer's nature is by no means a perfect one either, which makes itself felt in his book; but his gush, his better humour, his abundant materials, and his mellowed and constructive skill—all these are great things . . .

To the Same

London, Saturday [?1853.]

. . . Fret not yourself to make my poems square in all their parts, but like what you can my darling. The true reason why parts suit you while others do not is that my poems are fragments—i.e. that I am fragments, while you are a whole; the whole effect of my poems is quite vague and indeterminate—this is their weakness; a person therefore who endeavoured to make them accord would only lose his labor; and a person who has any inward completeness can at best only like parts of them; in fact such a person stands firmly and knows what he is about while the poems stagger weakly & are at their wits end. I shall do better some day I hope—meanwhile change nothing, resign nothing that you have in deference to me or my oracles; & do not plague yourself to find a consistent meaning for these last, which in fact they do not possess through my weakness.

There—I would not be so frank as that with everyone.

To his Mother

Hampton, Monday [May 1853].

My dearest Mother,

All my spare time has been spent on a poem[1] which I have just finished, and which I think by far the best thing I have yet done, and that it will be generally liked, though one never can be sure of this. I have had the greatest pleasure in composing it—a rare thing with me, and, as I think, a good test of the pleasure what you write is likely to afford to others; but then the story

[1] *Sohrab and Rustum.*

is a very noble and excellent one. F., I am sure, will be delighted with it, and K. I have settled with Fellowes to publish this, and one or two more new ones, with the most popular of the old ones, next winter or spring, with a preface, and my name. I never felt so sure of myself, or so *really* and *truly* at ease as to criticism, as I have done lately. There is an article on me in the last *North British* which I will send you. Can it be by Blackie? I think Froude's review will come sooner or later, but at *present* even about this I feel indifferent. Miss Blackett told Flu[1] that Lord John Russell said, "In his opinion Matthew Arnold was the one rising young poet of the present day." This pleased me greatly from Lord John—if it is true. You ask about Alexander Smith. There are beautiful passages in him, but I think it doubtful how he will turn. Here is a long letter, and all about myself; however you will like that.—Ever your most affectionate

M. A.

To A. H. Clough

Derby, Nove^ber 25/53.

My dear Clough

Just read through Tennyson's Morte d'Arthur and Sohrab and Rustum one after the other, and you will see the difference in the *tissue* of the style of the two poems, and in its *movement*. I think the likeness, where there is likeness (except in the two last lines which I own are a regular slip) proceeds from our both having imitated Homer. But never mind—you are a dear soul. I am in great hopes you will one day like the poem—really like it. There is no one to whose apercus I attach the value I do to yours—but I think you are sometimes—with regard to *me* especially—a little cross and wilful . . .

To the Same

Coleby. November 30th [1853].

My dear Clough

I think "if indeed this one desire rules all"[2]—*is* rather Tennysonian—at any rate it is not good.

The resemblance in the other passage I cannot for the life of me see.

I think the poem has, if not the *rapidity*, at least the *fluidity* of Homer: and that it is in this respect that it is un-Tennysonian:

---

[1] Arnold's wife. [2] *Sohrab and Rustum*, l. 74.

and that it is a sense of this which makes Froude and Blackett [1] say it is a step in advance of Tennyson in this strain.

A thousand things make one compose or not compose: composition seems to keep alive in me a *cheerfulness*—a sort of Tuchtigkeit, or natural soundness and valiancy, which I think the present age is fast losing—this is why I like it.

I am glad you like the Gipsy Scholar—but what does it *do* for you? Homer *animates*—Shakespeare *animates*—in its poor way I think Sohrab and Rustum *animates*—the Gipsy Scholar at best awakens a pleasing melancholy. But this is not what we want.

> The complaining millions of men
> Darken in labour and pain—[2]

what they want is something to *animate* and *ennoble* them—not merely to add zest to their melancholy or grace to their dreams.—I believe a feeling of this kind is the basis of my nature—and of my poetics.

You certainly do not seem to me sufficiently to desire and earnestly strive towards—assured knowledge—activity—happiness. You are too content to *fluctuate*—to be ever learning, never coming to the knowledge of the truth. This is why, with you, I feel it necessary to stiffen myself—and hold fast my rudder.

My poems, however, viewed *absolutely*, are certainly little or nothing. . .

To his Wife

Oxford, Sunday [October 1854].

I am writing from Walrond's [3] rooms in Balliol. This time *thirteen* years ago I was wandering about this quadrangle a freshman, as I see other freshmen doing now. The time seems prodigious. I do not certainly feel thirteen years older than when I came up to Oxford. . . . I am going with Walrond to-day to explore the Cumner country, and on Thursday I got up alone into one of the little coombs that papa was so fond of, and which I had in my mind in the "Gipsy Scholar," and felt the peculiar *sentiment* of this country and neighbourhood as deeply as ever. But I am much struck with the apathy and *poorness* of the people

[1] J. F. B. Blackett, friend of Arnold and Clough: M.P. for Newcastle, 1852–6.
[2] *The Youth of Nature*, ll. 51–2.
[3] Theodore Walrond (1824–1887), close friend of Arnold and Clough, and their contemporary at Rugby and Balliol. See J. Curgenven: *Theodore Walrond*. Durham University Journal, Vol. XLIV, 1952.

here, as they now strike me, and their petty pottering habits compared with the students of Paris, or Germany, or even of London. Animation and interest and the power of work seem so sadly wanting in them. And I think this is so; and the place, in losing Newman and his followers, has lost its religious movement, which after all kept it from stagnating, and has not yet, so far as I see, got anything better. However, we must hope that the coming changes, and perhaps the infusion of Dissenters' sons of that muscular, hard-working, *unblasé* middle class—for it is this, in spite of its abominable disagreeableness—may brace the flaccid sinews of Oxford a little.

To Mrs. Forster

Fox How, October 10/54.

I have so much to say to you, you dear soul. It was odd—as your letter about the country you went through on the Italian side of the Alps was being read, it brought to my mind delightfully just what had been present to it when many of the poems of mine which are nearest to me were composed—and then came your sentence saying that what you had seen had brought these Poems to your mind. That was a correspondence to give one real pleasure—but there is no one and never will be any one who enters into what I have done as you have entered into it, dearest K,—and to whom I so want to communicate what I do. I have just finished a poem which I think is better than Sohrab and Rustum, though here I do not think they consider it so—and William too I think will like it. You will see it in November, I hope.

To the Same

London, December 12, 1855.

My darling K.,

I think "Balder" will consolidate the peculiar sort of reputation that I got by "Sohrab and Rustum," and many will complain that I am settling myself permanently in that field of antiquity, as if there was no other. But I have in part done with this field in completing "Balder," and what I do next will be, if I can do it, wholly different.

I have had a letter from Arthur Stanley[1] who remarks on the similes much as you do, so I daresay what you both say is true;

[1] Arthur Penrhyn Stanley (1815–1881); became Dean of Westminster, 1864. A life-long friend of the Arnolds he is commemorated in the memorial poem *Westminster Abbey*.

he likes "Balder" as a whole better than "Sohrab," but thinks it too short; and this is true too, I think, and I must some day add a first book with an account of the circumstances of the death of Balder himself.

I felt sure William would be interested from what I knew of his Scandinavian interests. Mallet, however, tell him, and his version of the Edda, is all the poem is based upon.

It is hard to think of any volume like that of mine having a sale in England just now, with the war going on, and the one cry being for newspapers; but I daresay the book will dribble away in a year's time or so.—Ever your most truly affectionate

M. A.

To his Mother

London, Sunday, January 3, 1858.

My dearest Mother,

You wished to see everything about *Merope*, so I send you these. They have lost no time in opening cry. The *Athenæum* is a choice specimen of style, and the *Spectator* of argumentation. The *Saturday Review* is not otherwise to be complained of than so far as it is deadly prosy. I am very anxious to see what Lewes [1] says about *Merope*, as I have a very high opinion of his literary judgment, but the *Leader* is silent this week. It is singular what irritation the dispute between classicism and romanticism seems always to call forth; but I remember Voltaire's lamentation that the " literæ humanæ," *humane* letters, should be so desperately *inhuman*, and am determined in print to be always scrupulously polite. The bane of English reviewing and newspaper writing is, and has always been, its *grossièreté*.—Ever your affectionate

M. A.

To W. E. Forster

Education Department Council Office,
Downing Street, London
January 11th, 1858.

As to Merope not exciting you—on the stage (for which these things are meant) I think the chief situations would excite you; and it is easy to over-write a situation for acting. For an unconscious testimony to this truth, see that masterpiece of bad criticism, the Times' remarks on Rachel's acting. But we must beware of taking our notions of excitement from the modern drama or from the modern novel—from Adrienne Lecouvreur or from

[1] J. H. Lewes (1817–1878), editor of the *Leader* 1850, and of the *Fortnightly Review* 1865.

Night & Morning. Certainly the Greek tragic drama does not excite & harrow us to the extent that these do; I think, neither does Shakespeare. Not one hundredth part of the excitement have I ever felt at seeing Lear or Othello on the stage that I have felt at the Corsican Brothers or Adrienne Lecouvreur.[1] And, perhaps, this is necessary. For in good tragedy the poet must controul his matter—and in the drama and novel the matter is uncontrollable. There is a kind of pity & fear (Kotzebue is a great master of it) which cannot be purified, it is the most agitating and overwhelming, certainly, but, for the sake of a higher result, we must renounce this. Pity & fear of a certain kind— say commiseration & awe and you will perhaps better feel what I mean—I think Merope does excite—as does Greek tragedy in general; I allow, however, that the problem for the poet is, or should be, to unite the highest degree of agitatingness on the part of his subject-matter, with the highest degree of controul and assuagement on the part of his own exhibition of it—Shakespeare, under immense difficulties, goes further in this respect than the Greeks, and so far he is an advance upon them.[2]

To Miss Arnold [3]

February 3, 1858.

. . . The *Leader* was very gratifying. A great many letters I have not sent you, and indeed it rather goes against the grain with me to send you newspapers, I am so dead sick of criticism. Had it been one of my earlier volumes, I should have sent you a multitude of letters, but with this I soon got tired, seeing it was not

---

[1] *Adrienne Lecouvreur*, an adaptation by Henry Herman of the popular play by Scribe and Legouvé; *Night and Morning* from *La joie fait peur* by Mme. de Girardin, and *The Corsican Brothers* from a play based on Dumas' novel *Les Frères Corses*—both adapted by Boucicault.

[2] Arnold writes in the same year to Mrs. Forster :

> You must remember that this form of drama is above all calculated for the stage—a sort of opera-stage—and that as much as the Elizabethan drama loses by being acted the Greek drama gains.

And of Swinburne's *Atalanta in Calydon* he wrote to John Conington (Professor of Latin at Oxford) on May 17, 1865 :

> Swinburne's poem is as you say : the moderns will only have the antiques on the condition of making it more *beautiful* (according to their own notion of beauty) than the antique—i.e. something wholly different. You were always good to "Merope," and I think there is a certain solidity in her composition which makes her look as well now as five years ago—a great test.

[3] Frances, younger sister of the poet. Referred to in the letters as Fan.

going to take as I wished. Instead of reading it for what it is worth, everybody begins to consider whether it does not betray a design to substitute tragedies *à la Grecque* for every other kind of poetical composition in England, and falls into an attitude of violent resistance to such an imaginary design. What I meant them was to see in it a specimen of the world created by the Greek imagination. This imagination was different from our own, and it is hard for us to appreciate, even to understand it; but it had a peculiar power, grandeur, and dignity, and these are worth trying to get an apprehension of. But the British public prefer, like all obstinate multitudes, to "die in their sins," and I have no intention to keep preaching in the wilderness.

The book sells well, but it must be remembered that a good many people read it from curiosity. Temple [1] writes me word that "he has read it with astonishment at its goodness."

To Madame du Quaire [2]

The Athenæum, February 9, 1858.

My dear Fanny,

I hope by this time you have *Merope*. I got Drummond Wolff to undertake the transmission of her. I am anxious to explain to you that you are not the least bound to like her, as she is calculated rather to inaugurate my Professorship with dignity than to move deeply the present race of *humans*. No one is more sensible of this than I am, only I have such a real love for this form and this old Greek world that perhaps I infuse a little soul into my dealings with them which saves me from being entirely *ennuyeux*, professorial, and pedantic; still you will not find in *Merope* what you wish to find, and I excuse you beforehand for wishing to find something different, and being a little dissatisfied with me; and I promise you, too, to give you a better satisfaction some day, if I live.

I often think of poor dear Johnny and the pleasure that he would have taken in *Merope*, he having much the same special fondness for this sort of thing that I have. Make Browning look at it, if he is at Florence; one of the very best antique fragments I know is a fragment of a Hippolytus by him.[3]

The poem is a great deal reviewed here, very civilly, but very expostulatingly . . .

[1] Frederick Temple (1821–1902), contemporary of Arnold and Clough at Balliol and subsequently Fellow. Headmaster of Rugby, 1857, Archbishop of Canterbury, 1896.
[2] Fanny du Quaire, sister of John F. Blackett, who is referred to later in the letter. She was also a friend of Browning.
[3] "Artemis Prologizes" in *Men and Women*.

To Mrs. Forster

Martigny, August 6, 1858.

. . . Kingsley's remarks were very *handsome*, especially coming from a brother in the craft. I should like to send you a letter which I had from Froude about *Merope*, just at the same time that your record of Kingsley's criticisms reached me. If I can find it when I return to England I will send it to you. It was to beg me to discontinue the *Merope* line, but entered into very interesting developments, as the French say, in doing so. Indeed, if the opinion of the general public about my poems were the same as that of the leading literary men, I should make more money by them than I do. But, more than this, I should gain the stimulus necessary to enable me to produce my best—all that I have in me, whatever that may be,—to produce which is no light matter with an existence so hampered as mine is. People do not understand what a temptation there is, if you cannot bear anything not *very good*, to transfer your operations to a region where form is everything. Perfection of a certain kind may there be attained, or at least approached, without knocking yourself to pieces, but to attain or approach perfection in the region of thought and feeling, and to unite this with perfection of form, demands not merely an effort and a labour, but an actual tearing of oneself to pieces, which one does not readily consent to (although one is sometimes forced to it) unless one can devote one's whole life to poetry. Wordsworth could give his whole life to it, Shelley and Byron both could, and were besides driven by their demon to do so. Tennyson, a far inferior natural power to either of the three, can; but of the moderns Goethe is the only one, I think, of those who have had an *existence assujettie*, who has thrown himself with a great result into poetry. And even he felt what I say, for he could, no doubt, have done more, *poetically*, had he been freer; but it is not so light a matter, when you have other grave claims on your powers, to submit voluntarily to the exhaustion of the best poetical production in a time like this. Goethe speaks somewhere of the endless matters on which he had employed himself, and says that with the labour he had given to them he might have produced half a dozen more good tragedies; but to produce these, he says, I must have been *sehr zerrissen*. It is only in the best poetical epochs (such as the Elizabethan) that you can descend into yourself and produce the best of your thought and feeling naturally, and without an overwhelming and in some degree morbid effort; for then all the people around you are more or less doing the same thing. It is natural, it is the bent of the time to do it; its being the bent of the time, indeed, is what makes the time a *poetical* one. But enough of this. . . .

To his Wife

Paris, August 21, 1859.

. . . Now I will go back a little. After writing to you on Friday, I strolled out a little, came back and dressed, and drove to Sainte Beuve's, which is an immense way off, close to the Brittany railway. He had determined to take me to dine *chez le Restaurant du Quartier*, the only good one, he says, and we dined in the cabinet where G. Sand, when she is in Paris, comes and dines every day. Sainte Beuve gave me an excellent dinner, and was in full vein of conversation, which, as his conversation is about the best to be heard in France, was charming. After dinner he took me back to his own house, where we had tea; and he showed me a number of letters he had had from G. Sand and Alf. de Musset at the time of their love affair, and then again at the time of their rupture. You may imagine how interesting this was after *Elle et Lui*. I will tell you about them when we meet. Sainte Beuve says I must read *Lui et Elle*, to finish the history, and then to complete it all, a few pages in the *Memoirs* of Mogador about Musset. As for G. Sand and him, Sainte Beuve says, "*Tout le mal* qu'ils ont dit l'un de l'autre est vrai." But de Musset's letters were, I must say, those of a *gentleman* of the very first water. Sainte Beuve rather advised me to go and see George Sand, but I am still disinclined "to take so long a journey to see such a fat old Muse," as M. de Circourt says in his funny English. All Sainte Beuve told me of her present proceedings made me less care about seeing her; however, if Berri was nearer, the weather less hot, and French travelling less of a bore, I should go—as it is I shall not. After all, by staying I shall get another visit to Cousin, which is some compensation. I stayed with Sainte Beuve till midnight, and would not have missed my evening for all the world. I think he likes me, and likes my caring so much about his criticisms and appreciating his extraordinary delicacy of tact and judgment in literature. I walked home, and had a wakeful night. . . .

To Mrs. Forster

December 24, 1859.

. . . I thought the other day that I would tell you of a Frenchman whom I saw in Paris, Ernest Renan, between whose line of endeavour and my own I imagine there is considerable resemblance, that you might have a look at some of his books if you liked. The difference is, perhaps, that he tends to inculcate *morality*, in a high sense of the word, upon the French nation as what they most want, while I tend to inculcate *intelligence*, also in a high sense of the word, upon the English nation as what they most want; but with respect both to morality and intelligence, I think we are singularly at one in our ideas, and also with respect both to the progress and the established religion of the present day. The best book of his for you to read, in all ways, is his *Essais de Morale et de Critique*, lately published. I have read few things for a long time with more pleasure than a long essay with which the book concludes—"Sur la poésie des races celtiques." I, have long felt that we owed far more, spiritually and artistically to the Celtic races than the somewhat coarse Germanic intelligence readily perceived, and been increasingly satisfied at our own semi-Celtic origin, which, as I fancy, gives us the power, if we will use it, of comprehending the nature of both races. Renan pushes the glorification of the Celts too far; but there is a great deal of truth in what he says, and being on the same ground in my next lecture, in which I have to examine the origin of what is called the "romantic" sentiment about women, which the Germans quite falsely are fond of giving themselves the credit of originating, I read him with the more interest . . .

To Miss Arnold

December 17, 1860

. . . By the time you come I hope to have finished the introduction to that [1] and to have got it printed, and to be well plunged in the Middle Age. I have a strong sense of the irrationality of that period, and of the utter folly of those who take it seriously, and play at restoring it; still, it has poetically the greatest charm and refreshment possible for me. The fault I find with Tennyson in his *Idylls of the King* is that the peculiar charm and aroma of the Middle Age he does not give in them. There is something magical about it, and I will do something with it before I have done. The real truth is that Tennyson, with all his temperament and artistic skill, is deficient in intellectual power; and no modern poet can make very much of his business unless he is pre-eminently strong in this. Goethe owes his grandeur to his strength in this, although it even hurt his poetical operations by its immense predominance. However, it would not do for me to say this about Tennyson, though gradually I mean to say boldly

[1] His Report for the Commissioners of Education on *The Popular Education of France*, etc., 1861.

the truth about a great many English celebrities, and begin with Ruskin in these lectures on Homer. I have been reading a great deal in the *Iliad* again lately, and though it is too much to say, as the writer in the *Biographie Universelle* says, that "none but an Englishman would dream of matching Shakespeare with the Greeks," yet it is true that Homer leaves him with all his un-equalled gift—and certainly there never was any such naturally gifted poet—as far behind as perfection leaves imperfection.

To Mrs. Forster

2, Chester Square, Feb'y, 1861.

So you find my tone in the Lectures too dogmatic? I shall be curious to see if the reviewers find the same thing. No one else has yet made this complaint, and you must remember that the tone of a lecturing professor to an audience supposed to be there to learn of him, cannot be quite that of a man submitting his views to the great world. The expression to speak ex cathe-dra in itself implies what is expected in one who speaks from a Professor's chair. Also it is not positively forms in themselves that are offensive to people—it is positive forms in defence of paradox; such as Ruskin's, that Claude is a bad colorist, or Murillo a second-rate painter. But Voltaire one reads with delight, for all his positive forms and stringent argumentation—because he is generally defending the common-sense side of a question against pedantry or prejudice—and that Homer is plain, noble, etc., etc., is certainly the common-sense view of Homer, and that hitherto generally received by the best judges. But enough of all this—certainly I must and will take care not to fall into an offensive tone of dogmatizing, on any subject, for that is always in bad taste, and therefore always excruciating.

To his Mother

Oxford, May 14, 1861.

... I have been at Wantage to-day—King Alfred's birthplace. A wonderful, quiet old Berkshire town, in the White Horse Vale at the foot of the downs. I started by the half-past seven train this morning, and then drove four miles from Farringdon Road. The Vale is nearly all grass fields, with trees in a park-like way about them, and every village quite clustered round with elms; and the line of the downs bounding it all has great character, and has always been a favourite object with me. Presently I am going to my old haunts among the Cumner hills, and shall come back with plenty of orchises and blue-bells. I left Wantage at half-past twelve, and am back here by two, having had a biscuit and some mulled claret at Didcot. Getting back so early is one's reward for getting up early. I am wonderfully changed about that, now that without the slightest effort I get up at six, and walk down more than half a mile to take the early train at half-past seven. It is a great thing in my favour (and that advantage I have always had) that I am utterly indifferent about the time of my breakfast, and can wait for it till such time as it pleases Providence to send it me. I always like this place, and the intellectual life here is certainly much more intense than it used to be; but this has its disadvantages too, in the envies, hatreds, and jealousies that come with the activity of mind of most men. Goldwin Smith,[1] whose attack on Stanley's Edinburgh article[2] has made much noise, is a great element of bitterness and strife, though personally a most able, in some respects even interesting, man; the result is that all the world here seems more perturbed and exacerbated than of old. If I was disposed to fly for refuge to the country and its sights and sounds against the rather hum-drum life which prevailed here in old times, how much more am I disposed to do this now, convinced as I am that irritations and envyings are not only negatively injurious to one's spirit, like dulness, but positively and actively . . .

To the Same

2 Chester Square, November 20, 1861.

. . . First of all, you will expect me to say something about poor Clough. That is a loss which I shall feel more and more as time goes on, for he is one of the few people who ever made a deep impression upon me, and as time goes on, and one finds no one else who makes such an impression, one's feeling about those who did make it gets to be something more and more distinct and unique. Besides, the object of it no longer survives to wear it out himself by becoming ordinary and different from what he was. People were beginning to say about Clough that he never would do anything now, and, in short, to pass him over. I fore-see that there will now be a change, and attention will be fixed

[1] See note p. 341. Arnold remarked in a letter to Clough (Sept. 6, 1853), 'Goldwin Smith has the funereal solemnity of an undertaker. I suppose he caught it from Conington.'

[2] *Essays and Reviews*, a collection of papers on religious topics treated from a broad-church standpoint appeared in 1860. Among the contributors were Frederick Temple, Mark Pattison and Jowett. It was the cause of much controversy: Stanley wrote a balanced article on it in the *Edinburgh Review*, April 1861.

on what there was of extraordinary promise and interest in him when young, and of unique and imposing even as he grew older without fulfilling people's expectations. I have been asked to write a Memoir of him for the *Daily News*, but that I cannot do. I could not write about him in a newspaper now, nor can, I think, at length in a review, but I shall some day in some way or other relieve myself of what I think about him.

I know no details except that he died at Florence.[1] I heard this in a note from Lingen [2] the day before his death appeared in the newspaper. His wife was with him. . . .

To Mrs. Clough

Chester Square [London] Jany 22nd, 1862.

My dear Mrs. Clough

I cannot tell you how glad I am to have the lines you have sent me. I shall take them with me to Oxford, where I shall go alone after Easter;—and there, among the Cumner hills where we have so often rambled, I shall be able to think him over as I could wish. Here, all impressions are half impressions, and every thought is interrupted. . . .

To a Friend

[*At the time of Clough's death.*]

Stanley will, I hope, draw up a short notice of Clough. I cannot say his death took me altogether by surprise—I had long had a foreboding something was deeply wrong with him. But the impression he left was one of those which deepen with time and such as I never expect again to experience.

To his Mother

December 17, 1862.

. . . I was pleased with this performance[3] on Colenso and Spinoza, however, and glad of the opportunity of saying what I had to say. I have not read Vaughan's sermons,[4] nor do I think it possible for

---

[1] Nov. 13, 1861.

[2] W. R. Lingen (1819–1905), Fellow of Balliol while Arnold was an undergraduate, and later Secretary to Education Office.

[3] 'The Bishop and the Philosopher', which Arnold contributed to *Macmillan's Magazine*, January 1863.

[4] C. J. Vaughan (1816–1897), headmaster of Harrow and Dean of Llandaff.

a clergyman to treat these matters satisfactorily. In papa's time it was; but it is so, it seems to me, no longer; he is the last free speaker of the Church of England clergy who speaks without being shackled, and without being obviously aware that he is so, and that he is in a false position in consequence; and the moment a writer feels this his power is gone. I may add, that if a clergyman does not feel this now, he ought to feel it. The best of them (Jowett, for example) obviously do feel it, and I am quite sure papa would have felt it had he been living now, and thirty years younger. Not that he would have been less a Christian, or less zealous for a national Church, but his attention would have been painfully awake to the truth that to profess to see Christianity through the spectacles of a number of second or third-rate men who lived in Queen Elizabeth's time (and this is what office-holders under the Thirty-nine Articles do)—men whose works one never dreams of reading for the purpose of enlightening and edifying oneself—is an intolerable absurdity, and that it is time to put the formularies of the Church of England on a solider basis. Or a clergyman may abstain from dealing with speculative matters at all; he may confine himself to such matters as Stanley does, or to pure edification, and then, too, he is in a sound position. But the moment he begins to write for or against Colenso he is inevitably in a false position. . . .

To the Same

2 Chester Square, April 25, 1863.

. . . I came back yesterday from Oxford. Stanley took advantage of my visit to ask some of the Puseyite party whom he wanted to ask, but could hardly ask without the excuse of a stranger to meet; we had a very pleasant and successful party of this kind. Henry Bunsen [1] was staying with Stanley, and him I always like. The weather was fine but with a detestable cold wind, so that a new poem about the Cumner hillside, and Clough in connexion with it, which I meant to have begun at Oxford this week, I could not begin. I have been accumulating stores for it, however. I enjoyed the country in spite of the wind, and send Fan a "Turk's Cap," which I think does not grow at the Lakes. There are white and purple, and in places they cover the meadows by the Thames. . . .

[1] Son of Baron Bunsen, the German scholar and diplomat. He was rector of Donnington, Salop.

To his Wife

Cambridge, July 26, 1863,
Sunday evening.

It is a fine, warm day, and I have never seen Cambridge look so beautiful. We dined in the hall of Trinity at four o'clock (think of that!), and sat in Combination Room till half-past six; then Pollock and I strolled through the fields to Granchester, the only pretty walk about Cambridge. The ground is broken, the Cam, really a pretty stream, and tolerably clear, flows beside you; the woods of Trumpington Park and the pretty church and cottages of Granchester close the horizon. I should so like to have strolled about with you this lovely afternoon at the backs of the colleges and heard your dear remarks. I have made up my mind that I should like the post of Master of Trinity. We strolled back from Granchester by moonlight; it made me melancholy to think how at one time I was in the fields every summer evening of my life, and now it is such a rare event to find myself there.

To his Mother

October 29, 1863.

. . . I was in poor force and low spirits for the first ten days after I returned; now I am all right again, and hope to have a busy year. It is very animating to think that one at last has a chance of *getting at* the English public. Such a public as it is, and such a work as one wants to do with it! Partly nature, partly time and study have also by this time taught me thoroughly the precious truth that everything turns upon one's exercising the power of *persuasion*, of *charm*; that without this all fury, energy, reasoning power, acquirement, are thrown away and only render their owner more miserable. Even in one's ridicule one must preserve a sweetness and good-humour. . . .

To the Same

The Athenæum, London,
December 24, 1863.

. . . While writing these last words I have heard the startling news of the sudden death of Thackeray. He was found dead in his bed this morning. If you have not seen it in the newspaper before you read this, you will all be greatly startled and shocked, as I am. I have heard no particulars. . . . Still, this sudden cessation of an existence so lately before one's eyes, so vigorous and full of life, and so considerable a power in the country, is very sobering, if, indeed, after the shock of a fortnight ago,[1] one still needs sobering. To-day I am forty-one, the middle of life in any case, and for me, perhaps, much more than the middle. I have ripened, and am ripening so slowly that I should be glad of as much time as possible, yet I can feel, I rejoice to say, an inward spring which seems more and more to gain strength, and to promise to resist outward shocks, if they must come, however rough. But of this inward spring one must not talk, for it does not like being talked about, and threatens to depart if one will not leave it in mystery. . . .

To the Same

Haverhill B.S., April 29, 1864.

My dearest Mother,

This is a place on the borders between Cambridgeshire, Suffolk, and Essex—not three very lovely counties, yet this is their prettiest region, and any country would be pretty now, with the fruit-trees all in blossom and spring in full flush everywhere, if it were not for the horrible and hateful north-east wind. Edward thinks my life is all ease. Now I will tell him of my two last days and to-day. The day before yesterday up at seven. Wrote letters and so on till breakfast. At half-past nine off in the Woods' waggonette (how is the beast of a word spelt?) to the Mark's Tey station for Ipswich. Ipswich at eleven. A great British school 250 boys, 150 girls, and 150 infants, and the pupil teachers of these schools to examine. I fell at once to work with the Standards. My assistant joined me from London at half-past twelve. I worked in the Girls' School, with the pupil teachers on one side the room and the Standards drafted in, one after the other, on the other side. My assistant in the Boys' and Infants' Schools. I had a perpetual stream of visitors from the town—people interested in the schools. Biscuits and wine were brought to me where I was, and I never left the room till four, except for five minutes to run to a shop and buy a stud I wanted. At four I departed, and reached Copford at half-past five. My assistant returned to London by the six o'clock train, and between us we finished that school in the day. Yesterday off by the same train back to Ipswich, took the Wesleyan school, 120 children, and at half-past one took the train to Hadleigh, getting a biscuit at the station. Reached Hadleigh at half-past two. Could get nothing but a taxed cart and pony, and a half-drunk cripple

---

[1] The sudden death of his father-in-law, Mr. Justice Wightman, who died on circuit at York, 9 December, 1863.

to drive—six miles by cross country roads to Boxford. Got there
at half-past three. By half-past four had polished them off—only
thirty children—and was back at Hadleigh at half-past five. Got
to Copford at half-past seven, in time for an eight o'clock dinner.
This morning off as before. A school of sixty children at this
little town. Began them at eleven and finished at one. Have
since remained in the school, receiving visits from the Managers
and writing letters, till I leave by the 3.15 train, which will get
me to London at 6.30. Next week I have the same sort of days
throughout, then I return to London, or rather to Woodford,
for good. . . .

To J. Dykes Campbell [1]

Fox How, September 22, 1864.

I am much tempted to say something about the Enoch Arden
volume. I agree with you in thinking "Enoch Arden" itself very
good indeed—perhaps the best thing Tennyson has done;
"Tithonus" I do not like quite so well. But is it possible for one
who has himself published verses to print a criticism on Tennyson in which perfect freedom shall be used? And without perfect
freedom, what is a criticism worth? I do not think Tennyson a
great and powerful spirit in any line—as Goethe was in the line
of modern thought, Wordsworth in that of contemplation, Byron
even in that of passion; and unless a poet, especially a poet at this
time of day, is that, my interest in him is only slight, and my
conviction that he will not finally stand high is firm. But is it
possible or proper for me to say this about Tennyson, when my
saying it would inevitably be attributed to odious motives?
Therefore, though the temptation to speak —especially because
I should probably say something so totally different from what
the writer in the *Spectator* supposes—is great, I shall probably
say nothing.

To his Wife

Hôtel Meurice, Paris, April 30, 1865.

. . . I am beginning to have a great deal to do, and to have a great
many invitations. To-night I dine at the Embassy, and go to the
Princesse Mathilde [2] afterwards. Her salon is the best in Paris,
for she has all the clever men as well as the Court circle. It was

---

[1] James Dykes Campbell (1838–1895), editor and biographer of
Coleridge.

[2] Daughter of Jérôme Bonaparte: married Prince Demidoff but
separated from him. She was a patron of art and letters and her salon
in Paris was famous. She died in 1904.

very pleasant at Circourt's last night; no one but he, I, and Waddington; . . . and the Bruyères, Circourt's place, is quite beautiful on the high, wild, wooded ground between St. Cloud and St. Germain. We had coffee out in the grounds afterwards, and the nightingales were overpowering. Circourt gave us a model of a hermit's dinner, as he called it; very simple, but everything in perfection. He goes to a watering-place in the Black Forest on Wednesday, I am sorry to say. The day before I dined with the Schérers at Versailles; Schérer[1] is one of the most interesting men I have seen in France. If you see the Bowyers tell them I saw Monsignore Chigi yesterday—the Papal Nuncio; he is charming, and has done for me everything I wanted. I am going to see the Père Félix on Wednesday, so I shall have plenty of the Roman Catholic side. Did I tell you that I was introduced to Mme. de Boissy,[2] Byron's Mme. Guiccioli, on Thursday night? She asked me to go to her house on Friday, but I was too late home from Versailles—not till twelve o'clock. The brilliant green of the whole valley of the Seine, with the bright white houses amongst it, is quite Southern. I had no notion this could be so beautiful. To-morrow I was asked to dine at Mme. de Blocqueville's, Davoust's daughter, of whom I told you; but I dine with F.[3]—you know how hospitable she is. On Tuesday I dine with Milsand, one of the *Revue des Deux Mondes* set. After that I shall make no engagement for the evening till I hear what you will do. . . .

To his Mother

Paris, May 1, 1865.

My dearest Mother,

Here is a dull first of May, but the clouds are very pleasant after so much hot sun. I have been a little out of sorts since I came back, and certainly have never cared so little for Paris; but I have now got plenty to do, and while that is so, one is at least preserved from low spirits. It was six years since I had been here, and the two salons which I most frequented formerly have disappeared; but one soon re-knits one's relations in a place like this, and I am beginning to find it very hard to get an evening to myself for the theatre; and the theatre here, both for acting and for a study of the language, is just what the English theatre is not, where the

[1] Edmond Schérer (1815–89), theologian and literary critic. Contributed brilliant articles, mainly on foreign writers, to the *Revue des Deux Mondes*. He had a lively interest in English politics and literature, and was a frequent visitor to England.
[2] Teresa Guiccioli married the Marquis de Boissy in 1851.
[3] Mme. du Quaire.

acting is detestable, and the mode of speaking is just what one ought *not* to adopt. On Friday I dined with the Schérers at Versailles. He is one of the most interesting men in France, and I think I have told you of him. He called his youngest boy *Arnold*, after papa, and a very nice boy, of about nine, he is. Schérer has made a pilgrimage to Fox How, and saw some of the family, but not you. He interests me, from his connexion with Vinet, who has been occupying me a good deal lately; but he belongs now to the most advanced school among the French Protestants, and is a good deal troubled, I imagine, both from without and from within. At his house I met several of the writers in the *Journal des Débats*. Sainte Beuve, who is just made a senator, called for me at half-past ten, and took me to the Princesse Mathilde's. She received me very kindly, and said she knew that in my knowledge of France and the French language and literature I was a "Français"; to which I replied that I had read the writings of M. Sainte Beuve, he being a great *protégé* of hers. The Prince Napoleon was there, and a quantity of official and diplomatic people, also several literary notabilities, but none I cared very much for. The house, which formerly was Queen Christina's, is magnificent. To-day I am going to the Institute, to work an hour or so in the library, and then to the College Louis le Grand, to hear some lessons. I have seen the Papal Nuncio, who is charming, and he has given me letters which will enable me to see the schools of the Jesuits, where the French Minister's letter avails me nothing. I have just seen an American, a great admirer of mine, who says that the three people he wanted to see in Europe were James Martineau, Herbert Spencer, and myself. His talk was not as our talk, but he was a good man. He says that my *Essays* are already reprinted and published in America, and that I shall get something for them, but we shall see. . . .

To Miss Arnold

The Athenæum [November 1865].

. . . The *North American Review* for July had an article [1] on me which I like as well as anything I have seen. There is an immense public there, and this alone makes them of importance; but besides that, I had been struck in what I saw of them on the continent in the last few months, both with their intellectual liveliness and ardour, with which I had before been willing enough to credit them, as one of the good results of their democratic régime's emancipating them from the blinking and

[1] On *Essays in Criticism*.

hushing-up system induced by our circumstances here—and also with the good effect their wonderful success had produced on them in giving them something really considerable to rest upon, and freeing them from the necessity of being always standing upon their toes, crowing. I quite think we shall see the good result of this in their policy, as well as in the behaviour of individuals. An English writer may produce plenty of effect there, and this would satisfy people like Bright who think successful America will do quite as well for all they want, or even better, than successful England; but it will never satisfy me. Whatever Mary may say, or the English may think, I have a conviction that there is a real, an almost imminent danger of England losing immeasurably in all ways, declining into a sort of greater Holland, for want of what I must still call ideas, for want of perceiving how the world is going and must go, and preparing herself accordingly. This conviction haunts me, and at times even overwhelms me with depression; I would rather not live to see the change come to pass, for we shall all deteriorate under it. While there is time I will do all I can, and in every way, to prevent its coming to pass. Sometimes, no doubt, turning oneself one way after another, one must make unsuccessful and unwise hits, and one may fail after all: but try I must, and I know that it is only by facing in every direction that one can win the day. . . .

To his Mother

2 Chester Square, S.W., April 7, 1866.

My dearest Mother,

Many thanks for your letter, and tell that dear old Edward that I keep his note as a memorial of his duckishness. Tell him that the diction of the poem [1] was modelled on that of Theocritus, whom I have been much reading during the two years this poem has been forming itself, and that I meant the diction to be so artless as to be almost heedless. However, there is a mean which must not be passed, and before I reprint the poem I will consider well all objections. The images are all from actual observation, on which point there is an excellent remark in Wordsworth's notes, collected by Miss Fenwick. The cuckoo on the wet June morning I heard in the garden at Woodford, and all those three stanzas you like are reminiscences of Woodford. Edward has, I think, fixed on the two stanzas I myself like best in "O easy access" and "And long the way appears." I also like "Where is the girl," and the stanza before it, but that is because

[1] *Thyrsis.*

they bring certain places and moments before me. I have heard nothing about the poem, except that Bradley [1] is greatly pleased with it. It is probably too *quiet* a poem for the general taste, but I think it will stand wear.

To J. C. Shairp [2]

The Athenæum, April 12, 1866.

My dear Shairp,

To prevent all mistakes, and leave you without excuse in case of misconduct, I write a line to tell you that we have let our house (2 Chester *Square*) and are going out of town on the 1st of May. But we shall not go far—perhaps to Woodford in Epping Forest, where I heard, two years ago, the cuckoo I have brought in in *Thyrsis*; and, wherever we go, our address may be got at the Privy Council Office, and you will be inexcusable if you do not get it and communicate with me. I will take care that we meet, if you do not, in your shabby way, slip through London unperceived.

It gives me great pleasure that you and Sellar like *Thyrsis*. *Multi multa loquuntur; ideo fides parum est adhibenda,* says Thomas à Kempis; but the voices I do turn to are the voices of our old set, now so scattered, who, at the critical moment of opening life, were among the same influences and (more or less) sought the same things as I did myself. What influences those before and after us have been or may be among, or what things they have sought or may seek, God knows. Perhaps the same as we, but we cannot know, cannot, therefore, be sure of understanding them and their criticisms on what we do.

Thyrsis is a very quiet poem, but I think solid and sincere. It will not be popular, however. It had long been in my head to connect Clough with that Cumner country, and when I began I was carried irresistibly into this form; you say, truly, however, that there is much in Clough (the whole *prophet* side, in fact) which one cannot deal with in this way, and one has the feeling, if one reads the poem as a memorial poem, that not enough is said about Clough in it; I feel this so much that I do not send the poem to Mrs. Clough. Still Clough *had* this idyllic side, too; to deal with this suited my desire to deal again with that Cumner country: anyway, only so could I treat the matter this time. *Valeat quantum.* . . .

¹ George Granville Bradley (1821–1903), headmaster of Marlborough, and later Dean of Westminster. Author of the famous *Latin Prose Composition.*
² John Campbell Shairp (1819–1885), Principal, and Professor of Latin at St. Andrews. Professor of Poetry at Oxford from 1877 till his death.

To his Mother

The Athenæum [February 1867].

You will have been interested in the notice of old Mr. Crabb Robinson. Not a fortnight ago I found him in this very room where I am now writing, and spoke to him. He asked me which of all my books I should myself name as the one that had got me "my great reputation," as he wanted to buy it. I said I had not "a great reputation," upon which he answered: "Then it is some other Matthew Arnold who writes the books." But the odd thing is this—I told him I would send him my Essays, upon which he replied: "No, no, I'll buy them; don't throw them away upon an old fellow like me: *I shall be dead in a fortnight.*" And so he was. He talked for about a quarter of an hour that evening, and very well; repeating several of Goethe's epigrams, and saying some interesting things about them. He was one of those who most called up the thought of old days, and passed away people, even to me; and how much more must he have done this to others, who knew him thirty years before I did. . . .

To the Same

The Athenæum, June 17, 1867.

. . . I have just returned from Oxford, having to inspect a school in London to-day. I am going to dine and sleep at the Forsters', and Flu and her two boys will not return to West Humble [1] from Oxford till quite late this evening. I shall join them to-morrow. We had a very successful visit to Oxford, though I sigh for the days when I had a little more liberty, and had not so many engagements made for me there. We arrived on Saturday about two, and after luncheon Tom [2] and I took the boys to Port Meadow, and Dick had a canoe, which he manages very well, and had long wanted to try on the river at Oxford. Tom and I pulled little Tom in a boat for some time, but rain was threatening, so we deposited Tommy at Medley Lock, where he amused

[1] West Humble, near Dorking, where the Arnolds resided from 1866 to 1868.

[2] Arnold's younger brother Thomas (the 'Philip' of Clough's *Bothie*). A convert to Rome he had been professor of English Literature at Newman's Catholic University in Dublin and later classical master at the Birmingham Oratory School. He left the Roman Catholic church and was from 1865 to 1876 taking private pupils in his house at Oxford. Having rejoined the church of Rome he was in 1882 appointed to the Chair of English Literature at University College, Dublin.

himself with examining the barges and boats, and strolled along the river while Dicky paddled himself. Then we came back, and Flu and I dressed for Balliol.[1] It was an immense party, and we dined at the high table in hall. The Lingens were there, and the Farrers, and Lady Airlie and her daughter, and Arthur Peel, the Member for Warwick (the late Sir Robert's youngest son), and his wife (a Dugdale), and Browning, and others from London, besides Mrs. Liddell and a great number of Oxford people. I was sent in first with Lady Airlie, and was altogether made a great deal of, which I always am in Oxford. Lady Airlie is very clever and very handsome. She is Lady Stanley of Alderley's eldest daughter. There was a great evening party afterwards, and Tom and his wife came. They put up the boys beautifully, and the pupils taking to them immediately, as young men generally do to boys, Tom and Dick were in great bliss. On Sunday morning I went to see the Toms, as he was going off to Burton-on-Trent. Then I corrected the proofs of my lecture, which will appear unchanged,—as a lecture and not as an essay— in the next *Cornhill*.[2] After luncheon to the Taylor Buildings, to see the pictures there which Dr. Acland and the Dean of Christ Church have been rearranging, and wanted me to see their rearrangement of[3]; then to another great dinner at Merton—the same party as the night before, only Roundell[4] the host and not Jowett. This time, to vary the assorting, Browning was sent in with Lady Airlie, and I with Mrs. Arthur Peel. After dinner an immense party in Merton hall. I think Flu has liked it very much. I was pleased to hear from Lady Brodie what great satisfaction my last lecture had given; she said she could hardly express her pleasure at the turn I had given to this final lecture, after all my liberties with Oxford and old Oxford notions in former lectures. Dick excited immense admiration. He is going in a four-oar with the pupils to-day. Now I must go to my school.—Your ever most affectionate   M. A.

[1] Browning refers to this party in a letter to Isabella Blagden of June 19, 1867.

[2] *Culture and its Enemies*, his final lecture as Professor of Poetry, appeared in the *Cornhill Magazine*, July 1867. Arnold had written to his mother on June 4,

> I tried to make this last lecture one in which I could keep to ground where I am in sympathy with Oxford, having often enough startled them with heresies and novelties. And I succeeded.

[3] The Taylorian and the adjoining University Galleries were erected from designs by Cockerell, 1841–48. Acland and Liddell were curators of the University Galleries. The Ashmole antiquities were later transferred to the galleries, and the whole collection incorporated under the title of Ashmolean Museum in 1908.

[4] Charles Savile Roundell, Fellow of Merton, 1851–74.

The Rev. E. P. Arnold [1]

Cambridge, July 23, 1867.

. . . It gives me great pleasure that you should like what I do, you dear old boy; and particularly I am glad you like this last lecture, the judgments on which have been very various. Perhaps none but Oxford men can know how much truth there really is in the praise I have given to Oxford for her sentiment. I find I am generally thought to have *buttered her up* to excess for the sake of parting good friends; but this is not so, though I certainly kept her best side in sight, and not her worst. The *Saturday* has a friendly article on the lecture; the *London Review*, if you ever see that publication, had an outrageous one. I shall be interested in hearing what you think of the poems; [2] some of them, I feel sure, will interest you. There are two or three bad faults of punctuation which you will observe and correct. "Empedocles" takes up much room, but Browning's desire that I should reprint "Empedocles" was really the cause of the volume appearing at all. . . .

To Mrs. Forster

January 4, 1868.

My dearest K.,

Poor little Basil [3] died this afternoon, a few minutes before one o'clock. I sat up with him till four this morning, looking over my papers, that Flu and Mrs. Tuffin might get some sleep, and at the end of every second paper I went to him, stroked his poor twitching hand and kissed his soft warm cheek, and though he never slept he seemed easy, and hardly moaned at all. This morning, about six, after I had gone to bed, he became more restless; about eleven he had another convulsion; from that time he sank. Flu, Mrs. Tuffin, and I were all round him as his breathing gradually ceased, then the spasm of death passed over his face; after that the eyes closed, all the features relaxed, and now as he lies with his hands folded, and a white camellia Georgina Wightman brought him lying on his breast, he is the sweetest and most beautiful sight possible.

And so this loss comes to me just after my forty-fifth birthday, with so much other "suffering in the flesh,"—the departure of youth, cares of many kinds, an almost painful anxiety about

[1] Edward Penrose, the poet's brother; fourth son of Dr. Arnold.
[2] *New Poems*, 1867.
[3] Basil Francis, Arnold's youngest child, born 1866, died 1868.

public matters,—to remind me that *the time past of our life may suffice us!*—words which have haunted me for the last year or two, and that we "should no longer live the rest of our time in the flesh to the lusts of men, but to the will of God." However different the interpretation we put on much of the facts and history of Christianity, we may unite in the bond of this call, which is true for all of us, and for me, above all, how full of meaning and warning. . . .

To his Mother

Harrow, December 24, 1868.

My dearest Mother,

I have been doing papers till the last moment, but I must put them aside to write to you and thank you and Edward, Susy and Fan for your letters and good wishes. Now I am within one year of papa's age when he ended his life; and how much he seems to have put into it, and to what ripeness of character he had attained! Everything has seemed to come together to make this year the beginning of a new time to me: the gradual settlement of my own thought, little Basil's death, and then my dear, dear Tommy's.[1] And Tommy's death in particular was associated with several awakening and epoch-making things. The chapter for the day of his death was that great chapter, the 1st of Isaiah; the first Sunday after his death was Advent Sunday, with its glorious collect, and in the Epistle the passage which converted St. Augustine. All these things point to a new beginning, yet it may well be that I am near my end, as papa was at my age, but without papa's ripeness, and that there will be little time to carry far the new beginning. But this is all the more reason for carrying it as far as one can, and as earnestly as one can, while one lives. . .

To the Same

Harrow, June 5, 1869.

. . . My book was out yesterday.[2] This new edition is really a very pretty book, but you had better not buy it, because I am going to give it Fan, and shall bring it with me to Fox How, and the order of arrangement in this edition is not quite the final one I shall adopt. On this final order I could not decide till I saw this collected edition. The next edition will have the final order,

[1] Arnold's eldest son Thomas, aged sixteen, died at Harrow, November 23, 1868.

[2] *Poems :* 1869 (Two volumes)—the first collected edition.

and then the book will be stereotyped. That edition I shall then have bound, and give you. I expect the present edition will be sold out in about a year. Macmillan tells me the booksellers are subscribing very well for it. My poems represent, on the whole, the main movement of mind of the last quarter of a century, and thus they will probably have their day as people become conscious to themselves of what that movement of mind is, and interested in the literary productions which reflect it. It might be fairly urged that I have less poetical sentiment than Tennyson, and less intellectual vigour and abundance than Browning; yet, because I have perhaps more of a fusion of the two than either of them, and have more regularly applied that fusion to the main line of modern development, I am likely enough to have my turn, as they have had theirs . .

To Miss Arnold

Harrow, October 9, 1870.

. . . As one's years increase, and the desire to fulfil certain projects while one has yet time becomes keener and more pressing, the interruption caused by the continual travelling-about which inspection requires becomes trying. Only by much more rigorously laying out what I mean to do than formerly, and sticking much more rigorously than formerly to what is thus laid out, instead of going off on any new fancy or scheme that may turn up, can I hope to get along without self-dissatisfaction and constant impatience. The times are wonderful, and will be still more so; and one would not willingly lose by negligence, self-mismanagement, and want of patience what power one has of working in them and having influence on them. But the power of self-management and turning one's circumstances to the best account is the hardest power in the world to acquire; half the wasted lives one sees are due to the want of it. I have been feeling this very much lately, and the great thing is not to stop at feeling it, but to act as is requisite for one who strongly feels it. . . .

To Cardinal Newman

Harrow, November 29th, 1871.

My dear Sir,—

Mr. Boyle promised me he would tell you that it had been in my mind to give myself the great pleasure of calling upon you when I was in Birmingham, but the time at my command was too short. I have ventured to send you the lecture[1] I then gave at Birmingham; partly what is said about Mahometanism at the end seems to me to coincide very much with a strain of remark in a reprinted article of yours on Milman which I have just been reading, and to be an unconscious homage to the truth of what you have there said; partly to give myself an opportunity of explaining, that the Spectator's assertion, in a review of your Essays, that some lines of mine were "a portrait of Mr. Newman," has its sole ground in the writer's own imagination. What is said in those lines is not what I should have said if I had been speaking of you, and I should not like you to think it was; at any rate, said of you it was not; I had quite another personage in mind.

I cannot forbear adding, what I have often wished to tell you, that no words can be too strong to express the interest with which I used to hear you at Oxford, and the pleasure with which I continue to read your writings now. We are all of us carried in ways not of our own making or choosing, but nothing can ever do away the effects you have produced upon me, for it consists in a general disposition of mind rather than in a particular set of ideas. In all the conflicts I have with modern Liberalism and Dissent, and with their pretensions and shortcomings, I recognize your work; and I can truly say that no praise gives me so much pleasure as to be told (which sometimes happens) that a thing I have said reminds people either in manner or matter, of you. . . .

To Miss Arnold

United Service Club, Pall Mall, October 2, 1874.

My dearest Fan,

You may believe that I thought of you and of Fox How, and of all the past, on Wednesday.[2] We call it the past, but how much one retains of it; and then it is not really the dead past, but a part of the living present. And this is especially true of that central

---

[1] The lecture referred to is *A Persian Passion Play* printed in the third edition of *Essays in Criticism* (1875).

In a subsequent letter to Newman, Arnold writes:

> There are four people, in especial, from whom I am conscious of having learnt—a very different thing from merely receiving a strong impression—learnt habits, methods, ruling ideas, which are constantly with me; and the four are—Goethe, Wordsworth, Sainte-Beuve, and yourself. You will smile and say I have made an odd mixture and that the result must be a jumble . . .

[2] The first anniversary of his mother's death.

personage of our past—dearest mamma. We retain so much of her, she is so often in our thoughts, that she does not really pass away from us. She constantly comes into my mind. Some words of Gull [1] in to-day's *Times* about what we hope and believe, which are almost word for word what I have said, made me think as I read them that I should have pointed that out to mamma. Then I took up the *Blackwood* article on School Board Religion, and found the Jews spoken of as a people who, with all their faults, had yet had so near a sense of "the Eternal Power that makes for righteousness," and then that the Bible had the merit of putting such a mass of people in contact with so much "of the best that has been thought and said in the world," and again I thought how I should have liked to call dearest mamma's notice to this. It will more and more become evident how entirely religious is the work I have done in *Literature and Dogma*. The enemies of religion see this well enough already. It is odd that while I was in my recent article blaming a new book, *Supernatural Religion*, for being purely negative in its Bible criticism, Morley in the *Fortnightly* was praising the book for this very thing, which he says is all we want at present, and contrasting my book unfavourably with it as not insisting enough on the negative side and on disproof. I am amused to see Strahan's handbill stuck in all the magazines and book-stalls, announcing Gladstone and me as his two attractions this month. But no one knows better than I do how little of a popular author I am; but the thing is, I gradually produce a real effect, and the public acquires a kind of obscure interest in me as this gets to be perceived. . . .

To the Same

Cobham, Sunday [November 1874].

My dearest Fan,

I send you Jowett's letter, which turned up in a sorting of letters and papers today. You may burn it when you have read it. I send you also Mr F.—— I have written to him to say that in case I publish a cheap edition of *Literature and Dogma*, which I am not disposed to do at present, I shall very likely cut out all which is not directly essential to the argument of the book. I write in the manner which is natural to me; the manner has, no doubt, its weak points. But ponderous works produce no effect; the religious world which complains of me would not

[1] Sir William Gull, physician in ordinary to Queen Victoria: the reference is to his address to the Medical School of Guy's Hospital.

read me if I treated my subject as they say it ought to be treated, and I want them, indeed, to read me as little as they please, but I do not mean them to prescribe a mode of treatment of my subject to me which would lead to my being wholly ineffective both with them and with every one else. For it is my belief, at any rate, that I give something positive, which to a great many people may be of the very greatest comfort and service. And this is in part an answer to what you say about treating with lightness what is matter of life and death to so many people. There is a levity which is altogether evil; but to treat miracles and the common anthropomorphic ideas of God as what one may lose and yet keep one's hope, courage, and joy, as what are not really matters of life and death in the keeping or losing of them, this is desirable and necessary, if one holds, as I do, that the common anthropomorphic ideas of God and the reliance on miracles must and will inevitably pass away. This I say not to pain you, but to make my position clear to you. When I see the conviction of the ablest and most serious men round me that a great change must come, a great plunge must be taken, I think it well, I must say, instead of simply dilating, as both the religious and the anti-religious world are fond of doing, on the plunge's utterness, tremendousness, and awfulness, to show mankind that it need not be in terror and despair, that everything essential to its progress stands firm and unchanged . . .

To Miss Kingsley

January 1875.

Dear Miss Kingsley,

I fear your mother is in no state to read letters; you must let me write one line to you. I kept watching the accounts of your dear father's illness with a boding heart. I feared the worst.[1] It has seemed of late years as if he had not fortune on his side, as when he was young. With all the more interest I followed the accounts of this illness, and not only I, but Mrs Arnold and my two girls. Your dear father interested and attached all with whom he came in contact. His fine talents and achievements in literature will now have full justice done to them again; the injustice which he and they had in some quarters to experience will be no longer busy. But it is not of his talents and achievements that I now wish to speak. I find myself more full of the thought of something in which he seemed to me unique. I think

[1] Charles Kingsley died January 23, 1875.

he was the most generous man I have ever known; the most forward to praise what he thought good, the most willing to admire, the most free from all thought of himself in praising and in admiring, and the most incapable of being made ill-natured, or even indifferent, by having to support ill-natured attacks himself. Among men of letters I know nothing so rare as this; it will always keep your father's memory surrounded, in my mind, with a freshness and an honour peculiarly his own . . .

To Miss Arnold

Cobham, Thursday, July 1876.

. . . The Bayreuth performance turns my mind longingly to very different matters, the Nibelungen ring, and Fafnir and Siegfried and Gudrune and Brunhilde, all of whom I had once hoped to touch in poetry. They and their story are all at full length in the series of operas Wagner is to give at Bayreuth, £45 a ticket, and they are all taken! . . .

To Henry Nettleship [1]

Athenæum Club, Pall Mall, S.W. February 5, 1877.

My dear Nettleship,

Your letter went to Cobham, and we are in London, at 3 Eccleston Square, till Easter.

My best thanks to Mr Fowler [2] and those who have thought of me for the Poetry Chair again. But I shall not offer myself as candidate. I am not sure that it is not well to give new men the chance of showing themselves in the Poetry Chair; but, apart from that, I feel certain that, if I stood, the religious question would be raised, and to have this question raised in an election to a Chair of Poetry would be, in my opinion, a bad thing for the University; to me myself it would be intolerable. And I think you will see that, a body like Convocation being the electors, it could hardly be but that the religious question would be raised if I came forward at present, either for the Poetry Chair or for any Chair at Oxford . . .

[1] Henry Nettleship (1839–1893), Fellow of Corpus, and Professor of Latin at Oxford.
[2] Sub-rector of Lincoln College and Professor of Logic: later President of Corpus. J. C. Shairp was elected to the Poetry Chair in 1877.

To the Rev. G. D. Boyle [1]

3 Eccleston Square, S.W., March 11, 1877.

. . . I had forgotten the poem about Charlotte Brontë and Harriet Martineau, but I will look it up. I think there were things not bad in it, but I do not want to overpraise a personage so antipathetic to me as H.M. My first impression of her is, in spite of her undeniable talent, energy, and merit—what an unpleasant life and unpleasant nature! . . .

To his Wife

Athenæum, May 7, 1877.

. . . Your better account of my dear old Edward [2] was indeed a pleasure to me. I hope and trust he has got out—not getting out must be terrible. "*When I am dying, qu'on place ma chaise sur l'herbe courte,*" says Obermann, and I quite share his feeling. . . . I think Fan and Edward would like to look at the *New Republic*; [3] they can get it at any library. It seems generally thought that my verses are well parodied, but I myself and my conversation are not well hit off. But then the writer did not know me personally, even by sight: and Ruskin, Jowett, Pater, etc., he knew.

To Miss Arnold

Cobham, Saturday [December 1877].

. . . It was not very interesting, the dinner with ——, but then I did not expect it would be. An evening of Bulgaria is too

---

[1] Vicar of Kidderminster, later Dean of Salisbury.

[2] Rev. Edward Penrose Arnold, younger brother of the poet, died 1878.

[3] *The New Republic,* or *Culture, Faith and Philosophy in an English Country House,* 1877, by W. H. Mallock. Arnold figures as Mr. Luke. The parody opens:

> Softly the evening descends,
> Violet and soft. The sea
> Adds to the silence, below
> Pleasant and cool on the beach
> Breaking; yes, and a breeze
> Calm as the twilight itself
> Furtively sighs through the dusk,
> Listlessly lifting my hair,
> Fanning my thought-wearied brow.
> Thus I stand in the gloom
> Watching the moon-track begin
> Quivering to die like a dream
> Over the far sea-line
> To the unknown region beyond.

much, and of course Forbes knows nothing else, and Gladstone can go on for hours about that or any other subject. There were only nine people. Lord —— rested his face on his hand, after he had stuffed himself, and went fast asleep. Forbes is a fine, iron-gray, soldier-like sort of man. Ruskin was there, looking very slight and spiritual. I am getting to like him. He gains much by evening dress, plain black and white, and by his fancy being forbidden to range through the world of coloured cravats. Huxley was there, too, and I was by Chenery, the new editor of the *Times*, who was not at all a bad neighbour. Gladstone was not animated, and I think even he must have felt himself a little over-Bulgarised. His position between Knowles and Forbes almost compelled him to talk Bulgaria to Forbes incessantly. After dinner Huxley and I talked to him a little about Ireland, which was interesting. I am sorry to say he seemed full of the deep opposition in Ireland to England and English policy— for the present at any rate—that to *go contrary* was the main impulse there. One of the many blessings, my dear Fan, which we owe to Puritanism is this impracticable condition of Ireland. I am glad to hear from Green, who is expanding his history, that the more he looks into Puritanism, and indeed into the English Protestant Reformation generally, the worse is his opinion of it all . . .

To Miss Arnold

Athenæum Club, Pall Mall, S.W., April 14, 1879.

. . . I am well forward with my school reports, and have nearly finished arranging my Wordsworth selection,[1] so I feel more of a free man than usual. It is delightful to have to occupy oneself with Wordsworth, and he will come out better and more effective in my arrangement, I think, than he has ever come out before. I have gone on the plan of throwing pieces of one poetical *kind* together, not of classifying them, in Wordsworth's own intricate way, according to the spiritual faculty from which they are supposed to have proceeded. I don't think any of his *best* work will be left out, though a great deal must be left out which is *good* work, especially of his later time. When I have sent my list off to the printer I shall set about my introduction—a short one, but I hope to do him justice. He can show a body of work superior to what any other English poet, except Shakespeare and Milton, can show; and his body of work is more interesting than Milton's, though not so great. This seems to me to be the simple

[1] *Poems of Wordsworth* (Golden Treasury Series), 1879.

truth. I hope this collection of mine may win for him some appreciation on the Continent also. I shall send the book to Schérer, and beg him to review it. Wordsworth's body of work, to keep to that phrase, is superior to the body of work of any Continental poet of the last hundred years except Goethe; superior to that of Schiller, Heine, Musset, Victor Hugo. This, again, seems to me to be the simple truth. But I must not run on. . . .

To the Same

Cobham, Sunday, May 15, 1880.

. . On Thursday I got a card from the Duchess of Norfolk for a party that evening, to meet Newman. I went, because I wanted to have spoken once in my life to Newman, and because I wanted to see the house. The house was not so fine as I expected. Newman was in costume—not full Cardinal's costume, but a sort of vest with gold about it and the red cap; he was in state at one end of the room, with the Duke of Norfolk on one side of him and a chaplain on the other, and people filed before him as before the Queen, dropping on their knees when they were presented and kissing his hand. It was the faithful who knelt in general, but then it was in general only the faithful who were presented. That old mountebank Lord —— dropped on his knees, however, and mumbled the Cardinal's hand like a piece of cake. I only made a deferential bow, and Newman took my hand in both of his and was charming. He said, "I ventured to tell the Duchess I should like to see you." One had to move on directly, for there was a crowd of devotees waiting, and he retires at eleven. But I am very glad to have seen him. I met Lady Portsmouth there, who is a relation of the Duke; she took charge of me, and carried me through the crowd to the chaplain, who knew who I was; else I should never have got at Newman at all. I met A.P.S. at dinner at the Buxtons' before I went, who was deeply interested and excited at my having the invitation to meet the Cardinal; he hurried me off the moment dinner was over, saying, "This is not a thing to lose!" . . .

To the Same

[November 1880.]

. . . I have been reading Chaucer a great deal, the early French poets a great deal, and Burns a great deal. Burns is a beast, with splendid gleams, and the medium in which he lived, Scotch peasants, Scotch Presbyterianism, and Scotch drink, is repulsive.

Chaucer, on the other hand, pleases me more and more, and his medium is infinitely superior. But I shall finish with Shakespeare's *King Lear* before I finally write my Introduction,[1] in order to have a proper taste in my mind while I am at work.

To Sir Mountstuart Grant Duff [2]

Pains Hill Cottage, Cobham, Surrey, July 29, 1882.

My dear Grant Duff,

I was glad to hear from you direct, and I wish all happiness to your little Iseult. She coincides with Swinburne's poem on the subject, which is just published, and which he has sent me with a pretty letter. He has taken the story, answering to the old Theseus story, of the black and white souls, and a very fine story it is for poetical purposes. Swinburne's fatal habit of using one hundred words where one would suffice always offends me, and I have not yet faced his poem, but I must try it soon. You should have read my "Word about America" in the *Nineteenth Century*;[3] I think you would have liked it. One had to trust a great deal to one's "flair", but I think my "flair" served me here pretty well. At any rate, Henry James, the novelist, being asked by Knowles to write a reply to it, said after reading it that he could not write a reply to it, it was so true, and carried him so along with it. You must also look at my Rede Lecture at Cambridge, where I had a crowded audience; the parallel between Oxford and Cambridge will interest you, if the rest does not. It will appear in the *Nineteenth Century* for August.[4] I am very glad you liked the lines on dear A.P.S.[5] They did not fetch the great public, but the judicious were pleased, and A.P.S. himself would have liked them. And now no more literature.

. . . .

I have said nothing about politics. Events and personages succeed one another, but the central fact of the situation always remains for me this: that whereas the basis of things amidst all chance and change has even in Europe generally been for ever so long supernatural Christianity, and far more so in England than in Europe generally, this basis is certainly going—going amidst the full consciousness of the continentals that it is going,

---

[1] The General Introduction to T. H. Ward's *The English Poets*, 1880. Reprinted as 'The Study of Poetry' in *Essays in Criticism, Second Series*, 1888.

[2] Governor of Madras, 1881–86.   [3] May 1882.

[4] 'Literature and Science', 1882; reprinted in *Discourses in America*, 1885.

[5] 'Westminster Abbey' in the *Nineteenth Century*, January 1882.

and amidst the provincial unconsciousness of the English that it is going. Ewald has a very profound sentence: "Eigentlich von der Verkehrtheit des Verhaltens gegen das Göttliche alles Unglück ausgeht." But a letter has no room for this sort of thing. . . .

To John Morley, M.P.

Fox How, Ambleside, August 10, 1883.

My dear Morley,

To my surprise, I have just had a letter from your great leader offering me a pension of £250 "as a public recognition of service to the poetry and literature of England." To my further surprise, those about me think I ought to accept it, and I am told that —— thinks the same. I have written to him, but have not yet got his answer.

I write to you, that, whatever his answer may be, I may be fortified by your opinion also, for I have an instinct which tells me that in matters of feeling you and I are apt to be in sympathy.

It seems to me that, the fund available for literary pensions being small, and literary men being numerous and needy, it would not look well if a man drawing already from the public purse an income of nearly £1000 a year took £250 a year more from the small public fund available for pensions to letters, science, and art.

I feel this so strongly that I should have at once refused, if it were not for those about me. Of course, I should be glad of an addition of £250, and if I find everybody thinking that my scruple is a vain one, I shall at least consider the matter very carefully, though really I do not feel at present as if I *could* accept the offer.

Let me have a line here as soon as possible, as I must send an answer to your Pericles.

Ever affectionately yours,
Matthew Arnold.

To Miss Arnold

Cobham, Sunday, October 18, 1885.

. . . I have been for three nights at Oxford this last week, staying at Corpus in the perfection of comfort; Fowler, the President, is a bachelor. The house is as pleasant and cheerful a one as —— is the reverse. I dined at the Oriel Gaudy on Thursday, and met two bishops, Stubbs [1] and Wordsworth; [2] the other two nights

---

[1] Bishop of Chester, later of Oxford.   [2] Bishop of Salisbury.

there were people to dinner in Corpus. I saw many things I had
never seen before: the Corpus plate which is unique in Oxford,
not having been melted down for Charles the First; the library
which is full of treasures; the long record of papa's admission as
a scholar in presence, as the fashion then was, of a notary public;
the spoons given by papa when he left the College—these and a
mustard-pot given by Keble are now put aside as curiosities and
not brought into use; finally, papa's rooms, which had formerly
been Bishop Jewell's. The college is a most interesting one;
its founder, Bishop Fox, who had accumulated a large sum to
found a convent of monks, was warned by the King's ministers
that monks had had their day and that property left for their
benefit would not be safe, so he founded a college for learning
instead—at the very beginning of the sixteenth century. Much
was said at Oxford about my coming for the Chair of Poetry, and
I believe a requisition will be sent to me. On Friday I got out to
Hinksey and up the hill to within sight of the Cumner firs. I
cannot describe the effect which this landscape always has upon
me—the hillside with its valleys, and Oxford in the great Thames
valley below. . . .

To his Wife

Munich, March 4, 1886.

. . . The day before yesterday, after sending my letter, I walked
about a little, and then went to the opera to see *Tristram and
Iseult*. I may say that I have managed the story better than
Wagner. The second act is interminable, and without any action.
The hero and the heroine sit on a sofa and sing to one another
about light and darkness, and their connexion with love. The
theatre was a brilliant sight, and the *prima donna* is a handsome
woman with some sweet notes in her voice; but at the end of the
second act, at about half-past ten, the piece having begun at
half-past six, I was quite worn out and came away. The third
act is better, I imagine. But even in that, less is made of the
story than might be made. . . .

NOTES TO THE POEMS

NOTES

List of Arnold's Poetry

The Strayed Reveller, and Other Poems. By A. London: B. Fellowes, Ludgate Street. 1849.

Empedocles on Etna, and Other Poems. By A. London: B. Fellowes, Ludgate Street. 1852.

Poems. By Matthew Arnold. A New Edition. London: Longman, Brown, Green, and Longmans. MDCCCLIII.
[Second Edition 1854. Third Edition 1857].

Poems. By Matthew Arnold. Second Series. London: Longman, Brown, Green, and Longmans. MDCCCLV.

Merope. A Tragedy. By Matthew Arnold. London: Longman, Brown, Green, Longmans, & Roberts. MDCCCLVIII.

New Poems by Matthew Arnold. London: Macmillan and Co. MDCCCLXVII.
[Second Edition 1868.]

Poems by Matthew Arnold. The First Volume: Narrative and Elegiac Poems. The Second Volume: Dramatic and Lyric Poems. London: Macmillan and Co. MDCCCLXIX.
[First Collected Edition: in two vols.]

Poems by Matthew Arnold. The First Volume: Early Poems, Narrative Poems, and Sonnets. The Second Volume: Lyric, Dramatic and Elegiac Poems. New and Complete Edition. London: Macmillan and Co. MDCCCLXXVII.
[Second Collected Edition: in two vols. Reissued with slight alterations in 1881.]

Selected Poems of Matthew Arnold. London: Macmillan and Co. 1878.

Poems by Matthew Arnold. London: Macmillan and Co. 1885.
Early Poems, Narrative Poems and Sonnets: Lyric and Elegiac Poems: Dramatic and Later Poems.
[The so-called Library Edition in three unnumbered volumes—containing Arnold's final arrangement of his poems. Reissued without change in 1888, the last edition to appear in the poet's lifetime.]

Poetical Works of Matthew Arnold. London: Macmillan and Co. and New York. 1890.

> [The complete one-volume edition. It includes two poems, "Horatian Echo" and "Kaiser Dead", which had appeared in periodicals but had not been collected during the poet's lifetime.]

The Poetical Works of Matthew Arnold. Edited by C. B. Tinker and F. H. Lowry. Geoffrey Cumberlege: Oxford University Press. 1950.

> [Oxford Standard Authors. Complete critical edition recording alterations of text. Contains the two Prize Poems, and the cancelled poems which Arnold excluded from his works. Also reprints the Prefaces of 1853 and 1854.]

PRIZE POEMS

Alaric at Rome. A prize poem recited in Rugby School June XII, MDCCCXL. Rugby: Coombe and Crossley. MDCCCXL.

Cromwell: a prize poem, recited in the Theatre, Oxford: June 28, 1843. By Matthew Arnold, Balliol College. Oxford: Printed and published by J. Vincent. MDCCCXLIII.

> [Arnold's "Newdigate". The poem is included in *Oxford Prize Poems*, 1846.]

Notes to the Poems

EARLY POEMS

Quiet Work

Introductory poem to Arnold's first volume *The Strayed Reveller, and Other Poems*, 1849, and there entitled "Sonnet". In 1869 it was given the title "Quiet Work". The text underwent numerous changes and revisions in the various editions before reaching its final form.

To a Friend

From *The Strayed Reveller*, 1849. The friend was probably Clough, to whom Arnold sent the last three lines of the octave in a letter of 1848. As Professor of Poetry at Oxford he quoted the famous line on Sophocles in his inaugural lecture *On the Modern Element in Literature* in 1857. Homer and Epictetus are the subjects of the octave.

Shakespeare

The sonnet was first printed in *The Strayed Reveller*, 1849. The Ms. (in the British Museum) is dated 1 August 1844.

In Harmony with Nature

From *The Strayed Reveller*, 1849—not reprinted till the edition of 1877. The mood contrasts with "Quiet Work", but resembles that of "Dover Beach" and passages in the later prose.

Mycerinus

The second poem of *The Strayed Reveller* volume, 1849: reprinted in *Poems*, 1853, and in all later collected editions. In 1853 Arnold added a note summarizing the source passage from Herodotus:

> After Chephren, Mycerinus, son of Cheops, reigned over Egypt. He abhorred his father's courses, and judged his subjects more justly than any of their kings had done. To him there came an oracle from the city of Buto, to the effect that he was to live but six years longer, and to die in the seventh year from that time.

The Church of Brou

The first allusion to this poem is an entry —"La Châtelaine architecte"—in an 1851(?) list of titles for proposed poems, now among the Arnold Mss. at Yale. As "The Church of Brou" it appeared in *Poems*, 1853. In the 1877 edition the first two parts were discarded and the third kept as a separate poem, "A Tomb among the Mountains", among the Narrative Poems. In 1881 the poem reassumed its original form and became one of the Early Poems. Arnold's doubts about the poem may well have been due to the criticism it received for inaccuracy in historical and geographical detail. The church, a fine example of late Burgundian Gothic, is not among the mountains near Chambéry but is on the outskirts of Bourg-en-Bresse some fifty miles away— nor are the Tombs themselves accurately described. Arnold passed through Bourg on his way to Geneva in the summer of 1858 (see letter to his wife 28 August 1858) but did not stop. The inspiration is purely literary—Edgar Quinet's "Des Arts de la Renaissance et de l'Eglise de Brou", 1839.

A Modern Sappho

First published in *The Strayed Reveller*, 1849, where it followed the poem later called "A Memory-Picture". Reprinted in the 1853 volume, but not again till the 1869 collected edition where it became one of the Elegies. In 1877 it was finally placed among the Early Poems. The poem strikes for Arnold an unusual note of passion, and is unusual too in being written from the woman's point of view. There may be some connection with the Marguerite experience. In the 1849 and 1853 editions there was an extra stanza, the third, afterwards cancelled:

> Is it hope makes me linger? The dim thought, that sorrow
> Means parting? that only in absence lies pain?
> It was well with me once if I saw him: to-morrow
> May bring one of the old happy moments again.

Requiescat

First published in *Poems*, 1853—and text left unchanged in subsequent editions.

Youth and Calm

First appeared in *Empedocles on Etna, and Other Poems*, 1852, as the second part of "Lines written by a Death-Bed". When reprinted in *New Poems*, 1867, the first sixteen lines were discarded. The cancelled lines were later inserted into "Tristram and Iseult" as part of the meditation on the dead Iseult of Ireland—the passage in Part II beginning "Yes, now the longing is o'erpast", etc. The poem as it now stands, but without the first four lines, was copied by Arnold into the Album of Rotha Quillinan, (Wordsworth's daughter) which is in the Wordsworth Museum at Grasmere. It is there dated 28 December 1851.

A Memory-Picture

From *The Strayed Reveller*, 1849, where the title was "To my Friends, who ridiculed a Tender Leave-Taking". In *Poems*, 1853, it became the opening poem of the "Switzerland" group, and in 1869 was given the title "A Memory-Picture". In *Poems*, 1877, it was detached from "Switzerland" and classed as an Early Poem. It is the first poem which mentions Marguerite. The text underwent frequent alterations. The second stanza cancelled in 1869 was not restored:

> But my Youth reminds me—"Thou
> Hast liv'd light as these live now:
> As these are, thou too wert such:
> Much hast had, hast squander'd much."
> Fortune's now less frequent heir,
> Ah! I husband what's grown rare.
>   Ere the parting kiss be dry,
>   Quick, thy tablets, Memory!

A Dream

From *Poems*, 1853, where it was the third of the "Switzerland" series. Rejected in the edition of 1869, but restored in 1881 and placed with the Early Poems.

Youth's Agitations

First appeared in *Empedocles on Etna, and Other Poems*, 1852, entitled "Sonnet". In *New Poems*, 1867, with the title changed to "Youth's Agitations", it was placed between "Youth and Calm" and "Growing Old"—with both of which poems it has obvious affinities. In 1877 it was transferred to the Early Poems.

Human Life

From *Empedocles on Etna, and Other Poems*, 1852. Not reprinted till *New Poems*, 1867; in the 1877 edition transferred to the Early Poems.

To a Gipsy Child by the Sea-Shore

From *The Strayed Reveller*, 1849. In *Poems*, 1869 (with some alterations) it followed "Rugby Chapel" as an elegy. In the 1877 edition, restored to practically its original form, it became one of the Early Poems.

In Utrumque Paratus

First appeared in *The Strayed Reveller*, 1849, and was thereafter dropped. Reprinted at Swinburne's request in *Poems*, 1869, where the last stanza was altered. The original ending was restored in the 1877 edition.

Resignation

The concluding poem of *The Strayed Reveller*, 1849; not reprinted till *Poems*, Second Series, 1855. In the 1869 edition Arnold added a note identifying the scenery with a walk over the Wythburn Fells:

> Those who have been long familiar with the English Lake-Country will have no difficulty in recalling, from the description in the text, the roadside inn at Wythburn on the descent from Dunmail Rise towards Keswick; its sedentary landlord of twenty years ago, and the passage over the Wythburn Fells to Watendlath.

A memorial stone erected near the inn records the date of the first walk as 1833, and the second as 1843. On some doubts about this dating see Sir Edmund Chambers' *Matthew Arnold. A Study.* 1947, pp. 41–3. The Arnolds had settled at Fox How near Ambleside in 1833.

Fausta is Jane, the poet's eldest and favourite sister—the "K" of his letters—who married W. E. Forster in 1850. She held the first place in Arnold's heart as the judge of his poems (see letter to his mother, 18 December 1861). Her husband was sponsor of the Education Act of 1870 and Secretary for Ireland under Gladstone.

NARRATIVE POEMS

Sohrab and Rustum

"The Death of Sohrab" appears among the titles in a list of poems proposed for the year 1851 (Yale Mss.). The poem was finished by May 1853 (see letter to Clough, May 1) and published in the volume of that year. During composition Arnold wrote of it to his sister Jane as "a thing that gives me more pleasure than anything I have ever done yet" (Letters, ed. G. W. E. Russell, I. 29); and writing to his mother he says it is "by far the best thing I have yet done . . . but then the story is a very noble and excellent one" (ibid. p. 30).

In his own note to the poem Arnold quotes at length from Sir John Malcolm's *History of Persia* and from Saint-Beuve's "Causerie" on Mohl's translation of Ferdousi. He also drew on Captain Alexander

Burnes' *Travels into Bokhara* (1834); and while writing he was of course deep in the study of Homer.

The myth of tragic combat between father and unknown son appears in various literatures: it is the theme of the Old High German *Hildebrandslied*.

Balder Dead

Composed in 1854 and published in *Poems*, Second Series, 1855. The story is taken from the Younger (or Prose) Edda as Arnold found it in Percy's translation of Mallet's *Northern Antiquities*. He changes details of the story and adds many Homeric and Virgilian touches. He thought it a better poem than "Sohrab and Rustum" and at one time intended to do more work in this field. See Letters: to Mrs. Forster, 12 December 1855 (p. 746) and to Miss Arnold, July 1876 (p. 772).

The Forsaken Merman

From *The Strayed Reveller*, 1849. Though it appeared in his first volume Arnold never placed "The Forsaken Merman" among the Early Poems in his later editions. It may, as Tinker and Lowry suggest, have been kept with the Narrative Poems owing to shortage of material in that group. The later and inferior "The Neckan" (1853) is a companion piece—both poems deriving from Danish ballad sources the story of the merman who wooed a mortal bride.

SONNETS

The group of fourteen sonnets appeared in *New Poems*, 1867. After some rearrangement in subsequent volumes the final order was fixed in the edition of 1877. In an unpublished letter to John Payne Knight (among the Arnold papers at Yale) Arnold said of the sonnet, ". . . in no form does the composer mark more clearly whether he is essentially poetical or prosaic"—quoted Tinker and Lowry *Commentary*, p. 135.

Austerity of Poetry

Giacopone da Todi (fl. 1268–98) was the author of the *Stabat Mater*. The anecdote about him which is the subject of this sonnet was derived from A. F. Ozanam's *Poëtes franciscains en Italie au treizième siècle* (1851).

Rachel

The three Rachel sonnets were first published in the *New Poems*, 1867; at least one was written as early as 1863. Rachel died 3 January 1858. Arnold first saw Rachel act in London, probably in 1846, and again during the winter of the same year in Paris where, for two months, he hardly missed one of her performances. See his essay "The French Play in London" (in *Irish Essays*) for an appreciation of Rachel's acting. The material for the sonnets comes from Mme. de Barréra's *Memoirs of Rachel* (1858). Readers of *Villette* will recall the deep impression Rachel's acting made on Charlotte Brontë. Harriet Martineau brought Miss Brontë to see Arnold in 1850. (See note to *Haworth Churchyard*.)

Worldly Place

In Arnold's note-book for 1863 the quotation from Marcus Aurelius is entered as the subject-matter for a sonnet. See also the essay on Marcus Aurelius in *Essays in Criticism* (1865).

Immortality

A typical expression of one aspect of Arnold's religious thought.

The Good Shepherd with the Kid

Derived, like the "Austerity of Poetry", from Ozanam. A note, added in 1869, identifies the "unpitying Phrygian sect" as the Montanists.

Monica's Last Prayer

Arnold's own note gives the source of this sonnet—St. Augustine's *Confessions*, Book IX. Chap. 11.

LYRIC POEMS

Switzerland

The Marguerite lyrics were first grouped together under the title "Switzerland" in the 1853 volume, as a series of six poems of which five had already appeared in earlier editions. In later editions Arnold kept changing the text, the order, the number and the titles—till a final arrangement of seven poems was reached in the edition of 1877. Two of the rejected poems were reprinted among Early Poems—"A Memory-Picture" in 1877 and "A Dream" in 1881.

Two letters to Clough written from Switzerland on 29 September 1848 and 23 September 1849 (see Letters, pp. 734 and 739) throw light on these poems. In the first Arnold speaks of lingering at the Hôtel Bellevue at Thun "for the sake of the blue eyes of one of its inmates"; and in the second, written a year later, he sends Clough lines which were to become part of the lyric "Parting" (ll. 25–35) addressed to Marguerite. All attempts to identify the real Marguerite and to trace her at the Hôtel Bellevue have failed; outside the poems the two letters to Clough are the only evidence for her existence.

There can be little doubt that the experience depicted in this group was a real one, and that it is reflected widely in his poetry. *A Modern Sappho*, the *Faded Leaves* group, *The Buried Life*, *Urania*, *Euphrosyne*, and two poems, *Destiny* and *Courage* (never reprinted by him after 1852)—all these and others suggest in different ways a kinship with the Marguerite group. On Marguerite as a pervading presence throughout the whole 1852 volume see an illuminating essay on the "Poetry of Matthew Arnold" by H. W. Garrod in *Poetry and the Criticism of Life* (Harvard University Press, 1931). An imaginary reconstruction of the episode has been made by Miss Isobel Macdonald in *The Buried Self* (1949).

The Strayed Reveller

The Strayed Reveller, and Other Poems, 1849. This, the title poem, was reprinted in all subsequent collected editions.

Fragment of an "Antigone"
Fragment of Chorus of a "Dejaneira"

The "Antigone" appeared in *The Strayed Reveller* volume in 1849, the "Dejaneira" not till *New Poems* of 1867, though like the other it is probably an early poem. Arnold was already at work on "Merope" in 1856. Of the "Dejaneira" Swinburne wrote, "That must be a noble statue which could match this massive fragment". The parts, in fact, proved better than the whole: his attempt in "Merope" to write a Greek drama in English was a failure.

Arnold's second son, "Budge", died in 1872, aged 18. Before the funeral Arnold wrote to his own mother, "How fond you were of him, and how I like to recall this! He looks beautiful, and my main feeling about him is, I am glad to say, what I have put in one of my poems, the 'Fragment of a Dejaneira' ".

In 1869 Arnold added a note identifying "The Hunter of the Tanagræan Field" as Orion, and explained his reference to "the sun-redden'd western straits"—"Erytheia, the legendary region around the Pillars of Hercules, probably took its name from the redness of the West under which the Greeks saw it."

Philomela

"Philomela" first appeared in *Poems*, 1853. The first draft of the poem, with considerable differences from the final version, survives in Ms. (in the possession of the Rev. Roger Wodehouse) and is printed by Tinker and Lowry, *Commentary*, p. 164. Eugenia (unidentified) appears also in "Horatian Echo" (one of the Early Poems omitted from this selection).

The story of Philomela, well known to both Greek and Latin writers, is told in full by Apollodorus (*Bibl.* 3. 193 ff.) and by Ovid (*Met.* 6. 424 ff.). Tereus, king of Thrace, having ravished Philomela sister of his wife Procne, in order to ensure her silence cut out her tongue and imprisoned her. Philomela worked the story of her wrongs into a piece of embroidery and had the web conveyed to Procne. To avenge her ravished sister, Procne killed her own son Itys and served him as a meal to his father Tereus. Tereus, pursuing the two sisters, was about to slay them in revenge when the Gods arrested him in the act and turned all three into birds—Tereus into a hoopoe, Procne into a nightingale and Philomela into a swallow.

So the story is told by the Greek writers and this is the version Arnold follows. The Latin writers make Philomela the nightingale and Procne the swallow, and Swinburne in *Itylus* follows them.

See also an essay by a later occupant of the Oxford Chair of Poetry, H. W. Garrod, on "The Nightingale in Poetry" in *The Profession of Poetry and Other Lectures* (Oxford 1929).

Calais Sands

The Ms. of "Calais Sands" (in the possession of Prof. Arnold Whitridge) is dated August 1850. The poem appeared in *New Poems*, 1867: its position was changed to precede the "Faded Leaves" group in the 1877 edition. Like the following group, this poem is connected with Arnold's courtship of Frances Wightman, whom he married in 1851.

Faded Leaves

Arnold arranged the "Faded Leaves" group in *Poems*, Second Series, 1855. All the poems except "Separation" had already appeared in the 1852 volume. Some evidence points to Miss Wightman as the inspiration of these poems: but it is hard not to feel the presence of Marguerite in these lyrics as well as in "Switzerland". For a discussion of the problem see Tinker and Lowry, *Commentary*, pp. 167 et seq.

Dover Beach

"Dover Beach" appeared in *New Poems*, 1867. The Sophoclean reference is not identifiable with certainty. It may be to the *Antigone*, ll. 583 et seq.: but parallels in the *Trachiniæ* and *Œdipus Coloneus* are possible.

Growing Old

"Growing Old" first appeared in *New Poems*, 1867. "It is difficult not to see in 'Growing Old' a deliberate challenge to 'Rabbi Ben Ezra' " (H. W. Garrod, essay on Arnold in *Fifteen Poets*, Oxford (1941), p. 457). Browning's poem had appeared in 1864.

Arnold was acutely conscious of the passing of youth and the waning of creative power. "What a difference there is between reading in poetry and morals of the loss of youth, and experiencing it!" (Letter to Clough, Oct. 28, 1852.)

The Progress of Poesy

First appeared in *New Poems*, 1867.

The Last Word

From *New Poems*, 1867.

Bacchanalia; or, The New Age

From *New Poems*, 1867.

Epilogue to Lessing's Laocoön

From *New Poems*, 1867.

The Youth of Nature, The Youth of Man

These companion poems first appeared in *Empedocles on Etna*, 1852. In his Note-Books Arnold refers to both poems as "pindarics". In *Poems*, 1853, *The Youth of Man* was broken into two short poems, entitled *Richmond Hill* and *Power of Youth*. In the 1855 volume it was restored to its original form.

Palladium

From *New Poems*, 1867.

Morality

From *Empedocles on Etna*, 1852.

A Summer Night

From *Empedocles on Etna*, 1852. The poem seems to recapture in tranquillity the scene and mood of the Marguerite group.

The Buried Life

First printed in *Empedocles on Etna*, 1852. The opening lines suggest a connection with the Marguerite series.

A Wish

First published in *New Poems*, 1867. Arnold wrote to his mother in December 1865: "I remember thinking in the cemetery at Rome, how well to die in a place like Rome and be buried in peace. . . . It is not death which is in my eyes hideous—but it is its ceremonial." (Passage from an unpublished letter quoted by Tinker and Lowry, *Commentary*, p. 200.)

The Future

The final poem of *Empedocles on Etna*, 1852.

ELEGIAC POEMS

The Scholar-Gipsy

The Scholar-Gipsy was first published in *Poems*, 1853. The poem had long been taking shape in Arnold's mind. His copy of Glanvil's *Vanity of Dogmatizing*, now at Yale, is inscribed with the date 1844, and the book is on his reading list for 1845. In a list of poems proposed for 1849 is a title "The first mesmerist", changed in a second list to "the wandering Mesmerist". The final title of "Scholar-Gipsy" he found in Glanvil, though the words were omitted from the condensed and altered passage from the *Vanity of Dogmatizing* which originally prefaced the poem:

> There was very lately a lad in the University of Oxford, who was by his poverty forced to leave his studies there; and at last to join himself to a company of vagabond gipsies. Among these extravagant people, by the insinuating subtilty of his carriage, he quickly got so much of their love and esteem as that they discovered to him their mystery. After he had been a pretty while exercised in the trade, there chanced to ride by a couple of scholars, who had formerly been of his acquaintance. They quickly spied out their old friend among the gipsies; and he gave them an account of the necessity which drove him to that kind of life, and told them that the people he went with were not such impostors as they were taken for, but that they had a traditional kind of learning among them, and could do wonders by the power of imagination, their fancy binding that of others: that himself had learned much of their art, and when he had compassed the whole secret, he intended, he said, to leave their company, and give the world an account of what he had learned.

Arnold's own view of the poem—characteristic of one aspect of his two-fold personality—is expressed in a letter to Clough, 30 November 1853 (see Letters, p. 745).

On the landscape background of this poem and of "Thyrsis" see an essay "The Scholar-Gipsy Country" by Sir Francis Wylie contributed as an appendix to the Tinker and Lowry *Commentary*.

Stanza 19. ll. 182 ff. (p. 179)

> *and amongst us one*
> *Who most has suffer'd:*

In 1883 when Arnold read this poem at Boston he stated that he had Goethe in mind in these lines, and that they were written after reading *Dichtung und Wahrheit* while he still felt the impression of its sadness. (*The Worcester Spy*, 26 November 1883, reprinted by Chilson Leonard in *Modern Language Notes*, XLVI, (1931), p. 119.) Tinker and Lowry suggest that it is equally possible he had Tennyson in mind. In 1850 Tennyson had both succeeded to the Laureateship and published "In Memoriam". The phrase "intellectual throne" (conscious echo or not) is Tennyson's own in "The Palace of Art".

Mr. J. C. Maxwell in a private communication has put forward the suggestion that Arnold may have been thinking also of Leopardi—whose thought, as expounded by Sainte-Beuve in an essay which Arnold certainly knew (*Portraits contemporains*, vol. IV), is akin to the mood of "The Scholar-Gipsy". Arnold expressed his own feeling for Leopardi in the essay in Byron (*Essays in Criticism*, Second Series). There is no doubt of the suffering in Leopardi, but he offered few anodynes. Goethe's claim to the rôle of "our wisest" can hardly be challenged, and it is difficult to set aside Arnold's own explicit statement. Possibly the stanza presents a composite portrait with features from all three poets.

Thyrsis

Thyrsis was published in *Macmillan's Magazine*, April 1866, and appeared in *New Poems*, 1867. Clough had died in Florence on 13 November 1861. Arnold paid his first tribute to his friend in the same month at the close of his Oxford lecture "On Translating Homer: Last Words". In January 1862 he wrote to Mrs. Clough of a visit to Oxford, "There among the Cumner hills where we have so often rambled, I shall be able to think him over as I could wish". In a list of works to be written in 1863 there is the entry "Clough and the Cumner hill-side"; in 1866 he wrote to his mother that the elegy had been forming itself in his mind for the past two years.

See also Letters: to his mother 20 November 1861 (p. 754), 7 April 1866 (p. 762), and to J. C. Shairp 12 April 1866 (p. 763).

In *New Poems*, 1867, "Thyrsis" was prefaced with a quotation which was subsequently dropped.

> Thus yesterday, to-day, to-morrow come,
> They hustle one another and they pass;
> But all our hustling morrows only make
> The smooth to-day of God.
> —*From* Lucretius, *an unpublished Tragedy.*

These lines are of interest as the only published fragment of a drama which Arnold had in mind all his life. Writing to his mother in 1866 he says (Letters, ed. G. W. E. Russell, I. 322):

> I am rather troubled to find that Tennyson is at work on a subject, the story of the Latin poet Lucretius, which I have been occupied with for some twenty years . . . every one, except the few friends who have known that I had it in hand, will think I borrowed the subject from him. So far from this, I suspect the subject was put into his head by P——, [Palgrave] who knew I was busy with it. I shall probably go on, however, but it is annoying. . . .

He was still thinking of it at the time of his retirement in 1886. In a letter to Swinburne, 26 July 1882, he writes:

> If my daily grind at school inspecting ever ceases I mean to try my hand at a project of mine more than thirty years old, a Roman play with Lucretius for its centre, and shall quite disregard Tennyson's having forestalled me with Lucretius in the meantime. But I dare say I shall die in harness, and do no more poetry.

For full text of this letter see "Matthew Arnold and Swinburne" by Edmund Gosse, *Times Literary Supplement*, 12 August 1920.

A few fragments of the drama survive in manuscript, and these have been printed in the Tinker and Lowry *Commentary*.

l. 4. *And from the sign is gone Sibylla's name*. Sir Francis Wylie (vide essay referred to in note to "The Scholar-Gipsy") has explained this puzzling allusion. Sybella Curr was the hostess of the Cross Keys inn in South Hinksey. She died in 1860, and is buried in the churchyard.

Memorial Verses

First published in *Fraser's Magazine*, June 1850, and subsequently printed in the 1852 volume. From 1869 onwards this poem was grouped with the Elegiac Poems. It was written at the request of Edward Quillinan, Wordsworth's son-in-law, and neighbour of the Arnolds at Fox How.

A Southern Night

The author's younger brother, William Delafield Arnold, Director of Public Instruction in the Punjab, died at Gibraltar on his way home from India, 9 April 1859. He is commemorated also in the "Stanzas from Carnac" (omitted from this volume). In the fourth and fifth verses of the present poem there is a reference back to the moonlight scene of "A Summer Night".

"A Southern Night" was a contribution to *The Victoria Regia*, an anthology of original contributions in verse and prose edited by Adelaide Ann Procter and published by Emily Faithfull at the Victoria Press for the Employment of Women in 1861. It was reprinted in *New Poems*, 1867.

The Victoria Press was one result of the new movement in the sixties for promoting the industrial employment of women. Founded by two courageous feminists, Bessie Parkes and Emily Faithfull, it opened on

25 March 1860. *The Victoria Regia*, one of its first publications, was introduced by Miss Faithfull as "a choice specimen of the skill attained by my compositors". Among other contributors were Tennyson, Thackeray, William Allingham, Coventry Patmore and Anthony Trollope. Both Dante Gabriel and Christina Rossetti contributed to later miscellanies issued by the Victoria Press.

Haworth Churchyard

This elegy was first published in *Fraser's Magazine*, May 1855, signed "A" and dated "April 1855". Charlotte Brontë had died on the last day of March. The meeting with Harriet Martineau and Charlotte Brontë took place in December 1850, and the poet describes it in a letter to Miss Wightman on 21 December (see *Letters*, p. 741). The book referred to is Rotha Quillinan's Album.

The poem was not reprinted till the edition of 1877, when various omissions were made, notably three stanzas dealing with Harriet Martineau's apparently impending death in 1855. She lived on till 1876. Arnold also omitted ll. 121–139 of the original, having already printed these as the lyric poem "Early Death and Fame" which follows the "Fragment of Chorus of a 'Dejaneira'" in *New Poems*, 1867. And in 1877 he added the Epilogue.

The description of the graves at Haworth is inaccurate. The Brontë vault is in the church, not in the churchyard: and Anne is buried at Scarborough, where she died in 1849. Arnold is not to be trusted on tombs: cf. his mistakes in "The Church of Brou".

He seems also to be mistaken in placing the meeting at the house of Ed. Quillinan. The letter to Miss Wightman implies that it took place at Fox How, and this is confirmed by Charlotte Brontë's own account of the meeting in a letter to James Taylor of 15 January 1851, printed by Clement Shorter in *Charlotte Brontë and her Circle*. (There may of course have been more than one meeting.) She found Arnold's manner displeasing from its seeming foppery, and "the shade of Dr. Arnold seemed to frown on his young representative". But she admitted he improved on acquaintance, and Arnold sent her a copy of his *Poems*, 1853.

Rugby Chapel

First printed in *New Poems*, 1867. Dr. Arnold had died in 1842. In 1852 Fitzjames Stephen reviewed *Tom Brown's Schooldays* in the *Edinburgh Review*, making some criticism of Dr. Arnold's work at Rugby. In 1867, after the publication of the poem, Arnold wrote to his mother: "It was Fitzjames Stephen's thesis . . . of Papa's being a narrow bustling fanatic, which moved me first to the poem. I think I have done something to fix the true legend about Papa . . ."

Stanzas from the Grande Chartreuse

These stanzas appeared in *Fraser's Magazine*, April 1855: reprinted in *New Poems*, 1867, and in 1877 grouped with the Elegiac Poems.

Arnold visited the Grande Chartreuse in Sept. 1851, while on his honeymoon.

Stanzas in Memory of the Author of "Obermann"

The Obermann stanzas appeared in *Empedocles on Etna*, 1852. For the profound influence of Senancour on Arnold see the essay on him published in the *Academy*, 9 October 1869, and reprinted in *Essays in Criticism*, third series.

This poem was translated into French prose by Sainte-Beuve and quoted in his *Chateaubriand et son groupe littéraire*, 1861, with a tribute to "le jeune poète anglais, fils d'un bien respectable père, et dont le talent réunit la pureté et la passion".

Etienne Pivert de Senancour was born in Paris, 1770. Studied for the priesthood, but broke away from the church and left France for Switzerland. Returned later to France, where he died in 1846. Author of *Obermann* (1804) and *Libres Méditations d'un Solitaire Inconnu* (1819).

Obermann Once More

Appeared in *New Poems*, 1867, and with considerable alterations in the second edition, 1868, when a long note on Senancour was added. In the later editions this note was transferred to the earlier Obermann poem.

DRAMATIC POEMS

Empedocles on Etna

The title poem of the 1852 volume. It was excluded from *Poems*, 1853 (Arnold giving his reasons in the famous Preface), and not reprinted till 1867, when it was included in *New Poems* at the request of Browning. Though Arnold dropped the drama in 1853, he still valued the lyrical parts of it. In the 1853 volume the song of Callicles (at the end of Act I) is included, entitled "Cadmus and Harmonia". In *Poems*, Second Series, 1855, he reprinted the four songs under the title of "The Harp Player on Etna".

Empedocles occurs in the list of poems to be composed in 1849, and in the same year J. C. Shairp wrote to Clough:

> He was working at an "Empedocles"—which seemed to be not much about the man who leapt in the crater—but his name and outward circumstances are used for the drapery of his own thoughts. I wish Matt wᵈ give up that old Greek form but he says he despises all the modern ways of going about art and will stick to his own one. Also I do not believe in nor feel with that great background of fatalism or call it what you will which is behind all his thought. But he thinks he sees his way.

(Clough Mss., quoted Tinker and Lowry, *Commentary*, p. 287.)

LATER POEMS

The group of Later Poems appeared in the 1885 edition. It consisted of three poems: "Westminster Abbey", a memorial tribute to his life-long friend Arthur Penrhyn Stanley, and (somewhat incongruously) two elegies on the Arnold family pets: "Geist's Grave" and "Poor Matthias". "Kaiser Dead", another dog poem, appeared in the *Fortnightly Review*, July 1887, and was added to this group in the 1890 one-volume edition after the poet's death. In these late occasional poems Arnold strikes a new note—tender, whimsical and personal.

Geist's Grave

First published in the *Fortnightly Review*, January 1881. Geist was the dachshund belonging to the poet's son Richard Penrose Arnold. Carter and Pollard suspect that a pamphlet issue of this poem bearing the date 1881 is one of the Wise forgeries.

Poor Matthias

Evidence of Arnold's fondness for the family pets is found throughout his letters. Matthias was the pet canary of his daughter Eleanor (later Lady Sandhurst). The poem was published in *Macmillan's Magazine*, December 1882, and writing to John Morley Arnold describes the "dirge" as "a simple thing enough, but honest". It provoked an immediate parody, and again writing to Morley on 6 December 1882, Arnold says, "Parody is a vile art, but I must say I read 'Poor Matthias' in the *World* with an amused pleasure. I wonder if it is that demon Traill". The verses ran:

> Poor Matthias! many a year
> Has flown since first upon our ear
> Fell that sweetly-doleful song
> With its ancient tale of wrong.
> Now those curls, were wont to stray
> O'er that brow so gravely gay,
> Thin have grown and streaked with gray,
> And the crown's cross tracery
> Mars that eye's lucidity.
> But the burden never falters,
> But the chorus never alters;
> Those smooth periods no more vary
> Than the song of your canary.
> Won't you give us something new?
> *That* we know as well as you.

INDEX OF TITLES AND FIRST LINES

INDEX